Lecture Notes in Computer Science

# Lecture Notes in Artificial Intelligence 16586

Founding Editor

Jörg Siekmann

AF790036

The series Lecture Notes in Artificial Intelligence (LNAI) was established in 1988 as a topical subseries of LNCS devoted to artificial intelligence.

The series publishes state-of-the-art research results at a high level. As with the LNCS mother series, the mission of the series is to serve the international R & D community by providing an invaluable service, mainly focused on the publication of conference and workshop proceedings and postproceedings.

Emmanuel G. Blanchard · Guanliang Chen ·
Min Chi · Seiji Isotani
Editors

# Artificial Intelligence in Education

## 27th International Conference, AIED 2026
## Seoul, South Korea, June 27–July 3, 2026
## Proceedings, Part VI

Springer

*Editors*
Emmanuel G. Blanchard
Le Mans University
Le Mans, France

Guanliang Chen
Monash University
Clayton, VIC, Australia

Min Chi
North Carolina State University
Raleigh, NC, USA

Seiji Isotani
University of Pennsylvania
Philadelphia, PA, USA

ISSN 0302-9743 ISSN 1611-3349 (electronic)
Lecture Notes in Artificial Intelligence
ISBN 978-3-032-29772-3 ISBN 978-3-032-29773-0 (eBook)
https://doi.org/10.1007/978-3-032-29773-0

LNCS Sublibrary: SL7 – Artificial Intelligence



This Springer imprint is published by the registered company Springer Nature Switzerland AG
The registered company address is: Gewerbestrasse 11, 6330 Cham, Switzerland

# Preface

Welcome to the 27th International Conference on Artificial Intelligence in Education, taking place from June 27–July 3rd, 2026 in Seoul, South Korea. AIED is ranked A in CORE[1] (top 13.09% of 825 ranked venues). AIED is clearly growing and attracting more submissions, this year with 1,241 initial submissions. For more than three decades, the AIED community has advanced a rich body of research at the intersection of computer science, learning sciences, cognitive science, and artificial intelligence. From early intelligent tutoring systems to contemporary data-driven and adaptive platforms, the field has consistently pushed the boundaries of how technology can support teaching and learning. These contributions have not only deepened our theoretical understanding of learning but have also shaped educational practice across diverse contexts worldwide. Today, we stand at a pivotal moment. The rapid emergence of Generative AI and increasingly capable learning technologies challenges long-standing assumptions about the role of AI in education. Systems are no longer confined to delivering content, scaffolding problem solving, or modeling student knowledge; they are now capable of engaging in dialogue, generating explanations, co-creating artifacts, and participating in complex, context-aware interactions. This transformation compels us to reconsider a fundamental question: what does it mean for AI to meaningfully participate in the learning process?

The theme of **AIED 2026, "From Tools to Teammates: Human–AI Synergy for Augmented Learning"**, reflected this shift. Over decades of innovation, the AIED community has developed powerful tools and insights that have transformed learning worldwide. As these foundations continue to shape the field, emerging technologies, especially Generative AI, demand that we rethink how AI engages with learners and educators. Our field is entering a new era in which AI must evolve from simply supporting human learning to enabling richer human–AI collaboration. As AI becomes deeply embedded in everyday educational practice, AIED 2026 called for systems that foster genuine human–AI partnerships. This year's theme highlighted research on human and AI agency, collaborative intelligence, and the co-evolution of humans and AI. We invited work that reimagines AIED systems not merely as instruments, but as adaptive teammates that complement teachers and learners, align with human goals, and dynamically participate in shared educational processes. Such systems raise new opportunities and challenges: how to design for trust, transparency, and alignment; how to balance autonomy and control; how to support equity and inclusion; and how to rigorously evaluate learning in settings where humans and AI jointly construct knowledge.

AIED 2026 brought together a diverse and interdisciplinary community of researchers, practitioners, and policymakers to explore these questions. The contributions in these proceedings reflect a wide spectrum of perspectives—ranging from theoretical frameworks and empirical studies to system design, deployment, and real-world

[1] https://portal.core.edu.au/conf-ranks.

impact. Collectively, they illustrate a field that is both grounded in its intellectual heritage and boldly looking ahead.

The main conference program comprised three tracks:

- **Track 1 – Technical Aspects of AIED** focused on the computer science and engineering foundations that drive innovation in the field, emphasizing contributions where the primary novelty is technical. This track brought together work on novel AIED architectures, system engineering, and computational approaches to cognition and reasoning, including advances in knowledge representation, domain modeling, and agentic as well as multi-agent systems. Submissions span cutting-edge methods in machine learning, deep learning, generative models, natural language processing, and multimodal and video-based systems, alongside data mining, feature engineering, and predictive modeling techniques. The track also highlighted the design and implementation of intelligent tutoring systems, including those tailored for special education and resource-constrained (frugal) settings. Contributions were expected to demonstrate rigor through computational evaluation metrics such as accuracy, validity, and reliability, advancing the technical backbone of AIED while enabling more robust, scalable, and adaptive learning technologies.
- **Track 2 – Human Aspects of AIED** centered on the learning sciences, pedagogical foundations, and human-centered perspectives that underpin meaningful educational innovation. The primary insights emerge from theories of learning, empirical studies of human behavior, and humanities-informed analyses of educational practice. Topics include investigations of human agency, co-regulation, and human–AI collaboration, as well as rigorous evaluations of AIED systems using quantitative, qualitative, or mixed methods. Submissions draw on cognitive, motivational, metacognitive, and affective theories to better understand how learners and educators engage with AI-enabled environments, alongside work on instructional design, collaborative and social learning, and informal or game-based contexts. By foregrounding learners, teachers, and educational phenomena, this track advanced a deeper understanding of learning processes and aimed to ensure that AIED technologies are grounded in robust pedagogical and human-centered principles.
- **Track 3 – Societal Aspects of AIED** addressed the ethical, equitable, and policy-oriented dimensions of AIED, emphasizing contributions that critically examine the broader societal impact of AIED technologies. This track invited work on algorithmic fairness, bias, transparency, and accountability, as well as issues of privacy, surveillance, and data governance in educational contexts. It highlighted the importance of cultural awareness and sensitivity, alongside research focused on low-resource settings, unplugged AIED, and efforts to bridge the AIED divide across socio-economic, gender, and racial lines. Contributions also explored ethical frameworks for the design and deployment of AIED systems, policy implications of AI integration in education, and approaches to fostering AI literacy and critical understanding among learners and educators. By foregrounding responsibility, inclusion, and societal impact, this track sought to ensure that advances in AIED contribute to equitable and trustworthy educational futures.

AIED 2026 attracted an exceptionally broad range of submissions. We received 1,241 submissions across all tracks, of which 922 met the eligibility criteria and were accepted for review. From the full paper submissions, 143 were accepted as full papers, and an additional 168 were accepted as short papers. The acceptance rates for both full and short papers were 16.5% and 15.3% respectively. More specifically, 69 full and 71 short were accepted for Track 1; 54 full and 74 short were accepted for Track 2, and 20 full and 20 short were accepted for Track 3.

Every paper and presentation at AIED 2026 underwent a rigorous, double-blind peer-review process designed to ensure the highest scholarly standards and fair evaluation. We ensured that each paper was reviewed by three reviewers, including at least one senior reviewer. This rigorous collaborative effort—fueled by leading scholars and seasoned experts—resulted in a premier program spanning the complete spectrum of AIED innovation.

Beyond the scholarly sessions and paper presentations compiled in these conference proceedings, AIED 2026 offered a rich program of keynote addresses, panel discussions, interactive demonstrations, and specialized sessions which are compiled in the supplementary CCIS volumes of the conference. Specifically, this year was part of the Festival of Learning, co-organized with sister conferences Educational Data Mining (EDM 2026) and ACM Learning @ Scale (L@S 2026), which were co-located in Seoul, South Korea. Attendees had the opportunity to participate in the Doctoral Consortium, Workshops and Tutorials, Late-Breaking Results sessions, and dedicated tracks for Practitioners, Industry and Policy (PIP). The BlueSky track also invited visionary reflections on past progress and future trajectories in AIED, while the WideAIED track amplified perspectives from underrepresented regions and communities. Additionally, the conference offered presentations on the latest publications in the International Journal of Artificial Intelligence in Education (IJAIED)[2]. As a member of the International Alliance to Advance Learning in the Digital Era (IAALDE)[3], AIED 2026 also hosted presentations of the best papers from other IAALDE conferences.

This conference would not have been possible without the unwavering commitment of the International Artificial Intelligence in Education Society, the Organizing Committee, the Program and Senior Program Committees, the sponsors and partners who support our mission, and the Festival of Learning organizers. Their passion and dedication to advancing intelligent educational systems are the foundation of AIED's continued success and innovation.

We invite you to share your insights, spark new debates, and connect with peers to help drive the future of education. Together, we are exploring AI's potential as a powerful catalyst for inclusive, personalized, and ethical education globally. Welcome to AIED

[2] https://www.sciencedirect.com/journal/international-journal-of-artificial-intelligence-in-education.

[3] https://alliancelss.com/.

2026: where we aren't just predicting the future; we are actively reimagining it through every new innovation.

June 2026

Emmanuel G. Blanchard
Guanliang Chen
Min Chi
Seiji Isotani

# Organization

## Conference General Co-chair

| | |
|---|---|
| Seiji Isotani | University of Pennsylvania, USA |

## Program Co-chairs

| | |
|---|---|
| Emmanuel G. Blanchard | Le Mans Université, France |
| Guanliang Chen | Monash University, Australia |
| Min Chi | North Carolina State University, USA |

## Workshop and Tutorials Co-chairs

| | |
|---|---|
| Engin Bumbacher | University of Teacher Education Vaud, Switzerland |
| Shiyan Jiang | University of Pennsylvania, USA |

## Doctoral Consortium Co-chairs

| | |
|---|---|
| Irene-Angelica Chounta | University of Duisburg-Essen, Germany |
| Yu Lu | Beijing Normal University, China |
| Ido Roll | Technion - Israel Institute of Technology, Israel |

## Late Breaking Results (Posters) Co-chairs

| | |
|---|---|
| Davide Taibi | Consiglio Nazionale delle Ricerche, Italy |
| Renzhe Yu | Columbia University, USA |
| Zheng Yuan | University of Sheffield, UK |

## Blue Sky Co-chairs

| | |
|---|---|
| Ivon Arroyo | University of Massachusetts Amherst, USA |
| Xiangen Hu | Hong Kong Polytechnic University, China |
| H. Chad Lane | University of Illinois Urbana-Champaign, USA |

## WideAIED Co-chairs

| | |
|---|---|
| Alexandra I. Cristea | Durham University, UK |
| Rafael Ferreira Mello | Federal Rural University of Pernambuco, Brazil |

## Practitioners, Industry and Policy (PIP) Co-chairs

| | |
|---|---|
| Christian M. Stracke | University of Bonn, Germany |
| Lixiang Yan | Tsinghua University, China |
| Diego Zapata-Rivera | Educational Testing Service, USA |

## Interactive Events (Demos) Co-chairs

| | |
|---|---|
| Yuheng Li | Hong Kong Polytechnic University, China |
| Miguel Portaz | Universidad Nacional de Educación a Distancia, Spain |
| Sreecharan Sankaranarayanan | Extuitive Inc., USA |

## DEIA Fellowship Chairs

| | |
|---|---|
| Ig Ibert Bittencourt | Federal University of Alagoas, Brazil |
| Valery Psyché | Université TÉLUQ, Canada |

## Lifetime Award Chair

| | |
|---|---|
| Bruce M. McLaren | Carnegie Mellon University, USA |

## Awards Co-chairs

| | |
|---|---|
| Gautam Biswas | Vanderbilt University, USA |
| Riichiro Mizoguchi | Japan Advanced Institute of Science and Technology, Japan |
| Olga C. Santos | Universidad Nacional de Educación a Distancia, Spain |

## Virtual Experiences Co-chairs

| | |
|---|---|
| Patricia A. Jaques | Federal University of Paraná, Brazil |
| Huiyong Li | Kyushu University, Japan |

## Publicity Co-chairs

| | |
|---|---|
| Cristian Cechinel | Universidade Federal de Santa Catarina, Brazil |
| Xinyuan Hao | University College London, UK |

## Proceedings Co-chairs

| | |
|---|---|
| Matthieu Branthôme | University of Rennes, France |
| Diego Dermeval | Federal University of Alagoas, Brazil |
| Jionghao Lin | University of Hong Kong, China |
| Namrata Srivastava | Vanderbilt University, USA |

## Website Chair

| | |
|---|---|
| Yuheng Li | Hong Kong Polytechnic University, China |

## Main Track

## Senior Program Committee Members

| | |
|---|---|
| Mohammed Abdel Razek | Al-Azhar University, Egypt |
| Bita Akram | North Carolina State University, USA |
| Laia Albó | Universitat de Vic, Spain |

| | |
|---|---|
| Vincent Aleven | Carnegie Mellon University, USA |
| Giora Alexandron | Weizmann Institute of Science, Israel |
| Laura Allen | University of Minnesota, USA |
| Ivon Arroyo | University of Massachusetts Amherst, USA |
| Roger Azevedo | University of Central Florida, USA |
| Ryan Baker | University of Pennsylvania, USA |
| Ayan Banerjee | Arizona State University, USA |
| Tiffany Barnes | North Carolina State University, USA |
| Abhinava Barthakur | University of South Australia, Australia |
| Brian Belland | Pennsylvania State University, USA |
| Yoav Bergner | New York University, USA |
| Gautam Biswas | Vanderbilt University, USA |
| Ig Ibert Bittencourt | Federal University of Alagoas, Brazil |
| Geoffray Bonnin | Université de Lorraine - LORIA, France |
| Conrad Borchers | Carnegie Mellon University, USA |
| Anthony F. Botelho | University of Florida, USA |
| François Bouchet | Sorbonne Université - LIP6, France |
| Kristy Elizabeth Boyer | University of Florida, USA |
| Bert Bredeweg | University of Amsterdam, Netherlands |
| Julien Broisin | Université de Toulouse, France |
| Christopher Brooks | University of Michigan, USA |
| Armelle Brun | LORIA - Université de Lorraine, France |
| Peter Brusilovsky | University of Pittsburgh, USA |
| Ilona Buchem | Berlin University of Applied Sciences, Germany |
| Simon Buckingham Shum | University of Technology Sydney, Australia |
| Okan Bulut | University of Alberta, Canada |
| Engin Bumbacher | University of Teacher Education Vaud, Switzerland |
| Dan Carpenter | North Carolina State University, USA |
| Paulo Carvalho | Carnegie Mellon University, USA |
| Cristian Cechinel | Universidade Federal de Santa Catarina, Brazil |
| Penghe Chen | Beijing Normal University, China |
| Irene-Angelica Chounta | University of Duisburg-Essen, Germany |
| Jaroslaw A. Chudziak | Warsaw University of Technology, Poland |
| Ruth Cobos | Universidad Autónoma de Madrid, Spain |
| Cesar Collazos | Universidad del Cauca, Colombia |
| Alexandra I. Cristea | Durham University, UK |
| Jennifer Cromley | University of Illinois Urbana-Champaign, USA |
| Mutlu Cukurova | University College London, UK |
| Maria Cutumisu | McGill University, Canada |
| Carrie Demmans Epp | University of Alberta, Canada |
| Vanessa Dennen | Florida State University, USA |

| | |
|---|---|
| Diego Dermeval | Federal University of Alagoas, Brazil |
| Michel Desmarais | Polytechnique Montréal, Canada |
| Daniele Di Mitri | DIPF I Leibniz Institute for Research and Information in Education, Germany |
| Vania Dimitrova | University of Leeds, UK |
| Blazenka Divjak | University of Zagreb, Croatia |
| Mohsen Dorodchi | University of North Carolina at Charlotte, USA |
| Shayan Doroudi | University of California, Irvine, USA |
| Vanessa Echeverria | RMIT University, Australia |
| Ralph Ewerth | University of Marburg and hessian.AI – Hessian Center for Artificial Intelligence, Germany |
| Yizhou Fan | Peking University, UK |
| Mingyu Feng | WestEd, USA |
| Shihui Feng | University of Hong Kong, China |
| Márcia Fernandes | Federal University of Uberlândia, Brazil |
| Rafael Ferreira Mello | Federal Rural University of Pernambuco/CESAR School, Brazil |
| Brendan Flanagan | Kyoto University, Japan |
| Reva Freedman | Northern Illinois University, USA |
| Francisco José García-Peñalvo | University of Salamanca, Spain |
| Dragan Gasevic | Monash University, Australia |
| Isabela Gasparini | Santa Catarina State University, Brazil |
| Sébastien George | LIUM, Le Mans Université, France |
| Michael Glass | Valparaiso University, USA |
| Janice Gobert | Rutgers University, USA |
| Sabine Graf | Athabasca University, Canada |
| Monique Grandbastien | LORIA, Université de Lorraine, France |
| Floriana Grasso | University of Liverpool, UK |
| Beate Grawemeyer | Coventry University, UK |
| Jason Harley | McGill University, Canada |
| Peter Hastings | DePaul University, USA |
| Yugo Hayashi | Ritsumeikan University, Japan |
| Neil Heffernan | Worcester Polytechnic Institute, USA |
| Tsukasa Hirashima | Hiroshima University, Japan |
| Sharon I-Han Hsiao | Santa Clara University, USA |
| Xiao Hu | University of Arizona, USA |
| Stephen Hutt | University of Denver, USA |
| Gwo-Jen Hwang | National Taiwan University of Science and Technology, Taiwan |
| Tomoo Inoue | University of Tsukuba, Japan |
| Shoya Ishimaru | Osaka Metropolitan University, Japan |
| Mirjana Ivanovic | University of Novi Sad, Serbia |

| | |
|---|---|
| Patricia Jaques | Universidade Federal do Paraná/Universidade Federal de Pelotas, Brazil |
| Johan Jeuring | Utrecht University, Netherlands |
| Yang Jiang | Columbia University, USA |
| Srecko Joksimovic | University of South Australia, Australia |
| Jelena Jovanovic | University of Belgrade, Serbia |
| David Joyner | Georgia Institute of Technology, USA |
| Akihiro Kashihara | University of Electro-Communications, Japan |
| Judy Kay | University of Sydney, Australia |
| Mohammad Khalil | University of Bergen, Norway |
| Hassan Khosravi | University of Queensland, Australia |
| Yeo Jin Kim | North Carolina State University, USA |
| Kirsty Kitto | University of Bergen, Norway |
| Rene Kizilcec | Cornell University, USA |
| Simon Knight | University of Technology Sydney, Australia |
| Irena Koprinska | University of Sydney, Australia |
| Vitomir Kovanovic | University of South Australia, Australia |
| Amruth Kumar | Ramapo College of New Jersey, USA |
| Tanja Käser | EPFL, Switzerland |
| Sébastien Lallé | Sorbonne University, France |
| Andrew Lan | University of Massachusetts Amherst, USA |
| Yunshi Lan | East China Normal University, China |
| H. Chad Lane | University of Illinois Urbana-Champaign, USA |
| Mikel Larrañaga | University of the Basque Country UPV/EHU, Spain |
| Hady Lauw | Singapore Management University, Singapore |
| Nguyen-Thinh Le | Humboldt Universität zu Berlin, Germany |
| James Lester | North Carolina State University, USA |
| Carla Limongelli | Università Roma Tre, Italy |
| Fuhua Lin | Athabasca University, Canada |
| Jionghao Lin | University of Hong Kong, China |
| Zitao Liu | Guangdong Institute of Smart Education, Jinan University, China |
| Chee-Kit Looi | Education University of Hong Kong, China |
| Yu Lu | Beijing Normal University, China |
| Vanda Luengo | Sorbonne Université - LIP6, France |
| Collin Lynch | North Carolina State University, USA |
| Sonsoles López-Pernas | University of Eastern Finland, Finland |
| Mirko Marras | University of Cagliari, Italy |
| Roberto Martinez-Maldonado | Monash University, Australia |
| Jeffrey Matayoshi | McGraw Hill ALEKS, USA |
| Noboru Matsuda | North Carolina State University, USA |

| | |
|---|---|
| Manolis Mavrikis | University of Edinburgh, UK |
| Agathe Merceron | Berliner Hochschule für Technik - Berlin State University of Applied Sciences, Germany |
| Wookhee Min | North Carolina State University, USA |
| Tanja Mitrovic | University of Canterbury, New Zealand |
| Riichiro Mizoguchi | Japan Advanced Institute of Science and Technology, Japan |
| Phaedra Mohammed | University of the West Indies, Trinidad and Tobago |
| Inge Molenaar | Radboud University, Netherlands |
| Steven Moore | Carnegie Mellon University, USA |
| Bradford Mott | North Carolina State University, USA |
| Chrystalla Mouza | University of Illinois Urbana-Champaign, USA |
| Kasia Muldner | Carleton University, Canada |
| Tomohiro Nagashima | Saarland University, Germany |
| Nia Nixon | University of California, Irvine, USA |
| Roger Nkambou | Université du Québec à Montréal, Canada |
| Benjamin Nye | University of Southern California, USA |
| Jaclyn Ocumpaugh | University of Houston, USA |
| Eduardo Oliveira | University of Melbourne, Australia |
| Luc Paquette | University of Illinois Urbana-Champaign, USA |
| Abelardo Pardo | University of Adelaide, Australia |
| Radek Pelánek | Masaryk University, Czechia |
| Niels Pinkwart | Humboldt-Universität zu Berlin, Germany |
| Vitaliy Popov | University of Michigan, USA |
| Sasha Poquet | University of South Australia, Australia |
| Kaska Porayska-Pomsta | University College London, UK |
| Valéry Psyché | Université TÉLUQ, Canada |
| Anna Rafferty | Carleton College, USA |
| Mladen Rakovic | Monash University, Australia |
| Steve Ritter | Carnegie Learning, Inc., USA |
| Maria Mercedes T. Rodrigo | Ateneo de Manila University, Philippines |
| Ido Roll | Technion - Israel Institute of Technology, Israel |
| Vasile Rus | University of Memphis, USA |
| Demetrios Sampson | Curtin University, Australia |
| Sreecharan Sankaranarayanan | Amazon.com, Inc., USA |
| Olga C. Santos | Universidad Nacional de Educación a Distancia, Spain |
| Mohammed Saqr | University of Eastern Finland, Finland |
| Filippo Sciarrone | Universitas Mercatorum, Italy |
| Lei Shi | Newcastle University, UK |
| Yang Shi | Utah State University, USA |

| | |
|---|---|
| Sean Siqueira | Federal University of the State of Rio de Janeiro, Brazil |
| Sergey Sosnovsky | Utrecht University, Netherlands |
| Namrata Srivastava | Vanderbilt University, USA |
| John Stamper | Carnegie Mellon University, USA |
| Angela Stewart | University of Pittsburgh, USA |
| Christian M. Stracke | University of Bonn, Germany |
| Daner Sun | Education University of Hong Kong, China |
| Bill Swartout | University of Southern California, USA |
| Davide Taibi | Italian National Research Council, Italy |
| Tamara Tate | University of California, Irvine, USA |
| Michelle Taub | University of Central Florida, USA |
| Marco Temperini | Sapienza - Università di Roma, Italy |
| Craig Thompson | University of British Columbia, Canada |
| Stefan Trausan-Matu | University Politehnica of Bucharest, Romania |
| Yi-Shan Tsai | Monash University, Australia |
| Maomi Ueno | University of Electro-Communications, Japan |
| Julita Vassileva | University of Saskatchewan, Canada |
| Olga Viberg | KTH Royal Institute of Technology, Sweden |
| Rosa Vicari | Universidade Federal do Rio Grande do Sul, Brazil |
| Xu Wang | University of Michigan, USA |
| Alistair Willis | Open University, UK |
| Beverly Woolf | University of Massachusetts Amherst, USA |
| Marcelo Worsley | Northwestern University, USA |
| Lixiang Yan | Tsinghua University, China |
| Lan Yang | Education University of Hong Kong, China |
| Amel Yessad | LIP6, Sorbonne Université, France |
| Zheng Yuan | King's College London, UK |
| Diego Zapata-Rivera | Educational Testing Service, USA |
| Xiaoming Zhai | University of Georgia, USA |
| Guojing Zhou | South China Normal University, USA |
| Xiaofei Zhou | University of Rochester, USA |
| Gaoxia Zhu | Nanyang Technological University, Singapore |
| Craig Zilles | University of Illinois Urbana-Champaign, USA |
| Gustavo Zurita | Universidad de Chile, Chile |
| Benedict du Boulay | University of Sussex, UK |

## Program Committee Members

| | |
|---|---|
| Noorhan Abbas | University of Leeds, UK |
| Sophie Abel | University of Wollongong, Australia |
| Abdelghafour Aboukacem | Mohammed VI Polytechnic University, Morocco |
| Hasan Abu-Rasheed | Goethe University Frankfurt, Germany |
| Tomoki Aburatani | Osaka Metropolitan University, Japan |
| Ifeoma Adaji | University of British Columbia, Canada |
| Seth Adjei | Northern Kentucky University, USA |
| Imran S. A. Khan | Laboratoire d'Informatique de l'Université du Mans (LIUM), France |
| Dishank Aggarwal | IIT Bombay, India |
| Mahir Akgun | Pennsylvania State University, USA |
| Nazia Alam | North Carolina State University, USA |
| Veljko Aleksić | University of Kragujevac, Serbia |
| Azza Abdullah S. Alghamdi | King Abdulaziz University, Saudi Arabia |
| Samah Alkhuzaey | Umm Al-Qura University, Saudi Arabia |
| Isaac Alpizar-Chacon | Utrecht University, Netherlands |
| Ainhoa Alvarez | University of the Basque Country, UPV/EHU, Spain |
| Ioannis Anastasopoulos | University of California, Berkeley, USA |
| Moriah Ariely | Weizmann Institute of Science, Israel |
| Pablo Arnau-González | Universidad de Valencia, Spain |
| Burcu Arslan | Educational Testing Service, USA |
| Yuya Asano | University of Pittsburgh, USA |
| Gabriel Astudillo | Pontificia Universidad Católica de Chile, Chile |
| Berk Atil | Boğaziçi University, Turkey |
| Shen Ba | Education University of Hong Kong, China |
| Costin Badica | University of Craiova, Romania |
| Michelle P. Banawan | Asian Institute of Management, Philippines |
| Amanda Barany | University of Pennsylvania, USA |
| Alvaro Becerra | Universidad Autónoma de Madrid, Spain |
| Beata Beigman Klebanov | Educational Testing Service, USA |
| Francisco Bellas | Universidade da Coruna, Spain |
| Avia Ben-Ari | Technion - Israel Institute of Technology, Israel |
| Luca Benedetto | University of Cambridge, UK |
| El Houcine Bergou | Mohamed VI Polytechnic University, Morocco |
| Ismail Berrada | Mohamed VI Polytechnic University, Morocco |
| Susan Beudt | German Research Center for Artificial Intelligence (DFKI), Germany |
| Gabriele Biagini | Università degli Studi di Firenze, Italy |

| | |
|---|---|
| Wolfgang Bitter | TIB – Leibniz Information Centre for Science and Technology, Germany |
| Maria Bolsinova | Tilburg University, Netherlands |
| Anis Boubaker | École de Technologie Supérieure, Canada |
| Mariah Bradford | Colorado State University, USA |
| Matthieu Branthôme | University of Rennes, IRISA, CNRS, France |
| Rex Bringula | University of the East, Philippines |
| George Buchanan | University of Melbourne, Australia |
| Jill Burstein | Duolingo, USA |
| Marina Buzzi | IIT-CNR, Italy |
| Minghao Cai | University of Alberta, Canada |
| Jie Cao | University of Oklahoma, USA |
| Jie Cao | University of Pittsburgh, USA |
| May Kristine Jonson Carlon | RIKEN Center for Brain Science, Japan |
| Alberto Casas-Ortiz | Universidad Nacional de Educación a Distancia, Spain |
| Héctor Ceballos | Tecnológico de Monterrey, Mexico |
| Jeevan Chapagain | University of Memphis, USA |
| Ziyan Che | Central China Normal University, China |
| Eason Chen | Carnegie Mellon University, USA |
| Fu Chen | University of Macau, China |
| Shigeng Chen | King's College London, UK |
| Shijun Cindy Chen | University of Hong Kong, China |
| Wei-Peng Chen | Fujitsu Labs of America, USA |
| Xinyue Chen | University of Michigan, USA |
| Youjie Chen | University of Hong Kong, China |
| Yixin Cheng | Monash University, Australia |
| Thomas K. F. Chiu | Chinese University of Hong Kong, China |
| Chih-Yueh Chou | Yuan Ze University, Taiwan |
| Elizabeth Cloude | Michigan State University, USA |
| Keith Cochran | DePaul University, USA |
| Jade Mai Cock | EPFL, Switzerland |
| Maria de Los Angeles Constantino González | Tecnológico de Monterrey Campus Laguna, Mexico |
| Evandro Costa | Federal University of Alagoas, Brazil |
| Steven Coyne | Tohoku University; RIKEN, Japan |
| Jeffrey Cross | Tokyo Institute of Technology, Japan |
| Stefano D'Urso | Universitas Mercatorum, Italy |
| Rafael D. Araújo | Universidade Federal de Uberlândia, Brazil |
| Wei Dai | University of Hong Kong, China |
| Yiling Dai | Hiroshima University, Japan |
| Syaamantak Das | Indian Institute of Technology Bombay, India |

| | |
|---|---|
| Mihai Dascalu | University Politehnica of Bucharest, Romania |
| Rahul Dass | Georgia Tech, USA |
| Eduardo Davalos Anaya | Trinity University, USA |
| Erwan David | Le Mans University, France |
| Richard Lee Davis | Stanford University, USA |
| Jeanine DeFalco | University of New Haven, USA |
| Oscar Deho | Charles Sturt University, Australia |
| M. Ali Akber Dewan | Athabasca University, Canada |
| Nicholas Diana | Colgate University, USA |
| Yannis Dimitriadis | University of Valladolid, Spain |
| Heejin Do | ETH Zurich, Switzerland |
| Konomu Dobashi | Aichi University, Japan |
| Fabiano Dorça | Universidade Federal de Uberlândia, Brazil |
| Zhangqi Duan | University of Massachusetts Amherst, USA |
| Cristina Dumdumaya | University of Southeastern Philippines, Philippines |
| Nicholas Duran | Arizona State University, USA |
| Martin Ebner | Graz University of Technology, Austria |
| Yo Ehara | Tokyo Gakugei University, Japan |
| Bobbie Eicher | Georgia Institute of Technology, USA |
| Nour El Mawas | Université de Lille, France |
| Lara Ceren Ergenç | King's College London, UK |
| Kelechi Ezema | University of Colorado Boulder, USA |
| Xiuyi Fan | Nanyang Technological University, UK |
| Zhilin Fan | Beijing Normal University, China |
| Paolo Fantozzi | LUMSA University, Italy |
| Abdolali Faraji | Leibniz Information Centre for Science and Technology (TIB), Germany |
| Alexandra Farazouli | Stockholm University, Sweden |
| Effat Farhana | Auburn University, USA |
| Cassia Fernandez | University of São Paulo, Brazil |
| Gloria Milena Fernandez-Nieto | University of Technology, Sydney, Australia |
| Alessio Ferrato | Roma Tre University, Italy |
| Carol Forsyth | Educational Testing Service, USA |
| Kazuma Fuchimoto | University of Electro-Communications, Japan |
| Mari Fukuda | Kyoto University, Japan |
| Nikki G. Lobczowski | McGill University, Canada |
| Kobi Gal | Ben-Gurion University of the Negev, Israel |
| Cristiano Galafassi | Universidade Federal do Rio Grande do Sul, Brazil |
| Selen Galiç | Hacettepe University, Turkey |
| Jie Gao | McGill University, Canada |

| | |
|---|---|
| Zhen Gao | McMaster University, Canada |
| Zhikai Gao | Western Carolina University, USA |
| Sai Gattupalli | University of Massachusetts Amherst, USA |
| Gabrielle Gaudeau | University of Cambridge, UK |
| Jadon Geathers | Cornell University, USA |
| Thierry Geoffre | University of Luxembourg, Luxembourg |
| Alireza Gharahighehi | imec - KU Leuven, Belgium |
| Ashok Goel | Georgia Institute of Technology, USA |
| Sebastian Gombert | DIPF \| Leibniz Institute for Research and Information in Education, Germany |
| Guher Gorgun | University of Alberta, Canada |
| Alex Goslen | North Carolina State University, USA |
| Vikram Goyal | IIIT-Delhi, India |
| Quanlong Guan | Jinan University, China |
| Jiong Guo | Northwest Normal University, China |
| Zhihan Guo | University of Hong Kong, China |
| Shivang Gupta | Carnegie Mellon University, USA |
| Ashish Gurung | Carnegie Mellon University, USA |
| Ella Haig | University of Portsmouth, UK |
| Songhee Han | University of Texas at Austin, USA |
| Jiangang Hao | Educational Testing Service, USA |
| Soroush Hashemifar | Iran University of Science and Technology, Iran |
| Carl Haynes-Magyar | University of Pittsburgh, USA |
| Liqun He | University College London, UK |
| Xinyu He | Central China Normal University, China |
| Owen Henkel | University of Oxford, UK |
| Davinia Hernandez-Leo | Universitat Pompeu Fabra, Spain |
| Ben Hicks | University of Technology Sydney, Australia |
| Camila Hidalgo | Technical University of Munich, Germany |
| Langdon Holmes | Vanderbilt University, USA |
| Joanna Holt | Amsterdam University of Applied Sciences, Netherlands |
| Anett Hoppe | Philipps-Universität Marburg & Hessian Center for AI; TIB Leibniz Information Centre for Science and Technology, Germany |
| Chenyu Hou | Nanyang Technological University, Singapore |
| Xinying Hou | University of Michigan, USA |
| Zhifei Hu | Durham University, UK |
| Kevin Huang | WestEd, USA |
| Lingyun Huang | Education University of Hong Kong, China |
| Xiaoshan Huang | McGill University, Canada |
| Samuel Hum | University of Illinois Urbana-Champaign, USA |

| | |
|---|---|
| Hui-Chun Hung | National Central University, Taiwan |
| Haerim Hwang | Chinese University of Hong Kong, China |
| Kevin Hwang | Glenelg High School, USA |
| Soo Hyoung Joo | Columbia University, USA |
| Eleni Ilkou | TIB Leibniz Information Centre for Science and Technology, Germany |
| Paul Inventado | California State University Fullerton, USA |
| Sehrish Iqbal | Monash University, Australia |
| Tsunenori Ishioka | National Center for University Entrance Examinations, Japan |
| Md Mirajul Islam | North Carolina State University, USA |
| Daneih Ismail | DePaul University, USA |
| Percy Jardine | Monash University, Australia |
| Vimukthini Jayalath | University of South Australia, Australia |
| Hyangeun Ji | Temple University, USA |
| Qiao Jin | North Carolina State University, USA |
| Yueqiao Jin | Monash University, Australia |
| Julian Marvin Jörs | Otto-von-Guericke-Universität Magdeburg, Germany |
| Jiyoon Jung | Valdosta State University, USA |
| Vishav Jyoti | IIT Gandhinagar, India |
| Shiming Kai | Columbia University, USA |
| Hamid Karimi | Utah State University, USA |
| Enkelejda Kasneci | Technical University of Munich, Germany |
| Stamos Katsigiannis | Durham University, UK |
| Mizue Kayama | Shinshu University, Japan |
| Priyanka Khare | North Carolina State University, USA |
| Beaumie Kim | University of Calgary, Canada |
| Chanmin Kim | Pennsylvania State University, USA |
| Min Kyu Kim | Georgia State University, USA |
| Badmavasan Kirouchenassamy | LIP6 - Sorbonne Université, France |
| Aleksandra Klasnja-Milicevic | University of Novi Sad, Serbia |
| Ekaterina Kochmar | Mohamed Bin Zayed University of Artificial Intelligence, United Arab Emirates |
| Elizabeth Koh | National Institute of Education, Nanyang Technological University, Singapore |
| Kento Koike | Tokyo University of Science, Japan |
| Kazuaki Kojima | Teikyo University, Japan |
| Maria Konte | Georgia Institute of Technology, USA |
| Sotiris Kotsiantis | University of Patras, Greece |
| Nikhil Krishnaswamy | Colorado State University, USA |
| Zuzana Kubincová | Comenius University, Bratislava, Slovakia |

| | |
|---|---|
| Naiming Liu | Rice University, USA |
| Qinyi Liu | University of Bergen, Norway |
| Shiqi Liu | Central China Normal University, China |
| Tianqiao Liu | TAL AI Lab, China |
| Zhichun Liu | University of Hong Kong, China |
| Ziyuan Liu | Singapore Management University, USA |
| Giosué Lo Bosco | Università di Palermo, Italy |
| Angelica Lo Duca | IIT-CNR, Italy |
| Xinyi Lu | University of Michigan, USA |
| Nicholas Lytle | Georgia Institute of Technology, USA |
| Bailing Lyu | University of Utah, USA |
| Boxuan Ma | Kyushu University, Japan |
| Qianou Ma | Carnegie Mellon University, USA |
| Konrad Maciborski | Polish-Japanese Academy of Information Technology, Poland |
| John Magee | Clark University, USA |
| George Magoulas | Birkbeck College, University of London, UK |
| Subhankar Maity | ECE Paris, France |
| Aditi Mallavarapu | North Carolina State University, USA |
| Ivana Marenzi | L3S Research Center, Germany |
| Leonardo Brandão Marques | Federal University of Alagoas, Brazil |
| Alejandra Martínez-Monés | Universidad de Valladolid, Spain |
| Wannisa Matcha | Prince of Songkla University, Thailand |
| Yuichiroh Matsubayashi | Tohoku University, Japan |
| Tatsunori Matsui | Waseda University, Japan |
| Lindsay Clare Matsumura | University of Pittsburgh, USA |
| Hunter McNichols | University of Massachusetts Amherst, USA |
| Guilherme Medeiros Machado | ECE Paris, France |
| Paola Mejia Domenzain | EPFL, Switzerland |
| Grzegorz Meller | KU Leuven, Belgium |
| Xianghui Meng | Columbia University, USA |
| Donatella Merlini | Università di Firenze, Italy |
| Marcus Messer | Imperial, UK |
| Jamie Mikeska | Educational Testing Service, USA |
| Marcelo Milrad | Linnaeus University, Sweden |
| Tsunenori Mine | Kyushu University, Japan |
| Sein Minn | Inria, France |
| Kamila Misiejuk | FernUniversität Hagen, Germany |
| Tsegaye Misikir Tashu | University of Groningen, Netherlands |
| Yoshimitsu Miyazawa | National Center for University Entrance Examinations, Japan |
| Mukesh Mohania | IIIT Delhi, India |

| | |
|---|---|
| Wesley Morris | Vanderbilt University, USA |
| Ana Mouta | University of Salamanca, Spain |
| Hanni Muukkonen | University of Oulu, Finland |
| Pedro J. Muñoz-Merino | Universidad Carlos III de Madrid, Spain |
| Shatha N. Alkhasawneh | Pompeu Fabra University, Spain |
| Takashi Nagai | Institute of Technologists, Japan |
| Nurun Nahar | University of Greater Manchester, UK |
| Nidhi Nasiar | University of Pennsylvania, USA |
| Tanya Nazaretsky | EPFL, Switzerland |
| Léo Nebel | Sorbonne Université, France |
| Seyed Parsa Neshaei | EPFL, Switzerland |
| Jeremy T. D. Ng | University of Hong Kong, China |
| Manh Hung Nguyen | Max Planck Institute for Software Systems, Germany |
| Yasuhiro Noguchi | Shizuoka University, Japan |
| Ange Adrienne Nyamen Tato | Université Laval, Canada |
| Xavier Ochoa | New York University, USA |
| Soon Young Oh | Michigan State University, USA |
| Santiago Ojeda-Ramirez | University of California, Irvine, USA |
| Jeroen Ooge | Utrecht University, Belgium |
| María Óskarsdóttir | Reykjavík University, Iceland |
| Erin Ottmar | Worcester Polytechnic Institute, USA |
| Abdelkader Ouared | LIUM: Laboratoire d'Informatique de l'Université du Mans, France |
| Ranilson Paiva | Universidade Federal de Alagoas, Brazil |
| Martha Palmer | University of Colorado Boulder, USA |
| Viktoria Pammer-Schindler | Graz University of Technology, Austria |
| Prajakt Pande | Southern Methodist University, USA, and Aarhus University, Denmark |
| Maciej Pankiewicz | University of Pennsylvania, USA |
| Zaki Pauzi | University College London, UK |
| Bernardo Pereira Nunes | Australian National University, Australia |
| Margaret Perkoff | University of Pennsylvania, USA |
| Tung Phung | Max Planck Institute for Software Systems, Germany |
| Yang Pian | Beijing Normal University, China |
| Benjamin Pierce | University of Pittsburgh, USA |
| Gerti Pishtari | University for Continuing Education Krems (Danube University), Austria |
| Eduard Pogorskiy | Open Files LTD, UK |
| Allison Poh | University of Massachusetts Amherst, USA |
| Miguel Portaz | Universidad Nacional de Educación a Distancia, Spain |

| | |
|---|---|
| Victor Prado | Federal University of Rio de Janeiro, Brazil |
| Vijay Prakash | Indian Institute of Technology Bombay, India |
| Ethan Prihar | EPFL, Switzerland |
| James Pustejovsky | Brandeis University, USA |
| Pipob Puthipiroj | Northwestern University, USA |
| Mar Pérez-Sanagustín | Université de Toulouse, France |
| Ronald Pérez-Álvarez | Universidad de Costa Rica, Costa Rica |
| Kun Qian | Columbia University, USA |
| Liu Qiang | Sichuan Chengdu Shude High School, China |
| Emanuel Queiroga | Federal University of Pelotas, Brazil |
| Napol Rachatasumrit | Carnegie Mellon University, USA |
| Anna Radtke | Center for Advanced Internet Studies, Germany |
| Yuvaraj Rajamanickam | Anna University, India |
| Yasitha Rajapaksha | North Carolina State University, USA |
| Ramkumar Rajendran | IIT Bombay, India |
| Ilana Ram | Technion Israel Institute of Technology, Israel |
| Sowmya Ramachandran | Stottler Henke Associates Inc, USA |
| Injila Rasul | University of Massachusetts Amherst, USA |
| Manikandan Ravikiran | Thoughtworks AI Research Labs/IIT Mandi, India |
| Traian Rebedea | University Politehnica of Bucharest, Romania |
| Marcelo Reis | Universidade Federal de Alagoas, Brazil |
| Valérie Renault | Le Mans University, France |
| Shannon Rios | University of Melbourne, Australia |
| Sina Rismanchian | University of California, Irvine, USA |
| Luiz Rodrigues | Federal University of Technology - Paraná, Brazil |
| Carlos Felipe Rodriguez-Hernandez | Tecnológico de Monterrey, Mexico |
| José Raúl Romero | University of Córdoba, Spain |
| Rinat B. Rosenberg-Kima | Technion - Israel Institute of Technology, Israel |
| Daniela Rotelli | Sorbonne Université, France |
| José A. Ruipérez Valiente | University of Murcia, Spain |
| Stefan Ruseti | University "Politehnica" of Bucharest, Romania |
| Sylvio Rüdian | Humboldt-Universität zu Berlin, Germany |
| John Sabatini | University of Memphis, USA |
| Isabella Saccardi | Utrecht University, Netherlands |
| Nicy Scaria | Indian Institute of Science, India |
| Daniele Schicchi | CNR ITD, Italy |
| Ratan Sebastian | TIB Leibniz Information Centre for Science and Technology, Germany |
| Martha Shaka | University of Dodoma, Tanzania |
| Kshitij Sharma | Norwegian University of Science and Technology, Norway |

| | |
|---|---|
| Paras Sharma | University of Pittsburgh, USA |
| Vyom Sharma | Hippocratic AI, USA |
| Ryan Shea | Columbia University, USA |
| Bruce Sherin | Northwestern University, USA |
| Wanruo Shi | Tsinghua University, China |
| Atsushi Shimada | Kyushu University, Japan |
| Kazutaka Shimada | Kyushu Institute of Technology, Japan |
| Machi Shimmei | Tohoku University, Japan |
| Jinnie Shin | University of Florida, USA |
| Hajime Shirouzu | National Institute for Educational Policy Research, Japan |
| Momin Siddiqui | Georgia Institute of Technology, USA |
| Abubakir Siedahmed | Worcester Polytechnic Institute, USA |
| Aditi Singh | Cleveland State University, USA |
| Daevesh Singh | Indian Institute of Technology Bombay, India |
| Jasbir Singh | University of Otago, New Zealand |
| Andy Smith | North Carolina State University, USA |
| David Smith | Virginia Tech, USA |
| Shashank Sonkar | Rice University, USA |
| Deniz Sonmez Unal | University of Pittsburgh, USA |
| Marcus Specht | Delft University of Technology, Netherlands |
| Frank Stinar | University of Illinois Urbana-Champaign, USA |
| Amy Stornaiuolo | University of Pennsylvania, USA |
| Abhijit Suresh | University of Colorado Boulder, USA |
| Juan Andrés Talamás Carvajal | Tecnológico de Monterrey, Mexico |
| May Marie P. Talandron-Felipe | University of Sciencc and Technology of Southern Philippines, Philippines |
| Danielle R. Thomas | Carnegie Mellon University, USA |
| Xiaoyi Tian | North Carolina State University, USA |
| Sutapa Dey Tithi | North Carolina State University, USA |
| Paula Toledo Palomino | São Paulo State College of Technology (FATEC) - Matão \| Center for Excellence in Social Technologies (NEES-UFAL), Brazil |
| Christos Troussas | University of West Attica, Greece |
| Anne Trumbore | University of Virginia, USA |
| Ashwin Tudur Sadashiva | Vanderbilt University, USA |
| Onuralp Ulusoy | Utrecht University, Netherlands |
| Sam Urmian | University of Bergen, Norway |
| Masaki Uto | University of Electro-Communications, Japan |
| Giacomo Valente | University of L'Aquila, Italy |
| Enrique Valero-Leal | Universidad Politécnica de Madrid, Spain |
| Gerben van der Hoek | SG Huizermaat, Netherlands |

| | |
|---|---|
| Kaixun Yang | Monash University, Australia |
| Kexin Yang | University of Pennsylvania, USA |
| Pingjing Yang | University of Illinois Urbana-Champaign, USA |
| Weipeng Yang | Education University of Hong Kong, China |
| Yin Nicole Yang | Education University of Hong Kong, China |
| Zhiwei Yang | Jinan University, China |
| Chengyuan Yao | Teachers College, Columbia University, USA |
| Mingrui Ye | King's College London, UK |
| Seyma N. Yildirim-Erbasli | Concordia University of Edmonton, Canada |
| Hao Yu | Boston University, USA |
| Annie Yuan | University of Sydney, Australia |
| Guangji Yuan | National Institute of Education, Nanyang Technological Universit, Singapore |
| Andres Felipe Zambrano | University of Pennsylvania, USA |
| Andrew Zamecnik | University of South Australia, Australia |
| Franck Zenasni | Université Paris Cité, France |
| Chenwei Zhang | University of Hong Kong, China |
| Jianwei Zhang | University at Albany, USA |
| Jiayi Zhang | University of Pennsylvania, USA |
| Shan Zhang | University of Florida, USA |
| Shugang Zhang | Ocean University of China, China |
| Yi Zhang | Beijing Normal University, China |
| Yujing Zhang | University of Hong Kong, China |
| Chenyan Zhao | University of Illinois Urbana-Champaign, USA |
| Chloe Qianhui Zhao | Carnegie Mellon University, USA |
| Linxuan Zhao | Monash University, Australia |
| Yiling Zhao | Stanford University, USA |
| Jinxin Zhu | Education University of Hong Kong, China |
| Min Zhuang | North Carolina State University, USA |
| Stefano Zingaro | Università di Bologna, Italy |

## International Artificial Intelligence in Education (IAIED) Society

## IAIED Management Board

### President

| | |
|---|---|
| Seiji Isotani | University of Pennsylvania, USA |

## Secretary

| | |
|---|---|
| Olga C. Santos | Universidad Nacional de Educación a Distancia, Spain |

## Journal Editors

| | |
|---|---|
| Vincent Aleven | Carnegie Mellon University, USA |
| Cristina Conati | University of British Columbia, Canada |
| Marcus Specht | Delft University of Technology, Netherlands |

## Finance Chair

| | |
|---|---|
| Benedict du Boulay | University of Sussex, UK |

## Membership Chair

| | |
|---|---|
| Benjamin D. Nye | University of Southern California, USA |

## Publicity Chair

| | |
|---|---|
| Irene-Angelica Chounta | University of Duisburg-Essen, Germany |

## IAIED Officers

| | |
|---|---|
| Xinyuan Hao | University College London, UK |
| Jionghao Lin | University of Hong Kong, China |

## IAIED Executive Committee

| | |
|---|---|
| Ig Ibert Bittencourt | Universidade Federal de Alagoas, Brazil |
| Min Chi | North Carolina State University, USA |
| Irene-Angelica Chounta | University of Duisburg-Essen, Germany |
| Cristina Conati | University of British Columbia, Canada |
| Alexandra I. Cristea | Durham University, UK |

| | |
|---|---|
| Neil Heffernan | Worcester Polytechnic Institute, USA |
| Seiji Isotani | University of Pennsylvania, USA |
| Noboru Matsuda | North Carolina State University, USA |
| Bruce M. McLaren | Carnegie Mellon University, USA |
| Tanja Mitrovic | University of Canterbury, New Zealand |
| Andrew M. Olney | University of Memphis, USA |
| Erin Walker | University of Pittsburgh, USA |
| Beverly Park Woolf | University of Massachusetts Amherst, USA |
| Diego Zapata-Rivera | Educational Testing Service, USA |

## International Alliance to Advance Learning in the Digital Era (IAALDE)

The IAIED Society is a member of the International Alliance to Advance Learning in the Digital Era (IAALDE) and belongs to its board. IAIED is currently represented at IAALDE by Seiji Isotani (University of Pennsylvania, USA) as president of IAIED.

## AIED 2026 Sponsors

### Platinum

Gates Foundation

Learning Commons

Google

### Silver

/*elice*/

### Bronze

Eedi

VitalSource

### Best Paper Award Sponsorship

Springer

# How Best to Harness AI's Great Potential to Improve Education? (AIED 2026 Keynote)

Vincent Aleven

Human-Computer Interaction Institute, Carnegie Mellon University, USA

**Abstract.** AI has tremendous potential to improve education. For example, a substantial amount of scientific evidence shows that AI-based tutoring systems can help students learn better than other forms of instruction. Also, some scientific evidence suggests that AI-based tutoring systems can help reduce inequalities in the educational system, even if not all available evidence points in this direction. Yet, in the USA, standardized test scores are stagnant, including in K-12 mathematics learning, where AI-based tutoring systems are often used. Nor is there evidence that existing inequalities within the educational system are shrinking. These results are beginning to lead to calls to outlaw the use of computers in classrooms, in the USA and elsewhere. How might we reconcile these seemingly opposing views from research and educational practice? More importantly, what might researchers do to help improve educational outcomes? We propose that it is important to focus on creating favorable circumstances for the use of AI-based tutoring systems. To this end, it is productive to view the smart classroom as a socio-technical ecosystem with many stakeholders: students, in the first place, and "facilitators" such as teachers, peers, human tutors, and parents/caregivers. By carefully designing human-AI interactions to support these stakeholders, we stand a good chance to harness AI's great potential to improve education and reduce educational inequalities. We illustrate this vision with several example projects and promising empirical results from our lab. In these projects, students use AI-based tutoring software and facilitators are helped by a variety of novel AI-based tools, including a mixed-reality analytics-based awareness tool for teachers, support for goal setting for students, and small-dosage AI-supported remote human tutoring.

## Biography

Dr. Vincent Aleven is a Professor of Human-Computer Interaction at Carnegie Mellon University. As the head of the Creating Adaptive Tutoring Software (CATS) Lab, he investigates how AI can enhance education. His lab focuses on prototyping new designs for the smart classroom, with projects ranging from optimizing the design of AI-based tutoring systems, to a real-time mixed-reality teacher awareness tool, to easy-to-use authoring tools for creating AI-based tutoring systems. His work builds on cognitive theory and theories of self-regulated learning and helps extend the empirical science of how people learn with adaptive learning technologies. He has over 300 publications, is co-editor-in-chief of the International Journal of Artificial Intelligence in Education, received over 25 major research grants, and won 12 best paper awards at international conferences.

# Contents

**Track 3 - Societal Aspects of AIED - Short Papers**

# Scaffolding Critical Engagement with GenAI: Transforming Ethnic Minority Preparatory Students' Collaborative Discourse in Prompt Engineering Tasks

Deliang Wang[1] and Cunling Bian[2](✉)

[1] Faculty of Education, The University of Hong Kong, Hong Kong, China
wdeliang@connect.hku.hk
[2] Department of Education, Ocean University of China, Qingdao, China
clbian@ouc.edu.cn

**Abstract.** Generative AI (GenAI) holds significant promise for advancing educational equity among ethnic minority students by broadening access to learning resources and mitigating linguistic barriers. However, these benefits are counterbalanced by the risk of cognitive laziness, whereby students may treat GenAI as an answer engine or shortcut rather than as a partner in thinking. This design-based research investigated how pedagogical scaffolding can shift students from passive consumption to critical co-creation with GenAI. The study involved 78 ethnic minority preparatory students in China participating in a three-week GenAI course that integrated a human-in-the-loop workflow and teacher modeling with contrasting cases to disrupt uncritical reliance on GenAI. We employed epistemic network analysis to examine collaborative discourse, thematic analysis to analyze student reflections, and paired-samples $t$-tests to assess changes in prompt self-efficacy. Results revealed a phenomenon of strategic repurposing: initially, students instrumentalized strategy talk to coordinate efficient copying; however, after the intervention, they realigned strategic planning to scaffold critical evaluation and peer co-construction. Qualitative findings further indicated that the teacher's scaffolding helped students overcome their initial authority bias and prompt paralysis, repositioning themselves as active gatekeepers of AI-generated content; these shifts were corroborated by a significant increase in students' prompt self-efficacy. The study suggests that, particularly for ethnic minority students, technical training alone is insufficient; educators should design targeted pedagogical interventions around human–AI collaboration to prevent cognitive complacency and cultivate epistemic agency.

**Keywords:** Educational equity · Ethnic minority students · Generative AI · Collaborative learning · Human-AI collaboration


E. G. Blanchard et al. (eds.), AIED 2026, LNCS 16586, pp. 1–15, 2027.
https://doi.org/10.1007/978-3-032-29773-0_1

## 1 Introduction

Prior to the advent of generative AI (GenAI), educational inequality was largely defined by the unequal distribution of resources [33]. Students from high socioeconomic status (SES) families typically enjoyed privileged access to high-quality educational materials and personalised tutoring [16], whereas their low-SES peers depended primarily on limited school-based provision [26]. This disparity is further exacerbated for ethnic minority students from under-resourced regions. Research indicates that these populations in China face a double disadvantage: significantly lower household income compared to the Han majority [6,12] and substantial linguistic barriers [22]. For many minority students, Mandarin (Putonghua) is a second language, and limited proficiency often impedes their performance in high-stakes examinations such as the Gaokao (i.e., unversity entrance examinations), placing them in a structurally underprivileged position even after they enter higher education [22,27].

The emergence of GenAI has been considered a promising solution to mitigate these forms of inequality by enabling more democratic access to high-quality, personalised educational support, regardless of a student's geographic, economic, or ethnic background [17]. Theoretically, a minority student in a remote region can now access the same AI tutor as a student in highly developed areas such as Beijing or Shanghai. However, recent scholarship cautions that the digital divide is shifting from an *access divide* to a *usage divide* [15]. While disparities in access may be narrowing, disparities in the quality and sophistication of use may be widening. Developed regions, such as Beijing and Shenzhen, have launched large-scale initiatives to provide students with systematic training in digital and AI literacy [1], enabling them to employ GenAI as a tool for critical inquiry and knowledge construction. In contrast, students in disadvantaged contexts, who lack such pedagogical support, are more vulnerable to cognitive reliance or laziness [8], using GenAI primarily as an answer engine or shortcut to bypass cognitive work rather than as a collaborative partner in thinking.

This risk is particularly salient for students enrolled in the ethnic minority preparatory program, a specialised affirmative action policy in China. This program admits minority students from under-resourced regions to elite universities with lower entrance scores, on the condition that they complete a one-year bridging curriculum prior to beginning their undergraduate majors [18]. While GenAI can, in principle, provide these linguistically disadvantaged students with unprecedented access to learning resources [17], it simultaneously creates a risk of cognitive laziness. Without carefully designed pedagogical guidance, students may become dependent on GenAI as a shortcut, rather than using it as a tool for exploration and inquiry [8]. Consequently, bridging the digital divide for this specific population requires more than providing technological access; it calls for empirical evidence on how to transform their interaction with GenAI from passive consumption to critical co-creation through targeted pedagogical interventions.

To address this imperative, it is first necessary to understand how students interact with GenAI in the absence of explicit guidance and then examine how scaffolding reshapes these interaction patterns. The present study therefore tracks the evolution of ethnic minority preparatory students' collaborative discourse over the duration of a three-week GenAI-intensive course. Specifically, we first examine their initial engagement with GenAI under naturalistic, minimally guided conditions to identify authentic challenges. We then introduce teacher scaffolding aimed at fostering more reflective and critical engagement with GenAI. By analysing the trajectory of students' discourse across these distinct phases, the study seeks to illuminate the mechanisms underlying the transformation from dependency to more active epistemic agency. The research questions (RQs) guiding this study are as follows:

- **RQ1**: How does students' collaborative discourse evolve from the initial unguided phase to the post-scaffolding phase?
- **RQ2**: How do students perceive the challenges of initial collaboration and the role of teacher scaffolding in shifting their engagement with GenAI?
- **RQ3**: Is the shift towards critical collaboration associated with improvements in students' prompt self-efficacy?

## 2 Related Work

### 2.1 Educational Dilemmas of Ethnic Minority Students in China

China is a unified multi-ethnic state comprising a Han majority (approximately 91.1% of the population) and 55 officially recognized ethnic minority groups, such as the Uyghur, Tibetan, and Hui, who predominantly reside in peripheral regions, including western and border areas [7]. While these groups possess rich and distinct cultural and linguistic heritages, they often face structural disadvantages within the mainstream education system. As highlighted in the introduction, many ethnic minority students come from under-resourced regions where economic capital is relatively scarce [14]. However, the dilemma extends beyond mere resource access to profound linguistic and pedagogical disconnects.

On the one hand, for many minority students, Mandarin (Putonghua) functions as a second language. The transition from learning in their mother tongue to Mandarin-medium instruction in K–12 and higher education imposes a substantial extraneous cognitive load [23,34]. Research indicates that the continuous effort required for linguistic transcoding competes with the cognitive resources needed for higher-order thinking, making deep comprehension and critical argumentation considerably more demanding for these learners than for their Han peers [27].

On the other hand, studies show that secondary education in many ethnic minority regions is often dominated by traditional, teacher-centred pedagogies that prioritize textbook memorization and exam preparation for high-stakes assessments (e.g., the Gaokao), rather than student-centred approaches that cultivate critical thinking and inquiry-based learning [22]. As a result, these students may develop passive epistemic beliefs, viewing learning primarily as the reception of static facts rather than the active construction of knowledge [4]. This ingrained habit of passivity likely poses a significant challenge when they enter university environments [27] and, later, workplaces where 21st-century skills—such as critical thinking and authentic problem-solving competencies—are emphasised.

### 2.2 The Benefits and Cognitive Risks of GenAI in Education

Recent empirical studies and meta-analyses have provided robust evidence for the positive impact of GenAI on student learning outcomes. Comprehensive reviews indicate that GenAI interventions yield moderate to large effect sizes on academic performance, significantly enhancing learning efficiency and achievement across various disciplines [10,11]. For example, GenAI has been found to positively influences students' lower-order cognitive skills (e.g., basic understanding) and identified as a promising approach for cultivating students' higher-order cognitive skills [32]. In collaborative contexts, such as digital storytelling, GenAI tools have proven effective in augmenting team creativity performance, serving as an ideation partner that helps students overcome creative blocks and generate high-quality content [31].

These performance gains, however, may be accompanied by unintended cognitive costs. Scholars caution that although GenAI can improve the quality of students' products, it may inadvertently encourage cognitive laziness or cognitive dependency [8]. Fan et al. [8] found that students working with GenAI reported significantly lower mental effort and reduced metacognitive monitoring compared with those using conventional tools, suggesting a tendency to offload cognitive work onto the AI. Likewise, Han et al. [13] observed that students—particularly those with a high need for cognitive closure—were inclined to accept AI-generated answers prematurely to avoid uncertainty, rather than engaging in critical evaluation. These findings point to a paradox: students may produce ostensibly better outputs while engaging less deeply with the underlying content, as GenAI replaces rather than productively scaffolds the rigorous cognitive processes required for deep understanding [2,8].

This risk of cognitive offloading is especially concerning for the ethnic minority preparatory students. Given their existing linguistic barriers and potentially entrenched passive epistemic beliefs, these learners may be particularly prone to treating GenAI as an authoritative answer engine rather than a dialogic partner in inquiry. If mainstream university students already struggle with cognitive laziness in GenAI-supported learning [8], the "double disadvantage" experienced by ethnic minority students is likely to magnify this vulnerability. Consequently, merely providing access to GenAI is inadequate; there is a pressing need for carefully designed pedagogical scaffolding that cultivates critical AI literacy and deliberately supports a shift from passive acceptance of AI outputs to reflective, critical co-creation [11,21].

# 3 Method

## 3.1 Context and Participants

This study was conducted with an intact class (N = 78) enrolled in an ethnic minority preparatory programme at an elite university in northern China. As a key affirmative action initiative, this program admits students from under-resourced ethnic minority regions with the aim of promoting educational equity and ethnic solidarity. Admitted students are required to complete a one-year bridging curriculum designed to strengthen their academic foundations before matriculating into their undergraduate majors.

All students in this class were invited to participate in a three-week course on GenAI, in which basic concepts of GenAI and prompt engineering were introduced. Students were required to complete collaborative prompt-engineering tasks. To this end, they were assigned to 13 groups, with each group comprising six ethnic minority students.

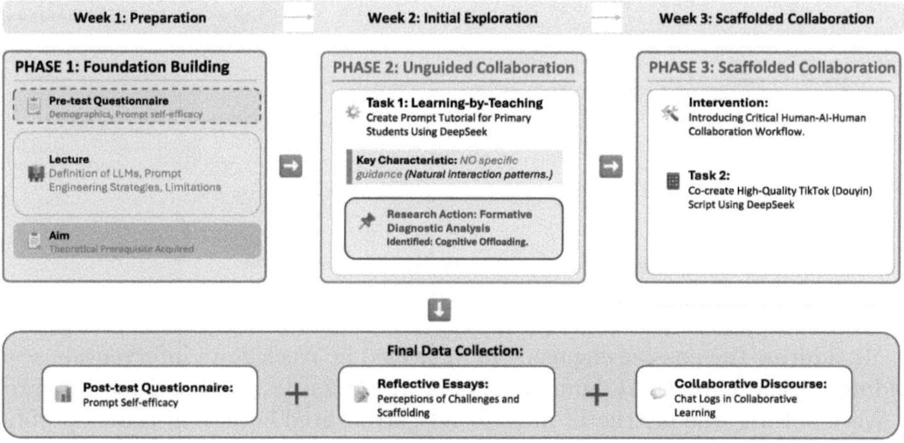


**Fig. 1.** Experimental procedures.

## 3.2 Experimental Procedures and Intervention

As Fig. 1 shows, the study adopted a design-based research approach spanning three weeks, structured into three phases: preparation, initial unguided exploration, and scaffolded collaboration. Each phase was implemented through a weekly two-hour workshop.

The primary objective of Week 1 was to establish a foundational understanding of GenAI among participants. To ascertain students' entry-level characteristics, a pre-test questionnaire was first administered to collect demographic information, prior GenAI experience, and initial self-efficacy in prompt engineering.

Subsequently, the instructor delivered a lecture covering the definition of LLMs, core strategies of prompt engineering, potential technical limitations such as hallucinations, ethical considerations, and illustrative use cases of LLMs. This phase ensured that all students possessed the theoretical prerequisites necessary to operate DeepSeek in the subsequent collaborative tasks.

In Week 2, students undertook their first collaborative task without any explicit pedagogical intervention regarding collaborative strategies. Each group was tasked with using DeepSeek to create a prompt-engineering tutorial for primary school students. This learning-by-teaching task was designed to cognitively challenge students to externalize and organize their understanding of prompting strategies. At the same time, this phase served as a diagnostic window to capture students' authentic, unguided interaction with GenAI and with peers. Immediately after Week 2, the research team reviewed the collaborative discourse and conducted a formative diagnostic analysis. This analysis revealed that several groups frequently copied DeepSeek's outputs with minimal discussion or critical verification.

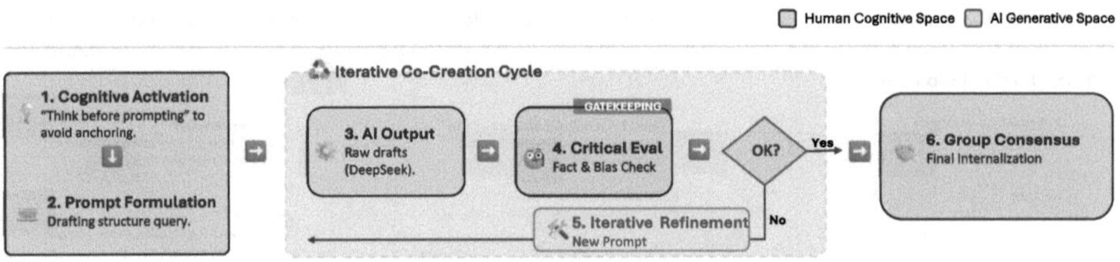


**Fig. 2.** The human-in-the-loop workflow.

To address the passive engagement identified in Week 2, an intervention scaffolding critical human–AI–human collaboration was designed and implemented in Week 3. First, the instructor introduced a structured human-in-the-loop workflow, as shown in Fig. 2. Drawing on the principle of cognitive activation, students were instructed to generate their own initial ideas before querying the AI. This step was explicitly intended to mitigate tendencies to offload cognitive effort to the AI [8] and to reduce anchoring effects. In addition, to foster critical evaluative literacy, the workflow required groups to treat AI outputs as provisional materials requiring fact-checking and scrutiny for potential bias, rather than as authoritative answers [32]. The workflow further emphasized iterative refinement, encouraging students to employ follow-up prompts to interrogate, adjust, and improve the AI's output [31].

Second, to facilitate the internalization of these strategies, the intervention employed instructor modelling with contrasting cases [24]. The instructor presented two simulated collaboration transcripts: a negative example illustrating passive copying and superficial agreement, and a positive example demonstrating critical discussion and iterative inquiry. By comparing these contrasting cases, students were guided to explicitly identify and emulate productive collaborative behaviours. Following this intervention, groups undertook a second authentic task: using DeepSeek to co-create a high-quality script for a specialised TikTok video. This task demanded greater creativity and contextual judgement, thereby providing a testing ground for the newly acquired critical collaboration strategies.

At the conclusion of Week 3, data collection was completed. Students filled out a post-test questionnaire assessing their prompt-engineering self-efficacy and submitted reflective essays describing the challenges they encountered during the initial collaboration, as well as their perceptions of how the instructor's scaffolding influenced their engagement with GenAI.

### 3.3 Data Collection and Analysis

**Collaborative Discourse Data**

*Coding Scheme.* To investigate how collaborative discourse evolved from the initial unguided phase to the post-scaffolding phase (RQ1), we applied a coding scheme to annotate students' engagement in group chat logs and then analyzed these annotations using epistemic network analysis (ENA).

The coding scheme, presented in Table 1, was developed based on the ICAP framework [5,29] and adapted to the specific context of human–GenAI collaborative learning [8,19,31]. It classifies each message into five hierarchical levels of engagement: off-topic, passive, active, constructive, and interactive.

Messages unrelated to the learning task were coded as off-topic (OT). *Passive* engagement is characterized by mechanical information sharing (P.Share) or uncritical acceptance (P.Acpt). *Active* engagement involves the activation of prior knowledge to manipulate or reorganize information, such as summarizing AI responses (A.Rprt) or asking operational questions (A.Qst), but without generating new inferences. *Constructive* engagement represents the core of critical engagement, where learners generate ideas that go beyond the information directly provided. This level includes three types of cognitive behavior: articulating abstract strategies for prompt engineering (C.Stra), critically evaluating the quality, style, or validity of AI outputs (C.Crit), and iteratively refining prompts based on reflection (C.Refi). Finally, *Interactive* engagement involves dialogic co-construction, where students build on (I.Build) or negotiate (I.Neg) peers' ideas in relation to the AI-generated content, rather than interacting solely with the tool. Following the "high-road" coding rule, the highest level of engagement evidenced in a message was assigned as its final code.

*Coding Procedure.* To ensure the reliability of the coding, two researchers first independently coded a randomly selected subsample of the dataset (approximately 20% of all messages). Discrepancies were discussed and resolved, leading to refinement of the coding manual. The two researchers then independently coded the remaining messages. Inter-rater reliability, calculated using Cohen's kappa, yielded a coefficient of $\kappa = 0.88$, indicating substantial agreement. All remaining disagreements were resolved through discussion.

**Table 1.** The coding scheme for analyzing collaborative discourse.

| Level | Code | Definition | Examples |
|---|---|---|---|
| Level 0: Off-Topic | OT (Off-Topic) | Content unrelated to the task (e.g., gossip, lunch, socializing). | "Are we going to the canteen later?" |
| Level 1: Passive | P.Share (Mechanical Sharing) | Copy-pasting AI text, sharing screenshots, or sending links without analysis. | [Sends a screenshot of DeepSeek] / "Here is the answer." |
| | P.Acpt (Uncritical Acceptance) | Blind agreement with AI or peers. Simple acknowledgments or stickers. | "Okay." / "Received." / [Sticker: Nodding] |
| Level 2: Active | A.Rprt (Active Reporting) | Summarizing, paraphrasing, or translating the AI's output. | "DeepSeek suggested three scenes: a classroom, a playground, and a dorm." |
| | A.Qst (Operational Questioning) | Questions focused on task logistics or tool operation rather than content depth. | "How do I input this prompt?" / "Did you send the screenshot yet?" |
| Level 3: Constructive | C.Stra (Strategy Talk) | Articulating abstract rules or strategies for prompting engineering. | "To get a good script, we must specify the target audience clearly in the prompt." |
| | C.Refi (Iterative Refinement) | Proposing specific changes to the prompt or refining the output based on reflection. | "Let's change the prompt to 'act as a funny blogger' to get a better hook." |
| | C.Crit (Critical Evaluation) | Explicitly judging the quality, style, or validity of the AI's output. | "This script is too formal; it doesn't sound like a Douyin video at all." |
| Level 4: Interactive | I.Build (Co-Construction) | Extending, elaborating, or challenging a peer's contribution. | "I agree with your idea to make the tone funnier, and we can ask DeepSeek to use internet slang." |
| | I.Neg (Negotiation) | Discussing conflicting views among group members or negotiating choices. | "You think we should use Script A, but I think Script B is better. Let's vote." |

*ENA.* ENA is a quantitative ethnographic method used to analyze patterns of co-occurrence among coded elements in discourse data [25]. It models and visualizes the structure and strength of connections among discourse elements as networks, and allows for comparison of these networks across different conditions [9,28,30].

In applying ENA to the collaborative discourse in this study, we specified four key components: codes, conversations, units of analysis, and stanzas. *Codes* corresponded to the engagement codes assigned to each message using the aforementioned scheme. *Conversations* referred to the messages exchanged among students within a given collaborative task. The *unit of analysis* was defined as the combination of week (Week 2 or Week 3) and group, such that each unit represented the discourse produced by a particular group in a given week. Finally, the *stanza* specified the window of co-occurrence for ENA modeling; in this study, we employed a moving stanza window of five consecutive messages.

**Reflective Data.** Students' reflective essays were analyzed using thematic analysis [3]. The first author repeatedly read the essays and generated initial codes related to the challenges experienced during the initial collaboration and the perceived role of teacher scaffolding in reshaping students' engagement with GenAI. Next, themes were inductively identified from these initial codes, refined, and clearly named. To ensure credibility, the second author reviewed the coding scheme to enhance its content validity. Revisions were made until both authors reached agreement on the scheme. Finally, the first and second authors independently applied the revised coding scheme to the full dataset. All remaining discrepancies were discussed and resolved.

**Prompt Self-efficacy Data.** Prompt self-efficacy data were collected using an adapted scale [20] designed to assess users' confidence in their ability to craft effective prompts for LLMs. The scale comprises eight items rated on a 5-point Likert scale ranging from 1 ("Strongly disagree") to 5 ("Strongly agree"). A paired-samples $t$-test was conducted to examine whether there was a significant improvement in students' prompt self-efficacy after the course.

## 4 Results

### 4.1 Collaborative Discourse

Figure 3 visualizes the epistemic networks of students' cognitive engagement during the unguided (Fig. 3a) and scaffolded (Fig. 3b) phases. In these sociograms, nodes represent cognitive codes, with their size proportional to the frequency of occurrence, while edges represent the relative strength of co-occurrence between behaviors. Thicker edges denote a higher probability that two cognitive behaviors appeared in close proximity, revealing the underlying structural patterns of student discourse.

As illustrated in Fig. 3a, the unguided discourse network reveals a paradoxical pattern regarding the role of strategic planning. While students frequently engaged in Strategy Talk (C.Stra), the strongest co-occurrences linked this high-level code directly to passive sharing (P.Share) and uncritical acceptance (P.Acpt). This counter-intuitive structural configuration suggests that without scaffolding, students' strategic discussions were instrumental rather than epistemic—aimed at efficiently generating content for immediate cognitive offloading rather than deep inquiry. The prominent connections between these nodes indicate a plan-and-paste loop, where strategy formulation served primarily to expedite the completion of the task via mechanical copying.

In stark contrast, the scaffolded network (Fig. 3b) demonstrates a fundamental topological shift towards high-order engagement. While P.Share and P.Acpt

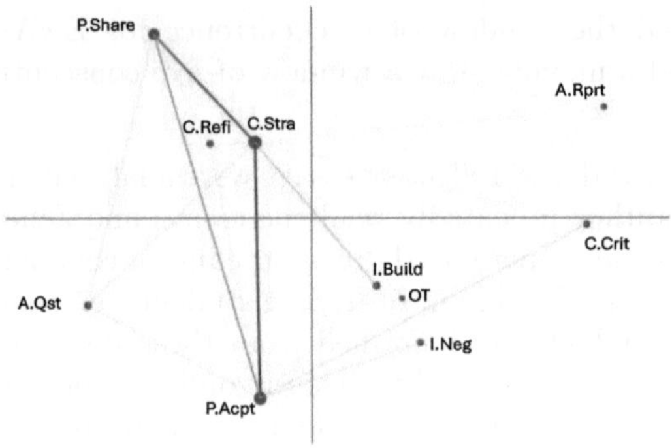


(a) The overall network of cognitive engagement in unguided collaboration.

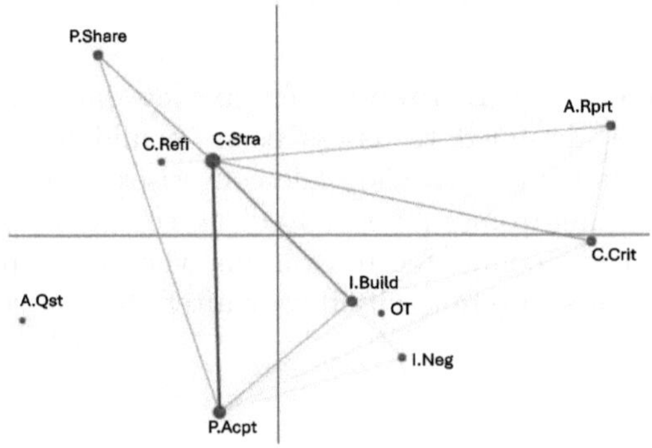


(b) The overall network of cognitive engagement in scaffolded collaboration.

**Fig. 3.** Students' epistemic network.

persist, the network structure has reconfigured around constructive and interactive nodes. Crucially, the connectivity of C.Stra transformed significantly; it formed a strong coherent cluster with Summarizing (A.Rprt) and Critical Evaluation (C.Crit), as well as linking to Co-construction (I.Build). This indicates that the intervention successfully repurposed strategy talk: instead of serving as a prelude to passive copying, strategies were deployed to guide the summarization and critical scrutiny of AI outputs. The emergence of the C.Stra—A.Rprt—C.Crit triad suggests a more sophisticated workflow where students articulated a strategy, summarized the AI's response to check alignment, and then critically evaluated its quality.

Figure 4 explicitly quantifies these structural transformations through the subtracted network. The dominance of red edges (representing associations stronger in the unguided phase) connecting P.Share and C.Stra visually highlights the "metacognitive disconnect" characteristic of the initial phase, where planning collapsed into passive execution. Conversely, the dense blue connec-

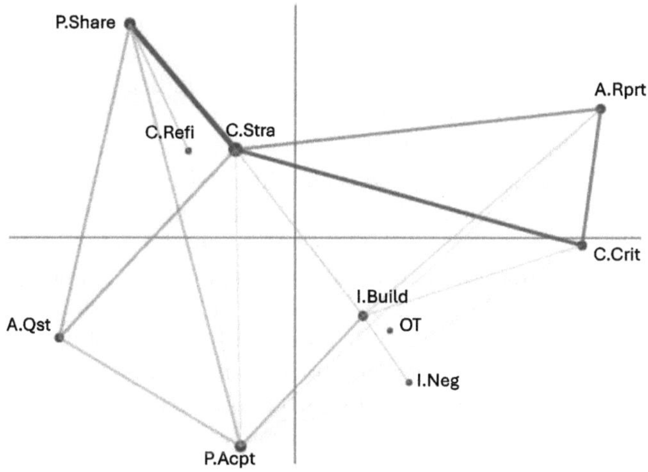


**Fig. 4.** The subtracted network showing differences in students' cognitive engagement between unguided collaboration and scaffolded collaboration. (Color figure online)

tions (representing associations stronger in the scaffolded phase) linking C.Stra, C.Crit, A. Rprt, and I.Build provide robust empirical evidence of the intervention's efficacy. These patterns suggest that teacher scaffolding did not merely increase the frequency of constructive behaviors but fundamentally altered the functional role of strategic planning, fostering a transition from passive consumption to critical co-creation with GenAI.

### 4.2 Students' Perceptions of Challenges and Scaffolding

The thematic analysis of students' reflections indicated that their initial passive reliance on GenAI arose from a combination of limited prompt literacy and a pronounced epistemic asymmetry between themselves and the tool. With respect to the challenges of unguided collaboration, students frequently reported a sense of "prompting paralysis": they did not simply lack operational knowledge of the tool, but struggled to translate vague, abstract intentions into explicit prompts that the LLM could process effectively. Several participants described the frustration of "knowing what to ask in mind but being unable to phrase it in a way the AI understood", which often resulted in irrelevant or only partially useful responses that they felt unable to revise or redirect.

More fundamentally, the analysis suggested that such cognitive offloading (e.g., direct copy-pasting of AI-generated text) was driven by an authority bias compounded by low academic self-efficacy. Students explicitly acknowledged that they tended to accept AI outputs because they perceived them as "more professional and organized" than their own writing, or because, under time pressure, the AI's responses appeared "good enough." In this sense, many students positioned GenAI as an epistemic authority to be deferred to rather than a tool to be interrogated and appropriated, which in turn created a psychological barrier to critical engagement.

Students' accounts of the scaffolding phase indicated that the teacher intervention—particularly the modeling with contrasting cases—functioned as an important turning point that reconfigured their collaborative norms with GenAI. They did not experience the scaffolding merely as technical training in prompt design, but as a deliberate challenge to their initial blind trust in algorithmic outputs. The juxtaposition of high- and low-quality collaboration examples helped students recognize their own passive practices (e.g., unconscious acceptance) as detrimental to learning. In response, many reported a shift in their perceived agency: they began to see themselves as active evaluators or gatekeepers of AI-generated content rather than passive recipients.

Following the intervention, several groups described establishing explicit norms to "cross-check possible AI hallucinations" and to engage in "iterative negotiation" with the tool by refining prompts and requesting revisions instead of accepting the first response. As one student reflected, the scaffolding encouraged them "not to accept the AI's answer directly, but to examine its logic and adapt it to our specific context." Overall, these reflections suggest that the pedagogical guidance helped re-centre human judgement and disciplinary knowledge as the primary drivers of the human–GenAI collaborative process.

### 4.3 Prompt Self-efficacy

Table 2 reports the results of the paired-samples $t$-test comparing students' prompt self-efficacy before and after the teacher intervention. Although 78 students participated in the study, complete pre- and post-test data were available for 71 students. The results show that, in the pre-test, students reported a mean prompt self-efficacy score of 3.757 ($SD = 0.654$), whereas in the post-test, the mean score increased to 3.991 ($SD = 0.589$). The paired-samples $t$-test ($t = 3.729$, $p < .001$) indicates that students' perceived prompt self-efficacy was significantly higher after the intervention than before it, suggesting a meaningful improvement in their confidence in crafting prompts.

**Table 2.** The results of the paired-samples t test.

| | N | Mean | SD | t | p |
|---|---|---|---|---|---|
| pre-test | 71 | 3.757 | 0.654 | 3.729 | < .001 |
| post-test | 71 | 3.991 | 0.589 | | |

## 5 Discussion and Conclusion

This study addresses the need to support underrepresented ethnic minority students in learning how to collaborate critically with GenAI. While GenAI can provide a powerful linguistic scaffold for these learners, our findings offer empirical evidence that access alone does not guarantee deep learning; without pedagogical guidance, it may inadvertently foster cognitive complacency. We conducted a three-week design-based research intervention with 78 ethnic minority preparatory students and examined (a) the evolution of collaborative discourse using epistemic network analysis, (b) students' perceptions using thematic analysis, and (c) changes in prompt self-efficacy using statistical analysis. With respect to discourse evolution, the study revealed a trajectory from instrumental to epistemic engagement: initially, students used GenAI primarily to enable passive copying, whereas after the intervention they increasingly engaged in critical evaluation and peer co-construction. The thematic analysis of students' reflective essays further indicated that their initial passive reliance on GenAI stemmed from a combination of limited prompt literacy and a pronounced epistemic asymmetry between themselves and the tool, whereas the teacher's scaffolding helped them overcome their initial authority bias and prompt paralysis and reposition themselves as active gatekeepers of AI outputs. This transition was corroborated by a significant increase in students' prompt self-efficacy. Overall, the findings underscore the necessity of metacognitive scaffolding for learners from diverse or under-resourced backgrounds. For ethnic minority students in particular, we argue that technical training alone is insufficient; educators should design targeted pedagogical interventions around human–AI collaboration to avoid cognitive complacency and cultivate epistemic agency.

Despite these contributions, several limitations should be acknowledged. First, the study was conducted within a specific context—an ethnic minority preparatory program in China—so the findings may not readily generalize to other populations or educational settings. Second, the three-week duration, although sufficient to observe immediate shifts in discourse and self-efficacy, does not guarantee the long-term maintenance of these critical collaborative habits. Future research should employ longitudinal designs to examine whether norms of critical human–AI collaboration persist as students transition into their undergraduate studies, and how these interaction patterns adapt to different disciplinary tasks and demands.

## References

1. Beijing Municipal Education Commission: Notice on issuing the "Beijing action plan for promoting artificial intelligence education in primary and secondary schools (2025–2027)" [beijing shi tuijin zhongxiaoxue rengongzhineng jiaoyu gongzuo fangan] (2025). https://jw.beijing.gov.cn/xxgk/2024zcwj/2024qtwj/202503/t20250307_4028227.html, policy Document No. 2 [2025] of the Beijing Education Office. (in Chinese)
2. Bhullar, P.S., Joshi, M., Chugh, R.: Chatgpt in higher education-a synthesis of the literature and a future research agenda. Educ. Inf. Technol. **29**(16), 21501–21522 (2024)
3. Braun, V., Clarke, V.: Using thematic analysis in psychology. Qual. Res. Psychol. **3**(2), 77–101 (2006)
4. Chan, K.W., Elliott, R.G.: Relational analysis of personal epistemology and conceptions about teaching and learning. Teach. Teach. Educ. **20**(8), 817–831 (2004)

5. Chi, M.T., Wylie, R.: The ICAP framework: linking cognitive engagement to active learning outcomes. Educ. Psychol. **49**(4), 219–243 (2014)
6. Chia, T., Hruschka, D.: Educational & income disparities among ethnic minorities of China. Int. J. Educ. Dev. **102**, 102846 (2023)
7. National Bureau of Statistics of China: Main data of the seventh national population census (2021)
8. Fan, Y., et al.: Beware of metacognitive laziness: effects of generative artificial intelligence on learning motivation, processes, and performance. Br. J. Edu. Technol. **56**(2), 489–530 (2025)
9. Gao, L., Li, X., Zheng, Y., Li, Y., Wang, D., Bao, H.: Discourse moves and socio-emotional interactions in collaborative argumentation: exploring how their co-occurrence impacts argumentation quality. Think. Skills Creat. **52**, 101525 (2024)
10. Gökoğlu, S., Erdoğdu, F.: The effects of genai on learning performance: a meta-analysis study. Educ. Technol. Soc. **28**(3) (2025)
11. Gu, J., Yan, Z.: Effects of genai interventions on student academic performance: a meta-analysis. J. Educ. Comput. Res. **63**(6), 1460–1492 (2025)
12. Gustafsson, B., Shi, L.: The ethnic minority-majority income gap in rural China during transition. Econ. Dev. Cult. Change **51**(4), 805–822 (2003). https://doi.org/10.1086/377191
13. Han, Z., Ying, R., Huang, C., Tsai, C.C., Wang, X., He, T.: Identifying students' metacognition patterns by their needs for cognitive closure in human-genai collaboration. Comput. Educ. 105422 (2025)
14. Hannum, E., Meiyan, W.: Geography and educational inequality in China. China Econ. Rev. **17**(3), 253–265 (2006)
15. Hendawy, M.: The intensified digital divide: comprehending genai. Internet Policy Rev. (2024)
16. Huang, J., Guo, B., Kim, Y., Sherraden, M.: Parental income, assets, borrowing constraints and children's post-secondary education. Child Youth Serv. Rev. **32**(4), 585–594 (2010)
17. James, T., Andrews, G.: Levelling the playing field through genai: harnessing artificial intelligence to bridge educational gaps for equity and disadvantaged students. Widening Participation Lifelong Learn. **26**(3), 250–260 (2024)
18. Liu, X.: Ethnic minority students' access, participation and outcomes in preparatory classes in China: a case study of a school of Minzu education. Asia Pac. J. Educ. **43**(1), 173–188 (2023)
19. Lukešová, A., Jennings, P.J.: Clue before correction: chatgpt-enhanced strategy for promoting autonomous and reflective language learning. Innov. Lang. Learn. Teach. 1–29 (2026)
20. Mun, I.B., Hwang, K.H.: Exploring the influence of prompt self-efficacy: accurate and customized information, perceived ease of use, satisfaction, and continuance intention to use chatgpt. Int. J. Hum.-Comput. Interact. 1–12 (2025)
21. Ouaazki, A., Bergram, K., Farah, J.C., Gillet, D., Holzer, A.: Generative AI-enabled conversational interaction to support self-directed learning experiences in transversal computational thinking. In: Proceedings of the 6th ACM Conference on Conversational User Interfaces, pp. 1–12 (2024)
22. Postiglione, G.A.: Education and Social Change in China: Inequality in a Market Economy: Inequality in a Market Economy. Routledge (2015)
23. Rong, M.: The development of minority education and the practice of bilingual education in xinjiang uyghur autonomous region. Front. Educ. China **4**(2), 188–251 (2009)

24. Schwartz, D.L., Chase, C.C., Oppezzo, M.A., Chin, D.B.: Practicing versus inventing with contrasting cases: the effects of telling first on learning and transfer. J. Educ. Psychol. **103**(4), 759 (2011)
25. Shaffer, D., Ruis, A.: Epistemic network analysis: a worked example of theory-based learning analytics. In: Handbook of Learning Analytics (2017)
26. Tranter, D.: Unequal schooling: how the school curriculum keeps students from low socio-economic backgrounds out of university. Int. J. Incl. Educ. **16**(9), 901–916 (2012)
27. Tsung, L.: Minority Languages, Education and Communities in China. Springer (2015)
28. Wang, D., Gao, L., Shan, D., Chen, G., Zhang, C., Kao, B.: When tutors simultaneously instruct students from the primary, middle, and high school levels in online one-on-one tutoring: investigating the interaction dynamics using AI, ENA, and LSA methods. J. Sci. Educ. Technol. 1–15 (2024)
29. Wang, D., Shan, D., Ju, R., Kao, B., Zhang, C., Chen, G.: Investigating dialogic interaction in K12 online one-on-one mathematics tutoring using AI and sequence mining techniques. Educ. Inf. Technol. **30**(7), 9215–9240 (2025)
30. Wang, D., Zhen, Y., Shan, D., Zhang, C., Kao, B., Chen, G.: More investment, more engagement? Analyzing dialogic behavior in online one-to-one tutoring among different payment mechanisms. Int. J. Educ. Dev. **117**, 103366 (2025)
31. Wei, X., Wang, L., Lee, L.K., Liu, R.: The effects of generative ai on collaborative problem-solving and team creativity performance in digital story creation: an experimental study. Int. J. Educ. Technol. High. Educ. **22**(1), 23 (2025)
32. Xia, Q., Zhang, P., Huang, W., Chiu, T.K.: The impact of generative ai on university students' learning outcomes via bloom's taxonomy: a meta-analysis and pattern mining approach. Asia Pac. J. Educ. 1–31 (2025)
33. Yang, J., Huang, X., Liu, X.: An analysis of education inequality in China. Int. J. Educ. Dev. **37**, 2–10 (2014)
34. Zhang, P., Adamson, B.: Multilingual education in minority-dominated regions in Xinjiang, People's Republic of China. J. Multiling. Multicult. Dev. **44**(10), 968–980 (2023)

## 2 Related Work

### 2.1 ADHD Assessment and Deficit-Oriented Frameworks

Current mainstream ADHD assessments tend to attribute a child's manifestations of inattention and hyperactivity directly to an internal, somatic dysfunction. This approach carries significant limitations by reducing complex behaviors—occurring within dynamic contexts like classrooms or family settings—to a purely physiological deficit. Critically, the diagnostic process can reify descriptive behaviors (e.g., easily distracted) into a static medical label (ADHD), which may then obscure the nuanced reasons and environmental triggers behind the child's actions [4,5].

In educational contexts, the consequences of this deficit-oriented framework are significant. It predisposes educators and systems to view neurodivergent children primarily as problems to be managed or fixed, rather than as learners requiring differentiated support. The assessment report can thus function as a definitive verdict, legitimizing the "problem student" label and potentially hindering the development of more inclusive educational practices [4,5,11]. Within China's hyper-competitive educational landscape (Involution), this effect is intensified. An ADHD diagnosis often compounds stigma with a perceived label of parenting failure, generating immense external pressure [2,4,11,12]. Research indicates that parental distress stems not only from caregiving challenges but, profoundly, from this overwhelming weight of social judgment. Consequently, traditional assessment can inadvertently undermine family resilience rather than serve as a supportive tool.

In summary, the deficit-centric narrative reinforced by current assessment systems forms the critical departure point for this study. We ask: when AI technology, often perceived as more scientific and authoritative, is integrated into this paradigm, does it risk perpetuating—or even exacerbating—these harms, or can it be designed to foster a perspective that recognizes a child's strengths and potential?

### 2.2 AI in Educational Assessment and Sociotechnical Issues

AI technologies, particularly deep learning-based student modeling, show great promise in predicting performance and diagnosing knowledge gaps for personalized learning [6,7]. However, a predominant focus on algorithmic precision has led to a relative neglect of the sociotechnical dilemmas AI assessment introduces in authentic educational settings.

First, technical precision does not guarantee stakeholder trust. As Vereschak et al. (2021) note, in high-stakes contexts like assessment, opaque black-box models struggle to gain user trust due to a lack of explainability [9]. This raises a pivotal, yet under-studied, question: beyond abstract accuracy metrics, what are the emotional and cognitive responses of parents and teachers when confronted with an AI-generated assessment report?

Second, AI intervention subtly reshapes educational relationships. Ethical frameworks caution that over-reliance on automated metrics can erode the professional judgment of educators and the situated understanding of parents [13]. Empirical work also suggests poorly designed systems can make teachers feel their expertise is sidelined [14], transforming assessment into a societal issue concerning agency, accountability, and fairness.

In conclusion, while existing literature identifies broad risks related to interpretability and ethics, a critical gap remains. Few studies empirically examine how these risks manifest to specifically heighten parental anxiety, reinforce teacher biases, and disrupt home-school communication within high-pressure, real-world contexts like China's special education environment. Our study aims to address this gap by exploring the complex sociotechnical impact and emotional ramifications of AI assessment as perceived by stakeholders.

### 2.3 Neurodiversity and Strength-Based Perspectives

To counter the above challenges, a paradigm shift is emerging from deficit models toward a Neurodiversity framework, which views cognitive variations like ADHD as natural forms of human diversity. Central to this shift is the Strength-Based Model, which focuses on identifying and cultivating an individual's unique cognitive assets [15].

However, translating this theory into practice faces resistance, particularly in cultural contexts emphasizing conformity. Lai and Aoki (2025) note that in such settings, neurodivergent traits face heightened stigma, and rhetorical advocacy is insufficient [16]. There is a pressing need for concrete tools that can render hidden cognitive strengths visible, thereby countering deep-seated pathological biases. This need directly motivates our work: to explore technological designs that create possibilities for recognizing strengths within standardized systems.

Currently, a significant design gap persists. As Spiel and Gerling (2021) critically review, most ADHD-focused technologies retain a correctionist agenda, training conformity rather than supporting agency [17]. Similarly, technologies in other domains often prioritize adapting the individual to the environment [18]. Such designs can perpetuate epistemic injustice by tacitly reinforcing a sense of inherent wrongness.

Therefore, despite theoretical advances, we lack tools for the high-stakes context of educational assessment that can translate strength-based theory into tangible, discussable evidence for parents and teachers. Existing systems tend to either solidify deficit labels or engage in corrective training. AssetLens, the conceptual probe developed in this study, is positioned to explore this gap. It is designed to investigate how a system that visually distills potential cognitive strengths from behavioral data might alter the narratives surrounding a child.

## 3 Methodology

This study does not focus on improving algorithmic performance, but on how AI-generated assessment results are understood and used by parents and teachers within China's high-pressure educational context, and how these results reshape perceptions of the child and home-school communication dynamics. We adopted a qualitative, exploratory approach, defining AssetLens as a design probe deployed via the Wizard-of-Oz (WoZ) simulation technique [19].

The choice of this method was based on two core considerations. First, ethical prudence. Although the subject of the assessment reports in this study is ADHD children, the direct research participants are the parents and teachers interpreting these reports. Directly testing immature automated algorithms involves potential risks. The Wizard-of-Oz method allows researchers to simulate ideal system feedback in a controlled environment, thereby effectively eliciting and observing authentic reactions while prioritizing the psychological safety of the participants (parents, teachers) and the children involved. Second, a focus on sensemaking rather than predictive accuracy. Our research goal is not to verify the accuracy of AI diagnosis, but to observe and deeply understand how parents and teachers interpret data, what emotional reactions they generate, and how they rethink and define the child's abilities when placed in a novel assessment context. Thus, AI here serves not only as the object of study but also as a medium to provoke reflection.

### 3.1 AssetLens System Description: Strength Visualization via Temporal Denoising

AssetLens is a conceptual AI assessment dashboard that reframes deficit-oriented data to reveal cognitive potential. Its core innovation is a temporal denoising logic, which distinguishes between errors caused by impulsive "behavioral noise" and those indicating genuine "cognitive gaps". As illustrated in Fig. 1, the system translates this logic through two key visualizations: (1) a Behavioral Noise Filter that semi-transparently overlays impulsive errors, directing focus to the underlying ability curve; and (2) a Multi-dimensional Strength Radar that maps cognitive assets (e.g., spatial reasoning) instead of a single deficit score. This design shifts the output from a static verdict to a dynamic pedagogical map. Table 1 summarizes this paradigm shift from a medical to a support-oriented model.

**Table 1.** Comparison between Traditional Report and AssetLens Approach

| Dimension | Traditional Report | AssetLens (Ours) |
|---|---|---|
| Focus | Deficits & Symptoms | Strengths & Potential |
| Format | Statistical Scores | Visual Trajectories |
| Outcome | Diagnostic Labels | Pedagogical Strategies |

*Note:* This comparison highlights the conceptual shift from a medical model (Traditional) to a pedagogical support model (AssetLens).

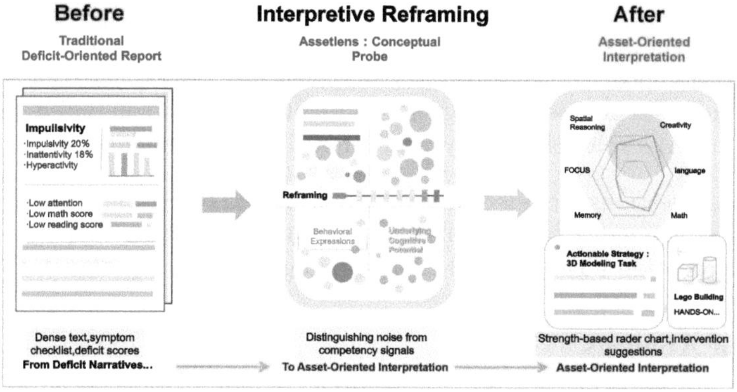


**Fig. 1.** Conceptual Framework of AssetLens: Transforming Deficit Data into Asset Insights through Temporal Denoising and Strength Visualization.

### 3.2 Participants

We recruited 16 stakeholders via snowball sampling in Tier 1 and 2 Chinese cities. The sample comprised two groups: (1) **Parents (N = 8)** of children (aged 6–12) with ADHD diagnoses or symptoms, who reported anxiety about traditional reports; and (2) **Teachers (N = 8)** with $\geq 3$ years of inclusive education experience. Children themselves did not participate; the focus was on adult interpretation. Participants are identified as P1 through P16 based on the chronological order of their interviews (e.g., P11 refers to the 11th participant, rather than the 11th parent).

### 3.3 Data Collection

Prior to the study, informed consent was obtained from all participants. All interview data and personal identifiers were strictly anonymized to ensure privacy. We conducted 16 semi-structured interviews (40–50 minutes each) in late 2025 [20]. To ensure consistency and mitigate ethical risks, we employed a standardized vignette approach [21], using a realistic persona ("Ming")—a student with ADHD traits whose high cognitive ability is often masked by executive dysfunction.

Based on Ming's behavioral data, the researcher (as Wizard) generated two distinct reports following a strict protocol: rapid incorrect responses were tagged as "behavioral noise" from impulsivity, while errors with correct logic were reclassified as cognitive potential. Participants interpreted these reports as if Ming were their own child/student.

A three-phase contrastive elicitation process was designed:

1. **Baseline Elicitation:** Participants reviewed a traditional diagnostic report for Ming, describing their initial reactions and expectations.

2. **Probe Intervention:** Under Wizard-of-Oz conditions, participants interacted with the *AssetLens* dashboard, observing how denoising filtered behavioral interference.
3. **Reflection & Sensemaking:** Participants directly compared both tools, discussing AI's role, credibility, and impact on their understanding.

The core questions included (but were not limited to): initial reactions ("What was your first feeling?"), interpretation ("Did your view change after denoising?"), and role-perception ("Do you feel AI is judging or defending the child?").

### 3.4 Data Analysis

This study employed **reflexive thematic analysis** [22] to identify emergent patterns. Following an inductive approach, the analysis—led by the author with an independent researcher acting as a **"critical friend"**—prioritized collaborative reflexivity. Coding decisions were iteratively debated to reach nuanced consensus, a process that continued until **thematic saturation** was achieved [23], ensuring themes were deeply grounded in participant narratives.

## 4 Findings

Through thematic analysis of the interview data, we developed three core themes that directly address our research questions (see Table 2 for the coding progression). These themes collectively illustrate a transformative journey: from the emotional burden imposed by deficit-focused assessments (Theme 1), through the cognitive reframing enabled by strength-based visualization (Theme 2), to the potential restructuring of home-school dialogue with AI as a mediator (Theme 3). This progression elucidates how a shift in assessment paradigm can reconfigure narratives about the child (RQ1) and reshape stakeholder roles and relationships to alleviate anxiety and build trust (RQ2).

### 4.1 Theme 1: From Diagnostic Certainty to Emotional Burden

Our first finding reveals a paradox within China's high-pressure educational context: the pursuit of diagnostic precision itself becomes a significant emotional burden. We term this the **Decontextualized Precision Paradox**: rigorous deficit quantification without context engenders despair and a fixed future trajectory.

For parents, the traditional diagnostic report for Ming was not a supportive diagnosis but a definitive verdict. P5 described heartbreak: "The report made me feel he was hopeless, like walking into a dead end." This anxiety is anchored in the unforgiving educational system ("Involution") [2,12]. P3 noted the pressure: "The education system forces children to climb step by step... now it is becoming more and more 'juan' (intensely competitive)." Within this frame, precise deficit quantification validated profound failure. As P6 reflected, such reports "only reveal a long and vague path of correction," amplifying uncertainty.

**Table 2.** Coding Process: From Raw Quotes to Emergent Themes

| Representative Quote (Raw Data) | Open Coding | Final Theme |
|---|---|---|
| "The report made me feel he was hopeless... It felt like a final verdict." (Parent P5) | Anxiety from verdict-like report; Hopelessness | **Theme 1: Diagnostic Certainty to Emotional Burden** |
| "I used to see only red crosses... But seeing the system's explanation, I realized his logic was right." (Parent P11) | Reframing errors as potential; Recognizing hidden strengths | **Theme 2: Strength-Oriented Perception Shift** |
| "With both sides looking at the trajectory map... we are analyzing together, not confronting each other." (Teacher P1) | AI as neutral mediator; Collaborative dialogue | **Theme 3: AI as Relational Mediator** |

*Note:* Quotes are translated and edited for conciseness.

Participants projected AI systems focused on diagnostic accuracy would exacerbate this burden. P7 offered a pointed critique: an algorithmic model can land as a "precise yet cold verdict... an overwhelming burden." This supports our argument that algorithmic authority, when categorizing deficits, functions as exclusion.

For teachers, a definitive diagnosis triggered defensiveness. P8 anticipated reports becoming tools for parents to transfer pressure onto teachers. Consequently, data fueled mutual blame rather than collaboration. The "problem student" label dominated interactions, reducing relationships to management and correction.

### 4.2 Theme 2: How Strength-Oriented Visualization Transforms the Perception of the Child

This theme demonstrates how AssetLens reframed stakeholders' perception of the child, triggering a cognitive shift from viewing the child as a collection of problems to recognizing a learner with distinctive cognitive strategies.

By simulating a distinction between behavioral noise and cognitive signals, AssetLens provided a novel attributional framework. This allowed stakeholders to reinterpret the same data. For example, P11 initially believed the child "knew nothing" from the traditional report. However, after seeing denoising analysis that highlighted spatial reasoning in incorrect but speedy answers, he realized: "I used to see only red crosses... But seeing that rating... I suddenly realized his logic was right." This reframed the child's intelligence, not merely corrected scores.

This shift fostered growth-oriented discourse. P5 found the strength-based presentation liberating, contrasting it with a terminal diagnosis. She noted it allowed her to view challenges as "a temporary, malleable state rather than a lifelong pathology," adding: "I no longer think he can never change; instead, I see room for his potential improvement." Such visualizations reinjected hope, critical for sustained engagement. While the cognitive-emotional shift was predominantly positive, a few parents expressed practical skepticism, noting that translating these conceptual strengths into actionable practices within the current high-pressure, grade-centric educational system remains deeply challenging.

For teachers, strength-oriented profiles sparked pedagogical imagination focused on leveraging abilities. P4 emphasized: "When I know where a student's strengths lie, my anxiety level drops to zero. I can then design activities to ignite their potential." This suggests strength-based assessment alleviates teacher anxiety and prompts a mindset shift from defensive management to empowered instructional design.

### 4.3 Theme 3: AI as Mediator From Authoritative Adjudication to Negotiated Boundaries

Our final finding highlights how AssetLens reshaped conceptions of assessment's social role. Unlike traditional reports perceived as definitive verdicts, participants described the strength visualization as a potential boundary object [24]—not replacing human judgment but creating space for negotiation and co-construction.

Whereas diagnostic scores were seen as unchallengeable authority, AssetLens's transparent reasoning (e.g., showing denoising processes) encouraged engaged critique. Stakeholders would not blindly obey its output but used it to start discussions. Teacher P16 noted she would distrust a black-box conclusion, but with AssetLens displaying behavioral trajectories, she saw it as a verification tool: "I would not trust it completely... If AI captured potential that I missed, that is exactly the beginning of the discussion, not the end." This reflective skepticism transformed AI's role from commander to discussion catalyst.

Participants anticipated such tools could shift home-school dialogue from blame to collaboration. Teacher P1 contrasted traditional unidirectional problem notification with joint examination of neutral evidence: "Previously, parents always felt teachers were picking on their child, but now, with both sides looking at the trajectory map... we are analyzing together, not confronting." This points to AI's potential as a relational scaffold for collaborative discourse [25].

The discussion also surfaced an institutional gap: specialized mediators exist in some contexts (e.g., the UK) but are often absent in China, forcing direct confrontation. Participants reflected that AssetLens could partially fulfill this mediating function. Parent P6 noted feeling "more equal facing AI because it has no emotions, just objective display." This suggests in high-pressure, support-scarce environments, well-designed AI visualization might serve as a digital mediator and trust-building scaffold.

## 5 Discussion

Grounding this study in China's high-pressure, high-stakes educational context—often termed Involution—was not a limitation but a deliberate and powerful lens. This environment, where standardized performance is paramount and deviation carries severe social cost, brings the socio-emotional consequences of assessment into sharp, urgent focus. Through the AssetLens design probe, we substantiate a core proposition: within such contexts, and arguably in special education broadly, the fundamental value of AI lies less in pursuing diagnostic precision and more in its catalytic potential to trigger a reconstruction of meaning. Our findings demonstrate that by reframing data presentation from deficits to strengths, AI can do more than alter information—it can transform the interpretive frameworks through which stakeholders understand a child's potential.

### 5.1 Reframing the Understanding of ADHD Educational Assessment

We acknowledge that emphasizing cognitive potential does not mean forcing a positive narrative 'at all costs.' AssetLens acts as a boundary object for reflection rather than a definitive diagnostic truth, aiming to balance realistic challenges with cognitive assets. Our study reveals two fundamental shifts in stakeholder perception catalyzed by the AssetLens probe. This suggests that the design goal of AI assessment systems might usefully move beyond generating diagnostic conclusions toward shaping processes of understanding and social interaction.

Existing AIED research often falls into the predicament we term the Decontextualized Precision Paradox: while pursuing more precise deficit prediction, researchers may inadvertently reinforce pathological labels. Our study indicates that such technical precision can translate into a significant emotional burden, as evidenced by the reactions to the traditional report in Theme 1. In contrast, the AssetLens probe points to an alternative role for AI: that of an epistemic tool that can facilitate reframing. The proposed mechanism is the visualization of a denoising process, which aims to shift focus from how many mistakes a child made to how the child thinks. This shift challenges data reductionism. For instance, Parent P3's engagement with the strength rating did not change the fact of inattention, but it altered his interpretive framework for that behavior. This implies a core design objective for AIED systems: to augment human understanding, helping stakeholders see beyond a deficit-based narrative.

Within the competitive context of our study, traditional reports were described as tools for allocating blame. Our findings in Theme 3 suggest that a strength-oriented visualization can act as a boundary object [24], potentially reshaping this dynamic. It does not provide a final verdict but a discussable artifact. As Teacher P8 noted, this fosters dialogue precisely because it invites scrutiny rather than demanding obedience. By providing a shared focus on data, such a system could lower defensive barriers, enabling a shift from adversarial blame to collaborative exploration of how to leverage a child's profile. The role of AI here is conceptualized not as a solution provider, but as a mediator of dialogue.

### 5.2 The New Role of AI: From Information Tool to Relational Mediator

In traditional AIED research, AI is often positioned as an efficient information tool for data transmission. However, our study suggests that in high-stakes special education contexts, its role may be more complex: it can be designed to actively participate in shaping relational dynamics, such as those between home and school.

Our findings indicate that the perceived potential of AssetLens to alleviate conflict lay not in providing more accurate data, but in offering a de-emotionalized focal point for interaction. As Teacher P1 noted, direct interpersonal communication is prone to being perceived as personal blame, whereas the visualization was seen as a neutral, third-party artifact. This points to a mechanism that could act as an emotional buffer, not by eliminating emotion, but by re-framing potential confrontations into collaborative data inquiry. This function was seen as particularly salient in contexts, like that of our study, which lack dedicated professional mediators.

Thus, the core value of an AIED system may lie less in pursuing autonomous decision-making, and more in its capacity to be designed as an invitation to human collaboration. The case of Teacher P8 is illustrative: her skepticism toward AI did not cause rejection but led her to describe how she would use it as a basis for cross-checking and discussion with parents. This reveals a critical insight: AI's value may be less in making perfect decisions and more in its potential to scaffold evidence-based dialogue—even by presenting data that provokes discussion. In this view, AI becomes embedded in the relational network as a scaffold for negotiation, providing a shared starting point for human sense-making.

### 5.3 Design Implications for AIED Systems

Based on our findings, we advocate for AIED research and practice to transcend the singular pursuit of predictive accuracy, particularly in high-stakes special education contexts. System design must centrally consider socio-emotional dimensions [9,13,26]. We propose a guiding principle: **prioritizing emotional safety over data granularity.**

Our study indicates that an excessive pursuit of precise deficit quantification can directly induce anxiety (Theme 1). Therefore, we suggest that a fundamental design ethic for such systems should be to avoid foreseeable emotional harm. In visualization design, this implies proactively avoiding stark pathological indicators (e.g., glaring red warnings) and considering phased presentation strategies. For instance, interfaces could first guide attention to a student's capability contours and strengths before constructively introducing areas for development. This positions AI not as a neutral data mirror, but as a communicative guide that manages information presentation with empathy.

Following this, we argue that AIED interaction design should shift from a paradigm of correction to one of construction. The interface does not merely convey information; it actively participates in constructing the child's digital identity. Traditional systems heavy with correction marks can construct an identity of failure. Conversely, as our probe suggests, highlighting strengths (Theme 2) can help construct an identity of a capable learner. Thus, future systems should explore the integration of strength-perspective modules—moving beyond tracking knowledge gaps to also aim to identify and visualize unique cognitive strategic strengths (e.g., spatial reasoning). Such an approach, documenting both growth and challenges, could help maintain stakeholder hope and reframe assessment as a forward-looking guide rather than a retrospective judgment.

Finally, building on these principles, we advocate for designs that open interpretative spaces rather than deliver closed verdicts. To counter the rigidity of algorithmic authority (Theme 1), systems should be designed as inherently negotiable. This means avoiding binary diagnostic labels and instead committing to transparent evidence chains (e.g., behavioral trajectory maps from Theme 3) while acknowledging data limitations. The core is to formally invite teachers and parents to integrate the system's output with their own observations and judgment, using it as a starting point for discussion. This safeguards human agency and professional responsibility in the educational assessment process.

### 5.4 Limitations

While this study, through a design probe, has revealed potential pathways for AI assessment to reshape understanding and relationships, its boundaries must be acknowledged.

First, **methodological scope**: The qualitative approach with a modest sample size (N = 16) enabled deep, thematic analysis and achieved theoretical saturation for the explored concepts. However, the findings are situated in specific stakeholder perceptions and are thus more apt for revealing mechanisms and possibilities than for statistical generalization. The long-term, behavioral impact of such systems on broader populations requires future large-scale, longitudinal study. Furthermore, employing a fixed presentation order and the hypothetical persona "Ming" limits ecological validity. While we focused on adults to protect vulnerable populations during this conceptual phase, future work must actively involve neurodivergent children in the co-design process [27].

**Second, Contextual Specificity:** The insights are deeply rooted in the high-pressure, high-stakes educational context of China ("Involution"). This context powerfully illuminated the Decontextualized Precision Paradox and the perceived value of a mediating tool. While this offers a rich case study, the manifestations and intensity of these dynamics may vary in cultures with different assessment philosophies or more robust institutional support systems. We therefore emphasize the need for, and anticipate, future cross-cultural comparative research to explore the transferability of this framework.

**Finally, Technical Implementation and Validity:** By design, this study employed a Wizard-of-Oz method to simulate an AI system's output. This was essential for ethically and safely probing reactions to the core conceptual reframing (strength-based visualization) without the risks of deploying an unvalidated algorithm. Consequently, the study evaluates a concept and its presentation logic, not a technical artifact. It cannot address challenges inherent to real system deployment, such as algorithmic reliability, the sustainability of user trust, or the integration of this logic into a functioning, data-driven pipeline. The logical next step is the development of a technically implemented prototype for longitudinal, in-context evaluation. Additionally, manually simulating the "temporal denoising" via Wizard-of-Oz may introduce researcher bias, and lacking a strict control group limits causal claims. Future implementations must validate algorithmic reliability and fairness.

## 6 Conclusion

This study critiques the deficit-oriented assessment paradigm and proposes AssetLens, a strength-based alternative. Our findings from China's high-pressure educational context reveal a Decontextualized Precision Paradox: the singular pursuit of AI diagnostic precision exacerbates anxiety and blame. Conversely, strength-oriented visualization reframes assessment from a pathological verdict into a developmental map, alleviating emotional burdens and activating pedagogical support.

Theoretically, we argue for redefining AI's role in special education from automated judge to socially embedded mediator. By demonstrating its potential as a boundary object [24] in home-school communication, AssetLens suggests a technical pathway for repairing trust in support-scarce environments. This underscores that responsible AI design must address socio-emotional dimensions. Future research should pursue longitudinal classroom studies and cross-cultural comparisons. We call for the AIED field to expand from algorithm optimization to epistemic and relational design—focusing on how technology shapes cognition and collaboration. Ultimately, educational AI's success might be measured not by how precisely it predicts deficits, but by how effectively it empowers stakeholders to collectively nurture a child's potential.

## References


1. Liu, H., Zhang, K., Wang, L., Chen, J.: Educational burden reduction, educational inequality, and enrollment pressure: evidence from China. Econ. Hum. Biol. **56**, 101459 (2025). https://doi.org/10.1016/j.ehb.2024.101459
2. Ma, X., Lin, Y., Yan, W., Jin, Z., Zhang, Y.: Parental ADHD knowledge and medical visit status of school-aged children in Shanghai. Child Adolesc. Psychiatry Ment. Health **18**, 91 (2024). https://doi.org/10.1186/s13034-024-00780-6
3. Nigg, J.T., Sibley, M.H., Thapar, A., Karalunas, S.L.: Development of ADHD: etiology, heterogeneity, and early life course. Annu. Rev. Dev. Psychol. **2**, 559–583 (2020). https://doi.org/10.1146/annurev-devpsych-060320-093413

4. Honkasilta, J., Koutsoklenis, A.: The (un)real existence of ADHD–criteria, functions, and forms of the diagnostic entity. Front. Sociol. **7**, 814763 (2022). https://doi.org/10.3389/fsoc.2022.814763
5. Te Meerman, S., Freedman, J.E., Batstra, L.: ADHD and reification: four ways a psychiatric construct is portrayed as a disease. Front. Psychiatry **13**, 1055328 (2022). https://doi.org/10.3389/fpsyt.2022.1055328
6. Abdelrahman, G., Wang, Q., Nunes, B.: Knowledge tracing: a survey. ACM Comput. Surv. **55**, 1–37 (2023). https://doi.org/10.1145/3569576
7. Qin, Q., Zhang, S.: Visualizing the knowledge mapping of artificial intelligence in education: a systematic review. Educ. Inf. Technol. **30**, 449–483 (2025). https://doi.org/10.1007/s10639-024-13076-1
8. Scarlatos, A., Baker, R.S., Lan, A.: Exploring knowledge tracing in tutor-student dialogues using LLMs. In: Proceedings of the 15th International Learning Analytics and Knowledge Conference, pp. 249–259. ACM, Dublin Ireland (2025). https://doi.org/10.1145/3706468.3706501
9. Vereschak, O., Bailly, G., Caramiaux, B.: How to evaluate trust in AI-assisted decision making? A survey of empirical methodologies. Proc. ACM Hum.-Comput. Interact. **5**, 1–39 (2021). https://doi.org/10.1145/3476068
10. Gaver, B., Dunne, T., Pacenti, E.: Design: cultural probes. Interactions **6**, 21–29 (1999). https://doi.org/10.1145/291224.291235
11. Butcher, L., Lane, S.: Neurodivergent (Autism and ADHD) student experiences of access and inclusion in higher education: an ecological systems theory perspective. High. Educ. **90**, 243–263 (2025). https://doi.org/10.1007/s10734-024-01319-6
12. Chen, S.-C., et al.: Parental challenges in raising preschoolers with attention-deficit/hyperactivity disorder in mainland China's first-tier cities: qualitative study using framework analysis. JMIR Form Res. **9**, e74047 (2025). https://doi.org/10.2196/74047
13. Holmes, W., et al.: Ethics of AI in education: towards a community-wide framework. Int. J. Artif. Intell. Educ. **32**, 504–526 (2022). https://doi.org/10.1007/s40593-021-00239-1
14. Mouta, A., Torrecilla-Sánchez, E.M., Pinto-Llorente, A.M.: Comprehensive professional learning for teacher agency in addressing ethical challenges of AIED: insights from educational design research. Educ. Inf. Technol. **30**, 3343–3387 (2025). https://doi.org/10.1007/s10639-024-12946-y
15. Jimerson, S.R., Sharkey, J.D., Nyborg, V., Furlong, M.J.: Strength-based assessment and school psychology: a summary and synthesis. Calif. Sch. Psychol. **9**(1), 9–19 (2004). https://doi.org/10.1007/BF03340903
16. Lai, E.C.L., Aoki, A., Seera, G.: Embracing neurodiversity: shifting from deficit-based model to strength-based model. East Asian Arch Psychiatry **35**, 123–127 (2025). https://doi.org/10.12809/eaap2518
17. Spiel, K., Gerling, K.: The purpose of play: how HCI games research fails neurodivergent populations. ACM Trans. Comput.-Hum. Interact. **28**, 1–40 (2021). https://doi.org/10.1145/3432245
18. Burtscher, S., Gerling, K.: Neurodivergence and work in human-computer interaction: mapping the research landscape. In: Proceedings of the 3rd Annual Meeting of the Symposium on Human-Computer Interaction for Work, pp. 1–14. ACM, Newcastle Upon Tyne United Kingdom (2024). https://doi.org/10.1145/3663384.3663386
19. Kelley, J.F.: An iterative design methodology for user-friendly natural language office information applications. ACM Trans. Inf. Syst. **2**, 26–41 (1984). https://doi.org/10.1145/357417.357420

20. Kallio, H., Pietilä, A., Johnson, M., Kangasniemi, M.: Systematic methodological review: developing a framework for a qualitative semi-structured interview guide. J. Adv. Nurs. **72**, 2954–2965 (2016). https://doi.org/10.1111/jan.13031
21. Hughes, R., Huby, M.: The application of vignettes in social and nursing research. J. Adv. Nurs. **37**, 382–386 (2002). https://doi.org/10.1046/j.1365-2648.2002.02100.x
22. Braun, V., Clarke, V.: Using thematic analysis in psychology. Qual. Res. Psychol. **3**, 77–101 (2006). https://doi.org/10.1191/1478088706qp063oa
23. Guest, G., Bunce, A., Johnson, L.: How many interviews are enough?: an experiment with data saturation and variability. Field Methods **18**, 59–82 (2006). https://doi.org/10.1177/1525822X05279903
24. Star, S.L., Griesemer, J.R.: Institutional ecology, 'translations' and boundary objects: amateurs and professionals in berkeley's museum of vertebrate zoology, 1907–39. Soc. Stud. Sci. **19**, 387–420 (1989). https://doi.org/10.1177/030631289019003001
25. Hinds, P.J., Bailey, D.E.: Out of sight, out of sync: understanding conflict in distributed teams. Organ. Sci. **14**, 615–632 (2003). https://doi.org/10.1287/orsc.14.6.615.24872
26. Jipguep-Akhtar, M.: Review of "race after technology: abolitionist tools for the new Jim code." Soc. Forces **98**, 1–3 (2020). https://doi.org/10.1093/sf/soz162
27. Druin, A.: The role of children in the design technology. University of Maryland (1999)

# BRIDGE the Gap: Mitigating Bias Amplification in Automated Scoring of English Language Learners via Inter-group Data Augmentation

Yun Wang[1(✉)], Xuansheng Wu[1], Jingyuan Huang[1], Lei Liu[2], Xiaoming Zhai[3], and Ninghao Liu[4]

[1] School of Computing, University of Georgia, Athens, GA, USA
{Yun.Wang1,Xuansheng.Wu,Jingyuan.Huang}@uga.edu
[2] Educational Testing Service, Princeton, NJ, USA
lliu001@ets.org
[3] AI4STEM Education Center, University of Georgia, Athens, GA, USA
Xiaoming.Zhai@uga.edu
[4] The Hong Kong Polytechnic University, Hong Kong, China
ninghliu@polyu.edu.hk

**Abstract.** In educational assessment, automated scoring systems increasingly rely on deep learning and large language models (LLMs). However, these systems face significant risks of bias amplification, where model prediction gaps between student groups become larger than those observed in training data. This issue is especially severe for underrepresented groups such as English Language Learners (ELLs), as models may inherit and further magnify existing disparities in the data. We identify that this issue is closely tied to representation bias: the scarcity of minority (high-scoring ELL) samples makes models trained with empirical risk minimization favor majority (non-ELL) linguistic patterns. Consequently, models tend to under-predict ELL students who even demonstrate comparable domain knowledge but use different linguistic patterns, thereby undermining fairness in automated scoring. To mitigate this, we propose BRIDGE, a **B**ias-**R**educing **I**nter-group **D**ata **GE**neration framework designed for low-resource assessment settings. Instead of relying on the limited minority samples, BRIDGE synthesizes high-scoring ELL samples by "pasting" construct-relevant (i.e., rubric-aligned knowledge and evidence) content from abundant high-scoring non-ELL samples into authentic ELL linguistic patterns. We further introduce a discriminator model to ensure the quality of synthetic samples. Experiments on California Science Test datasets demonstrate that BRIDGE effectively reduces prediction bias for high-scoring ELL students while maintaining overall scoring performance. Notably, our method achieves fairness gains comparable to using additional real human data, offering a cost-effective solution for ensuring equitable scoring in large-scale assessments.

Y. Wang and X. Wu—These authors contributed equally.


E. G. Blanchard et al. (eds.), AIED 2026, LNCS 16586, pp. 31–45, 2027.
https://doi.org/10.1007/978-3-032-29773-0_3

**Keywords:** Automated Scoring · Bias Amplification · English Language Learners · Algorithmic Fairness · LLM-based Data Augmentation

## 1 Introduction

Automated scoring systems powered by deep learning and large language models (LLMs) have been increasingly deployed in educational assessment [11,28,32], demonstrating strong performance and promising scalability for large-scale evaluations [10,34]. These systems are inherently data-driven, with predictive performance heavily dependent on the quality and representativeness of the training data [6,36]. However, such reliance creates a critical vulnerability in which imbalances in the training data are not just inherited but potentially amplified in model predictions [17,23]. This phenomenon, known as *bias amplification*, can widen group-level performance disparities in predicted scores beyond those warranted by actual proficiency differences [4,19,21]. It thereby undermines the fairness of automated scores in educational settings, particularly for underrepresented subgroups such as English Language Learners (ELLs) [31].

Such bias amplification can arise from the interaction between data-level *representation bias* and the empirical risk minimization (ERM) objective used to train deep models [13,17]. Representation bias occurs when certain parts of the target population are severely underrepresented in the training data [24]. In educational assessment datasets, ELLs constitute only a small proportion of the student population, with high-scoring ELL responses being even rarer [30,31]. This places high-performing ELL students in an extremely sparsely supervised region of the data distribution. Under the ERM paradigm, models prioritize majority patterns to minimize average loss, effectively down-weighting learning signals from underrepresented subgroups [13,22]. As a result, models may primarily learn scoring criteria from non-ELL exemplars, potentially assigning lower scores to ELL responses that employ different but valid linguistic strategies, even when their responses demonstrate comparable domain knowledge. This systematic underprediction can distort predictions for high-performing ELL students and widen group-level disparities beyond those present in the training data.

To mitigate bias amplification and its downstream fairness impacts, a natural strategy is to enlarge the training data for underrepresented subgroups [24]. Given that manually collecting new high-scoring ELL responses is difficult in practice, targeted synthetic data generation becomes a practical alternative. However, existing augmentation methods offer limited leverage when the target subgroup is extremely underrepresented, precisely the regime where augmentation is most needed. Most existing methods implicitly assume access to a nontrivial pool of subgroup examples to enable resampling or rewriting [2,5,7]. When such samples are scarce, classical resampling approaches can lead models to overfit the few minority samples rather than learning generalizable patterns [2,20]. Similarly, simple paraphrasing methods, including those based on LLMs, can increase apparent sample diversity, but they face a trade-off between diversity and fidelity [5,7,16]. Mild paraphrases often yield near-duplicate responses with limited additional learning signal, whereas aggressive rewrites can drift in meaning and inadvertently alter rubric-relevant content or normalize away subgroup-specific language patterns [25]. Moreover, such paraphrastic transformations are typically weakly constrained, making it hard to audit which aspects of the response are preserved or changed. This lack of transparency raises concerns about controllability and interpretability in assessment settings.

To address these challenges, we propose BRIDGE, an inter-group data augmentation framework designed for extreme underrepresentation scenarios, as illustrated in Fig. 1. Unlike resampling or paraphrasing methods whose effectiveness depends on having sufficient examples from the target subgroup, BRIDGE can generate high-quality training data even when the subgroup contains only a handful of samples. Our key insight, grounded in a modular view of student responses [1,18], is that semantic content indicates proficiency (i.e., high scores) while linguistic patterns reflect group status (e.g., ELL vs. non-ELL). Thus, although high-scoring ELL responses may be nearly absent, we have access to two abundant and complementary resources: high-scoring non-ELL responses that demonstrate group-invariant construct-relevant content, and other ELL responses that exhibit group-specific linguistic patterns. BRIDGE leverages construct-relevant content from high-scoring non-ELL responses and reformulates it within linguistic patterns characteristic of ELL students. This process generates synthetic responses that adhere to the scoring rubric while reflecting the linguistic characteristics of ELL, offering a more controlled and interpretable augmentation procedure than generic paraphrasing. To ensure the quality of the synthetic data, we further train a discriminator model to automatically filter candidate responses. The main contributions of this work are as follows:

1. Revealing and quantifying bias amplification in automated scoring models on high-scoring ELLs, with theoretical analysis from an ERM perspective.
2. Proposing BRIDGE, an inter-group data augmentation framework that mitigates extreme underrepresentation by blending high-score content with subgroup specific linguistic patterns without requiring additional real data.
3. Demonstrating on real educational datasets that BRIDGE reduces prediction bias while maintaining scoring performance, achieving fairness gains comparable to real-data augmentation.

## 2 Bias Amplification in Automated Scoring

This section formally defines the automated scoring task and the associated phenomenon of bias amplification. Section 2.1 formalizes the scoring task and introduces the Empirical Risk Minimization (ERM) paradigm. Section 2.2 introduces the concept of representation bias and analyzes how it interacts with ERM to impede learning from underrepresented groups. Finally, Sect. 2.3 characterizes the mechanism of bias amplification and defines a metric to quantify it.

### 2.1 Problem Formulation

We consider an automated scoring task where each example consists of a student response $x \in \mathcal{X}$, a holistic score $y \in \mathcal{Y} = \{0, 1, \ldots, K\}$ assigned by human raters,

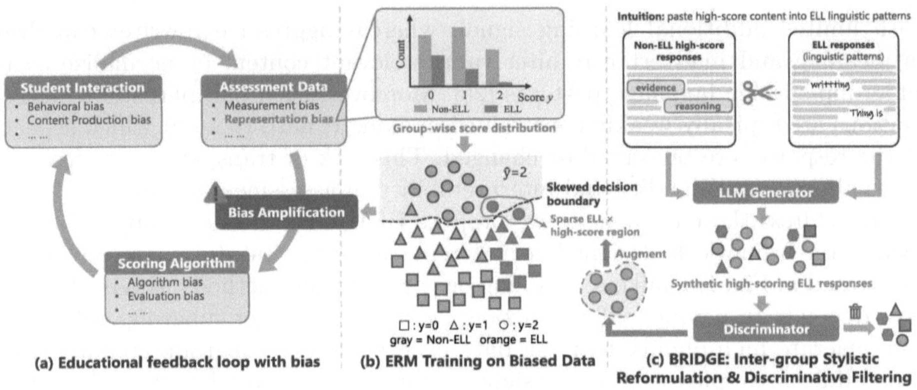


**Fig. 1.** Overview of the bias amplification loop and the BRIDGE framework. **(a) Bias Propagation:** Representation bias in training data creates a feedback loop that reinforces educational disparities. **(b) ERM Vulnerability:** Under ERM, the decision boundary for high scores is skewed by the majority non-ELL group, causing systematic underprediction of the sparse ELL high-score subgroup. **(c) BRIDGE Framework:** Our approach mitigates this by performing inter-group stylistic reformulation, extracting construct-relevant content from high-scoring non-ELL samples and injecting ELL-specific linguistic patterns, followed by a discriminator for quality control.

and a binary group label $g \in \mathcal{G} = \{\text{EL}, \text{NE}\}$ indicating the student's English learner status, where $K$ is the maximum score level, EL refers to ELLs, and NE to non-ELLs. Let $P$ denote the data distribution over $\mathcal{X} \times \mathcal{Y} \times \mathcal{G}$. The training set consists of $n$ i.i.d. examples $D = \{(x_i, y_i, g_i)\}_{i=1}^{n}$ drawn from $P$. We write $n_{\text{EL}}$ and $n_{\text{NE}}$ for the number of ELL and non-ELL responses in the training data.

A scoring model $f_\theta : \mathcal{X} \to \mathbb{R}$ maps an arbitrary response $x$ to a predicted score $\hat{y} = f_\theta(x)$ that approximates the human annotation $y$, where $\theta$ denotes the model parameters. The parameters are learned by minimizing the empirical risk over the training set:

$$\hat{R}(f_\theta) = \frac{1}{n} \sum_{i=1}^{n} \ell(f_\theta(x_i), y_i), \tag{1}$$

where $\ell$ denotes a standard loss function. This objective corresponds to the usual ERM paradigm [26].

From a fairness perspective, we are particularly interested in performance for high-scoring ELL students. Let $\tau$ denote a high-score threshold (for example, the top score level). We define the target subgroup as $\mathcal{S}_{\text{EL,high}} = \{i \mid g_i = \text{EL}, y_i \geq \tau\}$. Under the ERM objective in Eq. (1), all training examples are weighted equally in the loss. When $|\mathcal{S}_{\text{EL,high}}|$ is very small, the contribution of this subgroup to the overall objective becomes negligible.

### 2.2 Representation Bias Under ERM

Building on the ERM formulation in Sect. 2.1, we now analyze how representation bias in the training distribution interacts with ERM and impedes the model's learning from underrepresented groups. Informally, we say the training data exhibit **representation bias** when some subgroups are severely underrepresented [24], such as ELL students and in particular high-scoring ELL students, who constitute only a tiny fraction of the data. As we show below, the losses from these subgroups contribute only weakly to the ERM objective and its gradient.

We view each example $(x, y, g)$ as drawn from a joint data distribution $P$. For a given scoring function $f$, the population risk is $R(f) = \mathbb{E}_{(x,y,g)\sim P}\big[\ell(f(x), y)\big]$. Using the group label $g$, the population risk decomposes into a mixture of group-wise risks:

$$R(f) = \sum_{g\in\{\text{EL,NE}\}} P(g)\,\mathbb{E}\big[\ell(f(x), y) \mid g\big] = \sum_{g\in\{\text{EL,NE}\}} \pi_g\, R_g(f), \tag{2}$$

where $\pi_g = P(g)$ is the population ratio of group $g$ and $R_g(f) = \mathbb{E}\big[\ell(f(x), y) \mid g\big]$ is the group-wise risk.

Given the training set $D$ of size $n$ introduced in Sect. 2.1, the empirical risk in Eq. (1) admits a similar decomposition. Let $n_g = \big|\{i \mid g_i = g\}\big|$ denote the number of examples from group $g$, and define the empirical group-wise risk

$$\hat{R}_g(f_\theta) = \frac{1}{n_g}\sum_{i=1}^{n} \mathbb{1}\{g_i = g\}\ell\big(f_\theta(x_i), y_i\big). \tag{3}$$

Then

$$\hat{R}(f_\theta) = \frac{1}{n}\sum_{i=1}^{n} \ell\big(f_\theta(x_i), y_i\big) = \sum_{g\in\{\text{EL,NE}\}} \frac{n_g}{n}\,\hat{R}_g(f_\theta). \tag{4}$$

The gradient of the ERM objective decomposes accordingly:

$$\nabla_\theta \hat{R}(f_\theta) = \sum_{g\in\{\text{EL,NE}\}} \frac{n_g}{n}\,\nabla_\theta \hat{R}_g(f_\theta). \tag{5}$$

Under i.i.d. sampling, $n_g/n$ is a consistent estimator of $\pi_g$. Equation (5) shows that each group's contribution to the ERM gradient is proportional to its sample fraction. When a group is underrepresented, its gradient term is naturally down-weighted, and optimization is driven primarily by the majority group. Similar observations have been made in prior work on fairness under ERM and distributional robustness [13,15]. In our setting, this phenomenon is particularly severe for the high-scoring ELL subgroup $\mathcal{S}_{\text{EL,high}}$, which in our dataset constitutes only about 3.76% of ELL responses and less than 1% of all responses (see Sect. 4.1). As a result, its learning signal contributes negligibly to ERM optimization, and the high-score decision boundary is shaped largely by non-ELL examples.

### 2.3 From Representation Bias to Bias Amplification

Having established that ERM down-weights learning signals from underrepresented subgroups, we now characterize how this imbalance can lead to bias amplification. We define **bias amplification** as the phenomenon in which the disparities between groups in model predictions exceed those present in the training data [27,35].

To quantify bias amplification in automated scoring, we follow the idea of the directional bias amplification metric $BiasAmp_{\rightarrow}$ [27] and focus on the direction $A \rightarrow T$, i.e., how the protected attribute $A$ affects the prediction of the task outcome $T$ beyond what is present in the labeled data. In our setting, the English group label $g \in \{\mathrm{EL}, \mathrm{NE}\}$ serves as the protected attribute $A$, and the task is to predict whether a student will get a high score, formalized as the binary indicator $T = \mathbb{1}[y \geq \tau]$. Given a scoring model $f$, we obtain predicted scores $\hat{y} = f(x)$ and define the predicted high-score indicator $\hat{T} = \mathbb{1}[\hat{y} \geq \tau]$. For each group $g \in \{\mathrm{EL}, \mathrm{NE}\}$, we define the high-score rate in the labeled data and in the model predictions as $p_{\mathrm{true}}(g) = \Pr(T = 1 \mid g)$, $p_{\mathrm{pred}}(g) = \Pr(\hat{T} = 1 \mid g)$.

The **group disparity** in high-score rates in the labeled data and model is then $\Delta_{\mathrm{data}} = p_{\mathrm{true}}(\mathrm{NE}) - p_{\mathrm{true}}(\mathrm{EL})$, and $\Delta_{\mathrm{model}} = p_{\mathrm{pred}}(\mathrm{NE}) - p_{\mathrm{pred}}(\mathrm{EL})$, respectively. We define our bias amplification metric as the change in this disparity induced by the model training process:

$$\mathrm{BiasAmp}(f) = \Delta_{\mathrm{model}} - \Delta_{\mathrm{data}}. \tag{6}$$

Here $\mathrm{BiasAmp}(f) > 0$ means that the model amplifies the bias in the same direction as in the labeled data. $\mathrm{BiasAmp}(f) \approx 0$ indicates that the model largely preserves the disparity present in the labeled distribution, whereas $\mathrm{BiasAmp}(f) < 0$ corresponds to attenuation or even reversal of this disparity.

To theoretically substantiate how representation bias leads to bias amplification, we decompose $\mathrm{BiasAmp}(f)$ into its constituent classification error terms. For each group $g$, define the joint false-positive and false-negative rates $\mathrm{FP}_g = \Pr(T = 0, \hat{T} = 1 \mid g)$, $\mathrm{FN}_g = \Pr(T = 1, \hat{T} = 0 \mid g)$. Within a fixed group $g$, the true and predicted high-score rates can be expressed in terms of these quantities:

$$p_{\mathrm{true}}(g) = \Pr(T = 1 \mid g) = \Pr(T = 1, \hat{T} = 1 \mid g) + \mathrm{FN}_g, \tag{7}$$

$$p_{\mathrm{pred}}(g) = \Pr(\hat{T} = 1 \mid g) = \Pr(T = 1, \hat{T} = 1 \mid g) + \mathrm{FP}_g. \tag{8}$$

Hence $p_{\mathrm{pred}}(g) - p_{\mathrm{true}}(g) = \mathrm{FP}_g - \mathrm{FN}_g$. Intuitively, $\mathrm{FP}_g$ is the fraction of low-scoring responses in group $g$ that the model "upgrades" to high scores (over-predictions), whereas $\mathrm{FN}_g$ is the fraction of truly high-scoring responses that it "downgrades" (underpredictions). Thus $p_{\mathrm{pred}}(g) - p_{\mathrm{true}}(g)$ is exactly the net upward shift in the high-score rate induced by the model for group $g$.

Substituting $p_{\mathrm{pred}}(g) - p_{\mathrm{true}}(g) = \mathrm{FP}_g - \mathrm{FN}_g$ for $g \in \{\mathrm{NE}, \mathrm{EL}\}$ into the definition of $\mathrm{BiasAmp}(f)$ yields

$$\mathrm{BiasAmp}(f) = \left[\mathrm{FP}_{\mathrm{NE}} - \mathrm{FN}_{\mathrm{NE}}\right] - \left[\mathrm{FP}_{\mathrm{EL}} - \mathrm{FN}_{\mathrm{EL}}\right] \tag{9}$$

$$= \left[\mathrm{FP}_{\mathrm{NE}} - \mathrm{FP}_{\mathrm{EL}}\right] + \left[\mathrm{FN}_{\mathrm{EL}} - \mathrm{FN}_{\mathrm{NE}}\right]. \tag{10}$$

This decomposition shows that **bias amplification arises** when the model assigns more false-positive high scores to non-ELLs ($FP_{NE} > FP_{EL}$), while producing more false-negative errors for ELLs ($FN_{EL} > FN_{NE}$). This pattern is expected under representation bias and ERM-dominated training.

Under the representation bias characterized in Sect. 2.2, **the high-score decision boundary is shaped predominantly by non-ELL responses** [13]. During training, the model may conflate construct-relevant content with linguistic patterns typical of high-scoring non-ELL responses, effectively treating these group-specific patterns as a proxy for high proficiency. In contrast, high-scoring ELL responses often exhibit valid but sparsely represented linguistic features [8,29], so the model tends to under-predict high-scoring ELL responses at test time [13]. This mechanism naturally induces $FP_{NE} > FP_{EL}$ and $FN_{EL} > FN_{NE}$, and, combined with the decomposition above, implies $\text{BiasAmp}(f) > 0$.

## 3 Mitigating Bias Amplification with BRIDGE

Our analysis in Sect. 2 demonstrates that bias amplification arises from skewed decision boundaries under ERM. Left unaddressed, such biased predictions risk perpetuating a feedback loop (Fig. 1(a)) in which underprediction discourages minority students, leading to behavioral and content production biases that further reinforce representation bias. To break this cycle, we propose BRIDGE, a framework designed to intervene at the data level by augmenting the sparse $\mathcal{S}_{\text{EL,high}}$ subgroup. BRIDGE (Fig. 1(c)) operates in two stages: (i) an LLM-based generator performs inter-group stylistic reformulation to "paste" high-score content into ELL linguistic patterns; (ii) a discriminator filters synthetic candidates to ensure they are indistinguishable from authentic student responses.

### 3.1 Stage 1: Inter-group Stylistic Reformulation

The primary objective of the first stage is to synthesize high-quality responses that occupy the sparse $\mathcal{S}_{\text{EL,high}}$ region. While high-scoring ELL samples are rare, the complementary abundance of high-scoring non-ELL content and representative ELL linguistic patterns offers a viable path for synthesis. However, effectively leveraging these resources requires a principled decoupling justified by construct validity, which holds that domain-specific assessments should primarily target construct-relevant proficiency while minimizing construct-irrelevant variance arising from extraneous linguistic barriers [1,3,18,33]. Motivated by this principle, we conceptualize a student response $x$ as a modular composition of construct-relevant content $C(\cdot)$ and linguistic style $S(\cdot)$.

Empirical analyses of five datasets support this conceptualization. Even at the same score level, ELL responses $x_{\text{EL}}$ and non-ELL responses $x_{\text{NE}}$ remain linearly discriminable in the BERT latent space [9] (ROC AUC: 0.794–0.830). Crucially, identical scores are intended to reflect comparable content performance between ELL and non-ELL, and any residual content variations would typically average out across large samples. Thus, the persistent discriminability we observe suggests that the distinction resides not in the construct-relevant content, but in group-specific stylistic distributions. Building on this, BRIDGE formalizes the synthesis of high-quality ELL samples as a conditional generation task:

$$x_{\text{syn}} = G\big(C(x_{\text{NE}}), S(x_{\text{EL}})\big), \tag{11}$$

where $x_{\text{NE}} \in \mathcal{S}_{\text{NE,hi}}$ is the content donor and $x_{\text{EL}}$ is drawn from the ELL population. Specifically, the generator $G$ is instructed to "paste" the construct-relevant content of $x_{\text{NE}}$ into the authentic ELL linguistic patterns of $x_{\text{EL}}$, bridging the representation gap without introducing construct-irrelevant bias.

### 3.2 Stage 2: Discriminative Filtering for Authenticity

While Stage 1 reformulates high-score content into ELL patterns, outputs may still contain artifacts that deviate from the authentic distribution. Thus, we introduce a Discriminative Filtering stage to ensure authenticity of the augmented data. Specifically, we train a discriminator $D$ to distinguish between authentic responses and the synthetic candidates generated in Stage 1. For each candidate $x_{\text{syn}}$, the discriminator outputs an authenticity score $D(x_{\text{syn}}) \in [0, 1]$, representing the probability that the response originates from a real student rather than an LLM. We retain samples that exceed a predefined confidence threshold $\gamma$:

$$\mathcal{S}^*_{\text{syn}} = \{\, x_{\text{syn}} \mid D(x_{\text{syn}}) > \gamma \,\}. \tag{12}$$

By filtering out overly polished or hallucinated responses, this stage helps the augmented set $\mathcal{S}^*_{\text{syn}}$ better match the linguistic profile of the ELL population while providing the necessary high-score evidence.

## 4 Experiments

In this section, we evaluate the performance of the BRIDGE framework across five diverse science assessment items. Our experiments are guided by the following three research questions: **RQ1:** Does the ERM-based scoring model amplify prediction disparity for the sparse $\mathcal{S}_{\text{EL,high}}$ subgroup? **RQ2:** To what extent can BRIDGE reduce this bias amplification compared to existing augmentation methods? **RQ3:** Can BRIDGE maintain competitive overall scoring accuracy while improving fairness for the $\mathcal{S}_{\text{EL,high}}$ subgroup?

### 4.1 Datasets

Following prior work [12], we use Grade 8 student constructed-response data from the California Science Test (CAST), a state-administered assessment of science knowledge. Students write short answers that are scored by human raters on a 0/1/2 scale. We collapse the original seven English proficiency categories into a binary group label: the ELL group and the Non-ELL group. Across items, ELL students account for about 14.2% of responses (range ≈ 11.7%–17.0%).

**The Sparsity Challenge.** We focus on the intersectional subgroup $\mathcal{S}_{\text{EL,high}}$ (ELL students achieving score 2). This subgroup is rare, accounting for a median of 3.76% (mean = 8.28%) within the ELL population. In typical small to medium items containing about 200 ELL responses, about 60% of the items contain 10 or fewer $\mathcal{S}_{\text{EL,high}}$ samples. Consequently, a standard train/validation/test split (e.g., 60/20/20) would yield a test set with only a few $\mathcal{S}_{\text{EL,high}}$ samples (typically $\leq 3$ samples), making subgroup metrics statistically unreliable or even undefined.

**Simulated Low-Resource Scenario.** To investigate extreme sparsity during training while maintaining reliable evaluation, we select five large-scale items, each containing roughly 200,000 responses (30,000 ELL responses). For these items, the absolute count of $\mathcal{S}_{\text{EL,high}}$ samples is sufficient for testing (ranging from 713 to 3,658), while their within-ELL proportions mirror the sparse distributions of smaller items. For each item, we perform a two-stage stratified random split. Data are first divided into training (70%), validation (15%), and test (15%) sets. We then subsample 1% of the training data to simulate an extreme low-resource scenario. The remaining 99% of the training pool is reserved solely as a donor source for real-data (oracle) augmentation experiments. The validation and test sets remain fixed across all conditions to ensure reliable performance estimation.

### 4.2 Experimental Setup

**Scoring Models.** We fine-tune `bert-base-uncased` as a three-way sequence classifier over score level 0/1/2, with a maximum input length of 256 tokens. The model is trained with cross-entropy loss and optimized using AdamW (learning rate $2\times10^{-5}$, weight decay 0.01, batch size 16) and a linear learning-rate schedule with warm-up for up to 20 epochs. We employ early stopping with a patience of 3 epochs (minimum improvement: 0.001), retaining the checkpoint with the highest validation accuracy for test-set evaluation. All experiments are repeated over 10 random seeds to ensure statistical stability.

**BRIDGE Implementation.** To synthesize additional $\mathcal{S}_{\text{EL,high}}$ samples, we utilize GPT-4o [14] ($T = 0.8$) to perform the inter-group stylistic reformulation on the training split. Following the framework described in Sect. 3, we extract construct-relevant content from non-ELL high-scoring responses and reformulate it using ELL-specific linguistic patterns. Candidates are then passed through a lightweight discriminator trained on a mixture of authentic and synthetic responses for up to 10 epochs. We retain only synthetic samples exceeding an authenticity threshold of $\gamma = 0.6$, which are assigned the $\mathcal{S}_{\text{EL,high}}$ label and used as augmented training data in the subsequent experiments.

**Baselines.** We compare BRIDGE against three augmentation strategies while keeping the scoring architecture and optimization constant. (i) *Real-data augmentation (Oracle):* Adds additional authentic $\mathcal{S}_{\text{EL,high}}$ samples, drawn from the held-out 99% pool, to the 1% training set up to a fixed budget. This serves as an Oracle upper bound, representing the model's potential when provided with additional real human data. (ii) *Oversampling:* A standard baseline for addressing class imbalance. Randomly replicates existing $\mathcal{S}_{\text{EL,high}}$ samples within the 1% training set with replacement to meet the budget without introducing new linguistic content. (iii) *Paraphrasing*: An intra-group baseline using GPT-4o to rewrite available $\mathcal{S}_{\text{EL,high}}$ samples, relying solely on existing minority patterns without leveraging external content. All baselines differ exclusively in the construction of the additional $\mathcal{S}_{\text{EL,high}}$ training instances, ensuring observed performance gains are attributable to the augmentation strategy.

**Evaluation Metrics.** We evaluate models across two dimensions: scoring performance and group fairness. Scoring performance is measured by *Accuracy*, *Quadratic Weighted Kappa (QWK)*, *Mean Absolute Error (MAE)*, and *Macro-F1*, providing a holistic view of agreement and robustness. To quantify fairness, we report: (i) *MSG Gap:* Defined as the difference between the model's Non-ELL vs. ELL Mean Score Gap (MSG) and the corresponding MSG under human scores. Positive values indicate that the model widens the human MSG. (ii) *BiasAmp:* As defined in Sect. 2.3, this metric measures bias amplification for the $\mathcal{S}_{\text{EL,high}}$ subgroup by capturing the change in the Non-ELL vs. ELL disparity at the score 2 level between human and model scores. All metrics are reported as mean $\pm$ standard deviation over 10 random seeds.

### 4.3 Results and Analysis

**Quantification of Bias Amplification (RQ1).** To evaluate RQ1, we examine whether the vanilla scoring model (baseline) amplifies the Non-ELL vs. ELL disparity for the high-scoring subgroup $\mathcal{S}_{\text{EL,high}}$. For each dataset, we compute the high-score disparity in the training data, $\Delta_{\text{data}}$, and in the model predictions, $\Delta_{\text{model}}$, and obtain the bias amplification measure BiasAmp $= \Delta_{\text{model}} - \Delta_{\text{data}}$ defined in Sect. 2.3. As shown in Table 1, across the five datasets, the baseline model consistently exhibits positive bias amplification: BiasAmp ranges from 0.0073 to 0.0156 (mean $=$ 0.0119). In other words, the model further widens the between-group disparity in the probability of receiving the top score by about 3.4–9.0% relative to the disparity already present in the training data.

To ensure these findings are statistically meaningful rather than artifacts of random initialization, we perform significance tests over all runs for each dataset. We test the null hypothesis $H_0$ : BiasAmp $= 0$ against the one-sided alternative $H_1$ : BiasAmp $> 0$. Following normality checks, we apply either one-sample $t$-tests or Wilcoxon signed-rank tests as appropriate. Across all five datasets, the baseline model consistently exhibits significant bias amplification (all $p < 0.01$). These results provide robust evidence that scoring models systematically amplify existing group disparities for the $\mathcal{S}_{\text{EL,high}}$ subgroup under data sparsity.

**Comparative Analysis of Mitigation Strategies (RQ2).** To address RQ2, we compare the mitigation efficacy of BRIDGE against all baseline strategies. As summarized in Table 1, BRIDGE reduces both group-level disparity (MSG

**Table 1.** Bias mitigation performance of different data augmentation methods on five CAST datasets, each with 20 additional $\mathcal{S}_{\text{EL,high}}$ samples per method. Mean ± standard deviation over 10 random seeds. Best and second-best MSG Gap and BiasAmp are highlighted in **bold** and underlined, respectively.

| Dataset | Aug. Method | Fairness | | Performance | | | |
|---|---|---|---|---|---|---|---|
| | | MSG Gap↓ | BiasAmp↓ | Acc.(%)↑ | MAE↓ | QWK(%)↑ | F1(%)↑ |
| Dataset 1 | Baseline (no aug.) | 0.0279 ± 0.0134 | 0.0097 ± 0.0081 | 90.17 ± 0.48 | 0.0988 ± 0.0053 | 89.77 ± 0.64 | 88.68 ± 0.50 |
| | + Real-data (oracle) | 0.0100 ± 0.0129 | 0.0025 ± 0.0093 | 90.19 ± 0.48 | 0.0993 ± 0.0046 | 89.68 ± 0.34 | 88.58 ± 0.59 |
| | + Oversampling | 0.0279 ± 0.0092 | 0.0107 ± 0.0054 | 90.41 ± 0.42 | 0.0962 ± 0.0043 | 90.05 ± 0.40 | 89.01 ± 0.40 |
| | + Paraphrasing | 0.0268 ± 0.0137 | 0.0082 ± 0.0094 | 90.31 ± 0.32 | 0.0974 ± 0.0035 | 89.86 ± 0.39 | 88.77 ± 0.33 |
| | + Ours | **0.0079** ± 0.0139 | **−0.0014** ± 0.0085 | 90.22 ± 0.27 | 0.0994 ± 0.0031 | 89.53 ± 0.38 | 88.63 ± 0.27 |
| Dataset 2 | Baseline (no aug.) | 0.0125 ± 0.0045 | 0.0132 ± 0.0039 | 94.32 ± 0.32 | 0.0568 ± 0.0032 | 96.15 ± 0.21 | 92.81 ± 0.41 |
| | + Real-data (oracle) | 0.0120 ± 0.0089 | **0.0088** ± 0.0072 | 94.38 ± 0.25 | 0.0564 ± 0.0024 | 96.17 ± 0.16 | 92.86 ± 0.33 |
| | + Oversampling | 0.0145 ± 0.0056 | 0.0121 ± 0.0038 | 94.48 ± 0.18 | 0.0553 ± 0.0018 | 96.26 ± 0.12 | 92.99 ± 0.26 |
| | + Paraphrasing | 0.0155 ± 0.0056 | 0.0132 ± 0.0024 | 94.32 ± 0.32 | 0.0569 ± 0.0032 | 96.15 ± 0.21 | 92.78 ± 0.41 |
| | + Ours | **0.0094** ± 0.0086 | 0.0097 ± 0.0056 | 94.39 ± 0.41 | 0.0562 ± 0.0042 | 96.18 ± 0.27 | 92.89 ± 0.62 |
| Dataset 3 | Baseline (no aug.) | 0.0032 ± 0.0092 | 0.0073 ± 0.0066 | 91.28 ± 0.32 | 0.0874 ± 0.0033 | 93.43 ± 0.20 | 87.76 ± 0.51 |
| | + Real-data (oracle) | −0.0034 ± 0.0183 | 0.0034 ± 0.0130 | 91.27 ± 0.39 | 0.0876 ± 0.0039 | 93.39 ± 0.34 | 87.83 ± 0.53 |
| | + Oversampling | −0.0006 ± 0.0156 | 0.0036 ± 0.0111 | 91.41 ± 0.29 | 0.0861 ± 0.0030 | 93.47 ± 0.27 | 88.04 ± 0.40 |
| | + Paraphrasing | 0.0033 ± 0.0130 | 0.0075 ± 0.0109 | 91.38 ± 0.33 | 0.0864 ± 0.0033 | 93.48 ± 0.31 | 87.93 ± 0.47 |
| | + Ours | **−0.0037** ± 0.0117 | **0.0031** ± 0.0080 | 91.24 ± 0.28 | 0.0880 ± 0.0026 | 93.40 ± 0.20 | 87.70 ± 0.46 |
| Dataset 4 | Baseline (no aug.) | 0.0140 ± 0.0225 | **0.0156** ± 0.0126 | 88.71 ± 0.60 | 0.1131 ± 0.0060 | 92.79 ± 0.41 | 86.32 ± 0.71 |
| | + Real-data (oracle) | **0.0111** ± 0.0143 | 0.0170 ± 0.0092 | 88.78 ± 0.48 | 0.1126 ± 0.0047 | 92.84 ± 0.26 | 86.23 ± 0.83 |
| | + Oversampling | 0.0172 ± 0.0140 | 0.0200 ± 0.0069 | 89.00 ± 0.43 | 0.1104 ± 0.0042 | 92.97 ± 0.23 | 86.58 ± 0.74 |
| | + Paraphrasing | 0.0176 ± 0.0154 | 0.0223 ± 0.0069 | 88.70 ± 0.39 | 0.1133 ± 0.0037 | 92.79 ± 0.22 | 86.19 ± 0.66 |
| | + Ours | 0.0128 ± 0.0157 | 0.0170 ± 0.0050 | 88.92 ± 0.44 | 0.1111 ± 0.0043 | 92.93 ± 0.27 | 86.45 ± 0.55 |
| Dataset 5 | Baseline (no aug.) | 0.0134 ± 0.0154 | 0.0135 ± 0.0102 | 91.46 ± 0.29 | 0.0865 ± 0.0030 | 94.25 ± 0.21 | 88.35 ± 0.54 |
| | + Real-data (oracle) | 0.0122 ± 0.0088 | 0.0131 ± 0.0043 | 91.41 ± 0.29 | 0.0868 ± 0.0029 | 94.22 ± 0.22 | 88.43 ± 0.45 |
| | + Oversampling | 0.0113 ± 0.0081 | 0.0119 ± 0.0054 | 91.51 ± 0.26 | 0.0858 ± 0.0027 | 94.32 ± 0.16 | 88.37 ± 0.51 |
| | + Paraphrasing | 0.0194 ± 0.0064 | 0.0142 ± 0.0027 | 91.42 ± 0.28 | 0.0870 ± 0.0029 | 94.23 ± 0.19 | 88.22 ± 0.62 |
| | + Ours | **0.0009** ± 0.0173 | **0.0050** ± 0.0087 | 91.36 ± 0.27 | 0.0878 ± 0.0031 | 94.12 ± 0.25 | 88.25 ± 0.53 |

*Note.* F1 denotes the macro-averaged F1 score over score levels.

Gap) and high-score amplification (BiasAmp) across the majority of datasets. For instance, in Dataset 5, BRIDGE reduces the MSG Gap from 0.0134 to 0.0009, a 93.28% reduction in group-level disparity. Similarly, in Dataset 1, our method reduces the BiasAmp from 0.0097 to −0.0014, indicating that the model no longer under-predicts high-scoring ELLs. For datasets with larger initial bias amplification (e.g., Datasets 1 and 5), these reductions are statistically significant ($p < 0.01$), whereas for items with smaller baseline bias (e.g., Dataset 3), the numerical improvements are directionally consistent but statistically inconclusive.

Beyond these general improvements, BRIDGE demonstrates competitive performance against the Real-data aug. (Oracle), achieving numerically superior fairness metrics in Datasets 1, 3, and 5. For instance, in Dataset 5, BRIDGE achieves a BiasAmp of 0.0050, representing a 61.83% further reduction in high-score bias compared to the oracle (0.0131). We attribute this superiority to the fact that BRIDGE creates controlled examples by injecting prototypical Non-ELL high-score logic into ELL linguistic patterns. This targeted intervention helps the model learn to decouple surface-level language features from content quality, providing a more concentrated debiasing signal than the naturally occurring variations in authentic ELL samples.

Compared to intra-group baselines, BRIDGE exhibits crucial robustness in challenging scenarios. Oversampling and Paraphrasing show marginal or even negative effects across most datasets, confirming that intra-group augmentation lacks sufficient signal diversity when the target subgroup is sparse. Notably, in the most challenging scenario, Dataset 4, Oversampling and Paraphrasing yield "adverse effects", increasing BiasAmp by 28.21% and 42.95% respectively. In contrast, BRIDGE maintains comparable performance to the oracle baseline.

**Trade-Off Between Fairness and Scoring Performance (RQ3).** Regarding RQ3, Table 1 demonstrates that the substantial fairness gains of BRIDGE do not compromise overall scoring performance. Across all five datasets, BRIDGE introduces negligible changes to all performance metrics: Accuracy varies by −0.11% to +0.24%, QWK by −0.27% to +0.15%, Macro F1 by −0.11% to +0.15%, and MAE by −1.77% to +1.50%. These variations fall within the standard deviation of the baseline model, indicating that BRIDGE effectively mitigates bias amplification without degrading the model's scoring capability. This suggests that the fairness-performance tradeoff, a common bottleneck in bias mitigation methods, is not a significant concern for BRIDGE.

### 4.4 Ablation Study

To investigate the contribution of the Discriminative Filtering (Stage 2), we compare the full BRIDGE framework against a "generation-only" variant (w/o Stage 2). Our results indicate that Stage 1 (Inter-group Stylistic Reformulation) serves as the primary driver for bias mitigation, while Stage 2 provides critical quality control and robustness gains. For instance, in Dataset 5, Stage 1 alone achieves a 90.78% reduction in MSG Gap (from 0.0134 to 0.0012), with Stage 2 contributing a marginal further improvement to 0.0009, yielding an additional absolute improvement of 0.0003 (about 2.5% of the baseline). The necessity of Stage 2 becomes more apparent in scenarios where Stage 1's initial gains are constrained. For Dataset 1, Stage 1 reduces the MSG Gap by 44.90% (from 0.0279 to 0.0154), but Stage 2 is required to reach the final 0.0079 level, representing an additional 26.88% reduction relative to the baseline. In Dataset 3, Stage 1 alone yields negligible improvements to BiasAmp (0.0073 $\rightarrow$ 0.0071). Manual spot-checks suggest that the proportion of high-quality synthetic samples in Dataset 3 is lower than in other items. Consequently, the noise from low-fidelity outputs counteracts the augmentation signal. By filtering out such low-quality samples, Stage 2 enables a significant reduction in BiasAmp to 0.0031. In saturated scenarios like Dataset 2, the marginal impact of Stage 2 (a delta of only 0.0001 in MSG Gap and 0.0003 in BiasAmp) confirms its role as a reliability mechanism rather than a primary signal generator. Overall, these findings support our two-stage design: Stage 1 establishes the debiasing foundation, while Stage 2 ensures stylistic authenticity and stability.

## 5 Conclusion and Discussion

This work reveals and quantifies the phenomenon of bias amplification in ERM-based automated scoring models. To mitigate this, we propose BRIDGE, an inter-group data augmentation framework designed for extreme low-resource scenarios. By "pasting" construct-relevant content from high-scoring non-ELL responses into authentic ELL linguistic patterns and employing a discriminative filter to eliminate low-fidelity candidates, BRIDGE effectively fills the gaps in the training data distribution. Our experiments on real-world CAST datasets demonstrate that BRIDGE significantly reduces both group-level disparities and high-score bias amplification while maintaining overall scoring performance. Notably, BRIDGE achieves fairness performance comparable to augmentation using additional real data. This suggests that in practical settings where high-scoring ELL responses are inherently difficult to obtain, educational institutions can achieve bias mitigation without the prohibitive cost of collecting rare samples. These results highlight BRIDGE as a scalable, controllable, and cost-effective solution for ensuring algorithmic fairness in large-scale educational assessments.

Despite its efficacy, BRIDGE relies on the disentanglement of content and style, which may not fully hold in assessments where linguistic expression is part of the core construct. Additionally, this study is limited to short-answer science items, and its generalizability to long essays remains to be tested. Future research will extend BRIDGE to other data scarce educational contexts, explore finer-grained stylistic control, and investigate synergies with other fairness-enhancing strategies to build a more robust and equitable scoring ecosystem.

**Acknowledgments.** This work is supported by the Institute of Education Sciences (IES) under Grant No. R305C240010 and Grant No. R305A240356. The views and conclusions expressed in this paper are those of the authors and do not necessarily reflect the views of the funding agencies.

**Disclosure of Interests.** The authors have no competing interests to declare that are relevant to the content of this article.

## References

1. Abedi, J.: Psychometric issues in the ell assessment and special education eligibility. Teach. Coll. Rec. **108**(11), 2282–2303 (2006)
2. Alkhawaldeh, I.M., Albalkhi, I., Naswhan, A.J.: Challenges and limitations of synthetic minority oversampling techniques in machine learning. World J. Methodol. **13**(5), 373 (2023)
3. American Educational Research Association: American Psychological Association, National Council on Measurement in Education: Standards for Educational and Psychological Testing. American Educational Research Association, Washington, DC (2014)
4. Andersen, N., Mang, J., Goldhammer, F., Zehner, F.: Algorithmic fairness in automatic short answer scoring. Int. J. Artif. Intell. Educ. 1–38 (2025)

5. Chai, Y., Xie, H., Qin, J.S.: Text data augmentation for large language models: a comprehensive survey of methods, challenges, and opportunities. arXiv preprint arXiv:2501.18845 (2025)
6. Chaudhari, R., Patel, M.: Deep learning in automated short answer grading: a comprehensive review. In: ITM Web of Conferences, vol. 65, p. 03003. EDP Sciences (2024)
7. Chen, D., Yin, C.: Data augmentation for intent classification (2022). https://arxiv.org/abs/2206.05790
8. Crossley, S.A., McNamara, D.S.: Predicting second language writing proficiency: the roles of cohesion and linguistic sophistication. J. Res. Reading **35**(2), 115–135 (2012)
9. Devlin, J., Chang, M.W., Lee, K., Toutanova, K.: Bert: pre-training of deep bidirectional transformers for language understanding. In: Proceedings of NAACL-HLT (2019)
10. Dikli, S., Bleyle, S.: Automated essay scoring feedback for second language writers: how does it compare to instructor feedback? Assess. Writ. **22**, 1–17 (2014)
11. Emirtekin, E.: Large language model-powered automated assessment: a systematic review. Appl. Sci. **15**(10), 5683 (2025)
12. Guo, S., et al.: Artificial intelligence bias on english language learners in automatic scoring. In: International Conference on Artificial Intelligence in Education, pp. 268–275. Springer (2025)
13. Hashimoto, T., Srivastava, M., Namkoong, H., Liang, P.: Fairness without demographics in repeated loss minimization. In: International Conference on Machine Learning, pp. 1929–1938. PMLR (2018)
14. Hurst, A., et al.: GPT-4o system card. arXiv preprint arXiv:2410.21276 (2024)
15. Leino, K., Black, E., Fredrikson, M., Sen, S., Datta, A.: Feature-wise bias amplification. arXiv preprint arXiv:1812.08999 (2018)
16. Li, Z., Wu, X., Li, Y., Hu, L., Liu, N.: Less is enough: synthesizing diverse data in feature space of LLMs. arXiv preprint arXiv:2602.10388 (2026)
17. Mehrabi, N., Morstatter, F., Saxena, N., Lerman, K., Galstyan, A.: A survey on bias and fairness in machine learning. ACM Comput. Surv. (CSUR) **54**(6), 1–35 (2021)
18. Messick, S.: Validity. ETS Research Report Series **1987**(2), i-208 (1987)
19. Palermo, C.: Rater characteristics, response content, and scoring contexts: decomposing the determinates of scoring accuracy. Front. Psychol. **13**, 937097 (2022)
20. Park, S., Hong, Y., Heo, B., Yun, S., Choi, J.Y.: The majority can help the minority: context-rich minority oversampling for long-tailed classification. In: Proceedings of the IEEE/CVF Conference on Computer Vision and Pattern Recognition, pp. 6887–6896 (2022)
21. Plecko, D., Bareinboim, E.: Mind the gap: a causal perspective on bias amplification in prediction & decision-making. Adv. Neural. Inf. Process. Syst. **37**, 84384–84408 (2024)
22. Sagawa, S., Koh, P.W., Hashimoto, T.B., Liang, P.: Distributionally robust neural networks for group shifts: on the importance of regularization for worst-case generalization. arXiv preprint arXiv:1911.08731 (2019)
23. Schwartz, R., et al.: Towards a standard for identifying and managing bias in artificial intelligence, vol. 3. US Department of Commerce, National Institute of Standards and Technology (2022)
24. Shahbazi, N., Lin, Y., Asudeh, A., Jagadish, H.: Representation bias in data: a survey on identification and resolution techniques. ACM Comput. Surv. **55**(13s), 1–39 (2023)

25. Sourati, Z., Ziabari, A.S., Dehghani, M.: The homogenizing effect of large language models on human expression and thought. arXiv preprint arXiv:2508.01491 (2025)
26. Vapnik, V.: Principles of risk minimization for learning theory. In: Advances in Neural Information Processing Systems, vol. 4 (1991)
27. Wang, A., Russakovsky, O.: Directional bias amplification. In: International Conference on Machine Learning, pp. 10882–10893. PMLR (2021)
28. Wang, Y., Ding, Z., Wu, X., Sun, S., Liu, N., Zhai, X.: Autoscore: enhancing automated scoring with multi-agent large language models via structured component recognition. In: Proceedings of the AAAI Conference on Artificial Intelligence, vol. 40, pp. 40898–40906 (2026)
29. Weigle, S.C.: English language learners and automated scoring of essays: critical considerations. Assess. Writ. **18**(1), 85–99 (2013)
30. Welch, C., Dunbar, S., Ji, J., Vernon, A., Park, J.: Response time for english learners on large-scale writing assessments. Assess. Writ. **66**, 100979 (2025)
31. Wilson, J., Huang, Y.: Validity of automated essay scores for elementary-age english language learners: evidence of bias? Assess. Writ. **60**, 100815 (2024)
32. Xu, H., Gan, W., Qi, Z., Wu, J., Yu, P.S.: Large language models for education: a survey. arXiv preprint arXiv:2405.13001 (2024)
33. Zhai, X., Haudek, K.C., Stuhlsatz, M.A., Wilson, C.: Evaluation of construct-irrelevant variance yielded by machine and human scoring of a science teacher PCK constructed response assessment. Stud. Educ. Eval. **67**, 100916 (2020)
34. Zhai, X., Pellegrino, J.W.: Large-scale assessment in science education. In: Handbook of Research on Science Education, pp. 1045–1097. Routledge (2023)
35. Zhao, J., Wang, T., Yatskar, M., Ordonez, V., Chang, K.W.: Men also like shopping: reducing gender bias amplification using corpus-level constraints. arXiv preprint arXiv:1707.09457 (2017)
36. Zhu, X., Wu, H., Zhang, L.: Automatic short-answer grading via BERT-based deep neural networks. IEEE Trans. Learn. Technol. **15**(3), 364–375 (2022). https://doi.org/10.1109/TLT.2022.3175537

# Decomposing the Fairness Gap: Disentangling Data Scarcity from Validity Bias in AI-Driven Formative Assessment

Xuanyu Liu and Wen Zhu(✉)

Zhejiang University, Hangzhou 310058, China
1246656240@qq.com

**Abstract.** Intelligent learning systems increasingly rely on process evidence, such as clickstreams, for formative assessment. However, concerns persist that data-driven approaches may inadvertently encode socioeconomic disadvantages, reinforcing educational inequality. This study investigates the structural sources of assessment bias across socioeconomic status (SES) groups, questioning whether the gap stems from a "lack of data generation" (Endowment Effect) or "differences in predictive validity" (Coefficient Effect). Leveraging the Open University Learning Analytics Dataset (N = 31,482), we employed a methodological triangulation strategy combining Explainable Machine Learning (Random Forest + SHAP) and Econometric Oaxaca-Blinder Decomposition. Results reveal a significant "Poverty Penalty." While early behavioral engagement is a robust predictor, decomposition indicates that 73.1% of the assessment gap is attributable to the Coefficient Effect, whereas only 26.9% stems from the Endowment Effect. Propensity Score Matching confirms robust causal returns on engagement. We conclude that inequity is driven primarily by validity bias—algorithms undervaluing low-SES behavioral patterns—rather than data scarcity. Policy efforts must shift from "Fixing the student" (nudging for more data) to "Fixing the system" (calibrating models for Design Justice).

**Keywords:** Formative Assessment · Algorithmic Bias · Process Evidence · Oaxaca-Blinder Decomposition · Educational Equity

## 1 Introduction

Formative assessment, designed to support pedagogical decision-making through the continuous collection of learning evidence, is a cornerstone of personalized learning [1]. In digital learning environments, the convergence of Learning Analytics (LA) and Artificial Intelligence (AI) has shifted the assessment paradigm from periodic testing to the analysis of continuous Process Evidence—such as clickstreams and interaction trajectories. From the theoretical perspective of Self-Regulated Learning (SRL), micro-behavioral traces in Learning Management Systems (LMS) are not merely operational records but externalized manifestations of students' metacognitive strategies [2].

X. Liu and W. Zhu—These authors contributed equally to this work.


E. G. Blanchard et al. (eds.), AIED 2026, LNCS 16586, pp. 46–59, 2027.
https://doi.org/10.1007/978-3-032-29773-0_4

However, existing intelligent assessment algorithms often implicitly encode specific SRL patterns—typically linear, high-frequency interactions characteristic of advantaged groups—as "normative" standards. When students from low Socioeconomic Status (SES) backgrounds exhibit non-linear learning paths, this "Algorithmic Gaze" may misinterpret their behaviors as inefficiency, sparking ethical controversies regarding algorithmic fairness [3, 4]. While prior research has focused on equalizing predictive accuracy, the structural origins of this Assessment Bias remain under-explored. Bias may arise through two mechanisms: the Endowment Effect (Digital Activity Gap), where disadvantaged students generate fewer data points; and the more insidious Coefficient Effect (Validity Heterogeneity), where identical behavioral signals hold different predictive power across groups due to variations in cultural capital [5].

Addressing this gap, this study applies the Oaxaca-Blinder Decomposition to educational assessment. We construct a "Methodological Triangulation" framework using the Open University Learning Analytics Dataset (OULAD). This study makes three contributions: (1) Methodological Novelty: It marks the first application of econometric decomposition to disentangle "Data Scarcity" from "Validity Bias" in AI assessment; (2) Theoretical Reframing: It reveals that 73% of the gap stems from Validity Heterogeneity, challenging the traditional "Digital Divide" narrative; (3) Policy Paradigm Shift: It proposes moving from "Fixing the Student" to "Fixing the Algorithm" to achieve Design Justice.

## 2 Theoretical Framework

This study constructs an analytical framework based on three theoretical pillars: Formative Assessment theory provides the conceptual basis for identifying process evidence; Fairness theory offers ethical criteria for diagnosing assessment bias; and the Oaxaca-Blinder decomposition provides the analytical tool for quantifying structural sources of bias.

### 2.1 Formative Assessment and Process Evidence

Black and Wiliam (1998) emphasize that the fundamental purpose of assessment is to promote learning, not merely to judge outcomes. Formative assessment is characterized by continuity, diagnosticity, and guidance. In digital environments, we introduce the concept of "Process Evidence." In intelligent systems, students' interaction traces (e.g., clickstreams) constitute the operationalization of this evidence. Based on SRL theory [6], these behavioral data reflect learning engagement, cognitive strategies, and metacognitive monitoring. We define early course interactions (first 100 days) as the critical window for formative intervention, hypothesizing that early behavioral patterns effectively predict final academic achievement.

### 2.2 Algorithmic Fairness and Assessment Bias

Messick [7] posited that validity is not a property of the test itself, but of the inferences drawn from test scores. Fair assessment requires that inferences have equal validity across different groups. In the context of Educational AI, we focus on Validity Fairness—whether assessment signals hold equal predictive validity for different student populations. If the accuracy of model inference fluctuates systematically with SES background, validity bias occurs. Drawing on Baker and Hawn's [3] theory of algorithmic bias, assessment bias can operate through two distinct mechanisms: the Endowment Effect refers to disparities in the generation of process evidence (e.g., data scarcity); while the Coefficient Effect refers to differences in the predictive validity of identical behavioral signals across groups (e.g., the model's misinterpretation of low-SES behavioral patterns), which represents a deeper structural bias. The theoretical model of this study is formulated as:

$$Assessment\ Signal = f\,(Process\ Evidence, SES, Controls) \quad (1)$$

Through Oaxaca-Blinder decomposition, we quantify the gap as:

$$Gap = Endowment\ Effect\ (Data\ Scarcity) + Coefficient\ Effect\ (Validity\ Bias) \quad (2)$$

## 3 Methodology

### 3.1 Data and Preprocessing

We utilized the Open University Learning Analytics Dataset (OULAD) [8], containing detailed learning records of 32,593 students across 7 courses during 2013–2014.

To address Endogeneity and Survivorship Bias, we applied rigorous screening. First, we excluded students who withdrew before the course start date, retaining students with substantive learning behaviors. Second, we constructed an Early Engagement Window. Many studies use total semester clicks as predictors, leading to data leakage. To resolve this, we constructed the "early_clicks" variable, calculating clickstreams only from the first 100 days (approx. 1/3 of the course). This is based on the logic that only "early effort" capable of changing "final fate" holds predictive value for educational intervention.

### 3.2 Variable Construction

To quantify the structural sources of assessment bias, we constructed the following core variables, which are summarized in Table 1. For complete operational definitions, raw field mappings, and detailed coding rules, please refer to Table A1 in the Appendix.

In the regression models, we standardized early_clicks to clicks_std (mean = 0, standard deviation = 1). Therefore, regression coefficients and Odds Ratios (OR) are interpreted as the marginal effect of a "1-standard-deviation increase in process evidence."

### 3.3 Analytical Strategy

We adopted a progressive "Methodological Triangulation" strategy:

**Table 1.** Variable Definitions and Coding Rules.

| Category | Variable Name | Description and Coding Details |
|---|---|---|
| Dependent Variable | Final Result | A binary variable (1 = Pass/Distinction, 0 = Fail/Withdrawn), representing the final assessment outcome of the intelligent system. |
| Process Evidence | early_clicks | The total number of VLE interactions in the first 100 days of the course, serving as the core behavioral signal for formative assessment. |
| Grouping Variable | SES_score | An ordinal encoding based on imd_band (0 = most deprived, 9 = most affluent), used to distinguish between different socioeconomic status (SES) groups. |
| Controls | Prior_Education | The highest qualification held prior to enrollment (highest_education), ordinally encoded. Compared to in-course assignment scores (TMA1), this is a fully exogenous pre-determined variable, enabling stricter avoidance of endogeneity issues. |
| | Gender and Disability | Demographic control variables. |

**Phase 1: Signal Identification.** Descriptive statistics are first employed to demonstrate disparities in process evidence generation and assessment outcomes across different SES groups. Subsequently, Random Forest and SHAP is utilized for exploratory analysis. By calculating the Shapley Value of each feature, it is determined whether behavioral features-relative to background features-possess sufficient assessment value.
**Phase 2: Bias Decomposition.** The Oaxaca-Blinder Decomposition is applied to decompose the assessment gap between high SES and low SES groups into endowment and coefficient effects, precisely quantifying the relative contributions of "data scarcity" and "validity bias." Simultaneously, Logistic regression models (Baseline, Interaction, Fixed Effects) are constructed to test interaction effects, verifying whether significant differences exist in marginal returns across groups.
**Phase 3: Causal Verification.** Propensity Score Matching is adopted to match students with identical backgrounds but differing levels of process evidence generation. This constructs a "counterfactual" framework to verify whether behavioral engagement itself yields a robust causal return, thereby excluding interference from self-selection bias.

## 4 Results

This study is based on the Open University Learning Analytics Dataset (OULAD). After excluding early withdrawal samples, a total of 31,482 students were included for in-depth analysis of process evidence generation, socioeconomic status, and assessment outcomes.

### 4.1 The Process Evidence Gap: Unequal Signal Generation

Descriptive statistics first revealed significant group differences in process evidence generation. To avoid survivorship bias, Fig. 1 specifically presents student behavioral data from the "early course period (first 100 days)". Results show that students' family economic backgrounds (measured by imd_band) are significantly positively correlated with both the volume of behavioral signals sent to the system and their final assessment outcomes.

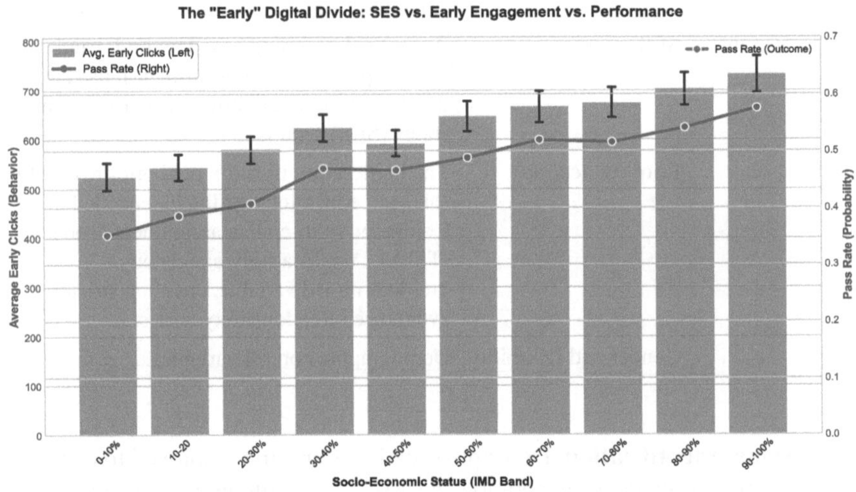


**Fig. 1.** The Early Digital Divide.

On one hand, there exists a significant process evidence gap. The bar chart in Fig. 1 (blue) shows that students from the most impoverished areas (0–10% IMD) had an average of only 524 early clicks (Avg. Early Clicks); whereas students from the most affluent areas (90–100% IMD) had early engagement as high as 733 clicks. The 95% CI error bars (black vertical lines) between the two groups show no overlap, indicating that this gap is highly statistically significant (independent samples t-test, $p < 0.001$). This "participation gap" demonstrates that disadvantaged students are inherently at a disadvantage when sending assessment signals to AI systems.

On the other hand, this difference in evidence generation directly maps onto the assessment gap. The line chart in Fig. 1 (red) shows that pass rates steadily increase with economic status. The pass rate for the poorest group is only 35.1%, while that of the wealthiest group reaches 57.5%. This result indicates that group differences indeed exist in intelligent assessment systems, and low-SES students face a significant "Poverty Penalty."

### 4.2 The Dominance of Process Evidence in Prediction

Although Sect. 4.1 revealed significant group differences, the second-stage machine learning analysis provided empirical support for the validity of process evidence as a basis for formative assessment. We trained a Random Forest Classifier (n_estimators = 100, max_depth = 10) to predict whether students would pass the exam, using an 80/20 train-test split, with the model achieving 80.6% accuracy on the test set. To identify key assessment signals, we introduced SHAP (SHapley Additive exPlanations) values for attribution analysis [9]. Figure 2 displays the average contribution of each feature to model predictions (Mean |SHAP value|).

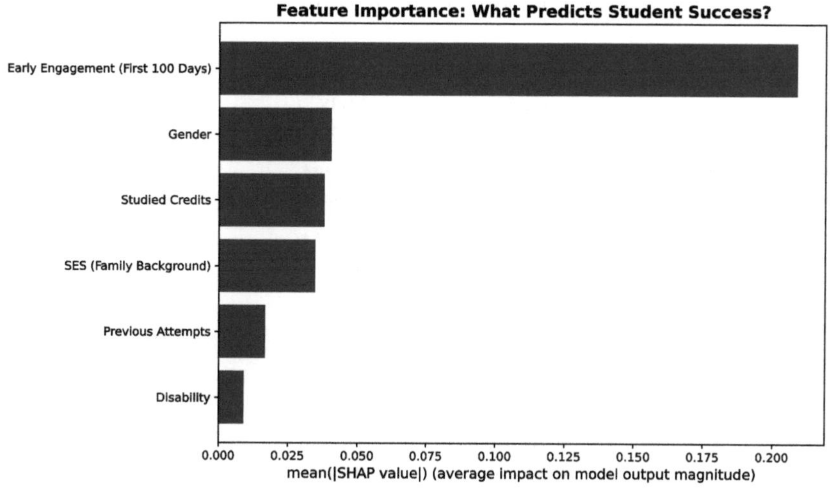


**Fig. 2.** Feature Importance.

The analysis results demonstrate the Dominance of Process Evidence. "early_clicks" (early behavioral signals) is the absolute core factor in predicting student assessment outcomes, with a SHAP importance value of approximately 0.30, far ahead of all other features. This means that in intelligent assessment systems, "clicking" behavior data (representing time investment and cognitive engagement) is the most critical variable determining assessment outcomes. This empirically validates the effectiveness of process behavioral data as a basis for formative assessment: "What you do" predicts academic success better than "who you are."

In contrast, background features contribute relatively weakly (Diminished Role of Background). The SHAP importance of "SES", representing family background, is only 0.028, even lower than "Gender" (0.041) and "Studied Credits" (0.029). This finding indicates that: Low-SES students have poorer assessment outcomes primarily because they generate less process evidence (fewer clicks). This preliminarily supports the "Endowment Effect" hypothesis—that assessment gaps may primarily stem from insufficient data generation.

### 4.3 Econometric Verification: Testing for Validity Heterogeneity

To further test whether validity heterogeneity exists—that is, whether the predictive power of process evidence systematically differs across groups—we employed a "Stepwise Regression" strategy, constructing three nested Logistic regression models (results summarized in Table 2). Model (1) Baseline includes only main effects, establishing the baseline correlation between process evidence and assessment outcomes; Model (2) Interaction introduces an interaction term (*SES*× *Engagement*) to test whether marginal return rates differ across groups; Model (3) Fixed Effects adds course, semester, and regional fixed effects to control for unobservable heterogeneity.

**Table 2.** Stepwise Logistic Regression Results.

| Variable | (1) Baseline | (2) Interaction | (3) + Fixed Effects |
|---|---|---|---|
| Constant | −0.020<br>(0.146) | −0.038<br>(0.142) | −0.142<br>(0.109) |
| SES (Family Background) | 0.078***<br>(0.005) | 0.082***<br>(0.006) | 0.073***<br>(0.005) |
| Early Engagement (Std) | 1.347***<br>(0.164) | 1.256***<br>(0.162) | 1.711***<br>(0.180) |
| Interaction (SES x Eng-) | | 0.022<br>(0.014) | 0.015<br>(0.015) |
| Prior Education (Std) | 0.243***<br>(0.034) | 0.243***<br>(0.034) | 0.324***<br>(0.013) |
| Gender (Male) | −0.549***<br>(.106) | −0.549***<br>(0.107) | 0.091**<br>(0.046) |
| Disability (Yes) | −0.302***<br>(0.056) | −0.301***<br>(0.056) | −0.299***<br>(0.053) |
| Control Variables | Yes | Yes | Yes |
| Module FE | No | No | Yes |
| Presentation FE | No | No | Yes |
| Region FE | No | No | Yes |
| Observations | 31,482 | 31,482 | 31,482 |
| Pseudo R-squared | 0.157 | 0.157 | 0.212 |

**p* < 0.1, ***p* < 0.05, *** *p* < 0.01. *Clustered standard errors (Module x Presentation) in parentheses*
*Fixed Effects include Module, Presentation, and Region.*

Based on the regression results in Table 2, we conducted in-depth analysis on three levels. First, regarding the Predictive Power of Process Evidence, Model (1) shows that early behavioral signals (standardized clicks_std) have an odds ratio as high as OR = 3.85, meaning that for every one standard deviation increase in process evidence, the odds of passing multiply by approximately 3.85; while the odds ratio for SES is only OR ≈ 1.08. This result confirms the central role of process evidence in assessment.

Second, regarding the Validity Heterogeneity Test, in Model (2) with the interaction term, the coefficient direction is positive ($\beta = 0.022$), but after applying Clustered Robust Standard Errors (Clustered SE by Module × Presentation), its statistical significance disappears (p = 0.111). In Model (3) with course, semester, and regional fixed effects added, the coefficient is similarly positive but not significant (β = 0.015, p = 0.299).

This result has important theoretical implications. The statistical non-significance means that the Marginal Return per unit of process evidence for high and low SES students may not show significant statistical differences—that is, the "slope validity" of behavioral signals is relatively stable across groups. However, this precisely proves that the source of assessment bias is not "slope differences" but rather massive "intercept differences." Low-SES students face an extremely low baseline starting point; even with the same signal conversion efficiency, due to their far-behind starting line, they still need to generate far more data than others to cross the assessment threshold. This also explains why such large coefficient effects appear in the Oaxaca decomposition.

Finally, regarding the Mediation Effect, to explore how SES affects assessment outcomes, we further conducted mediation effect testing [16]. Results show that after introducing process evidence, the direct effect coefficient of SES on assessment outcomes decreases. A more precise Sobel Test confirms a significant indirect effect: Indirect Effect = 0.026 (SE = 0.003, z = 9.69, $p < 0.001$, 95% CI [0.021, 0.032]). This means that part of SES's influence on assessment outcomes is transmitted through the mediating pathway of "insufficient process evidence generation."

### 4.4 Decomposing Assessment Bias: Oaxaca-Blinder Analysis

To precisely quantify the structural sources of assessment bias-specifically how much stems from "data scarcity" (Endowment Effect) versus "validity bias" (Coefficient Effect)—we employed the Oaxaca-Blinder decomposition method. This analysis is also based on "early_clicks" (clicks in the first 100 days) to ensure consistency with the main regression model and avoid endogeneity issues.

For the Oaxaca decomposition, we selected the "Low SES Group" (Top 20%, SES_score $\leq$ 1) and "High SES Group" (Bottom 20%, SES_score $\geq$ 8) for comparison. This classification strategy, compared to the extreme groups (10%) in Sect. 4.1, expands sample coverage, aiming to increase subgroup sample sizes to ensure the stability of regression coefficient estimates, while still preserving significant class differences. Under this grouping, the pass rate gap between the two groups is 18.78% (slightly lower than the 22.4% for the extreme 10% comparison in Fig. 1).

The classic Oaxaca-Blinder decomposition [10, 11] was primarily designed for continuous dependent variables. When the dependent variable is binary, two mainstream approaches exist: (1) Nonlinear decomposition methods [13, 14], conducted directly within the Logit/Probit framework; (2) Linear Probability Model (LPM) approximation, treating the binary dependent variable as a probability for OLS regression decomposition. This study adopts the latter approach for the following reason: LPM decomposition is widely used in practice for descriptive attribution (such as decomposing sources of achievement gaps in educational economics), and its results have good approximation properties near the mean [12]. Therefore, the decomposition results in this paper should be understood as a structural characterization of "sources of bias," rather than strict causal identification of marginal effects.

The analysis results reveal the structural sources of assessment bias (Fig. 3). As shown, the total gap in assessment outcomes between the high-SES and low-SES groups is 18.78%. Of this, the Endowment Effect accounts for 26.9%. This portion of the gap can be attributed to low-SES students' insufficient generation of process evidence—they send fewer behavioral signals to the system. If interventions could raise their data generation to high-SES levels, theoretically about 26.9% of the assessment gap could be eliminated.

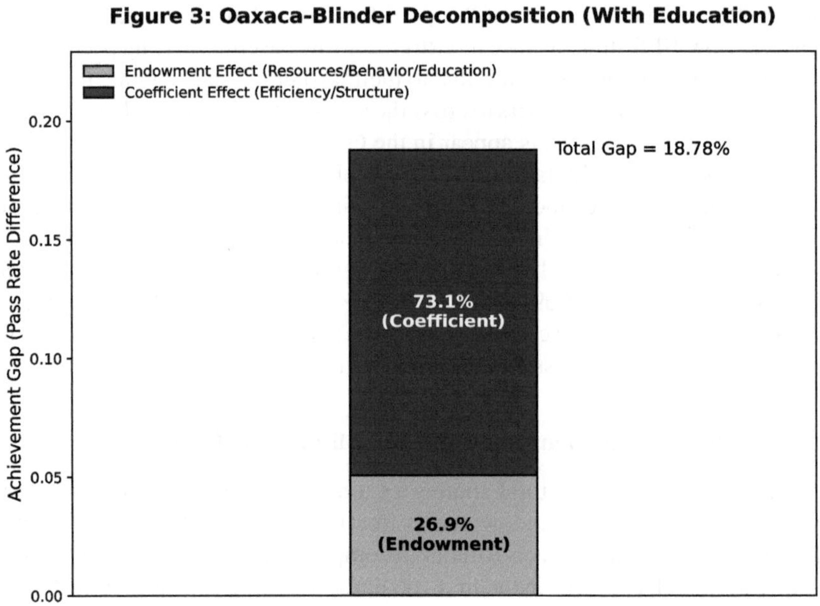


**Fig. 3.** Oaxaca-Blinder Decomposition.

However, the Coefficient Effect accounts for as much as 73.1%, which is the primary source of assessment bias. Combined with the non-significant interaction term results from Sect. 4.3, we can provide a more nuanced structural interpretation: The coefficient effect in Oaxaca decomposition is the sum of "Base Gap" (intercept difference) and "Return Gap" (slope difference). Since the regression model shows no significant difference in marginal return rates, this massive 73.1% gap is primarily driven by intercept differences. This means that even if low-SES students generate the same amount of process evidence, they still receive worse assessment outcomes—this is precisely the manifestation of Validity Heterogeneity. The algorithm assigns lower baseline weights to behavioral signals from low-SES students, forcing them to generate disproportionate amounts of data to receive equal system recognition.

It is worth noting that the Oaxaca "Endowment Effect" (26.9%) in this section and the "Mediation Effect" in Sect. 4.3, while both involving process evidence, answer different questions. The mediation effect quantifies "how much of SES's influence on assessment outcomes is transmitted through the process evidence pathway"; while the endowment effect quantifies "how much of the assessment gap between high and low SES groups can be attributed to between-group differences in mean process evidence."

The two complement each other, together characterizing the role of process evidence in assessment bias.

### 4.5 Causal Verification: Propensity Score Matching

To verify whether process evidence itself has genuine assessment returns-rather than merely being a proxy variable for ability or motivation-this study implemented Propensity Score Matching (PSM) analysis to eliminate self-selection bias. We adopted a two-step analytical strategy. The first step is Propensity Score Estimation, where we constructed a Logistic regression model to estimate each student's probability of belonging to the "high signal generation group" (i.e., propensity score e(X)):

$$\ln\left(\frac{e(X_i)}{1-e(X_i)}\right) = \alpha_0 + \alpha_1 SES_i + \alpha_2 PriorEducation_i + \alpha_3 Controls_i \tag{3}$$

Where *PriorEducation* is the highest education level before enrollment, which is a key variable for controlling prior cognitive ability. Additionally, the model controlled for SES, Gender, Disability, and *Region* (using dummy variable encoding).

We employed 1:1 Nearest Neighbor Matching algorithm, pairing samples based on estimated propensity scores. The specific implementation uses sklearn. neighbors. NearestNeighbors (algorithm = "ball_tree"), finding the control group sample with the closest propensity score for each treatment group sample. This study used matching with replacement to reduce matching bias [15].

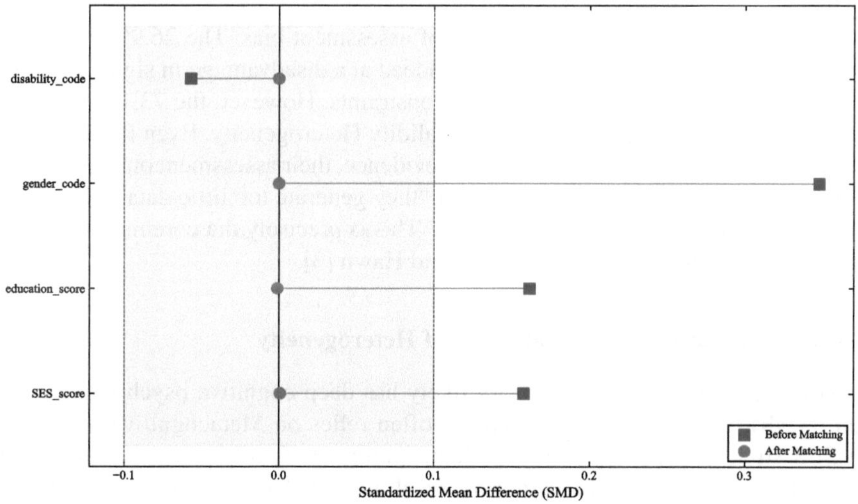


**Fig. 4.** PSM Covariate Balance.

The second step is Balance Check and ATT Calculation. As shown in Fig. 4, after matching (circular markers), the Standardized Mean Differences of key covariates all fall below 0.01, indicating that we successfully constructed more comparable "counterfactual" samples between the high-signal and low-signal groups. After satisfying the balance assumption, we calculated the Average Treatment Effect on the Treated (ATT). Estimation results show that the high signal generation group (Treatment Group) has an actual pass rate of 75.81%, while the matched control group (Matched Control Group) has a pass rate of 37.59%. This yields:

$$ATT = \overline{Y}_{T,matched} - \overline{Y}_{C,matched} = 0.7581 - 0.3759 = 0.382 \tag{4}$$

To ensure estimation reliability, we used Bootstrap methods (500 resamples) to calculate standard errors and confidence intervals: ATT = 0.382 (SE = 0.007, 95% CI [0.368, 0.396]). This result confirms that process evidence has independent causal returns on assessment outcomes—even after controlling for background, education level, and region, students who generate more behavioral signals still achieve significantly better assessment outcomes (approximately 38 percentage points improvement in pass rate).

Additionally, to verify the robustness of threshold selection, we also tested defining the high-signal group as Top 20% and Top 33%. Sensitivity analysis results show that while ATT effect sizes fluctuate slightly (ranging from 36% to 40%), they consistently remain highly significant ($p < 0.001$). This indicates that the causal returns of process evidence are robust and do not depend on specific threshold settings.

## 5 Discussion

### 5.1 The Structural Sources of Assessment Bias

Our empirical results reveal a dual source of assessment bias. The 26.9% Endowment Effect confirms that low-SES students are indeed at a disadvantage in signal generation (524 vs 733 clicks), likely due to external constraints. However, the 73.1% Coefficient Effect reveals the deeper structural issue: Validity Heterogeneity. Even if low-SES students generate identical amounts of process evidence, their assessment outcomes remain poorer. This implies the problem is not that "they generate too little data," but that "the algorithm weights their data less favorably." This is precisely the core manifestation of algorithmic bias warned against by Baker and Hawn [3].

### 5.2 Cognitive and Psychological Roots of Heterogeneity

The existence of validity heterogeneity likely has deep cognitive psychological roots. Based on SRL theory, successful learning often relies on Metacognitive Scaffolding. High-SES students typically inherit "Metacognitive Scripts" from their family environment that align with academic norms, resulting in behavioral data that exhibits the "linearity" and "consistency" preferred by algorithms [17].

In contrast, while low-SES students may possess equal motivation, lacking this implicit scaffolding may lead to behavioral patterns characterized by "trial-and-error exploration" or "fragmented jumps." Current algorithms fail to capture the potential value of these Non-standard SRL Strategies, erroneously downgrading their predictive weight. Thus, the Coefficient Effect essentially reflects the algorithm's Interpretative

Failure regarding diverse learning strategies. Furthermore, since training data is dominated by high-SES performance, the algorithm treats their patterns as the "Success Template." This leads to a paradox where low-SES students must generate disproportionate data to gain equal recognition—a form of "compensatory over-labor" necessitated because the algorithm "does not speak their learning language."

The policy implication is profound: The focus must shift from "Fixing the Student" to "Fixing the Algorithm." Merely urging disadvantaged students to generate more data is insufficient; we need to calibrate models to accommodate diverse behavioral patterns.

## 6 Conclusion and Implications

### 6.1 Theoretical Contribution

By introducing the Oaxaca-Blinder decomposition, this study provides a new theoretical lens for AI fairness. Our core finding is: Assessment Bias is a hybrid of "Endowment" (Data Scarcity) and "Coefficient" (Validity Bias), with the latter being the dominant contradiction. The 26.9% gap (Endowment) can be compensated by increasing data generation. However, the remaining 73.1% reveals the more insidious "Validity Divide"—the algorithm assigns different predictive weights to behavioral signals across groups. This implies that simply nudging students to "do more" is inadequate; the core issue lies in "how the algorithm interprets this data."

### 6.2 Policy Implications

Based on our findings, achieving equity requires a paradigm shift grounded in Design Justice [18]: moving from trying to "Fix the Student"—forcing them to generate data conforming to mainstream norms—to "Fixing the System"—proactively designing to include diverse behavioral patterns. We propose a "Dual Intervention" framework:

First, Data Generation Nudging, addressing the 26.9% endowment gap. System design should not assume all students possess equal "data generation capabilities" [19]. Future AI tutoring systems should incorporate Proactive Interaction Mechanisms, identifying students in "digital silence" and actively eliciting critical evidence through conversational prompts. Our PSM results (ATT = 0.382) suggest substantial marginal returns from enhancing information density for disadvantaged students.

Second, Inclusive Algorithmic Specifications, addressing the 73.1% validity gap. This requires resolving the algorithm's "interpretative failure" regarding non-standard SRL strategies:

(1) Counterfactual Data Augmentation: During training, simulate scenarios where "low-SES students succeed using existing fragmented strategies," forcing the algorithm to recognize the validity of non-linear paths.
(2) Context-Aware Metacognitive Scaffolding: Instead of merely predicting failure, systems should generate "Cognitive Elevators" (e.g., automated summaries, time management aids) to compensate for inherent disadvantages in cultural capital accumulation.

### 6.3 Limitations and Future Work

Despite the rigorous econometric approach employed, this study is subject to several limitations. First, the absence of qualitative data limits our ability to fully contextualize the findings; future research should integrate interview data to gain deeper insights into the actual learning strategies employed by low-SES students. Second, constrained by the data boundaries of the LMS, our "early_clicks" metric captures only on-platform behaviors, thereby omitting off-platform learning activities.

Finally, the interpretation of the "Coefficient Effect" within the Oaxaca decomposition requires caution. Although we theorize this component as validity heterogeneity, statistically, it represents the model's "Unexplained Component." This implies that the 73% gap may still conflate unobserved "endowment differences," such as high-SES students possessing greater access to offline tutoring resources or superior home learning environments. Due to data limitations, these potential resource advantages are statistically subsumed into the coefficient effect. Therefore, future studies incorporating richer offline contextual data could more precisely isolate pure algorithmic bias.

In conclusion, this study demonstrates that the Oaxaca-Blinder decomposition serves as an effective tool for auditing fairness in Educational AI, providing robust empirical support for the policy paradigm shift from "Fixing the Student" to "Fixing the Algorithm."

## Appendix A: Variable Coding Table

**Table A1.** Variable Definitions and Coding Rules.

| Variable Name | Original Field (OULAD) | Coding Rules and Logic | Range / Value |
|---|---|---|---|
| is_pass | final_result | Pass/Distinction→1;Fail/Withdrawn→0 | 0, 1 |
| SES_score | imd_band | 0–10% → 0; 10–20% → 1 ...... 90–100% → 9 | 0–9 |
| early_clicks | studentVle.sum_click | Sum of clicks where date ≤100 | ≥ 0 |
| clicks_std | early_clicks | Z-score standardization: $(x - \mu)/\sigma$ | Continuous |
| education_score | highest_education | No Formal quals→0; Lower Than A Level→1; A level→2; HE Qualification→3; Post Graduate→4 | 0–4 |
| education_std | education_score | Z-score standardization | Continuous |
| gender_code | gender | M → 1; F → 0 | 0, 1 |
| disability_code | disability | Y → 1; N → 0 | 0, 1 |
| studied_credits | studied_credits | Registered credits for the module (Raw value) | 30–600 |
| treatment (PSM) | early_clicks | Top25% → 1(High Engagement); Others → 0 | 0, 1 |

## References

1. Black, P., Wiliam, D.: Assessment and classroom learning. Assess. Educ. Prin. Policy Pract. **5**(1), 7–74 (1998)
2. Winne, P.H., Hadwin, A.F.: Studying as self-regulated learning. In: Hacker, D.J., Dunlosky, J., Graesser, A.C. (eds.) Metacognition in Educational Theory and Practice, pp. 277–304. Lawrence Erlbaum Associates, Mahwah (1998)
3. Baker, R.S., Hawn, A.: Algorithmic bias in education. Int. J. Artif. Intell. Educ. **32**(4), 1052–1092 (2022)
4. Yin, Z., Chinta, S.V., Wang, Z., Gonzalez, M., Zhang, W.: FairAIED: Navigating fairness, bias, and ethics in educational AI applications. arXiv preprint arXiv:2407.18745. (2024)
5. Bourdieu, P.: The forms of capital. In: Richardson, J. (ed.) Handbook of Theory and Research for the Sociology of Education, pp. 241–258. Greenwood, Westport (1986)
6. Zimmerman, B.J.: Becoming a self-regulated learner: an overview. Theory Pract. **41**(2), 64–70 (2002)
7. Messick, S.: Validity. In: Linn, R.L. (ed.) Educational Measurement, 3rd edn, pp. 13–103. Macmillan, New York (1989)
8. Kuzilek, J., Hlosta, M., Zdrahal, Z.: Open University learning analytics dataset. Sci. Data. **4**, 170171 (2017)
9. Lundberg, S.M., Lee, S.I.: A unified approach to interpreting model predictions. In: Guyon, I., et al. (eds.) Advances in Neural Information Processing Systems, vol. 30, pp. 4765–4774. Curran Associates, Inc, Long Beach (2017)
10. Blinder, A.S.: Wage discrimination: reduced form and structural estimates. J. Hum. Resour. **8**(4), 436–455 (1973)
11. Oaxaca, R.: Male-female wage differentials in urban labor markets. Int. Econ. Rev. **14**(3), 693–709 (1973)
12. Angrist, J.D., Pischke, J.S.: Mostly Harmless Econometrics: an empiricist's companion. Princeton University Press, Princeton (2009)
13. Fairlie, R.W.: An extension of the Blinder-Oaxaca decomposition technique to logit and probit models. J. Econ. Soc. Meas. **30**(4), 305–316 (2005)
14. Yun, M.S.: Decomposing differences in the first moment. Econ. Lett. **82**(2), 275–280 (2004)
15. Rosenbaum, P.R., Rubin, D.B.: The central role of the propensity score in observational studies for causal effects. Biometrika. **70**(1), 41–55 (1983)
16. Baron, R.M., Kenny, D.A.: The moderator–mediator variable distinction in social psychological research: conceptual, strategic, and statistical considerations. J. Pers. Soc. Psychol. **51**(6), 1173–1182 (1986)
17. Corbett, R., Kovanović, V., Gašević, D.: Bridging the gap: social class and the validity of learning analytics. J. Learn. Anal. **10**(2), 15–32 (2023)
18. Costanza-Chock, S.: Design Justice: community-led practices to build the worlds we need. The MIT Press, Cambridge (2020)
19. Thaler, R.H., Sunstein, C.R.: Nudge: improving decisions about health, wealth, and happiness. Yale University Press, New Haven (2008)

# From Barriers to Actions: A Thematic Analysis of Swedish K-12 Teachers' Perspectives on AI Integration


Yuki Nagae[1(✉)], Lechen Zhang[2], Jalal Nouri[3], and Linda Mannila[4]

[1] Stockholm University, Frescativägen 54, Stockholm 114 18, Sweden
yuki.nagae@edu.su.se
[2] University of Helsinki, Fabianinkatu 33, Helsinki 00014, Finland
[3] Stockholm University, Borgarfjordsgatan 12, Stockholm 164 25, Sweden
[4] University of Helsinki, Helsinki PB 68, 00014,, Finland



**Abstract.** While professional development (PD) programs aim to prepare teachers for AI integration, understanding what obstacles teachers perceive and what support they need to begin or expand AI use in their classrooms remains crucial for effective implementation. This study presents a thematic analysis of open-ended survey responses from Swedish K–12 educators who completed an AI-focused PD program. We analyzed 781 responses describing barriers to AI use and 816 responses articulating support needs. Using AI-assisted thematic analysis, we identified six barrier themes: student-related concerns, knowledge and competence gaps, time constraints, cost and access, technical infrastructure, and policy uncertainty. For support needs, six themes emerged: time for exploration, already using AI (teachers who reported no additional support needs), tools and access, training and education, practical examples, and collegial support. The prominence of student-related concerns, particularly about academic integrity and learning dependency, suggests that AI presents qualitatively different challenges than previous educational technologies. Therefore, we discuss implications for designing multi-level support systems that address barriers at the teacher, school, and policy levels.



**Keywords:** AI in Education · Teacher Professional Development · Implementation Barriers · Thematic Analysis · K–12 Education


## 1 Introduction

The rapid advancement of generative AI has created both opportunities and challenges for education systems worldwide. Teachers are increasingly expected to integrate AI tools into their practice, including lesson planning, instructional activities, assessment, and administrative tasks, while simultaneously teaching students to use AI responsibly [1]. The role of policy is to establish systems that support teachers within the changing educational environment, yet a significant gap remains between policy ideals and classroom realities [2].



E. G. Blanchard et al. (eds.), AIED 2026, LNCS 16586, pp. 60–73, 2027.
https://doi.org/10.1007/978-3-032-29773-0_5

Professional development programs have emerged as a primary mechanism for building teacher AI competencies [3]. Previous research, before AI emerged, has reported various barriers to educational technology adoption, including time constraints, resource constraints, insufficient training, and institutional resistance [4]. Moreover, AI presents unique challenges: rapidly evolving capabilities, ethical complexities related to academic integrity, concerns about student overreliance, and an uncertain policy landscape [5]. A systematic review of ChatGPT in K–12 settings found that while teachers recognize AI's potential for curriculum planning and differentiated instruction, concerns about academic integrity and student learning remain prominent [6]. Even after PD training, many teachers struggle to translate knowledge into practice. Understanding what prevents teachers from using AI and what support would enable them to begin is essential for designing effective implementation strategies.

This study addresses this gap through a thematic analysis of open-ended responses from Swedish K–12 educators who completed an AI-focused PD program. We examine two complementary research questions:

- RQ1. What barriers do teachers perceive as potentially hindering their use of AI in teaching?
- RQ2. What support do teachers need to begin or expand their AI integration?

By analyzing barriers and support needs together, we aim to inform the design of implementation support at multiple organizational levels.

## 2 Related Work

### 2.1 Barriers and Needed Support for Educational Technology Integration

Research on technology integration barriers has identified consistent themes across contexts. Ertmer's [7] distinction between "first"-order barriers, which are external, such as resources, training, support, and "second"-order barriers, which are internal, such as beliefs, attitudes, and knowledge, remains influential. More recently, Tsai and Chai [8] proposed a "third"-order barrier, which they called design thinking: teachers' capacity to create technology-enhanced learning experiences. Specifically for AI, as its impact on education became apparent and significant, several studies reported the challenges and concerns educators faced [2, 9]. Yet, only 35% of AI-in-education studies addressed teacher PD, highlighting a research gap [3].

As technology is driving the transformation of education, including curriculum development, teacher professional development, and changes in pedagogical practices, sustainable AI integration requires multi-level support: individual capacity building at the micro level, organizational resource allocation at the mezzo level, and system-level policy frameworks at the macro level. What is crucial at this point is the perspective of teachers who implement the technology in practice [3, 10–12]. Yet few studies have asked teachers directly what support they need to begin or expand to use AI in the classroom, instead inferring needs from observed barriers.

### 2.2 The Swedish Context

Sweden has been proactive in integrating digital technology. The National Agency for Education (Skolverket) has promoted digitalization actively and across a wide range [13]. Digital devices support individualized learning and are particularly used in special education, while some confusion has been reported during the implementation. The National Agency for Education has issued guidance on AI in schools in 2025 [14], and municipalities have launched various training initiatives. The PD program examined in this study is one such training effort that reaches teachers across multiple municipalities.

Despite these efforts, the implementation of generative AI remains uneven. Understanding teacher-perceived barriers and needs in this context can inform both Swedish policy and international efforts facing similar challenges.

## 3 Method

### 3.1 Context and Participants

Data were collected from a post-training evaluation survey administered to participants in an online AI PD program for Swedish K–12 educators between October 2024 and November 2025. The program's learning materials aligned with UNESCO's AI Competency Framework for Teachers [15] and were delivered through self-paced modules over approximately four weeks. The survey included two open-ended questions relevant to this study: "What barriers could potentially hinder your use of AI in teaching?" (Barriers) and "What do you need to get started with AI use?" (Support needs). These questions were purposely designed to be open-ended within a broader survey that also included quantitative measures (quantitative findings from an earlier phase of this dataset are reported in [16]). This format was selected to gather teachers' perspectives in their own words, enabling them to express concerns and needs that fixed response options might miss or limit. After removing incomplete and non-substantive responses (e.g., single characters, "don't know," or test entries), the analytic sample consisted of 781 barrier responses and 816 support need responses. Participants were 67.6% women and 30.1% men; age groups: 30–39 (24.3%), 40–49 (26.8%), 50–59 (28.4%); with over 15 years of teaching experience (30.7%). The sample included teachers (95.2%) and special educators (4.8%) from municipalities across Sweden.

### 3.2 Analysis Procedure

We employed an AI-assisted thematic analysis approach to analyze the open-ended survey responses, combining computational text classification with researcher-led interpretation and validation. This hybrid methodology aligns with emerging frameworks for leveraging large language models (LLMs) in qualitative research while maintaining human analytical control [17, 18]. This approach was chosen to manage the large volume of responses (N = 1597 barrier responses; N = 1669 support need responses, before data cleaning) while maintaining the interpretive depth characteristic of qualitative analysis. Recent methodological studies have demonstrated that such hybrid approaches can achieve high agreement with human coding while significantly reducing analysis time [19, 20].

**Phase 1: Initial Exploration and Framework Development.** We first reviewed a stratified sample of approximately 200 responses to develop an initial understanding of the data landscape. Through iterations, we identified preliminary thematic categories that captured the range of teachers' expressed barriers and support needs. This human-led phase established the conceptual framework that would guide subsequent computational coding, following recommendations that researchers maintain intellectual leadership throughout AI-assisted analysis [21].

**Phase 2: Codebook Development.** Based on the initial exploration, we developed a structured codebook with hierarchical organization: themes (broad conceptual categories), categories (specific dimensions within themes), and codes (discrete concepts identified through keywords and phrases).

For barriers, six themes were identified: Knowledge and Competence, Time Constraints, Student-Related Concerns, Cost and Access, Technical Infrastructure, and Policy Uncertainty. For support needs, six themes emerged: Training and Education, Tools and Access, Practical Examples, Time for Exploration, Collegial Support, and Already Using AI (teachers who reported no additional support needs).

Each code was operationalized through a set of Swedish keywords and phrases that would reliably identify relevant responses. For example, the code "Fear of student cheating" was operationalized through keywords such as "fusk" (cheating), "plagiat" (plagiarism), and "egen kunskap" (own knowledge). This deductive approach follows established practices for computational content analysis [22].

**Phase 3: Computational Classification.** We used a large language model (ChatGPT 4o) to assist with classifying responses according to our codebook. The AI system was provided with our codebook definitions and keyword lists, and tasked with classifying each response to the most appropriate code. Responses that did not clearly match any predefined code were classified as "Other/Unclear" for subsequent human review.

This approach is consistent with methodological frameworks that position AI as a "secondary coder" that consistently applies researcher-defined categories across large datasets [23, 24]. The computational classification functioned as a sophisticated keyword-based system where the AI applied our predetermined rules consistently across the full dataset. Importantly, the AI did not generate or interpret themes—it served as a coding tool applying researcher-defined categories.

**Phase 4: Human Validation and Refinement.** The research team reviewed all AI-generated classifications through several validation procedures.

1. Category-level review: We examined responses within each code to verify conceptual coherence and identify misclassifications. This aligns with recommendations for human-in-the-loop evaluation in AI-assisted qualitative workflows [25].
2. "Other/Unclear" analysis: Responses classified as unclear ($n = 143$ for barriers; $n = 121$ for support needs) were manually reviewed to identify any systematic patterns that might warrant additional codes or reclassification.
3. Frequency validation: We compared computational frequency distributions against our initial manual sample to verify consistency.

4. Quote selection: All illustrative quotes used in this article were selected by the research team based on their representativeness and clarity, then translated from Swedish to English with attention to preserving meaning and nuance.

**Phase 5: Interpretation and Synthesis.** The final interpretation of findings, including the identification of relationships between themes, theoretical implications, and practical recommendations, was conducted entirely by the research team. The AI assisted only with the mechanical task of classification; all analytical insights represent human interpretation. This separation between computational coding and human interpretation is essential for maintaining qualitative rigor [23, 24].

### 3.3 Methodological Considerations

This AI-assisted approach offers several advantages for large-scale qualitative research: consistent application of coding rules, efficient processing of large datasets, and complete documentation of the classification logic [19]. However, we acknowledge limitations inherent to computational approaches: keyword-based classification may miss nuanced expressions that a human coder would recognize, and such approaches are better suited to descriptive content analysis than to deeply interpretive work [26].

To enhance transparency and reproducibility, we have documented our complete codebook with all keywords and classification rules in the supplementary materials. This allows other researchers to examine, critique, and build upon our analytical framework, addressing calls for greater methodological transparency in AI-assisted qualitative research [27].

A further methodological limitation concerns the risk of missing emergent themes in the remaining data, given that the codebook was initially developed from approximately 200 responses. Future studies could address this by iteratively developing the codebook across the full dataset or by using inductive open coding before deductive classification.

We established trustworthiness through: (1) transparent documentation of the entire coding process and decision rules; (2) clear separation between computational classification and human interpretation; (3) validation of computational output against manual samples; (4) inclusion of "Other/Unclear" categories to avoid forcing responses into ill-fitting codes; and (5) availability of the complete codebook for external review.

## 4 Results

### 4.1 Barriers to AI Use in Teaching

Analysis of 781 responses revealed six distinct barrier themes, plus an "Other" category for responses that did not fit established themes or contained unclear content (Table 1). Each response was assigned to one primary theme based on the most salient content. The percentages are shown not to indicate the importance of each category relative to its quantity, but rather to demonstrate persuasiveness based on the number of responses.

The most prevalent barrier, mentioned by nearly a third of respondents, concerned students rather than teachers themselves. Teachers worried extensively about academic

**Table 1.** Barrier Themes.

| Theme | n | % |
|---|---|---|
| Student-related concerns | 241 | 30.9 |
| Knowledge and competence | 120 | 15.4 |
| Time constraints | 106 | 13.6 |
| Cost and access | 71 | 9.1 |
| Technical infrastructure | 64 | 8.2 |
| Policy uncertainty | 36 | 4.5 |
| Other/Unclear | 143 | 18.3 |
| Total | 781 | 100.0 |

integrity: "If it can be used for cheating" was a recurring concern. Beyond plagiarism, teachers expressed deeper anxieties about learning itself, fearing that "students become lazy and don't think for themselves." This theme extended to questions about whether AI use would develop or diminish student capabilities over time. Notably, this pattern inverts the typical finding in educational technology research, where teacher-centric barriers such as time and training dominate [4, 7]. Here, concerns about students outranked concerns about the teachers themselves.

Knowledge and competence gaps formed the second substantive theme. Teachers candidly acknowledged their own limitations: "Both I and the students need more knowledge to use AI correctly." This encompassed both foundational understanding of how AI works and practical know-how for classroom integration. Some teachers noted frustration with their current skill level: "I don't get good answers to my instructions," suggesting that prompt engineering itself poses a learning curve.

Time constraints emerged as a significant barrier, though teachers framed this not merely as busyness but as a structural problem. They needed "time to really immerse myself in the tools that exist" and noted that AI use created additional work: "Time and quality assurance—extra work to double-check everything."

Cost and access barriers reflected practical realities. Many teachers noted that "full versions cost money" and that their employers did not cover subscriptions. One teacher summarized the equity dimension: "We won't have access to the best tools because they're too expensive."

Technical infrastructure barriers included network limitations when "students work simultaneously," lack of student devices, and unreliable platforms.

Finally, policy uncertainty affected a smaller but notable group. GDPR compliance for student accounts, municipal platform restrictions, and the absence of national guidelines created hesitation. Teachers sought "concrete guidelines from the National Agency and politicians on how I'm expected to relate to AI."

The "Other" category (18.3%) included responses expressing general uncertainty, attitudinal barriers (e.g., "my own disinterest"), or concerns that did not fit neatly into established themes (e.g., "attitudes from colleagues toward AI").

## 4.2 Support Needs for AI Integration

Analysis of 816 responses identified six support need themes, plus an "Other" category (Table 2).

**Table 2.** Support Need Themes.

| Theme | n | % |
|---|---|---|
| Time for exploration | 219 | 26.8 |
| Already using (no needs) | 174 | 21.3 |
| Tools and access | 120 | 14.7 |
| Training and education | 96 | 11.8 |
| Practical examples | 52 | 6.4 |
| Collegial support | 34 | 4.2 |
| Other/Unclear | 121 | 14.8 |
| Total | 816 | 100.0 |

Time dominated teachers' articulated needs, but with a specific quality: they wanted time for exploration rather than time for training. Teachers requested "time to test myself before using it in lessons" and "time to try different apps." This suggests that traditional workshop-based PD may be insufficient; teachers need protected space to experiment without immediate performance pressure.

A striking finding was that 21.3% of respondents reported needing nothing at all. These teachers were already active users: "Nothing, I use it daily." Some attributed this to intrinsic motivation: "I'm already going. Own interest drives me." This group represents both a success story and a potential resource as early adopters who could support colleagues. While responses in this theme were characteristically brief, as described above, there were some requests to expand their use of AI: "Open up ChatGPT for me and others who are eager to really get started." Rather than signaling that professional development is unnecessary for this group, these responses suggest a need for institutional PD that moves beyond awareness-raising toward providing advanced tools, expanded access, and structured opportunities to deepen and share their existing practice.

Tools and access formed another substantial theme. Teachers who had begun using AI wanted institutional support to continue: "I'm already going. Want more paid versions (Canva, ChatGPT)." Others simply needed "access to AI for me and the students." The specificity of tool requests (ChatGPT, Copilot, Canva) indicated that teachers had already identified what they wanted to use; they just needed licenses.

Training and education needs emphasized ongoing development: "More training together with colleagues" and "continued education about what's possible."

Practical examples were requested by teachers seeking concrete demonstrations: "See more of how to use AI in a good way in mathematics."

Collegial support emerged as a distinct need for some teachers who valued peer learning over formal training. One teacher articulated: "I need time together with my colleagues where we can test this." Others emphasized collaborative approaches: "This is something that should be worked on collegially at the school." This theme reflected a desire for situated learning embedded in daily practice rather than isolated training events.

The "Other" category (14.8%) included responses that were too brief to classify, expressed multiple needs without clear priority, or contained idiosyncratic requests.

# 5 Discussion

## 5.1 The Primacy of Student Concerns

The most striking finding is that student-related concerns, not teacher-centric barriers, dominated responses. Nearly a third of teachers cited worries about cheating, reduced learning, or student dependency. This contrasts sharply with the educational technology adoption literature, which has historically emphasized teacher-focused barriers such as time, training, and resources [7, 28]. In Ertmer's [7] influential framework, barriers are categorized as first-order (external/resource-based) or second-order (internal/belief-based), yet our findings suggest a distinct category: concerns about how technology affects students.

This pattern aligns with emerging AI-specific research. Akgun and Greenhow [5] identified academic integrity as a central ethical challenge in K–12 AI integration, while Ng et al. [29] found that teachers' AI adoption decisions are heavily influenced by perceived risks to student learning. Interestingly, Chounta et al. [2] did not find student concerns as prominent among Estonian teachers in 2022, possibly because their data preceded widespread ChatGPT availability. Our findings suggest that generative AI has shifted teacher concerns from "Can I use this?" to "Should my students use this?"

This dual challenge teachers face, learning to use AI themselves while simultaneously managing student use, represents what Mishra and Koehler [30] might characterize as a novel form of technological pedagogical knowledge. Teachers must develop not only personal AI competencies but also pedagogical strategies for scaffolding appropriate student AI use. This suggests that PD programs should explicitly address classroom AI management, including academic integrity protocols and strategies for teaching critical evaluation of AI outputs, as recommended by Cotton et al. [20].

## 5.2 Time for Exploration, Not Just Training

Time emerged as the dominant support need, echoing decades of technology integration research [2, 4, 31]. However, our qualitative data revealed an important nuance: teachers specified needing time for exploration and experimentation, not merely training attendance. The distinction between "time for training" and "time to test myself before using it in lessons" carries significant implications for PD design.

This finding resonates with Darling-Hammond et al.'s [32] synthesis of effective professional development, which emphasizes sustained duration, active learning, and opportunities for practice. Similarly, Desimone's [33] conceptual framework identifies active learning and coherence as core features of effective PD. Workshop-based training, which is currently the dominant model for PD, may provide initial exposure but fails to support the iterative experimentation that integration requires.

Ertmer and Ottenbreit-Leftwich [28] suggested that teachers need low-risk environments to develop self-efficacy for technology integration. Our data support this: teachers wanted protected time to experiment without immediate pressure to apply classroom experiments. This process demonstrates that teachers need support with implementation, even after they have received training.

### 5.3 Early Adopters as Diffusion Agents

The 21% of teachers already using AI confidently represent an underutilized resource for system-wide adoption. Rogers' [34] diffusion of innovations theory characterizes such individuals as "early adopters" who play crucial roles in normalizing new practices. These teachers have overcome barriers that others still face and have developed practical strategies through experience.

Research on teacher learning communities supports leveraging peer expertise. Vescio et al. [35] found that professional learning communities improve both teaching practice and student outcomes when they include collaborative examination of practice. Vangrieken et al. [36] similarly identified collaboration as essential for teacher learning. Our finding that some teachers explicitly requested collegial support suggests latent demand for peer-learning structures.

Schools might formalize this collaborative environment among teachers by establishing model roles, called "champion," as successfully employed in other technology integration efforts [37]. Such distributed leadership approaches align with Spillane's [38] conception of leadership practice as stretched across multiple actors. Early adopters can guide teachers by translating formal PD content into classroom realities.

### 5.4 Multi-level Implementation Requirements

Our findings revealed that effective AI integration requires coordinated multi-level support: individual teachers at the micro level, organizational resource allocation within schools and across local government at the mezzo level, and system-level policy frameworks at the macro level. No single level can address all barriers.

At the micro level, our finding that student concerns dominate suggests the need for what Shulman [39] termed pedagogical content knowledge; in this case, AI pedagogical knowledge [40]. Teachers need not only AI skills but also pedagogical strategies to integrate AI appropriately into their subject contexts. Recent research that updates the TPACK framework with AI provides a conceptual foundation for this integration [40, 41].

At the mezzo level, our findings point to organizational and governance conditions that shape teachers' capacity to innovate. School leaders play a critical role in creating protected exploration time through relational trust and psychological safety, enabling experimentation without fear of judgment [34, 42]. At the same time, district- and municipal-level resource allocation remains decisive: consistent with longstanding critiques, technology integration falters when tools are provided without coordinated access and support infrastructure [4]. Teachers' specific requests for platforms such as ChatGPT and Copilot indicate clear pedagogical demand, but also reveal a solvable coordination problem at the organizational level.

At the macro level, teachers' requests for policy clarity echo research on policy implementation. Spillane et al. [43] showed that teachers interpret policy through existing beliefs and practices; vague guidelines allow wide variation in interpretation. Clear, practical guidance is being rewired to reduce uncertainty while preserving the risk of misinterpretation [15].

## 5.5 Implications for Practice

We propose the following recommendations to support AI integration (Table 3). Each barrier theme identified in Sect. 4.1 was aligned with the most directly relevant support need theme from Sect. 4.2, and the resulting recommended action was then assigned to a responsibility level — micro, mezzo, or macro — based on which actor has the practical authority and resources to implement it. For example, the most prevalent barrier, student-related concerns, was mapped to teachers' expressed need for practical examples and classroom protocols. Since addressing this requires both individual pedagogical decisions and school-level policy, responsibility was assigned to both the micro (teacher) and mezzo (school) levels. This logic was applied consistently across all six barrier themes, producing a structured set of actionable recommendations that connect the findings directly to implementation guidance at the appropriate organizational level.

These recommendations synthesize our empirical findings with the literature reviewed above and should be interpreted as the authors' interpretations rather than direct empirical results. At the same time, a systematic review of empirical studies on teachers' professional development needs for AI integration also supports the need for similar multi-level support [44].

**Table 3.** Proposed Recommendations for Supporting AI Integration.

| Barrier | Proposed Action | Responsibility Level |
|---|---|---|
| Student concerns | Develop classroom AI protocols; integrate AI literacy | Teacher + School |
| Knowledge gaps | Provide ongoing, hands-on PD with exploration time | School + Local Government |
| Time constraints | Allocate protected experimentation time | School + Local Government |
| Technical infrastructure | Ensure reliable devices and networks | Local Government + IT |
| Cost and access | Procure institutional licenses | Local Government |
| Policy uncertainty | Issue clear, practical guidelines | National + Local Government |

### 5.6 Limitations

Several limitations warrant consideration. First, open-ended responses varied in depth; brief responses were sometimes difficult to classify definitively, contributing to our "Other" categories.

Second, as no pre-intervention survey was conducted before the AI-focused PD program used in this study, it is not possible to determine whether or how teachers' perceptions changed as a result of the training, and causal claims about the program's effects on teacher attitudes or readiness cannot be made.

Third, single-label coding assigns each response to one primary theme based on salience, which may obscure responses containing multiple distinct barriers or support needs and overlook information regarding intersecting factors.

Fourth, the cross-sectional design captures a single point in time in a rapidly evolving landscape; longitudinal research could reveal how barriers shift as AI tools and policies evolve.

Fifth, while we proposed recommendations based on barrier-need correspondence, intervention studies are needed to test whether addressing identified needs actually reduces barriers and increases adoption.

Finally, the findings reflect Swedish conditions, where there is high digital infrastructure, strong teacher unions, and specific interpretations of the GDPR that may differ elsewhere. Cross-national replication would strengthen generalizability.

## 6 Conclusion

This thematic analysis identified six barrier themes and six support-need themes among Swedish K–12 educators (781 barrier responses, 816 support-need responses). Student-related concerns, particularly about academic integrity and learning outcomes, emerged as the most prevalent barrier, suggesting AI presents unique challenges beyond typical technology integration. Time for exploration was the most frequently articulated support need, indicating teachers require protected space to experiment rather than additional training sessions alone.

The 21% of teachers already using AI confidently represent both a success and a resource: their experiences can inform support for colleagues still working to overcome barriers. Our findings suggest that effective AI integration requires coordinated action across individual teachers, organizations such as schools and local government, and the national level.

**Acknowledgments. Competing Interests** The author, Jalal Nouri, is the founder of the research-oriented company, which provided the AI PD training program and collected data.

**Generative AI Use** We hereby declare to utilize ChatGPT-4o to proofread the text of this study. While ChatGPT-4o provided valuable suggestions about grammar and structure and enhanced overall readability, we have carefully reviewed all the proposed changes to ensure they align with the intended meaning and context of our original work.

**Data Availability.** The survey data analyzed in this study are available from the corresponding author upon reasonable request, subject to ethical approval and data protection requirements.

## References


1. Kasneci, E., et al.: ChatGPT for good? On opportunities and challenges of large language models for education. Learn. Individ. Differ. **103**, 102274 (2023)
2. Chounta, I.-A., Bardone, E., Raudsep, A., Pedaste, M.: Exploring teachers' perceptions of artificial intelligence as a tool to support their practice in Estonian K-12 education. Int. J. Artif. Intell. Educ. **32**, 725–755 (2022)
3. Tan, X., Cheng, G., Ling, M.H.: Artificial intelligence in teaching and teacher professional development: a systematic review. Comput. Educ. Artif. Intell. **8**, 100355 (2025)
4. Hew, K.F., Brush, T.: Integrating technology into K-12 teaching and learning: current knowledge gaps and recommendations for future research. Educ. Technol. Res. Dev. **55**, 223–252 (2007)
5. Akgun, S., Greenhow, C.: Artificial intelligence in education: addressing ethical challenges in K-12 settings. AI Ethics. **2**, 431–440 (2022)
6. Zhang, P., Tur, G.: A systematic review of ChatGPT use in K-12 education. Eur. J. Educ. **59**, e12599 (2024)
7. Ertmer, P.A.: Addressing first-and second-order barriers to change: strategies for technology integration. Educ. Technol. Res. Dev. **47**, 47–61 (1999)
8. Tsai, C.-C., Chai, C.S.: The "third"-order barrier for technology-integration instruction: implications for teacher education. Australas. J. Educ. Technol. **28** (2012). https://doi.org/10.14742/ajet.810
9. Velander, J., Taiye, M.A., Otero, N., Milrad, M.: Artificial intelligence in K-12 education: eliciting and reflecting on Swedish teachers' understanding of AI and its implications for teaching & learning. Educ. Inf. Technol. **29**, 4085–4105 (2024)
10. Zawacki-Richter, O., Marín, V.I., Bond, M., Gouverneur, F.: Systematic review of research on artificial intelligence applications in higher education—where are the educators? Int. J. Educ. Technol. High. Educ. **16**, 1–27 (2019)
11. Sperling, K., et al.: Perspectives on AI literacy in middle school classrooms: an integrative review. Postdigit. Sci. Educ. **7**, 719–749 (2025)
12. Chiu, T.K.F., Chai, C.-S.: Sustainable curriculum planning for artificial intelligence education: a self-determination theory perspective. Sustainability. **12**, 5568 (2020)
13. Skolverket [the Swedish National Agency for Education]: Fyra aspekter av digital kompetens [Four aspects of digital competence], https://www.skolverket.se/kompetensutveckling/stod-i-arbetet/fyra-aspekter-av-digital-kompetens. Last accessed 30 Jan 2026
14. Skolverket [the Swedish National Agency for Education]: Råd om AI, Chattbottar och liknande verktyg [Advice on AI, chatbots, and similar tools], https://www.skolverket.se/kompetensutveckling/stod-i-arbetet/rad-om-ai-chattbottar-och-liknande-verktyg. Last accessed 30 Jan 2026
15. Miao, F., Cukurova, M.: AI Competency Framework for Teachers. UNESCO (2024)
16. Nagae, Y., Zhang, L., Farias, L.H.: The effects of professional development training on teachers' AI literacy. In: Cristea, A.I., Walker, E., Lu, Y., Santos, O.C., Isotani, S. (eds.) Artificial Intelligence in Education, pp. 368–380. AIED 2025, Cham (2025)
17. Tai, R.H., et al.: An examination of the use of large language models to aid analysis of textual data. Int J Qual Methods. **23**, 4 (2024). https://doi.org/10.1177/16094069241231168
18. Marathe, M., Toyama, K.: Semi-automated coding for qualitative research: a user-centered inquiry and initial prototypes. In: Proceedings of the 2018 CHI Conference on Human Factors in Computing Systems, pp. 1–12. ACM, New York, NY, USA (2018). https://doi.org/10.1145/3173574.3173922
19. Zhang, H., et al.: Redefining Qualitative Analysis in the AI Era: utilizing ChatGPT for efficient thematic analysis (2023). https://doi.org/10.48550/arXiv.2309.10771

20. Xiao, Z., Yuan, X., Liao, Q.V., Abdelghani, R., Oudeyer, P.-Y.: Supporting Qualitative Analysis with Large Language Models: combining codebook with GPT-3 for deductive coding (2023). https://doi.org/10.48550/arXiv.2304.10548
21. Deterding, N.M., Waters, M.C.: Flexible coding of in-depth interviews: a twenty-first-century approach. Sociol. Methods Res. **50**, 708–739 (2021)
22. Krippendorff, K.: Content Analysis: an introduction to its methodology, p. 91320. SAGE Publications, Inc, 2455 Teller Road, Thousand Oaks California (2019)
23. Nguyen, D.C., Welch, C.: Generative artificial intelligence in qualitative data analysis: analyzing—or just chatting? Organ. Res. Methods. **29**, 3–39 (2026)
24. Blondeel, E., Everaert, P., Opdecam, E.: A practical guide to implementing ChatGPT as a secondary coder in qualitative research. Int. J. Acc. Inf. Syst. **56**, 100754 (2025)
25. Wang, Q., Erqsous, M., Barner, K.E., Mauriello, M.L.: LATA: a pilot study on LLM-assisted thematic analysis of online social network data generation experiences. Proc. ACM Hum. Comput. Interact. **9**, 1–28 (2025)
26. Mehta, S.D., et al.: Evaluation of large language models within GenAI in qualitative research. Sci. Rep. **15**, 34993 (2025)
27. Hayes, A.S.: "Conversing" with qualitative data: enhancing qualitative research through large language models (LLMs). Int J Qual Methods. **24** (2025). https://doi.org/10.1177/16094069251322346
28. Ertmer, P.A., Ottenbreit-Leftwich, A.T.: Teacher technology change: how knowledge, confidence, beliefs, and culture intersect. J. Res. Technol. Educ. **42**, 255–284 (2010)
29. Ng, D.T.K., Leung, J.K.L., Chu, S.K.W., Qiao, M.S.: Conceptualizing AI literacy: an exploratory review. Comput. Educ. Artif. Intell. **2**, 100041 (2021)
30. Mishra, P., Koehler, M.J.: Technological pedagogical content knowledge: a framework for teacher knowledge. Teach. Coll. Rec. **108**, 1017–1054 (2006)
31. Kopcha, T.J.: Teachers' perceptions of the barriers to technology integration and practices with technology under situated professional development. Comput. Educ. **59**, 1109–1121 (2012)
32. Darling-Hammond, L., Hyler, M.E., Gardner, M.: Efective Teacher Professional Development. Learning Policy Institution (2017)
33. Desimone, L.M.: Improving impact studies of teachers' professional development: toward better conceptualizations and measures. Educ. Res. **38**, 181–199 (2009)
34. Rogers, E.: The Diffusion of Innovations. The Free Press, New York (2003)
35. Vescio, V., Ross, D., Adams, A.: A review of research on the impact of professional learning communities on teaching practice and student learning. Teach. Teach. Educ. **24**, 80–91 (2008)
36. Vangrieken, K., Dochy, F., Raes, E., Kyndt, E.: Teacher collaboration: a systematic review. Educ. Res. Rev. **15**, 17–40 (2015)
37. Dexter, S., Richardson, J.W.: What does technology integration research tell us about the leadership of technology? J. Res. Technol. Educ. **52**, 17–36 (2020)
38. Spillane, J.P.: Distributed leadership. Educ. Forum. **69**, 143–150 (2005)
39. Shulman, L.S.: Those who understand: knowledge growth in teaching. Educ. Res. **15**, 4–14 (1986)
40. Ning, Y., Zhang, C., Xu, B., Zhou, Y., Wijaya, T.T.: Teachers' AI-TPACK: exploring the relationship between knowledge elements. Sustainability. **16**, 978 (2024)
41. Celik, I.: Towards intelligent-TPACK: an empirical study on teachers' professional knowledge to ethically integrate artificial intelligence (AI)-based tools into education. Comput. Human Behav. **138**, 107468 (2023)

42. Bryk, A., Schneider, B.: Trust in Schools: a core resource for improvement. Russell Sage Foundation Publications (2002). https://doi.org/10.7758/9781610440967
43. Spillane, J.P., Reiser, B.J., Reimer, T.: Policy implementation and cognition: reframing and refocusing implementation research. Rev. Educ. Res. **72**, 387–431 (2002)
44. Aravantinos, S., Lavidas, K., Komis, V., Karalis, T., Papadakis, S.: Artificial intelligence in K-12 education: a systematic review of teachers' professional development needs for AI integration. Computers. **15**, 49 (2026)

# How Students Interpret Representational Cues in AI-Generated Educational Illustrations

Jihyun Rho(✉) and Shamya Karumbaiah

University of Wisconsin-Madison, 1025 W Johnson Street, Madison WI 53706, USA
{jrho6,shamya.karumbaiah}@wisc.edu

**Abstract.** As generative AI systems are increasingly used to produce visual materials for educational contexts, students are more frequently encountering AI-generated illustrations that carry social and cultural meaning. While prior work has documented biases in AI-generated illustrations, less is known about how students interpret and reason about these representations when they appear in educational materials. This study examines how students make sense of social and racial cues embedded in AI-generated illustrations and how these interpretations relate to representational patterns in the images themselves. Using AI-generated illustrations derived from a children's book excerpt, we conducted focus group interviews with 21 Latine undergraduate students to explore how students interpreted identity and social hierarchy in the images. Drawing on a perception-based analytic lens, we show that students actively identified visual contrasts, negotiated stereotypes against lived experiences, and reasoned about implicit social hierarchies rather than passively accepting the images as neutral. To contextualize these interpretations, we conducted a computational analysis of the AI-generated illustrations to characterize salient representational cues that students repeatedly referenced. This analysis revealed patterned visual differences in skin tone across characters occupying different narrative roles, which aligned with students' interpretations of privilege and marginalization. Together, these findings highlight students' interpretive agency when critically engaging with AI-generated illustrations and demonstrate how algorithmic representations can become objects of critical sense-making. We discuss implications for the design of educational experiences that support students in critically engaging with AI-generated educational materials.

**Keywords:** Learner interpretation · AI-generated educational material · Critical AI literacy

## 1 Introduction

Generative AI (genAI) technologies are increasingly being used to produce visual content for educational settings [1]. In particular, educators and designers have begun to adopt genAI as a resource for supporting storytelling learning through the generation of illustrations [2]. These developments open new possibilities for engaging students, but they also raise important concerns. Prior research has shown that AI-generated visual content can unintentionally reproduce or amplify social biases, particularly those related to race,


E. G. Blanchard et al. (eds.), AIED 2026, LNCS 16586, pp. 74–88, 2027.
https://doi.org/10.1007/978-3-032-29773-0_6

ethnicity, and gender [3–5]. For example, studies have documented patterns such as the overpenetration of whiteness, the sexualization of women of color, and stereotypical portrayals of marginalized groups in AI-generated images [3].

Most existing investigations, however, examine these representational issues in broad media, technical, or auditing contexts [6, 7]. Comparatively less attention has focused on how such biases appear within educational narratives, where illustrations can play a formative role in shaping students' perceptions of identity, culture, and belonging [8, 9]. In educational settings, illustrations do not merely decorate text. They function as meaning-making resources that students actively interpret when reasoning about stories, relationships among characters, and social roles. Therefore, students do not remain passive recipients of illustrations. When encountering them, students draw on both perceptual cues in illustrations and their prior social knowledge to make sense of what they see [10]. Understanding how students interpret AI-generated illustrations, thus, require attention not only to the representational properties of the images themselves, but also students' interpretive reasoning.

In this study, we examine how students interpret social and racial cues embedded in AI-generated educational illustrations and how these interpretations relate to salient representational cues in the illustrations. Specifically, we focus on AI-generated illustrations derived from a children's book narrative and investigate students' interpretation alongside a targeted analysis of the visual cues present in the generated illustrations. Therefore, we address following research questions [RQ]:

RQ 1. How do students reason about visual cues and interpret social meanings in AI-generated educational illustrations?
RQ 2. What patterned representational cues emerge in AI-generated illustrations across narrative conditions?

By foregrounding students' interpretations while contextualizing them through a computational analysis of AI-generated illustrations, this study contributes to research on highlighting the role of interpretive agency in critically engaging with AI-generated educational materials.

## 2 Related Works

### 2.1 Learning with Educational Illustrations

Research on learning with visual materials has emphasized that illustrations in educational texts do more than accompany written content. In narrative-based learning materials, illustrations guide students' attention, foreground particular story elements, and support the understanding of characters and events [2, 11]. Indeed, studies comparing text-only versus text-plus-illustrations conditions have consistently found that the presence of illustrations enhances students' comprehension of story details [11], suggesting that visual cues can provide contextual information that supports meaning-making during reading.

Beyond improvement in comprehension, visual depictions of characters in illustrations influence students' perceptions of identity, belonging, and social roles, even when these attributes are not explicitly described in text. Prior work has documented how repeated visual patterns, such as consistent associations between certain appearances and social positions, can subtly reinforce social norms and hierarchies within educational illustrations [8, 9, 12, 13]. As a result, illustrations can shape students' understanding not only of story content, but also of broader cultural meanings related to race or ethnicity in narratives.

However, these effects do not arise solely from the illustrations themselves, but from how students engage with and interpret them. Understanding learning with illustrations therefore requires attending to students' interpretive processes, including how they notice, evaluate, and reason about visual cues embedded in illustrations.

### 2.2 Students' Interpretive Processes of Illustrations

Research on perception and social cognition emphasizes that interpretation of illustrations involves an active integration of perceptual features and prior knowledge [10, 14, 15]. Students draw on bottom-up cues, such as skin tone, facial features, or clothing, alongside top-down social knowledge shaped by cultural norms, stereotypes, and lived experiences. For example, for Latine individuals, perceived skin tone and societal colorism may affect how identity is perceived and experienced both within and outside their communities [16, 17]. This dual-process view highlights that perception is not a passive reception of visual input, but an interpretive act through which students construct social meaning.

In educational settings, this interpretive process becomes especially consequential when illustrations evoke identity-relevant cues. Prior studies have shown that students' interpretations of race and ethnicity in visual media including movie, commercial advertisement, or news media often reflect both societal stereotypes and personal experiences, leading to nuanced and sometimes conflicted reasoning [18–20]. For example, students may recognize stereotypical portrayals of their own ethnic community in social media while simultaneously resisting or questioning them based on their own community knowledge [19]. Such sensemaking processes reveal students' capacity to critically engage with representations rather than simply accepting them at face value.

This body of work positions students as active sense-makers who negotiate meaning when encountering visual representations. From a learning perspective, moments of tension, discomfort, or recognition can signal opportunities for reflection and critical engagement. From a learning perspective, examining how students interpret social meaning in AI-generated illustrations offers insight into how visual cues become learning resources for critical reflection and sensemaking in educational contexts.

### 2.3 Generative AI as a New Source for Educational Illustrations

Prior research has documented that genAI models often produce patterned visual outputs that reflect societal regularities present in their training data, including skewed representations of race, gender, and social roles [3, 5]. Empirical studies have shown that AI-generated images may overrepresent whiteness, homogenize marginalized identities, or associate particular appearances with stereotypical roles [6, 7, 21]. Importantly, this work has established that such representational tendencies emerge even when prompts do not explicitly specify identity-related attributes. However, most of this work has examined

AI-generated illustrations in isolation or within technical contexts. As a result, prior studies have primarily addressed what kinds of representational patterns generative AI systems can produce, while leaving open how students interpret and reason about these illustrations when they appear in educational settings.

As discussed in the previous sections, students actively integrate visual cues with prior knowledge when constructing social meaning from illustrations [10]. When illustrations are generated by AI systems and embedded within educational narratives, students encounter not only story content but also algorithmically produced visual cues that may implicitly signal identity, status, or social relationships. Therefore, rather than auditing AI systems for bias, our study situates AI-generated illustrations within an educational narrative and examines students' interpretations alongside salient representational cues in the illustrations. By connecting documented representational tendencies of generative AI with students' sensemaking processes, this work bridges research on AI-generated visual outputs and research on learning with illustrated materials.

# 3 Methods

## 3.1 Study Design Overview

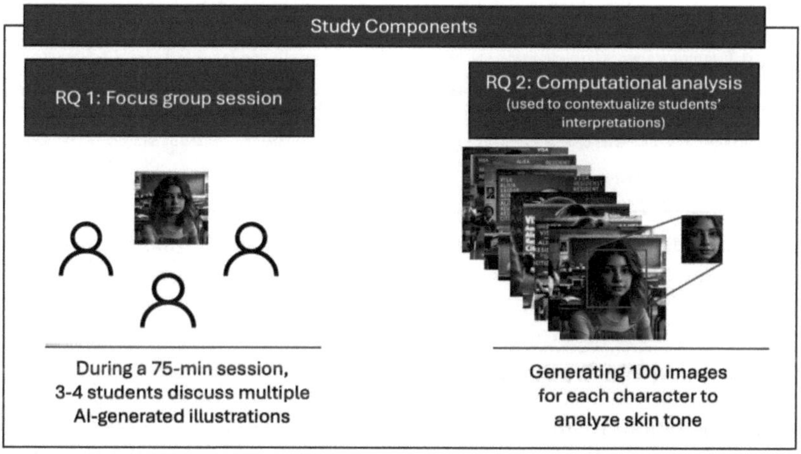


**Fig. 1.** Study design overview linking student interpretation (RQ 1) and computational analysis (RQ 2).

To examine how students interpret social and racial cues in AI-generated educational illustrations (RQ1) and how representational cues in the illustrations relate to these interpretations (RQ2), we adopted a learner-centered, sequential mixed-methods design as shown in Fig. 1. We first investigated students' interpretations of AI-generated illustrations embedded in a children's book narrative through focus group interviews. We then conducted a targeted computational analysis of the AI-generated illustrations to characterize salient representational cues that students referenced during interpretation.

### 3.2 Educational Narratives and Illustration Materials

We derived the illustration materials from *Stella Díaz Has Something to Say* [22], a children's book that portrays a Latina middle school student navigating school life in the United States. We selected a narrative excerpt (Fig. 2) that depicts a classroom interaction in which Stella experiences confusion and vulnerability related to her immigration status, while her classmate Jessica behaves unkindly toward her. We chose this excerpt because it implies social roles and power dynamics without explicitly specifying characters' ethnic backgrounds or citizenship status. This can create a space for participants in focus groups to engage in experience-based meaning-making. Also, the absence of explicit ethnic or citizenship labels allow visual depictions to play a central role in shaping interpretation. This excerpt served as the narrative context for all AI-generated illustrations.

Ms.Bell continues, "In just a little bit we are going to have a special ceremony for Don. Now everyone knows Don, right?"

"Don's the coolest!" says Ben Shaw.

Everyone agrees. Don, the school custodian, is always singing fun Beach Boys songs while he's cleaning. He also plays the craziest characters in the school plays, like Santa Claus in our holiday musical.

"Well, Don just became an American citizen, which is really hard! You have to take a big test. Not to mention all the years of waiting."

Jessica Anderson asks, "What was he before?"

Ms. Bell goes up to the board. She writes a bunch of words I haven't heard before.

In big letters, I see "visa," "alien," "resident," and "citizen."

"Great question. There are a few categories. Some people just come to visit. They get a piece of paper called a visa so they can stay awhile."

"Don't you buy things with a visa?" asks Jessica.

I lock eyes with her for a second, then quickly look away. Although I've been in the same class with Jessica since first grade, she makes me nervous. Everyone likes her, but I think she can be mean sometimes. Like when she laughed at me the first day of class for saying words wrong. Then another time, in first grade, she told everyone in our class that I had lice. Everyone believed her except for Jenny. The teacher even made me see the school nurse. And of course, I didn't have lice. Afterward, Jessica said she was sorry, but I never quite believed her. Ms. Bell chuckles.

"Yes, you do, but that's a different visa. For instance, people who come here for college get a student visa so they can stay here the entire time they are going to school. Then there are residents or legal aliens. They have green cards. They can stay here as long as they want, but they don't have as many rights as citizens."

My mouth drops open. I only have a green card. I know because Mom showed it to me when we got it in the mail. I was surprised that it wasn't green at all. I don't know too much about how we got it. I remember Mom was really stressed about it. I also remember waiting in line forever. The only part that was fun was getting fingerprints done. Oh, and taking bunches of pictures for it. But still, because of this green card, I'm an alien?

Ms. Bell continues, "After you've been a resident for a while you can apply to be a citizen. Then you can vote and be on a jury. You can even run for office!"

"What if you were born here?" asks Michelle.

"Then you're already a citizen. A natural citizen." I gulp again. This explains everything. I'm alien!

**Fig. 2.** An example of the excerpt from a children's book titled *Stella Díaz has something to say.*

### 3.3 AI-Generated Illustration Creation

To generate illustrations for the study, we used OpenAI's DALL·E 3 model via the official OpenAI API. For each illustration, we prompted the model using the format: *"Given this excerpt: [narrative excerpt], please generate a color image of [character name]."*

### 3.4 Focus Group Participants and Procedure

To examine learner interpretation (RQ1), we recruited 21 Latine undergraduate students from a predominantly white university in the Midwestern United States. All participants self-identified themselves as having Latin American or Caribbean heritage, though some were born in the United States.

We conducted five virtual focus group sessions, each lasting approximately 75 minutes and including four to five participants. Two of authors facilitated the sessions. We selected focus groups rather than individual interviews to foreground the socially negotiated nature of meaning-making around AI-generated images. The focus groups followed a semi-structured protocol informed by the perceptual framework outlined by Kawakami et al. [10]. At the start of each session, participants spent approximately three minutes reading the selected narrative excerpt. The facilitator then used a default prompt, "Given this excerpt: [narrative excerpt], please generate a color image of [character name]" to generate an AI illustration in real time and displayed the resulting image to participants. Participants were asked to evaluate the image and identify features they found notable. Guiding questions included, "Does this image suggest that the character belongs to your community?" and "What visual elements do you think the AI included to depict this character?" Follow-up probes explored participants' reasoning, such as "Why do you think the AI depicted the character this way?" and "How does this compare to how you imagine the character?" When participants expressed dissatisfaction with an image, they were invited to suggest alternative prompts, generate new illustrations, and discuss how the visual depictions changed. This iterative process allowed us to observe both participants' initial interpretive responses and their reflective engagement with the AI system. Each focus group session was video-recorded, and transcripts were generated using an automated transcription tool.

**Table 1.** Codes, code definitions, and corresponding examples.

| Code | Definition | Example |
|---|---|---|
| Bottom-up features | Perception of observable, physical attributes (e.g., skin tone, facial structure, hair texture) or cultural artifacts (e.g., clothing or accessories) of a character in a generated image. | "She has, like, brown eyes, like thicker eyebrows, and like, brown hair"<br>"I also noticed the bracelets, like she has all these multicolored bracelets on." |
| Top-down features | Statement drawing on culturally ingrained expectations, stereotypes, or personal experiences that influence the interpretation of a character in a generated image. | "Latina people are kind of stereotypes to look like with darker features, dark hair, dark skin…"<br>"My family in Mexico, they live in a small valley town that's like, also a ranch town, and that's a lot of the clothes that they wear are very similar, I guess." |

## 3.5 Analysis of Focus Groups

To analyze the focus group sessions, we reviewed the automatically generated transcripts for accuracy and conducted a thematic analysis [23] informed by prior work on social perception [10]. We developed two deductive codes before analysis (shown in Table 1): bottom-up features, referring to observable visual cues in the illustrations (e.g., skin tone, hair, clothing), and top-down features, referring to participants' prior knowledge, stereotypes, or personal experiences invoked during interpretation. Two researchers independently coded a subset of transcripts to refine code definitions and establish consistency. After reaching agreement, the coders applied the finalized codebook to the full dataset. We calculated inter-rater reliability using Cohen's Kappa (Kappa = .74), which indicated substantial agreement.

### 3.6 Computational Analysis of Representational Cues

To contextualize students' interpretations (RQ 2), we analyzed the AI-generated illustrations to identify salient visual cues that appeared repeatedly across conditions. We focused on skin tone because prior research has identified it as a socially salient and frequently referenced cue in racialized perception, and because students frequently discussed skin tone during the focus group sessions.

As shown in Fig. 3, we designed four experimental conditions that varied character names and implied social roles in the narrative. In this study, we operationalized social role based on the power dynamics described in the narrative. The character who occupied the bullying position (i.e., acting unkindly toward the other and displaying social dominance in the classroom interaction) was coded as occupying a relatively more privileged role. Conversely, the character who was bullied (i.e., experiencing confusion, vulnerability, or social exclusion) was coded as occupying a relatively more marginalized role. For character names, we drew on publicly available baby name data from New York City to reflect commonly recognized naming patterns associated with different ethnicity groups. Jessica and David were selected as names predominantly associated with White populations, while Stella and Mateo were selected as names predominantly associated with Latine populations. This manipulation allowed us to examine how AI-generated illustrations differed when the same narrative positioned characters as more privileged or more vulnerable, and when character names carried different identity associations [7]. Across all conditions, we generated 100 illustrations per character, resulting in a total of 800 AI-generated images.

To characterize skin tone computationally, we first detected faces in each illustration using an automated face detection method [24]. When an illustration contained multiple faces, we treated each detected face as a separate observation and selected the centrally positioned face as the focal target for analysis. We then extracted skin tone features using a computational model that represents apparent skin color along two dimensions: perceptual lightness and hue [25]. We selected these measures because they capture meaningful variation in skin appearance without relying on categorical racial labels. We compared lightness and hue values across narrative roles and character name conditions using statistical tests. Rather than treating these measures as definitive indicators of race, we used them to characterize visual differences that could plausibly inform students' interpretations.

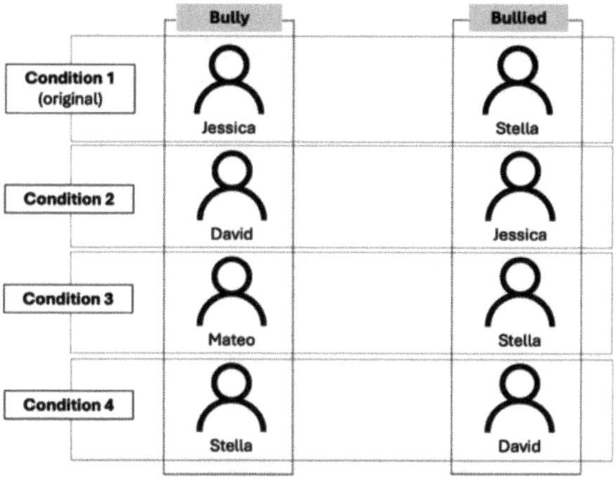


**Fig. 3.** We generated 100 AI-generated illustrations for each character across four conditions: (1) Jessica vs. Stella, (2) David vs. Jessica, (3) Mateo vs. Stella, and (4) Stella vs. David. In each condition, one character occupies a relatively more privileged position, while the other represents a more marginalized position.

# 4 Results

## 4.1 RQ 1: How Students Interpreted Social Meaning in AI-Generated Illustrations

Across focus group discussions, students consistently treated AI-generated illustrations (e.g., as shown in Fig. 4) as meaningful sources for interpreting characters' identities and social positions. Rather than describing images at a surface level, participants actively reasoned about social meaning by integrating visual cues in the illustrations with their prior knowledge and personal experience. We identified three recurring patterns in students' interpretive reasoning.

**Noticing and Interpreting Salient Visual Cues** Students frequently began their interpretations by attending to specific visual cues in the illustrations, including skin tone, facial features, hair texture, and clothing. Participants rarely described these features in isolation. Instead, they treated them as cues that carried social meaning. Students noted that AI-generated images often aligned with common stereotypes about Latine identity, such as darker skin or hair, while simultaneously emphasizing the diversity within Latine communities. During the focus group session, as one participant remarked after seeing Fig. 4(a), *"Latine people are kind of stereotyped to look like [Stella in this illustration who are] with like darker features, dark hair, dark skin.... "*, while another added, *"Latine people can come in all different colors and various skin tones."*

**Integrating Prior Knowledge and Lived Experiences** Students regularly connected visual cues to prior knowledge and personal experience. For example, several participants described feeling a sense of connection when characters' visual features resembled those of people in their own communities. One student, who identified herself as a "*white-passing Latina*," explained that Stella's skin tone in the left figure in Fig. 4(b), felt familiar, noting, "*I don't really think there's anything that distinguishes her from not being in [my] community.*" However, this sense of connectivity did not extend to all fair-skinned depictions and appearances. For example, students expressed a lack of connection with the representation of Stella in the right figure in Fig. 4(b). Based on their prior knowledge, they described the image as resembling styles unrelated to their community, such as "*Japanese anime*" or "Ghibli movie [style]." This critique highlights that while certain visual features (e.g., light skin) may be cues to invoke lived experiences or prior knowledge to build familiarity, other stylistic or exaggerated features can disrupt such sense of familiarity, making the image feel disconnected from their identity.

**Fig. 4.** Images of Stella: students show different responses to stereotypical depictions of Stella in (a) and two different depictions of Stella in (b).

**Negotiating Social Hierarchies and Stereotypes.** Students did not simply accept illustrated cues at face value. Instead, they actively negotiated their interpretations, especially when images appeared to suggest social hierarchies or stereotypical roles. Participants discussed whether certain characters appeared more privileged, confident, or marginalized, and debated whether these impressions aligned with or contradicted their expectations of the story. For example, when students prompted AI to generate an image of Stella and her classmate Jessica, who is bullying Stella, the resulting image portrayed the two characters as belonging to different ethnic groups. One student interpreted this contrast in terms of social privilege, commenting, "*[Jessica is] more ignorant because she may be more privileged [so she does not understand why Stella feels] confused by [her immigrant status in the classroom], and that's why [AI] made her look white-passing.*" This response illustrates how students linked visual differences in the illustration to assumptions about power and social position within the story. These discussions often involved explicit critique of the AI-generated illustrations. Students experimented with revising prompts to redraw characters in less privileged positions (e.g., "*Generate image of Stella and her friend in class without emphasizing ethnicity or skin tone*"). However, they found that these attempts reproduced implicit ethnic boundaries between characters again that aligned with their social roles in the narrative, as shown in Fig. 5.

**Fig. 5.** Images of Stella with Jessica showing implicit boundaries between ethnicities.

## 4.2 RQ 2: Representational Cues in AI-Generated Illustrations

To contextualize students' interpretations, we examined the AI-generated illustrations to identify representational cues that appeared repeatedly across conditions. We focused on cues that students frequently referenced during focus group discussions, particularly skin tone. We calculated the average value of lightness and hue values of each character's skin tone in different conditions (Fig. 2) in Table 2.

**Table 2.** Mean values for lightness and hue (values in parentheses are standard deviations).

| Condition | Character | Light | Hue |
|---|---|---|---|
| Condition 1: Original | Stella (bullied by Jessica) | 64.14 (12.87) | 42.70 (13.85) |
| | Jessica (bullying Stella) | 70.76 (10.05) | 45.41 (13.13) |
| Condition 2 | Jessica (bullied by David) | 66.65 (9.51) | 43.62 (16.43) |
| | David (bullying Jessica) | 69.07 (12.56) | 46.46 (16.43) |
| Condition 3 | Stella (bullied by Mateo) | 64.32 (10.89) | 43.74 (14.66) |
| | Mateo (bullying Stella) | 62.52 (9.81) | 53.46 (6.15) |
| Condition 4 | David (bullied by Stella) | 62.62 (13.77) | 43.89 (19.81) |
| | Stella (bullying David) | 74.43 (10.11) | 44.17 (21.71) |

**Differences in Skin Tone Across Narrative Roles** Analysis of the AI-generated illustrations revealed role-dependent differences in apparent skin tone across narrative roles, particularly when the same character appeared in contrasting narrative positions. Illustrations depicting characters positioned as more vulnerable in the narrative tended to show darker skin tones, whereas illustrations depicting characters in more dominant or privileged roles tended to show lighter skin tones. Specifically, when Stella appeared in a vulnerable role (i.e., being bullied by Jessica), the illustrations depicted her with significantly darker skin tones compared to when she appeared in a privileged role (i.e., bullying David), $t(198) = 6.864, p < .001$. In contrast, conditions in which David bullied Jessica or Mateo bullied Stella did not show statistically significant differences in skin tone between characters. These results suggest that changes in narrative role alone can shift how the same character is visually rendered, particularly along the dimension of perceptual lightness.

**Effects of Character Name and Role Manipulation** Beyond narrative role, character name was also associated with variation in how AI-generated illustrations depicted skin tone. When the same narrative context paired different character names with specific social roles, the resulting illustrations showed patterned differences in perceptual lightness. A two-way ANOVA revealed significant main effects of character name, $F(3, 792) = 16.37, p < .001$, and narrative role, $F(1, 792) = 50.29, p < .001$, as well as a significant interaction between character name and role, $F(3, 792) = 10.53, p < .001$. These results indicate that differences in perceptual lightness varied across character names and that the association between narrative role and skin tone differed depending on name-based cues. Cross-character comparisons further illustrate this interaction. For example, illustrations depicting Jessica in a bullying role tended to show lighter skin tones than illustrations depicting Stella in a victim role (mean difference = 6.53, $p < .001$). In contrast, characters such as Mateo and David appeared darker on average across roles. Mateo in a bullying role appeared darker than Stella in the same role (mean difference = –11.91, $p < .001$), and David as a victim appeared darker than Jessica as a victim (mean difference = –8.14, $p < .001$). Together, these patterns suggest that perceptual lightness in AI-generated illustrations varied in relation to both narrative role and name-based cues, with some role–name combinations showing more pronounced differences than others.

## 5 Discussion

This study examined how students interpret social meaning in AI-generated educational illustrations (RQ1) and how these interpretations relate to representational cues (i.e., skin tone) embedded in the images (RQ2). By foregrounding students' interpretation through computational analysis and situating AI-generated illustrations within an educational narrative, the findings extend prior research on illustrated learning materials and generative AI in education.

### 5.1 Students as Active Interpreters of AI-Generated Educational Illustrations

The findings demonstrate that students' engagement with AI-generated illustrations involved more than recognizing visual features or identifying representational issues. They rarely lingered at a purely perceptual level of interpretation. Visual cues such as skin tone, facial features, and stylistic elements quickly became resources for students' reasoning about AI-generated illustrations. Specifically, we found that students actively recognized and integrated these visual cues with their prior knowledge and lived experience. They then evaluated these visual cues. For example, when they noticed the implicit ethnic boundaries (i.e., different skin tone) in drawing characters positioned in different social roles, they engaged into deeper reflection and articulated a new prompt to challenge the representational cues in the current illustration. This finding suggests that students' active interaction with AI-generated illustrations can support as a critical sensemaking process where students are positioned as interpreters rather than passive recipients. As a result, students' interpretive activity functioned as a learning process through which they made sense of social meaning in AI-generated illustrations. Their critical engagement during discussion in the focus group sessions revealed their interpretive agency in evaluating, critiquing, and experimenting with the genAI, including attempting to revise prompts to explore alternative depictions. In this way, interpretation itself became a site of learning, where students reasoned about how AI-generated illustrations communicate social meaning.

## 5.2 Representational Cues on Students' Sense-Making for Illustrations

While students demonstrated strong interpretive agency, the computational analysis highlights how AI-generated illustrations structured the conditions under which interpretation occurred. Although the prompts did not explicitly specify ethnic attributes, the generated illustrations contained patterned visual cues that aligned with the features students noticed and discussed. This alignment is illustrated by the case of Jessica and Stella: students described Jessica as "white-passing when she occupied the bullying role and interpreted this visual contrast in terms of social privilege. The computational analysis confirmed that this perception was grounded in a measurable pattern. Jessica in the bullying role was rendered with significantly lighter skin tones than Stella in the bullied role (see Table 2). More broadly, the significant effects of both character name and narrative role on perceptual lightness indicate that such visual contrasts were not idiosyncratic impressions but reflected systematic representational regularities in the AI-generated illustrations.

Importantly, these patterned visual cues represent more than as isolated evidence of bias in AI outputs. Instead, they point to a learning-relevant concern. Such repeated visual patterns can narrow the space of possible interpretations available to students. When certain appearances consistently cooccur with particular social roles across illustrations, as observed in our computational analysis, these appearances can function as implicit signals that guide students' attention and inferences. Considering prior work showing that visual cues guide attention and inference, our findings extend this work by showing how AI-generated illustrations, through their patterned outputs, can foreground particular interpretations. During focus group sessions, even when students sought to alter representations, the AI often reproduced similar visual boundaries aligned with social roles. Thus, student interpretation may unfold within constraints shaped by the genAI's visual regularities, underscoring the need for pedagogical designs that examine such constraints, enabling students to reflect on AI-generated illustrations and limit the interpretations.

17. Telles, E., Paschel, T.: Who is black, white, or mixed race? how skin color, status, and nation shape racial classification in Latin America. Am. J. Sociol. **120**, 864–907 (2014)
18. Rivadeneyra, R.: Do you see what I see?: Latino adolescents' perceptions of the images on television. J. Adolesc. Res. **21**, 393–414 (2006)
19. Lutz, N., Aragon, C.: "We're not all construction workers": algorithmic compression of Latinidad on TikTok. Proc. ACM Hum.-Comput. Interact. **8**, 1–31 (2024)
20. Ramasubramanian, S.: The impact of stereotypical versus counterstereotypical media exemplars on racial attitudes, causal attributions, and support for affirmative action. Commun. Res. **38**, 497–516 (2011)
21. Jain, N., Olmo, A., Sengupta, S., Manikonda, L., Kambhampati, S.: Imperfect ImaGANation: implications of GANs exacerbating biases on facial data augmentation and snapchat face lenses. Artif. Intell. **304**, 103652 (2022)
22. Dominguez, A.: Stella díaz Has Something to Say. Roaring Brook Press (2018)
23. Braun, V., Clarke, V.: Using thematic analysis in psychology. Qual. Res. Psychol. **3**, 77–101 (2006). https://doi.org/10.1191/1478088706qp063oa
24. Bulat, A., Tzimiropoulos, G.: How far are we from solving the 2d & 3d face alignment problem?(and a dataset of 230,000 3d facial landmarks). In: Proceedings of the IEEE International Conference on Computer Vision (ICCV) (2017)
25. Thong, W., Joniak, P., Xiang, A.: Beyond skin tone: a multidimensional measure of apparent skin color. In: Proceedings of the IEEE/CVF International Conference on Computer Vision (2023)

# Evaluating the Impact of Workshop Interventions on AI Literacy and STEM Career Aspirations with Australian Secondary Students

Christian Bergh[1], Alexandra Vassar[1], Natasha Banks[2], Jessica Xu[1,2], and Jake Renzella[1](✉)

[1] University of New South Wales, Sydney, Australia
{c.bergh,jake.renzella}@unsw.edu.au
[2] Day of AI Australia, Sydney, Australia

**Abstract.** Artificial Intelligence (AI) is becoming increasingly important in K–12 educational environments, as well as in the daily lives of young people. Recent reports highlight an urgent need for systemic AI education to prevent a widening "intelligence divide" and to prepare the future workforce for a radically shifted labour market. As a result, fostering foundational AI literacy has emerged as a global priority. This study evaluates the impact of *Day of AI Australia*'s workshop-based intervention designed to improve AI literacy and conceptual understanding among Australian secondary students (Years 7–10). Using a mixed-methods approach with pre- and post-intervention surveys ($N = 205$), we analyse changes in student cohort's ability to identify AI in everyday tools, their understanding of AI ethics and training, and their interest in STEM-related careers. Baseline data revealed critical safety risks, with nearly one in five students (18.5%) admitting to sharing deepfakes and 7.3% creating them. Results indicate a significant increase in self-reported AI knowledge ($p < .001, r = .445$) and AI confidence ($p < .001, r = .279$) following intervention within the cohort. Students showed a significant improvement in recognising AI within popular platforms such as Netflix (+27.1%), Spotify (+16.2%) and TikTok (+12.8%), highlighting a transition from viewing these systems as simply algorithm-based to AI-driven. Post-workshop, self-reported interest in STEM careers increased ($p < .05$), though effect sizes were small. This suggests that alternatives to one-off workshops may be required to meaningfully shift long-term career aspirations. These findings contribute to the growing body of evidence on effective AI literacy frameworks and offer practical insights for scaling AI literacy programs.

**Keywords:** AI Literacy · K–12 · Secondary Education · Student Perceptions · STEM Aspirations · Large Language Models · Ethical AI · Australia · Workshop Intervention · Conceptual Change


E. G. Blanchard et al. (eds.), AIED 2026, LNCS 16586, pp. 89–102, 2027.
https://doi.org/10.1007/978-3-032-29773-0_7

## 1 Introduction

The rapid integration of Artificial Intelligence (AI) into daily life has prompted UNESCO to emphasise the need to prepare learners for AI-mediated futures [26]. In this report, Pedro et al. [26] highlight opportunities of AI-enabled education to improve equity, while stressing the need to strengthen learner capacities. Suggesting that schools must understand existing student engagement with AI and adjust curricula to ensure foundational AI literacy and future preparedness.

Understanding how students perceive AI is therefore essential for designing context-relevant AI literacy initiatives. This study focuses on Years 7–10 students (ages 12–17) from three New South Wales (NSW) government high schools in Australia, who completed pre- and post-intervention surveys as part of the Day of AI Australia curriculum. The surveys provide a view of learners' baseline AI knowledge, confidence using AI tools, ethical understanding (including privacy, bias and deepfakes) and attitudes toward AI's societal impact. Findings provide insight into how secondary school students interpret AI concepts and identify areas for further scaffolded learning, contributing to the growing body of literature on student AI perceptions [15,16,18].

This paper contributes empirical evidence on the short-term impact of a workshop-based AI literacy intervention implemented in three Australian government secondary schools (Years 7–10; $N = 205$ pre, $n = 163$ post). We provide (i) a construct-level profile of students' baseline AI literacy, tool-use patterns, and ethical understanding, and (ii) effect size estimates of post-intervention shifts in self-reported AI knowledge, confidence, and key conceptual statements (e.g., training, bias, privacy). We further show how the workshops broadened students' recognition of AI in everyday recommendation systems (e.g., Spotify, Netflix, TikTok), offering a practical lens for designing instruction connecting socio-technical AI concepts to adolescents' lived digital practices. Finally, we highlight the prevalence of deepfake creation and dissemination among participants, and discuss curriculum and policy implications for scaling AI literacy programs in context with heterogeneous teacher confidence and digital infrastructure.

The study is guided by the following research questions:

**RQ1** How do one-off AI literacy workshops impact students':
- (a) perceptions, understandings, misconceptions and confidence of AI?
- (b) aspirations toward Science, Technology, Engineering, and Maths careers?

**RQ2** How are Australian government secondary school students engaging with AI tools in their learning and broader digital practices?

## 2 Background and Literature Review

As AI technologies become increasingly integrated into daily life and work, research emphasises providing structured learning opportunities over incidental exposure [13,31]. Emerging studies highlight benefits of personalised learning

[17], improved feedback [27], and accessibility support for diverse learners [25]. 'Prompting literacy', has also been identified as a critical capacity for interacting productively with language models [14,34]. Studies in primary classrooms demonstrate how teachers have begun co-designing literacy and content lessons that integrate AI resources to support goal-aligned instruction [19].

Current literature has attempted to identify students' mental models and attitudes toward AI, but empirical data on how these perceptions shift following specific curricular interventions remains limited [23]. Surveys have indicated that students tend to have an overall positive perception of AI, often citing its potential to increase creativity [16,22]. They also indicate concern for ethics and privacy with AI, but show interest in methods of integrating AI into their learning processes [16,32].

Increasingly, AI literacy initiatives for K–12 students are operationalised through accessible, developmentally suitable pedagogical designs that are adaptable across school systems [1]. One approach utilises project-based learning to embed AI concepts in creative tasks, such as generating art, music, or text, fostering foundational understanding through direct interaction [21]. Another approach addresses equity and infrastructure barriers through "unplugged" curricula that teach AI concepts without digital devices, using structured analogies and games to support reasoning about classification, datasets, and model behaviour in low-resource settings. Unplugged methods yield positive learning gains in conceptual understanding, especially for younger students and schools with limited digital resources [8,33]. Beyond these technical foundations, a third pedagogical shift focuses on interdisciplinary socio-technical curricula. This approach moves beyond functional use to engage students with the ethical, civic and societal implications of AI algorithmic automation for communities and institutions [28]. However, despite these emerging global frameworks, empirical data on how these interventions influence the literacy and career aspirations of secondary students, particularly within the Australian context, is limited.

Australian AI education research is nascent, primarily focusing on policy, teacher perspectives or general digital access rather than student perspectives and practices [4,11]. Consequently, there is limited evidence to guide system-level decision-making [12] or address how local students perceive and interact with AI [5]. The study utilises workshops provided through the Day of AI Australia program, an initiative providing free curriculum-aligned resources to schools on machine learning, AI ethics, and natural language processing. Although educators value these accessible materials, scaling literacy programs across diverse settings is challenging with variable teacher confidence and digital infrastructure [29].

School-based AI literacy implementation remains fragmented [35], with effectiveness often contingent on teacher confidence, availability, quality of professional learning, and the alignment with local curricula [30]. Systemic barriers are further compounded by ethical concerns such as algorithmic bias, data privacy, and the opacity of generative models, potentially undermining educational foundations. [2]. Most existing evidence is from the United States and Europe, yet

**Table 1.** Summary of survey constructs, measurement scales, and item focus.

| Construct | Measurement Scale (Anchors) | Measurement Focus |
|---|---|---|
| Demographics | Categorical | Year level, gender, cultural identity. |
| AI Knowledge | Likert (None-Expert) | Subjective assessment of AI foundations. |
| Conceptual App. | Multi-select | Identifying AI in tools (e.g., Spotify, Netflix). |
| Understanding AI | Likert (Disagree-Agree) | Self assessment of understanding AI functions. |
| AI Confidence | Likert (Not at all-Extremely) | Self-efficacy in using/troubleshooting AI. |
| Tool Usage | Frequency (Never-Daily) | Engagement across 12 general and education apps. |
| Using AI | Multi-select | Identifying primary usage motivations and information sources for AI Literacy. |
| Deepfakes* | Multi-select | Identifying experience and understanding of deepfakes. |
| AI Attitudes | Likert (Disagree-Agree) | Ethics, privacy, bias, and societal impact. |
| STEM Careers | Likert (Uninterested-Interested) | Career intent in AI, CS, and Engineering. |
| Qualitative (Post-Survey) | Open-ended response | Reflections on utility and improvements. |

*Note: Deepfake was defined as:"Video, image or audio generated by, or altered with AI to make it appear as though someone said or did something they did not".

Australian implementation faces unique hurdles regarding digital equity. Uneven distribution of digital infrastructure, particularly limited internet access, and teacher expertise risk exacerbating existing educational inequalities [6,20]. Consequently, classroom integration necessitates addressing both infrastructure gaps and the risks associated with data governance and transparency.

## 3 Method

To evaluate differences between pre- and post-workshop samples, we administered pre- and post-intervention surveys consisting of Likert-scale items, multiple-choice questions, and open-ended reflections. The instrument was designed to capture baseline AI literacy and measure shifts in conceptual understanding and career intent. The survey constructs and their respective measurement scales are summarised in Table 1. Because surveys were collected anonymously on paper, pre- and post-intervention responses could not be paired at the individual level; therefore, results should be interpreted as differences between pre- and post-workshop samples rather than within-student change. The Day

**Table 2.** Summary of lessons and concepts covered.

| # | Lesson | Description |
|---|---|---|
| 1 | What is AI & How it Works | Experiment with AI models; discuss how AI learns from data, makes predictions |
| 2 | Ethics of AI | Examine the ethical implications of AI by analysing media examples, biases, and misinformation |
| 3 | AI Safety & Data Privacy | Examine platform practices, ethical risks of misinformation and deepfakes, and the value of personal data |
| 4 | AI & Misinformation | Evaluate and distinguish AI-generated content, understand misinformation and disinformation |
| 5 | AI in Careers & Industries | Explore how AI impacts different industries by analysing stakeholders, benefits and risks |

of AI Australia program introduces students to foundational concepts in AI through interactive lessons. Each lesson is described in Table 2.

Participants were recruited from three NSW government secondary schools, across metropolitan and regional contexts ($N = 205$), with a mix of students from lower to higher socio-economic backgrounds. The cohort was culturally diverse, including significant Indigenous representation (17% at one of the schools) and students who came from language backgrounds other than English (90% at one school). In accordance with the Ethics approval granted by the University of New South Wales Human Research and Ethics Committee, participation in all components of the study was voluntary and anonymous. The student cohort was made up of 66 year 7 students, 69 year 8 students, 21 year 9 students, and 48 year 10 students, and one student did not provide their year. Due to the inclusion of girls-only schools, the sample was majority female ($n = 136$), followed by male ($n = 56$), and students who did not wish to share their gender ($n = 13$). As the senior cohorts (Years 9–10) lacked male representation, data was analysed by total distribution rather than sex to avoid skewed correlations.

### 3.1 Procedure

The workshop intervention was delivered in a single-day format following a linear progression: **Pre-survey** → **Lessons 1–2** (Foundations & Ethics) → [**Lessons 3–4** (Safety & Literacy) *OR* **Lesson 5** (Careers)] → **Post-survey**. The variation in sequence was determined by school-specific scheduling. All survey instruments were administered and collected on-site by program staff for data integrity.

Data was cleaned before analysis. Participants who exhibited straight-lining behaviour (providing identical responses across all items, indicating surveys were not completed in good faith, potentially skewing analyses) were excluded from the final analysis. As the surveys were paper based, it was possible to mark more than one answer or leave questions blank. Responses that were left blank or had multiple selections were deemed invalid and excluded from analysis. Qualitative responses that were illegible were excluded. Written responses that were non-responses such as "none" were excluded.

Quantitative data were analysed using IBM SPSS Statistics (v30.0.0.0). Due to the non-normal distribution of the Likert-scale data, non-parametric tests specifically the Mann-Whitney U Test and Friedman Test were employed to evaluate pre- and post- intervention shifts. Once the Mann-Whitney U Test for Likert questions present in both pre- and post- surveys were completed, $r$ was calculated for effect size as $r = \frac{z}{\sqrt{N}}$. After conducting the Friedman Test a stepwise post-hoc analysis was conducted on the question asking how much time each student spends on each application. Each application was assigned to groups based on their stepwise subsets. A Wald Independent-Samples Proportions Test was conducted to identify any increase in whether or not they believe a set of applications uses AI.

Qualitative data was analysed using NVivo (v12.0.0.71). A thematic analysis was completed for three open ended survey questions; the first asks what students liked, the second asks what students found most useful, and the third asks what could be done to improve the lessons [7]. NVivo's Auto Code wizard was used to identify initial themes and codes. NVivo identified 27 codes for the first question, 18 for the second, and 24 for the third. Codes were grouped into high level themes and then went through three rounds of review for each question and were re-grouped, modified or eliminated each round. After review there were four themes for the first question responses, three for the second, and four for the third.

# 4 Results

## 4.1 Pre-survey

Prior to the start of the lessons, $N = 205$ student responses were collected (four responses were excluded due to uniform non-authentic answering patterns).

Students were asked to indicate the frequency with which they use specific AI-enabled applications, ranging from 'Rarely or Never' to 'Daily'. Figure 1 presents the distribution of usage across the 11 surveyed applications. Results reveal a clear hierarchy of engagement. AI integrated into social media platforms (Snapchat, TikTok, YouTube) is most used, with most students engaging daily or weekly basis. Generative productivity tools such as ChatGPT, Canva (Magic Write/Design), and Google Gemini show moderate usage, typically weekly use, while dedicated educational AI tools (NSWEduChat and Khanmigo) and companion bots (Replika) are 'Rarely or Never' used by students.

To validate observations, a Friedman Test was conducted to determine differences in usage, returning a significant result ($Q^2 = 667.724, p < .001$). A stepwise post-hoc analysis confirmed five homogeneous subsets, statistically distinguishing the high-frequency social media usage from general generative tools, which were in turn used significantly more often than specialised educational platforms.

Students were asked to indicate their motivations, if any, for using AI tools. As shown in Fig. 2, academic utility is the primary driver, with 'Schoolwork' reported by 65.9% of students. This was followed by 'Problem Solving' (39.5%) and 'Fun' (38.0%), suggesting that while students view AI as a utility for learning, recreational and creative exploration remain significant factors.

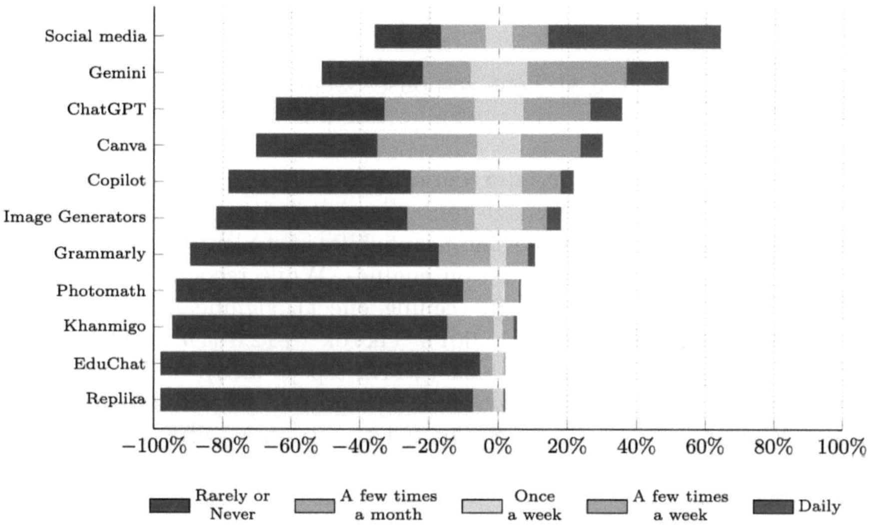


**Fig. 1.** AI tool usage reported by students $N=197$ (191 fully completed).

When students seek out information about AI, they indicated a heavy reliance on social media (74.1%), teachers (35.6%) and friends (34.6%) (Fig. 3). Additionally, students were asked if they learned about AI at school, with 42.1% reporting 'Yes', 28.4% reporting 'No', and 29.5% reporting 'Unsure'.

Responses regarding deepfakes indicate high exposure. Most students (82.4%) reported having seen deepfakes, and some reported sharing (18.5%) or creating (7.3%) them. Some (13.7%) reported seeing their friends create or share deepfakes. Crucially, gaps in safety knowledge exist; while half of the cohort (50.7%) indicated they knew how to report deepfakes and 14.1% having reported a deepfake, only 34.1% expressed confidence in knowing what to do if they were the subject of one and 6.8% indicated they have been a subject of a deepfake.

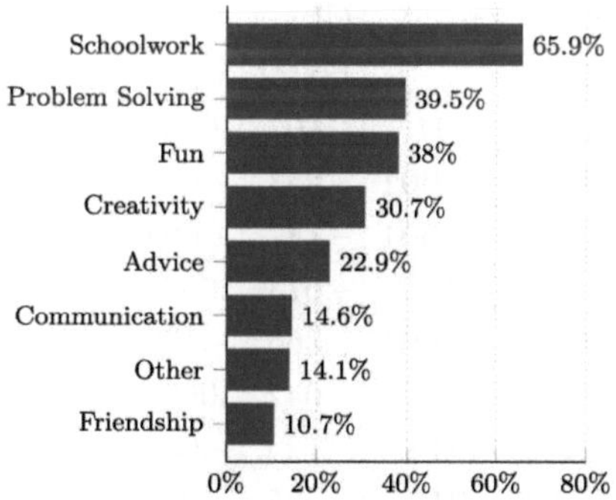


**Fig. 2.** Primary motivations for AI tool engagement among students.

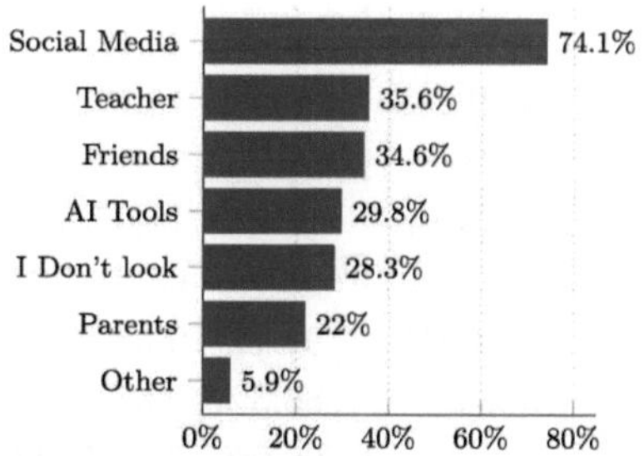


**Fig. 3.** Primary information sources for student AI literacy.

### 4.2 Post-survey

Post-workshops, $N = 163$ student responses were collected (seven responses were excluded due to survey straight-lining), and 35 students did not submit a post-workshop survey.

A primary objective of the intervention was to broaden student definitions of AI beyond generative text/image tools. As detailed in Table 3, independent samples proportions tests revealed significant shifts in students' ability to identify AI within algorithmic recommendation engines. While recognition of overt AI tools like ChatGPT remained high (ceiling effect), significant increases were observed for Netflix ($+27.1\%, p < .001$), TikTok ($+12.8\%, p < .001$), Spotify ($+16.2\%, p < .001$), and Face Unlock ($+11.2\%, p = .013$). This suggests the workshop challenged the misconception that "algorithms" are distinct from AI.

Mann-Whitney U Tests were conducted to evaluate shifts in self-reported knowledge and attitudes (Table 4). The intervention yielded the largest effect sizes in conceptual understanding. Students reported a significant increase in general 'AI Knowledge' ($r = .445$) and 'AI Confidence' ($r = .279$) with a medium and small effect size respectively. Additionally, medium effect sizes were also observed regarding their understanding of how AI systems are trained ($r = .399$) and their understanding of bias ($r = .302$). Alternatively, the intervention did not appear to impact the students' perception of AI, the only small effect change occurring in students' worry of AI's impact on job markets ($p = .049$, $r = .106$). Regarding career aspirations, the data indicates an uplift in interest across Artificial Intelligence ($p < .001$), Computer Science ($p = .005$), and Engineering ($p = .029$). However, the effect sizes for these career variables remained small ($r < .3$), suggesting that while the workshop successfully piqued interest, a single-day intervention may be insufficient to meaningfully alter long-term career trajectories compared to the immediate gains in content knowledge.

**Table 3.** Proportion of respondents identifying tools as using AI, with one-sided Wald Test results.

| | Proportion | | % Change | $z$ | $p$ | CI | |
|---|---|---|---|---|---|---|---|
| | Pre | Post | | | | Lower | Upper |
| Calculator | 28.8% | 30.1% | 1.3% | –.268 | .394 | –.107 | .080 |
| Spotify | 60.5% | 76.7% | 16.2% | –3.300 | **<.001** | –.253 | –.067 |
| TikTok | 82.9% | 95.7% | 12.8% | –3.830 | **<.001** | –.187 | –.064 |
| Microwave | 10.2% | 11.0% | .8% | –.247 | .402 | –.073 | .055 |
| Netflix | 38.5% | 65.6% | 27.1% | –5.166 | **<.001** | –.366 | –.170 |
| ChatGPT | 94.1% | 93.3% | –.9% | .352 | .362 | –.042 | .062 |
| Google | 86.3% | 93.3% | 6.9% | –2.139 | **.016** | –.129 | –.006 |
| Face Unlock | 60.0% | 71.2% | 11.2% | –2.230 | **.013** | –.206 | –.014 |

Note: For each proportion $N = 368 = (nPre = 205 + nPost = 163)$.
Significance level: .05

**Table 4.** Comparison of pre- and post-intervention AI knowledge & confidence scores, AI knowledge statements, and AI sentiment statements.

| Confidence/Statement/Career Interest | $n$ | | $U$ | $p$ | $z$ | $r$ |
|---|---|---|---|---|---|---|
| | Pre | Post | | | | |
| Knowledge about AI | 200 | 158 | 7945.0 | **<.001** | -8.428 | **.445** |
| Confidence in AI Tools | 179 | 154 | 9567.5 | **<.001** | -5.084 | .279 |
| Understand AI training | 201 | 160 | 8902.0 | **<.001** | -7.587 | **.399** |
| Understand AI bias/errors | 200 | 160 | 10636.5 | **<.001** | -5.725 | **.302** |
| Privacy skills (Social Media) | 201 | 157 | 11475.0 | **<.001** | -4.637 | .245 |
| Privacy skills (School Work) | 200 | 158 | 11997.0 | **<.001** | -4.122 | .218 |
| Importance of data consent | 199 | 157 | 12617.5 | **<.001** | -3.302 | .175 |
| Worried AI impacts my job | 187 | 157 | 12943.5 | **.049** | -1.965 | .106 |
| AI tools at school to help with learning | 187 | 156 | 14333.0 | .768 | -.296 | .016 |
| I feel pressured to use AI tools | 184 | 155 | 12695.5 | .068 | -1.827 | .099 |
| Worried teacher suspects AI | 184 | 156 | 13933.0 | .628 | -.484 | .026 |
| Effect of AI on society will be positive | 176 | 149 | 11973.0 | .090 | -1.695 | .094 |
| Career in Artificial Intelligence | 175 | 157 | 10848.0 | **<.001** | -3.443 | .189 |
| Career in Computer Science | 176 | 157 | 11424.5 | **.005** | -2.831 | .115 |
| Career in Engineering | 178 | 157 | 12094.5 | **.029** | -2.178 | .119 |

Note: Statistical significance was determined using the Mann-Whitney U Test ($N = nPre + nPost$).

Thematic analysis of open-ended responses ($N = 133$) reinforced the quantitative findings regarding knowledge acquisition. When asked what was "most useful" 85 (63.9%) students cited 'How AI works/trained'. Students identified the interactive elements and gamified components ($n = 52$, 39.0%) as the most engaging aspects of the curriculum. Similarly, suggestions for improvement focused on hands-on activities ($n = 60$, 45.1%), with students requesting "more activities and less talking," highlighting a preference for kinaesthetic learning over direct instruction in technical workshops.

## 5 Discussion

Students identified social media-integrated AI (Snapchat, TikTok and YouTube) as their most frequently used AI applications. This likely reflects the entrenched role of social media in teenage routines [9,24] (RQ2). Notably, this survey took place prior to new Australian legislation restricting social media access for those under 16 [10]. As accounts are closed or transitioned, teen engagement patterns may shift toward more task-specific or general AI tools.

Despite 65.9% of students self-reporting schoolwork as a primary motivation, 57.9% report that they are unsure or did not learn about AI at school (RQ2). This result highlights a gap in AI literacy within Australian school environments.

While students significantly improved at identifying AI in complex platforms like Spotify, Netflix, and TikTok, distinguishing AI from basic tools like calculators remains a challenge. A general increase in 'Yes' responses suggests potential response bias, yet this cannot explain the disproportional gains seen in identifying AI within social media and streaming platforms (RQ1a). This shift indicates a narrowing terminological disconnect; where these platforms were once marketed as "algorithms", students now increasingly recognise the underlying AI. As AI becomes increasingly invisible within daily-use software, students must be able to identify its presence to navigate these systems critically and ethically.

Qualitative feedback revealed a strong preference for hands-on activities, with students identifying interactive components as the most enjoyable workshops elements. To maintain student agency and attention, educational AI platforms should consider adopting engagement strategies from general-use applications to make niche educational tools more appealing to adolescents.

While the workshops achieved a statistically significant increase in STEM career interest, the effect size was low (RQ1b). This suggests that while a single-day intervention can spark curiosity, sustained, longitudinal engagement is required to meaningfully shift long-term career trajectories.

### 5.1 Implication for Policy

AI policy frameworks for education, including the *Australian Framework for Generative AI in Schools*, UNESCO's *Guidance for Generative AI in Education and Research*, and UNICEF's *Policy Guidance on AI for Children* emphasise the importance of ethical, inclusive, and curriculum-aligned AI literacy education. We find that while one-off workshop interventions can make significant headway in improving student perceptions and literacy, influencing career aspirations likely requires a more integrated, sustained approach. For policy-makers, this differentiation is important as it underscores that whilst these types of workshops are effective entry points, they must be supported by systemic curriculum integrations to drive workforce readiness. Education policy must be grounded in evidence that captures both immediate literacy gains, and long-term outcomes. As AI continues to reshape the global economy and workforce, policy must prioritise equitable access to ensure that the "intelligence gap" does not widen for students in disadvantaged or under-represented cohorts.

### 5.2 Limitations and Future Work

Due to the challenging nature of research of Australian government secondary schools, this study prioritised accessibility and low-friction participation, which influenced the research design and identified several avenues for future work. This most significancy manifested in the 35 student drop-off between pre- and post- responses from one school (N=136) which could introduce attrition bias in some findings of this study, future work should implement measures to mitigate drop-off.

Two of the three schools were all-girls institutions. While efforts were made to include diverse cohorts, some findings may not be generalisable. Future research should explicitly investigate balanced gender-based responsiveness to AI learning materials to determine if specific pedagogical approaches are more effective for different cohorts.

As student anonymity during paper-based data collection was required, pre- and post-intervention surveys could not be paired at the individual level. This necessitated cross-sectional analysis using Mann-Whitney U Test, rather than a longitudinal, paired-samples approach. Future studies could utilise paired methods to provide more granular understanding of impact on individuals.

Due to school-specific scheduling, there was a variation in the specific lessons each cohort completed (Subsect. 3.1), certain lessons may have contributed more significantly to the observed outcomes and possibly baseline differences between schools. Controlled experiments will provide clearer signals for future interventions.

Findings were based on self-reported measures of AI knowledge and confidence rather than objective performance data. Specifically, reported deepfake creation (7.3%) and sharing (18.5%) should be interpreted with caution as these figures may be influenced by acquiescence bias. Although several AI literacy constructs are currently in development, a gold standard quantitative tool has yet to emerge [3]. Future research could incorporate these frameworks to quantify gains in AI literacy beyond student perception. Further, given the number of outcomes tested in Tables 3 and 4, results with marginal statistical significance should be interpreted with caution, as they may be susceptible to Type I error in the absence of formal correction for multiple comparisons.

Finally, this study provides a snapshot of immediate impact, no claims can be made regarding the sustained impact or durability of these interventions on long-term knowledge retention, attitudes, skills, or career trajectories. Longitudinal research will better inform school-, state-, and national-level education policy both within Australia and internationally.

This study featured a high proportion of Indigenous participants at 17.1%, unevenly distributed across the three schools. The study did not isolate their specific perceptions or responsiveness to lessons. Opportunities exists for future work to prioritise Indigenous viewpoints to develop culturally responsive AI frameworks that promote equity and inclusion within the Australian educational landscape.

## 6 Conclusion

This study evaluated the efficacy of the Day of AI Australia's workshop interventions in fostering AI literacy and STEM career aspirations among Australian secondary students. Our findings demonstrate that targeted, short-duration workshops can facilitate statistically significant increases in self-reported AI knowledge ($p < .001, r = .445$) and self-efficacy. Notably, the interventions successfully equipped students to better identify AI within their daily lives. This shift is vital for developing a citizenry capable of navigating AI safely, ethically, and critically.

While the interventions resulted in increased interest toward AI, Computer Science, and Engineering careers ($p < .05$), the relatively small effect sizes suggest that singular interventions may serve more as a catalyst for interest, rather than a definitive driver of long-term career trajectories. This highlights the necessity for AI literacy to be integrated more deeply and systemically into Australian state curricula and the National Curriculum. Future research should focus on longitudinal studies to determine the persistence of literacy gains and whether sustained exposure leads to more robust shifts in long-term STEM participation. Ultimately, as AI reshapes the global labour market, providing equitable access to foundational AI education remains a primary lever for preventing a widening digital and intelligence gap within Australia and internationally.

**Acknowledgments.** Day of AI Australia and its research activities are funded by philanthropic donations and corporate partnerships.

**Disclosure of Interests.** Institution 2 is a registered Australian charity. Institution 1 and 2 have a legal collaboration. Institution 2 has previously received funding from Google.org and Microsoft, contributions have not funded this research.

## References

1. Ahmed, F.: The digital divide and AI in education: addressing equity and accessibility. AI EDIFY J. **1**(2), 12–23 (2024). https://researchcorridor.org/index.php/aiej/article/view/259
2. Alali, R., Wardat, Y.: Opportunities and Challenges of Integrating Generative Artificial Intelligence in Education. Int. J. Relig. **5**(7), 784–793 (2024). https://doi.org/10.61707/8y29gv34
3. Almatrafi, O., Johri, A., Lee, H.: A systematic review of AI literacy conceptualization, constructs, and implementation and assessment efforts (2019–2023). Comput. Edu. Open **6** (2024). https://doi.org/10.1016/J.CAEO.2024.100173
4. Blundell, C.N., Mukherjee, M., Nykvist, S.: Adopting generative AI in K-12 teaching and learning: Australian teachers' actions through the lens of innovation theory. Edu. Inf. Technol. **30**(16), 24009–24028 (2025). https://doi.org/10.1007/S10639-025-13699-Y
5. Bower, M., Henderson, M., Slade, C., Southgate, E., Gulson, K., Lodge, J.: What generative Artificial Intelligence priorities and challenges do senior Australian educational policy makers identify (and why)? Aust. Edu. Res. **52**(3), 2069–2094 (2025). https://doi.org/10.1007/S13384-025-00801-Z
6. Božić, V.: Artifical intelligence as the reason and the solution of digital divide. Lang. Edu. Technol. **3**(2), 96–109 (2023). https://langedutech.com/letjournal/index.php/let/article/view/53
7. Braun, V., Clarke, V.: Thematic analysis. APA handbook of research methods in psychology, Vol 2: Research designs: Quantitative, qualitative, neuropsychological, and biological, pp. 57–71 (2012). https://doi.org/10.1037/13620-004
8. Carrisi, M.C., Marras, M., Vergallo, S.: A Structured Unplugged Approach for Foundational AI Literacy in Primary Education. arXiv preprint (2025). https://arxiv.org/pdf/2505.21398

9. Cervi, L.: Tik Tok and generation Z. Theatre, Dance Perf. Train. **12**(2), 198–204 (2021). https://doi.org/10.1080/19443927.2021.1915617
10. Clare Armstrong: More than 4.7m social media accounts closed in two days after ban began, data reveals (2026). https://www.abc.net.au/news/2026-01-15/social-media-ban-data-millions-of-accounts-closed/106232768
11. Creely, E., Carabott, K., Carabott, K., Creely, E., Carabott, K.: Teaching and learning with AI: an integrated AI-oriented pedagogical model. Aust. Edu. Res. **52**(6), 4633–4654 (2025). https://doi.org/10.1007/S13384-025-00913-6
12. Elkhodr, M., et al.: A systematic review and multifaceted analysis of the integration of artificial intelligence and blockchain: shaping the future of australian higher education. Fut. Internet **16**(10) (2024). https://doi.org/10.3390/FI16100378
13. Gajos, K.Z., Mamykina, L.: Do people engage cognitively with AI? Impact of AI assistance on incidental learning. In: International Conference on Intelligent User Interfaces, Proceedings IUI, Vol. 22, pp. 794–806 (2022). https://doi.org/10.1145/3490099.3511138
14. Gattupalli, S., Maloy, R.W., Edwards, S.: Prompt literacy: A pivotal educational skill in the age of ai. Tech. rep., University of Massachusetts Amherst (2023). https://doi.org/10.7275/3498-WX48, https://hdl.handle.net/20.500.14394/22905
15. Hudec, M., et al.: Student perception of using artificial intelligence in education. In: 2025 Eleventh International Conference on eDemocracy & eGovernment, pp. 272–277. Institute of Electrical and Electronics Engineers (2025). https://doi.org/10.1109/icedeg65568.2025.11081680
16. Idroes, G.M., et al.: Student perspectives on the role of artificial intelligence in education: a survey-based analysis. J. Edu. Manag. Learn. **1**(1), 8–15 (2023). https://doi.org/10.60084/JEML.V1I1.58
17. Jiang, S., McClure, J., Tatar, C., Bickel, F., Rosé, C.P., Chao, J.: Towards inclusivity in ai: a comparative study of cognitive engagement between marginalized female students and peers. Br. J. Edu. Technol. (2024). https://doi.org/10.1111/bjet.13467
18. Kim, J., Cho, Y.H.: My teammate is AI: understanding students' perceptions of student-AI collaboration in drawing tasks. Asia Pac. J. Edu. **45**(3), 1013–1027 (2025). https://doi.org/10.1080/02188791.2023.2286206
19. Kosmas, P., Nisiforou, E.A., Kounnapi, E., Sophocleous, S., Theophanous, G.: Integrating artificial intelligence in literacy lessons for elementary classrooms: a co-design approach. Edu. Technol. Res. Dev. **73**(4), 2589–2615 (2025). https://doi.org/10.1007/S11423-025-10492-Z
20. Kucuk, S., Sisman, B.: Students' attitudes towards robotics and stem: Differences based on gender and robotics experience. Int. J. Child-Comput. Inter. **23-24**, 100167 (2020). https://doi.org/10.1016/J.IJCCI.2020.100167
21. Li, H., Xiao, R., Nieu, H., Tseng, Y.J., Liao, G.: "From unseen needs to classroom solutions": exploring AI literacy challenges & opportunities with project-based learning toolkit in K-12 education. In: Proceedings of the AAAI Conference on Artificial Intelligence, Vol. 39, no. 28, pp. 29145–29152 (2024). https://doi.org/10.1609/aaai.v39i28.35187
22. Lin, H., Chen, Q.: Artificial intelligence (AI)-integrated educational applications and college students' creativity and academic emotions: students and teachers' perceptions and attitudes. BMC Psychol. **12**(1), 487 (2024). https://doi.org/10.1186/S40359-024-01979-0
23. Marx, E., Leonhardt, T., Bergner, N.: Secondary school students' mental models and attitudes regarding artificial intelligence - a scoping review. Comput. Edu. Artif. Intell. **5**, 100169 (2023). https://doi.org/10.1016/J.CAEAI.2023.100169

24. Faverio, M., Sidoti, O.: Teens Social Media and Technology. Tech. rep., Pew Research Center (2024). https://www.pewresearch.org/internet/2024/12/12/teens-social-media-and-technology-2024/
25. Mitre, X., Zeneli, M.: Using AI to improve accessibility and inclusivity in higher education for students with disabilities. In: International Conference on Information Technology Based Higher Education and Training (2024). https://doi.org/10.1109/ITHET61869.2024.10837607
26. Pedro, F., Subosa, M., Rivas, A., Valverde, P.: Artificial intelligence in education : challenges and opportunities for sustainable development. Ministerio de Dducacion (2019). https://repositorio.minedu.gob.pe/handle/20.500.12799/6533
27. Qin, C., Zhang, M., Li, Z., Chen, L.: Shaping the future: How robot programming education changes the attitudes of robotics among rural primary school students in a developing country. Educ. Inf. Technol. (2024). https://doi.org/10.1007/s10639-024-13077-0
28. Ratner, S., Williams, R., Wonnacott, E.: Exploring AI in education through interdisciplinary collaboration. INTED2025 Proc. **1**, 5650–5655 (2025). https://doi.org/10.21125/INTED.2025.1443
29. Renzella, J., Banks, N., Vassar, A.: Building Global AI Literacy: Preparing Teachers for the Future of AI-Driven Classrooms. In: SIGCSE TS 2025 - Proceedings of the 56th ACM Technical Symposium on Computer Science Education, pp. 1727–1727 (2025). https://doi.org/10.1145/3641555.3705101
30. Scantamburlo, T., et al.: Artificial intelligence across europe: A study on awareness, attitude and trust. IEEE Trans. Artif. Intell. (2024). https://doi.org/10.1109/TAI.2024.3461633
31. Schiff, D.: Education for AI, not AI for education: the role of education and ethics in national AI policy strategies. Int. J. Artif. Intell. Edu. **32**(3), 527–563 (2021). https://doi.org/10.1007/S40593-021-00270-2
32. Smolansky, A., Cram, A., Raduescu, C., Zeivots, S., Huber, E., Kizilcec, R.F.: Educator and student perspectives on the impact of generative AI on assessments in higher education. In: L@S 2023 - Proceedings of the 10th ACM Conference on Learning @ Scale, pp. 378–382 (2023). https://doi.org/10.1145/3573051.3596191
33. Uema, M.A., Souza, T.d.P.C.d., Dermeval, D., Bittencourt, I.I., Isotani, S.: Designing for Meaningful Access: Towards a Framework for AI in Education Unplugged. Lecture Notes in Computer Science, Vol. 15880, pp. 307–320 (2025). https://doi.org/10.1007/978-3-031-98459-4
34. Xiao, R., et al.: Learning to Use AI for Learning: Teaching Responsible Use of AI Chatbot to K-12 Students Through an AI Literacy Module. PREPRINT (2025). https://arxiv.org/pdf/2508.13962
35. Yim, I.H.Y.: Artificial intelligence literacy in primary education: An arts-based approach to overcoming age and gender barriers. Comput. Edu. Artif. Intell. **7**, 100321 (2024). https://doi.org/10.1016/J.CAEAI.2024.100321

# Implementing a Statewide AI Curriculum: One Brazilian Experience

Cristiano Galafassi[1(✉)], Rosa Maria Vicari[2], Christian Brackmann[3], and Lucas Eishi Pimentel Mizusaki[4]

[1] Federal University of Pampa, Rio Grande do Sul, Brazil
cristianogalafassi@unipampa.edu.br
[2] Federal University of Rio Grande do Sul, Rio Grande do Sul, Brazil
rosa@inf.ufrgs.br
[3] Federal Institute of Education, Science and Technology Farroupilha, Rio Grande do Sul, Brazil
[4] Federal Institute of Education, Science and Technology of Rio Grande do Sul, Rio Grande do Sul, Brazil

**Abstract.** Since 2024, the Brazilian state of Piauí has incorporated a weekly Artificial Intelligence (AI) subject into the curriculum of public full-time high schools, where it is mandatory, with phased expansion by grade level through 2026. To support this statewide implementation, we developed an AI literacy curriculum aligned with Brazilian education standards. We adapted AI competency references to local constraints and emphasized both learning about AI and learning with AI through plugged and unplugged activitiesrationalized the curriculum through Open teacher-support resources, including a textbook for Basic Education (45 instructional sequences across 24 themes, 300+ pages) and 17 h of video lessons, all released under Creative Commons licensing. In parallel, we delivered an online distance-training program with synchronous sessions (recorded for asynchronous access), tutoring, and sustained teacher support throughout the school year. We present evidence from the first two years of the implementation, combining pre- and post-assessments and module-level evaluations, alongside participation and completion metrics. A total of over 650 unique teachers have been certified through the training across the first two years. The initiative currently reaches approximately 120,000 students across 494 full-time schools offering AI. We discuss design choices for resource-constrained settings and propose practical recommendations for scaling AI education across public-school systems.

**Keywords:** Artificial Intelligence Curriculum · AI Literacy · Basic Education

## 1 Introduction

Artificial Intelligence is increasingly embedded in everyday life, yet understanding remains limited regarding how AI systems work, what they can and cannot


E. G. Blanchard et al. (eds.), AIED 2026, LNCS 16586, pp. 103–116, 2027.
https://doi.org/10.1007/978-3-032-29773-0_8

do, and how they impact society. As AI becomes a vital tool for civic life and work, schools must cultivate AI literacy that is relevant both to academic learning and to students' daily lives, integrating it into the formal curriculum through feasible plugged and unplugged approaches. Because AI-mentioned services shape students' lives regardless of school infrastructure, combining unplugged and plugged activities can help connect concepts to real-world uses of AI.

Since 2024, the Brazilian state of Piauí has incorporated a weekly AI subject into the curriculum of public full-time high schools, making it mandatory and expanding grade-by-grade through 2026. This paper reports how this statewide implementation has been supported through the development of an AI literacy curriculum framework and Creative Commons–licensed Open Educational Resources (OER), alongside sustained teacher support. The teacher training followed a cascade model, equipping teachers to implement AI literacy activities with their high-school students within the weekly AI subject, which is mandatory in public full-time high schools; accordingly, the evidence reported here focuses on teacher learning and classroom practice. Student outcomes are not assessed directly; instead, we report teacher learning gains and evidence of classroom implementation.

We present the AI literacy curriculum framework we developed to support this statewide implementation. The framework aligns with Brazilian education standards and UNESCO's 2024 competency guidance, with adaptations to the Brazilian context, including planet-centered considerations and workforce-related competencies for students [1]. In particular, we shift the emphasis from human-centered AI to planet-centered AI, highlighting the natural resources required to sustain AI systems (e.g., water, electricity, and critical minerals). Brazil is home to several large data centers, which makes these considerations especially salient in our context [2]. Building on our previously delineated curriculum [3], we operationalized the framework through OER (instructional sequences, teacher guides, video lessons, and lesson plans) released under Creative Commons licensing [4], and through an online professional development program combining synchronous meetings (recorded for asynchronous access), tutoring, and sustained teacher support throughout the school year.

Our approach conceptualizes AI literacy through AI Thinking, inspired by Computational Thinking [5,6], which integrates "thinking with AI" (effective use for problem-solving and creation) and "thinking about AI" (understanding the foundations, limitations, and ethical and societal implications). Given connectivity and infrastructure constraints, the framework prioritizes unplugged strategies, drawing on Unplugged Computational Thinking [7].

This work is motivated by equity concerns: digital divides in access to technology [8] may evolve into an AI divide shaped by access to services and the ability to use them critically [9]. Finally, we present learning evidence and participation indicators from the first two years of implementation, combining pre- and post-assessments in year 1 with module-based evaluations in year 2. We also discuss design decisions, constraints, and recommendations for scaling AI education within public-school systems. This paper makes four contributions. First, we propose an AI literacy curriculum aligned with Brazilian education standards and grounded in an AI Thinking perspective. The curriculum balances learning about AI and learning with AI through plugged and unplugged activities under infrastructure and connectivity constraints. Second, the curriculum was operationalized as an open teacher-support package, combining a textbook and video lessons, released under Creative Commons licensing to enable reuse and adaptation at scale. Third, the initiative was designed and delivered as a statewide online teacher training program with synchronous sessions (recorded for asynchronous access), tutoring, and sustained pedagogical support throughout the school year. Fourth, evidence from the first two years of implementation is reported, combining pre- and post-assessments, module-level evaluations, and participation/completion metrics.

The remainder of the paper is organized as follows: we first present the theoretical and design foundations that guided the curriculum; we then describe the curriculum and its open educational resources, followed by the teacher training program that supported statewide adoption; next, we detail the evaluation design and report results from the first two years of implementation; finally, we discuss implications for large-scale AI literacy initiatives and outline directions for future work.

## 2 Theoretical Framework and Design

This section summarizes the theoretical basis and design principles that informed the statewide implementation, connecting prior work on AI literacy and K-12 curricula to the constraints and opportunities of public education systems.

**AI Literacy in K–12.** It is understood that the level of literacy in AI expected from students varies substantially across educational stages. In early childhood and elementary education, students are typically introduced to foundational AI concepts and simple mechanisms through age-appropriate activities [10], while high school students are expected to have a deeper understanding of AI, being able to use AI tools to solve school-related tasks, and critically evaluate predictions, recommendations, and decisions produced by AI systems [11]. Correspondingly, several K–12 proposals design AI curricula for adolescents grounded in Computational Thinking and connected to everyday AI applications [4]. [12] propose a discovery and inquiry-based learning approach incorporating storytelling activities for early childhood education. They argue that fundamental AI concepts can be taught to kindergarten students. AI literacy without using machines can also be used in preschool education, as it reduces screen exposure in early childhood (under 5), for which the World Health Organization recommends limiting sedentary screen time [13]. AI-powered applications can support inclusion in education by enabling personalization and accessibility. Examples include adaptive learning platforms that tailor content to students' pace and preferences [14], speech recognition and text-to-speech tools that assist learners with disabilities [15] and interactive environments such as augmented reality that provide additional supports [16]. Adaptive assessment and feedback systems, including Intelligent Tutor Systems, can also adjust task difficulty and provide real-time feedback [17,18]. While these applications are relevant to educational practice, this paper focuses on AI literacy, that is, the competencies required to understand, use, and critically engage with AI systems and their impacts.

**AI in Schooling: Opportunities and Risks.** A recent study [19] about AI and programming skills indicates these tools will enable users to solve complex problems beyond their skill level in areas such as software development. However, the authors highlighted that this improved performance does not translate into improved skill acquisition and can leave users with an illusion of competence. We can infer that, as AI becomes increasingly integrated with education, it risks turning into an obstacle to learning. Not only as a mere "shortcuts for answers", providing answers, it can also be poorly suited to specific contexts or contents. Depending on its training, it may generate incorrect content (hallucinations) and also present underlying biases and promote discrimination and racism [20]. There is a need to create and spread good AI practices for teaching and studying, guaranteeing its use as a supporting technology.

**AI Literacy Definition and Design Implications.** This UNESCO Chair (UNESCO Chair ID omitted for anonymization) employs the term "AI literacy", a concept still in development as seen in [21–24] to describe the emerging set of skills necessary to live in an AI-mediated world. These new competencies may complement or replace existing ones as interacting with AI becomes essential for work and full participation in civic and private life. They also raise critical ethical issues regarding the responsible use of AI.

From our implementation experience, we derive three design implications about teaching AI in schools. The first one is that a general AI curriculum can tackle innovations brought forward by technological development. One example is that, even though it was written before the large adoption of generative AIs, the curriculum was considered relevant and was the basis for classes on prompt engineering and ethics, and fake news. The second one was that, although there is a lack of teachers with computer sciences degrees (only 70 participated), AI can be taught at the basic education level and, as it is an interdisciplinary field, it thrives in an interdisciplinary teaching system, being either a subject of discussion (thinking about AI), or a tool for learning (thinking with AI). While the classes on AI were given in a specific discipline, teachers came from many backgrounds and used their original fields to plan and create their lessons. The third finding is that there is a need to think about unplugged AI, and promote activities without the need to use computers. This is not only necessary because there are still several schools that do not have access to digital hardware, but also because these activities are very powerful interdisciplinary tools and easily applied to the disciplines. One such activity, the decision tree [24], involves the students creating a decision tree about a subject they are studying. As one of the teachers said, "It was considered a success, since the students had the opportunity to apply the logic of the artificial intelligence in a practical and interactive activity".

# 3 Curriculum Framework

This section describes the curriculum framework adopted in the statewide implementation and how it was operationalized through open teacher-support resources.

## 3.1 Curriculum Framework

In this context, our group developed a curriculum aligned with the National Education Standards [25] to support AI literacy in basic education, building on the experiences with the curriculum for high school students. This initiative includes teacher guidance and age-appropriate educational materials, as well as recommendations for the critical, inclusive, ethical, and responsible use of AI in classrooms.

The curriculum is organized around five aspects of AI, derived from the four aspects of the UNESCO proposal [1], and categorizes the set of abilities addressed across the instructional sequences. We understand ethics as a transversal requirement across these aspects rather than as an isolated component. We also include both a planet-centered perspective, going beyond human-centered framings to examine societal and environmental impacts, and a personal and professional improvement dimension, given the effects of AI on the world of work and civic participation. The aspects are:

- **Planet Centered AI:** Recognize Artificial Intelligence systems in different contexts, understanding their characteristics, capabilities, and impacts on society, while differentiating them from human intelligence; Manage your data with responsibility, protecting your privacy; Understand that AI requires natural resources to function and that these resources must be used ethically; Understand that AI is steered by humans and that its creation and use depend on human action and leadership, considering legal aspects and impacts on the planet; Relate human responsibility and skills with the intentional and ethical use of AI.
- **AI Foundations:** Describe real problems and their solutions in natural language and math; Describe computable solutions or algorithms; Recognize problems and use simple techniques to organize information to solve them through classical algorithms; Create solutions by drawing paths (graphs) showing possible options; Use organizational techniques and symbolic reasoning to implement solutions; Understand the theoretical limits of Computers and Artificial Intelligence; Understand the relationship between AI and Statistics.

- **Use and Design of AI Systems:** Understand that AI needs data (from different sources) to function; Use multimodal AI systems in a critical and reflexive way; Relate data privacy to ethics in AI; Experiment with AI solutions for inclusion; Evaluate data and its quality, applying preprocessing methods; Identify computer requirements, physical or virtual; Analyze and evaluate answers generated by AI systems, investigating the process and exploring alternatives for improvement; Apply the AI lifecycle, creating a solution that guarantees ethical principles from conception to implementation, ensuring transparency, equity, and accountability at all stages; Recognize the ethical and legal implications of using AI computer systems in society.
- **Techniques and application:** Use simple algorithms to classify and group objects; Relate machine learning to AI; Understand the limits and ethical concerns when using AI solutions; Understand what Deep learning is and how AI solves complex problems; Describe and experiment with an AI that learns from examples; Describe and experiment with an AI that learns by itself; Describe and experiment with an AI that uses reinforcement learning; Compare different types of machine learning in everyday situations; Train an AI for specific objectives, respecting ethical and privacy concerns.
- **Personal and professional improvement:** Understand AI's impact on social relations; Understand the relationship between AI and labour; Prepare and present AI problems and solutions clearly, adapting it to different audiences; Propose solutions using mixed teams cooperation (humans and AIs); Evaluate and criticize the result of a task solved by mixed teams; Use data responsibly, ensuring privacy and demonstrating personal and social commitment in AI-driven societies.

The aspects and abilities are connected with five technical dimensions (Human-AI interaction, Perception, Representation and Reasoning, Machine Learning, and Social impact). For example, the ability "Use forms of organization and symbolic thinking to implement solutions" is mapped to Perception and to Representation and Reasoning. This matrix was created based on Bloom's Taxonomy, as reviewed by Ferraz and Beilhot (2010), to support progression and to inform the design of learning activities and assessments.

To translate these abilities into broader educational goals, we define five competencies adapted from [26], presented in Table 1. Through this organization, we have three complementary ways to think about the curriculum: the aspects provide thematic organization, the dimensions support technical grounding, and the competencies clarify overarching learning goals to guide lesson planning.

Through this organization, we have three complementary ways to interpret and design learning activities: the aspects provide thematic organization, the dimensions provide technical grounding, and the competencies provide broader educational goals to guide lesson planning and assessment.

In this context, the challenge for educators remains the same: to prepare individuals who are equipped to face the present moment. This moment is marked by changes in how we interact socially, in learning environments, in work groups, and in legal frameworks, as well as changes in the skills required professionally.

**Table 1.** List of competencies

| Code | Competency |
|---|---|
| C1 | Understand the principles of planet-centered AI, identifying risks, ethical implications, and its applications to society, analyzing challenges and impacts on social coexistence and human rights. |
| C2 | Demonstrate knowledge of the fundamentals of AI, including basic concepts and operational principles, using critical thinking to analyze its limitations, possibilities, and social and ethical impacts. |
| C3 | Evaluate AI systems with ethical solutions for real-world problems and create innovative applications, considering ethical aspects and exploring the potential of AI in different contexts. |
| C4 | Understand and apply concepts of AI and analyze their possibilities, limitations, ethical impacts, and applications in various contexts. |
| C5 | Relate Artificial Intelligence to the world of work, investigating how it transforms professions and contributes to the development of new skills. |

Technology enters people's daily lives almost invisibly, and must be made visible. Human history shows that, over time, some competencies become obsolete while others become essential. Education must address these shifts consciously, focusing on practices that enhance human capabilities. Education is about that too: competencies and skills, and what matters is that technology should be taught consciously, focusing on practices that serve humans, in other words, technology that enhances human capabilities.

### 3.2 Open Teacher-Support Resources

We operationalized the curriculum through open teacher-support resources released under a Creative Commons license, including a textbook for Basic Education (45 instructional sequences across 24 themes, 300+ pages) and 17 h of video lessons. The materials were designed to support plugged and unplugged activities and to help teachers from diverse disciplinary backgrounds adapt AI literacy lessons to local constraints. To support teachers in translating curriculum goals into classroom practice, we provided a lesson-plan template aligned with Brazilian national curriculum standards. Teachers were encouraged to adapt and author lesson plans tailored to the specific context of their schools. The template records the maturity level of the school and the teacher, the required resources, linked subjects (reflecting the cross-disciplinary nature of AI teaching), and important guiding questions to structure classroom discussion (e.g., "How does AI capture data?" and "How are or can these data be used?"). It also specifies lesson objectives and maps the targeted skills to the brazilian computing curriculum standards, supporting traceability between curricular goals and classroom activities.

## 4 Teacher Training Design

In 2024 and 2025, we developed a teacher professional development project in Piauí, Brazil, accompanying the phased rollout of the mandatory AI subject in public full-time high schools. The teacher training followed a blended approach, incorporating both plugged and unplugged AI methods. To achieve this, freely available AI technologies were utilized by different tech companies, focusing on everyday AI tools, such as those found on mobile phones, apps, and prioritizing cloud-based platforms. The goal of the training was to empower teachers to create their AI literacy content independently, regardless of the local context or the technology available at the time.

Piauí is a socioeconomically and geographically diverse state, and the public-school systems involved in the AI rollout operate under heterogeneous local conditions. Across municipalities, schools vary in connectivity quality, digital infrastructure, and access to devices, with more constrained conditions in many inland contexts. In addition, the teachers responsible for the subject come from different disciplinary backgrounds, which creates varying levels of familiarity with digital technologies and AI-related content. For this reason, both the curriculum and the teacher training model were designed to remain feasible across different school realities, combining unplugged and low-barrier plugged activities, mobile-friendly tools, recorded sessions, and ongoing tutoring support.

To design the training strategy, we use the proposal of [27] to invest time in providing individualized, one-to-one feedback with a holistic approach, engage with learners in asynchronous discussion forums, curate relevant supportive content resources, and deliver instructional content in efficient and versatile formats.

AI literacy followed the rollout progression: in the first year, the focus was on “understanding AI” (activities aimed to break the ice in the use of AI technologies); in the second year, the focus was on “applying AI” (training centered on technical aspects and classroom applications); and in the third year (2026, planned), the focus shifts to “creating with AI” (developing projects that involve the entire AI lifecycle).

The course lasted for three months each year and included weekly synchronous meetings. All sessions were recorded, allowing teachers to watch the synchronous lessons at their convenience, according to their schedules. Participants were divided into classes of no more than 30 teachers. Using an active learning methodology while cataloging several AI tools and activities, we also focused on a hands-on approach using practical class examples. Each class was supported by a tutor who answered questions in real time. After completing the training, teachers continued to receive ongoing support through tutoring sessions and monthly synchronous meetings to address questions and explore new AI topics and applications.

A local platform called “Mais Formação,” from a company based in Piauí, was used to deliver the training. The goal was to preserve data by ensuring it was stored in Brazil. Regarding the profile of teachers trained in the distance learning modality, their degrees covered a variety of high school disciplines (355 teachers), with 70 from computer science fields and 19 from areas not directly related to high school subjects.

## 5 Evaluation and Evidence from the First Two Years

We evaluated the first two years of implementation using a mixed evidence approach combining (i) a pre-test and post-test applied to teachers in year 1, (ii) module-level evaluations in year 2, and (iii) descriptive evidence of classroom enactment collected from school-shared artifacts and records (e.g., school social media). The analyses reported here focus on teachers who completed the teacher training and the associated assessments (N).

### 5.1 Teacher Learning Gains

Teachers completed a pre-test before starting the year-1 teacher training and a post-test after its completion. Both instruments were validated bu a group of 22 teachers who did not belong to the training sample. The analyses reported here focus on the 447 teachers who participated in the year-1 training cohort. As this was a large-scale implementation study, no control group was used. Results for the five assessed axes are presented in Table 2.

**Table 2.** Teachers' performance on AI main concepts before and after training

| | Computational Thinking | Pattern Recognition | Symbolic Reasoning | Statistical Reasoning | Machine Learning |
|---|---|---|---|---|---|
| Pre-test | 65.6% | 58.6% | 49.6% | 52.3% | 54.6% |
| Post-test | 89.7% | 77.7% | 76.0% | 71.0% | 76.3% |

Analyzing pre- and post-test scores with paired Student's t-tests for each axis, the observed differences are statistically significant at the 99% confidence level. Overall, the teacher training was associated with improved post-test performance across all assessed axes.

### 5.2 Module-Level Checks

In year 2, we complemented the pre/post evidence with module-level mastery checks embedded in the teacher training. The training was organized into seven modules, each concluding with a short multiple-choice assessment composed of ten items targeting the module's core concepts and classroom application points. To progress to the next module, teachers were required to achieve a minimum score of 7 out of 10. All questions related to AI literacy were assigned equal weight. Teachers who did not reach the threshold could retake the assessment until meeting the mastery criterion.

A total of 414 teachers participated in year 2. In Table 3, Teachers completing module (N) refers to the number of teachers who completed each module by reaching the $\leq 7/10$ criterion (i.e., obtained the passing score at least once). For each module, Passed on 1st attempt (%) is computed among module completers as the proportion of teachers who reached the passing score on their first attempt. Mean attempts reports the average number of attempts required by module completers to reach the passing score for the first time.

These module-level indicators provide complementary evidence about learning progression and feasibility under a mastery-oriented training design, beyond the end-of-course gains reported in Table 3.

**Table 3.** Module-level mastery check outcomes in year 2 (criterion: $\geq 7/10$)

| Module | Teachers assessed (N) | Passed on 1st attempt (%) | Median attempts |
|---|---|---|---|
| Module 1 | 414 | 79.71% | 1.40 |
| Module 2 | 396 | 71.21% | 1.41 |
| Module 3 | 383 | 68.66% | 1.35 |
| Module 4 | 374 | 85.29% | 1.09 |
| Module 5 | 372 | 77.69% | 1.23 |
| Module 6 | 369 | 84.28% | 1.05 |
| Module 7 | 359 | 86.62% | 1.02 |

Overall, the results indicate that the mastery threshold was attainable for most teachers, with first-attempt pass rates ranging from 68.66% (Module 3) to 86.62% (Module 7) and a low average number of attempts (approximately 1.02–1.41). Modules 2 and 3 show comparatively lower first-attempt pass rates and higher average attempts, suggesting that these modules may have posed greater conceptual or instructional demands and could benefit from additional scaffolding (e.g., worked examples, extra practice items, or clearer guidance tied to classroom applications). The gradual decrease in N across modules (from 414 in Module 1 to 359 in Module 7) also suggests cumulative workload effects over time, reinforcing the importance of pacing and support mechanisms in large-scale online training.

### 5.3 Classroom Enactment Evidence

Beyond test-based learning evidence, classroom enactment provides insight into how teachers translated training content into practice under real school constraints. Figure 1 illustrates complementary ways teachers introduced algorithmic reasoning and AI concepts by combining unplugged and low-barrier digital activities. On the right, students co-constructed and presented a large decision tree as an unplugged activity, making classification criteria explicit and discussable. On the left, teachers leveraged shared devices and whole-class projection to conduct plugged activities, including guided experimentation with Teachable Machine and small-group exploration of everyday AI applications on mobile devices. Together, these examples show how teachers adapted the curriculum to limited infrastructure while sustaining engagement and preserving core conceptual goals.

**Fig. 1.** Classroom enactment examples combining unplugged and plugged AI literacy activities under constrained infrastructure.

Figure 1 presents three complementary classroom enactments. In the top-left panel, students work in small groups using a shared mobile device to explore an everyday AI application, supporting discussion about how AI systems produce outputs from inputs in familiar contexts. In the bottom-left panel, the class uses Teachable Machine with a projected interface to collectively experiment with training and testing a simple classifier, enabling whole-group reflection on data, labels, and model behavior. In the right panel, students construct and present a decision tree as an unplugged activity, making classification criteria explicit and open to critique.

These enactments were not isolated classroom examples, but reflected the progression of the teacher training itself, which was carried out in parallel with school implementation. Early activities emphasized foundational AI concepts through low-cost and context-adapted tasks, such as identifying inputs and outputs in everyday AI applications, collectively training simple classifiers with shared devices and projected interfaces, and constructing decision trees as unplugged representations of classification logic. As the course advanced, teachers gradually incorporated activities involving data capture and introductory machine-learning ideas, adapting them to local school conditions. This parallel structure also allowed teachers to rely on ongoing tutor support and follow-up synchronous meetings as they translated course content into classroom practice.

### 5.4 Synthesis and Implications

Across two years of implementation, the teacher training supported measurable gains in core AI-related concepts (Table 2) and also led to diverse forms of classroom enactment documented in school contexts. Together, these results suggest that a curriculum grounded in AI literacy, supported by a structured teacher-support package and by plugged and unplugged strategies, can be enacted in practice by teachers from different disciplinary backgrounds.

Importantly, the classroom examples reinforce that enactment is not limited to tool use: teachers and students engaged with algorithmic ideas (e.g., decision trees) and with ethical questions central to AI literacy (e.g., misinformation), using formats that remain feasible under varying levels of infrastructure. These findings inform the discussion of design choices and recommendations for scaling AI education within public-school systems.

## 6 Conclusion and Future Work

Education is vital for society, as it supports personal development, social inclusion, and active citizenship, as well as innovation, creativity, and economic activities. In this context, ethics becomes indispensable for both the development and the use of AI. We need to understand what AI can offer and what it requires from us, particularly in terms of data, privacy, and power, so that we can decide which AI we want.

This project engaged teachers from various academic fields, fostering a cross-disciplinary approach to ensure that AI education is meaningful across diverse high school subjects. Initially, many teachers were hesitant to embrace technology. However, initial hesitation appeared to decrease as teachers engaged with unplugged activities and practical classroom applications. Rather than focusing only on using AI tools, the training emphasized understanding how AI works and its underlying mechanisms, aiming to support responsible and context-sensitive classroom practices.

In an era increasingly shaped by AI, expanding opportunities for teachers and students to engage critically, ethically, and creatively with these technologies is becoming an important educational priority. The curriculum framework presented here, grounded in AI Thinking and aligned with international references while responding to Brazilian constraints, represents an effort to broaden access to AI literacy through a structured and scalable approach.

As future work, building on the high school implementation and the evidence reported in this paper, our next steps are to further refine the curricular matrix, expand the set of activities and lesson suggestions associated with each ability, with special attention to unplugged AI as a recurring demand in teacher training.

We also plan to extend the approach to additional remote regions, strengthening support materials and implementation guidance to enable adaptation across contexts. Finally, a new training cycle is planned to support the next phase of rollout, emphasizing project-based activities that move toward "creating with AI" and, when feasible, projects that address broader AI lifecycle phases.

## References


1. UNESCO. AI Competency Framework for Students. UNESCO, Paris (2024)
2. Viana, M.E.F., da Costa Roma Scheidegger, O.F.: Infraestrutura computacional para a era da IA: desafios, políticas e oportunidades em data centers no brasil. BNDES Setorial **31**(60), 167–205 (2025)
3. Vicari, R.M., Brackmann, C., Mizusaki, L., Lopes, D., Barone, D., Castro, H.: Referencial curricular: Inteligência artificial no ensino médio (2022). Curriculum framework document
4. Vicari, R.M., Brackmann, C., Galafassi, C., Mizusaki, L.: IA@Escola. Lesson plans website (2024)
5. Papert, S.: Mindstorms: Children, Computers, and Powerful Ideas. Basic Books, New York (1980)
6. Wing, J.M.: Computational thinking benefits society. 40th Anniversary Blog of Social Issues in Computing (2014)
7. Brackmann, C.: Desenvolvimento do pensamento computacional através de atividades desplugadas na educação básica. Doctoral thesis, Universidade Federal do Rio Grande do Sul. LUME/UFRGS (2017)
8. Lythreatis, L., Singh, S.K., El-Kassar, A.: The digital divide: A review and future research agenda. Technol. Forecast. Soc. Change **175**, 121359 (2022)
9. Wang, C., Boerman, S.C., Kroon, A.C., Möller, J., de Vreese, C.H.: The artificial intelligence divide: who is the most vulnerable? New Media Soc. **27**(7), 3867–3889 (2025)
10. Jiahong, S., Zhong, Y., Ng, D.T.K.: A meta-review of literature on educational approaches for teaching AI at the K-12 levels in the asia-pacific region. Comput. Edu. Artif. Intell. **3**, 100065 (2022)
11. Shamir, G., Levin, I.: Teaching machine learning in elementary school. Int. J. Child-Comput. Inter. **31**, 100415 (2022)
12. Kandlhofer, M., Steinbauer, G., Hirschmugl-Gaisch, S., Huber, P.: Artificial intelligence and computer science in education: From kindergarten to university. In: 2016 IEEE Frontiers in Education Conference (FIE), pp. 1–9 (2016)
13. World Health Organization: Guidelines on Physical Activity, Sedentary Behaviour and Sleep for Children Under 5 Years of Age. World Health Organization, Geneva (2019)
14. Grant, P., Basye, D.: Personalized Learning: A Guide for Engaging Students with Technology. International Society for Technology in Education, Eugene, OR (2014)
15. Kerly, A., Ellis, R., Bull, S.: CALMsystem: Combining computer and human tutoring in an intelligent learning environment. Comput. Edu. **50**(3), 838–853 (2008)
16. Sánchez, J., Saldaña, D., Huertas, A.: Augmented reality for the teaching of basic sign language vocabulary to deaf students. Sensors **18**(6), 1766 (2018)
17. Baker, R.S., D'Mello, S.K., Rodrigo, M.M.T., Graesser, A.C.: Better to be frustrated than bored: The incidence, persistence, and impact of learners' cognitive-affective states during interactions with three different computer-based learning environments. Int. J. Human-Comput. Stud. **68**(4), 223–241 (2010)

18. Galafassi, C., Galafassi, F.F.P., Vicari, R.M., Reategui, E.B.: EvoLogic: toward an ITS for teaching propositional logic. Int. J. Artif. Intell. Edu. **33**(1), 35–58 (2023)
19. Prather, J., et al.: The widening gap: The benefits and harms of generative AI for novice programmers. In: Proceedings of the 2024 ACM Conference on International Computing Education Research, Vol. 1, pp. 469–486 (2024)
20. Nyland, J.J.A.O.L.: Racismo algorítmico: Uma revisão de literatura. Res. Soc. Dev. **12**(2), e1912239907 (2023)
21. Touretzky, D., Gardner-McCune, C., Martin, F., Seehorn, D.: Envisioning AI for K-12: What should every child know about AI? In: Proceedings of the AAAI Conference on Artificial Intelligence, Vol. 33, pp. 9795–9799 (2019)
22. Long, D., Magerko, B.: What is AI literacy? competencies and design considerations. In: Proceedings of the 2020 CHI Conference on Human Factors in Computing Systems, pp. 1–16 (2020)
23. Casal-Otero, L., Catala, A., Fernández-Morante, C., Taboada, M., Cebreiro, B., Barro, S.: AI literacy in K-12: a systematic literature review. Int. J. STEM Edu. **10**, 29 (2023)
24. Vicari, R.M., Brackmann, C., Mizusaki, L., Galafassi, C.: IA na Educação Básica. Novatec, 1 edn. (2023)
25. Brasil. Ministério da Educação. Base nacional comum curricular. Ministério da Educação (2018)
26. UNESCO. Recommendation on the ethics of artificial intelligence (2021)
27. Steele, J., Dyer, T., Jean Mandernach, B.: Five priorities to help learners in the online classroom. eLearn (9) (2023)

# Modernizing Ground Truth: Four Shifts Toward Improving Reliability and Validity in AI in Education

Danielle R. Thomas[1(✉)], Conrad Borchers[1], Kirk P. Vanacore[2], Kenneth R. Koedinger[1], and René F. Kizilcec[2]

[1] Carnegie Mellon University, Pittsburgh, USA
{drthomas,cborchers,koedinger}@cmu.edu
[2] Cornell University, Ithaca, USA
{kpv27,kizilcec}@cornell.edu

**Abstract.** Generative Artificial Intelligence (GenAI) is now widespread in education, yet the efficacy of GenAI systems remains constrained by the quality and interpretation of the labeled data used to train and evaluate them. Studies commonly report inter-rater reliability (IRR), often summarized by a single coefficient such as Cohen's kappa ($\kappa$), as a gatekeeper to "ground truth." We argue that many educational assessment and practice support settings include challenges, such as high-inference constructs, skewed label distributions, and temporally segmented multimodal data, which yield potential misapplication or misinterpretation of threshold-based heuristics for IRR. The growing use of large language models as annotators and judges introduces risks such as automation bias and circular validation. We propose four practical shifts for establishing ground truth: (1) treat IRR as a diagnostic signal to localize disagreement and refine constructs rather than a mechanical acceptance threshold (e.g., $\kappa > 0.8$); (2) require transparent reporting of rater expertise, codebook development, reconciliation procedures, and segmentation rules; (3) mitigate risks in LLM annotation through bias audits and verification workflows; and (4) complement agreement statistics with validity and effectiveness evidence for the intended use, including uncertainty-aware labeling (e.g., assigning different labels to the same item to capture nuance), criterion-related checks (e.g., predictive tests to check if labels forecast the intended outcome), and close-the-loop evaluations of whether systems trained on these labels improve learning beyond a reasonable control. We illustrate these shifts through case studies of multimodal tutoring data and provide actionable recommendations toward strengthening the evidence base of labeled AIED datasets.

**Keywords:** Reliability · Annotation · Generative AI · Model evaluation


E. G. Blanchard et al. (eds.), AIED 2026, LNCS 16586, pp. 117–131, 2027.
https://doi.org/10.1007/978-3-032-29773-0_9

## 1 Introduction

Humans often make notoriously flawed judgments. Research separates these human errors into two categories: *noise* and *bias* [18,22]. *Noise* is the random variability in judgments of the same or highly similar case [22], whereas *bias* is systematic directional error. While social bias and algorithmic fairness have received considerable attention [4,23], this work argues that *noise* is an underexamined but consequential obstacle for the AI in Education (AIED) community.

Education, at its best, is inherently noisy. Assigning grades, defining "student engagement," and identifying "giftedness" are tasks laden with subjective interpretation. For instance, consider the task of labeling a tutor's feedback: one expert educator might code a hint as "effective scaffolding," while another, with an equally valid pedagogical perspective, could see it as "giving away the answer." Yet, AIED often relies on inter-rater reliability (IRR) metrics, frequently summarized by a single coefficient such as Cohen's $\kappa$, which are often applied and interpreted as if they provide an objective gatekeeping test of "ground truth," even in settings involving high-inference constructs, skewed label distributions, or contextual judgment [15,28,43]. In such settings, disagreement does not necessarily indicate annotator error; it may reflect systematic differences in interpretation, underspecified constructs, or valid pedagogical ambiguity. Valid pedagogical ambiguity refers to the inherent complexity of educational interactions where multiple, equally defensible interpretations exist based on pedagogical perspectives or theoretical frameworks. Historically, the community has borrowed standards from machine learning, where disagreement is often treated as error to be minimized and high agreement is implicitly treated as a proxy for label quality [3].

A troubling trend in recent AIED literature is the treatment of reliability as a perfunctory checkbox rather than a rigorous scientific process. Many studies fail to report internal reliability measures entirely. For example, a meta-systematic review of AI in higher education found that 51.5% of the articles lacked any reliability metrics or coding protocols [6]. Even when included, reporting is often superficial, typically restricted to standalone agreement scores (e.g., [9,51,53]). Another problematic practice is "resolution by consensus," where researchers state that disagreements were discussed until a specific $\kappa$ threshold was achieved (e.g., [52]). Without detailing how disagreements were resolved, this process can amount to forcing consensus on complex constructs, effectively deleting valid pedagogical ambiguity from the data and making it difficult to determine if a model is learning the construct or merely annotators' biases. Without explicit documentation of how disagreements map to construct definitions, high post-hoc agreement may provide little evidence that the resulting labels support valid interpretation, rather than simply reflecting shared annotator heuristics.

Reconsideration of how our field labels and annotates data is timely. The rapid proliferation of Generative AI has ushered in a new era for AIED, promising scalable AI-driven tutoring systems [30]. In particular, multimodal interaction data, such as human-AI tutoring systems and classroom discourse analysis, are of increasing interest [2,45,51]. However, the learning efficacy of these systems depends on a fundamental bottleneck: the quality of human (and, recently, AI) annotations. If an AI model is trained on "ground truth" data labeled by inconsistent annotators, the resulting tool may simply codify and replicate that inconsistency [29]. A model trained on noisy or weakly specified labels may achieve high accuracy in reproducing annotator judgments, while failing to support the instructional mechanisms required to improve learning. Beyond immediate instructional efficacy, such models may be limited in their ability to support theory or yield interpretable estimates aligned with learning constructs. This aligns with cautions from EDM that models prioritizing prediction accuracy often fall short in providing interpretable, meaningful estimates useful for theory building [36]. Similarly, long-held warnings within qualitative psychology contend that the significance of a specific pattern is not strictly defined by its quantifiable prevalence, but instead by its capacity to capture a fundamental and meaningful element of the phenomenon being studied [7].

This challenge intensifies with the controversial emergence of large language models (LLMs) as judges, co-raters, or data augmentors [10]. Efficient yet contentious (c.f., [12,21]), LLMs complicate both the interpretation of agreement and the evidentiary role that agreement plays in validation, particularly when models act as annotators, judges, or data generators. We advocate replacing one-size-fits-all reliability metrics with methods that respect the inherent subjectivity of learning. To that end, we explain the unique landscape of AIED and contribute four shifts providing concrete actions to improve reliability practices: **1) Reframe IRR from a threshold to a diagnostic tool.** We argue for moving beyond mechanical acceptance thresholds (e.g., $\kappa > 0.8$) to using reliability metrics as signals for identifying productive disagreement and valid pedagogical ambiguity; **2) Contextualize and enforce transparent reporting.** We outline requirements for reporting rater characteristics, codebook evolution, and conflict resolution, while addressing AIED challenges like the "linking problem" in multimodal data; **3) Mitigate risks in LLM annotation.** We propose auditing methods to detect "beauty" and "authority" biases and call for verification frameworks (e.g., simulatability) when using LLMs as synthetic judges. **4) Prioritize validity over consensus.** We argue for moving beyond one-size-fits-all interpretations of reliability metrics towards clearer separation between reliability evidence, validity evidence, and evidence of instructional effectiveness.

## 2 Related Work

To assess consistency in human judgment, researchers commonly report interrater reliability (IRR), which quantifies the extent to which independent raters produce similar labels under a given coding scheme [11]. Metrics like Cohen's kappa ($\kappa$) estimate agreement beyond chance under specific assumptions about label distributions and rater behavior [28]. However, treating all disagreement as random noise is reductive; disagreement may reflect underspecified constructs, differences in pedagogical perspective, or contextual interpretation rather than unreliability. Disagreement often stems from systematic measurement error or valid ambiguity in high-inference and subjective tasks. Recent work argues that rather than eliminating this variance, researchers should treat "disagreement as data," analyzing differences in how multiple raters explain their annotation reasoning to better understand complex educational constructs and using ambiguity to guide opportunities for refinement [39].

Cohen's $\kappa$ is a common metric that improves upon simple percent agreement by accounting for chance, providing a standardized scale for reliability comparisons [28]. While traditional heuristics categorize $\kappa$ values in ranges from "poor" ($< 0.4$), "substantial" (0.61–0.80), to "almost perfect" (0.81–1.0) [25], some educational studies adopt heuristics, treating $\kappa$ values below 0.60 as potentially insufficient depending on task complexity and intended use [28]. However, the utility of a given $\kappa$ score is highly dependent on the downstream application of the annotated data. A low $\kappa$ does not automatically render a label useless. For applications that require stable, generalizable estimates across raters and contexts, persistently low agreement poses clear risks. By contrast, for applications such as curating illustrative cases for feedback or professional development, a "low $\kappa$, useful subset" scenario is possible. In such cases, the specific instances where raters do agree, even if infrequent, can represent highly useful data. Further, when raters from diverse pedagogical backgrounds reach a consensus on a difficult, high-inference construct, it likely signals an exceptionally clear and intelligible example of that construct. This highlights the importance of reporting rater characteristics, as such context is often necessary to interpret agreement estimates and assess whether consensus reflects construct clarity or shared perspective [34]. Other common IRR measures include Fleiss' $\kappa$, an adaptation of Cohen's $\kappa$ that can be used when there are more than two raters making judgments on a nominal scale; and Krippendorff's $\alpha$, a highly flexible and robust IRR metric that can handle any number of raters, different types of data (nominal, ordinal, interval, ratio), and can accommodate missing data [28]. These measures address different design constraints (e.g., number of raters, scale type), but none by themselves establish the validity of the underlying construct being annotated.

In AIED, IRR is often treated as a primary gatekeeping signal for labeled data quality. Low IRR can indicate substantial variability in judgment, though the source of that variability may include noise, construct ambiguity, or rater heterogeneity. High IRR alone can create a false sense of evidentiary sufficiency for validity [15,36,43]. A team of annotators can be perfectly reliable (high agreement) while sharing the same systematic bias or misconception (low validity). For example, limiting "student engagement" to "raising hands" introduces bias in the measurement step by distilling a rich state of the world into a narrow value [23]. While annotators may achieve high IRR, the AI will systematically miss quiet engagement, illustrating that reliability captures consistency of labeling, not whether the labels support valid interpretation of the intended construct.

## 3 The Unique Landscape of AIED

AIED data—ranging from student open-ended responses and behavioral clickstream data to biometric signals like eye-tracking and facial expressions—are fundamentally dual-purpose, differing from data in many other domains. It is used for both theory-building to uncover cognitive and social mechanisms of learning, similar to psychology [38], and to propel instructional action, such as providing real-time feedback in an intelligent tutoring system [24]. This dual responsibility necessitates a nuanced approach to measurement for both low- and high-inference tasks, presenting challenges that are amplified in AIED relative to many traditional machine learning benchmarks [37,43].

***AIED Contains a Wide Range of Low- and High-Inference Tasks.*** *Low-inference tasks* involve the tallying of direct, denotable behaviors that require minimal interpretation, such as "Did the tutor mention the student's name?" or "How many words did the student speak?" In these cases, traditional agreement metrics like Cohen's $\kappa$ are often high because the constructs are physically observable or easily inferrable. Conversely, educational constructs of interest, such as "confusion" (see Fig. 1), "conversational uptake," or "productive struggle," are often *high-inference tasks* [13], meaning they require contextual interpretation and grounding in higher-order concepts that are not directly observable from individual acts or behaviors. Unlike computer vision tasks where labeling an image as a "cat" is a low-inference perceptual task, labeling a student's ten-second pause as "deep thinking" versus "distraction" requires deep contextual and pedagogical interpretation. While a high-inference rating (e.g., a 1–5 scale of scaffolding quality) is often more strongly associated with downstream learning outcomes [34], it is significantly harder to reach a high IRR because humans bring different perspectives and experiences, which influence evaluation. Similarly, the context (e.g., cultural, social) of the data might make the annotation of high-inference tasks harder for raters. There are numerous high-inference tasks in AIED.

***Reliability Values Vary Widely by Use Case.*** Historical recommendations for $\kappa$ range widely from 0.4 to 0.8 [25], often failing to account for the distribution of the data itself. In high-inference domains where "ground truth" is uncertain and coding is holistic, such as affect detection, lower $\kappa$ scores are expected and often acceptable. For instance, the Baker Rodrigo Ocumpaugh Monitoring Protocol (BROMP), a rigorous field observation method for quantifying student engagement, sets its certification threshold at $\kappa > 0.6$ [34]. This reflects the reality that for subjective constructs like student affect, achieving "perfect" agreement is less critical than achieving sufficient aggregate reliability across a large volume of data. Conversely, for low-inference tasks with clear definitions, higher thresholds are both expected and necessary. This variance underscores that reliability is not an intrinsic property of the data alone, but depends on the construct definition, annotation design, and intended use. Table 1 illustrates examples of use cases, reported acceptable IRR, and the task inference level.

***AIED Often Uses Sequential and Multimodal Data.*** Educational data is frequently sequential and multimodal (e.g., classroom audio and video). Even when annotators agree that a specific pedagogical event occurred, they often disagree on its precise onset and offset times, a phenomenon known as the "linking problem" [19]. Standard reliability metrics often penalize these minor times-

**Table 1.** Use cases and applications containing reportedly acceptable IRR measures and inference level of task. Reported IRR thresholds vary widely across tasks.

| Use case/application | Acceptable IRR | Inference level of task |
|---|---|---|
| Agreement between a trainee and certified trainer needed to allow the trainee to begin coding data [34] | $\kappa = 0.6$ | Low to high inference. Behavior and affect coding schemes. Affective states are considered high-inference |
| Agreement between two human coders providing scores of learners open responses within online lessons on advocacy [44] | $\kappa = 0.55 - 0.93$ | Low to high inference. Assessing tutors' ability to respond to various tutoring situations varies in subjectivity |
| Agreement between human experts and foundation LLMs (e.g., Gemini 3 Pro, GPT-5) on coding Talk Moves in tutoring dialogues [47] | $\kappa = 0.38 - 0.58$ | High inference. LLMs struggled with tagging tutor moves that required sensitivity to social dynamics and metacognitive contexts |
| Agreement between multimodal LLMs and expert educators on grading handwritten student work [16] | $\kappa = 0.90$ (Arithmetic)<br>$\kappa \approx 0.47$ (Illustrations) | Low to high inference. Reliability drops from objective arithmetic (low) to interpreting student drawings (high) |

tamp offsets heavily, reporting "poor" reliability even when human judgments are conceptually aligned. This sensitivity to segmentation differences can create an illusion of low data quality in otherwise valid datasets, specifically in tasks involving visual-audio discrepancies. In such cases, low reliability values may be deemed acceptable for specific analytic purposes, or may indicate metric failure rather than annotator error. For example, researchers found a significant discrepancy between high raw agreement scores (often exceeding 90%) and low chance-corrected $\kappa$ scores for instructional activity labels in classroom videos [14]. The authors attribute this paradox to the timed-event nature of the data, where slight temporal misalignments deflate $\kappa$ scores despite conceptual consensus. This highlights why a rigid interpretation of standard measures, such as the widely cited guideline that $\kappa < 0.60$ is "unacceptable" [28], can be misleading in multimodal educational contexts. For complex, event-based data, relying solely on a single $\kappa$ value is often insufficient; researchers may need to consider a combination of metrics or adjust acceptability thresholds to account for the "linking problem" inherent to sequential analysis. Table 2 illustrates an example of the "linking problem" in real-life multimodal tutoring data.

**Table 2.** An example of temporal latency in multimodal tutoring. The lag between visual and audio events leads to misaligned annotations.

| Multimodal transcription | Student error? | |
|---|---|---|
| | Coder 1 | Coder 2 |
| [14:53] **[visual event]**: 'Sorry, incorrect...' feedback appears. The correct answer is -12g - 9.1 | X | X |
| [14:55] **[visual event]**: New problem loads: -4u +-6u + -2u -5u] | | |
| [14:55] **Tutor**: It's okay. Okay, what about this one? Can we combine or how many terms do we have or are in a relationship with somebody? | X | |
| [15:03] **Student**: We have four...actually three, cuz there's three that are negative and one that is positive. | | X |
| [15:08] **Tutor**: Okay, Does that mean we can combine them or we can't combine them? | | |
| [15:12] **Student**: We can. | | |
| [15:13] **Tutor**: Yeah, combine them. Perfect. | | |
| [15:15] **Tutor**: Okay. So what do we get when we put those all together? | | |
| [15:31] **Student**: 17u. | X | |
| [15:33] **[visual event]**: 'Sorry, incorrect...' appears. The correct answer is -17u. | X | X |
| [15:36] **Tutor**: Not quite. | | X |

### 3.1 Case Study Context: Multimodal Tutoring Data

Effective tutoring is among the most powerful influences on student learning [33], yet understanding effective tutor moves has been stalled by a lack of granular data [45]. Decades of research have lacked the large-scale, multi-modal datasets of tutoring and teaching (video, audio, transcripts, assessments, and metadata) necessary to unpack these dynamic interactions at the level of in-the-moment tutoring moves. We focus on multi-modal tutoring because the field is now seeing a proliferation of rich interaction data (e.g., National Tutoring Observatory, SafeInsights, SEERNet) that is increasingly processed by LLMs and AI agents to automate interpretation. Multi-modal tutoring interaction is particularly well suited for examining reliability challenges because the "ground truth" is rarely contained in a single modality. Figure 1 illustrates an example of multi-modal tutoring interaction data, which we use as a running example to ground our methodological arguments. The example shows how a student's verbal confusion ("I don't know what to do here") is paired with visual cues (e.g., shrugging, pointing to an equation) and processed into a transcribed, timestamped interaction. AI models operationalize these signals by inferring latent states (e.g., confusion), resolving ambiguous references (e.g., "here" to $x^2 = 225$), and classifying tutor moves, such as prompting self-explanation, affective support, and cognitive scaffolding. If annotation quality is evaluated solely through expert agreement statistics, we risk validating models that primarily mimic human consistency, including our biases and blind spots, rather than capturing the latent processes that drive student learning. This case highlights why agreement statistics alone are insufficient for validating annotations intended to support explanatory research and instructional intervention.

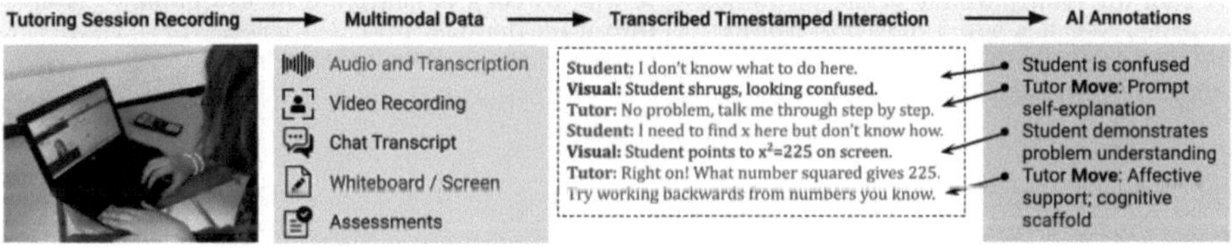


**Fig. 1.** A processing pipeline for multimodal tutoring data. Raw audiovisual recordings are transformed into transcripts enriched with AI-extracted features, highlighting the complexity of labeling pedagogical moves.

## 4 Four Shifts Toward Improving Reliability

### 4.1 Reframe IRR from Mechanical Threshold to a Diagnostic Tool

We propose reframing how IRR is used and interpreted in AIED: rather than treating a single coefficient as a threshold for acceptance (e.g., $\kappa > 0.8$), we emphasize diagnostic use that is sensitive to construct complexity, annotation design, and intended application. We aim to better align IRR uses with low-to-high inference educational constructs and the integration of LLMs. [11] provided a description of what IRR can and cannot do for qualitative case study research. We adapt this framing to AIED by highlighting common failure modes in multimodal and high-inference annotation and by linking agreement statistics to concrete design and reporting decisions. Table 3 summarizes common misinterpretations of IRR in AIED practice and contrasts them with defensible uses of agreement statistics as evidence about consistency, rather than as substitutes for validity or effectiveness claims.

**Table 3.** What inter-rater reliability (IRR) can and cannot do for AIED with examples from multimodal tutoring and educational discourse literature. Extended from [11] to reflect the nature of educational annotation and LLM integration.

| IRR is... | IRR is not... | Ex. |
|---|---|---|
| **A diagnostic tool** to determine the degree of consensus between coders as a basis for discussion that may enhance the findings or theory emerging from the data | **A mechanical threshold** (e.g., $\kappa > 0.8$) that must be cleared to prove a dataset is "ready" for machine learning | [48] |
| **A potential signal of productive disagreement**, where variance between human and/or LLM coders may warrant construct refinement or further validation | **A reason to eliminate disagreement**, as it may reveal the need for construct refinement, additional rater training, or complementary validity evidence | [35] |
| **A measure of consistency** for low-inference tasks (e.g., "Did the student ask a question?") to high-inference tasks (e.g., "Is the student engaged?") to ensure data quality for baseline AI models | **A guarantee of validity.** High agreement on a biased rubric (e.g., engagement = "quietness") only ensures the AI will accurately replicate that flaw | [1,34] |
| **A starting point** for understanding human coders and LLM agreement, used to assess variation | **An ending point** or sole indicator of AI accuracy. Matching a human coder does not mean the AI is "right" | [47] |
| **A tool for transparency** in the annotation pipeline, revealing how a codebook evolved through reconciliation to handle disagreements and edge cases | **A way to turn educational measurement into a mechanical task** that ignores the context of the teacher/tutor-student relationship | [1,5] |

## 4.2 Contextualize and Enforce Transparent Reporting

Reliability measures need to be reported and the process clearly described. A troubling trend in recent AIED literature is the treatment of reliability as a perfunctory checkbox rather than a rigorous scientific process. Many studies fail to report internal reliability measures entirely [6]. Even when included, reporting is often surface level, typically restricted to standalone $\kappa$ scores [9,51], leading to the common trope that "raters coded 20% of the data and agreement was good ($\kappa = 0.8$)." This reliance on simple percent accuracy masks the need for granular, chance-corrected measures necessary to accurately capture reliability (e.g., [27,53]). A particularly problematic practice is the "resolution by consensus" description, where researchers state that "disagreements were discussed until a $\kappa$ of 0.80 was achieved." Without detailing how these disagreements were resolved, this process often amounts to forcing consensus on high-inference constructs, effectively deleting valid pedagogical ambiguity from the dataset. This opacity prevents the field from understanding whether a model is learning the construct or merely the biases of the annotators. Similarly, when reviewing papers, reviewers should not automatically criticize work that reports lower than ideal reliability measures, if thorough explanation and justification is included.

AIED can benefit from greater reliance on domain expertise in construct definition, rater training, and adjudication—paired with transparent documentation of how expert judgments are elicited and reconciled. For many high-inference educational constructs, "ground truth" is unlikely to be adequately approximated by minimally trained crowd-workers; domain experts can improve construct specification and adjudication, especially when their roles and procedures are transparently documented. For instance, the Baker Rodrigo Ocumpaugh Monitoring Protocol (BROMP) enforces rigorous certification of human observers to ensure reliability before data collection even begins [34]. We argue that AIED should normalize this level of rigor. This entails two shifts: 1) **increased transparency**, reporting not just the final $\kappa$, but the demographics of the raters, the specific codebook definitions, and the nature of the disagreements found; and 2) **inclusion of experts**, by enrolling experienced educators or domain-experts not merely as annotators, but as co-authors whose pedagogical expertise defines the constructs we aim to capture.

### 4.3 Mitigate Risk in LLM Annotation via Auditing and Verification

LLMs are shifting data annotation from a manual task to an efficient human-AI collaboration, recasting them as active agents—especially in AIED where domain expertise is scarce [40]. We categorize their roles as an equal-party annotator, a judge, and a data augmentor.

***LLM as an Equal-Party Annotator.*** One recent use for LLMs is that of an equal-party annotator, where the LLM functions as a distinct rater alongside human raters. This approach is particularly attractive for scaling the coding of large educational datasets, such as classroom transcripts or MOOC discussion forum posts, where using purely human-coded data is cost-prohibitive and time consuming [35,40,47]. Research suggests that for context-independent and low-inference tasks (e.g., identifying explicit questions or social tags), LLMs can achieve high agreement with humans [20,31]. However, research indicates that for context-dependent constructs (e.g., "theorizing" or "reflection"), base models often struggle to reach acceptable reliability without extensive fine-tuning or the use of the largest frontier models [20,41]. Furthermore, traditional metrics like percent agreement often mask poor model performance. While LLMs can serve as a "first pass" coder to reduce cognitive load, they introduce risks of automation bias. [50] demonstrated that providing LLM pre-labels can actually decrease human accuracy when the model is incorrect, as annotators may uncritically adopt the AI's suggestion. Effective human and LLM collaboration may require a verification framework (e.g., the Lapras system), where a separate verifier model identifies low-confidence LLM labels for human re-annotation [1,50].

***LLM as a Judge.*** In the "LLM-as-a-judge" framework, AI models evaluate natural language responses like student essays or tutoring dialogues, offering a scalable, low-cost alternative to human annotation that has been shown to approximate crowd-workers agreement in some constrained settings [32]. This practice, however, introduces the critical risk of *circular validation*, a process where one AI's output is validated by another AI, creating a self-referential loop that can provide a false sense of accuracy [10]. Instead of verifying genuine correctness, such a loop often serves only to amplify the models' shared biases and flawed reasoning. LLM judges are also susceptible to systemic biases, such as "authority bias" (overvaluing citations) and "beauty bias" (favoring technical formatting) [10], or "position bias" in pairwise comparisons [26]. For instance, in multimodal math, models excel at rote arithmetic ($\kappa = 0.90$) but fail on conceptual illustrations ($\kappa \approx 0.47$), showing technical skill does not equal pedagogical "tacit knowledge" [17]. Beyond these biases, LLMs also show distinct "grading personalities," meaning high human-LLM agreement might merely reflect the human adapting to the training data [17]. For educational validity, an LLM's rationale must satisfy *simulatability*, meaning a human can predict its judgment from the explanation [50]. High agreement can mask flawed reasoning; even when LLMs achieve high IRR, their explanations often diverge from human reasoning in ambiguous cases [17]. This "right for the wrong reasons" phenomenon shows the danger of using score alignment as a sole proxy for pedagogical validity.

To justify replacing human annotators despite these risks, researchers have proposed various statistical procedures, such as the "Alternative Annotator Test" [8]. This test verifies whether an LLM offers a better alternative to recruiting a human by comparing the model with a small group of annotators (at least three) on a modest subset of data (50–100 examples). By demonstrating that the LLM aligns with the group consensus as well as or better than an individual human, researchers can assess whether an AI model offers a cost-effective substitute under defined assumptions about quality, risk, and oversight. These validity concerns extend beyond annotation to the use of LLMs for data augmentation, where models generate "synthetic ground truth" to address data scarcity [40]. While scalable, this practice creates a risk of "recursive training," where models amplify surface-level stylistic biases while losing pedagogical precision [41]. Consequently, LLM outputs should be evaluated using multiple complementary forms of evidence (targeted audits, agreement diagnostics, and predictive validity checks), to ensure alignment with educational mechanisms and outcomes.

### 4.4 Complement Agreement with Validity and Impact Evidence

To prioritize educational impact over statistical uniformity, we outline complementary sources of evidence that operate at three levels: representation, validation, and intervention. These evidence sources are not interchangeable; rather, they address distinct threats to validity and misuse at AIED pipeline stages.

***Multilabel Annotation.*** An annotation that allows for more than one label relaxes the assumption of a single, definitive "correct" label when constructs are ambiguous or multimodal evidence is incomplete. Instead, it allows for multiple valid interpretations by assigning several labels to a single data point. This method is particularly useful for capturing the complexity and "productive ambiguity" inherent in many educational tasks [43]. An example of applying this to multimodal tutoring data is shown in Table 4. Here, an annotator identifies student errors through multiple simultaneous valid lenses: *explicitly*, via visual system logs (e.g., "Sorry, incorrect" appearing on screen) and *implicitly*, via the tutor's verbal cues (e.g.,"not quite" or "it is okay"). The schema includes a confidence level, which allows the annotator to signal when the ground truth is ambiguous rather than forcing a low-confidence binary decision. This multilabel approach preserves the nuance of how errors manifest across different modalities, rather than relying on a single, potentially incomplete annotation.

**Table 4.** A multilabel annotation example of student math errors. The annotations capture ground truth across modalities by identifying *explicit* errors (visual events) and *implicit* errors (tutor cues). Confidence scores allow annotators to flag ambiguity.

| **Multimodal transcription** | **Student error? (0/1)** | **Implicit/ explicit (0/1)** | **Confidence level (0/1)** |
|---|---|---|---|
| [14:53][**visual event**]:'Sorry, incorrect...' feedback appears. The correct answer is -12g - 9.1 | 1 | 1 | 1 |
| [14:55][**visual event**]: New problem loads: -4u + -6u + -2u -5u] | 0 | | 1 |
| [14:55][**audio**] **Tutor**: It's okay. Okay, what about this one? Can we combine or how many terms do we have or are in a relationship with somebody? | 0 | | 1 |
| [15:03][**audio**] **Student**: We have four...actually three, cuz there's three that are negative and one that is positive. | 0 | | 0 |
| [15:08] **Tutor**: Okay, Does that mean we can combine them or we can't combine them? | 0 | | 1 |
| [15:12] **Student**: We can. | 0 | | 1 |
| [15:13] **Tutor**: Yeah, combine them. Perfect. | 0 | | 1 |
| [15:15] **Tutor**: Okay. So what do we get when we put those all together? | 0 | | 1 |
| [15:31] **Student**: 17u. | 1 | 0 | 1 |
| [15:33][**visual event**]: 'Sorry, incorrect...' feedback appears. The correct answer is -17u. | 1 | 1 | 0 |
| [15:36] **Tutor**: Not quite. | 1 | 0 | 1 |

***Expert-Based Approaches.*** Rather than using agreement among peer annotators as the benchmark, expert-based approaches treat expert judgment as a more credible reference standard for adjudicating difficult cases [17,34]. In [32], researchers implemented an expert-based re-annotation protocol where two experts independently reviewed and reached consensus on difficult cases where models disagreed. This reconciliation process created a high-confidence "gold standard" that was demonstrably more reliable than the original labels [31,50].

***Predictive Validity.*** Predictive validity ties the value of an annotation to its ability to forecast performance on an external, related measure. This concept is rooted in process-product research [37] and foundational AIED frameworks like Knowledge Component Analysis, where a model is validated by its ability to predict student error rates [24]. For example, an AI score on an open response gains validity if it accurately predicts the score on a corresponding MCQ [42,44].

However, predictive validity must be interpreted with caution. A high correlation with an outcome does not guarantee that the correct construct has been identified, e.g., incorrectly labeling "frustration" as "confusion" might still yield a predictive correlation with low performance because the two states are often collinear. Predictive validity should not be used in isolation but as a method to triangulate construct validity [38]. Researchers should verify that specific labels predict distinct outcomes (e.g., does the label predict the *specific* type of error?) to ensure the model is capturing the intended construct, not just a signal [36].

***Close-the-Loop (Intervention-Level) Evidence.*** Close-the-loop evidence assesses whether a given annotation scheme, and the AI system trained on it, produces improved student learning. For instance, Tutor CoPilot classifies pedagogical moves to give advice to tutors. It was evaluated by comparing student learning outcomes when tutors receive AI-generated advice versus control conditions. This "closes the loop" between the annotation, the AI system, and the desired educational outcome [49]. While this "closes the loop" between annotation and outcome, strong construct validity is still needed to ensure the learning gains are attributable to the specific pedagogical constructs the AI identified, not confounding factors [46]. By integrating these validity-centered frameworks, in addition to including traditional reliability estimates, researchers can move beyond simply measuring agreement. This shift prioritizes the goal of AIED: creating tools that are genuinely effective, not just consistent.

## 5 Next Steps for AIED & Conclusion

To move from the theoretical shifts proposed in this paper to a new standard of practice, the AIED community should consider: 1) **"uncertainty-aware" infrastructure** and 2) **an evolution in peer-review culture.** First, while privacy constraints often limit the sharing of raw data, the community could benefit from adopting standardized reporting frameworks that capture "productive ambiguity." Researchers should consider documenting de-identified edge cases and the specific rationales behind expert disagreements to illustrate construct complexity. As demonstrated in Table 4, integrating annotator confidence levels and multi-label schemas allows for a more nuanced understanding of "ground truth" that acknowledges the inherent subjectivity of high-inference tutoring interactions. Second, peer-review could gradually move toward prioritizing the transparent reporting of rater expertise and predictive validity evidence, such as demonstrating that the labels used to train a system effectively forecast learning outcomes. Rather than treating reliability as a mechanical gatekeeper (e.g., $\kappa > 0.8$), reviewers are encouraged to treat IRR as a diagnostic signal used to localize disagreement and refine pedagogical constructs (Table 3). This shift ensures that labels are validated not just by statistical agreement, but by their demonstrated alignment with meaningful instructional mechanisms and learning outcomes.

The rapid adoption of GenAI has increased the stakes of how we define and evaluate the quality of labeled data. By shifting the focus from mechanical consensus to diagnostic rigor, the AIED community can ensure that models are not merely mimicking human consistency, but are accurately capturing the complex, "noisy," and meaningful processes that drive learning. Our goal is not to replace established psychometric frameworks, but to translate and extend them for a new era of AI-driven education, characterized by high-inference constructs and multimodal data often annotated by LLMs.

**Acknowledgments.** This work was supported in part by the Learning Engineering Virtual Institute, the Gates Foundation, and the Chan Zuckerberg Initiative. The opinions, findings, and conclusions expressed are those of the authors.

## References

1. Ahtisham, B., Vanacore, K., Lee, J., Zhou, Z., Pietrzak, D., Kizilcec, R.F.: AI annotation orchestration: evaluating LLM verifiers to improve the quality of LLM annotations in learning analytics. arXiv preprint arXiv:2511.09785 (2025)
2. Aleven, V., et al.: Towards the future of AI-augmented human tutoring in math learning. In: International Conference on Artificial Intelligence in Education, pp. 26–31. Springer, Heidelberg (2023). https://doi.org/10.1007/978-3-031-36336-8_3
3. Ando, R.K., Zhang, T., Bartlett, P.: A framework for learning predictive structures from multiple tasks and unlabeled data. J. Mach. Learn. **6**(11) (2005)
4. Baker, R.S., Hawn, A.: Algorithmic bias in education. Int. J. Artif. Intell. Educ. **32**(4), 1052–1092 (2022)
5. Barany, A., et al.: Chatgpt for education research: exploring the potential of large language models for qualitative codebook development. In: International Conference on Artificial Intelligence in Education, pp. 134–149. Springer, Heidelberg (2024). https://doi.org/10.1007/978-3-031-64299-9_10
6. Bond, M., et al.: A meta systematic review of artificial intelligence in higher education. Educ. Technol. High. Educ. **21**(1), 4 (2024)
7. Braun, V., Clarke, V.: Using thematic analysis in psychology. Qual. Res. Psychol. **3**(2), 77–101 (2006)
8. Calderon, N., Reichart, R., Dror, R.: The alternative annotator test for LLM-as-a-judge: how to statistically justify replacing human annotators with LLMs. In: Association for Computational Linguistics, pp. 16051–16081 (2025)
9. Carpenter, D., et al.: Detecting off-task behavior from student dialogue in game-based collaborative learning. In: Bittencourt, I.I., Cukurova, M., Muldner, K., Luckin, R., Millán, E. (eds.) AIED 2020. LNCS (LNAI), vol. 12163, pp. 55–66. Springer, Cham (2020). https://doi.org/10.1007/978-3-030-52237-7_5
10. Chen, G.H., Chen, S., Liu, Z., Jiang, F., Wang, B.: Humans or llms as the judge? a study on judgement biases. arXiv preprint arXiv:2402.10669 (2024)
11. Cole, R.: Inter-rater reliability methods in qualitative case study research. Sociol. Methods Res. **53**(4), 1944–1975 (2024)
12. Davison, R.M., Chughtai, H., Nielsen, P., Trenz, M., Techatassanasoontorn, A.A., Andrade, A.D., et al.: The ethics of using generative ai for qualitative data analysis. Inf. Syst. J. **34**(5), 1433–1439 (2024)
13. Demszky, D., et al.: Measuring conversational uptake: a case study on student-teacher interactions. In: Proceedings of Computational Linguistics, pp. 1638–1653 (2021)
14. Foster, J.K., Youngs, P., van Aswegen, R., Watson, G.S., Acton, S.T.: Automated classification of elementary instructional activities. J. Learn. Anal. (2024)

15. Gwet, K.L.: Handbook of inter-rater reliability: The definitive guide to measuring the extent of agreement among raters. Advanced Analytics, LLC (2014)
16. Henkel, O., Roberts, B., Jaffe, D., Holt, L.: Seeing the big picture: evaluating multimodal LLMs' ability to interpret and grade. arXiv:2510.05538 (2025)
17. Henkel, O., Vanacore, K., Roberts, B.: When humans can't agree, neither can machines. In: Proceedings of the AI in Measurement and Education (2025)
18. Hilbert, M.: Toward a synthesis of cognitive biases: how noisy information processing can bias human decision making. Psychol. Bull. **138**(2), 211 (2012)
19. Holle, H., Rein, R.: Easydiag: a tool for easy determination of interrater agreement. Behav. Res. Methods **47**(3), 837–847 (2015)
20. Hou, C., Zhu, G., Zheng, J., Du, H., Ker, C.L.: Prompt-based and fine-tuned GPT models for context-dependent and-independent deductive coding. In: Proceedings of the 14th Learning Analytics and Knowledge Conference, pp. 518–528 (2024)
21. Jowsey, T., Braun, V., Clarke, V., Lupton, D., Fine, M.: We reject the use of generative ai for reflexive qualitative research. Qual. Inquiry (2025)
22. Kahneman, D., Sibony, O., Sunstein, C.R.: Noise: a flaw in human judgment. Hachette UK (2021)
23. Kizilcec, R.F., Lee, H.: Algorithmic fairness in education. In: The Ethics of Artificial Intelligence in Education, pp. 174–202. Routledge (2022)
24. Koedinger, K.R., Corbett, A.T., Perfetti, C.: The knowledge-learning-instruction framework. Cogn. Sci. **36**(5), 757–798 (2012)
25. Landis, J.R., Koch, G.G.: An application of hierarchical kappa-type statistics in the assessment of majority agreement among multiple observers. Biometrics (1977)
26. Li, H., et al.: LLMs-as-judges: a comprehensive survey on LLM-based evaluation methods. arXiv:2412.05579 (2024)
27. Li, Z., Akemoglu, Y., Lyu, J., Zheng, Q., Xiong, J.: ASD-HI: a parent-child interaction dataset for automated assessment of home intervention. In: International Conference on Artificial Intelligence in Education, pp. 48–62. Springer, Heidelberg (2025). https://doi.org/10.1007/978-3-031-98414-3_4
28. McHugh, M.L.: Irr: the kappa statistic. Biochemia medica **22**(3) (2012)
29. Messer, M., Brown, N.C., Kölling, M., Shi, M.: How consistent are humans when grading programming assignments? arXiv preprint arXiv:2409.12967 (2024)
30. Mittal, U., Sai, S., Chamola, V., Sangwan, D.: A comprehensive review on generative AI for education. IEEE Access **12**, 142733–142759 (2024)
31. Na, Y., Feng, S.: LLM-assisted automated deductive coding of dialogue data: leveraging dialogue-specific characteristics to enhance contextual understanding. In: International Conference on Artificial Intelligence in Education, pp. 248–262 (2025)
32. Nahum, O., Calderon, N., Keller, O., Szpektor, I., Reichart, R.: Are LLMs better than reported? In: Proceedings of the 2025 Empirical Methods in Natural Language Processing, pp. 26770–26797 (2025)
33. Nickow, A., Oreopoulos, P., Quan, V.: The impressive effects of tutoring on prek-12 learning: a systematic review of the experimental evidence (2020)
34. Ocumpaugh, J., et al.: Baker rodrigo ocumpaugh monitoring protocol (bromp) 2.0 technical and training manual. Teachers College (2015)
35. Petukhova, K., Kochmar, E.: Intent matters: enhancing AI tutoring with fine-grained pedagogical intent annotation. arXiv preprint arXiv:2506.07626 (2025)
36. Rachatasumrit, N., Carvalho, P., Koedinger, K.: Beyond accuracy: embracing meaningful parameters in educational data mining. In: Proceedings of the 17th International Conference on Educational Data Mining, pp. 203–210 (2024)

37. Rosenshine, B.: 5: Evaluation of classroom instruction. Rev. Educ. Res. **40**(2), 279–300 (1970)
38. Self, J.: Theoretical foundations for intelligent tutoring systems. J. Artif. Intell. Educ. **1**(4), 3–14 (1990)
39. Tajik, E., et al.: Disagreement as data: reasoning trace analytics in multi-agent systems. arXiv preprint arXiv:2601.12618 (2026)
40. Tan, Z., et al.: Large language models for data annotation and synthesis: a survey. In: Proceedings of the 2024 Conference on Empirical Methods in Natural Language Processing, pp. 930–957 (2024)
41. Thakur, A.S., Choudhary, K., Ramayapally, V.S., Vaidyanathan, S., Hupkes, D.: Judging the judges: evaluating alignment and vulnerabilities in LLMs-as-judges. In: Proceedings of the Fourth Workshop on Generation, Evaluation and Metrics ($GEM^2$), pp. 404–430 (2025)
42. Thomas, D.R., et al.: Improving open-response assessment with learnlm. In: International Conference on Artificial Intelligence in Education, pp. 220–227. Springer, Heidelberg (2025). https://doi.org/10.1007/978-3-031-98462-4_28
43. Thomas, D.R., Borchers, C., Koedinger, K.: Beyond agreement: rethinking ground truth in educational AI annotation. In: Proceedings of the Artificial Intelligence in Measurement and Education Conference (AIME-Con), pp. 345–351 (2025)
44. Thomas, D.R., et al.: Does multiple choice have a future in the age of genai? In: Proceedings of the Inter. Learning Analytics and Knowledge Conference, pp. 494–504 (2025)
45. Thomas, D.R., et al.: Advancing the science of teaching with tutoring data: a collaborative workshop with the national tutoring observatory. In: Proceedings of the ACM Conference on Learning@Scale, pp. 404–406 (2025)
46. Trochim, W.M., Donnelly, J.P., Arora, K.: Research methods: the essential knowledge base (2016)
47. Vanacore, K., Kizilcec, R.F.: How well do large language models recognize instructional moves? Establishing baselines for foundation models in educational discourse. arXiv preprint arXiv:2512.19903 (2025)
48. Vitale, J., Kocabagli, K.B., Sanghi, S., Van Camp, A., Miller, S., Coker, B.: From noisy classroom transcripts to actionable feedback: fine-tuning gpt-4o to detect teachers' opportunities to respond. In: International Conference on Artificial Intelligence in Education, pp. 149–162. Springer, Heidelberg (2025). https://doi.org/10.1007/978-3-031-98417-4_11
49. Wang, R.E., Ribeiro, A.T., Robinson, C.D., Loeb, S., Demszky, D.: Tutor copilot: a human-AI approach for scaling real-time expertise. arXiv:2410.03017 (2024)
50. Wang, X., Kim, H., Rahman, S., Mitra, K., Miao, Z.: Human-LLM collaborative annotation through effective verification of LLM labels. In: Proceedings of the 2024 CHI Conference on Human Factors in Computing Systems, pp. 1–21 (2024)
51. Wong, K., Wu, B., Bulathwela, S., Cukurova, M.: Rethinking the potential of multimodality in collaborative problem solving diagnosis with large language models. In: International Conference on Artificial Intelligence in Education. Springer, Heidelberg (2025). https://doi.org/10.1007/978-3-031-98417-4_2
52. Zhao, C., Silva, M., Poulsen, S.: Autograding mathematical induction proofs with natural language processing. J. Artif. Intell. Educ. (2025)
53. Zhuang, Y., Zhang, S.: Integrating chatgpt in mathematics teacher education: AI- based simulation role-playing to support practice-based teaching. Artif. Intell. Educ. **35** (2025)

# From Tool to Teammate? Negotiating Accountability and Disclosure in Academic Generative AI Use

Diane Vassallo(✉)

University of Malta, Msida, Malta
diane.vassallo@um.edu.mt

**Abstract.** Generative AI is becoming embedded in academic work, yet ethical boundaries and disclosure expectations remain inconsistently defined across contexts and contested. As these systems increasingly resemble collaborative partners rather than neutral tools, accountability questions become more complex, including what counts as acceptable assistance, who is responsible for errors, and what should be disclosed to different audiences. Drawing on focus groups with 15 university academics, this paper examines how academics in this context negotiate ethical boundaries for generative AI across academic tasks, how moral accountability and professional identity are performed in peer dialog, what transparency and disclosure norms emerge across key audiences, and how perceived competence trajectories may be associated with shifts in both boundary-setting and emotional positioning over time. Findings show that boundary-setting is strongly situational, with acceptability calibrated by task type, stakes, and visibility, and anchored in concerns about authorship, authenticity, responsibility, and credibility. Participants enacted moral accountability through tool reframing, verification, reliance minimization and self-presentational disclosure choices. Transparency norms were conditional and audience-dependent, shaped by uncertainty about institutional guidance and by anticipated judgement from colleagues, students and publishers. Adoption trajectories appeared to be associated with these negotiations: greater familiarity was often associated with increased confidence and more nuanced ethical rules, while lower perceived competence was associated with cautious use and heightened concern. The paper concludes with implications for responsible guidance in higher education, arguing for policy and professional learning that recognize the social dynamics of accountability and support calibrated, context-sensitive transparency.

**Keywords:** Generative AI · Higher Education · Accountability · Transparency and disclosure · Professional identity · Ethical boundary-setting


E. G. Blanchard et al. (eds.), AIED 2026, LNCS 16586, pp. 132–146, 2027.
https://doi.org/10.1007/978-3-032-29773-0_10

# 1 Introduction

Generative AI, especially large language models, is rapidly becoming embedded in everyday academic work [28,33]. Academics are using these tools to draft and revise text, summarize readings, generate ideas, and support routine teaching and administrative communication [27]. This creates an obvious appeal in environments shaped by heavy workloads and time pressure [33]. Embedding generative AI in academic work unsettles long-standing assumptions about what constitutes legitimate academic labor and where the boundary lies between acceptable assistance and substantive intellectual contribution [11]. Recent research suggests that this shift is not merely technical but also normative, reshaping how academic work is produced, evaluated, and trusted, with direct implications for authorship, originality, and responsibility [4,19,21].

Beyond questions of accuracy and efficiency, the use of generative AI is increasingly perceived as identity-relevant, raising concerns about credibility and what counts as legitimate academic work. Because these judgements are socially evaluated, emotional positioning of unease, reassurance and confidence may relate to both what academics do and what they feel comfortable disclosing. Building on prior survey evidence of anticipatory moral concern around generative AI use among academics [30], the present study examines how accountability and disclosure norms are negotiated in peer dialog among academics in one institutional context. While prior survey evidence captures anticipatory moral concern, there is still limited understanding of how academics construct ethical boundaries and disclosure expectations in real time when discussing their own use of generative AI with peers [24,26]. This matters because accountability in academic life is not only an internal judgment, but it is shaped through interaction, where academics anticipate evaluation, negotiate what counts as acceptable practice, and decide what is safe to disclose.

Drawing on four focus groups with 15 university academics, the present study addresses this gap by examining how ethical boundaries and disclosure norms are constructed through peer dialog in this setting. It examines how generative AI is framed in talk, not only as a tool but sometimes as a quasi-collaborative partner, and how this framing may be associated with boundary-setting across tasks, accountability performances, conditional transparency expectations, and competence-related shifts in emotional positioning over time. The study thus contributes interaction-sensitive evidence to inform more realistic, context-aware guidance for responsible use of generative AI in higher education.

## 1.1 Study Aims and Research Questions

Based on this study of 15 university academics at one institution, the study aims to explore how these academics collectively make sense of the use of generative AI as an ethical and identity-relevant issue, with particular attention to how norms of transparency and accountability are negotiated in peer dialog under uncertain and evolving expectations. The study is guided by four research questions:

RQ1: How do the academics in this study conceptualize and negotiate ethical boundaries for generative AI use across different academic tasks including teaching, research and administrative work, particularly around authorship, authenticity, responsibility and credibility?

RQ2: How do these academics perform moral accountability and protect professional identity when discussing generative AI use, including how they position unease, reassurance, confidence, or value-conflict through justification, reframing, minimization, and self-presentational disclosure choices?

RQ3: What transparency and disclosure norms emerge, and what accountability is anticipated, regarding generative AI use across key audiences, including students, colleagues, institutions and publishers in this context?

RQ4: How are perceived AI competence and adoption trajectories from novice to experienced associated with differences in ethical boundary-setting and emotional positioning (confidence, anxiety, guilt and comfort) as discussed by participants over time?

The next sections review related work, describe the methodology, and present findings on boundary-setting, accountability talk, disclosure norms, and adoption trajectories.

## 2 Literature Review

This literature review focuses on concepts that help explain how academics negotiate generative AI use in practice, particularly when expectations are uneven and socially evaluated. Throughout this paper, professional identity is understood as a dynamic and socially negotiated sense of self-in-role: the ongoing process through which academics define who they are, what they value and how they are recognized by others as legitimate members of their professional community [5, 13]. This framing treats identity not as a fixed attribute but as something performed and confirmed through interaction, making peer dialog a particularly salient site for its negotiation [29]. It synthesizes four strands of work that inform the present analysis: setting different AI boundaries for different academic tasks; authorship, authenticity and responsibility concerns when writing is produced with both human and AI input; conditional transparency norms shaped by audience and anticipated judgement; and competence trajectories (novice to more experienced use) that may be associated with shifts in both ethical positioning and emotional comfort over time.

The sections that follow examine these strands in turn, focusing on how academics articulate boundaries, manage accountability and disclosure, and recalibrate their positions as AI competence develops.

### 2.1 Ethical Boundary-Work and Task-Contingent Legitimacy

A consistent theme across emerging literature is that attitudes and acceptance of generative AI vary considerably across contexts, with educators recognizing both benefits and concerns related to academic integrity, assessment practices, and institutional support [9,24]. In practice, academics often distinguish between uses framed as relatively "surface" support like language improvement, formatting or ideation prompts, and uses perceived as more "substantive" because they shape interpretation, argumentation, or intellectual contribution [8]. This distinction reflects broader taxonomies of AI writing assistance that range from low-level linguistic edits to high-level cognitive contributions such as idea generation, argumentation, and synthesis [18]. These distinctions can be understood as professional boundary-setting, where actors seek to protect credibility by differentiating acceptable practices from those that threaten valued norms, and accountability [14].

Institutional guidance has focused unevenly on academic integrity and compliance [16,22]. Reviews highlight that even where perceived usefulness is high, concerns about integrity, accuracy, and skill development persist [24] with acceptability differentiated by task type and stage, for instance early-stage brainstorming versus later-stage production. Through a boundary-work lens, such distinctions protect professional credibility by defining legitimate academic contribution [14].

### 2.2 Authorship and Responsibility in Hybrid Production

Generative AI intensifies long-standing ethical questions about authorship and responsibility. Authorship is already a morally and politically complex category in higher education, involving credit, reputation, accountability and power [11]. The advent of generative AI has intensified these complexities, as institutions now explicitly frame authorship requirements around human oversight, individual learning evidence, and ethical responsibility [11], while foundational concepts of originality and intellectual property face reconceptualization [15]. Responsibility becomes complicated because academics remain accountable for errors and claims, even when the production process involves model-generated outputs that can appear authoritative while being difficult to verify and are sometimes inaccurate [20,21].

Verification and human oversight become recurring ethical anchors in defining responsible use [21]. Authorship and authenticity are negotiated through practical responsibility questions: who is answerable for mistakes, and what verification is sufficient [10,20]. These questions connect to disclosure, as when AI visibility shapes how audiences attribute responsibility to the human author [10,20].

### 2.3 Conditional Transparency and Disclosure Norms

Emerging research suggests that disclosure functions less as a simple compliance act and more as an accountability signal that shapes how audiences attribute responsibility, competence, and integrity. Disclosure decisions are therefore often described as contingent and strategic, balancing ideals of openness against anticipated judgement, increased scrutiny, or reputational cost across different academic relationships and outputs [9,10,26]. Empirical evaluations also suggest that current AI-text detectors are not sufficiently reliable for high-stakes enforcement, producing substantial error rates, including both false negatives and false positives that risk misattributing authorship [25,34]. This creates a practical mismatch between nuanced, audience-sensitive disclosure norms and blunt detector outputs, complicating attempts to formalize and enforce disclosure requirements [8]. Disclosure is a social act that positions integrity and competence before audiences who may judge AI use differently; however, we still know little about how such norms are negotiated in real time in peer dialog.

Identity theory is useful here because academics seek identity verification and confirmation from others that they match valued role expectations [29]. When institutional guidance is unclear or disciplinary norms are shifting, disclosure decisions are likely to become strategic. Evidence from higher-education settings shows that disclosure/non-disclosure can be shaped by anticipated judgement, scrutiny, or reputational cost, prompting calibrated explanations rather than full transparency [9,10,26]. This implies that "what should be disclosed" may be produced through social negotiation rather than merely derived from policy documents, making peer dialog a key site where local accountability expectations are articulated and stabilized. In practice, accountability in this context is not only an internal state but enacted through discourse, as academics perform responsibility through justification, verification claims, and selective disclosure [29].

### 2.4 Competence Trajectories and Changing Ethical Positions

While classical adoption models emphasize perceived usefulness and ease of use as drivers [12,31], perceived competence trajectories may also be associated with ethical positioning and emotional responses in professional contexts [2]. Empirically, a systematic review of teaching academics' attitudes and behaviours towards AI and GenAI reports generally positive views of efficiency alongside persistent concerns about integrity, accuracy, and skill development, and highlights that emotional dimensions remain underexplored [24]. These patterns are consistent with the expectation that, as familiarity and perceived competence increase, academics may move from initial uncertainty toward more calibrated, conditional use, potentially accompanied by shifts in affect from unease toward confidence [24]. Over time, increased experience may also enable more nuanced boundary rules (what is acceptable for which task, under which verification practices) and more refined disclosure reasoning (to whom, when, and why disclosure is appropriate), rather than simply increasing use in a linear way. Threat-avoidance perspectives suggest that perceived risks can override utilitarian benefits and sustain conservative adoption even when tools appear useful [24].

However, much existing evidence comes from surveys, policy analyses, or conceptual argumentation, leaving limited interaction-focused empirical work that shows how these judgements and norms are negotiated in peer dialog. This gap motivates qualitative, interaction-sensitive approaches that examine how academics publicly negotiate boundaries, enact moral accountability, and develop conditional transparency expectations as they make sense of generative AI in everyday academic practice.

# 3 Methodology

## 3.1 Study Design

This study used an online focus group design to examine how academics collectively make sense of generative AI use as an ethical, identity-relevant, and accountability-sensitive practice. Focus groups allow participants to respond to one another's accounts and construct shared (or divergent) norms, making them suitable for exploring how accountability is negotiated in peer dialog [17,23]. Across four groups, prompts encouraged reflection on task-based use (teaching, research, administration), ethical boundary-setting, audience-specific disclosure expectations, and changes over time as familiarity with AI develops.

## 3.2 Participants and Recruitment

Participants were 15 university academics recruited from a prior survey study [30]. Of 34 survey respondents who consented to follow-up contact, 16 confirmed interest and 15 participated across four online focus groups. Table 1 summarises participant attributes. The sample spanned multiple faculties including Education, Arts, Engineering, Health Sciences, and Social Wellbeing, with varied role profiles and self-reported familiarity with generative AI (range 1–5; $M = 3.5$).

**Table 1.** Overview of focus group participants ($N = 15$).

| Group | ID | Gender | Role | Faculty/School |
|---|---|---|---|---|
| FG1 | P1 | Female | Part-time Faculty | Economics, Management & Accountancy |
| | P2 | Non-binary | Senior Lecturer | Education |
| FG2 | P3 | Male | Senior Lecturer | Arts |
| | P4 | Female | Part-time Faculty | Education |
| | P5 | Male | Senior Lecturer | Education |
| | P6 | Male | Lecturer | Education |
| FG3 | P7 | Male | Part-time Faculty | Media and Knowledge Sciences |
| | P8 | Female | Part-time Faculty | Social Wellbeing |
| | P9 | Male | Full Professor | Education |
| | P10 | Female | Senior Lecturer | Education |
| FG4 | P11 | Male | Full Professor | Arts |
| | P12 | Female | Senior Lecturer | Engineering |
| | P13 | Female | Lecturer | Education |
| | P14 | Male | Lecturer | Education |
| | P15 | Female | Associate Professor | Health Sciences |

### 3.3 Data Collection Procedure

Four online focus groups were conducted via Zoom in January 2026. Each session lasted approximately 55–65 min and followed a semi-structured protocol consisting of six open-ended prompt areas covering: task-based AI use across teaching, research and administration; ethical boundary-setting; authorship and verification practices; audience-specific disclosure expectations; emotional positioning; and changes in practice over time. The protocol was developed from the survey instrument used in the prior study and reviewed by a colleague familiar with qualitative focus group methods prior to data collection. Participants were reminded that they could share only what they felt comfortable disclosing. Sessions were audio-recorded with participants' permission and transcribed using automated transcription, followed by manual checking to correct obvious errors and remove identifying details. Reflexive notes were recorded during and after sessions to capture emerging analytic observations and potential researcher assumptions.

### 3.4 Ethics and Data Protection

Ethical approval was obtained from the University of Malta Research Ethics Committee (Faculty of Education) prior to data collection (EDUC-2025-01422). Participants received an information sheet and provided informed consent. The consent process emphasized voluntary participation and the limits of confidentiality in group settings. To mitigate confidentiality risks, participants were asked at the start of each session to respect the privacy of other group members and to avoid sharing identifiable details about colleagues or cases. All transcripts were anonymized, and pseudonyms are used in reporting. Data were stored securely on encrypted institutional systems with access restricted to the researcher, consistent with GDPR principles of data minimization, purpose limitation, and restricted access.

### 3.5 Analytic Approach

Analysis followed reflexive thematic analysis, suited to identifying patterned meanings while recognizing the researcher's interpretive role [6,7]. Although the research questions were informed by the literature review strands, coding began inductively from the data, with themes subsequently interpreted in relation to the conceptual framework. The alignment between strands and themes thus reflects convergent patterns in the data rather than a fully deductive procedure. Analysis attended to task-contingent boundary-setting, accountability/identity work, disclosure norms, and competence trajectories. Following the phases of reflexive thematic analysis [6], transcripts were repeatedly read with reflexive note-taking, systematically coded and iteratively refined, and codes were clustered into themes that were reviewed against coded extracts and the full dataset before being defined and named. Rigor was supported through an audit trail

**Table 2.** Overview of themes and primary analytic building blocks (codes).

| **Theme** | What it captures | Primary contributing codes (from coding framework) |
|---|---|---|
| *"It depends": Boundary-setting is situational and task-contingent* | Acceptability calibrated by task type, stakes, visibility, and domain norms. | Task-based boundary-setting; Authorship/ownership; Responsibility/credibility. |
| *"Still my name on it": Moral accountability performances* | Justification/face-work through tool-framing, verification claims, minimization, and competence display. | Moral accountability performances; Identity protection; Responsibility/credibility; Moral emotions positioning. |
| *Conditional transparency: Audience-dependent disclosure norms* | Disclosure treated as contingent; shaped by anticipated judgement across audiences. | Disclosure expectations; Anticipated accountability; Identity protection; Responsibility/credibility. |
| *From apprehension to calibration: Competence trajectories* | Shifts from uncertainty to nuanced rules; competence linked to confidence/anxiety and disclosure reasoning. | Competence trajectories; Shifting ethics over time; Moral emotions positioning; Task-based boundary-setting. |

(protocol, memos, evolving codes and theme definitions) and attention to divergent cases; recognizing that focus group accounts can involve face-work, analysis treated qualifiers (e.g., "it depends") and moments of uncertainty or peer challenge as analytically informative [7].

# 4 Findings

Four focus groups (FG1–FG4) were analyzed using reflexive thematic analysis. Across the dataset, four themes captured how participants negotiated ethical boundaries, enacted moral accountability, articulated conditional transparency norms, and positioned themselves along shifting competence trajectories (Table 2). Theme 1 addresses RQ1 by examining how ethical boundaries are negotiated across academic tasks. Theme 2 addresses RQ2 by exploring how moral accountability and professional identity are performed. Theme 3 addresses RQ3 by analyzing transparency and disclosure norms across different audiences. Theme 4 addresses RQ4 by examining how competence trajectories may relate to ethical positioning and emotional responses over time.

## 4.1 Situational Boundary-Setting

Ethical acceptability was rarely treated as fixed. Participants described boundaries as contingent on domain, task type, and stakes, positioning some uses as acceptable support (e.g., language polishing) while treating others as riskier when closer to scholarly interpretation or high-stakes publication.

Participants explicitly framed this as contextual calibration: "It depends in what type of domain you are working on" (FG3, P8). This boundary work was not abstract; it often surfaced as practical distinctions between "helping" and "replacing," and between low-stakes communication and high-visibility academic outputs. Several participants linked acceptability to disciplinary norms and publishing expectations: "It also... depends on the field, and also the type of publication..." (FG4, P12). In teaching contexts, boundaries were often anchored in students' responsibility to demonstrate understanding, with AI positioned as permissible only when paired with sense-making and accountability: "what I would not find legitimate... [is when] students [don't] actually make sense of what kind of code the whatever AI platform they're using generates" (FG4, P13). This boundary logic extended to a concern about consistency between academics' own AI use and the rules they set for students. One participant made the tension explicit: "it's not okay for me as a lecturer to prepare my exam paper using ChatGPT, but then to say to students that ChatGPT is absolutely not okay. There's a question of fairness, of equity" (FG4, P11). Where teaching contexts made the stakes of AI use directly visible to students, boundary-setting was not only about task legitimacy but about modelling credible and consistent practice.

### 4.2 Moral Accountability as Performance

A second theme concerned how participants performed responsibility and protected professional identity while talking about their AI use. Across the focus groups, participants regularly emphasized human oversight and verification as moral anchors. Rather than claiming AI as an authorial contributor, they positioned it as subordinate to human judgement and accountability. A recurring accountability performance was "tool-framing" coupled with checking: "...it's a wonderful tool, as long as you check it" (FG1, P2). Participants also presented verification as a way of maintaining ownership and integrity: "It will always feel like my work... I check... extensively" (FG2, P4). Notably, emotional positioning was often folded into this accountability talk. Several participants explicitly rejected guilt by narrating AI as a normalized productivity tool, but this "guilt-free" stance was still typically paired with claims of responsibility and control: "...it's just another tool, and I use it guilt-free..." (FG2, P3). In teaching contexts, this responsibility framing shifted outward: "the only guilt I have is when we don't teach people how to use it properly" (FG2, P6).

Even when guilt was not foregrounded, the discourse showed repeated identity-protective moves, including minimizing reliance, emphasizing competence ("I can do this myself"), and portraying AI use as support rather than substitution. In this way, "moral accountability" appeared less as confession and more as self-presentational boundary maintenance, or a way of remaining credible while acknowledging the pragmatic appeal of AI.

### 4.3 Disclosure Norms and Anticipated Judgement

A third theme concerned how participants reasoned about transparency. Disclosure was not treated as a single universal expectation, instead, participants described it as shaped by who the audience is, what the relationship entails, and what sanctions or scrutiny might follow. The most explicit disclosure reasoning often appeared in teaching contexts, where participants positioned transparency as part of modeling responsible practice and setting expectations for students: "...encourage them to use it, as long as they're transparent as to how they use it" (FG1, P1). Some participants described disclosure as structured and built into assessment processes: "I generally disclose the way I use AI when I give them their assignment... [allocating] 10% of the marks [to] the way they used it" (FG3, P8).

At the same time, transparency was frequently discussed as socially risky because it could trigger suspicion or credibility loss. This was expressed through a language of evaluation, mistrust, and social consequences: "... it has... created a bit of a system of mistrust..." (FG3, P10). Publishing and peer-review contexts were also invoked as high-accountability settings where the reputational stakes of undisclosed AI involvement were perceived to be particularly salient. One participant contrasted publication with grant or proposal writing, treating the former as tightly tied to personal authorship and credibility, while positioning the latter as more acceptable for efficiency-oriented support because the "core idea" remained human-authored: "If you're publishing a paper, you're saying it's in your name... When it comes to applying for grants... the core of the idea is always... it's always been me... AI is just being used to write the text..." (FG1, P2).

Theme 3 shows that disclosure norms were conditional, not absolute. Participants oriented to transparency as a moral signal, but also as a reputational act whose consequences vary across students, colleagues, institutions, and publication contexts.

### 4.4 Competence Trajectories and Shifting Boundaries

A final theme captured how competence and learning trajectories appeared to be associated with both ethical boundary setting and emotional comfort. Participants often described movement from early uncertainty toward more confident, selective use as their skills improved. For some, increased competence prompted concrete changes to teaching practice: "all the stuff I had in my assessment, I removed, I changed totally, because [AI] can do an IPA transcription with its eyes closed... if [students] can't do it, they are not going to be able to check" (FG4, P12). Participants described training and experience as associated with shifts in how they viewed AI from "unknown risk" to something manageable and strategically useful: "...I've done the training... I'm much less apprehensive... now it's more positive" (FG4, P11). As competence increased, some participants described AI as empowering and supporting higher confidence, productivity, or even intellectual exploration (e.g., using AI as a critical interlocutor rather than a content generator): "... it is boosting my confidence... I'm using it as a thinking partner..." (FG2, P3). This confidence shift sometimes came with a narrative of crossing a threshold, becoming able to do tasks previously experienced as inaccessible or inefficient: "There's a glass ceiling, which now I've broken" (FG4, P15).

Importantly, higher competence was not simply associated with greater use; it was often accompanied by more nuanced ethical rules. As participants became more experienced, they articulated more refined boundaries (what is acceptable for which task), stronger verification practices, and more selective disclosure reasoning. Conversely, lower perceived competence was associated with more conservative use and heightened concern. In this way, based on participants' retrospective accounts, competence trajectories appeared to be tightly intertwined with both ethical calibration and emotional positioning over time.

## 5 Discussion

This study examined how academics negotiate ethical boundaries and disclosure expectations around generative AI in peer dialog, and how competence trajectories relate to ethical and emotional positioning. Findings show that boundary-setting is predominantly situational, calibrated by task type, stakes and visibility, especially where authorship, responsibility, and credibility are salient. "Responsible use" was enacted interactionally through tool-framing and verification claims. Disclosure emerged as conditional transparency: audience-dependent and socially consequential. Increased familiarity was associated with more nuanced ethical rules, while lower perceived competence aligned with cautious use. The discussion considers implications for guidance and professional learning.

### 5.1 Situational Boundary-Work

The finding that ethical boundaries were predominantly situational aligns with emerging accounts that generative AI intensifies uncertainty about what counts as legitimate academic labour [9,10,24]. Participants "it depends" logic resembles professional boundary-work, where acceptability is justified through context-specific distinctions that invoke valued norms and maintain credibility [29]. This fits broader accounts that AI in higher education forces more explicit articulation of tacit distinctions between 'surface' and 'substantive' assistance [4,8].

### 5.2 Accountability as Performance

A second contribution is demonstrating that 'responsible use' is enacted as an interactional performance [29], as much as it is articulated as a principle. Participants frequently used tool-framing ("it's a tool") alongside verification and oversight claims ("I check") to preserve a sense of human authorship and accountability. This supports the argument that generative AI challenges not only technical workflows but the normative foundations by which academic outputs are judged as trustworthy and attributable [4,19,21]. Where scholarly writing is bound up with competence, autonomy and intellectual independence, emphasizing oversight can function as a credibility-preserving narrative that keeps responsibility anchored in the human academic [1,29].

These patterns align with identity-based accounts, suggesting that academics seek social confirmation of competence, making peer settings salient for how practices are justified [29]. Verification talk and minimization of reliance resist identity threat while acknowledging tool use [32].

### 5.3 Conditional Transparency

The findings on disclosure reinforce the view that transparency is increasingly treated as an accountability signal, but disclosure remains unevenly specified and socially consequential [10,11]. Participants' audience-dependent reasoning suggests that disclosure is not merely a procedural add-on but a reputational act that can alter how competence, integrity, and responsibility are attributed. This echoes recent work arguing that higher education responses to generative AI are increasingly organised around trustworthiness and credibility, and questions of legitimacy and accountability [4,19]. Notably, similar patterns of conditional, audience-sensitive reasoning have been observed among students navigating uncertain institutional guidance on AI use in assignments, suggesting that the normative ambiguity academics experience mirrors that of the learners they teach [3]. It also resonates with concerns that disclosure can trigger scrutiny, incentivizing calibrated disclosure even when transparency is endorsed in principle [10].

The 'conditional transparency' pattern observed here can be interpreted through identity verification where academics may manage self-presentation in ways that preserve value identity claims, particularly under normative uncertainty [29]. This also helps clarify why norms were more straightforward in some teaching contexts (where transparency could be framed as modeling responsible practice) and more fraught in research and publication contexts (where reputational consequences and perceived sanctions may be higher). The key implication is that disclosure expectations are likely to stabilize not only through policy statements, but through local social negotiation, precisely the kind of interactional process captured in focus group dialog.

### 5.4 Competence Trajectories and Shifting Ethical Calibration

The fourth theme suggests that perceived competence is associated with ethical positioning and emotional comfort, aligning with adoption research recognizing that professional technology use involves social and emotional dynamics [2,12,31]. The shift from apprehension toward calibration suggests experience may be associated with more nuanced rules rather than simply increasing use.

Overall, these results suggest that competence development is not merely a training issue but a normative one. As participants described learning what tools can and cannot do, they reported greater confidence in ethical heuristics and more confident disclosure stances. These heuristics included rules such as: verify factual claims, only use AI for completable tasks, disclose substantial contributions and avoid AI for high-stakes assessment.

### 5.5 Implications for Policy and Practice

Findings suggest three implications for supporting responsible generative AI use in higher education. First, guidance should be task- and audience-sensitive, helping academics calibrate acceptable use by stakes, visibility, and error responsibility, with clear verification expectations. Second, transparency should be treated as a social accountability practice. Institutions and publishers can reduce uncertainty by clarifying disclosure requirements based on contribution type (interpretation/argumentation vs. formatting), stakes (publications vs. low-stakes communication), and audience (student-facing vs. internal use). Finally, professional learning should address verification practices, documentation, and credible disclosure strategies, especially for less confident users.

### 5.6 Limitations and Future Research

This study has several limitations. Most significantly, the focus group format creates conditions for strategic self-presentation. Participants may have emphasized responsible practices or downplayed reliance when speaking before peers and a researcher, and may have understated morally sensitive experiences. Because the data are cross-sectional and retrospective, causal claims cannot be made and competence trajectories are interpreted as perceived associations, not effects. While this performative dynamic is both a limitation and a design feature, revealing how accountability is enacted under peer scrutiny, it cannot confirm whether performances reflect everyday practice. Triangulation with observational methods or confidential individual interviews would strengthen transferability claims. The sample is also small and drawn from a single institutional context in Malta, so the findings are not intended to be statistically generalizable but to offer analytic insight into how accountability is negotiated in practice. The Maltese higher education context may have specific cultural, institutional, or regulatory features that shape these findings, and caution is warranted in assuming patterns transfer directly to other national or institutional contexts.

## 6 Conclusion

Generative AI is reshaping academic work not only by enabling new forms of assistance but by destabilizing how legitimacy, responsibility, and credibility are negotiated. Drawing on focus groups with 15 academics at a Maltese university, this study suggests that academics in this context calibrate ethical boundaries by task and stakes, perform moral accountability through verification and tool-framing, and develop conditional transparency norms shaped by audience and anticipated judgement. Competence trajectories appear to be associated with shifts in both ethical calibration and emotional comfort over time. Ultimately, findings from this study suggest that effective support for responsible generative AI use should treat boundary setting and disclosure as socially negotiated practices and provide context-sensitive guidance that matches the realities of academic work.

## References


1. Austin, A.E.: Preparing the next generation of faculty: graduate school as socialization to the academic career. J. High. Educ. **73**(1), 94–122 (2002)
2. Bagozzi, R.P.: The legacy of the technology acceptance model and a proposal for a paradigm shift. J. Assoc. Inf. Syst. **8**(4), 3 (2007)
3. Bearman, M., et al.: Time, emotions and moral judgements: how university students position genai within their study. High. Educ. Res. Dev. 1–15 (2025)
4. Bearman, M., Ryan, J., Ajjawi, R.: Discourses of artificial intelligence in higher education: a critical literature review. High. Educ. **86**(2), 369–385 (2023)
5. Beijaard, D., Meijer, P.C., Verloop, N.: Reconsidering research on teachers' professional identity. Teach. Teach. Educ. **20**(2), 107–128 (2004)
6. Braun, V., Clarke, V.: Using thematic analysis in psychology. Qual. Res. Psychol. **3**(2), 77–101 (2006)
7. Braun, V., Clarke, V.: Reflecting on reflexive thematic analysis. Qual. Res. Sport Exercise Health **11**(4), 589–597 (2019)
8. Chemaya, N., Martin, D.: Perceptions and detection of ai use in manuscript preparation for academic journals. PLoS ONE **19**(7), e0304807 (2024)
9. Chiu, T.K.: The impact of generative ai (genai) on practices, policies and research direction in education: a case of chatgpt and midjourney. Interact. Learn. Environ. **32**(10), 6187–6203 (2024)
10. Cotton, D.R., Cotton, P.A., Shipway, J.R.: Chatting and cheating: ensuring academic integrity in the era of chatgpt. Innov. Educ. Teach. Int. **61**(2), 228–239 (2024)
11. Dabis, A., Csáki, C.: AI and ethics: investigating the first policy responses of higher education institutions to the challenge of generative AI. Human. Soc. Sci. Commun. **11**(1), 1–13 (2024)
12. Davis, F.D.: Perceived usefulness, perceived ease of use, and user acceptance of information technology. MIS Q. 319–340 (1989)
13. Gee, J.P.: Identity as an analytic lens for research in education. Rev. Res. Educ. **25**, 99–125 (2000). http://www.jstor.org/stable/1167322
14. Gieryn, T.F.: Cultural Boundaries of Science: Credibility on the Line. University of Chicago Press (1999)
15. Hutson, J.: Rethinking plagiarism in the era of generative AI. J. Intell. Commun. **4**(1) (2024)
16. Kaşarcı, İ, Demircan, Z.A., Ercan, G.Ç., İnci, T.: Managing artificial intelligence ethics in higher education: a systematic framework for issues and policy recommendations. Int. J. Curr. Educ. Stud. **4**(2), 112–137 (2025)
17. Kitzinger, J.: Qualitative research: introducing focus groups. BMJ **311**(7000), 299–302 (1995)
18. Lin, Z.: Supercharging academic writing with generative AI: framework, techniques, and caveats. arXiv preprint arXiv:2310.17143 (2023)

19. Lodge, J.M., Thompson, K., Corrin, L.: Mapping out a research agenda for generative artificial intelligence in tertiary education. Australas. J. Educ. Technol. **39**(1), 1–8 (2023)
20. McGrath, C., Pargman, T.C., Juth, N., Palmgren, P.J.: University teachers' perceptions of responsibility and artificial intelligence in higher education-an experimental philosophical study. Comput. Educ. Artif. Intell. **4**, 100139 (2023)
21. Meyer, J.G., et al.: Chatgpt and large language models in academia: opportunities and challenges. BioData Mining **16**(1), 20 (2023)
22. Moorhouse, B.L., Yeo, M.A., Wan, Y.: Generative AI tools and assessment: guidelines of the world's top-ranking universities. Comput. Educ. Open **5**, 100151 (2023)
23. Morgan, D.L.: Focus Groups as Qualitative Research, vol. 16. Sage (1997)
24. Nikolic, S., et al.: A systematic literature review of attitudes, intentions and behaviours of teaching academics pertaining to ai and generative AI (genai) in higher education: an analysis of genai adoption using the utaut framework. Austral. J. Educ. Technol. (2024)
25. Perkins, M., Roe, J., Postma, D., McGaughran, J., Hickerson, D.: Game of tones: faculty detection of gpt-4 generated content in university assessments. arXiv preprint arXiv:2305.18081 (2023)
26. Qu, Y., Loo, H.E., Wang, J.: Generative artificial intelligence in higher education: emotional tensions and ethical declaration. Brit. J. Educ. Technol. (2025)
27. Ruediger, D., McCracken, C., Skinner, M.: Adoption of generative AI by academic biomedical researchers. JSTOR (2024)
28. Shata, A., Hartley, K.: Artificial intelligence and communication technologies in academia: faculty perceptions and the adoption of generative ai. Int. J. Educ. Technol. High. Educ. **22**(1), 14 (2025)
29. Stets, J.E., Burke, P.J.: Identity theory and social identity theory. Social Psychol. Q. 224–237 (2000)
30. Vassallo, D.: The ai guilt complex: moral emotions and ethical dilemmas in academic technology adoption. J. Acad. Ethics **24**(1), 53 (2026)
31. Venkatesh, V., Morris, M.G., Davis, G.B., Davis, F.D.: User acceptance of information technology: toward a unified view. MIS Q. 425–478 (2003)
32. Watermeyer, R., Lanclos, D., Phipps, L., Shapiro, H., Guizzo, D., Knight, C.: Academics' weak (ening) resistance to generative AI: the cause and cost of prestige? Postdigital Sci. Educ. **7**(4), 1171–1191 (2025)
33. Watermeyer, R., Phipps, L., Lanclos, D., Knight, C.: Generative ai and the automating of academia. Postdigital Sci. Educ. **6**(2), 446–466 (2024)
34. Weber-Wulff, D., et al.: Testing of detection tools for AI-generated text. Int. J. Educ. Integr. **19**(1), 1–39 (2023)

# Mapping AI Literacy: How Do DigComp 3.0 and OECD/EC AILit Inform K–12 Curriculum Integration Decisions?

Rubing Deng(✉), Hou Yee Tsi, Jiahui Zheng, and Sze Wai Mok

The University of Hong Kong, Hong Kong, Hong Kong
{angeldrb,louisa94,jiahuiz,Mokcindy}@connect.hku.hk

**Abstract.** As generative AI becomes embedded in students' learning and everyday practices, K–12 education faces a practical challenge: how to integrate AI literacy (AIL) into existing digital literacy (DL) provision while maintaining coherent progression and assessable learning outcomes. Hong Kong provides a timely policy context for this problem, with recent initiatives such as the 2023 AI curriculum module and the planned 2026 Digital Education Blueprint. To support curriculum decision-making under realistic constraints, this study conducts a comparative document analysis of two policy-level competence frameworks: Dig Comp 3.0 and the OECD/European Commission (OECD/EC) AI Literacy (AILit) framework. Using knowledge–skills–attitudes (KSA) as a shared analytic lens, this study developed a theme-based crosswalk to identify overlaps and gaps in learning requirements and derive an integration pathway. The crosswalk yielded 29 themes in total: 11 overlapping, 7 AILit unique, and 11 Dig Comp unique. Overlap was most extensive in the skills dimension, while the most consequential framework-specific gaps concerned knowledge. Most overlapping themes in Dig Comp 3.0 were also annotated as AI-implicit, indicating substantial AI-relevant capacity already embedded in DL-oriented competence expectations but not made explicit for curriculum work. On this basis, a three-layer integration pathway was proposed as an initial framework-derived heuristic, distinguishing where reinforcement within existing provision may be sufficient and where AI-specific learning goals require dedicated curricular design.

**Keywords:** AI literacy (AIL) · Digital literacy (DL) · Dig Comp 3.0 · OECD/EC AILit · K-12 curriculum integration · Comparative document analysis · Crosswalk mapping

## 1 Introduction

Generative AI and other AI systems are becoming increasingly visible in students' learning and everyday practices, raising new literacy demands in K–12 education. Under these conditions, students need more than operational familiarity with AI-enabled tools: they must understand basic mechanisms and limitations and be able to evaluate the quality, bias, and risks of AI-generated information [1–3]. A practical challenge for


E. G. Blanchard et al. (eds.), AIED 2026, LNCS 16586, pp. 147–162, 2027.
https://doi.org/10.1007/978-3-032-29773-0_11

schools, therefore, is how to integrate AIL into curricula while sustaining progression, often by embedding new expectations within existing DL and digital education structures [4–6].

Hong Kong offers a timely context for this integration problem. DL-related capabilities have long been developed through established ICT/IT curricula and school practices, supported by stable curriculum and assessment arrangements [7, 8]. In 2023, the Hong Kong Education Bureau introduced the Module on Artificial Intelligence for Junior Secondary Level, with recommended learning time and core content areas [9]. Policy momentum has continued: a K–12 Digital Education Blueprint is planned in 2026, alongside system-level initiatives highlighting an "AI literacy learning framework," curriculum alignment, and teacher professional development [10]. Taken together, these initiatives shift attention from whether AI education should occur to how AIL can be embedded in existing DL provision and developed into coherent progression [9, 10].

At the school level, integration is shaped by a tension between cross-curricular expectations and curricular hosting capacity. AIL is often framed as a cross-disciplinary priority [11, 12], yet the most stable entry point remains ICT/IT structures [7, 9]. Schools therefore need a viable "hosting structure" to carry AI-related learning over time [11]. Within this structure, integration must be feasible under limited curriculum time and sequencing constraints [9], generate assessable evidence of learning amid concerns about academic integrity and overreliance [12, 13], and be supported by teacher capacity and resourcing, since AI education involves judgement, responsibility, and ethical reasoning as well as application use [10]. Together, these conditions make AIL integration a more demanding curriculum problem.

Such decision support typically relies on reference frameworks for curriculum mapping, instructional design, and assessment alignment. In Hong Kong, Dig Comp has been used as a shared language for measuring and analysing DL-related outcomes [14, 15]. However, Dig Comp 3.0 mainly increases the visibility of AI at the framework level through AI-explicit and AI-implicit annotations. By itself, it does not provide curriculum-level decision rules for identifying which AI literacy requirements are already substantively covered within existing DL-oriented competence expectations and which require explicit curricular redesign [16]. By contrast, the OECD/EC AILit framework is more AI-specific and school-oriented, and organises learning goals through a knowledge, skills, and attitudes (KSA) structure [17]. Although Dig Comp 3.0 reports mapping work with AILit [16], publicly available information remains insufficient to identify overlaps, emphases, and gaps at the level of KSA themes, or to translate such comparisons into curriculum decision support. To address this gap, this study conducts a KSA-focused crosswalk between Dig Comp 3.0 and OECD/EC AILit and derives an integration pathway for curriculum decision-making under realistic constraints. Accordingly, this study is guided by two research questions:

RQ1: What overlaps and gaps exist between Dig Comp 3.0 and OECD/EC AILit at the level of KSA themes?
RQ2: How can crosswalk findings be translated into an integration pathway that supports curriculum decision-making for K–12 curriculum integration in Hong Kong?

# 2 Related Work

## 2.1 The Parallel Development of K–12 Digital Competence (DC) /DL and AIL

DL and DC have both become important in K–12 digital education [16, 18]. International frameworks consistently emphasise learners' abilities to access and evaluate information, communicate and collaborate, create digital content, and participate safely and responsibly in digital society [18, 19]. These terms, however, do not operate at the same analytical level.

In this paper, digital literacy (DL) is understood in the broader UNESCO sense as the ability to access, manage, understand, integrate, communicate, evaluate, and create information safely and appropriately through digital technologies [18]. DC, by contrast, is treated as a competence-based articulation of what learners should know, do, and value in digital environments, as formalised in Dig Comp 3.0 through itemised competence expectations organised across knowledge, skills, and attitudes [16, 25]. This distinction matters because "literacy" and "competence" are often used interchangeably, which can blur curricular intentions and weaken assessment alignment [5, 6, 24].

Accordingly, DL is treated here as a curriculum-facing construct, whereas DC is operationalised through descriptor-level competence statements that can be coded, compared, and mapped across frameworks. Dig Comp 3.0 is therefore used not as a definition of DL, but as an operational competence framework for analysing how DL-oriented expectations are structured and where AI-related requirements are visible, implicit, or absent [16].

Generative AI has brought AIL to the forefront of this agenda [20]. Although definitions vary, recent work points to recurring requirements: understanding AI concepts and limitations, using AI tools purposefully, evaluating the quality and potential biases of AI outputs, and engaging with ethical and societal implications [1, 20, 21]. These expectations are developmental, shifting from experience-based engagement in early grades to critical evaluation, responsible judgement, and more complex creation or design tasks in upper grades [22, 23]. AIL therefore overlaps partly with DL while placing more explicit emphasis on AI-specific requirements and risks [4].

## 2.2 DigComp 3.0 as an Itemised Baseline for DL Alignment

In this study, Dig Comp 3.0 is treated as an itemised DC baseline for DL-oriented curriculum mapping and assessment alignment, specifying intended learning outcomes that can anchor instructional design and evaluation [16, 19]. This orientation is particularly relevant in contexts where DL is embedded within established subject structures and where alignment across grades requires evidence-based coherence [5, 6].

Dig Comp 3.0 strengthens this itemisation logic by offering 523 intended learning outcomes organised through a KSA lens [16]. This level of granularity makes it possible to examine not only whether AI-related elements appear in a DL baseline, but also how they are distributed across learning requirements and how explicitly they are expressed. In Hong Kong, Dig Comp's value is not merely conceptual. It has been used as a shared language for measuring and analysing DL-related outcomes, creating a bridge between international framing and local evidence practices [14, 15]. This prior use provides a practical justification for treating Dig Comp 3.0 as a baseline in curriculum-facing analysis.

To address AI-related developments, Dig Comp 3.0 incorporates AIL through AI-explicit and AI-implicit annotations, enabling AI relevance to be located and tracked within the broader DL baseline [16]. However, this annotation system mainly increases framework-level visibility. It offers limited guidance on sequencing, integration workload, or evidence-chain design for implementation [6, 16]. As a result, Dig Comp 3.0 can indicate where AI relevance may exist, but it cannot directly answer a more curriculum-critical question: which AIL requirements are already substantively covered through existing DL-oriented competence expectations, and which require dedicated additions or redesign. This gap motivates the need for a focused crosswalk with an AI-specific framework.

### 2.3 OECD/EC AILit as an AI-Specific Framework for K–12 AIL

AIL frameworks developed for K–12 contexts typically foreground AI-specific understanding, evaluation, and ethical judgement as distinctive learning demands [1, 20]. In curriculum terms, this implies that a usable AIL framework must not only clarify AI-specific content but also articulate expectations that can be explicitly taught and assessed in relation to curricular goals [2]. The OECD/EC AILit framework represents a policy-oriented attempt to structure this agenda as itemised learning requirements. It organises learner engagement into four domains: Engaging, Creating, Managing, and Designing. It also adopts a KSA structure and provides grade-level scenario examples intended to strengthen classroom interpretability [17].

A further reason to examine AILit alongside Dig Comp 3.0 lies in their reported official linkage. Dig Comp 3.0 describes a mapping process with the AILit draft and suggests that AILit competence statements are adequately covered within Dig Comp [16]. However, the publicly available documentation provides limited item-level evidence showing how such coverage is established [16]. An independent and reproducible comparison is therefore needed to clarify overlaps, divergences, and gaps that affect curriculum design decisions.

At the same time, the comparison should be read with appropriate caution. The current AI literacy landscape includes multiple emerging frameworks, many of which remain in draft or pre-validation form. OECD/EC AILit is used here as a focused comparator rather than as a definitive statement of AI literacy in general. This is because it is school-oriented and makes AI-specific learning requirements explicit through itemised competences, a KSA structure, and grade-level scenarios [17].

### 2.4 Conceptual Framing and Analytic Lens for Cross-Framework Comparison

This study distinguishes framework-level alignment from curriculum-level integration. While annotations and mappings can support relevance judgements, curriculum integration requires decisions about how learning requirements are organised, how tasks are designed to make intended learning visible, and how assessment evidence can be generated and sustained over time [5, 6]. The present analysis therefore focuses not on whether AI is mentioned in a framework, but on how itemised learning requirements overlap or diverge in ways that imply different integration demands.

KSA is adopted as the shared analytic lens to support comparability. Both Dig Comp 3.0 and AILit explicitly structure competence requirements through KSA [16, 17], and this structure aligns with a policy-level consensus that competence involves the mobilisation of knowledge, skills, and attitudes [25]. Using KSA as the common dimension allows the analysis to move beyond broad relevance claims towards a more decision-relevant account of where overlaps and gaps occur across learning requirements. This, in turn, provides a clearer evidential basis for interpreting what embedded AIL integration would entail in curriculum terms.

The key curriculum question, then, is not simply whether AI-related competences appear in a framework, but how such alignment can be translated into sequencing, task design, and assessable evidence. A KSA-focused crosswalk is useful here because it permits comparison at the level of itemised learning requirements rather than broad conceptual claims.

## 3 Method

### 3.1 Research Design

This study adopts comparative document analysis to conduct a systematic side-by-side examination of two policy-level competence frameworks. Document analysis offers an efficient and non-intrusive approach for extracting comparable evidence from policy texts [26]. This design is well-suited to examining (a) how learning requirements are structurally organised and (b) what substantive expectations are specified at the item level. The analysis identifies convergences and divergences between the two frameworks and translates these relationships into decision-relevant implications for K–12 curriculum integration.

### 3.2 Selection Criteria and Data Sources

Dig Comp 3.0 [16] and OECD/EC AILit [17] were selected based on four criteria: authority and policy relevance as recent policy-level competence frameworks, applicability to K–12 education, structural comparability via KSA, and complementarity in scope, with Dig Comp providing a DL-related baseline and AILit offering AIL-specific depth. These criteria support a comparison that is analytically tractable while aligned with curriculum-facing concerns.

The primary data sources were the full texts of the two frameworks. For Dig Comp 3.0, the corpus comprised learning outcome descriptors, proficiency-level learning outcome descriptors, and the associated AI-explicit/AI-implicit annotations used to indicate AI relevance [16]. For AILit, the corpus comprised the complete 2025 publication, including competences, component-level descriptors, and illustrative learning scenarios [17].

To ensure consistency and granularity, explicit units of analysis were defined. The primary unit was the learning outcome descriptor, representing the most specific and actionable expression of an expected competence. In DigComp 3.0, these descriptors operationalise DL-oriented curriculum expectations through itemised digital competence statements and therefore serve as the most curriculum-actionable units for mapping and comparison. In AILit, the primary units were the descriptive statements specified under each competence component. Secondary units provided organisational structure for interpretation, including Dig Comp competence areas and statements, and AILit overarching competences and scenarios. Operationally, this means that DL is addressed at the level of curriculum-facing provision, whereas DC is examined through descriptor-level competence units that serve as the primary objects of coding and comparison in the crosswalk.

### 3.3 Analytic Procedure

The analytic procedure converted framework text into empirical findings for curriculum integration. As summarised in Fig. 1, it consisted of three stages: (a) constructing a coding framework, (b) developing a theme-level crosswalk, and (c) deriving a curriculum-oriented decision logic.

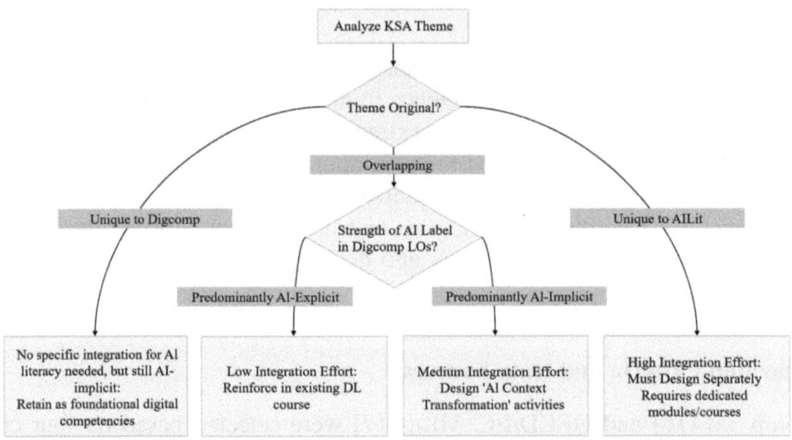


**Fig. 1.** Curriculum integration decision process based on framework comparison.

**Coding Framework** A two-stage coding procedure was implemented. First, all learning outcome descriptors were coded deductively using KSA as a shared meta-structure [16, 17]. Second, inductive thematic coding was applied within the KSA-coded units through iterative comparison and refinement. Each descriptor received a dual label, consisting of a K/S/A code and a theme code. Through this process, descriptor-level analysis was consolidated into a final thematic codebook, which served as the shared thematic vocabulary for cross-framework comparison. The final thematic codebook is presented in Table 1. In this table, theme codes combine the analytic dimension (K/S/A), crosswalk status (OV/AI/DG), and a mnemonic abbreviation of the theme label.

**Crosswalk Procedure and Matching Rules** Using the codebook, each theme was assessed to determine whether its semantic core and competency focus were represented in both frameworks or articulated in only one [26]. Themes were then classified into three mutually exclusive categories: AILit unique, overlapping, and DigComp unique. Three researchers conducted the matching independently and resolved disagreements through discussion until consensus was reached. Table 2 provides illustrative descriptor-level examples showing how selected knowledge descriptors informed overlap and gap judgements, including both direct overlap and borderline-related but non-overlapping cases.

**Deriving the Integration Pathway** Based on the crosswalk, a rule-based decision logic was developed (see Fig. 1). For each theme, the decision chain draws on crosswalk status and, where applicable, Dig Comp's AI-explicit and AI-implicit annotations to differentiate the type of curriculum action implied by the evidence: whether requirements are already stated explicitly, require contextual specification to make judgement assessable, or require dedicated design. Each assignment was documented with brief rationale notes.

**Table 1.** Consolidated thematic codebook and operational definitions

| KSA | Theme code | Theme label | Operational definition |
|---|---|---|---|
| K | K-OV-CAPLIM | AI Capabilities and Limitations | Recognize AI capabilities, limitations, risks, and wider impacts. |
| K | K-OV-BIAS | AI Reflects Human Choices and Perspectives (Bias) | Recognize bias in AI systems and outputs. |
| K | K-OV-SOCIETY | AI Role in Society / Ethics, Impact & Governance | Understand AI's societal, ethical, legal, and governance implications. |
| K | K-AI-NATURE | The Nature of AI | Explain AI's algorithmic, statistical, and probabilistic foundations. |
| K | K-AI-CONSTRUCT | AI Reflects Human Choices and Perspectives (Core Mechanism) | Explain how human decisions shape AI systems and outputs. |
| K | K-AI-WORK | AI Reshapes Work and Human Roles | Understand how AI reshapes work, roles, and responsibility. |
| K | K-DG-DATA | Foundational Data Concepts | Know foundational data concepts in digital environments. |

(*continued*)

**Table 1.** (*continued*)

| KSA | Theme code | Theme label | Operational definition |
|---|---|---|---|
| K | K-DG-COMM | Digital Communication Modalities | Know forms of digital communication across contexts. |
| S | S-OV-CT | Critical Thinking | Evaluate AI content for accuracy, fairness, and bias. |
| S | S-OV-PS | Problem Solving | Determine when and how to use AI appropriately. |
| S | S-OV-COMPTH | Computational Thinking | Decompose problems and instruct AI systems effectively. |
| S | S-OV-COMM | Communication | Explain AI use transparently and responsibly. |
| S | S-OV-COLLAB | Collaboration | Work effectively with humans and AI in shared tasks. |
| S | S-AI-SSA | Self and Social Awareness | Recognize AI's effects on self, others, and society. |
| S | S-AI-CREAT | Creativity | Create with AI while considering originality, attribution, and responsibility. |
| S | S-DG-INFOMGMT | Information Management | Manage, organise, retrieve, and transfer digital information. |
| S | S-DG-CONTENT | Digital Content Integration & Elaboration | Integrate, adapt, and elaborate digital content for varied purposes. |
| S | S-DG-CIVIC | Digital Citizenship Engagement | Participate in civic and community life through digital tools. |
| S | S-DG-MENTOR | Assisting & Mentoring Others | Support others in developing digital competences responsibly. |
| S | S-DG-TROUBLE | Technical Troubleshooting | Identify and resolve technical problems through diagnosis and iteration. |
| A | A-OV-RESP | Responsible | Demonstrate ethical and responsible engagement with AI and digital technologies. |
| A | A-OV-CURIOUS | Curious | Show openness to learning about AI and emerging technologies. |

(*continued*)

**Table 1.** (*continued*)

| KSA | Theme code | Theme label | Operational definition |
|---|---|---|---|
| A | A-OV-ADAPT | Adaptable | Demonstrate flexibility in evolving AI and digital environments. |
| A | A-AI-INNOV | Innovative | Show initiative in using AI to solve problems. |
| A | A-AI-EMPATH | Empathetic | Show awareness of AI's effects on people, communities, and environments. |
| A | A-DG-TRANSP | Transparent | Value openness about how content and system-assisted outputs are produced. |
| A | A-DG-PROACT | Proactive | Demonstrate vigilance and initiative in promoting responsible digital practice. |
| A | A-DG-INCL | Inclusive | Value inclusion and accessibility in digital environments and practices. |
| A | A-DG-ACCOUNT | Accountable | Demonstrate accountability in handling data, information, and technology-supported outputs. |

**Table 2.** Illustrative descriptor-level examples informing theme-level crosswalk judgement

| Evidence | Dual label | Judgement | Rationale |
|---|---|---|---|
| K2.5 + LO1.2.15 / 4.3.17 (AI bias) | K + AI Reflects Human Choices and Perspectives (Bias) | Overlapping | Shared core: System bias and non-neutral outputs. |
| K1.1–1.4 (AI mechanisms; probabilistic outputs) | K + the Nature of AI | AILit unique | AI-specific conceptual knowledge absent in Dig Comp. |
| LO1.3.24 / 1.3.25 (open/big data) | K + Foundational Data Concepts | Dig Comp unique (borderline-related) | General data literacy, not sufficiently AI-specific. |

**Note.** K codes refer to OECD/EC AILit and LO codes to Dig Comp 3.0

## 3.4 Trustworthiness

Several procedures were used to strengthen trustworthiness. Coding and matching involved multiple researchers, supported by regular consensus meetings. An audit trail documented codebook revisions, matching rationales, and decision inferences. Inter-coder agreement was assessed on a subset of the corpus before full-scale analysis, following established guidance for qualitative coding and reliability checks [27].

# 4 Results

## 4.1 Knowledge Themes

The knowledge dimension yielded three sets of themes (Fig. 2). Overlapping themes centred on AI's visible characteristics and societal implications, including capabilities and limitations, the potential to reflect and amplify bias, and related issues of ethics, copyright, and governance. AILit-unique themes, by contrast, captured knowledge needed to understand AI's internal logic and socio-technical foundations. These included the nature of AI itself, the human construction of AI systems through data and design, and AI-driven shifts in work patterns and human–machine collaboration. Dig Comp-unique themes were more general in orientation, focusing on background concepts that support digital activity, such as foundational data concepts and digital communication models.

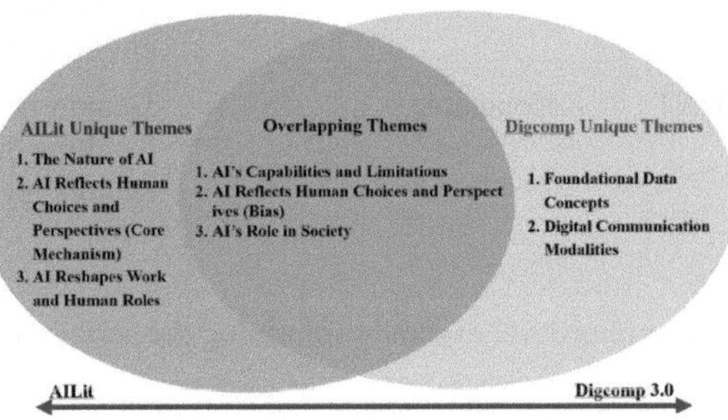


**Fig. 2.** Knowledge (K) theme comparison between Dig Comp 3.0 and OECD/EC AILit.

## 4.2 Skill Themes

The skills dimension also yielded three categories of themes (Fig. 3). Overlapping themes clustered around higher-order cognitive and social competences, including critical thinking, problem solving, computational thinking, communication, and collaboration. AILit-unique themes highlighted two additional areas: self and social awareness in interaction with AI, and human–AI creativity associated with co-creation. Dig Comp-unique themes, by contrast, emphasised a broader set of operational and supportive digital skills, including information management, digital content integration, civic participation, supporting others, and troubleshooting. Taken together, these themes point to a distinction between AI-oriented judgement and co-creation, on the one hand, and broader operational capacity in digital environments, on the other.

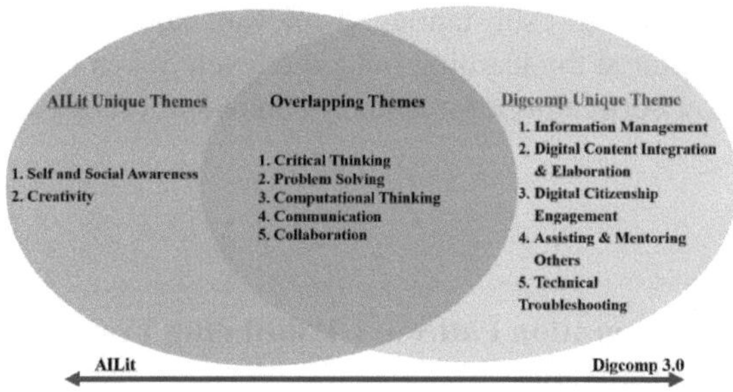


**Fig. 3.** Skill (S) theme comparison between Dig Comp 3.0 and OECD/EC AILit.

## 4.3 Attitude Themes

Attitudinal themes are summarised in Fig. 4. Overlapping themes included responsibility, curiosity, and adaptability. These indicate broad orientations that shape how learners engage with technology-rich environments. AILit-unique themes introduced two more distinctive dispositions: innovation, reflecting proactive use of AI to address challenges, and empathy, reflecting sensitivity to AI's differentiated social impacts. Dig Comp-unique themes foregrounded attitudes that support responsible participation across digital contexts, including transparency, proactivity, inclusiveness, and accountability in data and information management. Taken together, these themes suggest a value spectrum ranging from reflective judgement to active social participation.

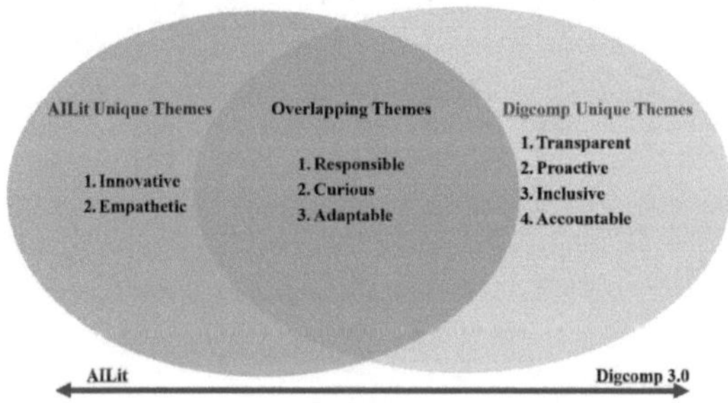


**Fig. 4.** Attitude (A) theme comparison between Dig Comp 3.0 and OECD/EC AILit.

## 4.4 Crosswalk Synthesis

As summarised in Table 1, the crosswalk yielded 29 themes across knowledge, skills, and attitudes: 11 overlapping, 7 AILit unique, and 11 Dig Comp unique. Two patterns stand out. First, overlap was most extensive in the skills dimension. Second, the most consequential framework-specific gaps concerned knowledge, particularly in relation to AI mechanisms, socio-technical construction, and changing human roles.

A further pattern concerns visibility. For most overlapping themes, the associated Dig Comp learning outcomes were predominantly AI-implicit. This suggests that the Dig

Comp baseline already contains substantial AI-relevant capacity, although that capacity is often not made explicit at the learning outcome level. Taken together, these patterns support the distinction between reinforcement, contextual redesign, and dedicated AI-specific design.

# 5 Discussion

## 5.1 A Three-Layer Integration Pathway: Translating Framework Comparison into Curriculum Decisions

Building on the crosswalk patterns reported in Sect. 4, the three-layer integration pathway is best understood as a framework-derived heuristic for curriculum decision support rather than a validated implementation model. It differentiates the level of curriculum effort implied when AIL is integrated into DL-oriented provision, ranging from reinforcement to contextual redesign and dedicated AI-specific addition [16]. The pathway reflects two empirical patterns in the crosswalk: shared themes are more concentrated in the skills dimension and therefore more likely to support reinforcement or contextual redesign, whereas the most consequential framework-specific gaps lie in knowledge and therefore more often require dedicated AI-specific curriculum design.

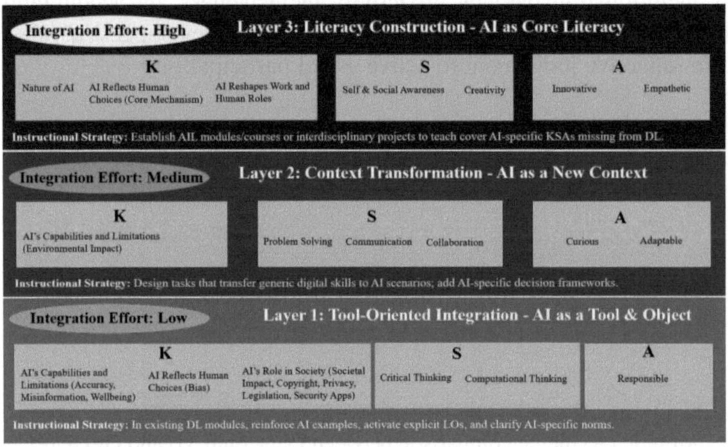


**Fig. 5.** Three-layer integration pathway for differentiated curriculum integration effort.

The key issue in competence-oriented curriculum implementation is often not whether a competence exists on paper, but how it is operationalised through sequencing, task design, and assessment evidence [5, 6]. AI-implicit labels may indicate potential relevance to AIL, but they do not clarify what additional pedagogical work is required to make that relevance instructionally visible and assessable. Figure 5, therefore, translates the crosswalk evidence into three levels of integration effort. Table 2 illustrates this logic at the descriptor level. Identifying bias in AI-generated information, for example, was classified as an overlapping knowledge theme, but in Dig Comp, the relevant learning outcomes were predominantly AI-implicit. For curriculum purposes, this places the theme in Layer 2. By contrast, themes such as *The Nature of AI* remain AILit unique and point more clearly towards Layer 3 [1, 2].

## 5.2 Layer 1 and Layer 2: Activating and Transforming Digital Literacy Foundations

A central implication of the crosswalk is that AIL is most feasibly advanced by building on established digital competences, although the curriculum work required varies across themes. This follows from two patterns in the results: overlap is most extensive in the skills dimension, and many AI-relevant expectations already appear in Dig Comp as AI-implicit rather than absent. In school contexts, this suggests that AIL can often be developed within existing DL provision rather than treated as a wholly separate curriculum strand [4].

Layer 1 captures cases where AI relevance is already explicit or can be surfaced with minimal disruption. Here, curriculum teams can reinforce existing learning targets by treating AI as an illustrative case or object of analysis. AI-generated outputs, for example, can be used when teaching information credibility, privacy, copyright, and digital safety.

Layer 2 addresses a more demanding challenge: competence is shared across frameworks, but it must be re-specified so that AI-related judgement becomes observable and assessable. This is consistent with OECD evidence that generative AI tools may improve task performance without necessarily producing corresponding learning gains [21]. In Layer 2, competences such as problem solving, critical evaluation, communication, and collaboration need to be reframed as situated performance in AI-mediated contexts. This includes selecting tools appropriately, evaluating outputs against task-specific criteria, documenting reasoning, and managing ethical trade-offs. Layer 2 therefore marks the pedagogical core of embedded integration.

## 5.3 Layer 3: Why AI-Specific Literacy Must be Built, Not Assumed

Layers 1 and 2 build on transferable foundations, but the crosswalk also identifies learning requirements that cannot be secured through reinforcement or contextual extension alone. AILit-unique themes cluster around AI's internal mechanisms, its socio-technical construction, and distinctive values and dispositions. This pattern is consistent with K–12 accounts of AIL that treat understanding AI concepts and limitations as a core requirement [2], and with the way AILit frames AI learning goals for school contexts [17].

The educational risk of omitting this layer is substantial. If integration focuses mainly on tool use and generic competence application, students may become capable AI users while remaining unable to explain system mechanisms, data dependencies, or the ways structural bias can be produced and amplified. Such "black box" use is insufficient for responsible participation, particularly when AI outputs shape what students read, write, and decide [3]. The AILit-unique attitudinal themes, especially innovation and empathy, further suggest that AIL also involves dispositions towards constructive use and towards careful consideration of differentiated social impacts [17]. These outcomes require sustained inquiry and explicit curriculum design rather than incremental lesson-level additions.

### 5.4 Implications for Curriculum Integration in Hong Kong: A Layered Implementation Strategy

Interpreted as a framework-derived implementation heuristic, the pathway in Fig. 5 supports curriculum decision-making in Hong Kong by clarifying how AIL expectations may be integrated into DL-oriented provision under different levels of instructional effort. This implication does not presume that local ICT or IT curricula have already adopted Dig Comp 3.0 as an explicit organising framework. Rather, the pathway is intended to inform curriculum review and alignment processes, whether Dig Comp-referenced or locally structured. It indicates where reinforcement, task redesign, or dedicated learning time is likely to be most needed [9, 10].

At the system level, the pathway supports staged curriculum updating and resourcing. Layer 1 provides a low-disruption baseline by integrating AI-visible learning points into existing DL modules and assessment routines. Layer 2 is central because it identifies where AI-implicit competences require contextual task redesign. This emphasis aligns with local concerns about academic integrity and overreliance, and it helps ensure that judgement and justification become observable and assessable [12, 21]. Layer 3 justifies dedicated attention to AI-specific concepts and socio-technical foundations that are unlikely to emerge through transfer alone [12].

At the school level, the pathway supports prioritisation under constraints of time, assessment, and teacher capacity. Schools may begin with Layer 1 adjustments, use Layer 2 tasks to make AI-mediated judgement assessable, and extend selectively towards Layer 3 where resources permit [11]. This points to four priorities: phased progression, teacher learning, targeted resourcing for the transition layer, and assessment practices that make AI-mediated judgement visible. In practice, these priorities are likely to be shaped by uneven teacher familiarity with AI, limited curriculum time, and the difficulty of generating assessable evidence for AI-mediated judgement within existing school routines.

## 6 Limitations and Future Work

This study has several limitations. First, it compares only two policy-level frameworks, so the findings should be read as contingent on the currently published version of OECD/EC AILit rather than as a final account of AI literacy framework alignment more generally. Second, the analysis is based on document evidence rather than classroom enactment. The proposed pathway should therefore be understood as a framework-derived implementation heuristic rather than a validated implementation model. A next step would be to examine it through curriculum expert review, teacher design tasks, and school-based implementation cases. Third, theme development and matching remain interpretive despite multi-coder procedures. Although the practical discussion is anchored in Hong Kong, the crosswalk may also offer a tentative reference for other curriculum systems facing similar integration questions.

## 7 Conclusion

This study examined how AIL can be embedded within DL provision through a KSA-focused crosswalk between Dig Comp 3.0 and OECD/EC AILit. Overlap was most extensive in the skills dimension, while the most consequential framework-specific gaps concerned knowledge. Many overlapping themes in Dig Comp 3.0 were also predominantly AI-implicit, indicating latent alignment that remains under-specified for curriculum work. On this basis, a three-layer integration pathway was proposed as an initial framework-derived heuristic for supporting AIL integration in Hong Kong. It may also offer a reference point for other curriculum systems seeking to embed AIL within existing DL-oriented provision under similar constraints.

**Acknowledgments.** This work developed from a group project in EDUR8600 at The University of Hong Kong (Semester 1, 2025–2026). We thank Prof. Nancy Law for her inspiration and guidance in shaping this paper, the course instructor, Prof. Jionghao Lin, for his teaching and feedback, and our peers for their helpful comments.

**Disclosure of Interests** The authors have no competing interests to declare that are relevant to the content of this article.

## References

1. Long, D., Magerko, B.: What is AI literacy? competencies and design considerations. In: Proceedings of the 2020 CHI Conference on Human Factors in Computing Systems, pp. 1–16 (2020)
2. Ng, D.T.K., Leung, J.K.L., Chu, S.K.W., Qiao, M.S.: Conceptualizing AI literacy: an exploratory review. Comput. Educ.: Artif. Intell. **2**, 1–11 (2021)
3. Almatrafi, O., Johri, A., Lee, H.: A systematic review of AI literacy conceptualization, constructs, and implementation and assessment efforts (2019–2023). Comput. Educ. Open. **6**, 1–18 (2024)
4. Ng, D.T.K., Leung, J.K.L., Su, M.J., Yim, I.H.Y., Qiao, M.S., Chu, S.: AI Literacy in K-16 Classrooms. Springer, Switzerland (2022)
5. Reichert, F., Zhang, D.J., Law, N.W.Y., Wong, G.K.W., de la Torre, J.: Exploring the structure of digital literacy competence assessed using authentic software applications. Educ. Technol. Res. Dev. **68**(6), 2991–3013 (2020)
6. Wong, G.K.-W., Reichert, F., Law, N.: Reorienting the assessment of digital literacy in the twenty-first century: a product-lifecycle and experience dependence perspective. Educ. Technol. Res. Dev. **71**(6), 2389–2412 (2023)
7. Curriculum Development Council: Hong Kong Examinations and Assessment Authority: Information and Communication Technology Curriculum and Assessment Guide (Secondary 4–6). Education Bureau, HKSAR Government, Hong Kong (2021)
8. Hong Kong Examinations and Assessment Authority: Hong Kong Diploma of Secondary Education Examination 2025: Information and Communication Technology—School-Based Assessment Teachers' Handbook (Updated Aug 2023). Hong Kong Examinations and Assessment Authority (2023)
9. Hong Kong Education Bureau: AI Curriculum Unit for Junior Secondary Schools. Education Bureau, The Government of the Hong Kong Special Administrative Region, Hong Kong (2023)

10. The Government of the Hong Kong Special Administrative Region: The Chief Executive's: Policy address: supplement 07—promote the integrated development of education, technology and talents (digital education blueprint and AI literacy measures). The Government of the Hong Kong Special Administrative Region, Hong Kong. **2025** (2025)
11. Chiu, T.K.F.: AI literacy and competency: definitions, frameworks, development and future research directions. Interact. Learn. Environ. **33**(5), 3225–3229 (2025)
12. Legislative Council: Latest progress of promoting digital education in schools. Paper. Panel on Education, Legislative Council of the Hong Kong Special Administrative Region (LC Paper No. CB (3)1050/2025(04)), Hong Kong (2025)
13. The Government of the Hong Kong Special Administrative Region: Application of artificial intelligence in primary and secondary education. Press release / Legislative Council written reply (2025)
14. Law, N., et al.: Hong Kong Students' Digital Citizenship Development 2019–2021: Findings from a Longitudinal Study. The University of Hong Kong, Hong Kong (2022)
15. Pan, Q., Reichert, F., Liang, Q., de la Torre, J., Law, N.: Measuring digital literacy across ages and over time: development and validation of a performance-based assessment. Educ. Inf. Technol. **30**(15), 22065–22100 (2025)
16. Cosgrove, J., Cachia, R.: Dig Comp 3.0: European Digital Competence Framework, 5th edn. Publications Office of the European Union, Luxembourg (2025)
17. Organisation for Economic Co-operation and Development, & European Commission Empowering learners for the age of AI: an AI literacy framework for primary and secondary education. OECD (2025)
18. UNESCO Institute for Statistics: A global Framework of Reference on Digital Literacy Skills for Indicator 4.4.2. UNESCO Institute for Statistics (2018)
19. Vuorikari, R., Kluzer, S., Punie, Y., et al.: Dig Comp 2.2: the Digital Competence Framework for Citizens—With New Examples of Knowledge, Skills and Attitudes. Publications Office of the European Union, Luxembourg (2022)
20. Yang, Y., Zhang, Y., Sun, D., He, W., Wei, Y.: Navigating the landscape of AI literacy education: insights from a decade of research (2014–2024). Humanit. Soc. Sci. Commun. **12**(1), 1–12 (2025)
21. OECD: OECD Digital Education Outlook 2026: Exploring Effective Uses of Generative AI in Education. OECD Publishing, Paris (2026)
22. Ng, D.T.K., Su, J., Leung, J.K.L., Chu, S.K.W.: Artificial intelligence (AI) literacy education in secondary schools: a review. Interact. Learn. Environ. **32**(10), 6204–6224 (2024)
23. Yim, I.H.Y., Su, J.: Artificial intelligence literacy education in primary schools: a review. Int. J. Technol. Des. Educ. **35**, 2175–2204 (2025)
24. Spante, M., Hashemi, S.S., Lundin, M., Algers, A.: Digital competence and digital literacy in higher education research: systematic review of concept use. Cogent Educ. **5**(1), 1–21 (2018)
25. Council of the European Union: Council recommendation of 22 may 2018 on key competences for lifelong learning (2018/C 189/01). Off. J. Eur. Union. **189**, 1–13 (2018)
26. Bowen, G.A.: Document analysis as a qualitative research method. Qual. Res. J. **9**(2), 27–40 (2009)
27. Miles, M.B., Huberman, A.M., Saldaña, J.: Qualitative Data Analysis: A Methods Sourcebook. SAGE, Thousand Oaks (2014)

# A Benchmark for Gender Bias in Large Language Model Feedback on Student Essays

Yishan Du[1(✉)], Conrad Borchers[2], and Mutlu Cukurova[1]

[1] UCL Knowledge Lab, Institute of Education, University College London, London, UK
{yishan.du.24,m.cukurova}@ucl.ac.uk

[2] Carnegie Mellon University, Pittsburgh, PA, USA
cborcher@cs.cmu.edu

**Abstract.** As teachers increasingly turn to generative AI in their educational practice, we need robust methods to benchmark large language models (LLMs) for pedagogical purposes. This article presents an embedding-based benchmarking framework to detect LLM bias in formative feedback. Using 600 authentic student essays from the AES 2.0 corpus, we constructed controlled counterfactuals along two dimensions: (i) implicit cues via lexicon-based swaps of gendered terms within essays, and (ii) explicit cues via gendered author background in the prompt. We investigated six representative LLMs (i.e. GPT-5 mini, GPT-4o mini, DeepSeek-R1, DeepSeek-R1-Qwen, Gemini 2.5 Pro, Llama-3-8B). We first quantified the response divergence with cosine and Euclidean distances over sentence embeddings, then assessed significance in differences via permutation tests, and, finally, visualised structure using dimensionality reduction. In all models, implicit manipulations reliably induced larger semantic shifts for male to female counterfactuals than for female to male. Only the OpenAI and Llama models showed sensitivity to explicit gender cues. These findings show persistent gender biases in LLM feedback to learners. Qualitative analyses further revealed consistent linguistic differences (e.g., more autonomy-supportive feedback under male cues vs. more controlling feedback under female cues). We conclude the paper with a discussion on the implications of these findings for fairness auditing of pedagogical LLMs and outline practical guidance for prompt design and deployment to safeguard equitable feedback.

**Keywords:** Large Language Models · Benchmarking · Gender Bias · Feedback

## 1 Introduction and Related Work

Generative Artificial Intelligence (GenAI) is increasingly applied in educational scenarios, such as in AI-supported writing assessment [30]. Given the emerging


E. G. Blanchard et al. (eds.), AIED 2026, LNCS 16586, pp. 163–178, 2027.
https://doi.org/10.1007/978-3-032-29773-0_12

potential of the large language models (LLMs) to enable timely and personalised feedback, teachers largely adopt LLMs to automate essay feedback [20]. A recent survey in the U.S. reported that one in four teachers already used GenAI tools to assess student work [16]. Yet, alongside this rapid uptake, concerns about LLMs' pedagogical precision and potential to exacerbate bias are mounting. For instance, a growing body of research has documented gender bias in LLM-based educational applications, raising concerns that such systems may amplify stereotypical gender inequalities through routine educational use [6]. These risks are particularly salient for assessment-related use cases, where models are often applied to pedagogically consequential downstream tasks under rich contextual prompts; this makes rigorous, context-sensitive auditing essential before LLMs are applied in assessment and feedback practices at scale [15]. However, to this day, there is no established benchmarking methodology to investigate gender bias of LLMs in educational applications [21]. To fill this gap, this paper explored an analytics-driven approach to benchmarking LLMs in education in the context of studying gender bias in LLM feedback to student essays. The proposed method, leveraging sentence embeddings that capture semantic differences in model behavior, allows for rigorous auditing of LLM biases for educational applications. Beyond quantifying the strength of bias, we show the potential of our method in generating embedding-based bias analytics (e.g., model response clustering).

### 1.1 Gender Bias in LLMs and the Need for A Benchmark

By gender bias, we refer to systematic preferences or prejudices towards one gender over others [8]. In principle, when all other input information remains consistent except for gender, unbiased LLMs should provide feedback without systematic variance. Yet, studies havc documented that gendered associations lead to systematic shifts even for the latest LLMs. For instance, [4] demonstrated that GPT-4, despite safeguards against explicit bias, continues to produce implicit gendered associations. [10] showed that GPT-4o significantly associates male students with agentic traits, while female students with communal leadership traits. [28] found that LLMs generate different explanations depending on demographic attributes, including gender, even when the educational topic is held constant. For pedagogical benefits, empirical evidence also suggests that men report holding more positive stances than women from ChatGPT-mediated learning [23].

Gender bias increasingly takes implicit forms, manifesting in subtle and context-dependent ways [25]. For instance, in essay writing, an education scenario with rich contextual information, gendered expressions can spontaneously emerge as students tend to draw on familiar gender roles to structure writing, and frequently include gender-themes or cases consistent with their gender identities [24]. Besides, in typical LLM-assisted assessment and feedback workflows, the drive for personalisation often leads teachers to supply richer student context [1], including gender-related cues such as forms of pronouns or background descriptors [18]. Thus, seemingly neutral inputs, such as prompt wording [21] or the readability and style of student essays [22], can systematically shape model feedback both *explicitly* and *implicitly*. Such asymmetries in feedback influence how learners perceive their agency and competence [27], which in turn can shape their intrinsic motivation and learning outcomes [14].

The persistence of opaque gender bias in LLM applications, together with teachers' frequent use of AI-generated feedback with minimal revisions [29] in practice, heightens the need for robust methods to detect bias in data and model outputs, which are essential to support the development of fair GenAI systems and to protect equity in educational applications of GenAI [3].

### 1.2 Bias Paradigms and Measurements

In the context of educational applications, three broad paradigms of algorithmic bias have emerged: similarity-based, causal, and statistical [17]. Among these, causal fairness, operationalised through counterfactual consistency [26], is particularly suited for measuring gender bias in LLMs [17]. From a quantitative measurement perspective, gender bias in language vector space models manifests in the geometric relationships. For instance, attribute words or social role descriptors systematically lean towards "male" or "female" semantic directions within the vector space [12]. Embedding-based approaches, which measure projection similarity and distances along gender dimensions, thus provide a promising avenue for detecting harms such as representation. A recent research study in AIEd community has demonstrated the use of sentence embeddings and analysed model responses through cosine similarity [7]. This work has highlighted the potential of embedding-based techniques for counterfactual evaluation and to assess how small input changes alter model behaviour. This approach is promising for probing gender bias: by systematically testing whether outputs shift in response to gender-related cues, it could enable bias detection. Yet, such applications remain largely unexplored in the detection of LLMs' gender bias. And because of the inherent stochasticity of LLM outputs, further robust control is needed.

Moreover, as critics highlight, current bias measurements in education still rely on template-based or synthetic probes, where researchers insert gender demographic markers into controlled, artificially constructed sentences to test model responses. They often fail to reflect the complexity and subtlety of real-world educational scenarios. Besides, present methods lack causal attributions and mostly rely on correlational evidence without counterfactual probing, making it difficult to establish whether observed differences reflect systematic gender bias [21]. Given that bias can surface both through explicit and implicit associations [5], there remains a pronounced lack of established benchmarks.

### 1.3 Research Questions

Our work builds on the causal fairness paradigm and introduces a novel embedding-based benchmarking approach that computes cosine similarity and semantic distance to detect implicit and explicit gender bias in educational scenarios. We focus on the critical use case of generating feedback on students' essay writing and employ counterfactual evaluation to quantify shifts in model responses. This approach allows us to move towards probing causal attributions, provide an educationally meaningful benchmark that captures subtle, real-world forms of gender bias in LLMs, and offer insights for teachers, researchers, and practitioners in the responsible and equitable application of AI in education at scale.

More specifically, it answers the following research questions:

- **RQ1:** To what extent do implicit gender-associated cues in essays trigger differential feedback from LLMs?
- **RQ2:** To what extent do explicit gender signals about authors trigger differential feedback from LLMs?

## 2 Methods

### 2.1 Study Context and Dataset

This study is situated in the context of using LLMs to generate feedback on student writing, where enriched gender-associated information may be either deliberately or inadvertently conveyed to LLMs through the student background provided by prompts or information in essay texts. We drew on an open-source dataset, the Automated Essay Scoring (AES) 2.0 dataset [11][1], to gain student writing data. This dataset contains approximately 24,000 student-written argumentative essays aligned with classroom inductive tasks (e.g., elaborating opinion regarding driverless cars). These tasks are naturally conducive to gendered language, as students often ground their reasoning in everyday cases (e.g., men/women driving to work). Besides, it offers authentic writing samples that include examples grounded in everyday experiences, which may naturally contain implicit identity-related signals. From the initial corpus, we retained 600 student essays containing gender-related vocabulary; such terms accounted for 0.84% of total words in essays. Table 1 illustrates representative writing tasks and excerpts.

**Table 1.** Examples of writing prompts and corresponding gendered expressions.

| Writing Task Topic | Writing Excerpt |
|---|---|
| Dream to become a cowboy/cowgirl | *"All he cares about is Seagoing Cowboys, he wants to be one. Well maybe if he is one then he might actually be happy..."* |
| Support or oppose driverless cars | *"Imagine a woman is late to work and her hair is a mess... But if she owns a driverless car, the woman could..."* |

[1] https://kaggle.com/competitions/learning-agency-lab-automated-essay-scoring-2/data.

## 2.2 Experiment Design and Data Processing Pipeline

**Experiment Design.** As discussed above, we adopt the causal fairness paradigm, which evaluates whether a model's outputs change counterfactually when a sensitive attribute (e.g., gender) is altered while all other factors remain constant. We operationalize this principle through two cue presentations by varying the locus of manipulation. We study two realistic pathways through which gender-associated information may be deliberately or inadvertently conveyed to LLMs in essay-feedback workflows: implicit cues embedded in the essay text itself when students draw on gendered language in writing [24]; and explicit cues introduced via student background provided in prompts, as done by teachers for enhancing personalisation [1]. To be specific, (i) Implicit condition: cues are introduced by manipulating the essay text. Specifically, we replace gender-associated words to construct counterfactual essay pairs, yielding two directional contrasts, M vs. M-F (male original → female counterfactual) and F vs. F-M (female original → male counterfactual). (ii) Explicit condition: cues are introduced by manipulating the prompt background information, where the author identity is specified as male, female, or neutral (M/F/N). In addition, we include a robustness baseline (M′), where original essays are re-prompted without manipulation to establish a natural variability benchmark for each LLM studied (shown in Fig. 1).

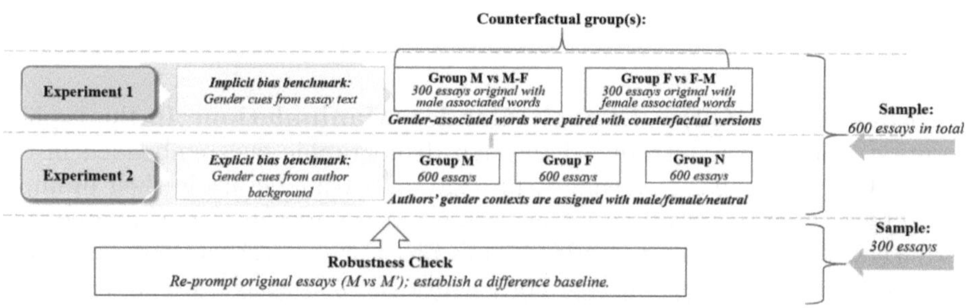


**Fig. 1.** Overview of experimental design.

**Experiment 1 (RQ1) - Implicit Gender Manipulation:** In the implicit condition, we constructed a lexicon of gender-synonymous word pairs based on prior work on gender-neutral embeddings and bias in NLP [31] which curated the lexicon by combining U.S. Bureau of Labor Statistics data on occupational gender distributions with rule-based substitutions and Mechanical Turk annotations and further extended the list through Cartesian products of seed words and demonstrated both occupational and contextual gender information. These pairs primarily covered identity terms (e.g., kinship, pronouns) and occupational words, which frequently appear in student writing. Using this lexicon, we generated counterfactual essays by swapping gendered words with their counterparts.

Two groups were created. In both groups, no explicit gender information was added, ensuring that only implicit lexical gender cues varied (see Table 2). We also manually checked all implicit replacements to ensure semantic coherence and grammatical correctness.

- *Group M vs. M-F*: 300 essays originally containing male-associated words were paired with counterfactual versions in which those words were replaced with female-associated terms.
- *Group F vs. F-M*: 300 essays containing female-associated words were paired with counterfactual male versions.

**Table 2.** Paragraphs example from original and counterfactual essays

| M group: | M–F group: |
|---|---|
| *"All* **he** *cares about is Seagoing* **Cowboys**; **he** *wants to be one. Well, maybe if* **he** *is one then* **he** *might..."* | *"All* **she** *cares about is Seagoing* **Cowgirls**; **she** *wants to be one. Well, maybe if* **she** *is one then* **she** *might..."* |
| **F group:** | **F–M group:** |
| *"Imagine a* **woman** *is late to work and* **her** *hair is a mess*; **she** *threw random clothes on, and all* **her** *work papers are ..."* | *"Imagine a* **man** *is late to work and* **his** *hair is a mess*; **he** *threw random clothes on, and all* **his** *work papers are ..."* |

**Experiment 2 (RQ2) - Explicit Gender Manipulation:** In the explicit condition, gender was introduced through demographic cues embedded in the prompt. Given teachers' tendency to provide contextual details in their prompts guided by prompt engineering training [9], we incorporated student-related contextual cues into the prompt (student name, pronouns, and school context, shown in Table 3) of the student author. For each of the 600 essays, we created three prompt variants: *Group M*, with male identity cues, *Group F*, with female identity cues, and *Group N*, with neutral identity cues. All prompts were paired with the same feedback request.

**Table 3.** Explicit gender cues in group M, F, N

| M | F | N |
|---|---|---|
| *"You are here to support in generating feedback on students' writing essays from an* **all-boys** *school. Your student,* **John**, *submitted the following essay for* **his** *assignment"* | *"You are here to support in generating feedback on students' writing essays from an* **all-girls** *school. Your student,* **Emily**, *submitted the following essay for* **her** *assignment"* | *"You are here to support in generating feedback on students' writing essays from a* **mixed gender** *school. Your student,* **Alex**, *submitted the following essay for* **their** *assignment"* |

**Robustness Check:** Model outputs differences may arise from two sources: (i) random variation introduced by the stochastic nature of LLM generation, and (ii) systematic content differences based on what learners write about. To address the random variation confound, we conducted a robustness check through re-prompting with original essays. Specifically, a subset of 300 original essays (Group M′) was re-submitted to the LLMs without any gender manipulation. By comparing the two sets of feedback on the same set of essays with identical information, we constructed a difference baseline that reflects the natural variability of LLM responses based on stochasticity and content differences.

**Data Processing Pipeline.** We operationalise the above counterfactual experimental groups within an auditing pipeline building on Borchers and Shou [7] and improving it with a robust baseline variation control. For each condition, we query LLMs with a shared feedback prompt, embed generated feedback, and test whether distances between matched counterfactual outputs exceed chance variation using permutation tests. In addition, we run a re-prompting baseline ($M'$) to benchmark natural output variability and support interpretation of gender-conditioned shifts. The pipeline is presented in Fig. 2. We constructed an open-source code repository for this benchmark pipeline[2].

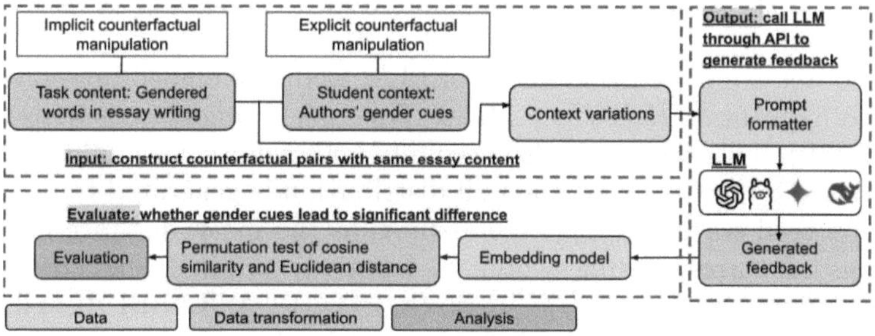


**Fig. 2.** Data processing pipeline.

Six selected LLMs are tested: GPT-5 mini, GPT-4o mini, DeepSeek-R1, DeepSeek-R1-Qwen, Gemini 2.5 Pro, and Llama-3-8B. Our model choices are grounded in availability via APIs and classic applications in education scenarios: (1) small, cost-effective distilled models, (2) mid-sized open-source models trained by professional datasets, and (3) proprietary, state-of-the-art models. For all models, the temperature was set to default values. This corresponds to how teachers usually interact with the models in web-based interfaces.

### 2.3 Bias Evaluation Metrics with Embedding

**Embedding Model.** We represent textual outputs as high-dimensional embedding vectors using OpenAI's `text-embedding-3-large` model, which maps each text to a 3072-dimensional vector space.

[2] https://github.com/Yishandu13/llm-gender-bias-edu-benchmarking.

Embeddings cluster similar texts within closer distances as well as preserve directional relationships that correspond to systematic semantic distinctions. Gendered word pairs (e.g., man: husband woman: wife) consistently form opposing poles in the embedding space [12], illustrating that the difference between male and female terms defines a gender direction within the embedding space. Formally, given a set of essays $E$, for each essay $e \in E$ we construct counterfactual pairs that differ only in gender-associated information. Let the embeddings of LLM-generated feedback be represented as:

$$M_0 = \{e(x_1), \ldots, e(x_n)\}, \quad M_1 = \{e(y_1), \ldots, e(y_n)\}$$

where $e(\cdot) \in \mathbb{R}^{3072}$ is the embedding function.

**Distance Metrics and Permutation Test** Adopting the testing approach from prior benchmarking work [7], we then statistically tested the directional and distance relationships through *cosine similarity* and *Euclidean distances* and employed a *non-parametric permutation test* to assess the statistical significance of groupwise differences in similarity or distance.

Cosine distance captures semantic drift, while Euclidean distance captures absolute displacement. Larger distances indicate greater divergence between counterfactual generations. For each group pair, the observed mean distance was compared against a null distribution generated by randomly permuting group labels. The null hypothesis is formalized as $H_0 : f(x \mid M_0) \approx f(y \mid M_1)$ (gender cues do not alter the distribution of LLM feedback embeddings), versus the alternative hypothesis $H_1 : f(x \mid M_0) \not\approx f(y \mid M_1)$ (gender cues systematically shift feedback). This approach also accounts for semantic variability introduced by quoted text in feedback, as the null distribution is generated from all essays.

The observed statistic ($T_{\text{obs}}$) was defined as the mean distance between the embeddings of corresponding sentences from the original and counterfactual groups, calculated as $T_{\text{obs}} = \frac{1}{n}\sum_{j=1}^{n} d(e(x_j), e(y_j))$. And **Null distribution** is constructed by concatenating both groups, randomly permuting labels, splitting into pseudo-groups of equal size, recomputing mean distances across $B$ iterations (here $B = 5000$), and generating a distribution of permuted statistics ($T_{\text{perm}}$) and whose mean ($\bar{T}$). A two-tailed $p$-value was calculated: $p = |T_{\text{perm}} - \bar{T}| \geq |T_{\text{obs}} - \bar{T}|$. A low $p$-value ($p < 0.05$) leads to the rejection of the null hypothesis.

## 3 Results

The comprehensive results are shown in Table 4. Overall, the gender manipulation induced detectable differences for most models, with all baseline tests revealing no significant differences through the cosine similarity metric.

### 3.1 RQ1: Implicit Gender Cues Trigger Differential LLM Feedback

In the **implicit condition**, significant group differences were consistently observed for M vs M-F comparisons across all models ($p's < .001$), indicating that the null hypothesis $H_0$ should be rejected for all models and subtle

**Table 4.** Statistical comparisons results.

| Condition | Comparison | Model | 1-Cosine Similarity | | | Euclidean Distance | | |
|---|---|---|---|---|---|---|---|---|
| | | | $T_{obs} - T_{perm}$ | *p*-value | Cohen's *d* | $T_{obs} - T_{perm}$ | *p*-value | Cohen's *d* |
| Implicit | M vs M-F | GPT-5 mini | 0.0094 | <.001*** | 0.257 | 0.0175 | <.001*** | 0.303 |
| | | GPT-4o mini | 0.0091 | <.001*** | 0.283 | 0.0173 | <.001*** | 0.327 |
| | | DeepSeek r1 | 0.0084 | <.001*** | 0.294 | 0.0169 | <.001*** | 0.345 |
| | | DeepSeek qwen | 0.0076 | <.001*** | 0.281 | 0.0141 | <.001*** | 0.308 |
| | | Gemini 2.5 Pro | 0.0107 | <.001*** | 0.288 | 0.0177 | <.001*** | 0.335 |
| | | Llama 3 8B | 0.0075 | <.001*** | 0.269 | 0.0141 | <.001*** | 0.316 |
| | F vs F-M | GPT-5 mini | –0.0002 | 0.136 | 0.005 | –0.0005 | 0.073 | 0.011 |
| | | GPT-4o mini | –0.0013 | 0.066 | 0.004 | –0.0005 | 0.051 | 0.011 |
| | | DeepSeek r1 | –0.0001 | 0.325 | 0.025 | –0.0002 | 0.185 | 0.032 |
| | | DeepSeek qwen | –0.0002 | 0.081 | –0.026 | –0.0004 | 0.062 | –0.015 |
| | | Gemini 2.5 Pro | –0.0003 | 0.062 | –0.001 | –0.0005 | 0.046 | 0.008 |
| | | Llama 3 8B | –0.0003 | 0.061 | 0.017 | –0.0004 | 0.048 | 0.024 |
| Explicit | M vs F | GPT-5 mini | 0.0070 | <.001*** | 0.200 | 0.0099 | <.001*** | 0.195 |
| | | GPT-4o mini | 0.0164 | <.001*** | 0.618 | 0.0242 | <.001*** | 0.580 |
| | | DeepSeek r1 | –0.0001 | 0.890 | 0.000 | –0.0004 | 0.821 | 0.000 |
| | | DeepSeek qwen | –0.0001 | 0.910 | 0.000 | –0.0003 | 0.821 | 0.000 |
| | | Gemini 2.5 Pro | –0.0002 | 0.880 | 0.000 | –0.0004 | 0.790 | 0.000 |
| | | Llama 3 8B | 0.0295 | <.001*** | 1.192 | 0.0429 | <.001*** | 1.116 |
| | M vs N | GPT-5 mini | 0.0044 | <.001*** | 0.147 | 0.0063 | <.001*** | 0.144 |
| | | GPT-4o mini | 0.0131 | <.001*** | 0.558 | 0.0198 | <.001*** | 0.527 |
| | | DeepSeek r1 | –0.0001 | 0.905 | 0.000 | –0.0003 | 0.832 | 0.000 |
| | | DeepSeek qwen | –0.0002 | 0.889 | 0.000 | –0.0003 | 0.805 | 0.000 |
| | | Gemini 2.5 Pro | –0.0001 | 0.899 | 0.000 | –0.0003 | 0.806 | 0.000 |
| | | Llama 3 8B | 0.0234 | <.001*** | 0.915 | 0.0343 | <.001*** | 0.869 |
| | F vs N | GPT-5 mini | 0.0056 | <.001*** | 0.196 | 0.0085 | 0.000 | 0.192 |
| | | GPT-4o mini | 0.0163 | <.001*** | 0.680 | 0.0246 | 0.000 | 0.640 |
| | | DeepSeek r1 | –0.0001 | 0.920 | 0.000 | –0.0003 | 0.848 | 0.000 |
| | | DeepSeek qwen | –0.0001 | 0.936 | 0.000 | –0.0002 | 0.861 | 0.000 |
| | | Gemini 2.5 Pro | –0.0001 | 0.917 | 0.000 | –0.0003 | 0.828 | 0.000 |
| | | Llama 3 8B | 0.0205 | <.001*** | 1.058 | 0.0313 | 0.000 | 1.005 |

*Note.* Robustness baseline ($M$ vs. $M'$; 1–cosine; $B$=5000): All models show no significant difference. Gemini 2.5 Pro ($p$=0.0176, $d$=0.0124) and Llama 3 8B ($p$=0.0112, $d$=0.0163) are marginally significant with minimal effect sizes within the Euclidean Distance metric; all baseline effects are substantially smaller than experimental contrasts.

gendered lexical substitutions led to significant differences in LLM feedback. The effect sizes ($0.2 < d < 0.5$) fall in the small-to-medium range, suggesting a consistent magnitude of the observed difference. By contrast, F vs F-M comparisons yielded consistently non-significant results ($p's > .05$) across models, suggesting that analysis across all models failed to reject the null hypothesis $H_0$ and female-associated substitutions had no measurable effects on semantic distances. Within the Euclidean distance metric, Gemini 2.5 pro and Llama-3-8B were marginally significant, and the others were not, but both showed a consistent trend. This contrast is surprising but was robust across all models. Visual inspection of the permutation distributions revealed a consistent trend across all models (shown in Fig. 3). In the M vs. M-F comparison, the observed statistics (red dashed line) systematically shifted to the right-hand side of the permutation distribution (blue histogram), well beyond the permutation mean (green dashed line) to a large extent. In the F vs. F-M comparison, the observed statistics were located to the left of the permutation mean, indicating smaller-than-expected distances when replacing female-associated words.

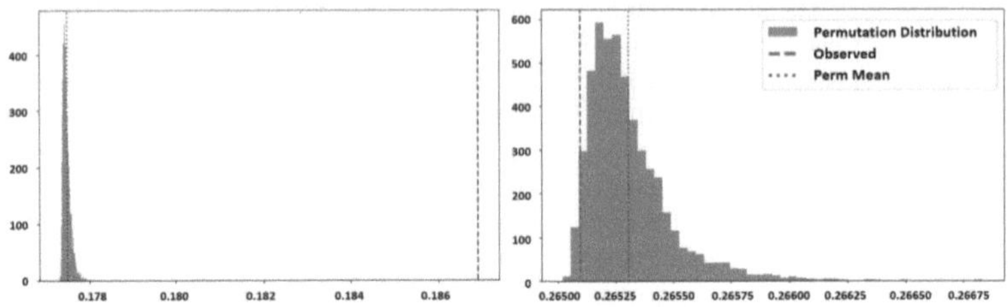


The main Fig. presents permutation analysis results for GPT-5 mini (left: M vs. M-F; right: F vs. F-M; n perm=5000). Other models shared similar similarity patterns with GPT-5 mini.

**Fig. 3.** 1-cosine similarity permutation analysis result of implicit condition. The main Fig. presents permutation analysis results for GPT-5 mini (left: M vs. M-F; right: F vs. F-M; n perm = 5000). Other models shared similar similarity patterns with GPT-5 mini.

By further inspecting representative clusters that showed the clearest separation in the t-SNE projection (M vs. M-F), we found that female-coded counterfactual essays tended to elicit a more interactive feedback stance (examples from Llama-3-8B are shown in Fig. 4). Compared with the male-coded originals, these responses used more second-person address (e.g., "you") and a more conversational tone, suggesting that the gender cue primarily shifted how directly the model engaged the learner.

### 3.2 RQ2: Explicit Gender Cues Trigger Differential LLM Feedback

In the **explicit condition**, LLMs showed mixed results. GPT-5 mini, GPT-4o mini, and Llama-3-8B were the LLMs (out of the six LLMs tested) that demonstrated significant differences in all comparisons ($p < .001$), including those involving the neutral group (M-N and F-N), while analysis of other models showed no evidence of bias under explicit manipulations. Notably, this difference was consistent across M-F and F-M pairs (unlike implicit manipulations above), with comparatively large effect sizes ranging from small to large ($d_{\text{GPT-5 mini}} = 0.195$, $d_{\text{GPT-4o mini}} = 0.58$, $d_{\text{Llama 3-8b}} = 1.116$). Overall, the M-F comparisons yielded the largest effect sizes, though in GPT-4o mini, the F-N contrast slightly exceeded the M-F effect, both falling within the medium range. Statistical tests failed to reject $H_0$ for DeepSeek-R1, DeepSeek-R1-Qwen, and Gemini 2.5 Pro. The permutation visualizations again highlighted systematic patterns. GPT-4o mini, GPT-5 mini, and Llama-3-8B showed observed statistics shifted to the right-hand side of the permutation distributions. By contrast, other models exhibited nearly Gaussian-shaped permutation distributions, with the observed values closely aligned with the permutation means.

Examining the dispersed t-SNE clusters in the explicit setting (M/F/N), we observed a clearer shift in pedagogical framing. Male-coded prompts were more often associated with agency-supportive guidance (e.g., you could/might consider...), whereas female-coded prompts more frequently contained controlling or directive formulations (e.g., imperatives and prescriptive steps) (examples from GPT-4o mini are in Fig. 5). This pattern indicates that explicit identity cues can differentially structure how strongly feedback supports learner agency.

## 4 Discussion

As educators increasingly rely on LLMs for automated essay feedback, there is a growing need to audit these systems for gender bias, which has been extensively documented in prior work [4,6,10]. We address this need by introducing a new application of randomisation tests over embedding spaces to audit fairness in educational LLM outputs. Grounded in the causal fairness paradigm, we

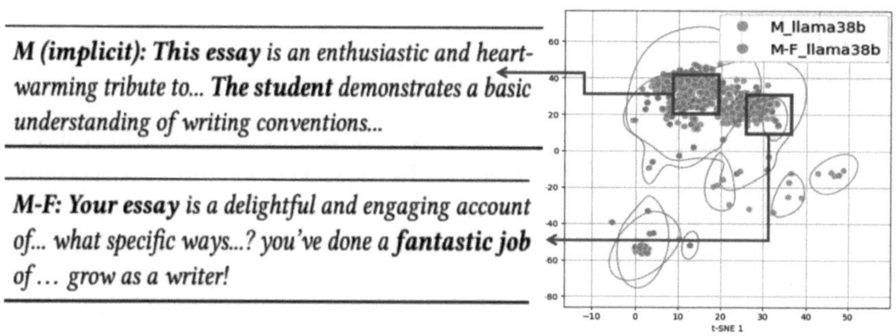


**Fig. 4.** Representative feedback text from group M and M-F.

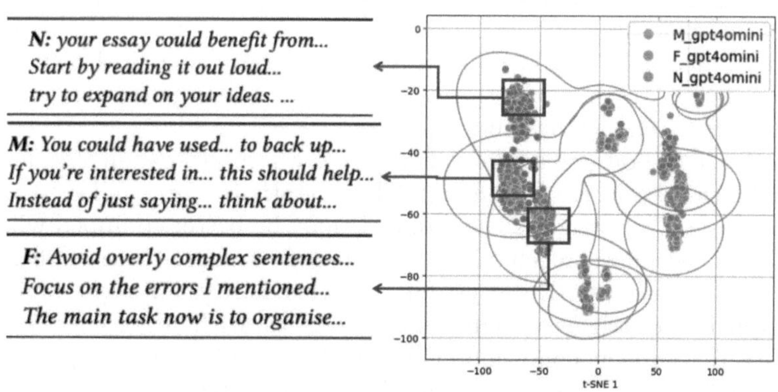


**Fig. 5.** Representative feedback text from group M, F and N.

propose a benchmarking methodology that combines cosine-based semantic distance with non-parametric permutation testing to measure gender-conditioned semantic drift while holding lexical and contextual factors constant. We apply this method to detect and characterise gender bias in LLM-generated feedback within a high-dimensional vector space. In contrast to existing approaches, our method is designed for realistic educational settings where demographic signals are pervasive and cannot be cleanly isolated [21], and where bias is often implicit, subtle, and context dependent [25]. As such, this work offers a timely methodological contribution for evaluating fairness in educational LLM applications.

Our results confirm that contemporary models still exhibit measurable gender bias [4,10]. The consistent divergence across models shows that this bias is real rather than speculative, intensifying concerns given teachers' documented practice of passing on AI-generated feedback with little modification [29]. Absent effective benchmarking, the widespread adoption of LLMs for assessment risks embedding and scaling gender bias within educational practice.

In answering the RQs, we find that model behaviour differs sharply in its treatment of implicit and explicit gender cues. First, we uncovered a striking and robust finding that implicit manipulations of M vs. M-F comparison consistently yielded systematic divergence across all models. This is confirmed by permutation tests and a robust baseline difference check. This demonstrates that subtle, semantically neutral word substitutions (e.g., replacing "he" with "she") can systematically alter AI-generated feedback with small-to-medium effect sizes, proving that bias is deeply embedded within model parameters and activated by everyday student writing. Conversely, the same models showed no significant divergence in the F vs. F-M condition. The observed asymmetry, striking but shown to be robust across our checks, could be caused by the original dataset composition underlying the M-F and F-M comparisons differing in ways that are not fully symmetric (see cases in Table 2). Besides, the asymmetry aligns with a growing body of evidence documenting asymmetric gender biases in LLMs. Prior research has identified patterns such as a stubborn adherence to masculine defaults, where models often fail to shift to feminine forms when combining male-stereotyped professions with feminine pronouns [19]. Besides, a greater flexibility in attributing male-stereotyped concepts to females than the reverse, suggesting an uneven "inclusivity" [13]. Our findings contribute a critical new empirical insight by demonstrating that this asymmetry also manifests systematically in LLM-generated feedback on student essays.

Second, the response to explicit gender cues was model-dependent. For half of the models (DeepSeek series, Gemini 2.5 Pro), statistical tests failed to reject the null hypothesis. This suggests these models may be better equipped with safety guardrails or safeguard mechanisms that reduce sensitivity to explicit demographic cues in prompts. However, for the other half (GPT-4o/5-mini, Llama-3-8B), explicit cues triggered significant divergence with larger effect sizes compared with the implicit condition. Thus, explicit gender bias, despite extensive mitigation efforts, remains consequential in certain LLM models.

The mixed response to explicit cues, coupled with the robust implicit bias, demonstrates that even when LLMs are used carefully, these models exhibit bias that practitioners cannot mitigate. This supports critiques that simplistic fairness tests are insufficient, underscoring the need for more sophisticated, context-rich evaluation frameworks.

Whether triggered implicitly or explicitly, these differences constitute meaningful biases, and they have consequences for how learners are positioned. For example, our data reveal that feedback for female-cued essays was often more directive (e.g., "Avoid overly complex sentences"), whereas feedback for male-cued essays encouraged agency (e.g., "You could develop..."). This pedagogical asymmetry, by offering differential levels of intellectual autonomy, can subtly shape a student's sense of agency, thereby influencing their identity and self-efficacy [6]. Besides, we also found that feedback for texts with female-associated cues (group M-F and group F) was consistently more personal, affective, and interactive, using more second-person pronouns and varied sentence types like exclamations. However, it was also more directive. This pedagogical divergence risks reinforcing stereotypical identities. It suggests that LLMs might coach students perceived as male towards intellectual independence and critical argumentation, while guiding students perceived as female towards diligence, compliance, and mechanical correctness. Such biased feedback also risks undermining students' sense of belonging and competence—core prerequisites for intrinsic motivation under self-determination theory, and thus for meaningful learning outcomes [2]. Therefore, it is not enough to measure bias through sentiment or toxicity. Considering these subtle differences shape learners' motivation, agency, and perceived competence, evaluations must also extend to the pedagogical framing of feedback.

**Limitations and Future Work:** First, our analyses primarily quantify divergence in embeddings and identify textual patterns, but deeper semantic interpretation (potentially more qualitatively) and explainable AI approaches are needed to uncover the underlying mechanisms that interpret and drive biases. Second, deeper error analysis is needed to clarify the mechanisms underlying these effects. Besides, comparison of divergence in manipulated essays with that in grading responses could help to better understand when models become sensitive to gender cues. Controlled sub-experiments that vary the extent of counterfactual manipulation could also further identify the conditions under which these asymmetric effects emerge. The extent to which cultural context or situational framing in prompts modulates bias remains underexplored. Our prompt variation frameworks can also be used to enable future work to study such nuances. More broadly, extending this framework to additional datasets and to other protected attributes would help assess the generalisability of the findings. Finally, while our findings highlight risks for learners, future work is needed to bridge these insights with practical debiasing strategies and teacher training strategies for mitigating AI bias's impact. We are currently planning and will run teacher-in-the-loop experiments with English writing instructors to begin bridging the audit insights to classroom practice and prototype practical mitigation strategies.

## 5 Conclusion

The primary contribution of this study is the demonstration that robust benchmarking of educational LLMs can be effectively achieved through the proposed benchmarking approach here. We introduced and validated a benchmarking framework for auditing gender bias in AI-generated feedback to students. Explicit student author information influenced biased feedback in three of the six LLMs, while subtle gender-coded language within student essays elicited biased responses across all six LLMs. These results indicate that gender bias in educational LLM feedback is both model-dependent and systematically triggered by linguistic cues, underscoring the necessity of bias-sensitive evaluation protocols in the design and deployment of LLM-based AI systems in educational practice. When such feedback is transmitted to learners without critical review (a common practice of teachers [29]), it is likely to generate downstream harms, including the internalisation of biased evaluations that shape students' perceived competence, agency, and academic identity in inequitable ways. Embedding bias-sensitive benchmarking into the design, development, and deployment lifecycle of educational LLMs is therefore essential to ensure that AI-mediated feedback systems support, rather than erode, equity in educational practice.

## References


1. Abolnejadian, M., Alipour, S., Taeb, K.: Leveraging ChatGPT for adaptive learning through personalized prompt-based instruction: A CS1 education case study. In: Extended Abstracts of the CHI Conference on Human Factors in Computing Systems. CHI EA '24. Association for Computing Machinery (2024)
2. Adams, N., Little, T.D., Ryan, R.M.: Self-determination theory. In: Development of Self-Determination Through the Life-Course, pp. 47–54. Springer, Dordrecht (2017)
3. Atwood, J., Lahoti, P., Balashankar, A., Prost, F., Beirami, A.: Inducing group fairness in LLM-based decisions. arXiv e-prints (2024)
4. Bai, X., Wang, A., Sucholutsky, I., Griffiths, T.L.: Measuring implicit bias in explicitly unbiased large language models. In: NeurIPS 2024 Workshop on Behavioral Machine Learning (2024)
5. Bai, X., Wang, A., Sucholutsky, I., Griffiths, T.L.: Explicitly unbiased large language models still form biased associations. Proc. Natl. Acad. Sci. U.S.A. **122**(8), e2416228122 (2025)
6. Bartl, M., Mandal, A., Leavy, S., Little, S.: Gender bias in natural language processing and computer vision: a comparative survey. ACM Comput. Surv. **57**(6), 1–36 (2025)
7. Borchers, C., Shou, T.: Can large language models match tutoring system adaptivity? A benchmarking study. In: International Conference on Artificial Intelligence in Education, pp. 407–420. Springer, Cham (2025). https://doi.org/10.1007/978-3-031-98417-4_29

8. Cantini, R., Cosenza, G., Orsino, A., Talia, D.: Are large language models really bias-free? Jailbreak prompts for assessing adversarial robustness to bias elicitation. In: International Conference on Discovery Science, pp. 52–68. Springer, Cham (2024). https://doi.org/10.1007/978-3-031-78977-9_4
9. Chen, B., Zhang, Z., Langrené, N., Zhu, S.: Unleashing the potential of prompt engineering for large language models. Patterns (2025)
10. Choi, J., Nixon, N.: Agentic men, communal women? Exploring gender bias in LLM-based leadership identification for collaboration analytics. In: International Conference on Artificial Intelligence in Education, pp. 11–18. Springer, Cham (2025). https://doi.org/10.1007/978-3-031-98465-5_2
11. Crossley, S.A., Tian, Y., Baffour, P., Franklin, A., Benner, M., Boser, U.: A large-scale corpus for assessing written argumentation: PERSUADE 2.0. Assess. Writ. **61**, 100865 (2024)
12. Durrheim, K., Schuld, M., Mafunda, M., Mazibuko, S.: Using word embeddings to investigate cultural biases. Br. J. Soc. Psychol. **62**(1), 617–629 (2023)
13. Fulgu, R.A., Capraro, V.: Surprising gender biases in GPT. Comput. Human Behav. Rep. **16**, 100533 (2024)
14. Howard, J.L., Bureau, J., Guay, F., Chong, J.X., Ryan, R.M.: Student motivation and associated outcomes: a meta-analysis from self-determination theory. Perspect. Psychol. Sci. **16**(6), 1300–1323 (2021)
15. Karumbaiah, S., Ganesh, A., Bharadwaj, A., Anderson, L.: Evaluating behaviors of general purpose language models in a pedagogical context. In: Artificial Intelligence in Education (AIED 2024), Proceedings, Part II. Lecture Notes in Computer Science, vol. 14830, pp. 47–61. Springer, Heidelberg (2024). https://doi.org/10.1007/978-3-031-64299-9_4
16. Kaufman, J.H., Woo, A., Eagan, J., Lee, S., Kassan, E.B.: Uneven adoption of artificial intelligence tools among US teachers and principals in the 2023–2024 school year. RAND (2025)
17. Kizilcec, R.F., Lee, H.: The Ethics of Artificial Intelligence in Education, pp. 174–202. Routledge. Algorithmic fairness in education (2022)
18. Lee, J., Hicke, Y., Yu, R., Brooks, C., Kizilcec, R.F.: The life cycle of large language models in education: a framework for understanding sources of bias. Br. J. Edu. Technol. **55**(5), 1982–2002 (2024)
19. Manna, C., Alishahi, A., Blain, F., Vanmassenhove, E.: Are we paying attention to her? investigating gender disambiguation and attention in machine translation. arXiv preprint arXiv:2505.08546 (2025)
20. Meyer, J., et al.: Using LLMs to bring evidence-based feedback into the classroom: AI-generated feedback increases secondary students' text revision, motivation, and positive emotions. Comput. Educ. Artif. Intell. **6**, 100199 (2024)
21. Rodrigues, L., Xavier, C., Costa, N., Gašević, D., Mello, R.F.: Is gpt-4 fair? An empirical analysis in automatic short answer grading. Comput. Educ. Artif. Intell. 100428 (2025)
22. Rony, S.B.Q., Fei, T.X., Arsovski, S.: Educational justice: reliability and consistency of large language models for automated essay scoring and its implications. J. Appl. Learn. Teach. **8**(1), 67–77 (2025)
23. Seifert, T., Tzamir-Levi, T.: Risk or promise: educators' perspectives on student use of chatgpt. In: Cristea, A.I., Walker, E., Lu, Y., Santos, O.C., Isotani, S. (eds.) Artificial Intelligence in Education: 26th International Conference, AIED 2025, Palermo, Italy, 22–26 July 2025, Proceedings, Part V. Lecture Notes in Computer Science, vol. 15881, pp. 164–170. Springer, Cham (2025). https://doi.org/10.1007/978-3-031-98462-4_21

24. Sun, H., Luo, X., Pae, H.K.: Changing gendered language in English academic writing? Epicene pronoun usage in learners' research manuscripts and gender-inclusive practices in journal guidelines. Chang. Engl. 1–15 (2025)
25. Torres, N.: Contrastive adversarial gender debiasing. Natural Lang. Process. J. **8**, 100092 (2024)
26. Vig, J., et al.: Investigating gender bias in language models using causal mediation analysis. Adv. Neural. Inf. Process. Syst. **33**, 12388–12401 (2020)
27. Warr, M., Oster, N.: Analyzing AI-generated feedback: a mixed-methods examination of ChatGPT's responses to student writers. In: Society for Information Technology & Teacher Education International Conference, pp. 3034–3043. Association for the Advancement of Computing in Education (AACE) (2025)
28. Weissburg, I., Anand, S., Levy, S., Jeong, H.: LLMs are biased teachers: evaluating LLM bias in personalized education. In: Findings of the Association for Computational Linguistics: NAACL 2025, pp. 5650–5698 (2025)
29. Xavier, C., et al.: Empowering instructors with AI: evaluating the impact of an AI-driven feedback tool in learning analytics. IEEE Trans. Learn. Technol. (2025)
30. Yang, K., Raković, M., Gašević, D., Chen, G.: Does the prompt-based large language model recognize students' demographics and introduce bias in essay scoring? In: International Conference on Artificial Intelligence in Education, pp. 75–89. Springer, Heidelberg (2025). https://doi.org/10.1007/978-3-031-98417-4_6
31. Zhao, J., Wang, T., Yatskar, M., Cotterell, R., Ordonez, V., Chang, K.W.: Gender bias in contextualized word embeddings. In: Proceedings of the 2019 Conference of the North American Chapter of the Association for Computational Linguistics: Human Language Technologies, pp. 629–634 (2019)

# Supporting the Text Entry of Nêhiyawêwin for Lifelong Learners

Daniela Teodorescu[1], Guher Gorgun[2], Delaney Lothian[3], Jialiang Yan[1], Josie Matalski[1], Yalmaz Abdullah[1], Hongwei Wang[1], Minghao Cai[1], and Carrie Demmans Epp[1(✉)]

[1] EdTeKLA Group, University of Alberta, Edmonton, Canada
{dteodore,jialian6,jmatalsk,yalmaz,hongwei2,minghaocai, cdemmansepp}@uablerta.ca

[2] Educational Psychology, University of Georgia, Athens, GA, USA
gorgun@uga.edu

[3] National Research Council Canada (NRC), Edmonton, Canada
delaney.lothian@nrc-cnrc.gc.ca

**Abstract.** Reconciliation and language revitalization efforts are ongoing in former colonial states. As part of these efforts, many locations are being renamed using local Indigenous language(s), and Indigenous languages are being increasingly used in signage and educational settings. These policy and practice changes mean that all members of society need help in navigating their use of an unfamiliar language that has few supports. To facilitate people's use of local Indigenous languages and support those who want to learn these languages, we conducted a study of predictive text for a morphologically complex Indigenous language (nêhiyawêwin). This study aimed to determine the level at which predictions should be made because existing predictive-text approaches are misaligned with the linguistic characteristics of this and other Indigenous languages that are morphologically complex, which suggests that word-level prediction will not benefit learners. As a first step towards providing appropriate cognitive supports for learners, we studied people's performance and preferences when interacting with a system that supported word, character, and morpheme-level predictions. This within-subjects study ($n = 50$) showed that word-level prediction was sub-optimal. The joint consideration of user performance and preferences indicated that the character-level and a morpheme-character hybrid best supported text entry for this morphologically-rich language.

**Keywords:** Indigenous Language Technologies · Predictive Text · Language Revitalization · Assistive Technologies

## 1 Introduction

Many of us regularly use predictive text as a cognitive support and efficiency tool [1]. It works well for for high-resource languages (e.g., Chinese, French,


E. G. Blanchard et al. (eds.), AIED 2026, LNCS 16586, pp. 179–193, 2027.
https://doi.org/10.1007/978-3-032-29773-0_13

English), but most of the world's languages do not benefit from the support of these technologies. This lack of support is especially noticeable when trying to learn low-resource and Indigenous languages [2,14,25,26]. This lack of tooling [22] leaves learners dependent on the few paper-based resources that exist. It also hinders language revitalization efforts. Plains Cree or nêhiyawêwin is one such language that is spoken in Canada and the United States, and its learners want tools to support their language use and learning [23].

Like many of the Indigenous languages spoken in North America, nêhiyawêwin is linguistically distinct from majority languages like English. It is morphologically complex (agglutinative and polysynthetic), making existing approaches to predictive text inappropriate [10,35,36,40]. In nêhiyawêwin, words are constructed by appending word-parts (i.e., morphemes) [15] and text can look like a single word when it is a full sentence (e.g., 'you all eat' is 'ki-mîciso-nâwâw'). These characteristics result in an exponential number of word forms and make standard (single-word prediction) infeasible.

In addition to nêhiyawêwin's under-supported linguistic characteristics, nêhiyawêwin is an extremely low-resource, endangered language [38]. Recently, there has been a move to make Indigenous languages more visible by including them on signage and by returning location names to their pre-colonial origins. This creates a need for tools that support the lifelong learning of residents in these regions as well as those who want to reclaim their heritage and identity.

As part of language revitalization efforts, speech-synthesis and recognition technologies [11,12] and educational games [24] have been developed to promote the learning of Indigenous languages. Some work has additionally investigated cognitive supports for working across the two writing system's that are commonly used to represent nêhiyawêwin in text [30]. For the majority of these examples and the present work, the need for a tool was identified while working with communities or community members.

## 2 Cognitive Supports for Text Entry

In a lifelong-learning setting cognitive support tools, like predictive text, are beneficial because they support recall and reduce errors while making text entry faster [4,7]. The extant literature reports on the use of different units of prediction according to each language's morphology and the resources available for that language (Please see OSF for a full comparison of prior approaches).

Languages, such as nêhiyawêwin, that are agglutinative or morphologically complex may benefit from subword-level (e.g., morpheme) or character-level predictions due to the exponential number of word forms that are possible. However, which approach is appropriate for a particular language and context remains an open question, with mixed results reported across agglutinative languages: character-level predictions performed well for Turkish [36] but were were worse than syllable- or morpheme-level representations when working with Korean [40].

The use of morpheme-level prediction is relatively common when developing language models for Indigenous languages that are spoken across the Americas

[19,19,21,32]; this includes nêhiyawêwin. However, these models have yet to be put into a support tool for learners of the language, meaning we do not know whether such models will support people's use or acquisition of the language. This motivates our exploration of different prediction granularities that include character, morpheme, and word-level predictions.

Given the status of the literature and the number of resources that are available, we developed models for various levels of prediction (character, morpheme, word, and a character-morpheme hybrid) to explore which is preferred. We go beyond the reported studies of Indigenous text prediction by conducting a user study ($n = 50$) to answer the following questions:

**RQ1.** Which type of predictive text, if any, supports quick and accurate text entry?
**RQ2.** Which type of predictive text, if any, is perceived as more mentally demanding?
**RQ3.** Which type of predictive text, if any, is preferred by learners?

# 3 Methods

We developed predictive-text models and performed a mixed-methods within-subject study to determine which unit of prediction is both effective and liked when entering nêhiyawêwin text. The model conditions and stimulus sets were counterbalanced using a Graeco-Latin square design to control for order, potential fatigue, and learning effects [8]. See OSF for materials.

## 3.1 Study Procedures

All participants underwent the same procedures with the order of materials and conditions counter-balanced. They each completed an English typing-speed test, which served as a control measure. Like with the study conditions, the timing of this control measure was counterbalanced: half performed it at the start and half at the end of the study.

Participants were assigned to one of 50 rows in the Graeco-Latin square. They then completed a questionnaire about their experience with nêhiyawêwin and underwent a training phase. During training, they were given a set of 2 nêhiyawêwin words to enter per model condition.

Following training, participants were given 5 typing blocks. Each block used one of the model conditions (character-level, morpheme-level, hybrid, word-level, and a baseline with no predictive model) and one of the stimulus sets. Participants were shown instructions for a block at the beginning of that block. They then completed 18 typing trials and answered questions about their experience. The top-5 predictions were shown through a drop-down (Fig. 1). The user could press tab to select the most likely prediction or select from other predictions by using the mouse, the up arrow key, or the down key. Users pressed the *enter* key when they thought they had entered the provided stimulus item.

Participants could take a break between blocks. After completing text entry for all conditions, they completed a questionnaire and received their honorarium.

**Fig. 1.** An example of the predictive-text interface for the character-level (left), morpheme-level (centre), and hybrid prediction approaches (right).

**Predictive-Text Conditions.** The evaluated conditions include a non-adaptive baseline and four predictive text settings. The n-gram language models that supported prediction were trained using the Cree Corpus data [37]. Explicit permission was obtained from Indigenous creators and communities, as appropriate, when developing this corpus and our use of it for supporting language learning and creating language technologies is consistent with the purpose for which the data were collected.

The models that drove the adaptive conditions were trained and tuned with intrinsic model performance evaluated through perplexity. A test of model performance that used a held-out set indicated the character-based model performed best (i.e., had the lowest perplexity), followed by the morpheme-level and the word-level models. This pattern is expected given the vocabulary size of the training data for each of these linguistic levels. Please see OSF for full model training, tuning, and testing information.

- **Baseline**: In this condition, there is no language model providing recommendations. The participant types the entirety of their message.
- **Character-level model** ($n = 6$): This model uses the preceding 1–5 characters to predict the next character.
- **Morpheme-level model** ($n = 6$): This model uses the preceding 1–5 morphemes to predict the next morpheme.
- **Word-level model** ($n = 1$): This model suggests the most probable word based on the characters entered.
- **Hybrid model**: This model suggests predictions with the highest probability from those made by both the character- and morpheme-level models.

### 3.2 Instruments and Measures

**Stimuli for the English and Nêhiyawêwin Typing Tasks.** Table 1 provides descriptive statistics for all stimuli.

For each language, items were chosen based on the number of characters and the number of syllables in the word. The selection of stimuli for nêhiyawêwin also controlled for letter, morpheme, and word frequency.

To ensure participants did not have to type anything that is offensive or inappropriate, the meanings of nêhiyawêwin words were checked. Words that had violent or inappropriate meanings, given cultural contexts, were replaced with words that had similar linguistic properties. When we were uncertain of a word's meaning, we checked with a nêhiyawêwin speaker before replacing words.

English typing speed was measured for reference by having participants enter real and pseudo-words from the TOWRE [39].

**Table 1.** The number of characters for the text users entered.

| | Min | Max | Mean | Median |
|---|---|---|---|---|
| *Typing Speed Test - English* | | | | |
| Real words | 5.00 | 10.00 | 7.78 | 8.00 |
| Pseudo words | 4.00 | 11.00 | 7.67 | 8.00 |
| Combined | 4.00 | 11.00 | 7.72 | 8.00 |
| *Stimulus Sets - nêhiyawêwin* | | | | |
| Set 1 | 5.00 | 14.00 | 9.11 | 9.00 |
| Set 2 | 4.00 | 12.00 | 8.67 | 9.00 |
| Set 3 | 5.00 | 14.00 | 8.83 | 9.00 |
| Set 4 | 6.00 | 14.00 | 8.94 | 8.50 |
| Set 5 | 4.00 | 14.00 | 8.89 | 9.00 |

**Text-Entry Measures.** As a measure of efficiency, the **typing speed** per character for a prompt was calculated. This is the difference between the time from when the *enter* key was pressed and that from when the first key was pressed. This value is divided by the number of characters in the prompt and is calculated for each trial. We report speed as seconds per character.

Because the typing-speed measure does not directly account for errors in a submitted response, we counted the number of **errors per word** (trial). We averaged this across trials per model type for each participant.

We employed a measure of keystrokes used to capture the **manual effort** required as the ratio of the number of keystrokes entered to the number of keystrokes the prompt should require. Each normal character counted as 1 keystroke, while special characters (e.g., $\hat{a}$, $\hat{\imath}$, $\hat{o}$) counted as 3 keystrokes since they require additional effort on an English-language QWERTY keyboard. Selecting a suggestion is 1 keystroke.

We calculated the manual effort for each trial. When this value is 1, there is no gain. When the value is less than 1, the manual effort required is reduced. When the value is greater than 1, there is increased manual effort.

**Suggestion usage** was also measured as the ratio of the number of suggestions selected to the number of suggestions shown during a trial.

**Questionnaires.** These were used to collect demographic information and preferences as well as information about task workload and participant experience. We sub-selected relevant items from the NASA-TLX [13]: we used the items for perceived *mental demand*, *performance*, *frustration*, and *overall* effort.

### 3.3 Participants

This study was approved by our institutional research ethics board. Participation took approximately 30 min and participants received a $15 honorarium.

A total of 51 persons completed the study. One was not a touch typist; the participant instead looked at the keyboard most of the time so we excluded their data and recruited another participant who then completed that row of the Graeco-Latin square. We report data from the 50 participants whose data was retained. Of these, 27 were women, 22 were men, and one declined to provide gender information. Their average age was 23.6 years ($SD = 4.4$, range: 19-45).

All participants self-identified as native-English speakers and said that English was the language they were most comfortable speaking. Many participants ($n = 26$) had multilingual backgrounds and some ($n = 3$) had experience with nêhiyawêwin, with only one having prior exposure to nêhiyawêwin in their home environment. This level of exposure is typical in the surrounding area despite nêhiyawêwin being the most widely-spoken Indigenous language in the region.

### 3.4 Analysis

We used inferential statistics to determine whether there were performance differences in participant text entry across conditions. The Graeco-Latin square design assumes the model is additive, thus there should be no interaction effects between predictors [18]. We checked whether the additivity assumption held; it did, so we proceeded with analyses using the Latin Square Design ANOVA [5].

Participant performance data that did not meet the normality assumption (i.e., error per word) were rank transformed. We then conducted an ANOVA test for each outcome variable using the same set of predictors (i.e., model type and stimulus set). When the ANOVA identified significant main effects, we reported pairwise comparisons using the Tukey HSD test, which controls for Type 1 error when making multiple pairwise comparisons [17].

To determine whether there was a difference in participants' perceptions of the workload involved in entering nêhiyawêwin text, we used a linear-mixed effects model. This model was fitted to predict each of the NASA-TLX items measured. Stimulus set and model type were fixed effects, and participants were entered as a random intercept.

## 4 Results

### 4.1 Which Condition Supports Quick and Accurate Text Entry?

Participant performance on various measures can be seen in Table 2. From this and the statistical tests reported below, the hybrid-level model was the fastest

**Table 2.** Participant performance by model and stimulus set

| | Typing Speed | | Errors/Word | | Manual Effort | | Suggestion Usage | |
|---|---|---|---|---|---|---|---|---|
| | *M* | *SD* | *M* | *SD* | *M* | *SD* | *M* | *SD* |
| *Condition* | | | | | | | | |
| Baseline | 0.80 | 0.438 | 0.02 | 0.902 | 1.33 | 0.699 | N/A | N/A |
| Character | 0.90 | 0.529 | 0.03 | 0.121 | 1.27 | 0.706 | 0.06 | 0.142 |
| Morpheme | 0.96 | 0.611 | 0.02 | 0.105 | 1.44 | 0.989 | 0.01 | 0.043 |
| Word | 0.93 | 0.548 | 0.05 | 0.151 | 1.28 | 0.940 | 0.05 | 0.086 |
| Hybrid | 0.89 | 0.499 | 0.03 | 0.118 | 1.32 | 0.698 | 0.05 | 0.128 |
| *Stimulus Set* | | | | | | | | |
| 1 | 0.94 | 0.590 | 0.04 | 0.136 | 1.39 | 0.990 | 0.03 | 0.077 |
| 2 | 0.89 | 0.507 | 0.02 | 0.099 | 1.34 | 0.867 | 0.03 | 0.099 |
| 3 | 0.85 | 0.492 | 0.03 | 0.114 | 1.34 | 0.774 | 0.03 | 0.089 |
| 4 | 0.89 | 0.534 | 0.03 | 0.130 | 1.33 | 0.842 | 0.03 | 0.099 |
| 5 | 0.90 | 0.522 | 0.03 | 0.116 | 1.24 | 0.548 | 0.05 | 0.123 |

while facilitating correct text entry, likely because participants in this condition used recommendations.

Participants' **typing speed** in nêhiyawêwin was approximately three times slower than their English typing speed ($M = 0.28$, $SD = 0.174$). When comparing their performance across the nêhiyawêwin tasks, we found an effect of model type ($F(4, 4491) = 12.05, p < .001, \eta^2 = .01$) and stimulus set ($F(4, 4491) = 4.07, p = .005, \eta^2 = .0003$). Post-hoc analyses showed the baseline condition was faster than each of the predictive text conditions (all $p < .001$), and the hybrid model was faster than the morpheme-based model ($p = .002$), which was the slowest. Participant performance was only measurably different for one pair of stimuli: Set 3 was entered more quickly than Set 1 ($p = .001$).

Participant **error rates** in nêhiyawêwin were similar to those for English ($M = 0.02$, $SD = 0.096$) for most conditions, and there was an effect of model type ($F(4, 4491) = 7.87, p < .001, \eta^2 = .0006$) and stimulus set ($F(4, 4491) = 4.62, p = .001, \eta^2 = .0004$) on errors per word. They submitted more errors when using the word model than they did when they had no predictive text ($p < .001$) or were using the hybrid ($p < .001$), character ($p < .001$), and morpheme ($p < .001$) models. Participants made fewer errors when entering words from Stimulus Set 2 than Set 1 ($p = .030$) and submitted more errors on Stimulus Set 5 than on both Set 2 ($p = .002$) and Set 3 ($p = .023$).

Participants expended more effort than required when entering text across all conditions: the average **manual effort** score exceeded 1 in all cases. There was a small difference in manual effort used across conditions ($F(4, 4491) = 5.96, p < .001, \eta^2 = .0005$) and stimulus sets ($F(4, 4491) = 4.08, p = .002, \eta^2 = .0003$). Post-hoc analyses revealed that manual effort was higher for the morpheme model than the character ($p < .001$), hybrid ($p = .026$), and word models ($p < .001$). Stimulus Set 1 also required more manual effort than Set 5 ($p < .001$).

### 4.2 Which Type of Predictive Text Is More Mentally Demanding?

Measures of participant workload for each model and stimulus condition are in Table 3. There was a significant main effect of condition for overall workload, mental demand, and frustration. There were no interaction or stimulus set effects. Post-hoc analyses revealed participants reported higher levels of mental demand ($p = .012$), frustration ($p < .001$), and overall workload when they were in the morpheme condition than when they were in the word condition ($p = .001$). Furthermore, participants reported higher levels of frustration for the morpheme condition than the baseline ($p = .003$), and higher levels of frustration for the character-level model than the word-level one ($p = .027$).

**Table 3.** Participants' perception of mental workload by model and stimulus set

| | Mental Demand *M (SD)* | Performance *M (SD)* | Frustration *M (SD)* | Overall *M (SD)* |
|---|---|---|---|---|
| *Condition* | * | — | *** | ** |
| Baseline | 6.92 (4.130) | 15.58 (4.581) | 4.14 (3.918) | 8.56 (3.072) |
| Character | 7.40 (4.540) | 15.26 (3.917) | 5.10 (4.330) | 8.96 (3.035) |
| Morpheme | 7.76 (4.547) | 15.16 (4.292) | 5.70 (4.718) | 9.36 (3.093) |
| Word | 6.02 (4.187) | 15.60 (4.651) | 3.84 (3.419) | 8.21 (2.470) |
| Hybrid | 7.04 (4.598) | 15.56 (3.924) | 4.60 (3.933) | 8.82 (2.941) |
| *Stimulus Set* | — | — | — | — |
| 1 | 7.04 (4.746) | 15.06 (4.515) | 4.98 (4.502) | 8.80 (3.210) |
| 2 | 7.32 (4.177) | 15.76 (4.043) | 4.46 (3.566) | 8.93 (2.675) |
| 3 | 6.50 (3.792) | 15.44 (4.343) | 4.48 (3.955) | 8.55 (2.651) |
| 4 | 7.26 (4.416) | 15.24 (4.281) | 4.84 (3.992) | 8.85 (2.892) |
| 5 | 7.02 (4.947) | 15.66 (4.255) | 4.62 (4.330) | 8.79 (3.283) |
| *Interaction* | — | — | — | — |

*Note.* * $p < .05$, ** $p < .01$, *** $p < .001$,—is Non-significant.

### 4.3 Which Type of Text Entry is Preferred by Learners?

While many participants (52%) indicated they are likely to use the predictive text and are likely to recommend it to others (56%), most (62%) reported using the predictive text only occasionally: only 6% reported using recommendations almost every time and 32% reported using them never or almost never. These perceptions were aligned with their usage statistics (Table 2).

We found an effect of model type ($F(4, 4491) = 78.55, p < .001, \eta^2 = .06$) and stimulus set ($F(4, 4491) = 8.27, p < .001, \eta^2 = .0006$) on suggestion usage. Participants used more of the model-provided suggestions in the character condition than they did in the hybrid ($p < .001$) and morpheme ($p < .001$) conditions. They also used more suggestions in the hybrid and word conditions than they did in the morpheme condition ($p < .001$). Participants used more suggestions for Stimulus Set 5 than they did for any other stimulus set ($p < .001$).

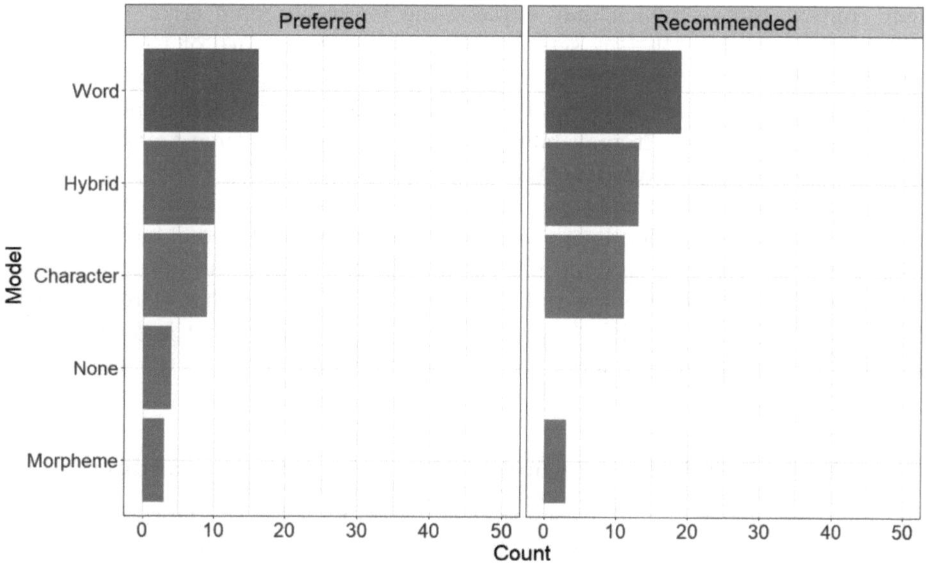


**Fig. 2.** Preferred and recommended predictive text models.

The morpheme model was the slowest, least preferred, and least recommended (see Fig. 2). Participants preferred and recommended the word model, followed by the hybrid and character models which had the highest recommendation usage even though the word condition resulted in slower text entry and more errors.

## 5 Discussion

For the case of novice learners of nêhiyawêwin, the word-based approach to providing predictive supports for text entry performed poorly, whereas the hybrid modelling and character-level approaches facilitated text entry. This, however, was inconsistent with stated participant preferences and recommendations, as they favored the word-based approach over others.

### 5.1 Which Text-Entry Method Supports Quick, Accurate Entry?

The finding that morpheme-level predictions were the slowest and required the most effort fails to match expectations based on the linguistic characteristics of nêhiyawêwin [9]. It also provides evidence for the need to evaluate predictive text for low-resource languages with learners, instead of relying on intrinsic evaluations of model performance (e.g., [20,21]).

The higher manual effort required for text entry in the morpheme condition was likely due to participants transforming selected morphemes so that they fit their context of use, which may explain the lower observed error rate in the morpheme condition. In this setting, the incomplete nature of the prediction may have drawn learner attention to potential mismatches between the text they were entering and the target text. This increased attention could facilitate language learning [31]. It may have also given them the time to perform the cognitive processing needed to catch errors.

Like the word-level predictions, the hybrid and character models were faster than the morpheme model. It appears that the hybrid model combines the benefits of both the character and morpheme-based models. In terms of typing speed, it facilitated quicker text entry and it resulted in error rates that were similar to the fastest of the two models (i.e., character-level model). That is, the integration of the character-level model compensated for limitations in the predictions of the morpheme-level model.

### 5.2 Which Text-Entry Method is More Mentally Demanding?

The increase in participant frustration and workload for the morpheme-based prediction method is aligned with the higher manual effort and slower typing speed seen for this version of nêhiyawêwin predictive text. There were no other differences in workload despite the presence of performance differences across conditions. This misalignment is consistent with prior research that found the text-entry approaches that enabled the fastest input were sometimes perceived as more demanding [28].

The observed differences between measured and perceived effort suggest the outputs of the predictive text models were responsible for the varied experiences, with shortcomings in how predictions were ranked or data limitations preventing adequate morpheme-level predictions. This interpretation is consistent with findings from a word-completion study [21]. In this case, suggestions did not always appear as expected based on the morphological analyses in the training data. For example, the model identified "nitisiyihkâson" as beginning with the morpheme "nitisiyi-" rather than it being composed of the target morphemes "ni-t-isiyihkâso-n". This error led to incorrect predictions being provided until all but the last two characters had been typed.

### 5.3 Which Text-Entry Mehtod is Preferred?

When participants were asked to explicitly provide their preferences, most selected the word condition. Given their weaker performance when using this version, their preference for word prediction is likely due to familiarity as this is the unit of prediction for their dominant language [9]. However, their behavioural data showed they used more recommendations from the character model (which is more dynamic), followed by the word and hybrid models. The hybrid and character-level models were the next most preferred after the word condition, showing an alignment in user preferences and behaviours after accounting for familiarity. Participants were also faster when using these models, they expended less manual effort, and submitted fewer errors.

Due to the focus of performing prediction at the morpheme level in the literature [9], it should be noted that participants were least likely to prefer or recommend this type of predictive text. Moreover, they used any other form of prediction at least five times more than they did morpheme-level predictions. Together, these indicate a need to refocus model development efforts on units of prediction that will be used. Given learner preferences for prediction at the word level, their use of these predictions, and their familiarity with this approach, it would be good to move towards this model as additional data become available.

### 5.4 Future Work: Supporting nêhiyawêwin Speakers and Learners

Both lifelong learners with limited previous exposure to nêhiyawêwin and first language (L1) speakers who are unaccustomed to writing in the language need cognitive supports for producing and accessing texts [23]. Since nêhiyawêwin is a predominantly oral language [6], many L1 speakers have oral fluency but have not been taught how to read or write in the language and many younger speakers want language technologies to support their learning and use of the language [23]. In order to create the specific language technologies they want, we must first develop useful language models. This is one step in that direction.

In contrast to the general population, L1 speakers and home-language learners of nêhiyawêwin may be differentially impacted by seemingly simple choices about what constitutes a morpheme given the role that morphological awareness plays in language teaching and learning [3], especially for morphologically complex languages like nêhiyawêwin [27,29]. This is because L1 speakers may have a different understanding of the structure of nêhiyawêwin, requiring different versions of the language model to be trained. These language models would need to be trained with data that has been preprocessed so that the morphemes used are closely aligned with how nêhiyawêwin morphological decomposition is taught within each community. For example, the morphological breakdown of "kinakatitin" (I leave you) can be taught as ki-nakat-itin [27] or "ki-nakat-iti-n" [33,34], which complicates language technology development. In this context, a morpheme-based model could support students as a reference and cognitive support for building and correctly spelling words when used as part of an educational program.

### 5.5 Limitations

This study investigated how novice lifelong learners responded to a form of cognitive support for an understudied and underserved language. While this provides insight into technology use for supporting Indigenous language learning, additional work should be conducted to better understand the impacts of these technologies on all possible user groups.

The small differences seen in performance across stimulus sets were not systematic across measures. This implies that other linguistic or contextual factors, beyond those we controlled for, influenced text entry. One such factor might be overlap between stimulus character sequences and those from a participant's L1, which could interfere with their nêhiyawêwin typing [16]. Despite these differences, our study was sufficiently powered to find important effects that challenge current disciplinary assumptions around how to support predictive text for low-resource, morphologically-complex languages.

## 6 Conclusion

We investigated which form of prediction provided the best support for lifelong learners of nêhiyawêwin, an endangered Indigenous language spoken in North America. We evaluated four predictive-text conditions (e.g., character, morpheme, word, and a hybrid of character and morpheme) and a baseline, where no suggestions were displayed. Our findings indicated that the commonly touted approach, morpheme-level predictions, frustrated users and slowed their text entry. In contrast, predictions at the character level and an approach that used a hybrid that combined morpheme- and character-level predictions was the most supportive of learner text entry.

**Acknowledgments.** This research was supported in part by the Natural Sciences and Engineering Research Council of Canada and the Social Sciences and Humanities Research Council of Canada. We would also like to thank Eddie Santos, Rebecca Knowles, and Patrick Littell from the NRC's Indigenous Language Technologies project for their advice and their support in using existing tools.

**Disclosure of Interests.** The authors have no competing interests to declare that are relevant to the content of this article

## References

1. Arnold, K.C., Chauncey, K., Gajos, K.Z.: Predictive text encourages predictable writing. In: International Conference on Intelligent User Interfaces, pp. 128–138. Association for Computing Machinery (2020). https://doi.org/10.1145/3377325.3377523
2. Blasi, D., Anastasopoulos, A., Neubig, G.: Systematic inequalities in language technology performance across the world's languages. Presented at the (2022). https://doi.org/10.18653/v1/2022.acl-long.376

3. Carlisle, J.F.: Fostering morphological processing, vocabulary development, and reading comprehension. In: Wagner, R.K., Muse, A.E., Tannenbaum, K.R. (eds.) Vocabulary Acquisition: Implications for Reading Comprehension, pp. 78–103. Guilford Press, New York (2007)
4. Chen, M.X., et al.: Gmail smart compose: real-time assisted writing. In: ACM SIGKDD International Conference on Knowledge Discovery & Data Mining, pp. 2287–2295. Association for Computing Machinery (2019). https://doi.org/10.1145/3292500.3330723
5. Chilton, N.W.: The latin square design in clinical experimentation. J. Dent. Res. **34**(3), 421–428 (1955). https://doi.org/10.1177/00220345550340031801
6. Daniels-Fiss, B.: Learning to be a nêhiyaw (Cree) through language. Diaspora Indigenous Minor. Educ. **2**(3), 233–245 (2008). https://doi.org/10.1080/15595690802145505
7. Darragh, J.J., Witten, I.H.: Adaptive predictive text generation and the reactive keyboard. Interact. Comput. **3**(1), 27–50 (1991). https://doi.org/10.1016/0953-5438(91)90004-L
8. Fisher, R.A.: The Design of Experiments, 8th edn. Hafner Publishing Company, Inc., New York (1966). https://doi.org/10.1002/bimj.19690110215
9. Garay-Vitoria, N., Abascal, J.: Text prediction systems: a survey. Univ. Access Inf. Soc. **4**(3), 188–203 (2006). https://doi.org/10.1007/s10209-005-0005-9
10. Garay-Vitoria, N., Abascal, J., Gardeazabal, L.: Evaluation of prediction methods applied to an inflected language. In: Sojka, P., Kopeček, I., Pala, K. (eds.) Text, Speech and Dialogue, pp. 397–403. Springer, Heidelberg (2002). https://doi.org/10.1007/s10209-005-0005-9
11. Geng, M., et al.: Evaluating speech foundation models for automatic speech recognition in the low-resource Kanyen'kéha language. In: Interspeech, pp. 2063–2067. ISCA (2025). https://doi.org/10.21437/Interspeech.2025-1215
12. Geng, M., Littell, P., Pine, A., Penáć, Tessier, M., Kuhn, R.: Supporting SENĆOŦEN language documentation efforts with automatic speech recognition. In: Lachler, J., et al. (eds.) Workshop on the Use of Computational Methods in the Study of Endangered Languages, pp. 29–39. Association for Computational Linguistics (2025). https://aclanthology.org/2025.computel-main.4/
13. Hart, S.: NASA Task Load Index (TLX). Technical report, Human Performance Research Group, NASA AMes Research Center (1986)
14. Hutchinson, B., Louro, C.R., Collard, G., Cooper, N.: Designing speech technologies for Australian aboriginal english: opportunities, risks and participation. In: ACM Conference on Fairness, Accountability, and Transparency, pp. 108–124. Association for Computing Machinery (2025). https://doi.org/10.1145/3715275.3732010
15. Jurafsky, D., Martin, J.H.: Speech and Language Processing: An Introduction to Natural Language Processing, Computational Linguistics, and Speech Recognition with Language Models, 3rd edn. (2024). https://web.stanford.edu/~jurafsky/slp3/
16. Karimiabdolmaleki, M., Farias Wanderley, L., Cutumisu, M., Rezazadeh, M., Demmans Epp, C.: Negative language transfer identification in the English writing of Chinese and Farsi native speakers. Int. J. Artif. Intell. Educ. (2025). https://doi.org/10.1007/s40593-025-00468-8
17. Keselman, H., Rogan, J.C.: The Tukey multiple comparison test: 1953–1976. Psychol. Bull. **84**(5), 1050 (1977). https://doi.org/10.1037/0033-2909.84.5.1050
18. Kohli, R.: Assessing interaction effects in Latin square-type designs. Int. J. Res. Mark. **5**(1), 25–37 (1988). https://doi.org/10.1016/0167-8116(88)90014-6

19. Kosyak, S., Tyers, F.: Predictive text for agglutinative and polysynthetic languages. In: Serikov, O., et al. (eds.) Workshop on NLP Applications to Field Linguistics, pp. 77–85. International Conference on Computational Linguistics (2022). https://aclanthology.org/2022.fieldmatters-1.9/
20. Kriukova, O., Arppe, A.: Word-level prediction in plains cree: first steps. In: Mager, M., Ebrahimi, A., Rijhwani, S., Oncevay, A., Chiruzzo, L., Pugh, R., von der Wense, K. (eds.) Workshop on Natural Language Processing for Indigenous Languages of the Americas, pp. 15–23. Association for Computational Linguistics (2024). https://doi.org/10.18653/v1/2024.americasnlp-1.3
21. Lane, W., Harrigan, A., Arppe, A.: Interactive word completion for Plains Cree. Presented at the (2022). https://doi.org/10.18653/v1/2022.acl-long.232
22. Littell, P., et al.: Indigenous language technologies in Canada: assessment, challenges, and successes. In: Bender, E.M., Derczynski, L., Isabelle, P. (eds.) International Conference on Computational Linguistics, pp. 2620–2632. Association for Computational Linguistics (2018). https://aclanthology.org/C18-1222/
23. Lothian, D., Akçayir, G., Demmans Epp, C.: Accommodating Indigenous people when using technology to learn their ancestral language. In: Workshop on Supporting Lifelong Learning at the International Conference on Artificial Intelligence in Education, vol. 2395, pp. 16–22. CEUR-WS (2019). http://ceur-ws.org/Vol-2395/paper3.pdf
24. Lothian, D., Akcayir, G., Sparrow, A., Mcleod, O., Demmans Epp, C.: SoundHunters: increasing learner phonological awareness in Plains Cree. In: Bittencourt, I.I., Cukurova, M., Muldner, K., Luckin, R., Millán, E. (eds.) Artificial Intelligence in Education, pp. 346–359. Springer, Heidelberg (2020). https://doi.org/10.1007/978-3-030-52237-7_28
25. Magueresse, A., Carles, V., Heetderks, E.: Low-resource languages: a review of past work and future challenges (2020). https://arxiv.org/abs/2006.07264
26. Nigatu, H.H., Canny, J., Chasins, S.E.: Low-resourced languages and online knowledge repositories: a need-finding study. In: Conference on Human Factors in Computing Systems, pp. 1–21. Association for Computing Machinery (2024). https://doi.org/10.1145/3613904.3642605
27. Okimāsis, J.L.: Cree, Language of the Plains. University of Regina Press (2004)
28. Quinn, P., Zhai, S.: A cost-benefit study of text entry suggestion interaction. In: CHI Conference on Human Factors in Computing Systems, pp. 83–88. Association for Computing Machinery (2016). https://doi.org/10.1145/2858036.2858305
29. Ratt, S., Martin, H.: Mâci-Nêhiyawêwin/Beginning Cree. University of Regina Press (2016)
30. Santos, E.A., Harrigan, A.: Design and evaluation of a smartphone keyboard for Plains Cree syllabics. In: Beermann, D., Besacier, L., Sakti, S., Soria, C. (eds.) Joint Workshop on Spoken Language Technologies for Under-resourced languages and Collaboration and Computing for Under-Resourced Languages, pp. 88–96. European Language Resources association (2020). https://aclanthology.org/2020.sltu-1.12/
31. Schmidt, R.W.: The role of consciousness in second language learning. Appl. Linguis. **11**(2), 129–158 (1990)
32. Schwartz, L., et al.: Neural polysynthetic language modelling. In: Final Report of the Neural Polysynthetic Language Modelling Team at the 2019 Frederick Jelinek Memorial Summer Workshop (2020). https://arxiv.org/pdf/2005.05477.pdf
33. Shirt, M., Wellman, T. (eds.): UnBQ okiskinwahamawâkan otwêstamâkêwasinahikan Student Dictionary. University nuhelot'ine thaiyots'i nistameyimâkanak Blue Quills (2019)

34. Shirt, M., Wellman, T. (eds.): tânisîsi kâ-ôsîtahk pîkiskwêwinisa Morphology Dictionary. University nuhelot'ine thaiyots'i nistameyimâkanak Blue Quills (2022)
35. Silfverberg, M., Lindén, K., Hyvärinen, M.: Predictive text entry for agglutinative languages using unsupervised morphological segmentation. In: Computational Linguistics and Intelligent Text Processing, pp. 478–489. Springer, Heidelberg (2012). https://doi.org/10.1007/978-3-642-28601-8_40
36. Tantug, A.C.: A probabilistic mobile text entry system for agglutinative languages. IEEE Trans. Consum. Electron. **56**(2), 1018–1024 (2010). https://doi.org/10.1109/TCE.2010.5506034
37. Teodorescu, D., Matalski, J., Lothian, D., Barbosa, D., Demmans Epp, C.: Cree corpus: a collection of nêhiyawêwin resources. Presented at the (2022). https://doi.org/10.18653/v1/2022.acl-long.440
38. Wagner, I.: New Technologies, Same Ideologies: Learning from Language Revitalization Online (2017). http://hdl.handle.net/10125/24730
39. Wagner, R., Torgesen, J.K., Rachotte, C.: Test of Word Reading Efficiency - (TOWRE-2), 2nd edn. Pearson (2011)
40. Yu, S., Kulkarni, N., Lee, H., Kim, J.: Syllable-level neural language model for agglutinative language. In: Faruqui, M., Schuetze, H., Trancoso, I., Yaghoobzadeh, Y. (eds.) Workshop on Subword and Character Level Models in NLP, pp. 92–96. Association for Computational Linguistics (2017). https://doi.org/10.18653/v1/W17-4113

# Toward Fair and Scalable Assessment of Socially Shared Regulation of Learning with Large Language Models

Yang Jiang[1(✉)], Yi Song[1], Ido Roll[2], Jiangang Hao[1], Chunyi Ruan[1], and Lei Liu[1]

[1] ETS Research Institute, Princeton, NJ 08541, USA
yjiang002@ets.org
[2] Technion – Israel Institute of Technology, Technion City, 3200003 Haifa, Israel

**Abstract.** Effective collaborative learning depends on learners' ability to collectively regulate their learning processes through socially shared regulation of learning (SSRL). Despite its central role in collaboration quality and learning outcomes, SSRL remains challenging to assess due to its multidimensional, dynamic, and interactional nature. Recent advances in large language models (LLMs) offer promising opportunities to automate discourse-based assessment, yet questions remain regarding their validity, robustness, and fairness across student populations. This study investigates the feasibility of using LLMs, specifically GPT-4o and GPT-5, to automatically code SSRL behaviors in collaborative discourse from a scenario-based science task, comprising 5830 student chat turns. Using a theory-driven coding framework, we compare LLM-based coding across prompt designs and model types, evaluate the consistency of LLM performance across underserved and non-underserved school contexts, and examine how SSRL behaviors differ between these student populations. Results show that LLM-based coding achieves strong agreement with human annotation, approaching human–human reliability, with context-enriched prompting yielding improved performance than general prompting. Importantly, LLM performance is stable across school contexts. Analyses further reveal meaningful differences in SSRL behaviors, with teams from an underserved school context demonstrating more cognitive information sharing behaviors, while teams from a non-underserved context engage more frequently in metacognitive planning and affective regulation. These findings highlight the potential of LLMs for scalable and equitable assessment of collaborative regulation and inform the design of responsible, adaptive AI systems that support collaborative learning for diverse learners.

**Keywords:** Socially Shared Regulation of Learning · Collaboration · Regulation · ChatGPT · Generative AI · Assessment · Context · Fairness · LLM-Based Coding

## 1 Introduction

Self-regulated learning (SRL) is a critical 21st-century competency that supports lifelong learning [39]. Learners with strong SRL skills can set goals, plan strategically, monitor progress, and adapt strategies across diverse contexts [29]. As collaboration


E. G. Blanchard et al. (eds.), AIED 2026, LNCS 16586, pp. 194–209, 2027.
https://doi.org/10.1007/978-3-032-29773-0_14

becomes increasingly central to education and beyond [16], regulation occurs not only at the individual level but also through social interaction. In collaborative settings, effective learning depends on how group members jointly regulate their learning processes, referred to as socially shared regulation of learning (SSRL; [10]). SSRL involves the active and collective coordination of cognitive, motivational, affective, and behavioral regulation strategies to achieve shared goals [10, 30]. Research has shown that SSRL is positively associated with group performance and academic achievement and shapes the quality of collaboration [9, 30, 38].

Despite its importance, SSRL is challenging to measure given its complex, multidimensional, and process-oriented nature [20, 22]. Traditional approaches for measuring SSRL include self-report surveys [20, 33], which often fail to capture the dynamic aspects of regulation as it unfolds in real time. While discourse data (e.g., student chats) provides more authentic and fine-grained evidence of regulatory behaviors, it typically requires manual qualitative coding, a process that is labor-intensive, time-consuming, and difficult to scale [12, 16]. These limitations pose significant barriers to scalable measurement and real-time adaptive support in learning environments.

Recent advances in large language models (LLMs) offer promising opportunities to automate the qualitative coding of complex learning processes. LLMs have demonstrated strong performance in analyzing educational discourse, especially when guided by well-designed prompts [6, 12, 16, 25, 26]. However, SSRL is a highly complex, context-sensitive construct involving multiple facets (e.g., cognition, affect, motivation, metacognition), often expressed implicitly across dialogic turns and distributed among group members. It remains unclear whether LLMs can reliably capture such nuanced regulatory behaviors, and how prompt design influences model performance.

Educational data is deeply shaped by learners' backgrounds, school environments, and communication norms. Students from different socioeconomic and educational contexts often have unequal access to learning resources and opportunities, which may influence how they regulate their learning and engage in collaboration [7]. These differences raise important concerns about the fairness and generalizability of AI-based coding approaches. While prior research has examined algorithmic bias in predictive models across demographic subgroups [3, 18, 27], empirical investigations of the consistency in LLM-based coding, particularly for shared regulation in collaborative learning, remain limited. To address this gap, our study systematically investigates the consistency of automated coding across underserved and non-underserved student populations, while also examining how learners from these contexts differ in their engagement in regulatory processes during collaboration. Understanding both the robustness of automated coding and differences in student behavior informs the responsible use of AI in educational research and the design of effective context-sensitive AI-driven supports.

In the present study, we investigate the use of LLMs to automate the coding and assessment of SSRL in collaborative discourse. Using a theory-driven SSRL coding framework, we evaluate LLM performance relative to human coders, examine how prompt design—particularly the inclusion of guidance to leverage local conversational context—and model type affect coding reliability. We further assess whether LLM-based coding performs consistently across student populations by comparing LLM performance on discourse from underserved and non-underserved school contexts. Finally, building on LLM-coded data, we explore whether students from distinct educational contexts engage in SSRL processes differently during collaboration. The research questions (RQs) we aim to address include:

RQ1: How accurately can LLMs identify SSRL skills in students' collaborative discourse compared to trained human raters? How do prompting strategies and model choice affect the performance of LLM-based SSRL coding?
RQ2: Does LLM-based coding show consistent performance when applied to collaborative discourse from underserved and non-underserved student populations?
RQ3: Are there differences in the SSRL skills and behaviors manifested by students from underserved versus non-underserved schools?

By integrating SSRL theory with LLMs, this study contributes to AIED research by demonstrating the potential of LLMs for scalable and fair SSRL assessment, highlighting the importance of prompt design, and providing empirical evidence to inform the design of AI tools for supporting diverse student populations in collaborative learning.

## 2 Related Work

### 2.1 Socially Shared Regulation of Learning in Collaboration

SSRL refers to the regulatory processes that occur at the group level in collaborative learning, where learners collectively plan, monitor, evaluate, and regulate their learning activities as a cohesive unit [10, 30]. Rather than residing solely within individuals, regulation in SSRL is jointly constructed and enacted through interaction, as group members negotiate goals, coordinate strategies, and manage shared understanding. Like SRL, SSRL encompasses multiple interrelated dimensions, including cognitive (e.g., explaining, problem solving), metacognitive (e.g., planning, monitoring), as well as motivational and affective processes (e.g., encouragement, emotional expression) [34]. Although these processes are partly internal, they are also socially shaped and manifested through discourse, making interactions central to understanding how regulation unfolds in collaborative contexts. Empirical studies have shown that effective SSRL is associated with higher-quality collaboration, deeper cognitive engagement, and improved learning outcomes [9, 30, 38].

Furthermore, both regulation and collaboration are shaped by learners' backgrounds and learning contexts, and thus may not be enacted uniformly across groups. Prior studies indicate that differences in prior knowledge, learner characteristics, and familiarity with collaborative norms influence how students regulate their learning [17, 36] and collaborate [1, 19]. Despite these insights, empirical research that systematically examines subgroup differences in SSRL—particularly across different school and educational contexts—remains limited. Addressing this gap informs the design of adaptive AI-supported collaborative learning systems that are responsive to diverse regulatory practices, and requires analytic approaches that can scale to diverse populations and support comparative analyses of SSRL processes across contexts, which is the focus of the present study.

## 2.2 Using Large Language Models for Automated SSRL Assessment

Discourse data such as chat logs is a critical data source for examining the dynamic collaborative learning and regulation processes [1]. Traditionally, such data has been analyzed through manual qualitative coding, which supports nuanced interpretation but is difficult to scale as datasets grow in size and complexity [16]. In response, researchers have explored automated approaches for analyzing discourse data to improve efficiency and scalability [8, 12, 31, 35]. Early work leveraged machine learning models with natural language processing (NLP) features to detect constructs related to SRL [21, 37] and collaborative problem solving (CPS, [8, 31]). For example, Zhang et al. [37] built detectors of four SRL behaviors using features extracted from student responses to questions and interaction logs in a digital learning environment, achieving AUC ranging from.76–.89 and were stable across different student populations. More recently, Sun and Liu [35] used n-gram features and traditional machine learning models to code SSRL behaviors in classroom collaboration data. However, these approaches often rely on extensive feature engineering and supervised models, still requiring substantial labeled data and limiting generalizability across tasks and contexts [16].

More recent work has applied LLMs to qualitative coding by directly prompting them with task instructions, coding schemes, and sometimes examples, enabling annotation with minimal task-specific training data. Studies have shown that LLMs can reliably code a range of educational constructs when supported by well-designed prompts [12, 16, 24–26]. For instance, our previous work [16] showed that GPT-4o achieved agreement comparable to human raters in coding CPS behaviors, though performance varied across constructs. Liu et al. [24] evaluated multiple prompting strategies when using GPT-4 for qualitative coding and found that their effectiveness depends strongly on the nature of the target construct. For example, zero-shot prompting tends to work best for well-defined, straightforward constructs, whereas few-shot prompts with contextual information such as background, conversational purpose, or the surrounding text are particularly beneficial for complex constructs sensitive to discourse context. Extending this line of work to SSRL, Li et al. [23] examined three LLMs (GPT-4o, GPT-o1, and DeepSeek-R1) for coding asynchronous peer discussions into one of four metacognitive regulation phases: Off-topic, acceptance, sharing, and co-construction. Their results showed that few-shot prompting outperformed zero-shot approaches, and that incorporating chain-of-thought reasoning further improved performance. However, the models still struggled with ambiguous and nuanced cases, highlighting the challenges of capturing implicit contextual meanings.

These challenges are particularly pronounced in SSRL, which is multifaceted and context-dependent, often involving dealing with contextual complexity, particularly when utterances are short, fragmented, or highly interdependent. Na and Feng [26] used multi-LLM ensemble prediction and iterative consistency-checking mechanisms that leverage adjacency relations (e.g., question–answer pairs) to resolve contextually inconsistent codes when coding dialogue characteristics such as communicative acts and communicative events among utterances. Their work highlights the importance of incorporating contextual reasoning when applying LLMs to discourse analysis. Building on these insights, the present study applies context-enriched prompting to detect SSRL in collaborative learning discourse, an area in which the use of LLMs has received relatively little attention.

### 2.3 Fairness and Robustness in LLM-Based Coding

Fairness is a core value in education. Prior research has shown that AI methods such as machine learning models may exhibit bias and limited robustness and generalizability across student populations and educational contexts [3, 27]. For example, Ocumpaugh et al. [27] demonstrated that affect detectors trained on data from one demographic group (e.g., urban students) did not generalize well to others (e.g., suburban or rural). Similar challenges have been documented in transferring models across countries and educational systems [28, 32], further underscoring the sensitivity of educational data to contextual and cultural factors. Despite these concerns, relatively few studies have examined whether LLM-based coding performs consistently across student populations. Emerging evidence is mixed. For example, Ashwin et al. [2] cautioned that LLMs may introduce subtle bias when annotating interview data, whereas Hao et al. [11] reported no significant performance differences across gender and racial groups in ChatGPT-based coding of collaborative problem solving. However, evidence regarding the fairness and robustness of LLM-based coding across different school contexts remains limited. Addressing this gap is critical for the responsible and equitable deployment of LLMs in collaborative learning systems and for informing ethical practice in AIED.

## 3 Methodology

### 3.1 Participants

Data for this study was collected from 200 eighth-grade students from two middle schools in the United States. Students worked in dyads (100 teams) to solve scenario-based science problems in a classroom setting, communicating via text-based chats on an online platform [19]. Across all teams, students produced a total of 5830 chat turns. Three teams were excluded from analysis because they did not engage in any chat during the task. The final sample therefore consisted of 194 students (97 dyads).

Of the 97 dyads, 43 teams (86 students) were from an underserved, urban school, and 54 teams (108 students) were from a non-underserved, suburban school. The two schools differed substantially in socioeconomic and academic contexts. According to publicly available data from the National Center for Education Statistics and state education agency reports, fewer than 20% of students at the non-underserved school were eligible for free or reduced-price lunch, and student performance on statewide assessments in English Language Arts (ELA), Mathematics, and Science was at or near the state average. In contrast, at the underserved school, more than 80% of students were eligible for free or reduced-price lunch. Student performance on statewide assessments in ELA, Mathematics, and Science at this school was well below the state average, with the majority of students not meeting state proficiency expectations. Detailed demographics of the participants, including eligibility for free or reduced-price lunch, gender, race/ethnicity, and English Language Learner status, are reported in Table 1. All study procedures were reviewed and approved by the appropriate Institutional Review Board (IRB).

**Table 1.** Participant demographics by school context.

| Demographic Variable | Underserved | Non-underserved |
|---|---|---|
| Eligible for free or reduced-price lunch | 93.2% | 25.0% |
| Received accommodations in end-of-year assessments | 9.6% | 0% |
| English language learner | 2.7% | 0% |
| Female | 56.2% | 40.7% |
| Race/ethnicity | 46.6% African American, 47.9% Hispanic, 4.1% Asian, 1.4% Mixed Race | 97.2% White, 1.9% Hispanic, 0.9% Hawaiian/Pacific |

### 3.2 Collaborative Task

A scenario-based science task focused on molecular physics, specifically the structures and properties of matter (see Fig. 1), was developed and delivered through the ETS Platform for Collaborative Assessment and Learning (EPCAL, [13]). Working in dyads, participants collaborated via a chat box while interacting with a science simulation on the phenomenon of condensation and completing a sequence of problems. Eight of the problems were multiple-choice or constructed-response questions, which required students to interpret the scenario, apply molecular-level concepts, and explain or justify their reasoning. In addition, the task included a modeling activity, where students collaboratively created visual representations of molecular structures or processes using an embedded drawing tool.

### 3.3 Assessing SSRL Using LLMs

**SSRL Coding Framework and Human Annotation.** To evaluate students' SSRL processes, we developed a coding framework that captures regulatory behaviors across five dimensions: cognitive, metacognitive, motivational, affective, and social regulation. The framework was grounded in prior theoretical models and empirical studies on SRL and SSRL (e.g., [10, 22, 30]) and was adapted to reflect the collaborative, chat-based problem-solving context of this study. Each chat utterance was coded into one of nine SSRL skills spanning the five dimensions (see Table 2). The categories were designed to systematically capture how teams jointly construct understanding, coordinate strategies, regulate motivation and affect, and manage social interaction during collaboration.

Two trained human raters independently coded approximately 19% of the total chat turns (1,114 utterances from 24 randomly selected teams; 12 teams per school), achieving strong inter-rater reliability (Cohen's $\kappa = 0.824$). Discrepancies were resolved by a trained adjudicator to produce final consensus codes. During annotation, human raters had access to the conversational context within each collaborative session and were instructed to interpret each utterance in relation to surrounding turns, following standard practice in qualitative analysis of collaborative discourse.

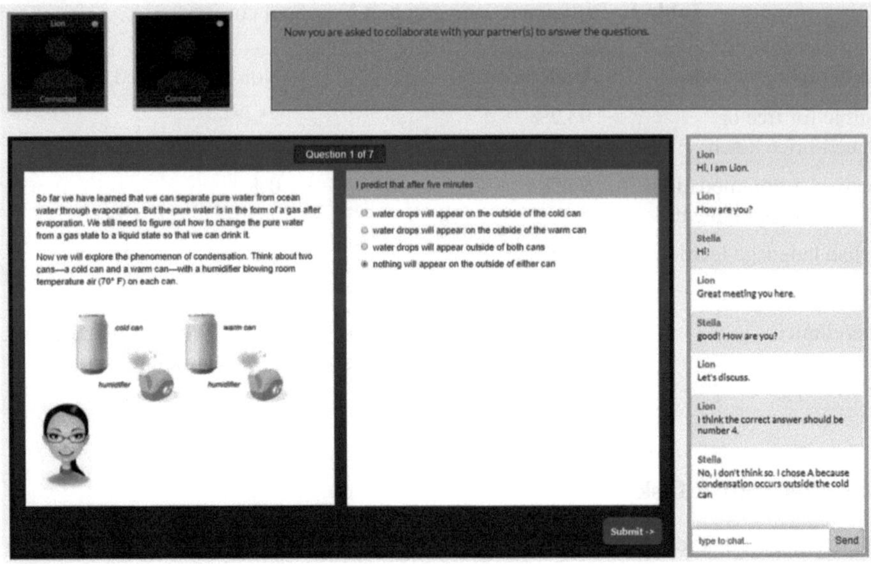


**Fig. 1.** Screenshot of scenario-based science task.

**LLM-Based Coding.** We used two LLMs, GPT-4o (version: 2024-05-13) and GPT-5 (version: 2025-08-07), to automatically detect SSRL skills using a prompting approach incorporating few-shot examples and chain-of-thought strategies. The prompt was structured based on prior work on prompt engineering for discourse annotation (e.g., [12, 24, 26]) and iteratively refined through group discussion. The final prompt consisted of several components: (a) role and task description, specifying the model's role and objective, study context, and the collaborative science task; (b) SSRL coding framework, including definitions for each category and associated subskills; (c) step-by-step reasoning instructions that guide systematic decision making (chain-of-thought approach); (d) a few example utterances illustrating each SSRL code (few-shot approach); and (e) specifications for input and output formats, including a structured output schema for predicted codes.

Following [26], we instructed LLMs to follow a stepwise reasoning procedure that mimics human chain-of-thought to: (1) identify the primary communicative function of the utterance given its local context, (2) determine whether the utterance was task-relevant or primarily social, and finally (3) assign the most appropriate SSRL skill.

We created two prompt variants to examine the effects of context-sensitive prompting on model performance. The *context-enriched prompt* explicitly emphasized the role of conversational context, including a dedicated section on contextual coding guidelines that instructed the model to interpret each utterance in relation to surrounding turns (three preceding and three following). In this version, the model was directed to attend to nearby utterances and to apply rules adapted from human coder training, recognizing that utterances, particularly short or ambiguous ones (e.g., "ok," "yeah," "thanks") may serve different functions depending on the conversational context. For example, brief

**Table 2.** SSRL coding framework.

| Dimension | SSRL Skill/Code | Definition |
|---|---|---|
| Cognitive | Sharing information | Student shares task-relevant information (e.g., individual response) or prior experience/knowledge with teammate. |
| | Eliciting | Chats that elicit task-relevant information or feedback from teammate. |
| | Elaborating | Chats that expand or add detail to ideas by making connections or providing further explanations. |
| Metacognitive | Planning | Students set goals, develop plans, and develop an understanding of the task. |
| | Monitoring | Student monitors their own, teammate's, or team's comprehension, progress, or collaboration. |
| | Evaluating | Chats that evaluate one's or others' understanding of the task, concepts, or problem-solving approach, or reflecting on the difficulty level of a task or what worked or could be improved after completing a task or item. |
| Motivational | Expressing/regulating motivation | Chats that involve expression or regulation of motivation, such as self-efficacy, motivational regulation, goal orientation/interest/task value. |
| Affective | Expressing/regulating emotions | Chats that express or regulate emotions |
| Social | Maintaining communication | Content-irrelevant social-oriented communications, including rapport building communication, off-topic communication, and inappropriate communication. |

acknowledgments were interpreted based on the utterances they responded to or preceded, rather than being coded in isolation. This design was intended to approximate the contextual information available to human annotators, and the choice of window size (three surrounding turns on each side) was informed by prior research [24] and human annotators' practices during training and coding. In contrast, the *general prompt* did not include explicit contextual coding guidelines.

All coding was conducted via the Azure OpenAI Service, which provided security and guardrails to protect student data. Chat logs were processed one collaborative session at a time, ensuring that the full conversational context within each session was available during coding. All model hyperparameters were set to default, except that a fixed random seed was used to ensure reproducibility, and that the temperature was set to 0 for GPT-4o.

### 3.4 Data Analysis

To evaluate the performance of LLM-based coding (RQ1), we computed two inter-rater reliability metrics: percent of agreement and Cohen's Kappa [5]. These metrics were used to infer the agreement between the LLM and human coders across SSRL categories and were compared against the inter-rater reliability observed between human raters. Model performance was further compared across different prompting strategies (general vs. context-enriched) and models (GPT-4o vs. GPT-5) to examine their effects on coding reliability.

We further fitted generalized linear mixed-effects models (GLMMs) to examine whether LLM coding performance differed across school contexts (RQ2). In these models, the dependent variable was agreement on a given chat turn between the LLM and human coder (coded as 1 for agreement vs. 0 for disagreement), with school context (underserved vs. non-underserved) included as a fixed effect. To account for the nested and hierarchical structure of the data, where multiple chat turns were produced by the same student and students were nested within teams, we included random intercepts for teams and for students nested within teams [15]. All mixed-effects models were implemented in R using the lme4 package [4].

To address RQ3, we examined differences in students' engagement in SSRL skills across school contexts using the LLM-coded full dataset (5,830 chat turns). For each team, we computed measures such as the total number of chat turns, time on task, average chat length, and the proportion of chat turns belonging to each SSRL category. These team-level measures were then compared between schools using two-tailed Mann–Whitney U tests to account for non-parametric distributions. We reported Cohen's $d$ [5] as a measure of effect size, with values of $d = 0.2$, 0.5, and 0.8 interpreted as small, medium, and large effects, respectively.

## 4 Results and Discussion

### 4.1 LLM Performance in Coding SSRL

To address RQ1, we examined the extent to which LLM-based coding of SSRL skills aligned with human coding (Table 3). As a benchmark, agreement between human raters was high ($\kappa = .824$), indicating strong reliability and establishing a solid reference for evaluating LLM performance. In general, ChatGPT achieved moderate to strong agreement with human raters, with $\kappa$ values ranging from.638 to .776 across models and prompting strategies. GPT-5 consistently outperformed GPT-4o under both prompt designs and achieved its highest reliability when using the context-enriched prompt, approaching human–human agreement levels. These results indicate that LLMs, particularly newer-generation models such as GPT-5, can identify complex, theory-driven constructs like SSRL in collaborative discourse with a level of reliability that approaches that of trained human coders. They are consistent with recent work demonstrating the potential of LLMs as effective proxies for human annotation when supported by well-designed prompts (e.g., [16, 24–26]), particularly in contexts where extensive human coding is costly or infeasible.

At the same time, the remaining gap between LLM–human and human–human agreement reflects the complexity and contextual sensitivity of SSRL as a construct. Regulatory behaviors in collaborative settings are often implicit and highly dependent on conversational context, posing challenges even for advanced language models.

For both models, performance was higher with the context-enriched prompt than with the general prompt, indicating that explicit incorporation of conversational context guidelines improves SSRL classification. This effect was especially pronounced for GPT-5, suggesting that the newer-generation model may be better able to leverage contextual information when guided appropriately. Examination of class-level performance (i.e., for each SSRL skill) and the confusion matrices further revealed that contextual coding guidelines led to notable improvements in the detection of maintaining communication ($\kappa = .900$ vs. .774), sharing information ($\kappa = .774$ vs. .630), expressing/regulating motivation ($\kappa = .698$ vs. .601), and expressing/regulating emotions ($\kappa = .646$ vs. .581). The model- and prompt-level differences suggest the importance of both model capability and prompt design, and reinforce the central role of contextual information in analyzing collaborative discourse, particularly for regulation-related behaviors that are inherently context dependent.

**Table 3.** Performance of LLM-based coding.

| Comparison | Prompt Design | Agree | Kappa |
|---|---|---|---|
| Human-human | | 86.7% | .824 |
| Human-GPT4o | General | 72.5% | .638 |
| | Context-enriched | 73.4% | .649 |
| Human-GPT5 | General | 77.5% | .705 |
| | Context-enriched | 83.0% | .776 |

Note. Percent of agreement and Cohen's Kappa were calculated based on double-coded chat turns.

## 4.2 LLM Coding Performance Across Student Populations

To address RQ2, we examined whether the performance of LLM-based SSRL coding differed for discourse generated by teams from different school contexts. Mixed effects model results (Table 4) indicated that agreement between human raters was marginally significantly higher for the non-underserved school (91.3%, $\kappa = .883$) than for the underserved school (83.5%, $\kappa = .783$), $p = .056$. The odds of agreement were nearly twice as high for chats from the non-underserved school (odds ratio = 1.90). This pattern suggests that SSRL-related discourse produced by students in the non-underserved context may be consistently more interpretable by human raters, potentially reflecting differences in discourse style, clarity, explicitness of regulatory behaviors, or alignment with the coding framework. For example, it is possible that chats from underserved schools may include shorter, more context-dependent, or more socially nuanced utterances, which can increase coding difficulty in the absence of strong contextual scaffolding. These results highlight the importance of continued validation across diverse populations and suggest that future work should examine how task design, discourse norms, and prompt scaffolding might further support reliable SSRL detection in underserved contexts.

A similar trend was observed for human–LLM agreement; however, after accounting for the nested structure of the data, agreement between LLMs and human coders was not significantly associated with school context. To further contextualize these results relative to human performance, we included human–human agreement as a covariate in the mixed-effects model. After controlling for human–human agreement, human–LLM agreement remained not significantly predicted by school context ($z = 0.77, p = .444$). The absence of statistically significant differences in human–LLM agreement suggests that LLM-based SSRL coding is relatively stable across student populations, and that school context does not substantially moderate LLM coding accuracy, particularly for newer-generation models such as GPT-5. Notably, for GPT-5 under the general prompt, agreement levels were highly similar across schools ($\kappa = .712$ for underserved vs. .697 for non-underserved). In contrast to the marginally significantly higher agreement among human raters in the non-underserved school, LLM-based SSRL coding does not appear to introduce systematic agreement differences across school contexts beyond variability already present in human interpretation.

**Table 4.** Performance of LLM-based coding by school context.

| | | Underserved | | Non-underserved | | | |
|---|---|---|---|---|---|---|---|
| Comparison | Prompt Design | Agree | Kappa | Agree | Kappa | *Odds Ratio* | *p* |
| Human-human | | 83.5% | .783 | 91.3% | .883 | 1.90 | .056 |
| Human-GPT4o | General | 67.8% | .581 | 79.2% | .721 | 1.57 | .124 |
| | Context-enriched | 69.5% | .603 | 79.0% | .716 | 1.36 | .382 |
| Human-GPT5 | General | 77.9% | .712 | 76.8% | .697 | 1.08 | .757 |
| | Context-enriched | 80.4% | .743 | 86.8% | .822 | 1.49 | .249 |
| | Number of chat turns | 653 | | 461 | | | |

*Note.* Odds ratios and *p*-values from generalized linear mixed-effects models were reported.

### 4.3 Differences in SSRL Behaviors Across Student Populations

The differences in inter-rater reliability observed between schools may reflect differences in how SSRL behaviors are expressed across contexts, which we examine in RQ3. On average, teams from the underserved school spent significantly more time on the collaborative task than teams from the non-underserved school, with a medium effect size ($d = -0.66, p = .011$; see Table 5). This suggests that underserved teams may have required more time to complete the task, possibly due to differences in prior science knowledge (as indicated by state assessment performance) or coordination demands during collaboration. Although no significant difference was observed in the number of chat turns produced by teams, students from the non-underserved school generated significantly longer chat turns, as indicated by a higher average word count per turn. In other words, students from an underserved context communicated through shorter, fragmented utterances, whereas those from the non-underserved school tended to consolidate ideas within individual turns, which may be related to different literacy skills as indicated by ELA performance in the state assessment. Shorter chat turns may increase ambiguity in interpretation, potentially contributing to the lower inter-rater agreement observed among human raters for discourse from underserved teams.

**Table 5.** Differences in task engagement and SSRL behaviors by school context.

| | Underserved | | Non-underserved | | | |
|---|---|---|---|---|---|---|
| Variable | *M* | *SD* | *M* | *SD* | *Cohen's d* | *p* |
| Number of chat turns | 73.86 | 105.32 | 46.11 | 35.71 | −0.37 | .520 |
| Average word count per turn | 3.67 | 2.00 | 4.62 | 2.17 | 0.45 | .008 |
| Time on task (in minutes) | 31.89 | 15.86 | 23.95 | 7.56 | −0.66 | .011 |
| Pct. Cognition | 21.3% | 16.6% | 15.6% | 14.5% | −0.37 | .074 |
| Pct. Sharing information | 12.8% | 11.7% | 7.0% | 8.5% | −0.57 | .011 |
| Pct. Eliciting | 5.9% | 6.4% | 7.0% | 6.2% | 0.17 | .346 |
| Pct. Elaborating | 2.6% | 6.4% | 1.6% | 3.2% | −0.20 | .761 |
| Pct. Metacognition | 28.3% | 19.7% | 39.2% | 22.2% | 0.51 | .011 |
| Pct. Planning | 4.9% | 5.5% | 10.6% | 11.0% | 0.64 | .008 |
| Pct. Evaluating | 1.1% | 2.3% | 1.5% | 2.7% | 0.12 | .554 |
| Pct. Monitoring | 22.3% | 16.4% | 27.1% | 17.3% | 0.29 | .131 |
| Pct. Expressing/regulating motivation | 1.6% | 2.8% | 2.2% | 4.5% | 0.15 | .953 |
| Pct. Expressing/regulating emotions | 2.4% | 5.4% | 3.9% | 4.9% | 0.30 | .027 |
| Pct. Maintaining communication | 46.4% | 31.6% | 39.1% | 31.9% | −0.23 | .214 |

*Note.* Effect size of the difference and the *p* value of the Mann Whitney U test comparing the variables between groups were reported.

At the level of SSRL behaviors, teams from the underserved school exhibited a marginally higher proportion of cognitive regulation behaviors during collaboration, driven primarily by a significantly higher proportion of information-sharing utterances. In contrast, teams from the non-underserved school engaged in a significantly larger proportion of metacognitive regulation, particularly planning behaviors, in which students communicated to develop a shared understanding of the task, set goals, and develop plans. This pattern could be partially explained by the differences in academic performance across schools and aligns with prior research showing associations between metacognitive regulation, prior knowledge, and task performance [36]. In comparison, the greater emphasis on information sharing among underserved teams may reflect a need to establish shared understanding in contexts characterized by more heterogeneous prior knowledge or lower confidence in common ground.

Differences also emerged in the affective dimension of SSRL, with students from the non-underserved school exhibiting a significantly higher proportion of chat turns involving the expression or regulation of emotions. Such affective expressions—including encouragement, frustration, or emotional reflection—may play an important role in sustaining engagement and coordinating collaborative work [34], particularly in extended problem-solving tasks.

## 5 Conclusions and Implications

This study examined the feasibility and robustness of LLM-based coding for automatically capturing complex SSRL skills in collaborative discourse, focusing on the effect of prompting strategies and the consistency of LLM performance across school contexts. Results showed that LLM-based coding—especially when using newer-generation models such as GPT-5 and context-enriched prompting—achieved strong agreement with human raters, approaching human–human reliability. These findings demonstrate the potential of leveraging LLMs to automatically monitor, model, and support shared regulation processes in real time or at scale. Such capabilities are especially valuable for large classrooms, online learning environments, and informal learning settings where manual discourse analysis is impractical. Moreover, explicitly guiding LLMs to attend to local conversational context improved coding performance, highlighting the importance of prompt design for reliable automated assessment of complex skills such as SSRL.

In addition, the study addresses a gap in the literature by examining the fairness and consistency of AI-based coding across student populations. Although human raters showed higher agreement when coding discourse from the non-underserved school—likely due to differences in discourse length and explicitness—LLM-based coding did not introduce additional systematic disparities. Instead, LLM performance remained relatively stable across underserved and non-underserved schools, providing empirical evidence supporting the responsible and equitable deployment of LLMs in collaborative learning systems. When carefully designed and validated, LLMs can support reliable and fair assessment of complex learning processes across diverse contexts—an enduring goal in AIED.

Meanwhile, meaningful differences emerged in how students engaged in SSRL behaviors across school contexts. Teams from an underserved background engaged more frequently in cognitive regulation, particularly information sharing to establish shared understanding, whereas teams from the non-underserved school exhibited more metacognitive regulation, such as planning, as well as greater expression and regulation of emotions. Understanding these differences is essential for designing adaptive AI-driven scaffolding and interventions that respond to students' diverse regulatory needs rather than assuming uniform patterns of collaboration.

Together, these findings suggest that LLMs can serve as scalable and reliable tools for automated assessment of SSRL, opening pathways for adaptive, personalized scaffolding (e.g., through AI-driven conversational agents). Future work will examine how SSRL behaviors relate to collaborative task performance and whether these relationships differ across student populations, as well as explore the temporal dynamics of SSRL using learning analytics methods to better understand how regulation unfolds over time. In addition, the context-enriched prompt used in this study relies on incorporating surrounding discourse (including subsequent turns), which aligns with the contextual information human coders typically use but may limit direct real-time deployment. Future research should therefore investigate approaches that rely solely on preceding context to enable more robust real-time monitoring and scaffolding applications.

**Disclosure of Interests.** The authors have no competing interests to declare that are relevant to the content of this article.

## References

1. Andrews-Todd, J., Jiang, Y., Steinberg, J., Pugh, S.L., D'Mello, S.K.: Investigating collaborative problem solving skills and outcomes across computer-based tasks. Comput. Educ. **207**, 104928 (2023)
2. Ashwin, J., Chhabra, A., Rao, V.: Using large language models for qualitative analysis can introduce serious bias. Sociol. Methods Res. **52**, 00491241251338246 (2023)
3. Baker, R.S., Hawn, A.: Algorithmic bias in education. Int. J. Artif. Intell. Educ. **32**(4), 1052–1092 (2022)
4. Bates, D., Mächler, M., Bolker, B., Walker, S.: Fitting linear mixed-effects models using lme4. J. Stat. Softw. **67**(1), 1–48 (2015)
5. Cohen, J.: A coefficient of agreement for nominal scales. Educ. Psychol. Meas. **20**, 37–46 (1960)
6. Cui, W., Hao, J., Jiang, Y., Kyllonen, P.C., Kerzabi, E.: Automated coding of communication data using large language models: a comparison of hierarchical and direct prompting strategies. Front. Educ. **11**, 1764154 (2026)
7. Floden, R.E.: The measurement of opportunity to learn. In: Methodological Advances in Cross-National Surveys of Educational Achievement, pp. 231–266. National Academy Press, Washington, DC (2002)
8. Flor, M., Andrews-Todd, J.: Towards automatic annotation of collaborative problem-solving skills in technology-enhanced environments. J. Comput. Assist. Learn. **38**(5), 1434–1447 (2022)
9. Haataja, E., Dindar, M., Malmberg, J., Järvelä, S.: Individuals in a group: metacognitive and regulatory predictors of learning achievement in collaborative learning. Learn. Individ. Differ. **96**, 102146 (2022)
10. Hadwin, A.F., Järvelä, S., Miller, M.: Self-regulation, co-regulation and shared regulation in collaborative learning environments. In: Schunk, D.H., Greene, J.A. (eds.) Handbook of Self-Regulation of Learning and Performance, 2nd edn, pp. 83–106. Routledge, New York (2018)
11. Hao, J., Cui, W., Kyllonen, P., Kerzabi, E.: Automated coding of communication data using LLM: consistency across subgroups. J. Educ. Meas. **63**, e70049 (2026)

12. Hao, J., Cui, W., Kyllonen, P., Kerzabi, E., Liu, L., Flor, M.: Automated coding of communications in collaborative problem-solving tasks using ChatGPT. J. Educ. Meas. **62**(4), 809–837 (2025)
13. Hao, J. et al.: EPCAL: ETS platform for collaborative assessment and learning. ETS Res. Rep. Ser. **2017**(1), 1–14 (2017)
14. Hayes, A.S.: "Conversing" with qualitative data: enhancing qualitative research through large language models. Int J Qual Methods. **24**, 16094069251322346 (2025)
15. Janssen, J., Erkens, G., Kirschner, P.A., Kanselaar, G.: Multilevel analysis in CSCL research. In: Puntambekar, S., Erkens, G., Hmelo-Silver, C. (eds.) Analyzing Interactions in CSCL, pp. 187–205. Springer, New York (2011)
16. Jiang, Y., Hao, J., Cui, W., Kerzabi, E., Kyllonen, P.: Uncovering transferable collaboration patterns across tasks using large language models. In: Proceedings of the 26th International Conference on Artificial Intelligence in Education (AIED 2025), LNCS, pp. 320–335. Springer, Cham (2025)
17. Jiang, Y., Clarke-Midura, J., Keller, B., Baker, R.S., Paquette, L., Ocumpaugh, J.: Note-taking and science inquiry in an open-ended learning environment. Contemp. Educ. Psychol. **55**, 12–29 (2018)
18. Jiang, Y., Hao, J., Fauss, M., Li, C.: Detecting ChatGPT-generated essays in a large-scale writing assessment: is there a bias against non-native English speakers? Comput. Educ. **217**, 105070 (2024)
19. Jiang, Y., Martín-Raugh, M., Yang, Z., Hao, J., Liu, L., Kyllonen, P.C.: Do you know your partner's personality through virtual collaboration or negotiation? Comput. Hum. Behav. **141**, 107608 (2023)
20. Kok, X.F.K.: Measuring socially shared regulation of learning: a review and critique of existing self-report surveys. Metacogn. Learn. **20**(1), 36 (2025)
21. Kovanović, V. et al.: Understanding students' self-reflections through learning analytics. In: Proceedings of the 8th International Conference on Learning Analytics and Knowledge, pp. 389–398 (2018)
22. Li, Y. et al.: Interactions for socially shared regulation in collaborative learning: an interdisciplinary multimodal dataset. ACM Transac. Interact. Intell. Syst. **14**(3), 1–34 (2024)
23. Li, M., Qin, W., Tang, Z., Fang, X., He, T., Cao, X.: Automating SSRL detection in asynchronous OCL via LLMs. In: Proceedings of the 7th International Conference on Computer Science and Technologies in Education (CSTE 2025), pp. 548–551. IEEE (2025)
24. Liu, X. et al.: Qualitative coding with GPT-4: where it works better. J. Learn. Anal. **12**(1), 169–185 (2025)
25. Long, Y., Luo, H., Zhang, Y.: Evaluating large language models in analysing classroom dialogue. Npj Sci. Learn. **9**, 60 (2024)
26. Na, Y., Feng, S.: LLM-assisted automated deductive coding of dialogue data. In: Proceedings of the International Conference on Artificial Intelligence in Education, LNCS, pp. 248–262. Springer, Cham (2025)
27. Ocumpaugh, J., Baker, R., Gowda, S., Heffernan, N., Heffernan, C.: Population validity for educational data mining models: a case study in affect detection. Br. J. Educ. Technol. **45**(3), 487–501 (2014)
28. Ogan, A. et al.: Collaboration in cognitive tutor use in Latin America. In: Proceedings of ACM SIGCHI Conference on Human Factors in Computing Systems, pp. 1381–1390 (2012)
29. Panadero, E.: A review of self-regulated learning: six models and four directions for research. Front. Psychol. **8**, 422 (2017)
30. Panadero, E., Järvelä, S.: Socially shared regulation of learning: a review. Eur. Psychol. **20**(3), 190–203 (2015)

31. Pugh, S.L., et al.: Say what? Automatic modeling of collaborative problem-solving skills from student speech in the wild. In: Proceedings of the 14th International Conference on Educational Data Mining (EDM 2021), pp. 55–67 (2021)
32. San Pedro, M.O.C., Baker, R., Rodrigo, M.M.: Detecting carelessness through contextual estimation of slip probabilities. In: Proceedings of the 15th International Conference on Artificial Intelligence in Education, LNCS, pp. 304–311. Springer (2011)
33. Sharma, K., Nguyen, A., Hong, Y.: Self-regulation and shared regulation in collaborative learning. Br. J. Educ. Technol. **55**(4), 1398–1436 (2024)
34. Singh, C.A., Muis, K.R.: An integrated model of socially shared regulation of learning. Educ. Psychol. **59**(3), 177–194 (2024)
35. Sun, W., Liu, J.: Leveraging Speech Data and Text Classification for Identifying Socially Shared Regulation, Proceedings of the Future of Education Conference (2025)
36. Taub, M., Azevedo, R., Bouchet, F., Khosravifar, B.: Predicting SRL strategies from prior knowledge. Comput. Hum. Behav. **39**, 356–367 (2014)
37. Zhang, J., Andres, J.M.A.L., Hutt, S., Baker, R.S., Ocumpaugh, J., et al.: Using machine learning to detect SMART model cognitive operations. J. Educ. Data Min. **14**(3), 76–108 (2022)
38. Zhou, X., Tsai, C.W.: Effects of socially shared regulation of learning on computational thinking. Educ. Inf. Technol. **28**(7), 8135–8152 (2022)
39. Zimmerman, B.J., Schunk, D.H. (eds.): Self-Regulated Learning and Academic Achievement. Lawrence Erlbaum Associates, Mahwah, NJ (2001)

# From Ethical Discourse to Empirical Evidence: How Ethical Concerns are Operationalized in Studies on Generative AI in Higher Education

Revekka Kyriakoglou[1(✉)], Anna Pappa[1], Valéry Psyché[2], Sébastien Lallé[3], Guilherme Medeiros Machado[4], Nour El Mawas[5], Sonia Proust-Androwkha[6], Lamprini Chartofylaka[7], and Anis Boubaker[8]

[1] LIASD, Université Paris 8, Paris, France
revekka.kyriakoglou@univ-paris8.fr
[2] Université TÉLUQ, Québec, Canada
[3] LIP6, CNRS, Sorbonne Université, Paris, France
[4] LyRIDS, ECE - Engineering School, Paris, France
[5] CREM, Université de Lorraine, Metz, France
[6] Université de Sherbrooke, Québec, Canada
[7] Université des Antilles, Guadeloupe, France
[8] RAISE, École de Technologie Supérieure, Montréal, Québec, Canada

**Abstract.** The rapid adoption of generative artificial intelligence (GenAI) in higher education has raised widespread ethical concerns, particularly in computer science (CS) education. While issues such as academic integrity, fairness, bias, and responsibility are frequently discussed, it remains unclear how these concerns are empirically examined in existing research. This paper presents a systematic analysis of how ethically relevant concerns are addressed in peer-reviewed empirical studies on GenAI use in higher CS education. Using a structured selection protocol, we analyze a corpus of empirical studies published since the public release of large language models, focusing on how concerns such as academic integrity, fairness, bias, responsibility and student autonomy are defined, studied, and methodologically grounded. Our analysis reveals a substantial gap between ethical discourse and empirical practice: although ethics is often mentioned, only a small subset of studies integrates ethically relevant concerns as a core analytical dimension with explicit empirical grounding. Most studies rely on indirect proxies or address ethics implicitly, without clear operational definitions or evaluative frameworks. Based on these findings, we propose an empirically grounded categorization of ethical concerns as addressed in current research and outline methodological directions for more robust integration of ethics into future empirical studies on GenAI-supported CS education.

**Keywords:** Generative AI in Higher Education · Empirical Ethics · Ethical Operationalization · Educational Research


E. G. Blanchard et al. (eds.), AIED 2026, LNCS 16586, pp. 210–224, 2027.
https://doi.org/10.1007/978-3-032-29773-0_15

## 1 Introduction

In higher education, and particularly in computer science (CS) programs, GenAI tools have become part of students' everyday learning practices. Large language model-based systems are now routinely used to generate code, debug programs, and obtain explanations of theoretical concepts, often outside formally designed instructional settings [58]. This rapid integration into day-to-day academic work has occurred largely in the absence of shared pedagogical and ethical frameworks governing their use. In the context of CS education, this absence of shared frameworks has particularly significant ethical implications. Programming courses aim not only to produce functional code, but also to foster core competencies such as computational thinking [59], problem decomposition, abstraction, and systematic reasoning. Recent empirical studies suggest that increasing reliance on GenAI systems can alter how these competencies are exercised, shifting attention toward surface-level task completion [43,61] and challenging traditional assumptions about authorship, assessment, and cognitive effort in CS education.

Institutional responses to GenAI use in CS education remain heterogeneous, ranging from outright bans and increased reliance on plagiarism detection mechanisms to redesigned assessment formats and deliberate integration of GenAI as a pedagogical resource [29]. However, many of these responses are developed in the absence of robust empirical evidence regarding the ethical implications of GenAI use, particularly with respect to academic integrity, fairness, transparency, and student autonomy. In programming education, where plagiarism detection is already technically complex [14], GenAI further blurs the boundary between legitimate assistance and misconduct. Although ethical concerns are frequently invoked in research on GenAI in CS education, they are rarely treated as central objects of empirical investigation. Existing studies predominantly focus on user perceptions, short-term learning outcomes, or tool performance, while ethical dimensions, such as bias, fairness, equity, and data responsibility, are often addressed incidentally or retrospectively.

In this study, we do not treat ethics itself as a direct measurable variable. Ethics is understood here as a normative domain concerned with what ought to be done, including questions of fairness, responsibility, harm, accountability, privacy, and appropriate conduct [35]. Therefore, our focus is not on measuring ethics as such, but on examining how empirical studies translate ethically relevant concerns into measurable constructs, indicators, perceptions, behaviors, or institutional responses.

Rather than proposing new ethical principles or curricular guidelines, this study investigates how published research on GenAI in higher CS education empirically operationalizes ethically relevant concerns. We conduct a systematic empirical analysis of peer-reviewed studies to address the following research question: *To what extent are ethically relevant concerns explicitly integrated into the design, analysis, and evaluation of empirical studies on GenAI adoption in higher CS education?*

The main contributions of this paper include: A systematic review of existing literature, focusing on how empirical studies have addressed the ethically relevant concerns of GenAI in education. A categorization framework to help organize and classify papers dealing with ethics in educational GenAI. Key perspectives for researchers aiming to incorporate ethics into their future empirical work.

## 2 Related Work

Several prior syntheses have examined the integration of GenAI in CS education, primarily focusing on pedagogical opportunities, technical challenges, and assessment-related issues. These works typically organize existing research around themes such as accuracy, authenticity, and evaluation practices, and discuss their implications for teaching and learning in CS [2,44,46,47]. While ethical concerns are often implicitly connected to these themes, they are rarely treated as a distinct object of empirical analysis.

A complementary perspective is provided by prior syntheses that examine benefits, risks, and potential harms associated with GenAI use in CS education. For instance, [47] analyze recent studies using a SWOT framework, highlighting strengths such as code generation and feedback, alongside challenges related to plagiarism, bias, and over-reliance. Similarly, [7] foreground ethical risks and unintended consequences of GenAI adoption. Agbo et al. [2] examined the pros and cons found in studies on GenAI in CS education, and highlighted a few issues that relate to ethical considerations such as biases and lower critical thinking. Another systematic review [1] focused specifically on the impact of GenAI in CS education related to cognitive processes (including over-reliance), equity of access, and critical thinking skills, providing actionable findings related to these dimensions These reviews typically include discussions of perspectives on ethical challenges, such as the need for better integration of GenAI into pedagogical frameworks, promoting equitable and fair access, raising awareness among stakeholders, or advocating for regulation. However, despite explicitly discussing issues with ethical implications, these works do not systematically examine how such concerns are empirically operationalized within study designs, analyses, or evaluation frameworks.

Beyond these secondary analyses, a limited number of empirical studies explicitly foreground ethical dimensions of GenAI use in education. Some focus on educators' perspectives on computing ethics and curriculum design [5], while others examine specific ethical concerns, such as academic integrity, authorship, transparency, or responsibility, most often through survey-based approaches in higher education contexts [18,22]. These studies, however, tend to address ethical issues in isolation and with limited connection to concrete programming practices or learning processes.

More broadly, reviews conducted at the level of general education or other domains, such as medical education, underscore the need for regulatory frameworks [20], but also highlight the importance of discipline-specific analyses capable of capturing contextual constraints and practices [32,39]. In CS education, where programming practices, assessment formats, and notions of authorship play a central role, such domain-specific considerations are particularly salient.

Building on this body of work, the present study adopts a different analytical perspective by examining how ethically relevant concerns are translated into empirical research practice. Rather than synthesizing uses, perceptions, and benefits of GenAI, we focus on how ethical considerations are defined, operationalized, and empirically examined across studies on GenAI in higher CS education.

## 3 Methodology

### 3.1 Study Design and Analytical Perspective

This study adopts a systematic empirical analysis of published research to examine how ethical relevant concerns are operationalized in studies on the use of GenAI in higher education. Rather than mapping general research trends or usage patterns, the methodology focuses on how studies translate ethical concerns into empirical analytical forms: that is, how concerns such as academic integrity, fairness, bias, privacy, responsibility, and student autonomy are defined, integrated into study designs, examined through explicit constructs or indicators, and interpreted within evaluative frameworks. In this sense, the analysis does not treat ethics itself as a directly measurable variable, but examines how empirical research makes ethically relevant issues investigable. This framing is consistent with work that approaches ethics in GenAI not as a singular measurable entity, but as a reflective process organized around principles, responsibilities, standards, and context-sensitive decision-making [12].

To ensure transparency and reproducibility in the identification and selection of studies, the analysis follows a structured selection and reporting protocol informed by the PRISMA Extension for Scoping Reviews (PRISMA-ScR) guidelines [56]. This framework is used to systematically document corpus construction, screening, and filtering decisions throughout the study.

### 3.2 Corpus Identification and Study Selection

A comprehensive search strategy was developed to identify peer-reviewed empirical studies examining the use of GenAI in the teaching and learning of CS in higher education. Searches were conducted in four major bibliographic databases commonly used in computing and education research: Web of Science, arXiv, Érudit, and IEEE Xplore. Additional databases, including Academic Search Complete and Education Source, were also explored but did not yield further publications meeting the inclusion criteria.

The search strategy combined three components using the Boolean operator AND: (i) GenAI-related terms, (ii) CS education terms, and (iii) higher education context terms. GenAI keywords included both generic descriptors (e.g., *generative AI*, *large language model*, *chatbot*) and specific tool names (e.g., *ChatGPT*, *Copilot*, *Gemini*). Education-related keywords targeted CS (e.g., *computer science education*, *computer education*, *CS*), while higher education keywords referred to university-level settings (e.g., *higher education*, *university*, *college*,

**Table 1.** Overview of study identification and selection process

| Stage | Description | Records |
|---|---|---|
| Identification | Records initially retrieved from bibliographic databases (arXiv, Web of Science, Érudit, IEEE Xplore) using keyword-based search queries related to GenAI, CS education, and higher education | > 1000 |
| Initial filtering | Peer-reviewed journal and conference papers, written in English, published between Dec. 2022 and Apr. 2025, situated in higher education contexts | 658 |
| Title and abstract screening | Records screened for relevance to GenAI use in higher CS education | 342 |
| Full-text assessment | Full texts assessed for empirical contribution and methodological adequacy | 225 |
| Included empirical studies | Empirical studies meeting inclusion criteria after full-text screening | 105 |
| Ethical operationalization subset | Studies in which ethical considerations are substantively integrated into the empirical design, analysis, or results | **45** |

*undergraduate*, *graduate*). The search was limited to peer-reviewed journal articles and conference papers published in English between December 2022 and April 2025, and focused exclusively on higher education contexts.

Bibliographic records were imported into Zotero to remove duplicates and complete missing metadata, then exported in EndNote XML format and uploaded to Covidence to manage the screening and selection process. Following the application of eligibility criteria, 658 records were retained for title and abstract screening. This screening resulted in 342 records deemed potentially relevant, which then underwent full-text assessment. Each full text was independently reviewed by two team members; in cases of disagreement, one or two additional reviewers were consulted. The inclusion criteria targeted empirical studies examining the use of GenAI in higher education CS contexts. The full identification and selection process is summarized in Table 1.

### 3.3 Identification and Analysis of Empirical Ethical Integration

The second stage of the analysis focused on identifying studies that substantively integrated ethical considerations into their empirical research. As an initial support step, a keyword search was conducted on the full texts of the 105 retained studies using the following terms: *ethic**, *moral**, *responsible AI*, *trustworthy AI*, *bias**, *fair**, *transparency*, *accountability*, *privacy*, and *integrity*. This search was used solely to facilitate the identification of potentially relevant content and did not constitute a selection criterion on its own.

Each potentially relevant article was then reviewed in full by one researcher to assess whether ethical considerations were empirically integrated into the study

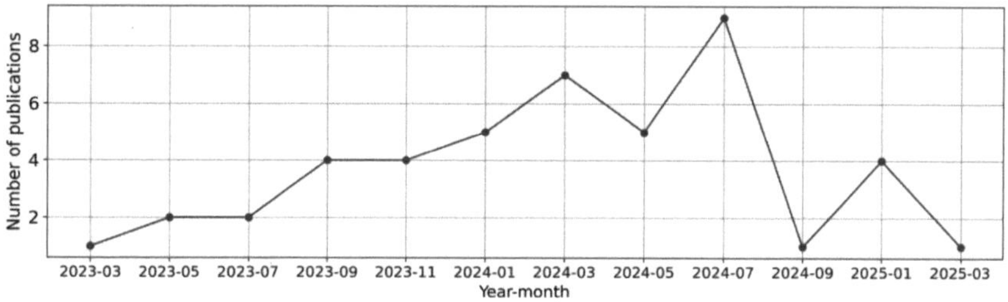


**Fig. 1.** Temporal distribution of publications (bimonthly).

design, analysis, or results, rather than being confined to discussion sections or future work. In cases of uncertainty, inclusion decisions were discussed and resolved collectively within the research team. Following this process, 45 studies were retained for in-depth analysis.

These studies were subsequently ezxamined using a collaborative thematic analysis to identify recurring ethical concerns and patterns of empirical integration. Through iterative discussion and refinement, this process led to the identification of six ethical categories. Each article was assigned to one or more categories based on how ethical considerations were empirically defined and examined. The resulting categorization is reported in Sect. 4.2.

### 3.4 Data Availability

The full corpus of the 105 empirical studies, along with bibliographic metadata and selection documentation, is publicly available via the Open Science Framework (OSF) at: Ethic_Scoping_Review_Data_CS_Education.

## 4 Results

### 4.1 Corpus Characteristics

Most publications in the analyzed corpus (29 papers, 64.4%) originate from conference venues, while the remaining 16 papers (35.6%) are journal articles. Regarding disciplinary focus, 37.8% (17 papers) are published in venues centered on educational sciences, 31.1% (14) in multidisciplinary venues combining educational sciences and CS/AI, 15.6% (7) in CS venues, and 8.9% (4) in AI-focused venues, with the remaining 6.7% (3) belonging to other fields.

The temporal distribution of publications is shown in Fig. 1. No publication predates March 2023, and publication counts remain low throughout 2023. An upward trend becomes visible from early 2024, with the highest publication levels observed in mid-2024 (bimonthly peak of 9 publications). This trend is followed by a decline toward the end of 2024 and early 2025.

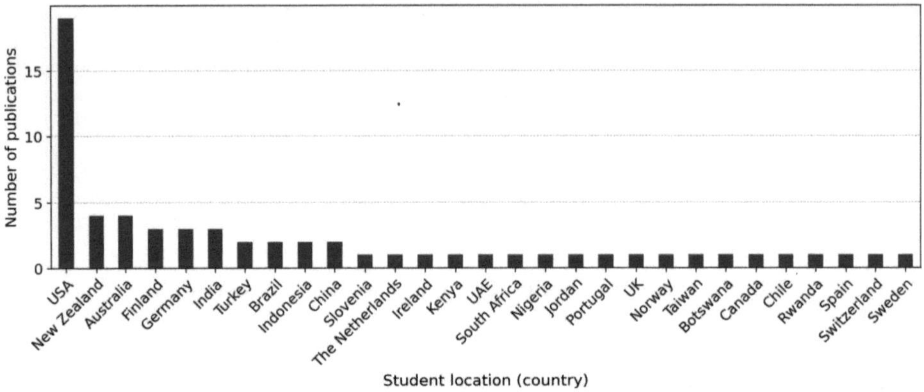


**Fig. 2.** Geographical distribution of the students and teachers involved in the studies.

We observed limited diversity in the investigated populations, with most empirical work focusing on students and educators from a restricted set of geographical regions and institutional contexts. Overall, the majority of the 45 studies were conducted in Western contexts. Specifically, 44% of the studies involved participants from North America, 33% from Europe, 19% from Asia, 14% from Australasia, 9% from the Middle East, 5% from South America, and 5% from Africa. Percentages exceed 100% as several studies included participants from multiple geographical regions; in particular, 16% of the studies involved participants from more than one country. The distribution of reported participant countries is shown in Fig. 2. Among studies reporting gender information, male students accounted for up to 70% of the reported sample sizes.

### 4.2 Ethical Considerations Addressed in Empirical Studies

Although ethical concerns related to the integration of GenAI tools in higher CS education are increasingly discussed in the literature, they are unevenly addressed in empirical research practice. Within the 105 studies, 45 explicitly refer to ethical issues; however, only ten [23,24,26,34,41,42,51,53,57,58] integrate ethical considerations into the study design, analysis, or empirical findings. In the remaining 35 studies, ethical aspects are mentioned only superficially or are confined to discussion or future work sections.

To characterize how ethical concerns are empirically addressed across this subset, we identified six thematic categories reflecting distinct ethical dimensions. For each article, the most prominent ethical focus was retained. The identified categories are: *"Ethical Guidelines, Policies, and Education for GenAI Use"; "Accuracy, Reliability, and Quality of GenAI Output"; "Academic Integrity and Misconduct"; "Over-reliance and Learning Interference"; "Bias, Fairness, and Equity in GenAI"; and "Data Privacy, Student Data Protection, and Perceived Risks"*. The distribution of the 45 articles across these categories is shown in Fig. 3, and the corresponding studies are listed in Table 2.

**Table 2.** Categorization of the 45 included papers by their primary ethical focus, ordered by frequency.

| Identified Ethical Category | $n$ | References |
|---|---|---|
| Ethical Guidelines, Policies, and Education | 11 | [3,4,9,19,40–42,51–53,55] |
| Accuracy, Reliability, and Quality of Output | 10 | [16,17,23,25,31,36,38,50,54,62] |
| Over-reliance and Learning Interference | 8 | [6,8,15,21,28,29,45,60] |
| Academic Integrity and Misconduct | 7 | [11,13,14,26,27,30,57] |
| Bias, Fairness, and Equity in GenAI | 7 | [24,33,34,37,43,49,58] |
| Data Privacy, Protection, and Perceived Risks | 2 | [10,48] |

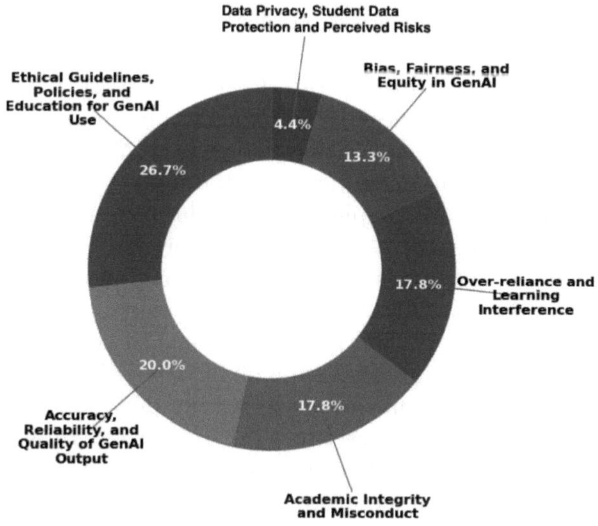


**Fig. 3.** Distribution of studies across ethical themes and learning-related categories.

The *Ethical Guidelines, Policies, and Education for GenAI Use* category encompasses studies proposing institutional and pedagogical frameworks to guide responsible GenAI adoption in CS education. These works refer to professional guidelines, such as the ACM Code of Ethics, as well as university-level policies addressing acceptable and unacceptable uses of GenAI tools. They emphasize the importance of explicit guidance and ethical education in supporting both students and instructors when engaging with GenAI-supported practices.

The *Accuracy, Reliability, and Quality of GenAI Output* category focuses on empirical evaluations of the quality of GenAI-generated code and feedback in educational settings. Reported concerns include students' loss of trust when feedback is imprecise or inconsistent [36], the need for human oversight to identify and correct erroneous outputs [31], and mismatches between generated content and students' knowledge levels [25]. In response, some studies explore approaches for generating automated feedback that more closely approximates human instructor input [38].

Papers categorized under *Academic Integrity and Misconduct* primarily address concerns related to plagiarism and academic dishonesty in the context of GenAI use in CS education. Several studies report cases in which students submit GenAI-generated code or text as their own work, raising challenges for traditional notions of authorship and originality [13]. In response, some authors explore automated approaches for detecting GenAI-assisted plagiarism [11,14], while explicitly noting the limitations of such methods given the rapid evolution and variability of generative models. Other studies focus on pedagogical or assessment-oriented strategies, such as requiring students to submit both a GenAI-generated response and their own solution to the same task, enabling instructors to more effectively assess students' understanding and originality [30].

The *Over-reliance and Learning Interference* category highlights concerns that students, particularly novices in introductory programming courses, may become overly dependent on GenAI-generated code [21,29], potentially hindering the development of conceptual and metacognitive skills [15]. These studies warn that frequent reliance on auto-completion and code suggestion tools may encourage surface-level problem solving and reduce opportunities for deeper learning, underscoring the need for careful pedagogical framing and instructor guidance.

The *Bias, Fairness, and Equity in GenAI* category addresses ethical concerns related to unequal access and representational biases in GenAI-supported learning environments. Several studies highlight the risks of reinforcing social inequalities, as GenAI tools may be more readily accessible to students with greater financial or institutional resources [33,37]. Others raise concerns about media literacy and information diversity [34,43,49], noting that reliance on a single GenAI system may limit exposure to alternative perspectives and sources.

The *Data Privacy, Student Data Protection, and Perceived Risks* category includes studies examining how privacy- and data protection-related concerns are perceived by students and educators in GenAI-supported learning contexts [10,48]. These studies report uncertainty regarding how personal and academic data are handled by GenAI tools, as well as concerns about institutional responsibility and the adequacy of existing policies. Rather than analyzing technical surveillance mechanisms, these studies emphasize perceived risks and the need for data protection–compliant access and clearer institutional guidance.

In what follows, we examine in detail the ten studies listed at the beginning of this section that integrate ethical considerations directly into their empirical research design, analysis, or findings. Several of these studies investigate students' perceptions of the ethical implications of GenAI use through qualitative or survey-based approaches, revealing awareness of GenAI biases as well as concerns about misinformation, plagiarism, and potential negative effects on learning [24,53,58]. One study adopts a mixed empirical approach, combining survey data, interviews, and policy-oriented analysis to examine ethical challenges such as academic integrity, responsible use, and institutional responses, explicitly framing these issues through established ethical frameworks [41].

Other studies focus on ethical risks related to over-reliance, learning interference, and students' ability to evaluate AI-generated outputs, grounding these concerns in empirical observations of student interactions with GenAI tools [34,42,51]. Ethical considerations related to authorship, plagiarism, and misuse of GenAI are examined through controlled studies and large-scale course data, highlighting measurable effects on student behavior and learning outcomes [26].

A small number of studies operationalize ethical concerns through the design and evaluation of assessment mechanisms intended to verify authorship and promote responsible use of GenAI [57]. Others integrate ethical considerations by explicitly framing student interaction with GenAI through advance disclosure of system limitations and risks, or by embedding principles of scientific integrity and responsible conduct in the study protocol [23].

Across these ten studies, student perspectives are predominant. Only two explicitly include faculty perspectives alongside student perspectives [41,58]. These studies report substantial instructor concerns regarding the potential impact of GenAI on student learning and academic integrity, as well as anticipated changes to assessment practices. Student perspectives, in contrast, reveal more heterogeneous attitudes, combining perceived relevance for future careers with concerns about over-reliance, learning outcomes, and assessment fairness [34,51].

## 5 Discussion

**Findings.** The results reveal several recurring gaps in empirical evidence that addresses the ethical implications of GenAI in higher CS education. These include the marginal consideration of teachers as ethical stakeholders, the scarcity of longitudinal investigations, limited empirical grounding of ethical claims, and restricted geographical and demographic diversity between studied populations.

Although ethical concerns are frequently mentioned in empirical studies of GenAI use in CS education, only a small subset integrates ethics as a primary object of empirical investigation. These studies predominantly focus on academic integrity, over-reliance, and learning interference, often motivating calls to rethink assessment practices through approaches such as in-person examinations, specification grading, or alternative forms of evaluation. From the student perspective, attitudes toward GenAI range from enthusiasm to concerns about skill erosion, over-dependence, and reduced personal achievement. By contrast, issues related to equity, bias, and inclusion remain comparatively underexplored.

When considered in relation to the literature discussed in Sect. 2, these findings highlight a persistent gap between the prominence of ethical discourse surrounding GenAI in CS education and the limited number of studies that empirically operationalize ethical concerns. While prior work frequently discusses ethical risks at a conceptual or normative level, our analysis shows that such concerns are seldom integrated into empirical research designs, analyses, or evaluative frameworks. Distinguishing between superficial references to ethics and studies that treat ethics as a substantive empirical dimension provides a clearer picture of the current evidence base.

Beyond this distinction, our present analysis extends existing work by proposing an empirically grounded categorization of ethical issues addressed in GenAI-supported CS education and by identifying concrete blind spots in the literature. In particular, the limited inclusion of faculty perspectives, the lack of longitudinal and cross-cultural studies, and the minimal attention to equity-related dimensions suggest that current empirical research captures only a partial view of the ethical challenges associated with GenAI integration.

Some authors argue that future work should promote more equitable and inclusive uses of GenAI by ensuring accessibility across socioeconomic contexts and accounting for cultural and algorithmic biases [13]. Our findings indicate, however, that such recommendations are rarely reflected in empirical study designs. Addressing these gaps will require closer collaboration between CS educators and AI researchers, as well as methodological approaches capable of capturing long-term and context-sensitive ethical effects.

Overall, this analysis suggests that ethical awareness surrounding GenAI in CS education is developing, but remains insufficiently supported by empirical evidence. Strengthening this empirical foundation therefore constitutes a key challenge for future research aimed at supporting responsible, equitable, and pedagogically sound integration of GenAI in higher education.

**Limitations.** This study is subject to limitations related to its scope and methodological choices. The analysis is restricted to peer-reviewed journal articles and conference papers, excluding other potentially relevant sources such as technical reports, policy documents, or practitioner-oriented publications. In addition, although the selection and analysis procedures were systematic, identifying and categorizing ethical considerations involves a degree of interpretative judgment, particularly when ethical issues are addressed implicitly rather than through explicit empirical constructs. Finally, the corpus reflects the state of empirical research at the time of data collection, and subsequent publications can expand or refine the patterns identified. Within these bounds, the study provides a structured snapshot of how ethics is currently treated as an empirical dimension in research on GenAI-supported CS education.

**Perspectives.** The findings of this study indicate that the advancement of GenAI research in CS education requires moving beyond declarative or normative references to ethics toward empirically grounded approaches that make ethical concerns observable, measurable, and analytically tractable. Rather than treating ethics as a contextual backdrop, future empirical work should integrate ethical dimensions—such as academic integrity, over-reliance and learning interference, bias and fairness, data protection, and responsibility—into core research questions, study designs, and evaluation criteria.

At the institutional level, there is a need for longitudinal and multi-context investigations capable of capturing how ethical concerns evolve over time and across educational settings, as well as how policies and guidelines related to GenAI are enacted, negotiated, and experienced in practice. Such studies would help clarify how institutional responses shape, enable, or constrain the ethical uses of GenAI in CS education.

At the instructor level, future research should more explicitly examine ethical responsibilities associated with the integration of GenAI into teaching and assessment practices, including issues of student confidentiality, data protection, and transparency. Ethical effects of GenAI do not operate at the same level for instructors and students, and understanding how these differentiated responsibilities are managed in practice remains an important open research question.

At the student level, further empirical work is needed to examine how ethical concerns relate to learning trajectories, skill development, and perceptions of agency over time, beyond short-term self-reported attitudes.

Overall, strengthening the empirical treatment of ethics would allow future research to move ethical considerations from peripheral commentary to analytically central components of studies on GenAI-supported CS education.

**Acknowledgements.** This study was funded by the AICT project (Grant ANR-24-CE38-2478-01), the COPCOT project (Project-ANR-22-CE38-0003), and *"AAP Recherche MEC-PLLM"* of the Université Paris 8 des Créations.

## References

1. Adejumo, A.A., Oyelere, S.S., Sanusi, I.T., Suhonen, J.: A systematic review of the impact of genai on learning performance, ai hallucinations, and problem-solving in computer science education. Comput. Educ. Artif. Intell. 100570 (2026)
2. Agbo, F.J., Olivia, C., Oguibe, G., Sanusi, I.T., Sani, G.: Computing education using generative artificial intelligence tools: a systematic literature review. Comput. Educ. Open **9**, 100266 (2025)
3. Amoozadeh, M., et al.: Trust in Generative AI among Students: an exploratory study, pp. 67–73. ACM (2024)
4. Araujo, S.M., Cruz-Correia, R.: Incorporating ChatGPT in medical informatics education: mixed methods study on student perceptions and experiential integration proposals. JMIR Med. Educ. **10** (2024)
5. Barkhuff, G.: Ethical computing education in the age of generative ai. In: Proceedings of ACM Conference ICER V. 2, pp. 46–47 (2025)
6. Bassner, P., Frankford, E., Krusche, S.: Iris: an AI-driven virtual tutor for computer science education, pp. 394–400. ACM (2024)
7. Bernstein, S., Rahman, A., Sharifi, N., Terbish, A., MacNeil, S.: Beyond the benefits: a systematic review of the harms and consequences of generative ai in computing education. In: Proceedings of the 25th Koli Calling ICCER, pp. 1–18 (2025)
8. Bobadilla, S., Glassey, R., Bergel, A., Monperrus, M.: SOBO: a feedback bot to nudge code quality in programming courses. IEEE Softw. **41**(2), 68–76 (2024)
9. Budhiraja, R., Joshi, I., Challa, J.S., Akolekar, H.D., Kumar, D.: It's not like Jarvis, but it's pretty close!" - Examining ChatGPT's Usage among Undergraduate Students in Computer Science, pp. 124–133. ACM (2024)

10. Carmi, G.: Learning with generative AI: an empirical study of students in higher education. Educ. Sci. **15**(12) (2025)
11. Chen, B., Lewis, C., West, M., Zilles, C.: Assoc comp machinery: plagiarism in the age of generative AI: cheating method change and learning loss in an intro to CS course, pp. 75–85 (2024)
12. Deng, X.N., Joshi, K.D.: Promoting ethical use of generative ai in education. DATA BASE Adv. Inf. Syst. **55**(3), 6–11 (2024)
13. Denny, P., et al.: Computing education in the era of generative AI (2023)
14. Denzler, B., Vahid, F., Pang, A., Salloum, M.: Style anomalies can suggest cheating in CS1 programs, pp. 381–387. ACM (2024)
15. Dickey, E., Bejarano, A., Garg, C.: AI-Lab: a framework for introducing generative artificial intelligence tools in computer programming courses. SN Comput. Sci. **5**(6), 720 (2024)
16. Santos, D., Cury, O.L., D.: Challenging the confirmation bias: using ChatGPT as a virtual peer for peer instruction in computer programming education. In: 2023 IEEE Frontiers in Education Conference (FIE), pp. 1–7 (2023)
17. Er, E., Akçapinar, G., Bayazit, A., Noroozi, O., Banihashem, S.K.: Assessing student perceptions and use of instructor versus AI-generated feedback. Br. J. Edu. Technol. **56**(3), 1074–1091 (2025)
18. Đerić, E., Frank, D., Vuković, D.: Exploring the ethical implications of using generative ai tools in higher education. In: Informatics, vol. 12, p. 36. MDPI (2025)
19. Ferreira, J.M.M.: A strategy for ai-supplemented teaching and learning. In: 2024 IEEE Global Engineering Education Conference, pp. 01–10. IEEE (2024)
20. García-López, I.M., Trujillo-Liñán, L.: Ethical and regulatory challenges of generative AI in education: a systematic review. In: Frontiers in Education, vol. 10, p. 1565938. Frontiers Media SA (2025)
21. Hou, I., et al.: "All Roads Lead to ChatGPT": how generative AI is eroding social interactions and student learning communities (2025)
22. Hsiao, C.H., Tang, K.Y.: Beyond acceptance: an empirical investigation of technological, ethical, social, and individual determinants of genai-supported learning in higher education. Educ. Inf. Technol. **30**(8), 10725–50 (2025)
23. Huo, H., et al.: Accelerating learning with AI: improving students' capability to receive and build automated feedback for programming courses, pp. 1–9. 2024 World Engineering Education Forum - Global Engineering Deans Council (2024)
24. Hutson, J., Jeevanjee, T.: Perceptions and aspirations of undergraduate computer science students towards generative AI: a qualitative inquiry. J. Biosens. Bioelectron. Res. **2**(3) (2024)
25. Jury, B., Lorusso, A., Leinonen, J., Denny, P., Luxton-Reilly, A.: Evaluating LLM-generated worked examples in an introductory programming course. In: Proceedings of the 26th Australasian Computing Education Conference, pp. 77–86 (2024)
26. Karnalim, O., Toba, H., Johan, M.C., Handoyo, E.D., Setiawan, Y.D., Luwia, J.A.: Plagiarism and AI assistance misuse in web programming: unfair benefits and characteristics. In: 2023 IEEE International Conference on Teaching, Assessment and Learning for Engineering (TALE), pp. 1–5 (2023)
27. Kosar, T., Ostojić, D., Liu, Y.D., Mernik, M.: Computer science education in ChatGPT era: experiences from an experiment in a programming course for novice programmers. Mathematics **12**(5), 629 (2024)
28. Lai, C., Lin, C.: Analysis of learning behaviors and outcomes for students with different knowledge levels: a case study of intelligent tutoring system for coding and learning (ITS-CAL). Appl. Sci. Basel **15**(4) (2025)

29. Lau, S., Guo, P.: From "Ban it till we understand it" to "Resistance is futile". In: ACM Conference on International Computing Education Research, pp. 106–121 (2023)
30. Liu, Y.: Leveraging the power of AI in undergraduate computer science education: opportunities and challenges. In: 2023 IEEE Frontiers in Education Conference (FIE), pp. 1–5 (2023)
31. Logacheva, E., Hellas, A., Prather, J., Sarsa, S., Leinonen, J.: Evaluating contextually personalized programming exercises created with generative ai. In: ACM Conference on International Computing Education Research, pp. 95–113 (2024)
32. Lucas, H.C., Upperman, J.S., Robinson, J.R.: A systematic review of LLMs and their implications in medical education. Med. Educ. **58**(11), 1276–1285 (2024)
33. Maher, M.L., Tadimalla, S.Y., Dhamani, D.: An exploratory study on the impact of AI tools on the student experience in programming courses: an intersectional analysis approach. In: IEEE Frontiers in Education Conference, pp. 1–5 (2023)
34. Nguyen, S., Babe, H., Zi, Y., Guha, A., Anderson, C., Feldman, M.: How beginning programmers and code LLMs (Mis)read each other. In: Proceedings of the CHI Conference on Human Factors in Computing Systems, pp. 1–26. ACM (2024)
35. Ortega-Bolaños, R., Bernal-Salcedo, J., Germán Ortiz, M., Galeano Sarmiento, J., Ruz, G.A., Tabares-Soto, R.: Applying the ethics of AI: a systematic review of tools for developing and assessing ai-based systems. Artif. Intell. Rev. **57**(5), 110 (2024)
36. Ouyang, F., Guo, M., Zhang, N., Bai, X., Jiao, P.: Comparing the effects of instructor manual feedback and ChatGPT intelligent feedback on collaborative programming in China's higher education. IEEE Trans. Learn. Technol. **17**, 2173–2185 (2024)
37. Oyelere, S.S., Aruleba, K.: A comparative study of student perceptions on generative AI in programming education across Sub-Saharan Africa. Comput. Educ. Open, **8** (2025)
38. Phung, T., et al.: Automating human tutor-style programming feedback: leveraging GPT-4 tutor model for hint generation and GPT-3.5 student model for hint validation, pp. 12–23. ACM (2024)
39. Porayska-Pomsta, K., Holmes, W., Nemorin, S.: The ethics of AI in education. In: Handbook of Artificial Intelligence in Education, pp. 571–604. Edward Elgar Publishing (2023)
40. Prakasha, G.S., Sanskriti, R., Ishani, B.: User experiences of ChatGPT among engineering students, teachers, and working professionals in India. J. Educ. Online **21**(2) (2024)
41. Prather, J., et al.: The robots are here: navigating the generative AI revolution in computing education, pp. 108–159. ACM (2023)
42. Prather, J., et al.: "It's Weird That it Knows What I Want": usability and interactions with copilot for novice programmers. ACM Trans. Comput.-Hum. Interact. **31**(1), 4:1–4:31 (2023)
43. Prather, J., et al.: The widening gap: the benefits and harms of generative AI for novice programmers, vol. 1, pp. 469–486. ACM (2024)
44. Proust-Androwkha, S., et al.: Beyond programming assistance towards the integration of generative AI into computer science education: a scoping review. In: Proceedings of the International Conference on Artificial Intelligence in Education, pp. 380–389. Springer, Cham (2025)
45. Rajala, J., Hukkanen, J., Hartikainen, M., Niemelä, P.: "Call me Kiran" – ChatGPT as a tutoring chatbot in a computer science course, pp. 83–94. ACM (2023)

46. Reihanian, I., Hou, Y., Chen, Y., Zheng, Y.: A review of generative ai in computer science education: challenges and opportunities in accuracy, authenticity, and assessment. In: ICCSCI, pp. 144–158. Springer, Cham (2024)
47. Roberts, J., Mohamed, A.: Generative AI in cs education: literature review through a swot lens. In: Proceedings of the 26th Western Canadian Conference on Computing Education, pp. 1–6 (2024)
48. Rudra, S., et al.: Use and perception of genai in higher education: insights from the erasmus+ project 'teaching and learning with ai'(talai). In: Proceedings of the 17th ICCSE, pp. 319–330 (2025)
49. Shin, J., et al.: Understanding optimal interactions between students and a chatbot during a programming task. In: Winter Simulation Conference, pp. 3106–3117 (2024)
50. Shoufan, A.: Exploring students' perceptions of ChatGPT: thematic analysis and follow-up survey. IEEE Access **11**, 38805–38818 (2023)
51. Silva, C.A.G.D., Ramos, F.N., De Moraes, R.V., Santos, E.L.D.: ChatGPT: challenges and benefits in software programming for higher education. Sustainability **16**(3), 1245 (2024)
52. Singh, H., Tayarani-Najaran, M-H., Yaqoob, M.: Exploring computer science students' perception of ChatGPT in higher education: a descriptive and correlation study. Educ. Sci. **13**(9) (2023)
53. Smith, C.E., et al.: Early adoption of generative artificial intelligence in computing education: emergent student use cases and perspectives in 2023, pp. 3–9. ACM (2024)
54. Speth, S., Meißner, N., Becker, S.: Investigating the use of AI-generated exercises for beginner and intermediate programming courses: a ChatGPT case study. In: 35th CSEE&T, pp. 142–146. IEEE (2023)
55. Styve, A., Virkki, O.T., Naeem, U.: Developing critical thinking practices interwoven with GenAI usage in an intro. Prog. Course, pp. 01–08 (2024)
56. Tricco, A.C., et al.: Prisma extension for scoping reviews (prisma-scr): checklist and explanation. Ann. Intern. Med. **169**(7), 467–473 (2018)
57. Vintila, F.: AVERT (authorship verification and evaluation through responsive testing): an LLM-based procedure that interactively verifies code authorship and evaluates student understanding. In: 21st International Conference on Information Technology Based Higher Education and Training, pp. 1–7 (2024)
58. Weber, J.L., Neda, B.M., Juarez, K.C., Wong–Ma, J., Gago–Masague, S., Ziv, H.: Beyond the hype: perceptions and realities of using LLMs in CSE at an R1 university. In: 2024 IEEE EDUCON, pp. 01–08 (2024)
59. Wing, J.M.: Computational thinking. Commun. ACM **49**(3), 33–35 (2006)
60. Xue, Y., Chen, H., Bai, G.R., Tairas, R., Huang, Y.: Does ChatGPT help with introductory programming? An experiment of students using ChatGPT in CS1. In: 2024 IEEE/ACM 46th International Conference on Software Engineering: Software Engineering Education and Training (ICSE-SEET), pp. 331–341 (2024)
61. Yilmaz, R., Karaoglan Yilmaz, F.G.: The effect of generative artificial intelligence (AI)-based tool use on students' computational thinking skills, programming self-efficacy and motivation. Comput. Educ. AI **4**, 100147 (2023)
62. Zhang, Z., Dong, Z., Shi, Y., Price, T., Matsuda, N., Xu, D.: Students' perceptions and preferences of GenAI feedback for programming. In: Proceedings of the ACM Conference on Learning at Scale, pp. 23250–23258 (2024)

# Territorial Fairness in Large-Scale Academic Risk Prediction: Comparing National and State-Level Machine Learning Models in Brazil

Tobias Vieira Francisco[1,2], Abílio Nogueira Barros[2], Felipe Vieira Roque[2], Tiago Paulino[2], Augusto Schmidt[2], Flavia Galvani[3], Rafael Oliveira[2,5], Leonardo Brandão Marques[2], Diego Dermeval[2], Pedro Barreto[4], Anita Gea Martinez Stefani[4], Marisa de Santana da Costa[4], Emanuel Marques Queiroga[2,5], Elthon Oliveira[2], Ig Ibert Bittencourt[2], Cristian Cechinel[2,6](✉), and Thales Vieira[2]

[1] Instituto Federal de Educação, Ciência e Tecnologia Sul-Rio-Grandense (IFSul), Pelotas, Brazil
tobiasfrancisco@ifsul.edu.br
[2] Núcleo de Excelência em Tecnologias Sociais (NEES), Universidade Federal de Alagoas (UFAL), Alagoas, Brazil
{abilio.barros,felipe.roque,tiago.paulino,augusto.schmidt, rafael.oliveira,leonardo.marques,diego.matos,elthon.oliveira,ig.ibert, thales.vieira}@nees.ufal.br
[3] Blavatnik School of Government, University of Oxford, Oxford, UK
flavia.galvani@bsg.ox.ac.uk
[4] Ministério da Educação (MEC), Brasília, Brazil
{pedrobarreto,anitastefani,marisacosta}@mec.gov.br
[5] Universidade Tecnológica Federal do Paraná (UTFPR), Dois Vizinhos, Brazil
[6] Centro de Ciências, Tecnologias e Saúde, Universidade Federal de Santa Catarina, Araranguá, Brazil
cristian.cechinel@ufsc.br

**Abstract.** Early identification of students at academic risk is a central challenge for large and decentralized educational systems. In countries such as Brazil, pronounced regional disparities raise concerns not only about predictive performance, but also about whether machine learning models generalize equitably across territories. This study examines the role of regionalization in academic risk prediction by comparing national and state-level models trained under a unified experimental pipeline using longitudinal administrative data from over six million upper secondary student enrollments across all Brazilian states. Multiple supervised learning algorithms are evaluated, with Random Forest selected for detailed analysis due to its robust overall performance. Territorial fairness is assessed through an operationalization of Equal Opportunity and Equalized Odds based on state-level true and false positive rates. Results show that while national and state-level models achieve similar aggregate performance, substantial disparities persist in Recall across


E. G. Blanchard et al. (eds.), AIED 2026, LNCS 16586, pp. 225–239, 2027.
https://doi.org/10.1007/978-3-032-29773-0_16

states. State-level models improve local risk detection in a small subset of states, often at the cost of increased false positives. These findings indicate that regional specialization is not uniformly beneficial and should be understood as a context-dependent trade-off between improved local detection and governance complexity. By separating territorial fairness auditing from performance-based model comparison, this study provides an evidence-based framework for reasoning about regionalization in large-scale educational risk prediction.

**Keywords:** Learning Analytics · Academic Risk Prediction · Algorithmic Fairness · Territorial Equity

## 1 Introduction

Upper secondary school non-completion, including dropout, grade repetition, and chronic absenteeism, remains a persistent challenge for educational systems worldwide, with long-term social and economic consequences for individuals and societies [20]. In Brazil, this phenomenon is particularly pronounced, reflecting structural inequalities, regional disparities, and institutional constraints that limit the effectiveness of universal educational policies [17]. Prior research has shown that school disengagement is a cumulative process shaped by academic, behavioral, family, and contextual factors that often emerge early in students' educational trajectories [15]. In response, Learning Analytics (LA) and Educational Data Mining (EDM) have gained prominence as approaches for supporting data-driven decision-making in education [18]. By leveraging administrative, behavioral, and academic data, machine learning models have demonstrated strong potential for early identification of students at risk of adverse academic outcomes, including dropout and failure [11]. Large-scale studies in national contexts such as Denmark, Uruguay, and Brazil have shown that such models can be trained using routinely collected data, achieving meaningful predictive performance even under severe class imbalance [16].

Despite these advances, much of the existing evidence is derived from institution- or district-level analyses that implicitly assume relatively homogeneous educational contexts [6]. In contrast, national education systems—particularly in large and socioeconomically diverse countries—exhibit substantial territorial heterogeneity in school infrastructure, student profiles, and policy implementation [8]. In Brazil, historical, economic, and administrative differences across states are reflected in both data distributions and model behavior, raising concerns that a single nationwide model may obscure local patterns and yield uneven performance across regions [17]. The use of machine learning in education also raises critical questions related to fairness, equity, and responsible data use [13]. Recent work has shown that models trained on aggregated data can inadvertently reinforce existing inequalities when disparities in predictive errors across groups or contexts are not explicitly examined [3]. These concerns are especially salient in public education systems, where predictive models increasingly inform policy decisions and the allocation of limited resources [17].

In Brazil, large-scale educational data infrastructures such as the Sistema Gestão Presente (SGP) [2] have enabled the integration of administrative and behavioral data at a national scale. This infrastructure plays a central role in supporting public policies such as the *Pé-de-Meia* program, a conditional cash transfer initiative aimed at reducing dropout, which relies on these data to monitor student participation and enforce eligibility criteria. Beyond policy enforcement, the availability of such integrated datasets creates opportunities for the development of predictive models capable of identifying students at risk of adverse academic outcomes at early stages. This, in turn, supports more targeted and data-driven intervention strategies, aligning learning analytics approaches with large-scale policy implementation in highly heterogeneous educational systems.

In this paper, we examine the generalization behavior of machine learning models for academic risk prediction in a territorially heterogeneous educational system. We adopt a two-scale modeling strategy, training a national-level model using data from all Brazilian states and state-level models using the same pipeline restricted to individual states. Using a fairness-oriented diagnostic perspective, we operationalize Equal Opportunity and Equalized Odds through state-wise True Positive and False Positive Rates to assess whether the national model generalizes uniformly across regions. This framework supports a structured analysis of territorial disparities and informs a performance-governance trade-off analysis, identifying when state-level specialization may offer meaningful advantages beyond aggregate predictive performance. The remainder of this paper is structured as follows. Section 2 reviews related work on predictive modeling in education. Section 3 describes the experimental design and evaluation framework. Section 4 presents and discusses the empirical findings, and Sect. 5 concludes the paper with final remarks and directions for future work.

## 2 Related Work

The use of Learning Analytics (LA) and Educational Data Mining (EDM) to predict academic risk and school dropout has grown substantially over the past decade. Early contributions established the role of analytics in supporting evidence-based and learning-centered decision-making in education [7], while subsequent surveys documented the widespread adoption of machine learning techniques for predicting academic performance, failure, and dropout across secondary and higher education settings [1].

Several large-scale studies have demonstrated the feasibility of applying predictive models at national or multi-district levels using administrative educational data. In Uruguay, Queiroga et al. [16] reported a nationwide learning analytics initiative in K–12 education, employing Random Forest models to predict grade repetition and dropout using data from more than 258,000 students. Similarly, Sara et al. [19] conducted a national study in Denmark using registry data from over 36,000 upper secondary students, achieving high predictive performance with Random Forest models. In the United States, Christie et al. [5] described a machine learning–based early warning system deployed across 32 states, covering millions of educational records and integrating XGBoost models directly into school management platforms. In South Korea, Lee and Chung [12] analyzed national data from more than 165,000 students, showing that tree-based and boosting methods outperformed alternative approaches for dropout prediction, particularly under severe class imbalance.

Beyond technical feasibility, prior work has emphasized the importance of aligning predictive modeling with educational decision-making processes. Lakkaraju et al. [11], in collaboration with large U.S. school districts, highlighted that commonly reported performance metrics such as AUC and accuracy may not fully capture the operational needs of educators, underscoring the relevance of selecting evaluation criteria that reflect intervention priorities.

Despite these advances, important gaps remain in the literature. In particular, systematic analyses comparing centralized (e.g., national-level) and decentralized (e.g., state- or district-level) modeling strategies are still limited, especially in contexts characterized by strong territorial heterogeneity [6]. Moreover, while large-scale studies often report aggregate performance, they rarely examine how predictive errors are distributed across regions or consider fairness-related implications of model generalization. Addressing these gaps is essential for informing governance-aware modeling strategies in decentralized educational systems.

## 3 Methodology

This section describes the materials and methods employed to analyze the generalization behavior of machine learning models for academic risk prediction in a territorially heterogeneous context. The methodology is organized into three main components: (A) data collection, (B) preprocessing and modeling, and (C) evaluation and analysis. Figure 1 summarizes the overall experimental framework.

### 3.1 Data Collection, Feature Selection, and Preparation

The construction of the dataset (see Table 1 for variable names and descriptions) was based on the consolidation of two main sources of information: the Sistema de Gestão Presente and the 2024 Basic Education Census. The SGP operates as the Basic Education Data Platform, integrating administrative and behavioral data from multiple education networks to provide a unified view of students' educational trajectories. As a centralized infrastructure, it supports large-scale monitoring initiatives in Brazilian public education. In this study, it serves as the primary source for constructing the analytical dataset used in model development.

The dataset comprises attendance records associated with high school enrollments, covering the first, second, and third grades, reported monthly throughout the 2024 academic year, with the exception of January. The data were extracted directly from the SGP, the system responsible for collecting and consolidating

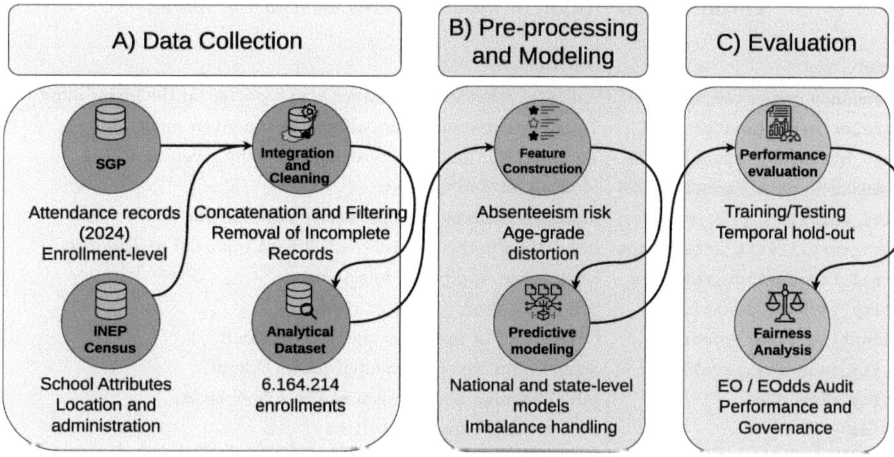


**Fig. 1.** Overview of the proposed approach, comprising data collection, preprocessing and modeling, and evaluation stages.

information on high school students across the national territory [2]. Records are organized at the enrollment level and include students regularly enrolled in the Brazilian state school network in 2024, totaling 6,170,183 enrollment records.

We aggregate enrollment attendance data at the school level to compute absenteeism metrics, defined as sustained student absence over the academic year. The proportions of students in each absenteeism level follow the framework proposed by [10]: Low ($> 95\%$), indicating high attendance; Moderate (91–95%), indicating few absences; Significant (81–90%), reflecting frequent absence; High (71–80%), indicating a concerning pattern; and Severe ($\leq 70\%$), representing a high risk of school dropout. Based on these proportions, variables were created to describe each school's student composition according to the adopted absenteeism criteria. Using these measures, a derived feature was created (`entity_risk_abs`) to indicate overall school-level absenteeism risk. Schools with more than 50% of enrollments classified as Low or Moderate were labeled as class 1, whereas schools with more than 50% of enrollments classified as Significant, High, or Severe were labeled as class 0, characterizing high absenteeism levels. A set of features incorporated into the dataset refers to the Age–Grade Distortion Rate (TDI). A student is considered to be in an age–grade distortion condition when they are two years or more above the expected age for the grade attended [9]. Based on this criterion, three features were created: `in_tdi`, `pp_tdi_serie`, and `pp_mat_tdi`. Information related to school location, including region, federative unit, and location type (urban or rural), was obtained from the 2024 Basic Education Census published by the Instituto Nacional de Estudos e Pesquisas Educacionais Anísio Teixeira (INEP). After integrating all data sources through dataset concatenation, 5,969 records were removed due to incompleteness, corresponding to approximately 0.10% of the original dataset.

**Table 1.** Description of input features used in the model

| Feature Name | Description |
|---|---|
| attendance_reported_{month} | Indicates whether attendance was reported in the given month. |
| hours_offered_{month}_2024 | Total instructional hours offered in the given month. |
| hours_attended_{month}_2024 | Total instructional hours attended in the given month. |
| attendance_rate_{month}_2024 | Monthly attendance rate. |
| multi_enroll | Indicates student multiple active enrollments. |
| multi_enroll_with_attendance | Indicates whether another enrollment reported attendance. |
| enroll_termination_reason | Reason for enrollment termination. |
| entity_{school_location} | School location (urban or rural). |
| student_in_{year}_year | Grade level in upper secondary education. |
| entity_{edu_gov_level} | School adm. level (municipal/state/federal). |
| entity_risk_abs | Indicates high absenteeism at the school level. |
| in_tdi | Indicates age–grade distortion. |
| pp_tdi_serie | Percentage of students with age–grade distortion. |
| pp_mat_tdi | Percentage of enrollments with age-grade distortion in the school. |
| no_region_entity_{region} | School macro-region indicators. |
| no_uf_entity_{uf} | State (federative unit) indicators. |

The final dataset comprises a total of 6,164,214 enrollments. Of these, 623,901 enrollments (10.12%) correspond to students associated with multiple enrollments (`multiple_enrollments`) during the academic year. Among them, 623,450 enrollments (10.11%) reported at least one occurrence in which enrollments associated with the same student recorded attendance within the same month (`multiple_enrollments_with_attendance`). Regarding administrative dependency, the dataset is predominantly composed of enrollments from state-administered schools (`entity_state`), totaling 6,129,921 enrollments (99.44%). Municipal schools (`entity_municipal`) account for 25,101 enrollments (0.41%), while federal schools (`entity_federal`) represent 9,192 enrollments (0.15%). Concerning school location, 5,814,378 enrollments (94.33%) are associated with urban schools (`entity_loc_urbana`), whereas 349,836 enrollments (5.67%) correspond to rural schools (`entity_loc_rural`).

The distribution of enrollments across upper secondary grades indicates that 2,391,491 enrollments (38.78%) correspond to students enrolled in the first year (`student_in_1_year`), 2,017,858 enrollments (32.74%) in the second year (`student_in_2_year`), and 1,754,865 enrollments (28.48%) in the third year (`student_in_3_year`).

The target variable was defined at the enrollment level using administrative information that captures the student's enrollment status at the end of the academic year, as recorded in the SGP. This variable reflects the officially reported reason for enrollment termination and serves as a proxy for academic risk within the public education system. Prior to label construction, records associated with administrative inconsistencies and cases in which the final status indicated death were excluded, as these situations are not informative for modeling educational risk. The remaining enrollment outcomes were then grouped according to whether they reflected successful academic progression or trajectories associated with potential vulnerability. Outcomes corresponding to approval or confirmed completion, either through regular progression or alternative certification pathways, were labeled as not at risk (class 0). All other outcomes, including dropout, abandonment, failure, transfers, suspensions, and reclassification events, were labeled as at risk (class 1), as they represent conditions in which continued educational engagement is disrupted or uncertain.

### 3.2 Modeling and Evaluation

Five algorithms were selected: Logistic Regression (LR), Random Forest (RF), Gradient Boosting (GB), AdaBoost (AB), and Multilayer Perceptron (MLP). Logistic Regression was adopted as the baseline model, as it represents a low-complexity linear approach widely recognized for its simplicity and interpretability [14]. In contrast, the MLP was included as an approximate upper bound of performance due to its higher expressiveness and ability to model complex non-linear relationships, which are often associated with predictive gains in large-scale educational settings [11]. The dataset was partitioned into training and testing subsets using a stratified split with a 90%/10% ratio. Within the training set, five-fold cross-validation was applied using the `cross_validate` function, evaluating the metrics Accuracy, Precision, Recall, F1-score, and AUC-ROC.

As a methodological choice, no systematic hyperparameter optimization techniques were employed. This decision reflects the comparative nature of the study, whose primary objective is not to maximize the absolute performance of a specific model, but to isolate the effect of territorial segmentation by ensuring that both nationwide and state-level models are evaluated under identical configurations. Using the same pipeline and parameters across all scenarios enables a controlled comparison, in which observed differences in performance and fairness can be attributed to the modeling strategy rather than to differences in optimization or calibration.

Random Under Sampling (RUS) was applied exclusively to the training data. This approach is expected to introduce less distortion to the data characteristics. RUS was performed independently for each state-level subset in order to preserve local class balance and reflect regional data distributions. However, in states with smaller student populations, state-level RUS may attenuate rare-pattern signals associated with high-risk cases, potentially affecting local prevalence estimation and calibration, with possible implications for fairness-related outcomes. This trade-off represents a known threat to validity and is partially mitigated by the consistent application of the same resampling strategy across all models and by the comparative focus of the analysis.

Model training and evaluation were conducted longitudinally through eleven independent training cycles, in which all algorithms were trained on cumulative datasets defined by monthly cutoffs of school attendance records (from February to December). This design simulates the progressive accumulation of information over the academic year, allowing analysis of how predictive performance evolves as additional behavioral evidence becomes available [16]. After identifying the algorithm with the highest average performance at the national level, a second experimental phase applied the same classifier to train state-specific models using datasets derived from the national training and test partitions, ensuring methodological consistency and preventing data leakage. The performance of these state-specific models was then compared against that of the national model when evaluated on the corresponding state-level subsets, enabling a controlled assessment of the effects of regional specialization in a territorially and socioeconomically heterogeneous educational system [5].

# 4 Results and Discussion

This section presents and discusses the results of the proposed predictive models for identifying students at risk. We first report the performance of the national-level model trained using data from all Brazilian federative units. Next, we analyze the results of state-level models, highlighting differences in predictive performance across regions. Finally, we evaluate the generalization ability of the national and state models by examining their cross-level applicability and robustness. The findings are discussed regarding the implications for large-scale educational monitoring and early identification of at-risk students.

## 4.1 Overall Predictive Performance

First, we present a comparative analysis of five supervised classification algorithms, trained on the national-level dataset to predict students at academic risk. Random Forest achieved the most robust and balanced performance across all evaluated metrics, including Accuracy, F1-score, and AUC-ROC, while maintaining lower variance across cross-validation folds. As illustrated in Fig. 2, RF

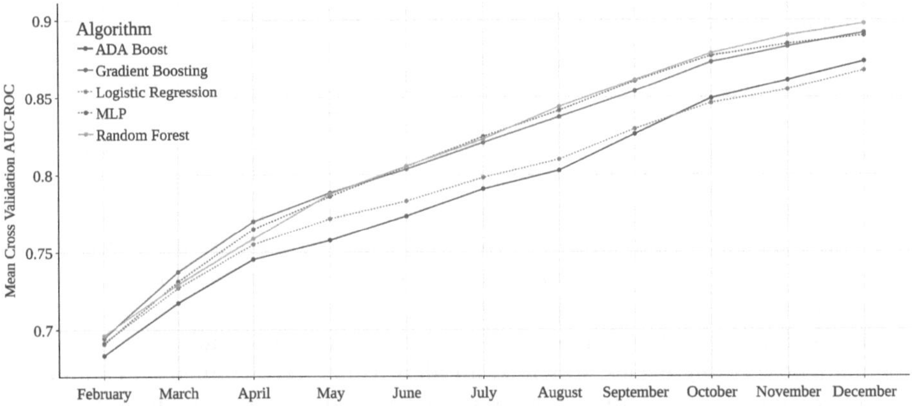


**Fig. 2.** Longitudinal Mean AUC-ROC performance by algorithm at the national level.

showed consistently strong performance across the academic year, with improvements becoming increasingly evident as more monthly data accumulated.

After selecting RF as the best-performing algorithm at the national level, a second experimental stage evaluated its behavior under regional specialization. In this phase, the national RF model was applied to state-level test datasets and compared against models trained exclusively with data from each respective federative unit. Across all months and experimental folds, the national and state-level models exhibited very similar overall performance. Aggregate metrics such as AUC, F1-score, and Recall showed no consistent dominance of one modeling strategy over the other when averaged across states. This proximity in global performance indicates that, from a purely predictive standpoint, both approaches are viable and that performance differences are subtle.

Nonetheless, a closer inspection reveals variation across states and metrics. While AUC and F1-score remain relatively stable, Recall presents larger dispersion between national and state-specific implementations (as can be seen in Fig. 3). Given that Recall directly reflects the model's ability to correctly identify students at risk, these variations warrant deeper investigation beyond aggregate performance summaries, especially in early warning system (EWS) contexts [12].

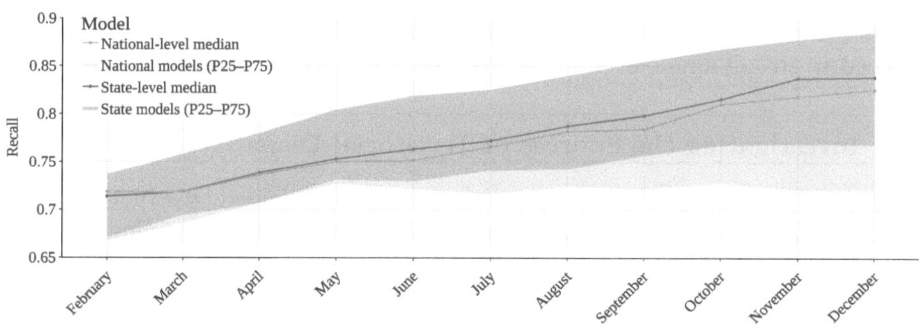


**Fig. 3.** Median Recall over time for the national and state-level models. The shaded region indicates the range of Recall values across states.

## 4.2 Territorial Fairness: Operationalizing Equal Opportunity

We evaluate the generalization behavior of national and state-level predictive models through a fairness-oriented analysis of EO across Brazilian states. Rather than adopting EO and Equalized Odds (EOdds) in their classical group-based fairness formulations, this study operationalizes a notion of *territorial fairness*. In this context, states are treated as comparison groups, and fairness is assessed through disparities in error rates across territories.

EO is operationalized through the True Positive Rate (TPR) computed independently for each state. This choice aligns with the study's prioritization of

Recall and reflects the normative importance of ensuring that students with similar risk profiles have comparable probabilities of being correctly identified, regardless of their state of residence [17]. Disparity in EO is quantified as the difference between the maximum and minimum state-level true positive rates, as defined in $\Delta_{EO} = \max_s(TPR_s) - \min_s(TPR_s)$, where $TPR_s$ denotes the true positive rate observed in state $s$. The results indicate a substantial territorial gap. The observed $\Delta EO$ reaches approximately 0.26, meaning that the probability of correctly identifying at-risk students differs by up to 26% points between states. In practical terms, disparities of this magnitude indicate that students in some states are substantially less likely to be correctly identified as at risk compared to others.

### 4.3 Equalized Odds and False Positive Trade-Offs

To complement the EO analysis, EOdds is examined by jointly considering TPR and False Positive Rate (FPR). Consistent with the extended evaluation pipeline, EOdds is summarized using the average odds disparity, defined as $\Delta EOdds = \frac{\Delta TPR + \Delta FPR}{2}$. Post-processing results show a $\Delta FPR$ of approximately 0.20 and an average $\Delta EOdds$ of roughly 0.23. These values indicate that disparities are not confined to missed detections but also involve uneven exposure to false alarms across states. Importantly, this reinforces that fairness considerations cannot be reduced to Recall alone, even when Recall is the prioritized metric.

### 4.4 Investigating the Sources of Territorial Disparity

To assess whether observed EO disparities could be explained by structural characteristics of the data, statistical analyses were conducted examining the relationship between $\Delta EO$ and two factors: (i) state-level risk prevalence and (ii) sample size. To test (i), we compute the Spearman rank correlation between state-level TPR and the proportion of students in each state who are truly at academic risk. The association between EO disparity and the prevalence of risk was weak and did not reach statistical significance (Spearman's $\rho = 0.229$, $p = 0.25$). This suggests that differences in underlying risk distribution alone do not account for the observed territorial gaps in TPR.

In a similar way, the association between EO disparity and sample size (ii) was tested by applying the Spearman rank correlation between state-level TPR and the number of at-risk students in states. In contrast to the previous finding, the presented correlation was moderate and statistically significant (Spearman's $\rho = 0.434$, $p = 0.023$). While this result indicates that data volume may influence fairness outcomes, it does not fully explain the magnitude or direction of disparities. States with larger samples do not systematically achieve either higher or lower fairness gaps, suggesting that additional contextual or structural factors are at play.

### 4.5 Analyzing Performance-Governance Trade-Offs Across Models

To further investigate whether territorial disparities identified in the fairness audit could be mitigated through regional specialization, we performed a paired comparison between national and state-level models at the state level. This analysis focuses on differences in True Positive Rate (TPR, corresponding to Recall for the positive class) and False Positive Rate (FPR), computed as state–national differences and evaluated using the Wilcoxon signed-rank test applied to monthly hold-out Recall values. While this step does not constitute a direct fairness assessment, it examines whether state-level models yield statistically robust gains in risk detection relative to the national model, given the additional analytical and governance complexity associated with specialization.

**Table 2.** Operational model selection under recall-false-alarm trade-offs

| State | National TPR | State-level TPR | $\Delta$TPR | $\Delta$FPR | Recall $p$-value | Decision |
|---|---|---|---|---|---|---|
| Acre | 0.7011 | 0.7193 | 0.0182 | 0.0125 | 0.0049 | No diff |
| Alagoas | 0.7661 | 0.7713 | 0.0052 | 0.0108 | 0.0312 | No diff |
| Amapá | 0.7152 | 0.7168 | 0.0016 | −0.0150 | 0.2754 | No diff |
| Amazonas | 0.8578 | 0.8484 | −0.0094 | −0.0118 | 0.4785 | No diff |
| Bahia | 0.7543 | 0.7607 | 0.0065 | −0.0011 | 0.0010 | No diff |
| Ceará | 0.8555 | 0.8389 | −0.0165 | −0.0235 | 0.0010 | No diff |
| Espírito Santo | 0.8665 | 0.8555 | −0.0110 | −0.0148 | 0.0420 | No diff |
| Federal District | 0.8266 | 0.8292 | 0.0025 | −0.0002 | 0.6152 | No diff |
| Goiás | 0.7876 | 0.7853 | −0.0022 | −0.0005 | 0.8262 | No diff |
| Maranhão | 0.7536 | 0.7631 | 0.0095 | 0.0069 | 0.0010 | No diff |
| Mato Grosso | 0.8488 | 0.8397 | −0.0091 | −0.0095 | 0.0049 | No diff |
| Mato Grosso do Sul | 0.8271 | 0.8322 | 0.0051 | 0.0027 | 0.0010 | No diff |
| Minas Gerais | 0.8174 | 0.8212 | 0.0038 | 0.0019 | 0.0098 | No diff |
| Pará | 0.6965 | 0.7188 | 0.0222 | −0.0104 | 0.0029 | State-level model |
| Paraíba | 0.7630 | 0.7626 | −0.0003 | −0.0049 | 0.0137 | No diff |
| Paraná | 0.8215 | 0.8219 | 0.0004 | 0.0015 | 0.0059 | No diff |
| Pernambuco | 0.7782 | 0.7813 | 0.0031 | −0.0028 | 0.0400 | No diff |
| Piauí | 0.7378 | 0.7516 | 0.0138 | 0.0012 | 0.0049 | No diff |
| Rio de Janeiro | 0.7305 | 0.7309 | 0.0004 | 0.0030 | 0.1416 | No diff |
| Rio Grande do Norte | 0.7970 | 0.7917 | −0.0053 | −0.0005 | 0.0098 | No diff |
| Rio Grande do Sul | 0.7799 | 0.7796 | −0.0004 | 0.0001 | 0.7480 | No diff |
| Rondônia | 0.7260 | 0.7706 | 0.0445 | 0.0221 | 0.0049 | State-level model |
| Roraima | 0.6228 | 0.6267 | 0.0039 | 0.0139 | 0.0312 | No diff |
| Santa Catarina | 0.6097 | 0.6325 | 0.0228 | 0.0226 | 0.0029 | State-level model |
| São Paulo | 0.8475 | 0.8465 | −0.0010 | −0.0020 | 0.0049 | No diff |
| Sergipe | 0.7040 | 0.7634 | 0.0594 | 0.0435 | 0.0010 | State-level model |
| Tocantins | 0.6817 | 0.6877 | 0.0061 | 0.0052 | 0.0020 | No diff |

As shown in Table 2, only a small subset of states exhibits statistically significant improvements in Recall when using state-level models, with gains ranging from approximately 2 to 6% points. However, these improvements are frequently accompanied by increases in False Positive Rate (FPR), making explicit the trade-off between enhanced risk detection and higher false-alarm rates. To complement the tabular comparison, Fig. 4 visualizes these differences by positioning states according to $\Delta$TPR and $\Delta$FPR (state minus national). Shaded regions, defined empirically using the median absolute deviation, delineate zones of meaningful advantage and trade-off, providing an operational perspective on when regional specialization yields balanced gains and when it imposes additional governance costs. For most states, differences between national and state-level models are not statistically significant, and in several cases the national model slightly outperforms its specialized counterpart. These results indicate that regional specialization should not be interpreted as a uniformly superior modeling strategy. Instead, its advantages are context-dependent and must be evaluated jointly under EO and EOdds criteria, consistent with recent discussions on equitable ML deployment in education [13].

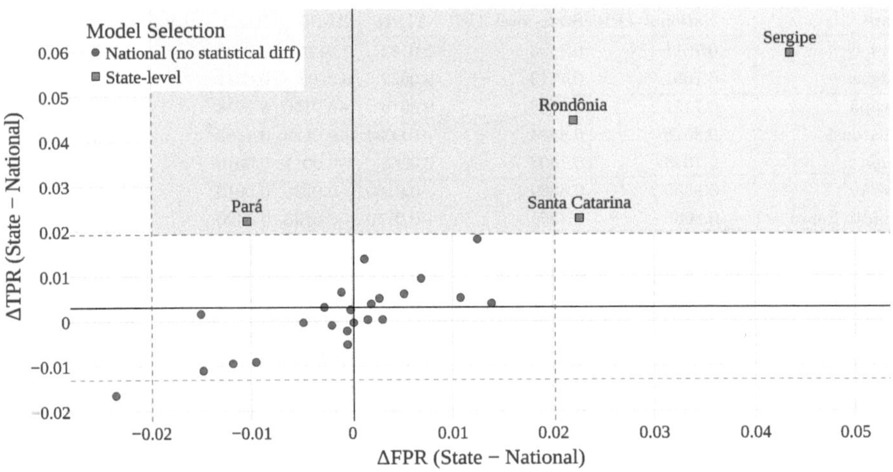


**Fig. 4.** Performance-governance trade-offs between national and state-level models.

## 4.6 Implications for Model Selection and Governance

The results suggest that there is no single modeling approach that can be considered best across the majority of states. Although national and state-level models achieve comparable overall performance, substantial territorial disparities persist, particularly when fairness is evaluated through Recall-based EO.

These disparities are not fully explained by sample size or risk prevalence, underscoring that fairness-aware governance requires analyses that go beyond conventional performance summaries.In this context, EO and EOdds serve as **diagnostic tools** to audit territorial generalization, while the national-versus-state comparison supports an **operational decision framework**. Rather than selecting models solely based on average performance, the proposed approach prioritizes Recall—reflecting the educational imperative to minimize missed detections of students at risk—while explicitly accounting for the operational costs associated with increased false positives [4,16]. This distinction clarifies that fairness considerations guide *where to look*, whereas deployment decisions determine *when to intervene.*

From a policy and implementation perspective, these findings suggest that centralized models can serve as a stable default in large-scale educational systems, but should be complemented by targeted regional specialization when fairness diagnostics and statistical evidence jointly indicate clear benefits. By separating territorial fairness auditing from performance-driven model selection, this study reframes model deployment as a governance problem that balances equity, effectiveness, and feasibility in highly heterogeneous educational contexts.

When contrasted with prior work on large-scale dropout prediction and early warning systems, our results reinforce a recurring observation in the literature: predictive performance alone is often insufficient to support deployment decisions in heterogeneous educational systems. Large-scale studies at national or multi-district levels have demonstrated the effectiveness of centralized predictive models, typically evaluated through aggregate metrics such as AUC and F1-score [5,11,12]. However, despite acknowledging contextual and institutional heterogeneity, these studies primarily report average performance and provide limited analysis of how predictive errors are distributed across territorial units or regions [19]. This limitation becomes especially salient in countries with strong regional diversity and large geographic extent, such as Brazil, where socioeconomic conditions, school infrastructures, and student trajectories vary substantially across states [17]. Such structural differences are reflected in the variability and specificity of the data itself, directly impacting model behavior across regions. While regional analyses have been explored in other national contexts [8], these studies primarily focus on uncovering local patterns or improving predictive accuracy, without explicitly framing regional disparities as a fairness problem.

In contrast, this study advances the state of the art by explicitly integrating territorial fairness into the model selection process at an unprecedented national scale. By operationalizing EO and EOdds through state-level TPR and FPR, we assess whether a national model generalizes equitably across regions, rather than merely whether it performs well on average. This approach moves beyond the binary question of whether state-level models outperform a national one and instead provides evidence-based criteria to determine *when* specialization may be analytically justified. In doing so, model selection is reframed as a fairness-sensitive assessment that accounts for territorial heterogeneity, rather than a purely predictive optimization task.

## 5 Final Remarks

This study examined the behavior of large-scale machine learning models for academic risk prediction in a territorially heterogeneous educational system. By comparing national and state-level modeling strategies under a unified experimental pipeline, we showed that similar aggregate performance can conceal substantial regional variability in model behavior. The adoption of a territorial fairness perspective, operationalized through Equal Opportunity and Equalized Odds based on Recall, enabled a systematic assessment of how well a national model generalizes across states, reframing fairness as a governance-relevant property, rather than as a classical protected-attribute constraint.

Despite practical and methodological challenges inherent to this type of analysis, such as the country's continental scale, pronounced regional diversity, highly variable data distributions, and the computational constraints of large-scale experimentation; the proposed framework demonstrates that fairness-oriented diagnostics can be effectively integrated into model comparison. Even in the absence of fine-grained contextual variables and under limited validation flexibility, the combination of territorial fairness auditing and governance-aware performance analysis provides a principled way to reason about model selection in decentralized educational systems, moving beyond aggregate accuracy toward more context-sensitive and equitable analytical decisions.

Future work should explore fairness-aware modeling strategies based on hybrid and cascading architectures that combine national models with progressively localized components, potentially extending specialization beyond the state level to intra-state regions. Additional efforts should assess the role of class balancing techniques in mitigating territorial disparities. Finally, longitudinal analyses of fairness indicators remain necessary to evaluate the stability of territorial gaps over time and their responsiveness to policy or behavioral changes.

**Acknowledgment.** This work was supported by the Brazilian Ministry of Education (MEC) under grants TED13914 and TED11476; by the Brazilian National Council for Scientific and Technological Development (CNPq) under grant No. 445016/2024-8; by the project Ia. Edu – National Institute of Artificial Intelligence in Unplugged Education (grant No. 4084883/2024-5); and by the Research Support Foundation of the State of Alagoas (FAPEAL) under grant No. FAPEAL60030.0000001481/2025.

**Disclosure of Interests.** The authors have no competing interests to declare

## References

1. Balaji, P., Alelyani, S., Qahmash, A., Mohana, M.: Contributions of machine learning models towards student academic performance prediction: a systematic review. Appl. Sci. **11**(21), 10007 (2021)
2. Barros, A.N., et al.: Ensuring data quality in national educational databases: Insights from Brazil's centralized database of high school students' data. In: Conference on Digital Government Research, vol. 1 (2025)
3. Bulut, O., Wongvorachan, T., He, S., Lee, S.: Enhancing high-school dropout identification: a collaborative approach integrating human and machine insights. Discov. Educ. **3**(1), 109 (2024)
4. Christenson, S.L., Thurlow, M.L.: School dropouts: prevention considerations, interventions, and challenges. Curr. Dir. Psychol. Sci. **13**(1), 36–39 (2004)

5. Christie, S.T., Shi, A., Gobert, L., Rosen, C.: Machine-learned school dropout early warning at scale. In: Proceedings of the 12th International Conference on Educational Data Mining (2019)
6. Coleman, C., Baker, T., Stephenson, E.: A better cold-start for early prediction of student at-risk status in new school districts. In: Proceedings of the 12th International Conference on Educational Data Mining (2019)
7. Ferguson, R.: Learning analytics: drivers, developments and challenges. Int. J. Technol. Enhanc. Learn. **4**(5/6), 304–317 (2012)
8. Hernández-Leal, E., Duque-Méndez, N.D., Cechinel, C.: Unveiling educational patterns at a regional level in colombia: data from elementary and public high school institutions. Heliyon **7**(9) (2021)
9. Instituto Nacional de Estudos e Pesquisas Educacionais Anísio Teixeira: Dicionário de indicadores educacionais: fórmulas de cálculo. Instituto Nacional de Estudos e Pesquisas Educacionais Anísio Teixeira, Brasília (2004). https://download.inep.gov.br/publicacoes/institucionais/estatisticas_e_indicadores/dicionario_de_indicadores_educacionais_formulas_de_calculo.pdf
10. Kearney, C.A.: Integrating systemic and analytic approaches to school attendance problems: synergistic frameworks for research and policy directions. In: Child & Youth Care Forum, vol. 50, pp. 701–742. Springer, Cham (2021)
11. Lakkaraju, H., et al.: A machine learning framework to identify students at risk of adverse academic outcomes. In: Proceedings of the 21st ACM SIGKDD International Conference on Knowledge Discovery and Data Mining, pp. 1909–1918 (2015). https://doi.org/10.1145/2783258.2788620
12. Lee, S., Chung, J.Y.: The machine learning-based dropout early warning system for improving the performance of dropout prediction. Appl. Sci. **9**(15), 3093 (2019). https://doi.org/10.3390/APP9153093
13. Mangal, M., Pardos, Z.A.: Implementing equitable and intersectionality-aware ml in education: a practical guide. Br. J. Edu. Technol. **55**(5), 2003–2038 (2024)
14. Márquez-Vera, C., Cano, A., Romero, C., Noaman, A.Y.M., Fardoun, H.M., Ventura, S.: Early dropout prediction using data mining: a case study with high school students. Expert. Syst. **33**(1), 107–124 (2016)
15. Parr, A.K., Bonitz, V.S.: Role of family background, student behaviors, and school-related beliefs in predicting high school dropout. J. Educ. Res. **108**(6), 504–514 (2015)
16. Queiroga, E.M., et al.: Early prediction of at-risk students in secondary education: a countrywide k-12 learning analytics initiative in Uruguay. Information **13**(9), 401 (2022). https://doi.org/10.3390/info13090401
17. Queiroga, E.M., et al.: Data-driven strategies for achieving school equity: insights from Brazil and policy recommendations. IEEE Access **12**, 101646–101659 (2024)
18. Romero, C., Ventura, S.: Educational data mining and learning analytics: an updated survey. WIREs Data Min. Knowl. Discov. **10**(3), e1355 (2020)
19. Sara, N.B., Halland, R., Igel, I.G., Alstrup, S.: High-school dropout prediction using machine learning: a danish large-scale study. In: Proceedings of the 23rd European Symposium on Artificial Neural Networks, Computational Intelligence and Machine Learning (2015)
20. UIS — UNESCO Institute for Statistics: Global education digest 2012—opportunities lost: The impact of grade repetition and early school leaving (2012)

# What Children's AI Literacy Books Teach: A Content Analysis Using the AI4K12 Framework

Feiwen Xiao(✉), Jiayi Zhang, Andrés Felipe Zambrano, and Shiyan Jiang

University of Pennsylvania, Philadelphia 19104, PA, USA
{feiwenx,joycez,azamb13,jiang33}@upenn.edu

**Abstract.** Although many books introducing artificial intelligence (AI) to young children are now available, their quality and educational value have not been systematically or empirically examined. This study addresses this gap by analyzing how AI literacy books conceptualize and communicate foundational AI ideas, practices, and values to young learners. Guided by the AI4K12 "Five Big Ideas in AI" framework, we conducted a mixed-methods content analysis of 57 English-language AI literacy books for children ages 5–8. Results revealed an uneven distribution of AI Big Ideas introduced by these books. Societal Impact, Learning, and Natural Interaction were emphasized, whereas Perception, Representation and Reasoning, which capture foundational technical mechanisms, were comparatively underrepresented. To examine the variation across books, we calculated per-book relative frequencies and conducted a cluster analysis, which revealed five recurring book profiles dominated by different combinations of Big Ideas. These findings suggest that children's AI literacy books prioritize socially meaningful narratives over explanations of how AI systems function internally, highlighting important gaps and design implications for developmentally appropriate AI education resources.

**Keywords:** AI Education · AI literacy Book · Children · Computing Education

## 1 Introduction

As artificial intelligence (AI) becomes increasingly embedded in everyday technologies, young children now regularly encounter AI systems such as Siri, Alexa, social robots, interactive media, and intelligent agents [1]. In the absence of formal instruction at school or home, their understanding of AI is primarily shaped by these informal interactions [2, 3]. Many AI-powered platforms portray machines as human-like, intentional, or even omniscient. Although such anthropomorphic designs can boost engagement, they also risk reinforcing misconceptions by leading children to confuse programmed behavior with human agency or to overestimate AI's autonomy and accuracy [4, 5]. Developing AI literacy in early childhood is, therefore, critical for preparing children for an AI-infused future. Early AI education not only supports accurate conceptual understanding [6, 7] but also fosters inquiry, reasoning, and problem-solving skills [8]. However, most existing AI literacy initiatives target middle and high school students, leaving this line of research largely unexplored for young children [6].


E. G. Blanchard et al. (eds.), AIED 2026, LNCS 16586, pp. 240–254, 2027.
https://doi.org/10.1007/978-3-032-29773-0_17

Children's books represent a particularly promising medium for early AI literacy. Storytelling has long been recognized as a pedagogically powerful and developmentally appropriate tool for helping young learners understand abstract and complex STEM concepts through contextualization, analogy, and emotional engagement [9–11]. By embedding technological mechanisms within concrete situations and characters, books can spark curiosity while providing conceptual footholds for young readers [12]. Recently, a surge of AI-themed children's books claiming to teach AI concepts has entered the market, yet little is known about what AI concepts and values these books actually communicate.

Grounded in the AI4K12 "Five Big Ideas" framework [13–15], this content analysis addresses this gap by examining how contemporary children's AI literacy books represent foundational AI concepts. Specifically, this study asks: How are the AI4K12 Five Big Ideas and concepts represented in children's AI literacy books (RQ1)? And what types of books emerge based on their AI4K12 big ideas profiles (RQ2)? By systematically analyzing concept coverage across books, this work aims to illuminate what children's books do and do not teach about AI, and to inform the design and selection of future AI literacy materials for young learners.

## 2 Literature Review

### 2.1 Children's AI Literacy

With the increasing omnipresence of AI technologies in children's everyday lives, growing attention has been directed toward preparing young learners with foundational AI literacy. Early discussions of AI literacy emphasized basic understanding of AI concepts and techniques [16]. Long and Magerko [17] expanded the construct and conceptualized AI literacy as a basic literacy that non-technical individuals should possess, encompassing not only how AI systems function, but also their limitations, appropriate use, and ethical and societal implications. Although a single, unified definition of AI literacy has yet to emerge, there is growing consensus regarding the importance of equipping the next generation with the knowledge and dispositions needed to navigate an AI-infused world. Such preparation is increasingly viewed as essential both for supporting informed participation in everyday life and for fostering future readiness in education and the workforce.

As interest in AI literacy for K–12 learners has expanded, multiple frameworks have been proposed to clarify learning goals and guide educational practice. For instance, Ng and colleagues [18] framed AI literacy as a critical component of twenty-first-century digital literacy in both work and everyday contexts, with an emphasis on ethical awareness and responsible use of AI. However, such frameworks often do not specify learning goals across different developmental stages. In contrast, a leading effort in K-12 AI education is the AI4K12 initiative [13], which provides content-oriented guidance explicitly organized by grade bands. Drawing on perspectives from artificial intelligence, computer science education, and learning sciences, AI4K12 articulates Five Big Ideas in AI: 1) Perception, 2) Representation and Reasoning, 3) Learning, 4) Natural Interaction, and 5) Societal Impact. It emphasizes developmentally appropriate progressions of AI concepts, suggesting that even K-2 students can explore foundational ideas such as how computers perceive the world or interact naturally with humans through age-appropriate activities.

In the context of early childhood education, AI literacy has increasingly been recognized as an important component of preparing children for an AI-driven future [6, 7]. Although young children may not yet engage with AI at a technical level, research suggests they can develop age-appropriate mental models of AI when instruction is grounded in concrete experiences, familiar contexts, and developmentally appropriate representations [19]. Accordingly, emergent research has explored a range of instructional approaches to support children's AI literacy, including unplugged activities that model AI processes without screens [20], digital storytelling that embeds AI concepts within narrative contexts [21], play-based learning experiences with social robots and tangible tools [8], and scaffolded family-based discussions around AI-enabled technologies encountered in everyday life [20]. This body of work demonstrates both the feasibility and promise of fostering foundational AI literacy in early childhood through pedagogically appropriate and contextually meaningful learning experiences.

### 2.2 Children's Books as Unplugged Learning Media for AI Literacy

Children's books have long been recognized as powerful learning resources in early childhood and elementary education, particularly for introducing complex or abstract ideas in developmentally appropriate ways [11]. In early learning contexts where screen time is often limited or discouraged, books function as a form of unplugged learning media, enabling children to engage with disciplinary ideas through narrative, illustration, and shared discussion rather than direct interaction with digital technologies. Prior research in computing education suggests that storybooks can serve as effective entry points for young learners by contextualizing technical ideas within familiar experiences, concrete scenarios, and emotionally engaging narratives [22].

More recently, researchers and educators have begun to explore children's books as resources for introducing AI concepts. For example, Arn and Huang [12] designed AI-themed picture books to promote children's critical reflection on human–AI relationships and to foster ethical awareness of AI tools. Their work leveraged co-design partnerships among technical experts, illustrators, and educators, highlighting the potential of storybooks to communicate complex sociotechnical ideas in accessible ways. In parallel, a growing number of commercially available children's books aim to familiarize young readers with AI-related concepts such as robots, data, machine learning, and human–AI interaction. Notable examples include the AI+Me series[1], which explicitly aligns with the AI4K12 Five Big Ideas in AI by dedicating individual books to each Big Idea, such as Perception, Learning, Natural Interaction, as well as titles published by Rocketbabyclub[2] that emphasize the mathematical foundations underlying AI systems, such as patterns, classification, and decision rules. Together, these books suggest increasing public and educational interest in using story-based formats to introduce AI literacy concepts to young children.

[1] https://ai4k12.org/book-series-ai-and-me/

[2] https://bookscouter.com/publisher/rocket-baby-club

Despite this growing interest, there is no systematic research examining children's books as a class of AI literacy resources. Most existing studies focus on curriculum interventions, tool-based learning environments, or interactive technologies, leaving children's books largely unexamined as informal yet influential learning media. Moreover, little is known about how AI-themed children's books align with established AI literacy frameworks, which AI concepts they emphasize or omit. Given the central role of storybooks in early childhood classrooms and family learning, this gap demands closer examination.

# 3 Method

## 3.1 Book Selection

We collected a corpus of children's AI literacy books explicitly designed to introduce AI concepts. Books were identified through online marketplaces (e.g., Amazon, Barnes & Noble), publisher websites using a combination of related keywords and synonyms, for example, "artificial intelligence," "machine learning," "AI," "robot/robotics," "technology for kids". All these search terms were paired with age-related descriptors such as "children," "kids," "storybook", or "picture book." Inclusion criteria were: (1) books intended for children aged 5–8, (2) English-language publications, and (3) explicit reference to AI-related ideas in titles, descriptions, or narratives. In total, 57 books published between 2019 and 2025 met these criteria and were included for analysis. This timeline was selected because 2019 marks the official release of the AI4K12 "Five Big Ideas" framework, which has since guided many educational initiatives in AI literacy.

## 3.2 Coding Procedure and Analysis

To analyze how AI concepts were represented in the books, we conducted a content analysis grounded in the Five Big Ideas guideline for the K-2 stage[3]. The AI4K12 **Five Big Ideas** in AI (i.e., Perception, Representation and Reasoning, Learning, Natural Interaction, and Societal Impact) served as the primary analytic categories. Based on the official guideline, each Big Idea is operationalized through a set of **concepts**. For instance, under the Big Idea 5 Societal Impact, concepts included Ethical AI, AI for social good, AI and culture, AI and economy.

To code the content, we first segmented each book into instances, with each instance covering at least one AI concept, which typically comprises one or several consecutive paragraphs or short exchanges that together convey a complete conceptual idea. Each instance constitutes a coding unit. Two trained coders independently coded 10% of the corpus to establish interrater reliability. This initial round of coding yielded strong agreement across all the concept-level coding categories (Cohen's $\kappa = 0.90$), indicating a high level of consistency in code application. All discrepancies were resolved through discussion, leading to refinements and clarifications of the coding guidelines. Following this calibration process, the two coders divided the remaining books and coded them independently. To ensure continued reliability and consistency, the coders cross-checked

[3] https://ai4k12.org/gradeband-progression-charts/

one another's codes per week, discussing any ambiguous cases and reaching consensus when necessary. This iterative process helped maintain alignment in code interpretation across the full corpus. Throughout the coding process, the coders also recorded analytic memos highlighting notable or illustrative examples to provide contextual information and support later interpretation. Descriptive analysis of the coded data was conducted to examine the distribution of AI4K12 Big Ideas and concepts across the corpus in order to address **RQ1**.

### 3.3 Cluster Analysis

To examine whether distinct types of children's books emerge from the corpus, we conducted a cluster analysis (**RQ2**). For each book, we calculated the percentage (relative frequency) of instances that discuss each concept and big idea. Using the relative frequencies of the five big ideas, we conducted a cluster analysis to identify the main types of books. The optimal number of clusters was determined using silhouette analysis [23], which evaluates clustering solutions by maximizing the cohesion of items within clusters while simultaneously maximizing the separation between clusters. Solutions ranging from three to ten clusters were examined, and the number of clusters that yielded the highest silhouette score was selected; this resulted in a five-cluster solution, corresponding to the number of big ideas. Finally, for each cluster, we averaged the relative frequencies of each big idea to characterize the general structure and dominant topics discussed within each cluster.

## 4 Results

### 4.1 Distribution of AI4K12 Big Ideas

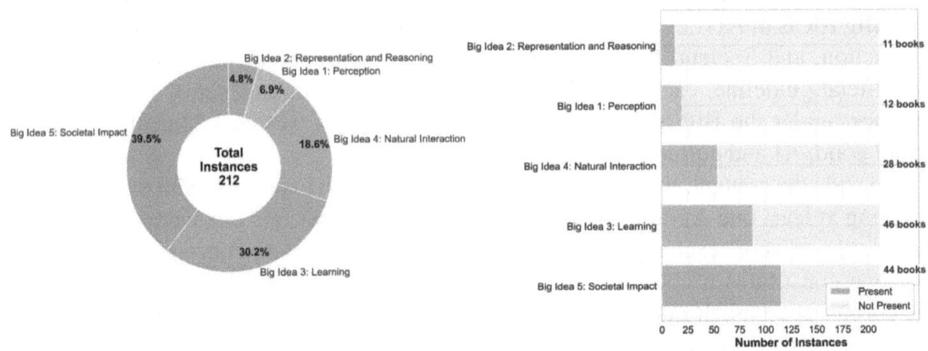


**Fig. 1.** Distribution of instances under each Big Idea.

Across the entire corpus of 57 books, we identified 212 instances that fall under the five big ideas, with an average of 3.72 instances per book, ranging from 1 to 11 instances per book. As shown in Fig. 1, representations of AI concepts were unevenly distributed across the Big Ideas. Societal Impact was the most frequently represented Big Idea, accounting for 39.5% of all coded instances, followed by Learning (30.2%) and Natural Interaction (18.6%). In contrast, Perception (6.9%) and Representation and Reasoning (4.8%) were comparatively underrepresented. These findings suggest that children's AI literacy books tend to emphasize AI's societal roles and consequences, as well as how AI systems learn from data, while providing limited coverage of foundational technical mechanisms such as how AI systems sense the world (Perception) or internally represent and reason with information (Representation and Reasoning). This highlights a tendency to foreground AI's functions and implications over its underlying computational processes.

## 4.2 Book Profile Based on Clustering Analysis

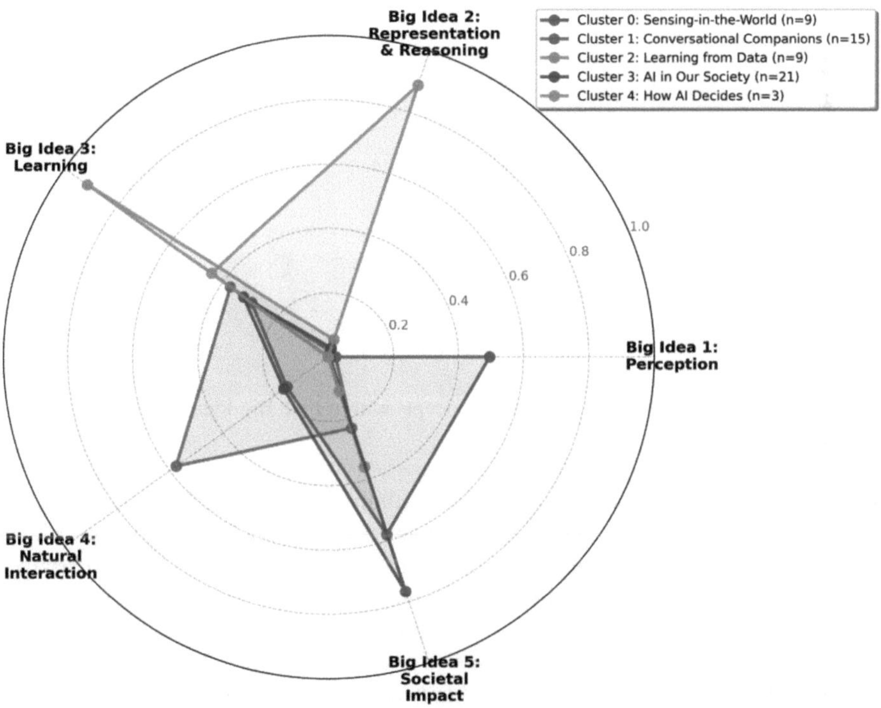


**Fig. 2.** AI4K12 Big Idea profiles by book cluster. Radar plots show the mean relative frequency of each Big Idea within clusters; legend reports cluster labels and *n* books.

Cluster analysis identified five distinct clusters (Fig. 2), each characterized by different dominant Big Ideas and varying concept-level emphasis. This suggests that the books form distinct AI literacy profiles rather than uniformly covering individual Big Ideas. The largest group, cluster 3 (n = 21), was strongly dominated by Societal Impact (M = 0.766), with smaller contributions from Learning (0.32) and Natural Interaction (0.167).

Cluster 1 (n = 15) foregrounded Natural Interaction (0.576) and Learning (0.372), representing books that frame AI primarily as interactive and language-based agents. Cluster 2 ("Learning from Data", n = 9) concentrated almost entirely on Learning (0.913), with moderate Societal Impact (0.359) and little to no Perception or Natural Interaction. Cluster 0 (n = 9) showed relatively stronger Perception (0.496) paired with Societal Impact (0.58), representing a smaller set of books that more explicitly describe how AI perceives the world. Finally, Cluster 4 (n = 3) was a rare profile dominated by Representation and Reasoning (0.889). The results reinforce the corpus-level distribution: most children's AI books prioritize Societal Impact, Natural Interaction or Learning, while explicit attention to Perception appears in fewer titles, and Representation and Reasoning is represented in a very small subset.

### 4.3 Distribution of Concepts Within Big Ideas (Fig. 3)

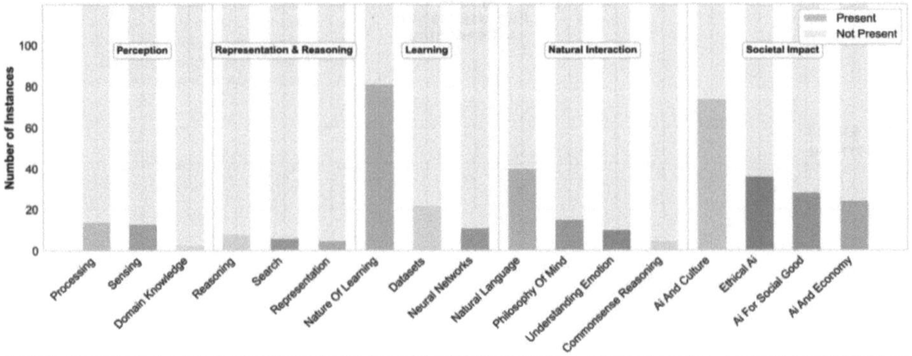


**Fig. 3.** Distribution of concepts within Five Big Ideas.

**Societal Impact.** Within Big Idea 5, AI and Culture dominated (74 instances; 34.91%) and was present in 40 books, indicating that many texts situate AI in everyday social and cultural contexts. Other concepts appeared less frequently, with Ethical AI (36 instances; 16.98%) in 26 books, AI for Social Good (28 instances; 13.21%) in 22 books, and AI & the Economy (24 instances; 11.32%) in 17 books. When introducing or defining AI, 40 books used AI in daily life as a starting point (75 instances). They foregrounded concrete and familiar embodiments of AI in children's everyday life, such as smart speakers (e.g., Amazon Echo), voice assistants (e.g., Siri), and self-driving cars, often accompanied by explanations of the benefits these technologies provide. For instance, in a book *What is Artificial Intelligence?* (cluster 3) [24], AI capabilities are presented across multiple pages through statements such as "AI can talk to you and answer your questions," paired with illustrations of a child asking a smart speaker about the weather. Similar narrative–visual pairings are used to depict AI applications in domains such as space exploration and agriculture, reinforcing AI's usefulness across diverse contexts. This representational strategy not only makes AI visible and relatable, but also implicitly frames AI primarily in terms of its positive functions and benefits.

**Learning.** Big idea 3 was the second most represented one. Nature of Learning emerged as the dominant concept, accounting for 81 instances (38.21%). Additional concepts such as model training, datasets, features, and bias in datasets appeared with moderate frequency, whereas representations of neural network structure or adjustment were relatively rare. The majority of the books used human learning metaphors to explain the AI learning process.

One example comes from the book *Machine Learning for Kids (cluster 0)* [25] which uses parallel visual metaphors to explain AI learning by aligning it with children's everyday experiences. Across a sequence of illustrations, the book moves from explicit instruction to increasing machine capability and finally to data-driven learning through experience. In the opening scene (Fig. 4), a child draws an apple while a computer produces the same image by following step-by-step commands (e.g., "Draw apple," "Color red"), framing computers as entities that act by following instructions. A subsequent scene depicts a child and a robot side by side, accompanied by the statement "Computers are getting smarter!", shifting the emphasis from rule execution to improvement over time and reinforcing a human-like learning trajectory. This metaphor is further developed in scenes that ask "How do we get smarter?" and answer "More data helps us learn and build!" Both a child and a robot are shown interacting with a data-rich environment containing sensors, satellites, and labeled objects, with data visually presented as the source of learning. A final street-crossing scene explicitly maps human decision-making onto machine learning, stating that computers, like people, "gather data, process, and make decisions," and that algorithms perform better with more data. This book presents AI learning as progressive improvement through accumulated experience, using human learning as the primary explanatory metaphor.

**Fig. 4.** Human drawing with rule-based computer behavior (source: book *Machine Learning for Kids*).

Although this approach makes data-driven learning intuitive and developmentally accessible, it also abstracts away internal computational mechanisms such as model architecture, representation learning, or parameter updates. These findings suggest that children's AI literacy books portray learning as a defining feature of AI, but tend to emphasize high-level, experience-based explanations grounded in human analogy rather than detailed accounts of underlying learning processes.

**Natural Interaction.** As for Big Idea 4, representations within this category were dominated by the Natural Language, which accounted for 40 instances (18.87%), primarily reflecting language applications such as conversational agents and voice-based systems (21 books, 36 instances). These representations typically portrayed AI systems as entities that can talk, listen, and respond to users' questions, emphasizing fluent communication and responsiveness rather than the processes underlying language understanding. Concepts related to philosophy of mind or consciousness (11 books; 15 instances; 6.91%) and understanding emotion (9 books; 10 instances; 4.61%) also appeared, suggesting that some books discuss whether AI can think, feel, or communicate meaningfully with humans. In these cases, books often raised questions about whether AI can think, feel, or possess human-like awareness, or depicted AI systems as recognizing and responding to human emotions in socially appropriate ways. For instance, in *Hello, AI! A Kid's Interview with Artificial Intelligence* (cluster 1) [26], natural interaction is presented through a conversational exchange between a child and an AI agent. When the child expresses sadness and asks whether the AI can help, the AI responds with emotionally supportive language, offering jokes or stories, and acknowledging the child's feelings, while also explicitly stating its limitations by encouraging the child to seek comfort from parents, teachers, or other trusted humans. Through this dialogue, the AI is framed as a socially responsive and emotionally aware conversational partner, yet not as a replacement for human relationships.

**Perception.** Big Idea 1 accounted for 30 concept-level instances (14.15%) across 12 books. When present, representations most frequently focused on processing (14 instances; 6.60%; 10 books) and sensing (13 instances; 6.13%; 9 books), often emphasizing how AI systems collect and transform sensory inputs. In contrast, domain knowledge related to perception was rarely addressed (3 instances; 1.42%; 2 books), suggesting limited attention to how prior knowledge shapes AI perception. Most books mentioning this Big Idea depict AI "seeing" through cameras or "hearing" through microphones, describing sensors as the inputs that help computers notice features in the environment.

**Representation and Reasoning.** Big Idea 2 appeared in 19 instances (8.96%) across 11 books, making it the least represented big idea. Concepts related to reasoning were most common (8 instances; 3.77%; 7 books), followed by search (6 instances; 2.83%; 5 books) and representation (5 instances; 2.36%; 3 books). Overall, these books offered relatively sparse and fragmented depictions of how AI systems represent knowledge or engage in structured problem solving.

When reasoning did appear, it was typically presented through simplified problem-solving scenarios rather than explicit representations or algorithmic processes. Only one book, *How AI Learns?* (cluster 4) [27] from the AI+ME series, provided a relatively complete and explicit depiction of AI representation and reasoning aligned with AI4K12 expectations. The book models AI reasoning using a decision-tree structure, framing classification as a guessing-game process. The visual representation begins with an initial binary question (e.g., "Does it swim?"), with answers ("yes" or "no") determining the next question the AI asks (e.g., "Does it have scales?" or "Does it fly?"). Through this branching structure, the book makes the process of how an AI system maintains internal representations of features visible and uses these features to reason step by step toward a classification decision.

Importantly, the illustration emphasizes that the AI uses previous answers to choose subsequent questions, highlighting core ideas of feature-based representation, conditional reasoning, and search through a state space. By externalizing the reasoning process in a tree-like diagram, the book offers children a concrete visualization of how AI systems narrow possibilities and make decisions based on structured representations of information. However, such explicit treatment of representation and reasoning was rare across the corpus. The scarcity of similar examples suggests that most children's AI literacy books provide limited opportunities for learners to engage with how AI systems internally organize information and reason over it, despite the centrality of these mechanisms to AI functionality.

## 5 Discussion

This study provides an empirical account of how AI-themed children's books conceptualize foundational AI ideas when analyzed through the AI4K12 framework. Across the corpus, representations were heavily concentrated in Societal Impact, Learning, and Natural Interaction, whereas Perception and especially Representation and Reasoning were comparatively underrepresented. These patterns suggest that children's AI literacy books primarily teach AI through what AI does in the world (e.g., helping, communicating, benefiting society) and how AI "gets smarter" from data, rather than through how AI works internally. From an early childhood education perspective, this distribution is not inherently problematic, as books are a narrative medium that naturally foreground functions and social meaning. However, it does shape the mental models that children are likely to develop. In the following, we discuss the implications of these patterns for early AI literacy development.

Across the corpus, children's AI books overwhelmingly foreground AI's functions and societal roles, positioning AI primarily as a helpful and pervasive technology embedded in everyday life. This function-first orientation supports accessibility by anchoring abstract ideas in familiar experiences [28], but it also implicitly frames AI as a finished and largely benevolent artifact rather than a designed system shaped by human choices [29]. By emphasizing what AI does over how it works, these books tend to position children as users or observers of AI systems, rather than as sense makers capable of interrogating AI behavior [30]. Future children's AI literacy books should complement functional narratives with moments that explicitly surface AI as a constructed system, making visible that AI behavior results from design decisions. Future research could examine how early exposure to function-centered versus design-centered AI narratives in children's books shapes children's epistemic agency, particularly their capacity to question, explain, and critique AI systems as constructed and revisable rather than fixed and inevitable.

Additionally, the strong reliance on concrete examples and observable AI behaviors aligns with established understandings of young children's learning needs [4, 31]. However, the near absence of explicit treatment of perception, representation, and reasoning suggests a missed epistemic opportunity. Prior research demonstrates that children can engage meaningfully with invisible mechanisms when supported by external representations, diagrams, and structured narratives [32]. The rarity of books that externalize internal AI processes, such as decision trees or feature-based reasoning, indicates that these concepts are largely excluded by design rather than by necessity. For future design iterations, different stakeholders, including educators, AI experts, and illustrators, should collaborate to ensure that children's AI books leverage visualizations, branching diagrams, and simplified models to make internal AI processes perceptible, allowing children to reason about how AI systems arrive at decisions. Future research could investigate how the introduction of explicit visualizations of internal AI processes in children's narratives influences children's ability to reason about invisible mechanisms, particularly their understanding of causality, decision making, and system behavior.

Notably, human-centered metaphors dominate explanations of AI learning, framing AI as "getting smarter" through experience in ways analogous to children's own learning. While such metaphors lower cognitive barriers and foster intuitive understanding [33], they also risk obscuring fundamental differences between human cognition and algorithmic optimization [34]. By emphasizing experience accumulation without unpacking representational structures or parameter adjustment, these narratives may inadvertently anthropomorphize AI and mask its limitations [35]. Designers should retain human learning metaphors as entry points while explicitly contrasting them with explanations that clarify what AI does not do, helping children develop more differentiated and accurate mental models of AI learning. Future research could explore how different uses of human learning metaphors, with or without explicit contrasts to algorithmic processes, shape children's conceptual boundaries between human intelligence and machine learning, including their susceptibility to anthropomorphism and misconceptions about AI capabilities.

Furthermore, ethical themes such as bias and fairness appeared with moderate frequency, most books framed AI primarily through benefits and offered limited attention to risks, limitations, or negative consequences. Portrayals were also often narrow or dated: generative AI was largely absent, constraining discussion of issues unique to these systems (e.g., authorship, misinformation, and human–AI responsibility). Even when ethics was raised, it was rarely connected to underlying technical mechanisms, such as data selection, feature representation, or model design. As a result, ethical discussions often remained at the level of outcomes rather than causes, limiting children's opportunities to reason about responsibility and accountability [36]. This separation of ethics from technical foundations may constrain children's capacity to understand how social values become embedded in AI systems [17]. Future AI books should integrate ethical questions directly into explanations of learning, perception, and representation, illustrating how technical choices give rise to societal consequences and ethical tradeoffs. Future research could study how integrating ethical issues with explanations of technical mechanisms in children's AI narratives influences children's causal reasoning about bias, responsibility, and accountability in sociotechnical systems.

Moreover, representation and reasoning emerged as the least represented Big Ideas, despite their centrality to AI functionality and decision making [37]. The scarcity of explicit reasoning models suggests that children are rarely invited to engage with AI as a system that organizes information, evaluates alternatives, and makes conditional choices. Yet the few counterexamples demonstrate that such concepts can be made accessible through concrete visual structures and simplified problem spaces. To support children's epistemic agency, AI books should treat representation and reasoning as core narrative elements rather than optional technical details, allowing children to see AI systems not only as tools that act, but as systems whose behavior can be examined, questioned, and redesigned [38]. Future research could examine how early exposure to explicit representations of AI reasoning processes in children's narratives influences the development of children's epistemic agency, particularly their capacity to explain, question, and critically reason about AI decision making.

Finally, the cluster analysis suggests that children's AI books do not simply vary in completeness, but instead organize around coherent narrative pathways that privilege particular ways of knowing AI. The books tend to specialize in specific conceptual framings, such as AI as a societal actor, a conversational partner, a data-driven learner, a sensing system, or a reasoning agent, thereby introducing AI literacy through thematic entry points that foreground certain epistemic stances while backgrounding others [39]. These profiles may shape how children come to orient themselves toward AI well before encountering more integrated or technically explicit explanations, raising important questions about how early narrative specialization influences the sequencing, coherence, and transfer of AI literacy across developmental stages [40]. Designers could intentionally sequence books across complementary AI literacy profiles to scaffold a more coherent and developmentally progressive understanding of AI over time. Future research could explore how exposure to different profiles and their ordering shapes longitudinal trajectories of AI understanding and the integration of technical and societal reasoning about AI systems.

## 6 Limitation

One limitation of this study lies in the analytic scope afforded by the AI4K12 framework. As a comprehensive and widely adopted framework for defining foundational AI knowledge in K–12 education, AI4K12 provides a powerful lens for systematically examining the presence and balance of core AI concepts in children's books. At the same time, because the framework is explicitly designed to foreground the technical and computational foundations of AI systems, it may not fully capture pedagogically intentional representational choices rooted in narrative or sociocultural meaning-making. Consequently, the underrepresentation of certain Big Ideas in our analysis should not be interpreted as a deficiency of the books themselves, but rather as evidence of a productive tension between technical definitions of AI literacy and the narrative affordances of children's literature. Future research could complement AI4K12 with additional lenses drawn from literacy studies, childhood studies, or sociotechnical theory to capture a broader range of how AI is communicated and made meaningful for young learners. Additionally, the study captures whether AI ideas are present, but not how accurately or accessibly they are conveyed. As a result, brief or inaccurate depictions are treated the same as more carefully explained ones. Future work could incorporate complementary frameworks to better capture how AI is meaningfully communicated to young learners.

## References


1. Druga, S., Williams, R., Breazeal, C., Resnick, M.: "Hey Google is it OK if I eat you?": initial explorations in child-agent interaction. In: Proceedings of the 2017 Conference on Interaction Design and Children, pp. 595–600. ACM, Stanford California USA (2017). https://doi.org/10.1145/3078072.3084330
2. Famaye, T.: AI is not just a robot; it's more than a robot. Understanding Children's AI Competencies in an AI Literacy Workshop
3. Williams, R. (Scientist in media arts and sciences): PopBots: leveraging social robots to aid preschool children's artificial intelligence education, https://dspace.mit.edu/handle/1721.1/122894 (2018)
4. Cai, Z., Xing, Y.G., Yamamoto, Y., Wang, X.C.: From Piaget to Posthumanism: Critical Review of Conceptualization of AI in Early Childhood Education, https://www.researchsquare.com/article/rs-5969987/v1 (2025). https://doi.org/10.21203/rs.3.rs-5969987/v1
5. Druga, S., Williams, R., Park, H.W., Breazeal, C.: How smart are the smart toys?: children and parents' agent interaction and intelligence attribution. In: Proceedings of the 17th ACM Conference on Interaction Design and Children, pp. 231–240. ACM, Trondheim Norway (2018). https://doi.org/10.1145/3202185.3202741
6. Su, J.: Kindergarten parents' perceptions of the use of AI technologies and AI literacy education: positive views but practical concerns. Educ. Inf. Technol. **30**, 279–295 (2025). https://doi.org/10.1007/s10639-024-12673-4
7. Su, J., Yang, W.: Artificial intelligence (AI) literacy in early childhood education: an intervention study in Hong Kong. Interact. Learn. Environ. **32**, 5494–5508 (2024). https://doi.org/10.1080/10494820.2023.2217864
8. Williams, R., Park, H.W., Breazeal, C.: A is for artificial intelligence: the impact of artificial intelligence activities on young children's perceptions of robots. In: Proceedings of the 2019 CHI Conference on Human Factors in Computing Systems, pp. 1–11. ACM, Glasgow Scotland Uk (2019). https://doi.org/10.1145/3290605.3300677
9. Banister, F., Ryan, C.: Developing science concepts through story-telling. School Sci. Rev. **82**, 75–84 (2001)
10. Azis, Y., Metafisika, K., Ayu Lestari, F.A., Asistiana, L.: Analysis of validity, practicality, and readability of islamic STEAM activity storybook for early childhood. Al-Athfaal. **5**, 63–75 (2022). https://doi.org/10.24042/ajipaud.v5i1.11964
11. Furner, J.M.: Using children's literature to teach mathematics: an effective vehicle in a STEM world. Eur. J. STEM Educ. **3**(3), 14 (2018). https://doi.org/10.20897/ejsteme/3874
12. Arn, L., Huang, E.M.: "Robots can do disgusting things, but also good things": fostering children's understanding of AI through storytelling. ACM Trans. Comput. Educ. **24**, 1–55 (2024). https://doi.org/10.1145/3677613
13. Touretzky, D., Gardner-McCune, C., Martin, F., Seehorn, D.: Envisioning AI for K-12: what should every child know about AI? AAAI. **33**, 9795–9799 (2019). https://doi.org/10.1609/aaai.v33i01.33019795
14. Touretzky, D., Gardner-McCune, C., Seehorn, D.: Machine learning and the five big ideas in AI. Int. J. Artif. Intell. Educ. **33**, 233–266 (2023). https://doi.org/10.1007/s40593-022-00314-1
15. Kong, S.C., Abelson, H. (eds.): Computational Thinking Education in K-12: Artificial Intelligence Literacy and Physical Computing. The MIT Press, Cambridge, Massachusetts; London, England (2022)
16. Burgsteiner, H., Kandlhofer, M., Steinbauer, G.: IRobot: teaching the basics of artificial intelligence in high schools. In: AAAI, vol. 30, (2016). https://doi.org/10.1609/aaai.v30i1.9864

17. Long, D., Magerko, B.: What is AI literacy? Competencies and design considerations. In: Proceedings of the 2020 CHI Conference on Human Factors in Computing Systems, pp. 1–16. ACM, Honolulu HI USA (2020). https://doi.org/10.1145/3313831.3376727
18. Ng, D.T.K., Leung, J.K.L., Chu, S.K.W., Qiao, M.S.: Conceptualizing AI literacy: an exploratory review. Comput. Educ.: Artif. Intell. **2**, 100041 (2021). https://doi.org/10.1016/j.caeai.2021.100041
19. Kleinknecht, E., Blumberg, F.C., Flynn, R.M.: Making a case for artificial intelligence literacy skills for school-age children. In: Papadakis, S., Kalogiannakis, M. (eds.) Education, Development and Intervention: Toward Participatory and Integrated Solutions, pp. 201–212. Springer Nature Switzerland, Cham (2024). https://doi.org/10.1007/978-3-031-60713-4_13
20. Druga, S., Christoph, F.L., Ko, A.J.: Family as a third space for AI literacies: how do children and parents learn about AI together? In: CHI Conference on Human Factors in Computing Systems, pp. 1–17. ACM, New Orleans LA USA (2022). https://doi.org/10.1145/3491102.3502031
21. Ng, D.T.K., Leung, J.K.L., Su, M.J., Yim, I.H.Y., Qiao, M.S., Chu, S.K.W.: AI Literacy in K-16 Classrooms. Springer International Publishing, Cham (2022). https://doi.org/10.1007/978-3-031-18880-0
22. Sableski, M.-K.: Stretching STEM: using Picturebooks to connect STEM and literacy. Child. Libr. **17**, 23–26 (2019). https://doi.org/10.5860/cal.17.3.23
23. Kaufman, L., Rousseeuw, P.J.: Finding Groups in Data: An Introduction to Cluster Analysis. John Wiley & Sons (2009)
24. Shade, E.: What is Artificial Intelligence? Upgrade with AI, for Kids ages 4-8: A Fun and Easy Guide to Explore the Future with Robots, Games, and Smart Technology. Independently published
25. Dhoot, D.: Machine Learning for Kids (Tinker Toddlers): STEAM Book to Kick-Start Your Future Genius! Tinker Toddlers
26. Ripacs, P.: Hello, AI! A Kid's Interview with Artificial Intelligence: A Friendly Chat Between a Curious Kid and Artificial Intelligence -
27. ReadyAI: AI+Me: Big Idea 3 - Machine Learning: How AI Learns. Independently published
28. Papert, S.A.: Mindstorms: Children, Computers, and Powerful Ideas. Basic Books (2020)
29. Kalluri, P.: Don't ask if artificial intelligence is good or fair, ask how it shifts power. Nature. **583**, 169–169 (2020). https://doi.org/10.1038/d41586-020-02003-2
30. Kafai, Y., Proctor, C., Lui, D.: From theory bias to theory dialogue: embracing cognitive, situated, and critical framings of computational thinking in K-12 CS education. ACM Inroads. **11**, 44–53 (2020). https://doi.org/10.1145/3381887
31. Piaget, J., Inhelder, B.: The Psychology of the Child. Basic Books (2008)
32. diSessa, A.A.: Metarepresentation: native competence and targets for instruction. Cogn. Instr. **22**, 293–331 (2004). https://doi.org/10.1207/s1532690xci2203_2
33. Gentner, D.: Structure-Mapping: A Theoretical Framework for Analogy
34. Dreyfus, H.L.: What Computers Still Can't Do: A Critique of Artificial Reason. MIT Press (1992)
35. Darling, K.: Extending legal protection to social robots: the effects of anthropomorphism, empathy, and violent behavior towards robotic objects. In: Calo, R., Froomkin, A.M., Kerr, I. (eds.) Robot Law. Edward Elgar Publishing (2016). https://doi.org/10.4337/9781783476732.00017
36. Biagini, G.: Towards an AI-literate future: a systematic literature review exploring education, ethics, and applications. Int. J. Artif. Intell. Educ. **35**, 2616–2666 (2025). https://doi.org/10.1007/s40593-025-00466-w
37. Frankish, K., Ramsey, W.M.: The Cambridge Handbook of Artificial Intelligence. Cambridge University Press (2014)

38. Morales-Navarro, L., Gan, M.A., Yu, E., Vogelstein, L., Kafai, Y., Metaxa, D.: Learning AI auditing: a case study of teenagers auditing a generative AI model. Proc. ACM Hum. Comput. Interact. **9**, CSCW439:1–CSCW439:29 (2025). https://doi.org/10.1145/3757620
39. Gee, J.P.: Social Linguistics and Literacies: Ideology in Discourses. Routledge, London; New York (2008)
40. Schwarz, C.V. et al.: Developing a learning progression for scientific modeling: making scientific modeling accessible and meaningful for learners. J. Res. Sci. Teach. **46**, 632–654 (2009). https://doi.org/10.1002/tea.20311

# Community Futures: Hybrid and Situated Critical AI Literacy


Supratim Pait[1](✉), Sylvia Janicki[1], Yuhan Hou[1], Michael Nitsche[1], and Noura Howell[2]

[1] Digital Media, Georgia Institute of Technology, Atlanta, USA
{spait3,sjanicki3,yhou312,mn81}@gatech.edu

[2] University of Southern Denmark, Odense, Denmark
nouh@mmmi.sdu.dk



**Abstract.** "Community Futures" presents a hybrid digital-physical workshop framework for Critical AI Literacy (CAIL) through making, performance, and design futuring. It focuses on site-specific, embodied positioning to counter over-generalizing AI output and supports a critique of AI through shared expressive activity. This approach is outlined in detail and was tested (n = 37, children aged 9–12) in a workshop combining GenAI co-creation and material puppetry in a design futuring activity. Through a mixed-methods analysis, we report how the children's lived experiences served as a "ground truth," and the performative expression enabled them to imagine local futures where generic algorithmic narratives failed to reflect local civic and environmental complexities. This paper contributes to critical AI education by proposing a novel adaptable hybrid framework of making, performance, and design futuring that is situated in children's local environment.



**Keywords:** Child-Computer Interaction · Critical AI Literacy · Tangible AI Education · Design Futuring


## 1 Introduction

Artificial Intelligence (AI) increasingly shapes how children create, learn, and imagine. As Generative AI (GenAI) systems become embedded in classroom tools, creative platforms, and everyday technologies, the need for AI literacy for youth has expanded beyond teaching technical mechanisms toward cultivating *critical* and *contextual* understanding. AI literacy frameworks emphasize not only skills for interacting with AI, but also the capacity to assess AI's limitations, biases, and social impacts. These are competencies essential for children navigating AI-mediated futures [25]. They call for children as agents capable of critiquing, shaping, and resisting algorithmic narratives [21].

Two persistent challenges limit these necessary AI literacy efforts. First, most tools remain **predominantly virtual**, presenting AI through interfaces such as chat windows, prompt boxes, or simulations [22]. These tools rarely provide any



E. G. Blanchard et al. (eds.), AIED 2026, LNCS 16586, pp. 255–269, 2027.
https://doi.org/10.1007/978-3-032-29773-0_18

*physical* or *embodied* relationships, even though tangible encounters such as craft, physical models, and embodied interactions can anchor abstract AI concepts in children's sensory, emotional, and narrative worlds [26]. Likewise, different forms of making support personal meaning-making, storytelling, collaborative sense-making, and recognition of AI's imperfections [12,23,28,33]. Yet, researchers highlight the "absence of physical kits" and call for more tangible, embodied modes of AI learning [22].

Second, AI literacy approaches frequently rely on global datasets that **lack local context** and fail to resonate with children's lived experiences. This results in "cultural flattening," where generic algorithmic narratives misrepresent or erase local heritage, social values, and situated identities [4,7]. Children struggle to situate these kinds of results in their own daily lives and inherently have less ability to critically reflect on them.

Our approach combines **design futuring** through embodied interaction with a specific environment that students are familiar with. Anchoring AI engagement in a familiar environment, in our case, a creek behind the students' school, provides a strong foundation for design futuring activities, which span from design fiction to critical design and fabulation. They prompt children to imagine alternative socio-technical futures and examine values, possibilities, and consequences [17]. Prior work with children shows that speculative activities help surface ethical tensions, plural perspectives, and civic concerns [32,33] as they offer powerful pathways for cultivating critical AI literacy [23].

Our work investigates:

- **RQ1 (Situatedness):** How does grounding AI interaction in a specific, familiar local environment influence children's ability to identify and understand AI's limitations?
- **RQ2 (Hybrid Method):** How does integrating material practices (e.g., puppetry) with Generative AI empower children to resist AI-driven narratives and articulate complex ecological futures?

Through **Community Futures**, a multi-day workshop with children (n = 37) aged 9–12, we examine how this combination of making and performing, paired with situated GenAI interactions, fosters *Situated Critical AI Literacy* through design futuring activities.

These workshops demonstrate how combining *tangible*, *embodied*, and *speculative* methods within a *situated* context can transform children's engagements with GenAI—from passive consumption into critical, playful negotiation and creative resistance. Our contribution expands the landscape of AI literacy by offering a hybrid, place-based framework for cultivating criticality rooted in children's own environments, material-engagements, and imaginations.

## 2 Related Work

Critical AI literacy requires frameworks that go beyond teaching children how AI works to supporting their understanding of what AI *does* in the world, how it intersects with culture, community, and place. Thus, we argue for a combination of (1) critical, child-centered AI literacy with (2) embodied, tangible, and playful modes of learning toward (3) participatory design futuring.

### 2.1 Critical AI Literacy: Child Agency and Embodied Interaction

Child–Computer Interaction requires attention to power, politics, and values in children's technological worlds [19]. Likewise, AI literacy research has moved from technical comprehension to *critical awareness*, emphasizing the need for children to understand AI's limitations, biases, and ethical implications [25]. This shift aligns with *computational empowerment*, which reframes learning as a process through which children become capable of critiquing and reshaping technological systems [21]. Children readily encounter the limitations of AI and negotiate their own sensemaking around AI's agency [10], which can highlight the importance of equity, cultural inclusion, and global diversity for such sensemaking [9]. This frames AI literacy as a practice defined by questions of *agency*: children must not only gain access to the AI as an operational tool, but also develop and recognize their own agency in relation to this tool.

### 2.2 Embodied, Tangible, and Playful AI Literacy

Forms of bodily engagement can deepen conceptual understanding and collaborative sensemaking [24] and hands-on exploration support children's reasoning [10,32,33]. Embodiment has become a central design strategy to translate abstract AI concepts into performable, manipulable interactions [26]. This is exemplified in projects such as *Tangible Diffusion*, which combines physical building blocks with diffusion models [13], or *Stage Wizard*, which combines LLMs paired with physical staging of objects for narrative generation [14]. *Creat'AI* uses tangible props and hand-made objects to teach AI concepts through embodied narrative co-creation [28]. As a special form of embodied expression, performance and drama empower children to tackle social issues and rehearse alternatives [34]. In AI contexts, performance allows learners to *stage* AI outputs, exposing where model assumptions clash with character logic, social dynamics, or situated realities. Collectively, this work reframes AI interaction as a *material practice* that is a *social, embodied, and public* process. Children shape AI not only through text but through gesture, placement, and manipulation.

### 2.3 Participatory Design Futuring

Participatory Design (PD) positions children as *protagonists* with authority to shape design goals, processes, and outcomes [20]. PD futuring applies this to an ensemble of critical and speculative practices, including speculative design [11], critical design [18], reflective design [31], Afrofuturist speculative design [15], and fabulation [29]. These approaches aim to open *plural, contestable futures*, rather than promoting a singular narrative of progress [17].

Children have used design-futuring to explore environmental change [8], social robots [33], and AI-mediated education and care [32]. These projects can make sociotechnical futures negotiable from children's standpoints [32]. Through them, children can operationalize fairness-by-design into meaningful design features [2] and identify concerns and articulate modes of agency grounded in their real practices [3]. Such futuring works best when it is situated and its criticality is anchored in contexts children understand intimately. This points toward localisation as an essential layer of critical AI literacy.

### 2.4 Localised AI Literacy: Culture, Community, and Environment

Child-centered AI research emphasizes children's developmental relation to AI [16]. Systems like *StoryPrompt* illustrate how narrative co-creation with GenAI supports creativity and literacy [12]. Participatory workshops can engage children to critically analyze AI as a cultural tool, identifying bias and misalignment with their contexts [7]. Accordingly, fairness-by-design work recommends tangible and culturally relevant tools [2]. Integrating children's lived experiences and situated knowledge has the potential for critical engagement [30]. For example, for underserved youth, AI learning is most effective when it leverages local cultural capital, communal, and creative forms of knowledge [6]. Even very young children can shift to relational, interdependent understanding when problems are grounded in familiar places [32]. That is whay our method of PD inherently calls for culturally sensitive practices attuned to local values [2], which often clash with LLMs' tendency to reproduce social biases [4]. Emphasizing shared experiences, environments, and communal cultural settings form the final layer for our CAIL approach.

## 3 The Community Futures Workshop

Our approach combines key criteria that emerged from the related work. Methodologically, it targets critical AI literacy through participatory design futuring grounded in plurality. Its practices combine tangible making and performance with situated engagement rooted in the local community and environment.

We developed **Community Futures**, a workshop design that engages in tangible making and performing situated future scenarios. Our focus on local communities—in this case, a public school and its students—meant that this workshop was situated in a specific socio-ecological context. This setting was the local creek behind the school. This location was chosen in collaboration with the school teachers, who were already exploring the creek as part of their learning curriculum. This included regular visits to the park and collecting environmental data from the creek. At the same time, the creek remained part of the children's daily experiences with nature, and as such, it could serve as a shared reference point. Situating the inquiry in a local creek familiar to the children created a power dynamic where the children held local knowledge that the AI models (trained on global, generalized datasets) lacked. This framework invites children to resist and re-author algorithmically generated futures. It surfaces AI's limitations through a situated framing (RQ1) and introduces our hybrid approach (RQ2) as a mode toward *Situated Critical AI Literacy.*

### 3.1 Tools and Materials

For our design futuring activities, we developed a hybrid toolkit combining digital Generative AI platforms with crafting, storytelling, and performance.

**MagicSchool AI** [27] served as the classroom-approved GenAI platform that empowered children to generate and iterate content at different stages. We employed three distinct tools within this platform: **ChatBot (LLM):** for generating "News from the Future" headlines and answering open-ended queries about the creek's ecosystem. **Image Generator (Diffusion Model)** (based on Adobe Firefly [1]) allowed children to upload their photos of the creek as a base layer for the AI. This grounded the image generation in the actual site and produced visualizations for their "Big Idea" scenarios. **Create a Skit!** within MagicSchool AI offered a structured narrative generation tool used to draft the initial scripts for the performance.

**Storytelling and performance materials** supported children in the generation of their scenes and the final puppet performances of their skits. We designed a **"Community Futures" Booklet** that scaffolded the process, providing space for prompting, sketching, and reflection. A breakdown of these activities is covered in more detail below. Finally, we provide **Puppet Prototyping Kits** that include cardboard, felt, markers, and recycled materials. Most of these materials were already available in the classrooms.

### 3.2 Workshop Design

An introductory Likert scale questionnaire was provided in the booklet introduction, asking them to rate their current understanding of AI and Gen-AI features like image generation, LLMs and Bias in AI.

**Phase 0: Introduction:** The first workshop session started with a 30-minute interactive presentation introducing core concepts of Artificial Intelligence. This segment covered the basics of Large Language Models (LLMs) and Image Generation, explicitly framing AI not as a "magic box" but as a tool trained on human data that can make mistakes ("hallucinations") and contain biases.

**Phase 1: Understanding The Creek:** Children were asked to reflect on their current, cumulative experiences and knowledge of the creek. Using the *Booklet*, they documented their ideas about the creek, why they thought the creek was important according to them, identifying civic challenges (e.g., pollution, invasive species) they wanted to address. This activity aimed to establish a human-centered baseline of "truth" about the creek before using AI tools.

**Phase 2: The "Big Idea":** Groups formulated a **"Big Idea"** for the *future* of the creek. The teams were encouraged to imagine radical futures based on the prompt: *"Our community imagines the creek might become [state] due to [cause] in the future."* These big Ideas ranged from utopian ("Luxury Resort") to "Dark Ecological" futures ("Acid Creek," "Nuclear Waste Dump").

**Phase 3: GenAI Text and Image Generation:** This phase introduced AI tools for visualizing children's Big Ideas. First, children used MagicSchool's Chatbot (LLM) to generate news headlines, both positive and negative, from the year 2050 based on their Big Idea. This enforced a balanced view of the future (utopian vs. dystopian). Second, groups used MagicSchool's image generator to visualize their scenario, starting from a photo of their real creek taken during their previous class visit. Children used specific prompts to refine the images (e.g., "Make the creek more [X], make the creek less [Y]"). This iterative prompting helped probe frictions where children negotiated with AI outputs.

**Phase 4: Tangible: Puppet Making and Script Generation:** To enact their future Big Idea scenarios, children created physical characters using craft materials and scripts using Magic School AI. Each participant created a character with a specific stance regarding the Big Idea (Support, Disagree, or Mediator). Each stance might have multiple characters depending on group size. Using MagicSchool's "Create a Skit" tool, groups generated a dialogue for their characters. Children crafted puppets of their characters through hands-on making with materials such as cardboard, felt, googly eyes, pipe cleaners, and markers. Scripts were printed out on paper, and groups were explicitly instructed to make any changes to the scripts if they wanted to; e.g., some groups physically crossed out lines, rewrote endings, and added or removed dialogue (Fig. 1).

**Fig. 1.** *(Left)* Children's workdesk showing the "Community Futures" booklets, their handmade puppets, and their generated scripts. *(Right)* Children perform using puppets in front of visuals they generated about the creek's future, depicting an envisioned future in which the fish have to leave the creek due to oily water as the creek is being replaced by a new Golfing Space.

**Phase 5: Performance and Reflection:** The workshop concluded with a performance of the edited skits and a collective reflection from each group after their performance. Groups acted out their stories for their big ideas. After the performances, the researcher asked the group about their experiences of working with generative AI, the challenges, and the improvisations they did, if any.

Children completed a post-workshop survey measuring shifts in familiarity with **LLMs**, **Image Generation**, and **AI Bias** (Likert scale 1–5). They also answered open-ended questions about their experience working with Gen-AI, such as, "What did you change about the story generated by AI and why?"

### 3.3 Participants and Setting

We tested the design in a study conducted in partnership with a public elementary school. As noted, the school is located adjacent to a creek, a site which children pass daily, play in, and observe. Participating students were part of the school's special STEAM learning initiative. The workshops were held for 58 students across two days (Day 1 = 28 Students, Day 2 = 30 Students). Each day offered the same workshop to a different set of students. Parental consent for data usage was obtained for 37 children aged 10–11 across both days. The cohort was diverse in gender and interest in STEAM, with many children self-identifying as having low prior familiarity with AI concepts (see Sect. 4 for a quantitative breakdown). Children were organized into teams of about 4–5 members. School teachers were present and assisted during the workshops. All workshops were conducted in the school facilities. Each workshop session lasted about 5 h and included breaks for snacks and rest. The study was approved by the university's ethics board as well as the local public school system's Office of Research and Evaluation.

**Data Collection.** A mixed-method approach captured data from both the process and the outcome of the workshops. No video recording was done in accordance with school policies. Audio was captured using voice recorders during the workshop for desks where we had parental consent as well as participant assent for study participation.

1. **Booklet Responses**: The booklet asked children to document key workshop steps (e.g., their "Big Idea") and included **Pre- and Post-Questionnaires** asking children to rate their familiarity with "LLMs," "Image Generation," and "AI Bias" on a 5-point Likert scale. Post activity questions included "What did you change and why?" They also asked children to reflect on AI, their understanding of the creek, and their idea of community.
2. **Artifact Analysis:** MagicSchool logged the AI outputs (text and images) and iterations. We captured the hard copies of children's edited scripts, including their highlighted changes and photographs of the physical puppets.
3. **Post Workshop Reflections:** children's collective responses as a group were collected in a shared reflection and transcribed from audio recordings.

**Analysis.** The data included workbooks that included individual questionnaires, workshop notes from children, AI logs, field notes, and still images, as well as audio recordings of the final presentations and post-performance reflections.

Workbook data was transcribed for coding and was analyzed using thematic Analysis [5]. Two researchers initially coded the workbook data using a top-down, deductive approach, and established an equal understanding through consensus/ discussion of the data to refine a shared code book.

We found codes for instances of resistance (rejecting AI suggestions), alignment (accepting AI suggestions), and improvisations (modifying AI suggestions). Quantitative survey data were analyzed using paired t-tests to identify significant shifts in pre- vs. post- questionnaires.

## 4 Findings

Our discussion integrates quantitative and qualitative findings to examine how children engaged with GenAI in a situated, hybrid workshop, using making practices and performance to revise and resist AI outputs.

### 4.1 Quantitative Evaluation

We evaluated the workshop's impact on AI familiarity through workbook-based pre- and post-workshop assessments. Of the 37 children, 31 completed both pre- and post-workshop surveys using a 5-point Likert scale assess familiarity with 3 core AI constructs—Large Language Models (LLMs), Image Generation, and AI Bias. These specific concepts were selected due to their integration in the workshop's activities. LLMs were used for collaborative script generation, Image Generation facilitated speculative visualization of future creek scenarios, and AI Bias was introduced in the introductory session. This allowed us to measure any perceptual shift specifically tied to the children's hands-on engagement with generative AI and materials.

We used paired-sample t-tests to measure shifts in understanding before/after the intervention. All categories showed statistically significant gains (Cohen's d $> 0.9$), indicating a significant impact on self-reported AI understanding.

**Large Language Models (LLMs):** Childrens' perceived familiarity with LLMs increased by 77.6%. The mean reported score increased from $M = 1.87$ ($SD = 1.26$) to $M = 3.32$ ($SD = 1.17$) out of 5. This shift was highly significant ( $p < .001$) with a large effect size ($d = 0.93$).

**Image Generation:** Children reported near-ceiling familiarity post-workshop, moving from $M = 3.87$ ($SD = 0.88$) to $M = 4.68$ ($SD = 0.54$) out of 5, the most significant statistical improvement in the study ($p<.001$, $d = 1.23$).

**AI Bias:** Familiarity with this term increased by 55.9% ($M = 2.19, SD = 1.19$; $M = 3.42, SD = 1.15$). The result was statistically significant ($p < .001$) and yielded a large effect size ($d = 1.13$).

## 4.2 Localised Context: Situated Anchor and Groundedness

Before engaging with GenAI, children had already established a baseline of "ground truth" rooted in their lived experiences with the local creek. The creek had been part of school activities and a shared place for the children to experience. During the workshop, children articulated connections to the creek and the importance of the creek as a place with ecological, social, and affective meanings, revealing a grounded understanding of the local environment. Not all children framed change as necessary. Only a small number described the creek as perfect (P1), indicating their wish for preserving the creek's existing state.

At an ecological level, children described the creek as a living system that sustains animals, vegetation, and water flow. When describing the site's importance, more than half the children (18 of 37) referenced the animal ecosystem or habitat, others highlighted water source (N = 14), or ecological balance (N = 6). Children also identified environmental harm based on their encounters at the site. This included water contamination such as "the pollution" of "oily water" (P4). Others emphasized "water quality" more broadly (P9, P10), reflecting a concern for ecological viability. Beyond this, physical neglect such as "trash" (P8) was identified as a critical issue, anchoring the children's environmental concerns in their sensory, situated knowledge.

Socially, childrens' desired futures for the creek were rooted in their understanding of the site as a community space, fostering social interaction and play. For instance, they described the creek as a place where "kids love to play and hang out together" (P6) and one that "brings people together" (P13) where they can "be calm" (P35). Several children recognized that the creek also served as shelter for people experiencing homelessness (P37, P8) and signaled a desire for infrastructure that "keeps our community happy and not gloomy" (P22).

Affective emotions and experiences further grounded children's relationships with the creek, with many describing it through feelings of calm, peace, and familiarity. Children frequently characterized the creek as a peaceful spot (P21, P23) or emphasized its sensory qualities, such as "peaceful noises" (P1), suggesting that the tranquil atmosphere was central to how the creek was experienced. Emotional attachments were often tied to routine and memory. One child referenced "morning visits" (P35), while another highlighted personal "fond memories" associated with the site (P14), indicating how repeated encounters fostered familiarity and care. Others expressed affective connection through exploration and play, describing the creek as a place for "adventure" (P10) or for "finding cool stuff" (P21). These statements reflect an attachment to the creek through complex embodied and emotional experiences.

The creek was perceived as a place shaped by ecological vitality, everyday social use, and affective experience. This indicates that the creek as a site already had significance to participating children before any turn to AI systems. We argue that this establishes a "ground truth" of the creek for children, which establishes shared values and perceived qualities of the location.

### 4.3 Questioning "Cheesy" and "Unrealistic" AI

Children initially used AI to generate dramatic scenes about their "Big Idea" for the creek. When generating the script, AI's outputs aligned with some children's expectations and were described as "exactly what we wanted" (P3, P4). Some children also expressed appreciation for the AI-generated skits, noting that "the AI made the story a little more funny and detailed" (P33). However, children also critiqued AI's narrative and emotional authenticity, calling outputs "cheesy" or "corny." The label "cheesy" stood out as a frequently used descriptor by 16 out of 37 participants. This was not just a critique of the AI's writing style, but also of the narrative logic and character behavior. Children rejected AI's "smooth" resolution of conflict, particularly when it defied the logic of their characters. For instance, when an AI-generated script included a "group hug" at the conclusion of a debate, P36, who was performing as a fish puppet, stated that "fish can't do that." Similarly, P1 rejected the same trope, explaining it simply "didn't fit the character." Children prioritized their own character ideas over AI's suggestions.

Script editing offered opportunities for these required adjustments. Children improvised over the generated script to inject humor, specificity, and realism back into the dialogue. P10 described this as removing "cheesy lines" and replacing them with lines that "gave more info," opting for narrative clarity and description. P13 similarly "added some funny bits" to steer the story away from being what they described as "extremely unrealistic." These edits served to ground the generic AI script in the specific, often messy reality of the children's own visions. Children articulated ownership over their narratives as AI components were "not exactly what we wanted" (P14) or that specific narrative parts "weren't really our style" (P37).

In this critique, children also identified ethical implications of the AI's "cheesiness." P24 realized the machine's "sugar-coated" perspective was problematic because it erased human disagreement. P16 remarked, "I think AI doesn't ever show how it's okay to disagree." By rejecting these endings through their re-written performance, children were not just editing scripts; they were resisting a "flattened" version of AI's output where conflict is artificially smoothed over.

### 4.4 Inauthentic Beautification

Children reported the AI's image generation consistently "beautified" the creek, creating a visual mismatch with their own knowledge of the creek. The AI "tried to make the creek [picturesque]" and rendered it "really enchanted and beautiful." P24 observed that the tool "showed me way more beautiful images than what it is," while P11 felt it made the creek look "more colorful." These observations position AI as an unreliable visual narrator of place, prioritizing an idealized aesthetic over the specific reality of the site. This was perceived by children as a form of deception or "sugar-coating." P15 noted that while the image was technically "good," it was "all sunshine and rainbows" when they were "thinking more polluted." P26 similarly observed the AI "made the creek beautiful even though it was polluted." These responses highlight how children's knowledge of the creek served as the ground truth basis for critiquing the inauthentic "pretty" images.

The rejection of this idealized aesthetic extended to a desire for "uglier," more truthful representations, in which it would be better to "try to make the creek not pretty" (P33). For these children, a "scary" or "polluted" image was preferable because it was closer to their experiences. We argue that the children's lived experience helped them understand the complex reality of the creek, leading them to more critically reject AI's aesthetics.

# 5 Discussion

Statistically significant increases in children's self-reported familiarity with key AI topics (Sect. 4.1) show that children overall gained higher awareness of key AI literacy components. They also experimented with prompt generation, iterative image generation, and AI text interfaces. However, for our approach, the main contribution to highlight is the means of embodied and critical engagement.

## 5.1 Design Futuring for Critical AI Literacy

Design futuring activities in our workshops—including exercises such as "Good / Bad News 2050" and formulating the "Big Idea"—did more than scaffold imagination. They helped highlight prevalent issues situated in place (pollution sources, climate, community labor), while surfacing specific lived, local concerns. Speculative workshops have shown potential as means to critical AI literacy [23]. In our workshops, we used **design futuring** through **place-based, hybrid material** activities, which connected children with a specific site (creek) through the use of performative and tactile mediums (puppetry and performance). This combination enabled children to imagine while anchoring their speculations in their own lived experiences of place. Utilizing design futuring in this way enabled children to move beyond generic AI narratives and articulate nuanced, situated imaginations and critiques.

## 5.2 Grounded in Place and Environment

A central consideration in our approach was that the targeted environment—the creek—was already known to the children. Their prior knowledge enabled children to critically evaluate AI outputs. Children identified AI-generated scripts as too conflict-averse and images of the creek as too beautified, because these images and scripts departed from the creek they had smelled, heard, and traversed. Their experiences of "oily water," "trash," "water quality," "animals," "peaceful sounds," or "morning visits" were foundational in questioning AI-generated work. In other words, the lived experience of place sets a comparison against which to critically evaluate AI outputs. Answering our first research question, how grounding AI interaction in a specific, familiar local environment might influence children's ability to identify and understand AI's limitations, we argue that precisely these individual and shared experiences were key to a critical reflection. This counters a detached AI generalization of future environments, such as whitewashed urban centers devoid of realistic human traces and cultural effects. A place-based approach also helped surface sensitive social realities (e.g., "homelessness") as we found that children did not hesitate to name it as a condition of the creek. Not only did such an approach open up a critical perspective toward AI as a generative "too pretty" technological solution, but it also surfaced these multi-layered connections through the reflective exercises. Rather than resolving conflicting perspectives, our approach invites children to recognize and engage with the site's diversity as well as the complexity of their lived experiences as a basis for critiquing AI's lack of relational context. Grounded, lived experience becomes a counterpoint to the AI's abstract generality.

### 5.3 Material Practice: Hybrid Making and Performance as Literacy

Our hybrid approach re-framed AI prompting as a material, participatory, and performative practice. Puppets, props, and staging imposed frictions during the workshops that surfaced questions grounded in specific scenarios, such as "what *can* a body do?", "where *would* trash collect?", "who *would* disagree?" or "how *would* my character react?" These concerns were often individual to each participant, but organized within their group into the shared performance that provided a collective speculative future where all the characters would come together.

Children did not simply accept the AI's script. Instead, they physically wrote over the text, crossed out lines, and added new dialogue to better suit their vision. This hybrid practice was achieved both individually and collaboratively. Children were able to craft their own character independently, but collectively decided how to rewrite their story in a group and acted it out together in a coordinated way. Children did not only recognize the AI-generated options as "cheesy" or "too pretty" but also took control and developed alternatives as they changed scene outlines, added causal detail, reprompted to reduce "shininess," and re-shaped scenes to form their own expressions.

In response to our second research question, how integrating material practices with GenAI might empower children to resist AI-driven narratives and articulate complex ecological futures, the workshops showed children confidently departing from AI materials through their creative material practices. Whether those were in the making of their puppet characters or the physical performance itself - children were able to claim ownership of their creations without AI components taking over the process (as documented in 4.3).

We argue that **making and performance provide core mechanisms** for CAIL, not enrichment or purely motivational tools. Realizing what **constraints** material bodies and public stages impose offers embodied perspectives that a chat window cannot provide. The workshops demonstrate that through building deliberate moments where children must perform what they believe, leads to them identifying and addressing inconsistencies with AI's elements.

## 6 Limitations

Although our quantitative findings show significant increases in self-reported AI familiarity, we recognize the limitations of this measurement approach. The 5-point Likert scales capture perceived confidence rather than learning competencies, and statistical relevance is constrained by applying parametric tests to ordinal data. Time constraints also prevented a comparative baseline control group test. Future iterations must integrate performance-based assessments to more accurately evaluate children's conceptual understanding of complex topics like algorithmic bias and model limitations.

Additional limitations include the study's short-duration, single-site design, specific age range (9–12), and restrictions enforced by the school approved GenAI tools. To a large extent, these limitations were tied to the specific shared knowledge and coherence of the group. Future research should employ longitudinal studies and control groups to better measure the transferability and long-term retention of these place-based critical skills. It should also explore efficiency of our approach with other target audiences and varying institutional contexts.

## 7 Conclusion

**Community Futures** introduces a hybrid framework for *Situated Critical AI Literacy*: a multi-step futuring approach integrating AI tools, storytelling, performance, and tangible making in a workshop for middle school children. This design supports a critical lens towards AI through embodiment and situated engagement. Findings show how children's own experiences in their local environments served as a vital "ground truth" to challenge Generative AI. Children successfully identified AI limitations (RQ1) as they critiqued "beautified" or "cheesy" outputs that contradicted their sensory and social knowledge of the site. Furthermore, hybrid integration of materials and expressivity via puppetry and performance (RQ2) enabled children to generate alternatives to algorithmic outputs and foreground their own voices. We argue that the call for embodiment and situated shared experiences can translate to wider designs and remain a rich reference for the development of future AI educational approaches.

**Acknowledgments.** This material is based upon work supported by US National Science Foundation (NSF) award 2335974 and Foundations and Applications of Generative AI award from the Institute for Data Engineering and Science (IDEaS) at Georgia Tech. The authors thank Mary Lin Elementary School, Atlanta, and Ms.Carter for support with the workshops.

## References

1. Adobe: Adobe firefly (2024). https://www.adobe.com/products/firefly.html
2. Atabey, A., Wilson, C., Urquhart, L.D., Schafer, B.: Fairness by design: cross-cultural perspectives from children on AI and fair data processing in their education futures. In: Proceedings of ACM CHI (2025). https://doi.org/10.1145/3706598.3714402
3. Babai, N., Gazulla, E.D., Iivari, N., Kinnula, M.: Navigating the future of data-driven systems: children's perspectives on data and agency. In: Proceedings of ACM IDC (2025). https://doi.org/10.1145/3713043.3728844
4. Bender, E.M., Gebru, T., McMillan-Major, A., Shmitchell, S.: On the dangers of stochastic parrots: can language models be too big? In: Proceedings of ACM FAccT (2021). https://doi.org/10.1145/3442188.3445922
5. Braun, V., Clarke, V.: Using thematic analysis in psychology. Qual. Res. Psychol. (2006)
6. Cao, H.J., Choi, K., Park, C., Lee, H.R.: AI literacy for underserved students: leveraging cultural capital from underserved communities for AI education research. In: Proceedings of ACM CHI (2025). https://doi.org/10.1145/3706598.3713173
7. Dangol, A., et al.: Mediating culture: cultivating socio-cultural understanding of AI in children through participatory design. In: Proceedings of ACM DIS (2024). https://doi.org/10.1145/3643834.3661515
8. Demneh, M.T., Darani, Z.H.: From remembering to futuring: preparing children for anthropocene. J. Environ. Stud. Sci. (2020)
9. Druga, S., Vu, S.T., Likhith, E., Qiu, T.: Inclusive AI literacy for kids around the world. In: Proceedings of FabLearn 2019 (2019)
10. Druga, S., Williams, R., Breazeal, C., Resnick, M.: "Hey Google is it OK if I eat you?": initial explorations in child-agent interaction. In: Proceedings of ACM IDC (2017)
11. Dunne, A., Raby, F.: Speculative Everything: Design, Fiction, and Social Dreaming. MIT Press (2013)
12. Fan, M., et al.: StoryPrompt: exploring the design space of an AI-empowered creative storytelling system for elementary children. In: Proceedings of ACM CHI EA (2024)
13. Han, K., Tang, K., Wang, M.: Tangible diffusion: exploring artwork generation via tangible elements and AI generative models in arts and design education. In: Proceedings of ACM TEI (2024). https://doi.org/10.1145/3623509.3633394
14. Han, K., Tang, K., Wang, M.: Stage wizard: enhancing tangible storytelling with multimodal LLMs. In: Proceedings of ACM TEI (2025). https://doi.org/10.1145/3689050.3704429
15. Harrington, C.N., Klassen, S., Rankin, Y.A.: "All that you touch, you change": expanding the canon of speculative design towards black futuring. In: Proceedings of ACM CHI (2022). https://doi.org/10.1145/3491102.3502118
16. Honauer, M., Frauenberger, C.: Exploring child-AI entanglements. In: Proceedings of ACM IDC (2024). https://doi.org/10.1145/3628516.3661155
17. Howell, N., Schulte, B.F., Twigger Holroyd, A., Fatás Arana, R., Sharma, S., Eden, G.: Calling for a plurality of perspectives on design futuring: an un-manifesto. In: Proceedings of ACM CHI EA (2021). https://doi.org/10.1145/3411763.3450364
18. Iivari, N., Kuutti, K.: Critical design in interaction design and children: impossible, inappropriate or critical imperative? In: Proceedings of ACM IDC (2018)

19. Iivari, N., Sharma, S., Ventä-Olkkonen, et al.: Critical agenda driving child–computer interaction research—Taking a stock of the past and envisioning the future. Int. J. Child-Comput. Interact. (2022)
20. Iversen, O.S., Smith, R.C., Dindler, C.: Child as protagonist: expanding the role of children in participatory design. In: Proceedings of ACM IDC (2017)
21. Iversen, O.S., Smith, R.C., Dindler, C.: From computational thinking to computational empowerment: a 21st century PD agenda. In: Proceedings of PDC (2018)
22. Jia, K., Yu, J.: Technologies for children's AI learning: design features and future opportunities. In: Proceedings of ACM CHI (2025). https://doi.org/10.1145/3706598.3713443
23. Kenny, S., Antle, A.N., Russell, G., Kitson, A., Veldhuis, A.: Beyond the algorithm: speculative approaches to critical AI literacies with diverse youth. In: Proceedings of ACM IDC (2025). https://doi.org/10.1145/3713043.3727052
24. Li, Y., et al.: A meta-analysis of tangible learning studies from the TEI conference. In: Proceedings of ACM TEI (2022). https://doi.org/10.1145/3490149.3501313
25. Long, D., Magerko, B.: What is AI literacy? Competencies and design considerations. In: Proceedings of ACM CHI, pp. 1–16 (2020). https://doi.org/10.1145/3313831.3376727
26. Long, D., et al.: Fostering AI literacy with embodiment & creativity: from activity boxes to museum exhibits. In: Proceedings of ACM IDC (2023). https://doi.org/10.1145/3585088.3594495
27. MagicSchool: Magicschool AI (2024). https://www.magicschool.ai
28. Marçal, C., Baptista, A.C., Nicolau, H., Campos, P.F., Pires, A.C.: Creat'AI: using tangible storytelling to teach AI to children. In: Procedings of ACM IDC (2025)
29. Rosner, D.K.: Critical Fabulations: Reworking the Methods and Margins of Design. MIT Press (2018)
30. Salac, J., Landesman, R., Druga, S., Ko, A.J.: Scaffolding children's sensemaking around algorithmic fairness. In: Proceedings of ACM IDC (2023). https://doi.org/10.1145/3585088.3589379
31. Sengers, P., Boehner, K., David, S., Kaye, J.J.: Reflective design. Critical Computing 2005 (2005)
32. Sharma, S., Howell, N., Ventä-Olkkonen, L., Iivari, N., Eden, G., et al.: Promoting criticality with design futuring with young children. In: Proceedings of ACM NordiCHI (2024). https://doi.org/10.1145/3679318.3685335
33. Sharma, S., Klemettilä, P., Tanaka, J.: A robot teacher " is very good for learning, but not for human relationships": Japan. Children's Critic. Perspect. Towards Ethical AI Futures. In: Proceedings of ACM CHI (2025). https://doi.org/10.1145/3706598.3713204
34. Ventä-Olkkonen, L., Iivari, N., Sharma, S., et al.: All the world is our stage: empowering children to tackle bullying through theatre of the oppressed in critical design and making. In: Proceedings of ACM NordiCHI (2022). https://doi.org/10.1145/3546155.3546705

# What Constitutes AI Harms and/or Unfairness? An Empirical Analysis of Teacher Deliberation with a Fairness Elicitation Scaffold

Shamya Karumbaiah(✉), Yaxuan Yin, and Harry Brighouse

University of WisconsinMadison, Madison, WI 53706, USA
{shamya.karumbaiah,yaxuan.yin,mhbrigho}@wisc.edu

**Abstract.** Which values matter, when, and why are highly contextual. Yet, conversations on values such as AI fairness often exclude stakeholder expertise. Consequent conceptualization and operationalization suffer from value misalignment. To bridge this gap between AI development and downstream use in education, we explore a method (reflective equilibrium) and a practical tool (fairness elicitation scaffold) that supports stakeholders such as educators to construct fairness conceptions ground up (e.g., what is (un)fair, for whom, why?). In this paper, we present empirical evidence by analyzing data collected from 29 teachers in two distinct educational contexts: United States and the Philippines. Our analysis revealed that there is a statistically significant increase in teachers' recognition of AI's potential to reinforce bias or unfair treatment with the scaffold. Teachers in this study understood fairness in educational AI as conditional and context-sensitive rather than rule-based, drawing on their knowledge of students, classroom dynamics, and instructional goals to weigh learning benefits against potential harms. Unequal learning outcomes were sometimes viewed as fair—particularly when they supported equity goals—but became contested when paired with additional harms or competitive stakes. These findings suggest that fairness in educational AI must account for how benefits and harms are distributed in specific contexts. Overall, our study underscores the need for bottom-up, participatory approaches that treat fairness as an ongoing reasoning process led by educational stakeholders. Future studies will investigate how stakeholders prioritize competing fairness values across contexts and how these priorities evolve through reflective deliberation.

**Keywords:** Fairness · Harms · Deliberation · Teachers · Context

## 1 Introduction

As artificial intelligence (AI) and other technological interventions in education become more sophisticated, evidence suggests that some tools—particularly those designed around human-AI partnerships—can improve learning outcomes


E. G. Blanchard et al. (eds.), AIED 2026, LNCS 16586, pp. 270–284, 2027.
https://doi.org/10.1007/978-3-032-29773-0_19

[8]. This has sparked interest in large-scale AI implementation in education, which in turn raises critical questions about fairness and equity: are the harms and benefits of using AI for teaching and learning distributed equitably? These questions are deeply contextual, with answers varying by student populations, learning goals, sociopolitical settings, and the specific values that teachers and other stakeholders bring to AI adoption [24].

Yet, dominant frameworks that shape the development of responsible and fair AI systems rarely consider the unique ethical concerns in education [7], be it those from the tech industry [15], federal agencies (AI Risk Management Framework by the National Institute of Standards and Technology (NIST); [22]) or multilateral organizations (Organisation for Economic Co-operation and Development (OECD); [16]). These frameworks operate at a level of generality that makes direct application to education difficult: education involves distinctive relationships of power and trust (between teachers, students, parents, and institutions), developmental considerations, and equity stakes that generic principles do not adequately capture [20]. Even ethical, responsible, and human-centered principles can fail when applied to problematic use cases to begin with—an issue often referred to as "putting lipstick on a pig" [12].

Gross generalizations of deeply contextual fairness value and a lack of rigorous conceptualization [2] in these frameworks lead to invalid operationalizations [10]. For instance, questions such as "What system behaviors are fair? For whom? Why?" are often overlooked in favor of oversimplified technical notions of fairness (e.g., assuming homogeneity in student groups based on flawed, static demographic labels; [9]). Consequently, even well-intentioned AI bias audits and mitigation efforts may produce outputs that are misaligned with the social justice goals of real-world educational stakeholders. Moreover, different responsible AI values often conflict in non-trivial ways [23]. For instance, ensuring fairness may raise privacy concerns in sharing individual student demographics such as race, gender, special education, and English learner status. Likewise, fairer AI models may sacrifice performance, or better-performing AI models may be less transparent [11].

In sum, dominant frameworks on responsible AI offer a high-level, conceptual scaffolding for considering values; however, their application is limited in situated contexts like education and we lack the tools and methods for operationalizing these values in practice [6].

To bridge this gap, in this paper, we present empirical evidence for the efficacy of a *fairness elicitation scaffold* (elaborated in Sect. 2.1) in supporting teacher deliberation (Sect. 2.2) on different fairness notions. There are better, and worse, ways of conceptualizing fairness. The aim of the scaffold is not to settle which are the better ways. Instead, it aims to make it easier for the deliberator to arrive at their own judgments, and to avoid misunderstanding of others who make different judgments. We analyze how teachers use the scaffold to make sense of different conceptions of fairness, in the context of thinking about AI for teaching and learning. We discuss how the scaffold could also be used by researchers to elicit fairness notions from educational stakeholders such as teachers when designing fairness measures and auditing frameworks. Our analysis is guided by the following research questions: *How do teachers deliberate on AI harms and/or unfairness using the fairness elicitation scaffold?*

## 2 AI Fairness Deliberation: A Method and Scaffold

### 2.1 The AI Fairness Elicitation Scaffold to Disambiguate Conceptions of AI Fairness

We developed an *AI fairness elicitation scaffold* to support educational stakeholders in deliberating and articulating how they understand fairness in the context of AI-supported learning. Rather than prescribing a definition of fairness, the scaffold presents a set of structured scenarios that vary how learning benefits, harms, risks, and time horizons are distributed across groups. Participants are prompted to reflect on which configurations they view as problematic, for whom, and why.

The scaffold assumes a working definition of learning that is specified within each scenario (e.g., performance on a knowledge assessment) and asks participants to reason about how anticipated benefits and harms are distributed across groups. In our study, participants considered an AI intervention for automated feedback on student essays that was expected to improve learning outcomes. They were invited to reflect on whether their judgments depended on which groups were compared (e.g., students from different regions or linguistic backgrounds), the magnitude of differences in benefit or harm, or whether certain thresholds or conditions shaped their evaluation.

To support this deliberation, the scaffold consists of six core cases that capture common benefit–fairness tensions in educational contexts:

1. *[Benefit, No Harm]* Using an AI intervention only makes one group's learning better and not the other, without reducing the learning of the other.
2. *[Benefit, Harm]* Using an AI intervention makes one group's learning better and makes the other group's learning worse compared to a feasible alternative intervention.
3. *[Unequal Benefit]* Using an AI intervention makes everyone's learning better off than before but improves learning more for one group than the other and
   (a) *[absolute value]* actual learning is the outcome of interest.
   (b) *[relative value]* attaining positional goods as a result of learning (e.g., college admission) is the outcome of interest i.e., relative or competitive value of the learning.
4. *[All-Things-Considered Benefit]* Using an AI intervention makes a group's learning worse in the short-term but better in the long-term.
5. *[Unequal Benefit to Redress Historical Bias]* Using an AI intervention makes everyone's learning better off than before but improves learning more for the historically disadvantaged group than the other.
6. *[Actual vs. Risk of Harm]* Using an AI intervention has a very high probability to make learning better off than before but:

(a) *[slight risk of failure]* there's also a low probability that learning will be harmed.
(b) *[slight risk of exposure to toxicity]* there is some small risk that students are exposed to racist, sexist, or xenophobic content.

Across these cases, benefits and harms are primarily defined in terms of academic learning outcomes, reflecting the central goals of schools and classrooms. However, participants were also encouraged to raise concerns that extend beyond learning performance when relevant to their reasoning. In particular, some discussions surfaced potential non-learning harms, including concerns related to students' dignity, procedural treatment, or recognition as epistemic agents. These considerations were not introduced as additional cases, but rather emerged as secondary concerns that participants invoked when interpreting the core scenarios [4,5]. Together, the scaffold supports comparative reasoning across cases while leaving space for participants to surface broader conceptions of unfairness and harm.

## 2.2 Reflective Equilibrium as a Method to Elicit AI Fairness Conceptions

"Fairness" is a concept about how benefits and burdens should be distributed, so it should not be surprising that people differ in their conceptions of it, which are liable either to generate, or reflect, different views about what the right distribution of burdens and benefits is, about what the right method is for determining that distribution, and/or whether they should be distributed at all. Simultaneously, people may also differ in their conceptions of what counts as benefits or burdens. We propose a method (reflective equilibrium) and a practical scaffold readers can use (ideally with others with whom they disagree) in attempting to make progress in determining what the correct (or at worst a good) conception—is, in their particular contexts.

Reflective equilibrium [1] is a method for moral reasoning that helps agents deliberate about questions of value when no fixed algorithm or authoritative ranking of values is available. Rather than prescribing particular moral conclusions, it provides resources for responsible agents—such as individuals, institutions, or governments—to reason for themselves. It begins with two fallible kinds of judgments: judgments about particular cases and judgments of general principles. When enough of these judgments are considered together, inconsistencies typically emerge. Since inconsistency implies falsehood, uncovering and resolving such conflicts is a central task of moral philosophy.

The method is not merely logical but evaluative. Once contradictions are identified, reasoners attempt to determine which judgments are least reliable and should therefore be revised or rejected. Judgments are considered less reliable when they align with self-interest, are inherited uncritically from social environments, are reasonably disputed by others, or are unstable over time. None of these conditions is decisive on its own, but they provide comparative reasons to favor some judgments over others when resolving inconsistencies. Crucially, reflective equilibrium allows for the temporary suspension of judgment rather than outright rejection. Further reflection on the reasons involved may justify retaining or reinstating a belief once it is better supported.

Although reflective equilibrium can be described as an individual reasoning process (akin to other fairness elicitation methods; [3]), it is ideally collaborative [21,25]. Our thought is that dialogue can be more productive when, rather than insisting that their conception is 'the correct one' or, worse, not even recognizing that their conceptions are different, participants start out with an understanding of how the conceptions they bring to the discussion differ from each other's. Everyone has insights that are due to their background, upbringing, environment, cultures, and particular experiences. And everyone has blindspots that are due to the same things. So the ideal reflective equilibrium involves multiple participants, as different in environment, culture, outlook, experience, and ideology as is compatible with effective communication, but all of whom are committed to honest and self-critical collective deliberation. The expectation is that in such a process it will be more common for better reasons and better ideas than for worse reasons and worse ideas to prevail.

## 3 Methods

### 3.1 Participants and Contexts

The study recruited 29 teachers from two educational contexts, the United States (n = 14) and the Philippines (n = 15). Participants were recruited through partner institutions and participated voluntarily. Teachers represented a range of subject areas and instructional settings, as shown in Table 1. Nearly all participants reported prior experience using AI-powered tools, with only one participant in the United States and one in the Philippines indicating no prior exposure. The most common uses involved generative text and chat tools ($N = 27$) for brainstorming, drafting, or refining materials, as well as writing support and lesson planning or curriculum development.

### 3.2 Procedure

Each workshop followed the same structured procedure across locations. Participants first completed a pre-survey that captured their initial judgments about fairness-related concerns in AI-supported instructional contexts. They were then organized into small groups of three to four teachers. Within these groups, participants discussed the scenarios from the *AI fairness elicitation scaffold.* Discussions centered on whether and why particular scenarios raised fairness-related concerns, and on how contextual factors shaped participants' reasoning. This phase provided a focused setting for exchanging perspectives and surfacing points of convergence, divergence, or uncertainty prior to broader deliberation.

The workshop then transitioned to a whole-group discussion structured as a facilitated fishbowl-style activity. Representatives from each small group shared

**Table 1.** Participant demographics by geographic context

| Characteristic | US (n = 14) | Philippines (n = 15) |
|---|---|---|
| Primary Role | | |
| K–12 Classroom Teacher | 11 | 5 |
| Higher Education Faculty/Instructor | 2 | 9 |
| Administrative/Support Role | 1 | 1 |
| Years of Teaching Experience | | |
| 1–3 years | 1 | 1 |
| 4–6 years | 1 | 1 |
| 7–10 years | 0 | 3 |
| 11–15 years | 2 | 4 |
| 16–20 years | 4 | 2 |
| More than 20 years | 6 | 4 |

salient perspectives with the full workshop, while facilitators prompted comparison across scenarios and encouraged reflection on similarities, differences, and unresolved tensions in participants' reasoning. The fishbowl format was designed to surface a range of viewpoints and reasoning strategies without requiring consensus or privileging particular positions.

Participants completed the post-survey at the conclusion of the workshop discussion. All sessions were audio recorded and transcribed for subsequent qualitative analysis.

### 3.3 Quantitative Measures and Qualitative Data

The pre–post surveys consisted of ordinal Likert-scale items designed to capture teachers' fairness-related judgments about AI interventions. Specifically, participants responded to the statement: *"Using AI tools can reinforce bias and/or unfair treatment of students in the following aspects of my teaching"*. Responses were collected across six instructional aspects: Assessment, Classroom Management, Discussion Facilitation, Lesson Planning, Personalized or Adaptive Instruction, and Teacher Reflection. Each item was rated on a four-point Likert scale ranging from *Strongly Disagree* to *Strongly Agree*.

Qualitative data consisted of transcripts from the facilitated workshop discussions. We analyzed the workshop transcripts using thematic analysis to identify recurring patterns in how teachers reasoned about unfairness and harm when evaluating AI interventions. The analysis focused on characterizing forms of reasoning and sensemaking rather than categorizing participants according to fixed fairness positions.

Members of the research team independently reviewed the transcripts to identify segments in which participants articulated fairness-related concerns. Through iterative discussion, the team refined a set of themes that captured common reasoning patterns observed across scenarios. Quotes presented in Sect. 4 are labeled with anonymized participant identifiers and geographic context.

# 4 Results

This section examines how teachers reasoned about unfairness and harm when evaluating AI interventions across structured classroom scenarios, drawing on both survey responses and workshop discussions. We report quantitative pre–post changes in survey responses (Sect. 4.1) and then present qualitative findings that trace recurring patterns in teachers' reasoning.

## 4.1 Pre–post Changes in Fairness-Related Judgments Across Aspects and Contexts

We first examined overall pre–post changes in teachers' fairness-related judgments using a Wilcoxon signed-rank test. The results indicated a significant positive shift from pre to post ($n = 29$, $p = 0.0039$), with a large effect size ($r = 0.62$). This effect reflected an imbalance in the direction of individual change, with more participants shifting toward stronger agreement with the survey statement regarding AI's potential to reinforce bias or unfair treatment. We next examined whether these response patterns differed by geographic location (US vs. Manila). Because responses were measured on an ordinal Likert scale and group sizes were modest, we used Mann–Whitney $U$ tests to compare independent groups. We found no significant difference between US and Manila participants at a single time point ($p = 0.30$). We further compared individual pre–post change scores across locations and again found no significant difference in either the magnitude or direction of change ($U = 110$, $p = 0.82$). Together, these results indicate that the observed pattern of pre–post change was similar across geographic contexts, suggesting that increased articulation of fairness-related concerns was not specific to one location.

To examine whether this pattern held across different instructional aspects, we conducted Wilcoxon signed-rank tests separately for each aspect. Across all six aspects, median responses remained unchanged from pre to post ($\text{Median}_{\text{pre}} = 3$, $\text{Median}_{\text{post}} = 3$), indicating that the central tendency of responses did not shift. However, Five of the six aspects showed statistically significant positive pre–post changes: Assessment ($p = 0.0039$), Classroom Management ($p = 0.0124$), Discussion Facilitation ($p = 0.0075$), Lesson Planning ($p = 0.0209$), and Personalized or Adaptive Instruction ($p = 0.0075$). Teacher Reflection exhibited a marginal effect that did not reach conventional significance ($p = 0.0522$). As shown in Fig. 1, these effects were not driven by uniform shifts across all participants, but by a consistent directional pattern: across instructional aspects, more participants increased their responses from pre to post than decreased them, while some reported no change. Downward shifts were rare. This pattern indicates that participation in the workshop was associated with a greater tendency for teachers to recognize or articulate potential fairness-related concerns across multiple areas of teaching.

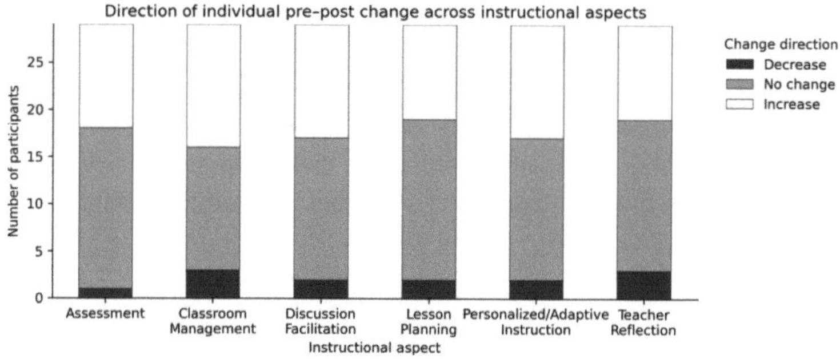


**Fig. 1.** Direction of individual pre–post changes across instructional aspects. Bars indicate the number of participants whose responses increased, decreased, or remained unchanged from pre to post. Across all aspects, upward changes were more common than downward changes, despite stable median responses.

### 4.2 Fairness Concerns are Minimal When Learning Benefits Do Not Create Harm

In scenarios where an AI intervention was described as improving learning outcomes without disadvantaging any group, participants largely expressed agreement that the intervention did not raise substantial fairness concerns. Our results show that teachers tended to treat the absence of harm or loss as a key condition under which learning benefits were seen as compatible with fairness.

For example, in cases where one group's learning improved while other groups' learning outcomes remained unchanged, participants often framed the intervention as acceptable or unproblematic. One teacher noted: *"If no one is actually losing anything and some students are benefiting, I don't really see where the fairness issue is."* (P04)

Similarly, participants frequently distinguished these scenarios from others involving explicit tradeoffs, emphasizing that fairness concerns arose primarily when improvements came at a cost to others: *"This feels different from the other examples, because here nobody is worse off. It's just extra support for some students."* (P12)

Cases involving unequal benefit intended to redress historical disadvantage also tended to elicit broad agreement, particularly when participants viewed the intervention as compensatory rather than exclusionary. Several teachers explicitly connected these scenarios to existing equity-oriented practices in education. As one participant explained: *"We already do things like this all the time—extra resources for students who've been underserved. So this doesn't feel unfair to me."* (P07)

Rather than interpreting unequal improvement as inherently problematic, participants in these cases often evaluated fairness in relation to broader educational goals, such as reducing achievement gaps or providing targeted support. Another teacher described this reasoning as follows: *"If the goal is to help stu-*

*dents who are behind catch up, then it makes sense that they might benefit more. That's kind of the point."* (P09)

Across these scenarios, participants rarely expressed uncertainty or hesitation. Instead, they articulated fairness judgments with confidence, often contrasting these cases with others that involved harm, risk, or competitive disadvantage. Taken together, these findings suggest that when learning benefits do not introduce harm or worsen outcomes for any group, teachers' fairness judgments tend to converge, treating benefit and fairness as aligned rather than in tension.

### 4.3 Learning Benefits Alone Do Not Resolve Fairness Disagreements

Across several scenarios, participants diverged in their fairness judgments when learning benefits were accompanied by harm, risk, or unequal consequences. In these cases, improvements in overall learning outcomes were not sufficient to produce consensus, and participants articulated competing interpretations of what fairness required.

In scenarios where an AI intervention improved learning for one group while disadvantaging another relative to a feasible alternative, some participants emphasized aggregate learning gains as the primary consideration. For example, one participant argued that increased overall performance justified adoption despite unequal effects: *"If most students are learning more, that still feels like a positive outcome overall, even if it's not perfect for everyone."* (P01)

In contrast, others rejected this reasoning, foregrounding harm to the worse-off group as a decisive fairness concern: *"I'm uncomfortable with the idea that one group is learning less just so another can learn more. That feels like we're sacrificing some students for efficiency."* (P08)

Disagreement was particularly pronounced in cases involving unequal benefit tied to relative or positional outcomes, such as college admission or competitive advancement. While some participants focused on absolute learning gains, others emphasized that relative advantages could exacerbate existing inequities. One teacher (P02) noted: *"Even if everyone improves, if one group gets a bigger boost, that's what matters in competitive settings. That advantage carries forward."*

Similarly, scenarios that introduced risk of harm, such as a small probability of exposure to biased or toxic content, surfaced contrasting risk tolerances. Some participants viewed low-probability harms as acceptable tradeoffs: *"There's always some risk with new tools. If the likelihood is small and the learning benefit is real, I'd still consider using it."* (P13) Others treated even minimal risks as unacceptable, particularly when harms implicated dignity or identity: *"Even a small chance of exposing students to racist content feels serious to me. That's not something I'm willing to gamble with."* (P08)

Across these cases, participants' disagreements did not stem from misunderstanding the scenarios but from different prioritizations of benefit, harm, and risk. While some framed fairness in terms of maximizing learning outcomes, others emphasized non-maleficence, protection of vulnerable students, or the broader social consequences of unequal or risky interventions. Together, these findings indicate that learning benefits alone do not resolve fairness questions when interventions introduce harm, tradeoffs, or unequal consequences.

### 4.4 Teachers Reason About Fairness Through Conditional Tradeoffs Rather Than Binary Judgments

Across multiple scenarios, participants rarely framed fairness judgments as simple decisions of agreement or disagreement. Instead, they engaged in conditional reasoning, articulating the circumstances under which an AI intervention might be acceptable, problematic, or require additional safeguards. These patterns were particularly salient in cases involving unequal benefit, delayed outcomes, or probabilistic risks.

In scenarios where an AI intervention produced unequal benefits but improved learning outcomes overall, participants frequently distinguished between absolute learning gains and relative or competitive consequences. Rather than treating these cases as uniformly fair or unfair, teachers reasoned through how outcomes would be interpreted in different institutional contexts. One participant explained: *"If we're just talking about students understanding the material better, then the unequal improvement might be okay. But if this affects who gets into college, that changes how I think about it."* (P11)

Similarly, in cases involving short-term harm in exchange for long-term benefit, participants emphasized temporal tradeoffs. Some expressed openness to temporary setbacks if longer-term learning gains were expected, while others questioned whether such tradeoffs were justifiable without strong evidence. As one teacher (P04) noted: *"I could maybe accept a short-term dip if I knew it really helped them later, but that's a big 'if.' I'd want to be sure before going down that road."*

Moreover, scenarios that introduced probabilistic risks, such as a small chance of exposing students to biased or harmful content, further illustrated participants' conditional reasoning. Rather than responding uniformly to the presence of risk, teachers weighed likelihood, severity, and the availability of mitigation strategies. One participant (P09) articulated this balancing process explicitly: *"It's not just whether there's a risk, but how likely it is and what kind of harm we're talking about. Those things matter a lot."*

Across these cases, expressions of uncertainty were common, but they did not signal indecision or confusion. Instead, participants used uncertainty to surface underlying concerns and clarify what information or conditions would be necessary to reach a judgment. As one teacher (P04) reflected during discussion: *"I don't have a clear yes or no here, but talking it through makes me realize what I'd need to know before feeling comfortable."*

Taken together, these findings indicate that teachers' fairness reasoning is fundamentally contextual and conditional, shaped by considerations such as time horizon, competitive stakes, and risk mitigation. Rather than applying fixed rules, participants treated fairness judgments as contingent on how benefits and harms unfold in specific educational settings. This pattern helps explain why median survey responses remained stable even as individual-level shifts were observed, reflecting refinement and articulation of reasoning rather than categorical changes in stance.

### 4.5 Comparing BenefitFairness Tradeoffs Helps Teachers Articulate Fairness Boundaries

As participants worked through multiple scenarios, they frequently referenced earlier cases to refine, qualify, or revise their fairness judgments. Rather than evaluating each scenario in isolation, teachers used comparison across cases to articulate the boundaries of what they considered acceptable or problematic. This comparative reasoning allowed participants to clarify which dimensions of benefit, harm, and risk were most salient to their fairness judgments.

Several participants explicitly contrasted cases where learning benefits were unaccompanied by harm with those involving tradeoffs earlier agreement as a reference point for later disagreement. One teacher (P14) noted: *"I was okay with the first example because no one was losing anything. But this one feels different, because now someone actually ends up worse off."*

Others used comparison to distinguish between different kinds of unequal benefit, particularly when reflecting on absolute versus relative outcomes. As one participant (P11) explained while revisiting an earlier case: *"At first I thought unequal improvement was fine, but then when I compared it to the college admissions example, I realized that context really changes how unfair it feels."*

In some instances, participants described how moving across scenarios helped them surface concerns that were initially implicit. One teacher (P08) reflected: *"I didn't think much about risk in the beginning, but after seeing the later cases, I realized that even a small chance of harm matters more to me than I expected."*

These cross-case reflections were not limited to shifts in agreement or disagreement. Instead, participants often used comparison to articulate conditional criteria, such as the role of safeguards, institutional context, or the reversibility of harm. As another participant (P03) summarized during discussion: *"Seeing all of these together makes me realize I don't have one rule for fairness. It depends on what kind of benefit it is and who's affected."*

Overall, comparison across cases functioned as a mechanism for sensemaking, enabling participants to move beyond initial reactions toward more articulated and differentiated fairness reasoning. Rather than converging on a single definition of fairness, teachers used the contrast between scenarios to clarify the conditions under which learning benefits aligned with or conflicted with their fairness concerns.

## 5 Discussion

We conducted a mixed-methods study combining surveys and workshops to examine how teachers reason about unfairness and harm when evaluating AI interventions in educational contexts. The study is analytically informed by reflective equilibrium, which we adopt as an orientation for eliciting and analyzing teachers' reasoning rather than as a normative endpoint. Reflective equilibrium highlights the role of comparison across cases in surfacing and refining judgments about complex ethical questions. In this study, this orientation informed both the design of the *AI fairness elicitation scaffold* (see Sect. 2.1) and our analytic focus on how participants compared scenarios to reason about whether and why particular outcomes raised fairness-related concerns.

Rather than evaluating the correctness of specific fairness principles or the fairness of particular AI systems, our approach focuses on empirically characterizing how teachers articulate and negotiate fairness-related concerns across structured scenarios. These scenarios systematically vary the configuration of learning benefits, risks, and time horizons, allowing us to examine how teachers' reasoning shifts across contexts and tradeoffs.

### 5.1 Fairness Reasoning as Conditional and Context-Sensitive, Not Rule-Based

Teachers in this study did not treat fairness as a fixed rule that could be applied uniformly across AI interventions. Instead, fairness reasoning emerged as conditional and context-sensitive, shaped by how anticipated learning benefits interacted with potential harms, risks, and burdens in particular classroom settings. This finding reinforces the need for bottom-up approaches to AI fairness that prioritize stakeholders' expertise rather than relying on decontextualized definitions of responsible AI values.

Educators are not passive recipients of AI technologies but active mediators of how AI systems are interpreted, implemented, and experienced in classrooms [17]. Prior work has shown that teachers' practices significantly shape AI effectiveness and student outcomes [8,24]. Our findings extend this work by showing that teachers also play a critical role in reasoning about fairness, drawing on their knowledge of students, instructional goals, and classroom dynamics to evaluate whether learning benefits are achieved at an acceptable cost.

Our results show that participants did not converge on a single fairness judgment. Instead, they refined the conditions under which learning gains should or should not count as fair. Fairness concerns were articulated relative to classroom context, student population, and instructional purpose, consistent with prior findings that answers to questions about fair AI use vary across learning goals and sociopolitical contexts [23]. These patterns suggest that fairness in educational AI cannot be meaningfully assessed without attending to the situated expertise of those who enact AI systems in practice.

### 5.2 When Benefits Legitimize Inequality, and When They Do Not

Our study shows that unequal learning outcomes were not inherently viewed as unfair. In several scenarios, teachers treated unequal benefit as legitimate or even desirable when it aligned with broader educational aims, such as remediation or addressing historical disadvantage. This reasoning reflects well-established distinctions in education and political philosophy between equality and equity, where differential treatment is justified to promote fair opportunity or redress prior injustice [18].

However, unequal benefit became contested when it was coupled with additional burdens or when the meaning of learning outcomes shifted. Scenarios involving direct harm to another group, increased exposure to risk, or competitive and positional stakes generated more disagreement. In these cases, teachers questioned whether learning gains for some could justify losses, risks, or diminished opportunities for others.

Teachers also distinguished between different interpretations of learning value. When learning was framed in absolute terms, unequal improvement was often tolerated or endorsed. When learning outcomes were tied to relative or competitive advantages, participants were more likely to view unequal benefit as problematic. This implication echoes work in education policy and sociology that highlights how the stakes attached to learning outcomes shape perceptions of fairness and harm [19].

### 5.3 Implications for Designing and Evaluating AI in Education

These findings suggest that evaluating fairness in educational AI systems requires attention beyond aggregate learning gains. Even when AI interventions improve outcomes, teachers attend closely to how benefits and burdens are distributed, who bears risk, and whether tradeoffs align with pedagogical goals. This reinforces critiques of performance-driven approaches to educational technology evaluation, which risk overlooking ethical and distributive consequences that matter in practice.

Second, our study highlights the value of deliberative and scenario-based approaches for fairness assessment. Rather than requiring binary judgments, tools that surface tradeoffs and support comparison across cases may better reflect how fairness reasoning operates in educational settings. This aligns with recent calls in AI governance and HCI for participatory, context-aware evaluation methods that foreground stakeholder reasoning [13,14].

Finally, these findings suggest that teacher-facing governance and professional development efforts should treat fairness as an ongoing reasoning process rather than a checklist. Supporting teachers in articulating and negotiating benefitburden tensions may be more productive than prescribing fixed fairness criteria, particularly as AI systems are deployed across diverse instructional contexts and student populations.

In conclusion, this paper examined how 29 teachers from two educational contexts, the United States and the Philippines, reason about unfairness and harm when evaluating AI interventions in education. Using a mixed-methods design, we show that fairness judgments are shaped not by learning benefits alone, but by how benefits interact with harms, burdens, risks, and instructional goals. Teachers articulated conditional, context-sensitive reasoning, endorsing unequal benefit in some cases while expressing concern when benefits were paired with harm, risk, or competitive stakes. Methodologically, this work contributes a practical, stakeholder-centered approach to fairness sensemaking by operationalizing reflective equilibrium through structured scenario comparison, highlighting the importance of bottom-up reasoning for responsible AI design and evaluation in education. Future work will study how demographic, institutional, or cultural factors may shape differences in fairness prioritization, how the deliberation process may introduce social desirability, the long-term stability of shifts in teacher perceptions, and how to elicit and operationalize fairness notions from teachers' deliberation.

**Acknowledgment.** Support for this research was provided by the Office of the Vice Chancellor for Research and Graduate Education at the University of Wisconsin-Madison with funding from the Wisconsin Alumni Research Foundation. We thank Shona Acquaye and Ajita Raghavendra for their valuable inputs. We also thank the AIED reviewers for their feedback and our teacher participants for sharing their valuable time and insights with us.

**Disclosure of Interests.** The authors have no competing interests to declare that are relevant to the content of this article.

## References

1. Brighouse, H.: Normative case studies and thought experiments: how they differ and why we need both. Educ. Theory **74**(3), 329–339 (2024)
2. Castro, C., O'Brien, D., Schwan, B.: Egalitarian machine learning. Res. Publ. **29**(2), 237–264 (2023)
3. Cheng, H.F., et al.: Soliciting stakeholders' fairness notions in child maltreatment predictive systems. In: Proceedings of the 2021 CHI Conference on Human Factors in Computing Systems, pp. 1–17 (2021)
4. Crawford, K.: The Atlas of AI: Power, Politics, and the Planetary Costs of Artificial Intelligence. Yale University Press (2021)
5. Fricker, M.: Epistemic Injustice: Power and the Ethics of Knowing. Oxford University Press (2007)
6. Guerdan, L., Saxena, D., Chancellor, S., Wu, Z.S., Holstein, K.: Measurement as bricolage: examining how data scientists construct target variables for predictive modeling tasks. ACM Hum.-Comput. Interact. **9**(7), 1–37 (2025)
7. Holmes, W., et al.: Ethics of AI in education: towards a community-wide framework. Int. J. Artif. Intell. Educ. **32**(3), 504–526 (2022)
8. Holstein, K., McLaren, B.M., Aleven, V.: Student learning benefits of a mixed-reality teacher awareness tool in AI-enhanced classrooms. In: Penstein Rosé, C., et al. (eds.) AIED 2018. LNCS (LNAI), vol. 10947, pp. 154–168. Springer, Cham (2018). https://doi.org/10.1007/978-3-319-93843-1_12
9. Hu, L.: What is "race" in algorithmic discrimination on the basis of race? J. Moral Philos. **21**(1–2), 1–26 (2023)
10. Jacobs, A.Z., Wallach, H.: Measurement and fairness. In: Proceedings of the 2021 ACM Conference on Fairness, Accountability, and Transparency, pp. 375–385 (2021)

11. Jakesch, M., Buçinca, Z., Amershi, S., Olteanu, A.: How different groups prioritize ethical values for responsible AI. In: proceedings of the 2022 ACM Conference on Fairness, Accountability, and Transparency, pp. 310–323 (2022)
12. Jung, J.Y., et al.: Making the right thing: bridging HCI and responsible ai in early-stage ai concept selection. In: Proceedings of the 2025 ACM Designing Interactive Systems Conference, pp. 2992–3012 (2025)
13. Karumbaiah, S., Yin, Y., Bharadwaj, A.: AIBAT: AI behavior analysis tool for teacher-driven contextual evaluation of language models in education. In: Cristea, A.I., Walker, E., Lu, Y., Santos, O.C., Isotani, S. (eds.) AIED 2025. LNCS, vol. 15877, pp. 56–71. Springer, Cham (2025). https://doi.org/10.1007/978-3-031-98414-3_5
14. Madaio, M.A., Stark, L., Wortman Vaughan, J., Wallach, H.: Co-designing checklists to understand organizational challenges and opportunities around fairness in AI. In: Proceedings of the 2020 CHI Conference on Human Factors in Computing Systems, CHI 2020, New York, NY, USA, pp. 1–14 (2020)
15. Microsoft: Responsible AI principles and approach (2025). https://www.microsoft.com/en-us/ai/principles-and-approach. Accessed 9 Oct 2025
16. OECD: OECD AI principles. Organisation for economic co-operation and development (2025). https://oecd.ai/en/ai-principles. Accessed 9 Oct 2025
17. Puntambekar, S.: Distributed scaffolding: scaffolding students in classroom environments. Educ. Psychol. Rev. **34**(1), 451–472 (2022)
18. Rawls, J.: A Theory of Justice. Harvard University Press (1971)
19. Reay, D.: What would a socially just education system look like? Sociology **46**(4), 587–599 (2012)
20. Selwyn, N.: The future of ai and education: some cautionary notes. Eur. J. Educ. **57**(4), 620–631 (2022)
21. Shen, H., Deng, W.H., Chattopadhyay, A., Wu, Z.S., Wang, X., Zhu, H.: Value cards: an educational toolkit for teaching social impacts of machine learning through deliberation. In: Proceedings of the 2021 ACM Conference on Fairness, Accountability, and Transparency, pp. 850–861 (2021)
22. Tabassi, E.: Artificial intelligence risk management framework (AI RMF 1.0) (2023)
23. Yin, Y., Karumbaiah, S., Acquaye, S.: Responsible ai in education: understanding teachers' priorities and contextual challenges. In: Proceedings of the 2025 ACM Conference on Fairness, Accountability, and Transparency, pp. 2705–2727 (2025)
24. Yin, Y., Karumbaiah, S., Lim, J., Acquaye, S., Schwartz, S.: Toward teacher-centered AI design: exploring the role of pedagogical values and contextual factors in k-12 teachers' perceptions of responsible AI. In: Proceedings of the 18th Computer-Supported Collaborative Learning, pp. 196–204 (2025)
25. Zhang, A., Walker, O., Nguyen, K., Dai, J., Chen, A., Lee, M.K.: Deliberating with AI: improving decision-making for the future through participatory AI design and stakeholder deliberation. Proc. ACM Hum.-Comput. Interact. **7**(CSCW1), 1–32 (2023)

# A Survey of AI Misconception and Adoption Among Indonesian K-12 Teachers

Alham Fikri Aji[1,4(✉)], Afifa Amriani[1], Rendi Chevi[1], Ayu Purwarianti[2], and Derry Wijaya[3,4]

[1] Mohamed bin Zayed University of Artificial Intelligence, Abu Dhabi, United Arab Emirates
alham.fikri@mbzuai.ac.ae
[2] Institut Teknologi Bandung, Bandung, Indonesia
[3] Boston University, Boston, USA
[4] Monash University, Jakarta, Indonesia
derry.wijaya@monash.edu

**Abstract.** Indonesia's fragmented geography and uneven infrastructure pose persistent challenges for adopting new educational technologies. While national initiatives aim to mainstream AI in K–12 schools by 2025, policy readiness does not automatically mean teachers are ready for the classroom. This study surveys Indonesian K–12 teachers to examine: (1) their understanding of AI, (2) how they and their students use AI, and (3) their views on the acceptability of AI in learning activities. Through semi-automated thematic analysis, we identify common misconceptions and use cases. Our findings reveal a notable mismatch: while teachers find AI use in education acceptable and support it for the sake of efficiency, they remain fully aware of the risks to learning depth and academic honesty. We also find that this high level of acceptance is currently coupled with a poor understanding of how AI actually works.

**Keywords:** AI Misconception · LLMs · Pedagogy · Indonesia

## 1 Introduction

Global educational landscape is undergoing a paradigm shift driven by the rapid adoption of AI technologies. International guidelines and policy recommendations increasingly stress that realizing AI's educational benefits depends on system readiness, particularly, the teacher's capacity, equitable infrastructure, and governance [8,19]. However, in many middle-income and structurally diverse education systems, AI adoption is advancing on ambitious policy timelines while teacher preparation and other enabling conditions remain uneven across regions and school sectors [14]. This mismatch creates a key implementation risk: self-reported "readiness" may not correspond to classroom-relevant understanding and judgment, limiting the ability to target professional development effectively


E. G. Blanchard et al. (eds.), AIED 2026, LNCS 16586, pp. 285–299, 2027.
https://doi.org/10.1007/978-3-032-29773-0_20

or anticipate downstream pedagogical harms. Moreover, without sustained support for teacher AI literacy, gaps in preparedness can widen existing digital divides rather than reduce them [4]. In this study, we refer to AI literacy as the teachers' demonstrated conceptual understanding of what AI systems, including Large Language Models (LLM)-based tools, can and cannot do, and their ability to make informed pedagogical decisions about how AI should be used in classroom practice.

Indonesia provides a salient case of these broader dynamics. The transition is being accelerated by aggressive government mandates, including the National Strategy for Artificial Intelligence 2020–2045 [12] and the 2025 Academic Draft on Coding and AI Education [11]. These policy frameworks seek to integrate AI and coding into the national curriculum beginning in the 2025–2026 academic year. As this deadline approaches, a critical question remains: *Are Indonesian teachers prepared for this pedagogical shift?*

Indonesia's geographical and socioeconomic diversity pose structural barriers to uniform technology adoption. Infrastructure gaps constrain national readiness: approximately 65% of schools reportedly lack stable internet and 35% operate without reliable electricity [1]. Systemic disparities further influence teacher capacity, as urban educators typically access better compensation and professional development than those in rural regions [6]. Consequently, opportunities to understand and ethically evaluate AI are likely uneven across regions.

As AI adoption intensifies, it remains unclear how teachers will navigate complex pedagogical decisions given uncertainties regarding their own AI conception and literacy. Research highlights risks of over-reliance, including reduced critical thinking [13,16,25]. Because teachers' conceptions determine how tools are operationalized, a lack of understanding regarding AI capabilities may reinforce passive learning rather than critical engagement. To address this, we survey Indonesian educators' readiness for AI adoption. While utilizing Indonesian data, the measurement approach and readiness tensions identified remain relevant to other systems facing similar constraints. The preliminary study is guided by the following research questions:

**RQ.1:** What (mis)conceptions do K-12 Indonesian teachers have towards AI?
**RQ.2:** What are the practical use cases of AI among K-12 Indonesian teachers?
**RQ.3:** How do teacher perceive associated benefits and risks of AI in education?
**RQ.4:** What are the teachers' pedagogical stances regarding the acceptability of student AI adoption in learning activities?

## 2 Background and Related Works

Indonesia's diverse K-12 system is governed by a national framework shaping institutional provision and teacher support. The National Education System Law (Law No. 20/2003) [20] permits multiple provider types (public and private), creating variation in curricula and resourcing. Teacher roles also vary; Law No. 14/2005 [21] defines teachers as professional educators, yet employment ranges from state positions (ASN) to non-ASN hires, impacting incentives and professional development access [22]. Despite national funding like the School Operational Assistance grant (BOS), infrastructure differs by locality, affecting technological readiness. These structural differences create a measurement challenge: since opportunities to practice AI pedagogy are uneven, assessment must distinguish perceived readiness from classroom-relevant competence.

Against this backdrop, the government has begun scaling teacher capacity in AI. In 2025, the Ministry reported deploying 2,915 facilitators to train 62,898 teachers across 53,568 schools. While an important step, this initiative underscores the gap between policy ambition and scale: Indonesia has 3,857,718 K–12 teachers across 276,415 schools. Given this size, accurately measuring AI literacy is essential for targeting professional development and monitoring whether training translates into competence.

Most evidence on Indonesian teachers' AI literacy relies on self-report instruments, which capture perceptions but are limited proxies for competence. Self-reports are vulnerable to bias and inconsistent interpretations, particularly given uneven AI exposure. Recent studies exemplify this. Drajati et al. (2025) [7] surveyed 176 EFL teachers using translated Artificial Intelligence Literacy Scale (AILS) items [28] and interviews; they found teachers least confident in using AI but confident in recognizing misuse, alongside resource constraints. Similarly, Batubara et al. (2025) [2] examined elementary teachers' readiness using adapted self-efficacy scales [9,28] and open-ended responses, reporting high perceptions but lower practical readiness, with concerns regarding privacy and bias.

Prior studies provide useful signals about teachers' perceived readiness for AI, but offer less insight into how teachers articulate their understanding of AI and its classroom use. Under pressure to adopt AI, fixed-response survey answers may reflect aspiration rather than how teachers actually describe AI, reported uses, and acceptable classroom boundaries. Our study addresses this gap by using open-ended items and task-specific pedagogical judgments to elicit how teachers understand AI concepts and justify classroom uses. This approach allows us to examine the substance of teachers' expressed understanding, not only their confidence ratings. These findings provide a foundation for designing differentiated professional development, evaluating training efficacy, and helping policymakers target support.

# 3 Methods

## 3.1 Participants Recruitment

We recruited participants through our professional word-of-mouth networks, reaching out directly to K–12 schools (elementary, junior high, and high school) across Indonesia to build an initial pool of potential teacher participants. At each school, a contact person circulated a study advertisement and an online registration via Google Form through which teachers could submit their interest in the study. The form briefly describe that we are recruiting teachers to study how AI being adopted within their teaching-learning activities and they are being asked to fill in several demographic informations: sex, age, subject they taught, education level, employment status, school's sector, and region.

To ensure more balanced representation across different socioeconomic backgrounds of teachers, we employed quota sampling when screening participants from the pool. Specifically, we set quotas for sex, school level, school region, and employment status. However, because the pool of registrants from outside West Java was limited, we did not apply quota constraints for that subgroup, instead, we invited participants from outside West Java via random sampling from the available pool. Screened participants were then invited to the study and received IDR 50,000 compensation for an approximately one-hour session, which is twice the average hourly rate in Indonesia.

### 3.2 Survey Design

We designed a mixed-format survey of 13 items spanning open-ended responses, multiple-response selections, and Likert-style ratings, divided into 3 sections. These sections aimed to probe teachers' AI (mis)conceptions and literacy (Q1–Q4), reported AI use in teaching-learning activities (Q5–Q12), and pedagogical judgments about the acceptability of students' AI usage in learning activities (Q13). Our survey items are in[1].

**Survey Items Rationale.** For Q1–Q4, we adapted and localized 3 open-ended questions from [15] that aimed to elicit the teacher's initial conceptions of AI in a minimally leading way. We further add a new question (Q2) to explicitly probe the teacher's mental models how popular LLM works. In Q5–Q6, we elicited concrete, self-reported examples of how teachers and students use AI in everyday learning contexts. Q7–Q8 then captured teachers' stance toward AI use by teachers versus students, along with the reasons underlying each stance as well as the conditions under which teachers would change their position. In Q9–Q12, we asked teachers to articulate perceived positive and negative impacts of AI use for teachers and students. Finally, we probed teachers' pedagogical decision about when student AI use is acceptable by eliciting task and stage-specific judgments rather than general attitudes. In Q13, teachers indicated which learning tasks they believe students use AI for. For each selected task, we asked teachers to rate the appropriateness of student AI use on a structured scale and to further evaluate AI use across fine-grained stages within that task. This branching, stage-level design was intended to probe teachers' boundaries of AI usage in a format that supports comparison across various learning activities.

**Refining Survey Items in Pilot Study.** We conducted a pilot study with six teachers recruited through our professional networks to validate and refine our initial questionnaire items, particularly those newly developed (Q5–Q13). After the teachers completed the survey, we invited them for an unstructured interview, providing feedback that informed several revisions. Notably, Q3 was

[1] We attached our survey items, prompts, rubrics, and other artefacts here: https://github.com/afaji/AIED2026-Indonesian-AI-misconception.

rephrased after teachers expressed confusion and felt it was assessing their technical knowledge of AI, it was rephrased to focus on their own understanding of what happened after one gave inputs to the AI. Discussions with teachers on their AI use in teaching and learning also strongly resonated with Q5–Q12, sparking engaging discussion between teachers and researchers, and confirming the items relevance and ability to capture diverse perspectives on teacher's AI use. Finally, Q13's nested, mixed-format design was refined based on insights that teachers' attitudes toward AI wildly vary across different learning activities, leading us to specify activity types more explicitly to better capture their stances.

### 3.3 Data Collection and Analysis

We conducted the data collection from September to November 2025. Each screened participant received a study invitation link, directing them to our online survey. Survey responses were stored in a tabular format, where each row corresponds to a participant and columns include: (1) item-level responses (open-ended text responses and structured selections and Likert ratings) and (2) demographic information, yielding a mixed-type tabular data.

**Analysis Overview.** We analyzed the dataset using a mixed-methods workflow. For structured items, we summarized the responses descriptively (e.g., frequencies and distributions) and used these variables to contextualize patterns in the qualitative findings. For open-ended items, we applied a human-in-the-loop NLP workflow to identify and label the major themes (topics) participants expressed, combining topic modeling with researcher review and LLM-assisted rubric development.

**Human-in-the-Loop NLP Workflow.** Following prior work on LLM-assisted topic modeling [29], we analyzed each open-ended question using a three-step workflow: (1) *topic generation* with Latent Dirichlet Allocation (LDA) [3], (2) *topic refinement* (collapse/split) with LLM support and human review [29], and (3) *topic representation* via an LLM-generated coding rubric [10]. We first ran LDA with 2–10 topics per question and selected the topic count using the $C_v$ coherence score [23]. We then reviewed the 20 most representative responses per topic to draft provisional labels. Next, ChatGPT (GPT-5.2) was used in a human-in-the-loop process to improve interpretability by proposing and validating merges/splits. After finalizing the topic set, ChatGPT generated operational definitions and a coding rubric for each label. Finally, GPT-5 mini applied the rubric at scale to assign a label to each response; researchers iteratively audited representative outputs and refined rubrics as needed for alignment. The average agreement rate between the LLM-assigned codes and human judgment, computed on 10% sample of the data across questions, is 95.6%; showing strong alignment between LLM and human judgments based on the rubric (see footnote 1).

**Filtering AI-generated Responses.** We hypothesize that AI-generated responses are the main concern threatening our data quality. Since automatic detectors are unreliable for short, non-English text [30], we used a two-stage human-in-the-loop filter informed by evidence that experienced LLM users better recognize AI-written text [24]. We first used a RegEx-based exclusion-first heuristic to surface candidate cases. The script returned no alert when a response showed cues that we treated as more characteristic of human-written Indonesian survey text, including reduplication such as "orang2", abbreviations such as "dll", "dst", or "dkk", non-standard spacing around punctuation, lowercase list items, lowercase or variably capitalized forms of "ai"/"ChatGPT", lowercase sentence starts, or missing sentence-final punctuation. Only responses without those cues were then checked for red flags, namely length greater than 400 characters, double newlines, numbered or bulleted list structure, non-ASCII characters or emojis, the formal pronoun "anda", and parenthetical explanations such as "Artificial Intelligence (AI)". Two authors then independently reviewed flagged cases, and we excluded a response only when both judged it to be AI-generated.

# 4 Result

## 4.1 Distribution of Teacher Participants

Total number of teachers we managed to reach out and completed the survey are 132, with 61.4% (n = 81) from West Java and 38.6% (n = 51) from outside of West Java. Due to quota sampling on West Java participants, we managed to gather decently balanced representation on sex (Male: 42.0%, Female: 58.0%), school level (Elementary: 30.8%, Junior High: 30.8%, High School: 38.0%, employment status (Full-time: 56.7%, Part-time: 43.2%), but not on school sector (Public: 65.4%, Private: 34.5%). For outside West Java the distribution is as follows, sex (Male: 39.2%, Female: 60.7%), school level (Elementary: 43.1%, Junior High: 11.7%, High School: 45.0%), employment status (Full-time: 88.2%, Part-time: 11.7%), school sector (Public: 90.1%, Private: 9.8%). We attach the complete demographic distribution in (see footnote 1). Among our 132 participants, 2 of them have been flagged as AI-generated and omitted from the final analysis.

## 4.2 RQ.1: Conceptions of AI Among Indonesian Teachers

To assess Indonesian teachers' conceptual understanding of AI, the survey began with two items on general AI and LLMs. Responses to **Q1: "Based on your current understanding, explain what is AI?"** clustered into three themes. **(T1) AI as a technology that mimics human** (55.4%): many responses described AI as "artificial intelligence that mimics human intellectual abilities." [r116]; **(T2) AI defined through practical uses** (40%): responses that emphasized utility, such as "applications that can make work easier" [r8]; and **(T3) AI framed primarily through risks, limitations, or governance as a key point** (4.6%): a small minority focusing on harms or misuse, for example "AI that leads to criminal acts" [r45].

Most responses were high-level and lack depth, suggesting limited understanding of how AI works. To probe teachers' literacy about AI mechanisms more directly, we asked **Q2: "Explain what ChatGPT does after receiving the instructions you type until it gives you an answer"**. Responses clustered into four themes: **(T1) High-level input-output interaction** (69.2%), the majority of respondents describe ChatGPT as simply processing instructions and returning a response; their answers were often vague, demonstrated a lack of understanding regarding how AI functions beyond the immediate user interaction, and largely restated the question (e.g., "process and produce text according to the instructions given" [r13] or "send the answer back to the user via a conversational interface" [r21]. A small proportion used **(T2) Technical jargons** (4.6%), mentioning concepts such as tokenization, generative AI, or decoding. Another substantial group reflected **(T3) Knowledge retrieval misconceptions** (21.5%), suggesting that ChatGPT primarily searches the internet or a database for information (e.g., "looking for information from the data center he has" [r115]). Lastly, a minority emphasized **(T4) Personalization and adaptation** (4.6%), focusing on the system's ability to learn user habits over time (e.g., "AI learns user habits" [r67]).

Responses in topics **T1** and **T4** are typically superficial, failing to explore the actual mechanics of LLMs and instead focusing on the interaction itself. Those in **T3** are misinformed, viewing ChatGPT as a search engine or database retrieval system. Although the small number of respondents in **T2** utilize technical keywords, their explanations often remain high-level, such as simply stating that the system "uses NLP techniques" [r8]. Our findings suggest uneven and often limited AI literacy within this survey population.

To understand teachers' AI conception in terms of its perceived impacts and everyday uses, we asked **Q3: "What are the reasons why people use AI in their personal and professional daily lives?"** Responses clustered into four themes. **(T1) Efficiency and productivity** (55.4%) was the most prevalent, focusing on AI's ability to "simplify and speed up work" [r1] and make tasks "practical, effective, and efficient" [r6]. Some respondents noted that AI helps "reduce the burden" of work [r53], while a small number framed its use in terms of avoiding effort or seeking fast responses (e.g., being "lazy to think" [r5] or wanting "quick answers" [r82]). **(T2) Information retrieval** (25.4%) framed AI as a sophisticated search tool for "finding information and data according to needs" [r3], identifying "solutions to problems" [r44], or obtaining quick references. **(T3) Content creation and ideation** (16.1%) highlighted creative and teaching-related uses, such as "making lesson plans, creating questions" [r4], "generating ideas or inspiration" [r42], and helping"arrange words" [r13] when respondents feel stuck. Finally, **(T4) Personal assistance and everyday needs** (3.1%), a smaller group emphasized convenience-oriented functions of AI, including managing schedules as a "virtual assistant" [r48], providing "entertainment and music recommendations" [r58], or serving as a "companion to share stories and seek advice" [r61].

To gauge respondents' awareness of AI's broader societal uses, we asked **Q4: "What do you think AI technology has been used for?"** Responses clustered into four themes. **(T1) Education & Academic** (45.4%) was most common, with respondents primarily identifying schools and office applications, such as producing "teaching materials, quiz creation, and administrative reports" [r48, r53], as well as supporting students with "college assignments" and summarizing study material [r108, r49]. **(T2) Creative & Digital Content Production** (16.2%) recognizing uses such as "editing photos and videos" [r29, r35], "graphic design" [r22], and generating "social media content, slogans, or animations" [r53, r101]. **(T3) Business & Services** (10.8%) captured consumer-facing and operational applications of AI, including "online shopping and marketplaces" [r1, r45], "chatbot customer services" [r101], "mobile banking" [r45], and "marketing and business analytics" [r49, r70]. Finally, in **(T4) Critical Sectors & Governance** (27.7%), a significant portion of respondents mentions AI use in high-stakes domains, including "medical diagnosis and remote surgery" [r49, r100, r104], "defense-related systems like radar and drones" [r7], and "security applications such as facial recognition" [r61, r104].

### 4.3 RQ.2: Practical Utility of AI in Education

Overall, these responses suggest that teachers' familiarity with AI is strongly anchored in their professional domain, particularly within academic administration and pedagogy, even when asked about general use cases. We next examine how AI is integrated into teachers' day-to-day professional teaching activities. In response to **Q5: "In your activities as a teacher, in what ways do you utilize AI?"**, the reported use cases clustered into four themes. **(T1) Teaching Planning and Design** (19.2%) captured use cases for AI, particularly LLMs, for drafting or designing teaching plans, including "teaching modules" [r18], "learning steps" [r37], worksheets, and lesson personalization. **(T2) Generating Teaching Materials** (32.3%), the most common response included the use of AI for producing teaching materials, such as slides, infographics, as well as "editing image or videos" [r15] and "creating poster" [r29]. **(T3) Grading and Assessment** (26.9%) the second most common response captured the use of AI to aid in grading, whether by directly using AI to grade or by using AI to generate rubrics or answer sheets (e.g., "automated grading" [r131]). Finally, **(T4) Information Curation and Administrative Tasks (21.5%).** described the use of AI as "teaching tools" [r76] to search for, summarize, translate, validate, simplify, or otherwise curate information to support teaching and related administrative work.

Finally, to examine teachers' awareness of students' AI use, we asked **Q6: "In what ways do you think students utilize AI?"** Teachers' perceptions clustered into five themes. **(T1) No Use or No Knowledge** (9.2%) captured, perhaps surprisingly, a small fraction of respondents who were unsure whether students used AI or believed they did not (e.g., "unaware as it is not implemented yet") [r15]. The most common theme was **(T2) Direct Answering** (44.6%), where teachers perceived the use of AI by students to obtain immediate answers for homework or assignments (e.g., "looking for answer when given assignments" [r117]). **(T3) Tutor-like support** (10.8%), a minority of respondents described AI as a learning assistant used to ask questions, obtain explanations, and understand concepts (e.g., "for learning reference sources, asking complex questions" [r4]). **(T4) Information Retrieval** (19.2%) reflected the use of AI to find or collect learning materials, information, or references (e.g., "learning material quizzes" [r54]). Finally, **(T5) Content Generation** (16.2%) included the use of AI for producing slides, reports, or images (e.g., "create poster" [r29]).

These findings indicate that AI is already embedded across multiple stages of the teaching pipeline, from lesson design to assessment. As a result, teacher support mechanisms need to evolve to reflect this reality. With the exception of a small minority, educators also recognize that students commonly use AI to obtain direct answers. Although many view this answer-seeking behavior unfavorably (as discussed in later sections), it does not appear to reduce their broader support for students' use of AI.

### 4.4 RQ.3: Percieved Benefit and Risk of AI Use in Education

**Support for AI Use in Education** Next, we asked respondents' views on AI use in education. Specifically, we asked **Q7: "Do you support the use of AI by teacher in learning activities?"** and **Q8: "Do you support the use of AI by students in learning activities?"**. Majority of respondents expressed support, with 96.2% supporting teachers' use of AI, and 84.6% supporting students' use. To understand the basis for teachers' AI use, respondents who supported it were then asked **Q9a: "I support the use of AI by teachers because..."**. Their explanations clustered into three themes. **(T1) Teacher Work Efficiency** (50.9%), majority of respondents emphasized reduced workload and time savings, particularly for administrative tasks and the preparation of teaching materials (e.g., "effectiveness; efficiency" [r7]). Another common response was **(T2) Improvement of Student Learning** (43%) that framed AI as enhancing the learning experience through innovation, personalization, and more "engaging learning experience" [r131]. **(T3) Conditional Support** (6.1%) expressed approval conditional upon specific safeguards, emphasizing that AI outputs must be verified and adapted to the pedagogical context (e.g., "they must be filtered to suit the conditions of the students" [r38]) and the need to avoid over-reliance. Overall, support for teachers' AI use centered on efficiency gains and personalization for improved learning experiences.

Likewise, teachers who supported students' use of AI were asked **Q10a: "I support the use of AI by students because..."**. Their responses clustered into six themes. **(T1) Information Access and Learning Resources** (27.3%) emphasized AI's ability to provide fast access to references and broader knowledge (e.g., "learning new things or content that is minimally covered at school." [r7]). **(T2) Understanding and Personalized Learning** (30%) favored the use of AI for explaining complex concepts and providing step-by-step guidance (e.g., "understading task given" [r31]). **(T3) Creativity and Idea Generation** (13.6%) expressed support as AI can help students brainstorm and explore new perspectives (e.g., "searching for creative for ideas" [r117]). **(T4) Engagement and Interactive Experience** (9.1%) described AI as making learning more interesting and interactive (e.g., "learning becomes more fun, enjoyable, and smart." [r94]), boosting student motivation. **(T5) Efficiency and Productivity** (10.9%) focused on completing tasks more quickly (e.g., "speed up the completion of tasks" [r8]). Finally, **(T6) Risks and Governance (9.1%).** expressed support conditional on supervision and ethical safeguards to prevent misuse, including plagiarism or overdependence (e.g., "because they generally or mostly use it to cheat" [r2]).

Perceived benefits of students' AI use similarly focus on efficiency, where AI helps students complete work faster through improved access to information and resources. Additionally, personalization emerges as a significant theme, ranging from enabling interactive learning to assisting brainstorming.

Among the minority of respondents who were undecided or did not support AI use, we asked follow-up questions: **Q10b: "I will support the use of AI by teachers if..."** and **Q9b: "I will support the use of AI by students if..."**. Across both questions, responses consistently emphasized the need for monitoring, governance, and clear guardrails to prevent misuse (e.g., "in the absence of adequate supervision, there is a risk of misuse" [r39]).

**Opposition and Perceived Risks.** This section explores the factors driving opposition to AI integration in education and the perceived risks respondents associated with its use. While support for AI was largely motivated by efficiency, opposition was most commonly framed around the detrimental effects of over-reliance. This over-dependency is perceived to foster complacency and skill degradation, negative outcomes that are intrinsically linked to the efficiency gains AI provides. In addition, while teachers value AI assistance in their daily activities, they expressed caution about the risk of inaccurate outputs.

To understand the specific grounds for resistance, we asked **Q11: "I will not support AI use by teachers if..."**. Responses clustered into six themes. **(T1) Quality Control and Pedagogical Fit** (26.4%) expressed concerns when AI is used without verification or adaptation to the classroom context (e.g., "if used without filtering the information presented by AI" [r28]), which may result in misleading content or misalignment with the curriculum. **(T2) Dependency and Shortcut Mentality** (24%) reflected concerns that AI would encourage over-reliance or a "shortcut" approach to teaching (e.g., when AI is "used as the primary source in learning without further developing it." [r36]). **(T3) Replacement of the Teacher's Role** (11.2%) is concerned with the risk of AI replacing the teacher's role or reduce essential human interaction (e.g., "it may reduce important aspects of education such as the development of social and emotional skills." [r19]). **(T4) Academic Integrity and Misuse** (6.4%) focused on unethical use of AI, including for cheating or when it results in a lack of originality in teacher-produced work (e.g., "simply copy-pasting without reading it first" [r33]). **(T5) Harmful Content and Social Harm** (19.2%) reflected concerns about hoaxes, hate speech, or content that violates social or religious norms (e.g., "ssed for unethical purposes" [r121]. Finally, **(T6) Governance and Implementation** (12.8%) included worries about data privacy (e.g., "AI collects private data when it is used" [r101]), insufficient competence to use AI, and practical barriers such as costs, as reasons to not support AI use.

We observed a parallel pattern in teachers' opposition to students' use of AI. When asked **Q12: "I will not support the use of AI by students if..."**, respondents expressed significant apprehension about skill erosion due to dependency, alongside heightened concerns about academic dishonesty. Responses clustered into four themes. **(T1) Academic Cheating and Plagiarism** (23.8%) reflected opposition when AI is used for dishonest purposes in assignments or exams, such as "creating research reports by copying 100% from AI" [r99]. **(T2) Dependency and Learning Erosion** (34.6%) captured concerns when AI replaces the actual learning process, resulting in shallow understanding, or students becoming "unable to think critically based on their own reasoning." [r24]. **(T3) Non-learning Misuse** (30.8%) described opposition when AI is used for off-topic, negative, or unsafe purposes, such as "seeking entertainment without age limits" [r94]. Finally, **(T4) Conditional Support and Guardrails** (10.8%) expressed that support depends on clear ethical guidelines, boundaries and supervision, and is withdrawn when "its use has no clear limits." [r63]

Overall, these findings point to a key tension: although support for AI is broad, it is tempered by substantial concerns about cognitive-skill erosion and academic integrity. Among the minority of teachers who fundamentally oppose AI use, their reasoning aligns closely with these risks. For example, one respondent noted, "Because this can make students accustomed to artificial intelligence, making students reluctant to think critically to solve the problems given" [r35].

## 4.5 RQ.4: Pedagogical Stances of Student AI Use

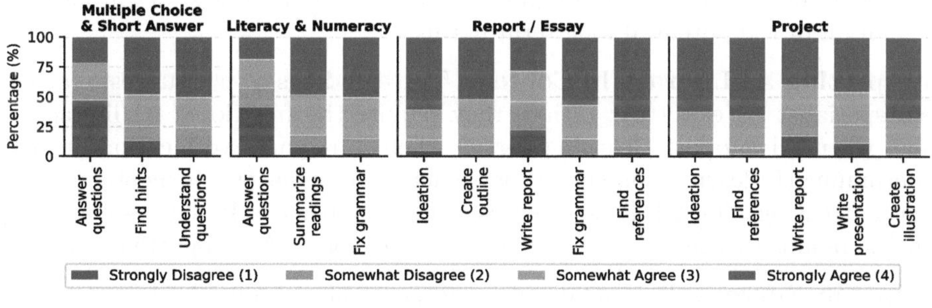


**Fig. 1.** Support of AI Use for Teachers and Students.

This section discusses teacher agreement regarding student AI use across various learning task, specifically: short-answer tasks, literacy/numeracy assignments, essays, and projects. We presented respondents with a multiple-response question, **Q13: "To your knowledge, what do students use AI for in their**

**learning activities?"**, which encompasses the four aforementioned options. For each task selected, we then employed a four-point Likert scale to assess the level of support for AI integration of activities correspond to each task in Fig. 1.

As discussed, teachers generally support students' use of AI. Figure 1 further reflects this supportive stance, with a few notable exceptions: the most contested uses are using AI for answer seeking in performance-based tasks (e.g., MCQs and literacy/numeracy tasks) and AI-written reports for report-based assignments. Even so, some teachers remain strongly supportive and opposition, especially to report writing, remains a minority view. Given growing concerns about AI's educational effects, pedagogical integrity should take priority over mere efficiency: using AI to produce direct answers can undermine learning, and even ideation requires careful use to avoid harms teachers identified.

## 5 Discussion

Our findings reveal a disconnect between AI adoption and AI literacy among Indonesian educators. While AI has rapidly penetrated the teaching profession, underlying conceptual models remain superficial or misinformed. This gap creates a critical tension because teachers are increasingly reliant on a "black box" they lack the literacy to evaluate. This literacy lag is particularly evident in the prevalence of high level or vague descriptions of AI mechanics, which suggests that while the tools are being utilized, their internal logic remains opaque.

Paradoxically, while educators are acutely aware of systemic risks such as academic dishonesty, cognitive over-reliance, and student laziness, their support for AI integration remains remarkably high. This approval persists even when teachers perceive student usage as primarily a shortcut for direct answer seeking. Such a stance suggests that the perceived utility of AI in managing workloads currently outweighs traditional pedagogical caution. This results in a permissive environment where AI is supported across most use cases, despite a clear recognition of the potential long term harms.

**Interpreting AI Literacy in Context.** These findings do not suggest teachers need specialist AI expertise; rather, they require the functional AI literacy to judge when AI supports learning versus when it requires verification or risks undermining the learning process. When teachers have inaccurate mental models, such as treating ChatGPT as a search engine, it negatively shapes classroom policies, monitoring practices, and the normalization of AI-supported activities.

**AI-Use in Surveys.** We found several respondents who used AI in the questions. In one of the questions, their answer included the phrase "As an AI language model developed by Google," which shows that they did not double-check the response and simply copied and pasted it. Another respondent had most of their responses flagged as suspicious, with the remaining two questions confirmed as AI-generated. One of these included markdown formatting which serves no purpose on our survey platform. We find this result interesting and ironic, as it anecdotally illustrates the negative side effects of AI that the respondents themselves confirmed, such as over-reliance, laziness, and the need for instantaneous results, including a failure to check for correctness for the sake of work efficiency.

**Recommendation.** Based on the misconceptions identified, we recommend a more practice-oriented approach to AI literacy and governance in Indonesian K–12 schools. Although the Ministry of Primary and Secondary Education provides initial training, many teachers still hold inaccurate mental models (e.g., treating ChatGPT as a search engine). At the same time, teachers are not unaware of risks: many explicitly mentioned harms such as dependency and dishonesty, yet some still support AI for direct answer seeking and many continue to support AI for report writing, reflecting how strongly perceived efficiency and convenience shape adoption decisions.

To close this gap, AI literacy programs should be longer and directly address misconceptions about accuracy, hallucinations, bias, and privacy [27]. Training should also require *demonstrated* responsible use through authentic tasks (e.g., producing an AI-supported lesson plans, documenting verification steps, and explaining how over-reliance will be mitigated), rather than relying on self-reported readiness so that learning quality remains the priority [5,18,26]. In parallel, guidance should be consolidated in a simple portal and written as short, operational documents with concrete "do/don't" examples [5,17], supported by follow-up checks such as scenario-based assessments or micro-certifications to verify classroom-relevant competence [26,27].

At the school level, clear rules are needed: teachers should state AI policies in the syllabus (permissible purposes, disclosure requirements, and prohibited uses [5]), and students should document their AI process to protect integrity. Schools should also form AI committees to adapt national guidance to local contexts and monitor risks [26], treating AI governance as an ongoing process rather than a one-time document [27]. Finally, given the persistent appeal of AI's convenience and the broad support for its adoption in Indonesia, even in high-risk use cases like answer seeking and report writing, teacher training in AI should shift from general awareness to intensive risk mitigation. Without explicit preparation for managing these trade-offs, strong support for AI may translate into classroom practices that inadvertently compromises pedagogical integrity.

**Limitations.** These findings should be interpreted with several limitations. The sample is not nationally representative, with limited data from private-school teachers outside West Java. Additionally, our recruitment method may introduce selection bias toward technology-engaged educators. Furthermore, the study relies entirely on self-reported survey responses rather than observed classroom behavior. Finally, our analysis is limited to descriptive patterns and does not include inferential subgroup comparisons.

## 6 Conclusion

In this study, we examined the AI conception, use cases, and pedagogical stances of 132 Indonesian K–12 educators through a mixed-methods survey. We found that while adoption and support for AI are high, actual technical understanding implied from the teacher's conceptions of AI remains superficial, with widespread misconceptions regarding AI and LLM functionality. Furthermore, teachers expressed a clear awareness of the impact on student critical thinking and academic honesty, though most teacher supports AI use including by students. We suggest that future professional development and policy frameworks must move beyond general awareness toward performance-based training that directly addresses these conceptual gaps and provides concrete strategies for risk mitigation.

## References


1. Badaruddin, M., Muhardi, F.K., Jofanda, H., et al.: Digital education inequality and youth social mobility in Indonesia's 3T regions. Perspect. Adv. New Gener. Glob. Local Econ. Horizons **1**(2), 31–41 (2025)
2. Batubara, H.H., Syukur, F., Junaedi, M., Purwanti, K.L., Shanie, A.: Teachers perceptions and readiness for mobile artificial intelligence integration in elementary education. Int. J. Interact. Mob. Technol. **19** (2025)
3. Blei, D.M., Ng, A.Y., Jordan, M.I.: Latent Dirichlet allocation. J. Mach. Learn. Res. **3**, 993–1022 (2003)
4. Daher, R.: Integrating ai literacy into teacher education: a critical perspective paper. Discov. Artif. Intell. **5**(1), 217 (2025)
5. Department for Education (UK): Generative artificial intelligence (AI) in education (2025). https://www.gov.uk/government/publications/generative-artificial-intelligence-in-education/generative-artificial-intelligence-ai-in-education. Accessed 12 Aug 2025
6. Dini, I., Kim, S., Nomura, S.: Teacher practices in Indonesia: results of the teach primary classroom observation study. World bank report, World Bank Group, Washington, D.C. (2024). http://documents.worldbank.org/curated/en/099090924033026750
7. Drajati, N.A., Cahyaningrum, D., Handayani, E.I.P., Handayani, A.: Understanding the artificial intelligence literacy between novice and experienced english teachers in Indonesia. TEFLIN J. **36** (2025)
8. Funa, A.A., Gabay, R.A.E.: Policy guidelines and recommendations on ai use in teaching and learning: a meta-synthesis study. Soc. Sci. Humanit. Open **11**, 101221 (2025)
9. Galindo-Domínguez, H., Maza, M.S.D.L., Campo, L., Iglesias, D.L.: Design and validation of a multidimensional scale for assessing teachers' perceptions toward artificial intelligence in education. Int. J. Learn. Technol. **20**, 294–315 (2025)
10. Hashemi, H., Eisner, J., Rosset, C., Van Durme, B., Kedzie, C.: LLM-rubric: a multidimensional, calibrated approach to automated evaluation of natural language texts. In: Ku, L.W., Martins, A., Srikumar, V. (eds.) Proceedings of the 62nd Annual Meeting of the Association for Computational Linguistics (Volume 1: Long Papers), pp. 13806–13834. Association for Computational Linguistics, Bangkok (2024)
11. Kemendikbud: Kemendikdasmen bahas pembelajaran coding dan ai untuk siswa sekolah dasar (2024). https://internal-portal.kemdikbud.go.id/siaran-pers/12290-kemendikdasmen-bahas-pembelajaran-coding-dan-ai-untuk-siswa-. Accessed 31 Jan 2026

12. KORIKA: Strategi nasional kecerdasan artifisial Indonesia 2020-2045 (2024). https://korika.id/2024/07/stranas-ka-2045/. Accessed 31 Jan 2026
13. Kosmyna, N., et al.: Your brain on chatGPT: accumulation of cognitive debt when using an ai assistant for essay writing task (2025)
14. Landa-Blanco, M.: Artificial intelligence in education: applications and limitations for teachers in low-and middle-income countries. In: Frontiers in Education, vol. 10, p. 1681836. Frontiers Media SA (2025)
15. Mertala, P., Fagerlund, J.: Finnish 5th and 6th graders' misconceptions about artificial intelligence. Int. J. Child-Comput. Interact. **39**, 100630 (2024)
16. Mollick, E.R., Mollick, L.: Assigning AI: Seven approaches for students, with prompts. The Wharton School Research Paper (2023)
17. NSW Department of Education: Guidelines regarding the use of generative ai (2025). https://education.nsw.gov.au/teaching-and-learning/education-for-a-changing-world/guidelines-regarding-use-of-generative-ai. Accessed 19 Sept 2025
18. OECD: OECD Digital Education Outlook 2026: Exploring Effective Uses of Generative AI in Education. OECD Publishing (2026)
19. Pedro, F., Subosa, M., Rivas, A., Valverde, P.: Artificial intelligence in education: challenges and opportunities for sustainable development (2019)
20. Republic of Indonesia: Law of the Republic of Indonesia Number 20 of 2003 on the National Education System (2003). https://peraturan.bpk.go.id/Details/43920/uu-no-20-tahun-2003
21. Republic of Indonesia: Law of the Republic of Indonesia Number 14 of 2005 on Teachers and Lecturers (2005). https://peraturan.bpk.go.id/Details/40266/uu-no-14-tahun-2005
22. Republic of Indonesia: Law of the Republic of Indonesia Number 20 of 2023 on the State Civil Apparatus (2023). https://peraturan.bpk.go.id/Details/269470/uu-no-20-tahun-2023
23. Röder, M., Both, A., Hinneburg, A.: Exploring the space of topic coherence measures. In: Proceedings of the Eighth ACM International Conference on Web Search and Data Mining, WSDM 2015, pp. 399–408. Association for Computing Machinery, New York (2015)
24. Russell, J., Karpinska, M., Iyyer, M.: People who frequently use chatGPT for writing tasks are accurate and robust detectors of ai-generated text. arXiv preprint arXiv:2501.15654 (2025)
25. Shen, J.H., Tamkin, A.: How AI impacts skill formation. arXiv preprint arXiv:2601.20245 (2026)
26. TeachAI: AI guidance for schools toolkit (2025). https://www.teachai.org/toolkit. Toolkit for developing and iterating school/system AI guidance
27. UNESCO: Guidance for generative ai in education and research (2023)
28. Wang, B., Rau, P.L.P., Yuan, T.: Measuring user competence in using artificial intelligence: validity and reliability of artificial intelligence literacy scale. Behav. Inf. Technol. **42**(9), 1324–1337 (2023)
29. Wang, H., Prakash, N., Hoang, N.K., Hee, M.S., Naseem, U., Lee, R.K.W.: Prompting large language models for topic modeling. In: 2023 IEEE International Conference on Big Data (BigData), pp. 1236–1241. IEEE (2023)
30. Wang, Y., et al.: M4: Multi-generator, multi-domain, and multi-lingual black-box machine-generated text detection. In: Graham, Y., Purver, M. (eds.) Proceedings of the 18th Conference of the European Chapter of the Association for Computational Linguistics (Volume 1: Long Papers), pp. 1369–1407. Association for Computational Linguistics, St. Julian's (2024)

# Mapping AI Literacy in Medical Education: A Review of Concepts and Teaching Practices

Yingbo Ma(✉) and Yukyeong Song

The University of Tennessee, Knoxville, TN, USA
{yma47,ysong51}@utk.edu

**Abstract.** As artificial intelligence (AI) is increasingly integrated into high-stakes professional workflows, including clinical decision-making, domain-specific AI literacy is becoming a critical requirement for responsible and ethical practice. In medical education, despite the growing number of AI literacy frameworks proposed for medical students, there has been no systematic synthesis that examines how AI literacy competencies for medical students are conceptualized across frameworks and reflected in teaching practice, making it difficult for educators to determine which competencies are commonly emphasized and how they should be prioritized in teaching practice. To address this gap, this paper reports a systematic review of AI literacy frameworks and teaching practices for medical students. The results show that while existing AI literacy frameworks for medical students share the common emphasis on foundational knowledge of AI and responsible AI use in clinical contexts, they differ in technical depth and the roles medical students are expected to play in AI-enabled healthcare. In contrast, current AI education teaching practices for medical students tend to prioritize fundamental concepts and coding-related skills, with limited attention to clinical integration and ethical considerations, reflecting a persistent theory-practice gap. This review contributes to the ongoing discussion on responsible AI in medical education by clarifying how AI literacy competencies for medical students are conceptualized in theory and integrated into teaching practice, offering insights to support the alignment of AI literacy education for medical students with ethical responsibilities and clinical practice in AI-enabled healthcare.

**Keywords:** AI literacy · AI education · Medical education · Systematic review · Responsible AI · Ethical AI

## 1 Introduction

Artificial intelligence (AI) literacy has gained significant momentum in general education, most notably in K12 through the establishment of national guidelines [1,2] and competency frameworks [5,29]. In medical education, however,


E. G. Blanchard et al. (eds.), AIED 2026, LNCS 16586, pp. 300–308, 2027.
https://doi.org/10.1007/978-3-032-29773-0_21

AI literacy development has followed a more complex trajectory shaped by the high-stakes nature of clinical decision-making and professional accountability, as AI-assisted decisions carry significant clinical and ethical weight [10]. As emerging innovations in AI increasingly transform medical practice and healthcare delivery, and AI-enabled devices become more deeply integrated into clinical workflows, AI literacy among medical students (i.e., future physicians) will become a critical requirement for safe and ethical clinical practice.

Despite multiple AI literacy frameworks and guidelines been proposed to define what competencies medical students should have about AI [4,6,15], these efforts have largely emerged independently and are shaped by differing assumptions about the role of physicians in AI-enabled healthcare and perspectives spanning medicine, computer science, and ethics. The lack of synthesis among these theoretical efforts leaves educators an incomplete understanding of how proposed competencies relate to one another or which are consistently emphasized across frameworks. In addition, how closely current teaching practices align with these proposed frameworks remains unknown, as few studies examine the adoption of AI literacy frameworks into traditional and often-overloaded medical curricula. To address these gaps, this study aims to systematically map how AI literacy is conceptualized and taught in medical education by examining both theoretical frameworks and teaching practices. Specifically, we seek to (1) identify common competency dimensions across AI literacy frameworks, and (2) analyze how these competencies are reflected in current educational implementations. This study has the following two research questions (RQs):

**RQ1:** What are the commonalities and differences among existing AI literacy competencies proposed for medical students?

**RQ2:** How is AI literacy for medical students currently being taught by educators, and to what extent do these teaching practices align with existing frameworks?

Findings from RQ1 indicate that existing frameworks share a common emphasis on foundational AI concepts and ethical and responsible AI use in clinical contexts, while differing in their prioritization of technical depth and expectations for practical engagement with AI. Findings from RQ2 suggest that current AI education for medical students primarily emphasizes foundational knowledge and basic coding skills, with limited coverage of other proposed competencies, revealing a persistent theorypractice gap. By synthesizing AI literacy competencies across existing frameworks and examining their translation into educational practice, this study provides a conceptual foundation to inform how AI literacy should be designed, prioritized, and integrated into medical education for responsible clinical practice.

## 2 Methods

We conducted a PRISMA-guided [21] systematic review to examine how AI literacy for medical students is conceptualized in theory and taught in real-world teaching practices. Seven databases across medicine, education, and computer science were searched (PubMed, Scopus, Web of Science, ERIC (Education Resources Information Center), Embase, ACM Digital Library, and IEEE Xplore) using the following search terms:

(*"AI"* OR *"artificial intelligence"* OR *"machine learning"* OR *"deep learning"* OR *"natural language processing"*) AND (*"teaching"* OR *"training"* OR *"curricul*"* OR *"program"* OR *"course"*) AND (*"medical student"* OR *"medical education"* OR *"medical training"*).

Search terms were iteratively refined through pilot searches and domain knowledge. While emerging terms such as *"large language models"* were not always explicitly included, they were captured through broader AI-related terminology. Searches were limited to publications from January 2016 through December 2025, yielding 2,784 records for screening. All records were imported into Covidence and screened independently by two authors in duplicate using a two-stage process (title/abstract screening followed by full-text review), with disagreements resolved through discussion and consensus. Studies were included if they focused on medical students and described either theoretical AI literacy frameworks or practical AI teaching practices.

Ultimately, 38 studies (20 for RQ1 and 18 for RQ2) were included and data were extracted using standardized forms followed a qualitative coding process. For RQ1, the explicitly defined AI literacy competencies for medical students were organized into four overarching AI literacy dimensions adapted from AI Literacy for the Public [19]: Know and Understand AI, (2)Use and Apply AI, (3)Evaluate and Create AI, and (4)AI Ethics. This framework was selected because it is widely adopted across AI literacy research and offers a comprehensive and domain-agnostic structure. Within each of the four dimensions, related competencies were first extracted and then iteratively grouped into sub-categories based on conceptual similarity and frequency of emphasis across the reviewed frameworks. For RQ2, AI topics covered in teaching practice were mapped to the synthesized AI literacy dimensions and sub-categories. Additional information was also extracted on instructional format, topics covered, and instructor background. Due to space constraints, the full list of included studies (n = 38) is provided as a material.

## 3 Results

**For RQ1, Table 1 presents an overview of the mapped key areas of AI literacy** and representative example conpetencies. Frequencies and percentages indicate how many of the 20 frameworks reference each key area.

Commonalities: all 20 frameworks emphasize **introductory knowledge of AI**, such as AI history, basic terminology, what AI can do and cannot do for physicians, and its relevance to clinical decision-making, while largely avoiding in-depth topics of specialized AI sub-fields. In addition, all frameworks agree that AI literacy should **prepare medical students as safe and responsible clinical users of AI**, with consistent emphasis on equipping medical students

**Table 1.** Conceptual mapping of key areas across existing 20 AI literacy frameworks proposed for medical students and representative examples.

| Four Aspects of AI Literacy [19] | Mapped Key Areas (Frequency, Percentage) | Example Competency from Literature |
|---|---|---|
| "Know and Understand AI" | Basic AI concepts, definitions, and terminology (**20, 100%**) | "understanding of theoretical AI concepts" [18]; "understand what large language models are" [27] |
| | Foundations from mathematics and computer science (**5, 25%**) | "mathematical concepts such as basis of linear algebra and calculus" [22], "data science, biostatistics" [7] |
| | Introductory-level AI methods and algorithms (**12, 60%**) | "a minimum level of training in AI algorithms (their pros and cons, benefits, and limitations) [6]" |
| | How AI systems work, training, workflows, and principles (**14, 70%**) | "can explain how AI systems are trained, organize basic workflow in accordance with the logic of AI" [9] |
| | Capabilities, limitations, and implications of AI in medicine (**20, 100%**) | "know what AI can and cannot do for their future research and practices" [7] |
| "Use and Apply AI" | Health data curation and management for clinical AI (**11, 55%**) | "data collection and curation and concerns about privacy, safety, and bias in AI models" [25] |
| | Clinical applications and use cases of AI tools (**20, 100%**) | "familiar with exemplary AI applications in different areas relevant to health care" [8] |
| | Critical and responsible selection and use of AI in practice (**17, 85%**) | "can choose the proper AI application for the problem encountered in healthcare" [9] |
| "Create and Evaluate AI" | Applied programming and data analysis for clinical AI (**5, 25%**) | "perform and co-create basic AI-related programming or data analysis tasks" [4] |
| | Evaluating and interpreting AI outputs (**14, 70%**) | "evaluate AI outputs against potential biases, hallucinations, and errors" [16] |
| "AI Ethics" | Ethical principles and responsibility in medical AI (**20, 100%**) | "effectively navigate the ethical complexities associated with AI technologies in medicine" [30] |
| | Bias, fairness, transparency, and explainability (**20, 100%**) | "understand potential biases and disparities that can harm patients" [25] |
| | Legal, regulatory, and governance considerations (**16, 90%**) | "be educated in ethical and legal issues" [6], "critically evaluate and draft AI policies" [16] |
| | Data rights, privacy, and informed consent (**15, 75%**) | "know how to handle patient data securely" [4], "explanation of AI technologies to patients" [30] |

with understanding of the black-box nature of AI models, as well as sources of data and model bias leading to the explainability and fairness issue of AI models. As future "users" of clinical AI applications, medical students need to know how these issues directly relate to core clinical values, and be fully transparent on informed consent when communicating with patients.

Differences: beyond the above-mentioned shared foundations, current AI literacy frameworks for medical students differ remarkably in how they prioritize other competencies. While most frameworks emphasize **the practical use of AI**, expectations regarding technical depth vary widely. Some frameworks limit technical requirements to conceptual understanding of clinical AI tools, different application scenarios of AI in medicine, and the basic flow of how they work, whereas others incorporate elements of data science, statistical reasoning, or use of AI tools into clinical practice. Competencies related to evaluating and interpreting AI outputs were reported in 70% of included studies, whereas competencies related to related to advanced technical development, such as mathematical foundations and data analysis skills, were only explicitly emphasized in 25% of studies, indicating that while these skills may be valuable for specialized roles, they are not widely treated as core requirements for general medical AI literacy.

**For RQ2, Table 2 presents a synthesized overview of how AI literacy for medical students is currently taught**, and the extent to which

**Table 2.** How AI literacy is currently taught to medical students and its alignment with existing frameworks.

| Dimension | Synthesized Patterns |
|---|---|
| Curriculum Integration | AI training is most often positioned as elective or extracurricular, with relatively few mandatory or fully embedded curricular implementations |
| Duration | Typically short-term, ranging from weekend workshops, multi-week modules to single-semester courses |
| Teaching Format | Predominantly lecture-based supplemented by discussions, with limited hands-on or project-based learning |
| Instructor Background | Primarily led by AI researchers, computer science, or informatics faculty, with few clinician-led modes |
| Clinical Contextualization | Clinical relevance is often limited with authentic clinical workflows or cases |
| Ethics and Regulation | Ethical, legal, and regulatory issues are commonly acknowledged but inconsistently integrated, often treated as discrete topics rather than design principles |
| Misalignment between theory and practice | Instruction emphasizes technical AI knowledge while under-representing competencies related to clinical application, ethical responsibility, and knowledge transfer to real-world settings |

these teaching practices align with existing frameworks. Analysis of 18 studies indicates that AI education for medical students is most often implemented as elective, extracurricular, or short-term instructional offerings rather than as fully embedded curricular components [13,24]. Instruction is predominantly lecture-based, occasionally supplemented by discussions or limited hands-on activities, with relatively few programs incorporating sustained project-based learning or authentic clinical workflows. Teaching commonly begins with didactic learning sessions delivered through in-person lectures, often supplemented by self-directed study using prerecorded materials or readings [12,23]. Instructor expertise represents another key characteristic shaping teaching practice. Most programs are led by university faculty or AI researchers, and **very few instructors have both clinical and AI expertise** [28].

Across programs, instructional content consistently covers introductory AI concepts, basic machine learning techniques, and selected applications of AI in medicine. Ten out of 18 programs also introduce technically advanced topics, such as neural networks and deep learning, and require students to engage in basic coding or model implementation tasks. While these technical components support skill development, they often exceed the technical expectations articulated in many AI literacy frameworks, which emphasize conceptual understanding and responsible use over algorithmic development. In contrast, competencies related to clinical integration, ethical reasoning, and real-world decision-making are less addressed in teaching practice. Although ethical, legal, and regulatory issues are commonly acknowledged, they are frequently treated as standalone topics rather than being consistently integrated throughout instruction.

## 4 Discussion

This study synthesizes the existing literature on AI literacy frameworks and AI education practices for medical students to examine how AI literacy is currently conceptualized and taught to medical students. The findings of RQ1 suggest that there is a consistent emphasis on foundational conceptual understanding of AI as well as ethical responsibility in high-stakes clinical contexts, including model opacity and bias, accountability, and the implications of AI-assisted decision-making. However, beyond these shared foundations, existing AI literacy frameworks for medical students differ remarkably in their emphasis on competencies related to technical depth and level of engagement with AI tools, suggesting that medical educators have different assumptions about the future roles medical students are expected to play in AI-enabled healthcare systems (e.g., end users, or more active participants in the evaluation and oversight of AI [11]). Such differences are not unexpected and reflect ongoing exploration of the appropriate scope of AI-related competencies for future physicians [3]. Importantly, more recent AI literacy frameworks increasingly emphasize competencies related to critical evaluation and ethical reasoning about AI systems, particularly in response to the increasing use of generative AI in clinical contexts [4,18].

Addressing RQ2, the predominance of elective, short-term, and non-mandatory AI instruction suggests that current AI education for medical students still treats AI as an add-on rather than as an integrated core component to medical curricula. Moreover, the observed theorypractice gap highlights a structural challenge of AI education for medical students. While current teaching practices successfully introduce medical students to foundational and advanced technical aspects of AI, they do not consistently reflect the broader set of competencies related to clinical application and ethical responsibility. The predominance of instructors from AI and computer science backgrounds may further exacerbate this gap, as technical expertise alone is insufficient to address questions such as clinical accountability and patient trust. Addressing this gap requires a shift from treating AI education as a technical add-on toward embedding it as a core component of clinical training. This includes integrating AI literacy into authentic clinical scenarios, designing learning activities that require students to evaluate and justify AI-assisted decisions, and fostering collaboration between clinicians and AI experts in curriculum design [14,20]. Such approaches can better prepare medical students to exercise informed judgment and accountability when working with AI systems in practice. Addressing this gap also involves the continued efforts from institutional policies and regulatory frameworks to position AI literacy for medical students as an integral component of professional competence for safe and responsible engagement with AI in clinical practice [27].

Similarly, in other high-stakes professional domains such as law [17] and public administration [26], AI literacy is also increasingly emphasized as an ability to interpret AI outputs within specific context, recognize potential ethical and societal consequences. For example, AI literacy in legal education has emphasized critical evaluation of AI-generated legal analyses, accountability for AI-assisted judgments, and the ethical use of generative tools in legal reasoning [17]. Therefore, this theorypractice gap identified in medical AI education reflects a broader challenge in AI education in high-stakes professional domains, underscoring the need to integrate technical understanding with contextual, ethical, and institutional considerations.

Building on our synthesis, we outline key competency areas to inform the future design of AI literacy in medical education. (1) Conceptual understanding: Medical students need a foundational understanding of how AI systems function, including their capabilities, limitations, and common failure modes. This includes awareness of data sources, model development processes, and the implications of AI-assisted decision-making in clinical contexts; (2) Practical and technical engagement: This includes interpreting outputs, recognizing uncertainty, and appropriately integrating AI recommendations into clinical workflows; (3) Critical evaluation: Students should be able to critically assess AI systems by identifying potential biases, evaluating reliability, and questioning outputs, particularly in situations involving ambiguity or conflicting evidence; (4) Ethical and professional responsibility: Students are expected to understand issues related to fairness, transparency, and patient safety, and to communicate AI-assisted decisions responsibly in ways that maintain patient trust. We also suggest that these competency areas can be considered across different stages of medical training. For example, in the pre-clinical stage, the focus is on developing foundational understanding and building confidence in interacting with AI systems. In the clinical stage, competencies become more practice-oriented, including the use of AI in clinical workflows, alongside increased attention to safety, risk, and accountability. In later stages, such as clinical research or advanced training, learners may engage more directly in evaluating or adapting AI tools, requiring deeper technical understanding and continued learning.

**Limitations.** There are a few important limitations of this study. First, this review synthesizes peer-reviewed literature and may not capture unpublished or institution-specific AI education initiatives. In addition, while this review examines alignment between proposed competencies and teaching practices, it does not evaluate the effectiveness of specific instructional approaches or learning outcomes. Finally, given the rapid evolution of AI technologies and the growing influence of generative AI in clinical contexts, it is important to continue examine how theoretical guidelines and teaching practices adapt to emerging AI technologies.

## 5 Conclusion

AI education for medical students needs to prepare future physicians not only to use AI tools, but also to critically evaluate their implications for ethical, clinical, and institutional practice. By synthesizing existing AI literacy frameworks and AI education practices for medical students, this study clarifies prevailing priorities in AI competency development and reveals a persistent gap between theoretical expectations and educational implementation. These findings provide a foundation for aligning medical AI education more closely with the professional responsibilities required for responsible engagement with AI-enabled healthcare.

**Acknowledgments.** This work was supported by the University of Tennessee at Knoxville faculty startup fund. We also sincerely thank the reviewers for their constructive feedback, which helped strengthen the clarity and contribution of this work.

## References

1. Ai4k12. https://ai4k12.org/
2. Ailit. https://ailiteracyframework.org/
3. Arvai, N., Katonai, G., Mesko, B.: Health care professionals' concerns about medical ai and psychological barriers and strategies for successful implementation: scoping review. J. Med. Internet Res. **27**, e66986 (2025)
4. Cai, C., et al.: Advancing AI literacy in medical education: a medical AI competency framework development. In: Cristea, A.I., Walker, E., Lu, Y., Santos, O.C., Isotani, S. (eds.) AIED 2025. LNCS, vol. 15881, pp. 116–123. Springer, Cham (2025). https://doi.org/10.1007/978-3-031-98462-4_15
5. Casal-Otero, L., Catala, A., Fernández-Morante, C., Taboada, M., Cebreiro, B., Barro, S.: Ai literacy in k-12: a systematic literature review. Inte. J. STEM Educ. **10**(1), 29 (2023)
6. Cussat-Blanc, S., Castets-Renard, C., Monsarrat, P.: Doctors in medical data sciences: a new curriculum. Int. J. Environ. Res. Public Health **20**(1), 675 (2022)
7. Grunhut, J., Marques, O., Wyatt, A.T.: Needs, challenges, and applications of artificial intelligence in medical education curriculum. JMIR Med. Educ. **8**(2), e35587 (2022)
8. Kalthoff, D., Prien, M., Götz, N.A.: "AI4Health"–development and conception of a learning programme in higher and continuing education on the fundamentals, applications and perspectives of ai in healthcare. In: Challenges of Trustable AI and Added-Value on Health, pp. 785–789. IOS Press (2022)
9. Karaca, O., Çalışkan, S.A., Demir, K.: Medical artificial intelligence readiness scale for medical students (MAIRS-MS)-development, validity and reliability study. BMC Med. Educ. **21**(1), 112 (2021)
10. Katznelson, G., Gerke, S.: The need for health ai ethics in medical school education. Adv. Health Sci. Educ. **26**(4), 1447–1458 (2021)
11. Labkoff, S., et al.: Toward a responsible future: recommendations for AI-enabled clinical decision support. J. Am. Med. Inform. Assoc. **31**(11), 2730–2739 (2024)
12. Laupichler, M.C., et al.: Effect of a flipped classroom course to foster medical students' AI literacy with a focus on medical imaging: a single group pre-and post-test study. BMC Med. Educ. **22**(1), 803 (2022)

13. Lee, Y.M., Cao, K., Leech, M., De Ponti, F.: Developing medical artificial intelligence leaders: international university consortium approach. Med. Educ. **55**(11), 1321 (2021)
14. Ma, Y., et al.: Promoting ai competencies for medical students: a scoping review on frameworks, programs, and tools. arXiv preprint arXiv:2407.18939 (2024)
15. McCoy, L.G., Nagaraj, S., Morgado, F., Harish, V., Das, S., Celi, L.A.: What do medical students actually need to know about artificial intelligence? NPJ Digit. Med. **3**(1), 86 (2020)
16. Mehta, N., Mehta, S., Rubenstein, A., Wood, S.K.: Not replaced, but reinvented: AI education pathways to prepare future physicians to lead healthcare transformation. Perspect. Me. Educ. **14**(1), 849 (2025)
17. Migliorini, S., Moreira, J.I.: The case for nurturing AI literacy in law schools. Asian J. Legal Educ. **12**(1), 7–24 (2025)
18. Mihalas, G.I., Cotoraci, C., Boru, C.: Integrating artificial intelligence in the medical curriculum: approaches and strategies. Stud. Health Technol. Inform. **329**, 1402–1406 (2025)
19. Ng, D.T.K., Leung, J.K.L., Chu, S.K.W., Qiao, M.S.: Conceptualizing ai literacy: an exploratory review. Comput. Educ.: Arti. Intell. **2**, 100041 (2021)
20. Ötleş, E., James, C.A., Lomis, K.D., Woolliscroft, J.O.: Teaching artificial intelligence as a fundamental toolset of medicine. Cell Rep. Med. **3**(12) (2022)
21. Page, M.J., et al.: The PRISMA 2020 statement: an updated guideline for reporting systematic reviews. BMJ **372** (2021)
22. Paranjape, K., Schinkel, M., Panday, R.N., Car, J., Nanayakkara, P.: Introducing artificial intelligence training in medical education. JMIR Med. Educ. **5**(2), e16048 (2019)
23. Pizzolla, I., Aro, R., Duez, P., De Lièvre, B., Briganti, G.: Integrating artificial intelligence into medical education: lessons learned from a Belgian initiative. J. Interact. Learn. Res. **34**(2), 401–424 (2023)
24. Sendak, M.P., et al.: Preliminary results of a clinical research and innovation scholarship to prepare medical students to lead innovations in health care. In: Healthcare, vol. 9, p. 100555. Elsevier (2021)
25. Tejani, A.S., Elhalawani, H., Moy, L., Kohli, M., Kahn Jr, C.E.: Artificial intelligence and radiology education. Radiol.: Artif. Intell. **5**(1), e220084 (2022)
26. Trajkovski, G.: Bridging the public administration-AI divide: a skills perspective. Public Adm. Dev. **44**(5), 412–426 (2024)
27. Triola, M.M., Rodman, A.: Integrating generative artificial intelligence into medical education: curriculum, policy, and governance strategies. Acad. Med. **100**(4), 413–418 (2025)
28. Tsopra, R., et al.: Putting undergraduate medical students in AI-CDSS designers' shoes: an innovative teaching method to develop digital health critical thinking. Int. J. Med. Inform. **171**, 104980 (2023)
29. Wang, N., Lester, J.: K-12 education in the age of AI: a call to action for K-12 AI literacy. Int. J. Artif. Intell. Educ. **33**(2), 228–232 (2023)
30. Weidener, L., Fischer, M., et al.: Proposing a principle-based approach for teaching ai ethics in medical education. JMIR Med. Educ. **10**(1), e55368 (2024)

# Identifying High-Confidence Social Biases in LLMs for Trustworthy Conversational Tutoring Agents

Aitor Arronte Alvarez(✉) and Naiyi Xie Fincham

University of Hawaii at Manoa, Honolulu, HI 96822, USA
{arronte,naiyixf}@hawaii.edu

**Abstract.** Conversational tutoring agents have been shown to improve learning engagement and student outcomes, and large language models (LLMs) are increasingly used in these systems to provide scalable, personalized feedback. However, LLMs may perpetuate or amplify stereotypical social biases, posing particular risks in educational settings. In this study, we evaluate LLMs in conversational tutoring scenarios to identify high-confidence social biases, instances in which models fail to detect biased judgments while expressing strong confidence in their assessments, potentially affecting their reasoning and the feedback they provide to learners. Results indicate that bias detection is substantially more challenging in conversational tutoring contexts than in benchmark-based evaluations, and that state-of-the-art LLMs are overconfident in their incorrect assessments of stereotypical bias statements. Moreover, model confidence strongly influences reasoning and feedback, highlighting the risks of overconfidence biased behavior in LLM-based tutoring agents.

**Keywords:** social biases · stereotypes · overconfidence · conversational tutoring agents · trustworthy AI

## 1 Introduction

Conversational tutoring systems have been associated with improved learning efficiency and cognitive engagement [4]. Recent advances in LLMs have enabled personalized, adaptive tutoring at scale [8,16], with learners perceiving these systems as supportive and helpful [2,9]. However, LLMs still produce hallucinations, exhibit social biases, and tend to be overconfident in their judgments [17].

While social biases in educational AI have received some attention [10,21], the confidence and uncertainty associated with model judgments, and the risks they pose in educational contexts, remain underexplored. As LLM-based tutoring agents become more widely adopted, evaluations must move beyond general-purpose benchmarks toward context-specific settings, though collecting educational data introduces additional ethical and privacy challenges [6,14].


E. G. Blanchard et al. (eds.), AIED 2026, LNCS 16586, pp. 309–317, 2027.
https://doi.org/10.1007/978-3-032-29773-0_22

In this paper, we examine how LLM confidence affects reasoning and student feedback when identifying stereotypical bias in student-tutor conversations, focusing on second language (L2) acquisition. We propose a method to generate tutoring dialogue datasets for bias evaluation by deidentifying authentic interactions and regenerating them with an LLM (DeepSeek), preserving linguistic and instructional structure while introducing controlled stereotypical content based on StereoSet categories [15]. We then evaluate multiple LLMs on this dataset to address the following research question: **How do state-of-the-art LLMs detect stereotypical bias in conversational tutoring contexts compared to benchmark datasets, and how does their confidence, when incorrect, affect their reasoning and feedback to students?** We investigate this question through a combination of computational and human evaluations.

## 2 Background and Related Work

### 2.1 Education, Social Biases, and AI

Language plays a central role in establishing power relations, projecting social biases, and reinforcing stereotypes [3]. These biases are often embedded in linguistic categories that frame social contexts and shape perceptions of others [18]. In educational settings, implicit associations related to race, ethnicity, gender, cultural background, or social status can significantly affect students' opportunities and outcomes [23].

With the rapid development of generative AI, particularly large language models (LLMs), millions now rely on these systems for cognitively complex tasks. In education, LLMs support personalized learning and generate instructional materials, lesson plans, and assessments. However, they can reproduce and amplify social biases present in their training data [5].

The combination of social bias and overconfidence is particularly concerning in educational contexts, where learners may lack the background knowledge needed to recognize stereotypes. As conversational agents are increasingly used to scaffold learning, large language models (LLMs) are being positioned as tutors, coaches, and learning assistants. When biased behaviors emerge in instructional dialogue, they can shape the feedback learners receive, the opportunities afforded to them, and their perceptions of competence and belonging, ultimately influencing academic trajectories [19]. Despite these risks, there is a lack of tutoring-specific datasets designed to evaluate such biases.

### 2.2 Confidence and Uncertainty in LLMs

For the safe, trustworthy, and effective integration of AI systems in critical domains such as education, confidence and uncertainty must be clearly communicated to stakeholders. Although LLMs rely on statistical predictions to generate responses, prior work shows that they often exhibit inconsistent or poorly calibrated expressions of confidence and uncertainty [17]. Existing approaches have focused on fine-tuning LLMs to better align uncertainty estimates using token-level probabilities [12]. However, token probabilities conflate multiple sources of uncertainty and offer limited interpretability. In contrast, verbalized expressions of confidence and uncertainty have been shown to better support human-AI collaboration [11].

Because fine-tuning is not always feasible, particularly for large or closed-source models, prompting-based approaches have gained prominence. These include self-consistency methods [20], which estimate confidence through agreement across multiple outputs, and self-correction techniques [13], which can improve response accuracy. However, self-correction can also affect expressed confidence, sometimes reducing it even when correctness improves [22].

Overall, eliciting and calibrating uncertainty in LLMs remains challenging. Models frequently exhibit overconfidence, and although both fine-tuning and prompting-based approaches offer potential solutions, each involves trade-offs. Fine-tuning is often impractical for large or closed models, while prompting-based methods may be unstable.

## 3 Methodology

### 3.1 Dataset Generation

To evaluate stereotypical bias in naturalistic language-learning scenarios, we collected studenttutor interaction data from an AI-powered EFL platform [2], comprising multi-turn practice dialogues on predefined topics from a speaking course at a Southeast Asian university. From two academic semesters, 4,210 conversations were retrieved. To address a gender imbalance in the original sample (70% female), stratified sampling was applied, yielding a more balanced distribution (55% female, 45% male). Conversations with fewer than 12 turns were then removed to ensure sufficient contextual depth, reducing the dataset to 1,844 dialogues, all of which underwent deidentification.

The Biased Conversational Tutoring Dataset, was generated using DeepSeek-V3.1 via its API, as it is currently the only model allowing the generation of stereotypical language. We first applied a prompt-based procedure to extract linguistic features from original tutoring conversations, covering discourse structure, interaction style, common errors, and proficiency level, then sampled instances from the StereoSet dataset [15], stratified by type (stereotypical, anti-stereotypical, neutral), target group, and contextual category. DeepSeek-V3.1 was then prompted to regenerate full studenttutor dialogues, as shown in Algorithm 1, that preserve the original linguistic characteristics while incorporating a single target turn aligned with the sampled StereoSet context (see Fig. 1).

Two expert annotators reviewed the 1,844 generated conversations using the Context Association Test (CAT) protocol [15], discarding 117 where the introduced turn was misaligned with the intended context or label. The final dataset comprises 1,727 valid studenttutor conversations: 610 stereotypical, 554 anti-stereotypical, and 563 neutral.

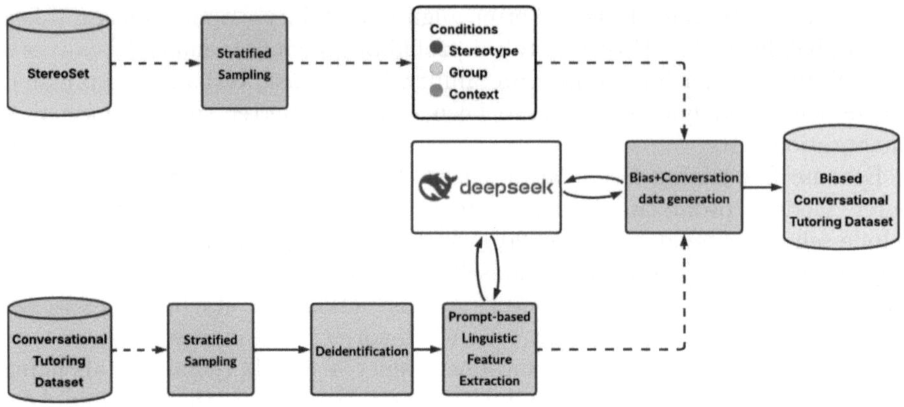


**Fig. 1.** Stereotypical conversational tutoring dataset generation process.

### 3.2 Experiments

Using the dataset generated in the previous subsection, we conduct a series of experiments to evaluate three state-of-the-art LLMs, GPT-5.1, Gemini 2.5 Pro, and Claude Sonnet 4.5.

**Experiment #1** evaluates model performance on stereotype detection across StereoSet and a generated tutoring dataset (1,689 matched samples). Models classify each input as stereotype, anti-stereotype, or neutral, then are prompted to reconsider their initial judgment as a form of self-verification, regardless of correctness. They then report confidence via an overall score 0–100 (Prompt 1), and class-specific distributions (Prompt 2). Performance is measured using accuracy, precision, recall, and $F_2$. A confidence-weighted bias score, the sum of misclassified instances weighted by model confidence, captures the confidence of incorrect predictions; lower is better.

**Experiment #2** uses the least biased model from Experiment #1 (lowest confidence-weighted bias score) to: (1) explain its reasoning using epistemic uncertainty markers, and (2) generate brief teacher-style feedback on the conversation's language, content, and potential issues. From the model outputs, 100 incorrect classifications are randomly sampled for human evaluation.

Two raters scored each instance on a 3-point Likert scale assessing coherence between expressed uncertainty and language in (a) the reasoning explanation and (b) the student feedback, where 1 = no coherence, 2 = partial coherence, and 3 = high coherence, using the following confidence intervals: very high ($\geq 90\%$), high ($\geq 80\%$, $< 90\%$), moderate ($\geq 70\%$, $< 80\%$), and low ($< 70\%$). The goal is to assess alignment between the model's verbalized confidence, its reasoning, and its tutoring feedback.

**Algorithm 1.** Biased Conversational Dataset Generation

```
Require: Conversational dataset D, benchmark dataset B with labeled instances
    (stereotype, target group, context), LLM L
Ensure: Biased conversational dataset D'
Initialize D' ← ∅
for each conversation d ∈ D do
    Extract linguistic features C ← EXTRACT(d, L)
    Sample (s, g, c) ~ B where s = stereotype, g = target group, k = context
    d' ← REGENERATE(d, C, s, g, k, L) {Uses C_d to preserve linguistic features; intro-
    duces one turn aligned with (s, g, c)}
    D' ← D' ∪ {d'}
end for
return D'
```

**Table 1.** Bias detection performance across models and datasets.

| Model | Dataset | Precision | Recall | $F_2$ | Accuracy |
|---|---|---|---|---|---|
| Claude Sonnet 4.5 | Tutoring | **0.613** | 0.544 | 0.514 | 0.543 |
| GPT-5.1 | Tutoring | 0.527 | 0.497 | 0.467 | 0.497 |
| Gemini-2.5-Pro | Tutoring | 0.563 | **0.550** | **0.534** | **0.549** |
| Claude Sonnet 4.5 | StereoSet | 0.723 | 0.660 | **0.672** | **0.677** |
| GPT-5.1 | StereoSet | 0.715 | 0.514 | 0.461 | 0.514 |
| Gemini-2.5-Pro | StereoSet | **0.749** | **0.667** | 0.646 | 0.667 |

# 4 Results and Discussion

## 4.1 Results

**Experiment #1.** Table 1 shows classification results across models and data sets. Sonnet and Gemini outperform GPT-5.1 on both datasets; however, the Biased Conversational Tutoring dataset proves to be consistently harder, with a mean relative degradation of 15.4% across metrics compared to StereoSet (Precision: −22.1%, Recall: −12.8%, $F_2$: −13.2%, Accuracy: −13.6%), indicating a substantial reduction in bias detection performance in naturalistic instructional contexts.

As shown in Table 2, all models exhibit high absolute confidence even when incorrect, particularly GPT-5.1 and Gemini-2.5-Pro. Significant differences in confidence means are observed across prompting strategies for both correct and incorrect predictions ($p < 0.05$). Prompt 1 elicits higher confidence when incorrect than Prompt 2 across models overall (91.6% vs. 84.4%), and while Prompt 2 best reduces confidence on incorrect responses, mean confidence stays high. Models revised their initial judgments in only 0.1% of verification checks, with no measurable impact on performance.

Table 3 shows that Sonnet 4.5 achieves the lowest confidence-weighted bias score, making it the least overconfident model on incorrect judgments. Neverthe-

**Table 2.** Average confidence for correct and incorrect predictions on the tutoring dataset. Lower incorrect and higher correct values indicate better confidence calibration.

| Model | Prompt | Correct | Incorrect |
|---|---|---|---|
| Claude Sonnet 4.5 | 1 | 89.40 | 89.90 |
| Claude Sonnet 4.5 | 2 | 85.39 | 82.82 |
| GPT-5.1 | 1 | 96.73 | 93.79 |
| GPT-5.1 | 2 | 93.25 | 87.14 |
| Gemini-2.5-Pro | 1 | 93.38 | 91.21 |
| Gemini-2.5-Pro | 2 | 86.87 | 83.10 |

**Table 3.** Average confidence-weighted bias score across models. Lower values indicate more appropriate uncertainty in biased or incorrect judgments.

| Model | Score |
|---|---|
| Claude Sonnet 4.5 | **82.5** |
| GPT-5.1 | 84.1 |
| Gemini-2.5-Pro | 82.9 |

less, and as depicted in Fig. 2, confidence remains high: 34% of its errors occur at very high confidence ($\geq$90%), 38% at high confidence ($\geq$80%, <90%), 24% at moderate confidence ($\geq$ 70%, <80%), and only 4% at low confidence (<70%).

Examining Sonnet 4.5's per-class performance (Table 4), anti-stereotype detection is the weakest, with very low recall (0.177) indicating a high rate of false negatives. Notably, the model is less confident in its correct anti-stereotype predictions than its incorrect ones (0.730 vs. 0.826). Stereotype detection also remains difficult, with uniformly high confidence in both correct and incorrect predictions (0.835 in both cases), suggesting limited calibration.

**Experiment #2.** Annotator evaluations showed substantial inter-rater agreement ($\kappa > 0.61$) across both dimensions. Reasoning and Feedback scores were positively correlated and statistically dependent ($\rho = 0.46$, $\chi^2 = 3.76$, $p < 0.05$), indicating a significant association between the coherence of model reasoning and student feedback.

When analyzing incorrect classifications, Sonnet 4.5 showed strong coherence between elicited confidence and verbalized reasoning (75% high, 23% partial, 2% incoherent) and generated feedback (68% high, 31% partial, 1% incoherent). Overall, results indicate strong alignment between the model's overconfidence, reasoning, and learner feedback.

### 4.2 Discussion

The results show that LLMs exhibit substantial overconfidence when judging stereotypes in conversational tutoring scenarios, overconfidence that, when incor-

**Table 4.** Per-class metrics and confidence for Claude Sonnet 4.5 on the biased conversational tutoring dataset.

| Class | Precision | Recall | F2 | Avg. Conf. (Correct) | Avg. Conf. (Incorrect) |
|---|---|---|---|---|---|
| Stereotype | 0.591 | 0.557 | 0.563 | 0.835 | 0.835 |
| Anti-stereotype | 0.757 | 0.177 | 0.209 | 0.730 | 0.826 |
| Neutral | 0.491 | 0.898 | 0.770 | 0.890 | 0.819 |

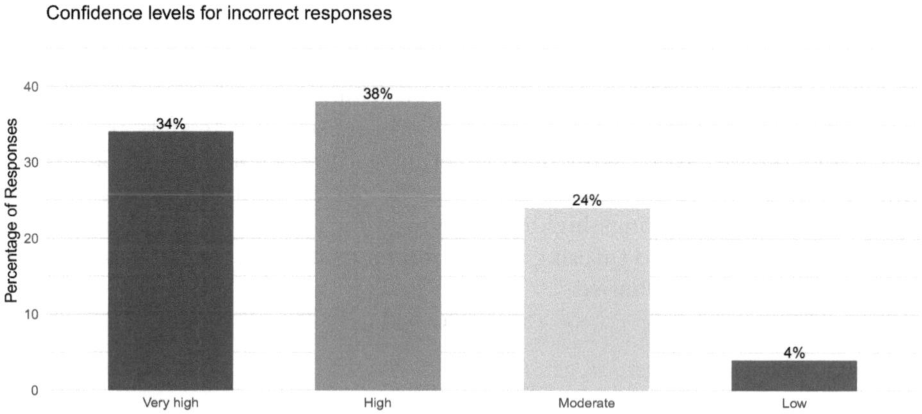


**Fig. 2.** Sonnet 4.5 confidence levels elicited when responses are incorrect.

rect, reinforces both their reasoning and student feedback. While prior work has documented inconsistent confidence expression in factual benchmarks [17], our findings suggest that social bias assessment, which demands interpretive rather than factual judgment, elicits even stronger overconfidence. Unlike in factual or reasoning tasks, where models often revise judgments when prompted to reflect [17], models here almost never changed their initial assessments, further underscoring this effect.

These findings highlight the need for contextualized, educationally grounded evaluations of social bias. Relying exclusively on general-purpose benchmarks risks systematic underestimation of potential harms in naturalistic settings. The dataset generation method proposed here addresses this gap by enabling bias evaluation under realistic instructional conditions and is broadly applicable to domains demanding interpretation and normative judgment, such as the humanities and social sciences.

As evaluation frameworks for pedagogically oriented AI continue to mature [14], greater emphasis should be placed on uncertainty quantification and confidence calibration. The traditional epistemic–aleatoric distinction [7] does not adequately capture the interpretive complexity of social biases in tutoring exchanges. Consistent with notions of hermeneutic uncertainty [1], educational AI should offer multiple reasoned interpretations with explicit uncertainty rather than singular authoritative judgments.

Finally, the internal consistency of overconfidence across reasoning and feedback is particularly concerning in tutoring agents, given their association with learning efficiency and student engagement. Such overconfidence may act as a bias amplification mechanism, either reinforcing stereotypical judgments or overlooking them. A promising mitigation strategy may be designing agents that present multiple plausible perspectives, fostering critical thinking and contextual understanding of cultural, social, and ethical issues.

## 5 Conclusions

We evaluated three LLMs on stereotype detection, uncertainty quantification, and feedback generation in conversational tutoring settings. Results reveal consistent overconfidence across models, affecting both reasoning and student feedback; a concern for learners who may lack the background to recognize biased explanations. These findings highlight the need for calibrated uncertainty communication in LLM-based tutoring agents and for evaluating social bias detection in realistic educational contexts.

## References


1. Delacroix, S., et al.: Beyond quantification: navigating uncertainty in professional ai systems. RSS: Data Sci. Artif. Intell. **1**(1), udaf002 (2025)
2. Fincham, N.X., Alvarez, A.A.: Using large language models (LLMs) to facilitate L2 proficiency development through personalized feedback and scaffolding: An empirical study. In: Proceedings of the International CALL Research Conference, vol. 2024, pp. 59–64 (2024)
3. Fiske, S.T.: Controlling other people: the impact of power on stereotyping. In: Social Cognition, pp. 101–115. Routledge, New York (2018)
4. Graesser, A.C., VanLehn, K., Rosé, C.P., Jordan, P.W., Harter, D.: Intelligent tutoring systems with conversational dialogue. AI Mag. **22**(4), 39–39 (2001)
5. Hofmann, V., Kalluri, P.R., Jurafsky, D., King, S.: AI generates covertly racist decisions about people based on their dialect. Nature **633**(8028), 147–154 (2024)
6. Huang, L.: Ethics of artificial intelligence in education: student privacy and data protection. Sci. Insights Educ. Front. **16**(2), 2577–2587 (2023)
7. Hüllermeier, E., Waegeman, W.: Aleatoric and epistemic uncertainty in machine learning: An introduction to concepts and methods. Mach. Learn. **110**(3), 457–506 (2021)
8. Kasneci, E., et al.: ChatGPT for good? On opportunities and challenges of large language models for education. Learn. Individ. Differ. **103**, 102274 (2023)
9. Labadze, L., Grigolia, M., Machaidze, L.: Role of AI chatbots in education: systematic literature review. Int. J. Educ. Technol. High. Educ. **20**(1), 56 (2023)
10. Lee, J., Hicke, Y., Yu, R., Brooks, C., Kizilcec, R.F.: The life cycle of large language models in education: a framework for understanding sources of bias. Br. J. Edu. Technol. **55**(5), 1982–2002 (2024)
11. Li, J., Yang, Y., Liao, Q.V., Zhang, J., Lee, Y.C.: As confidence aligns: understanding the effect of AI confidence on human self-confidence in human-ai decision making. In: Proceedings of the 2025 CHI Conference on Human Factors in Computing Systems, pp. 1–16 (2025)

12. Liu, S., et al.: Can LLMs learn uncertainty on their own? Expressing uncertainty effectively in a self-training manner. In: Proceedings of the 2024 Conference on Empirical Methods in Natural Language Processing, pp. 21635–21645 (2024)
13. Madaan, A., et al.: Self-refine: iterative refinement with self-feedback. Adv. Neural. Inf. Process. Syst. **36**, 46534–46594 (2023)
14. Maurya, K.K., Srivatsa, K.A., Petukhova, K., Kochmar, E.: Unifying AI tutor evaluation: an evaluation taxonomy for pedagogical ability assessment of LLM-powered AI tutors. In: Proceedings of the 2025 Conference of the Nations of the Americas Chapter of the Association for Computational Linguistics: Human Language Technologies (Volume 1: Long Papers), pp. 1234–1251 (2025)
15. Nadeem, M., Bethke, A., Reddy, S.: StereoSet: measuring stereotypical bias in pretrained language models. In: Zong, C., Xia, F., Li, W., Navigli, R. (eds.) Proceedings of the 59th Annual Meeting of the Association for Computational Linguistics and the 11th International Joint Conference on Natural Language Processing (Volume 1: Long Papers), pp. 5356–5371. Association for Computational Linguistics, Online (2021). https://doi.org/10.18653/v1/2021.acl-long.416, https://aclanthology.org/2021.acl-long.416/
16. Park, M., Kim, S., Lee, S., Kwon, S., Kim, K.: Empowering personalized learning through a conversation-based tutoring system with student modeling. In: Extended Abstracts of the CHI Conference on Human Factors in Computing Systems, pp. 1–10 (2024)
17. Pawitan, Y., Holmes, C.: Confidence in the reasoning of large language models. Harv. Data Sci. Rev. **7**(1) (2025)
18. Sap, M., Gabriel, S., Qin, L., Jurafsky, D., Smith, N.A., Choi, Y.: Social bias frames: reasoning about social and power implications of language. In: Proceedings of the 58th Annual Meeting of the Association for Computational Linguistics, pp. 5477–5490 (2020)
19. Van Poucke, M.: ChatGPT, the perfect virtual teaching assistant? Ideological bias in learner-chatbot interactions. Comput. Compos. **73**, 102871 (2024)
20. Wang, X., et al.: Self-consistency improves chain of thought reasoning in language models. In: The Eleventh International Conference on Learning Representations (2023)
21. Weissburg, I., Anand, S., Levy, S., Jeong, H.: LLMs are biased teachers: evaluating LLM bias in personalized education. In: Findings of the Association for Computational Linguistics: NAACL 2025, pp. 5650–5698 (2025)
22. Yang, Z., Zhang, Y., Wang, Y., Xu, Z., Lin, J., Sui, Z.: Confidence vs critique: a decomposition of self-correction capability for LLMs. In: Proceedings of the 63rd Annual Meeting of the Association for Computational Linguistics (Volume 1: Long Papers), pp. 3998–4014 (2025)
23. Zucker, S.H., Prieto, A.G.: Ethnicity and teacher bias in educational decisions. J. Instr. Psychol. **4**(3), 2 (1977)

# When LLMs Give Voting Advice: Bias, Coherence, and Educational Risk

Omed Abed[1,2], Rabia Basri[1], Patrick-Benjamin Bök[1(✉)], and Matteo Große-Kampmann[1,2(✉)]

[1] Rhine-Waal University of Applied Sciences, Kleve, Germany
{omed.abed,patrick-benjamin.boek, matteo.grosse-kampmann}@hochschule-rhein-waal.de, rabia.basri@hsrw.org

[2] Doctoral School of Applied Sciences NRW, Department Computer and Data Science, Bochum, Germany

**Abstract.** When used alongside Voting Advice Applications (VAAs), LLMs serve as informal civic learning systems, pairing stance labels with AI-generated explanations. We audit five commercial LLMs (Gemini 2.0 Flash Lite, Gemini 2.5 Pro, GPT-4o, Grok 3, Mistral Large) using four European VAAs (Germany, Netherlands, Luxembourg, Czech Republic), analyzing 7,400 responses. Reframing LLM bias as an educational AI problem, we assess explanation coherence via Natural Language Inference and a Semantic Consistency Index. We find pedagogically incoherent feedback. Reasoning contradicts the stated stance in 3.2% of a stratified subsample of 1,000 cases, with a bimodal coherence distribution suggesting two distinct explanation regimes. All models align most strongly with Green and Social Democratic parties, with cross-national differences indicating unequal civic-learning impacts shaped by language-resource and VAA design factors.

**Keywords:** Large Language Models · Pedagogical Coherence · Cross-Cultural Equity · Responsible AI

## 1 Introduction

Large language models (LLMs) are increasingly embedded in educational and civic information systems, reshaping how learners engage with political content [24]. When combined with Voting Advice Applications (VAAs), LLMs serve as informal civic learning systems: users may respond to policy statements and receive AI feedback (a categorical stance on a certain policy domain and an explanation). Systematic bias or incoherence in this feedback can produce *educational harm*. For example, a biased learning signal could distort civic understanding or stance. Especially when reasoning mismatches confuse learners and cultural/linguistic gaps lead to unequal learning outcomes. Prior work documents political biases in LLMs [14,28], and VAAs are increasingly used for civic


E. G. Blanchard et al. (eds.), AIED 2026, LNCS 16586, pp. 318–326, 2027.
https://doi.org/10.1007/978-3-032-29773-0_23

learning, also among younger voters [2]. However, existing audits typically examine single VAA contexts and do not explore how bias varies across countries, issue domains, or reasoning coherence [22].

We address three research questions: **RQ1** Do explanations coherently justify model stances? **RQ2** How do biases vary across cultural contexts, and what equity risks follow? **RQ3** What governance safeguards are needed for educational deployment? To answer these, we audit five commercial LLMs using four European VAAs, analyzing 7,400 responses for pedagogical coherence, stance–sentiment alignment, and cross-national bias patterns [24].

## 2 Background

Unlike other retrieval systems that return multiple potential candidates for a given query, LLMs generate a single synthesized response [20], with limited algorithmic or reasoning transparency [36]. In educational settings, outputs that pair a categorical label with a free-form explanation function as feedback. Learners treat the label as the answer and the explanation as the justification [35]. When the explanation is weakly connected to the label or internally inconsistent, the feedback signal can undermine trust and reinforce misconceptions. Prior work has shown systematic biases in search engines [9], recommender systems [11], and LLMs [30], but these studies do not examine explanation coherence in civic learning contexts. Voting Advice Applications (VAAs) are widely used instruments for voter education [3], Wahl-O-Mat was used 26 million times in the 2025 German federal election [7]. Their standardized design and transparent matching logic make them transparent testbeds for auditing LLM behavior in contrast to LLMs' opaque reasoning [4].

## 3 Methods

We evaluated five LLMs: Gemini 2.0 Flash Lite (Gemini 2.0) [17], Gemini 2.5 Pro (Gemini 2.5) [13], GPT-4o [26], Grok 3 [38], and Mistral Large [23], all top performers on LMSYS Chatbot Arena [21]. Experiments were conducted in June 2025. The full dataset is released as an open artifact[1]. We collected political statements from four European VAAs: **Wahl-O-Mat** (Germany, 38 statements, *Agree/Disagree/Neutral*) [6,7]; **StemWijzer** (Netherlands, 30 statements, *Agree/Disagree/Neither*) [8,27,32]; **SmartWielen** (Luxembourg, 38 statements, five-point scale) [33]; and **Volební Kalkulačka** (Czech Republic, 42 statements, binary *Yes/No*) [16].

### 3.1 Experimental Protocol

Statements were translated into English by two fluent speakers (10% of the statements were back-translated for validation). The 148 unique statements were each

[1] https://github.com/cloudresiliencelab/vaa-analysis.

presented to every model across 10 independent runs using a neutral prompt, yielding 7,400 responses. Categorical responses were mapped to $[-2, 2]$ (*Disagree*$= -2$, *Neutral* $= 0$, *Agree* $= +2$; *Rather No/Yes* $= \mp 1$) and processed with each VAA's matching process. Parties were mapped to political families using the 2024 CHES taxonomy [29]. Alignment scores were Z-score normalized within each VAA for cross-national comparison [1]. As a secondary check, we measured whether reasoning-text sentiment aligns with the categorical decision using a lexical bag-of-words proxy and VADER [15]. We note that sentiment is an imperfect proxy for political stance (see Limitations 5). Statements were assigned to seven EU policy domains, following the European Commission's categories [10], by two coders ($\kappa = 0.84$).

### 3.2 NLI-Based Semantic Consistency

Natural Language Inference (NLI) is a classification task that determines whether a *hypothesis* is entailed by, contradicts, or is neutral with respect to a *premise* [37]. We use zero-shot NLI (`facebook/bart-large-mnli` [19]) to assess whether model reasoning semantically supports categorical decisions. Each decision $y \in \{-2, \ldots, 2\}$ was verbalized as a hypothesis (e.g., "The model strongly agrees with the statement"), and posterior probabilities over ENTAILMENT, NEUTRAL, CONTRADICTION} were computed. From these, we derive a Semantic Consistency Index on a stratified subsample of 1,000 responses (200 per model, balanced across VAAs):

$$SCI_i = p_i^{(E)} - p_i^{(C)},$$

ranging from $-1$ (full contradiction) to $+1$ (full entailment) [12,18]. We label `high` (SCI $\geq 0.6$), `moderate` ($0.3 \leq$ SCI $< 0.6$), and `low` (SCI $< 0$) coherence. Reliability was assessed via label-shuffling baseline (1,000 permutations) [5].

## 4 Results

### 4.1 Quantitative Results

Across all VAAs, models exhibited a positive/optimistic framing tendency, including in disagreement contexts. Lexical sentiment matched the decision polarity in only 43% of cases, and 63% with VADER. Both rates indicate substantial stance-sentiment mismatch.

*Semantic Consistency.* Across $N = 7{,}400$ pairs, NLI entailment scores were tightly clustered (mean $\bar{s} = 0.592$, s.d. 0.103) and weakly discriminative across models, motivating our SCI analysis. On the stratified subsample ($n = 1{,}000$), mean SCI was 0.531 (95% bootstrap CI: [0.520, 0.541]), significantly above the shuffled-label baseline (0.475; $Z = +10.0$, $p < 0.001$, $d = +0.32$). The fraction with SCI<0 was 3.2% (32 of 1,000; 95% CI: [2.2%, 4.3%]), stable across resampled subsets (3.1–3.3%). Coherence tiers: 34.2% high (SCI $\geq 0.6$), 62.3% moderate, and 3.2% contradictory. Figure 1 reveals a bimodal distribution (peaks near $\approx 0.6$

and $\approx -0.4$), suggesting two explanation regimes. Per-model differences were notable: Gemini 2.0 showed the lowest incoherence (0.5%) and Grok 3 the highest (6.4%). Incoherence did not cluster by VAA ($\chi^2 = 2.34$, $p = 0.51$) or issue domain ($\chi^2 = 8.12$, $p = 0.15$).

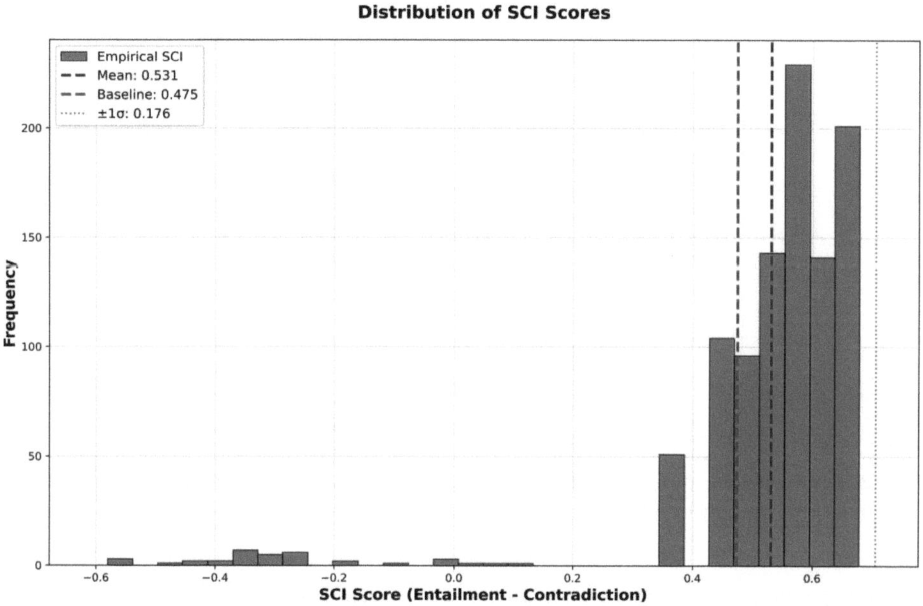


**Fig. 1.** SCI distribution (bimodal): primary peak near $\approx 0.6$ and secondary peak near $\approx -0.4$.

*Issue-Level Orientations.* Figure 2 summarizes Z-score normalized model positioning by policy domain. All models leaned left on economic redistribution, strongly pro-environment, and liberal on social progressivism. EU integration showed the greatest cross-model divergence. Equity-relevant domains revealed systematic cross-national variation: for instance, digital rights scores ranged from −0.52 (Germany) to 1.90 (Netherlands), suggesting unequal civic-learning impacts shaped by VAA design and language-resource factors. Raw mean responses differed by VAA (CZ 1.33, NL 0.98, LU 0.81, DE 0.55), but after Z-score normalization, these differences were effectively eliminated, indicating they largely reflect platform and item design rather than genuine cross-national model bias.

### 4.2 Cross-National VAA Analysis

Party alignment (Table 1) shows three patterns: (i) strongest alignment with Green (68.3%–72.4%), Liberal (63.0%–67.8%), and Social Democratic families

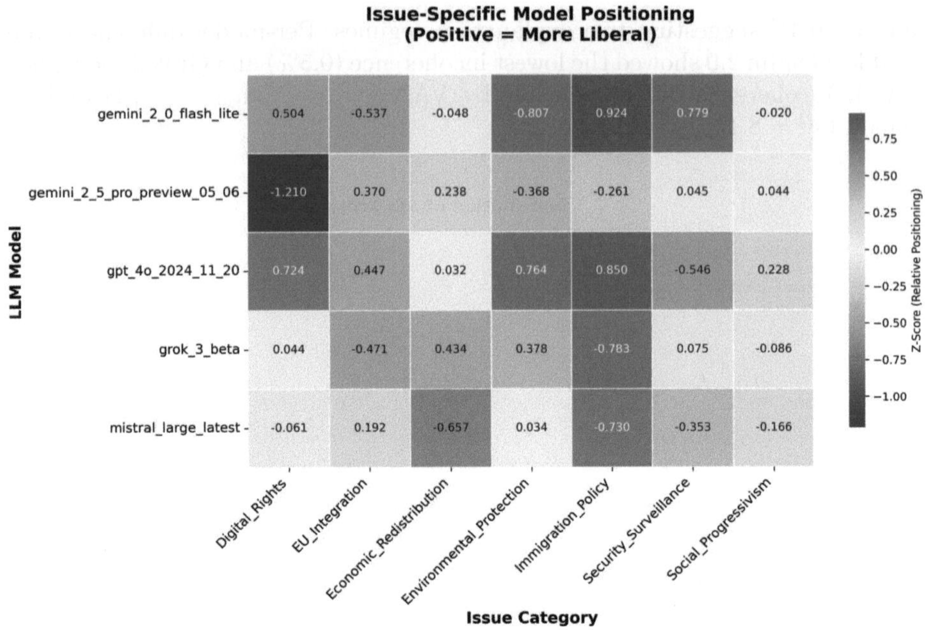


**Fig. 2.** Issue-specific model positioning (Z-score normalized). Positive = more liberal; negative = more conservative.

(55.4%–77.4%); (ii) uniformly low Radical-Right affinity (18.2%–35.3%); and (iii) country-specific variation, with GPT-4o consistently more centrist. An omnibus ANOVA confirmed significant cross-model differences ($F(4, 244) = 15.31$, $p < .001$), with the largest contrasts between GPT-4o and other models ($|d| > 0.9$).

## 5 Discussion

Our results show that the evaluated LLMs are not politically neutral. Across VAAs and countries, most models aligned most strongly with Green, Social Democratic, and pro-EU liberal parties, and showed consistently low affinity with nationalist and far-right parties. These tendencies are context-dependent and should not be treated as stable properties across languages, prompts, or time. Unlike search engines that surface multiple sources, LLMs typically provide a single synthesized response [20,25]. Consistent ideological framing can therefore shape users' beliefs and reduce epistemic diversity, e.g., among users with limited familiarity with local policy contexts, such as recently migrated people [31]. Neutrality is both a technical and normative challenge. Training data embeds human values, making value-free outputs implausible. A key design question is whether models should target a centrist stance or present multiple well-reasoned perspectives.

**Table 1.** Mean party alignment (%) by political family using CHES 2024 classifications. Values are averaged across four VAAs; n/a indicates no party in that category.

| Family | G2.0 | G2.5 | 4o | Grok3 | Mistral |
|---|---|---|---|---|---|
| Radical Left | 57.6 | 46.6 | 20.4 | 56.3 | 53.4 |
| Green | 68.3 | 64.0 | 45.1 | 69.7 | 72.4 |
| Social Dem. | 55.4 | 77.4 | 33.6 | 65.6 | 75.3 |
| Liberal | 66.9 | 63.0 | 47.4 | 67.5 | 67.8 |
| Christian Dem. | 54.1 | 38.5 | 24.2 | 52.9 | n/a |
| Conservative | n/a | 56.0 | 56.8 | 57.2 | 56.4 |
| Radical Right | 35.3 | 19.7 | 18.2 | 29.4 | 23.7 |
| Populist | 43.0 | 29.1 | 40.0 | 42.6 | n/a |
| Regionalist | 34.1 | n/a | 5.2 | 35.4 | n/a |

The SCI analysis reveals that, although most explanations are moderately coherent, the bimodal distribution and a 3.2% contradiction rate indicate a minority of outputs in which reasoning undermines the stated position. Manual inspection suggests that some low-SCI cases reflect limitations of NLI (e.g., hedged explanations). However, genuine contradictions and measurement artifacts can cause similar pedagogical harm. Cross-national variation in raw agreement rates likely reflects VAA design and language-resource differences rather than stable model properties, but translation into English may remove sociopolitical nuance.

For responsible educational deployment, we recommend: (i) displaying coherence indicators and flagging low-SCI outputs; (ii) requiring explicit stance labels rather than relying on sentiment framing; (iii) surfacing uncertainty when reasoning is ambiguous; (iv) disclosing cultural context and translation limits; and (v) conducting regular cross-national audits.

*Limitations.* We evaluated five models at a single time point using four VAAs whose item selection may embed normative assumptions. Forcing categorical responses and mapping to $[-2, 2]$ can obscure nuance. Sentiment-stance match rates depend on the analyzer used, and Z-score normalization yields comparative rather than absolute placement.

*Ethical Considerations.* This study involved no human subjects or interventions in real-world elections. For Smartwielen, we release only derived outputs, consistent with the terms of service [34].

## 6 Conclusion

Our cross-national audit shows that commercial LLMs are not politically neutral and that a non-trivial fraction of their explanations contradict one another. Their stated stances pose risks to civic learning. These issues are compounded by cross-national variation tied to VAA design and language-resource factors, raising equity concerns for educational deployment. Future work should extend this analysis longitudinally, include non-European contexts, and evaluate whether the proposed governance safeguards measurably improve outcomes.

**Acknowledgments.** This work was funded by the "Daimler und Benz Stiftung" grant: Ladenburger Kolleg (Project: KonCheck) and the Centre for Assistance and Participation at Rhine-Waal University of Applied Sciences. The authors used Claude Sonnet 4.6 and Grammarly to revise the text across all sections, correcting typos, grammatical errors, and awkward phrasing.

## References

1. Abdi, H.: Z-scores. Encycl. Meas. Stat. **3**, 1055–1058 (2007)
2. Abed, O., Große-Kampmann, M.: Towards protecting youth from mis-and disinformation. In: Workshop Proceedings of the 19th International AAAI Conference on Web and Social Media (2025). https://doi.org/10.36190/2025.20
3. Anderson, J., et al.: Matching Voters with Parties and Candidates: Voting Advice Applications in Comparative Perspective. ECPR Press (2014)
4. Badyal, N., Jacoby, D., Coady, Y.: Intentional biases in LLM responses. In: 2023 IEEE 14th Annual Ubiquitous Computing, Electronics & Mobile Communication Conference (UEMCON), pp. 0502–0506. IEEE (2023)
5. Brook Weiss, D., Roit, P., Klein, A., Ernst, O., Dagan, I.: QA-align: representing cross-text content overlap by aligning question-answer propositions. In: Moens, M.F., Huang, X., Specia, L., Yih, S.W.T. (eds.) Proceedings of the 2021 Conference on Empirical Methods in Natural Language Processing, pp. 9879–9894. Association for Computational Linguistics, Online and Punta Cana (2021). https://doi.org/10.18653/v1/2021.emnlp-main.778, https://aclanthology.org/2021.emnlp-main.778/
6. Bundeszentrale für Politische Bildung: Wahl-O-Mat 2025 (2025). https://www.wahl-o-mat.de/bundestagswahl2025/app/main_app.html
7. Bundeszentrale für Politische Bildung: Wahl-O-Mat zur Bundestagswahl 2025 übertrifft bisherigen Nutzungsrekord deutlich (2025). https://www.bpb.de/die-bpb/presse/pressemitteilungen/559822/wahl-o-mat-zur-bundestagswahl-2025-uebertrifft-bisherigen-nutzungsrekord-deutlich/
8. De Graaf, J.: The irresistible rise of stemwijzer. Voting advice applications in Europe: the state of the art, pp. 35–46 (2010)
9. Epstein, R., Robertson, R.E.: The search engine manipulation effect (seme) and its possible impact on the outcomes of elections. Proc. Natl. Acad. Sci. **112**(33), E4512–E4521 (2015)
10. European Commission: Areas of EU action (2025). https://commission.europa.eu/about/role/law/areas-eu-action_en
11. Flaxman, S., Goel, S., Rao, J.M.: Filter bubbles, echo chambers, and online news consumption. Public Opin. Q. **80**(S1), 298–320 (2016). https://doi.org/10.1093/poq/nfw006
12. Gekhman, Z., Herzig, J., Aharoni, R., Elkind, C., Szpektor, I.: TrueTeacher: learning factual consistency evaluation with large language models. arXiv preprint arXiv:2305.11171 (2023)

13. Google DeepMind: Gemini Pro (2025). https://deepmind.google/models/gemini/pro/
14. Hartmann, J., Schwenzow, J., Witte, M.: The political ideology of conversational AI: converging evidence on chatGPT's pro-environmental, left-libertarian orientation. arXiv preprint arXiv:2301.01768 (2023)
15. Hutto, C., Gilbert, E.: Vader: a parsimonious rule-based model for sentiment analysis of social media text. In: Proceedings of the International AAAI Conference on Web and Social Media, vol. 8, no. 1, pp. 216–225 (2014). https://doi.org/10.1609/icwsm.v8i1.14550, https://ojs.aaai.org/index.php/ICWSM/article/view/14550
16. Koho Volit: Volební kalkulačka (2025). https://web.archive.org/web/20250825165927/, https://www.volebnikalkulacka.cz/
17. Koray Kavukcuoglu: Gemini 2.0 is now available to everyone (2025). https://blog.google/technology/google-deepmind/gemini-model-updates-february-2025/
18. Laban, P., Schnabel, T., Bennett, P.N., Hearst, M.A.: SummaC: re-visiting NLI-based models for inconsistency detection in summarization. Trans. Assoc. Comput. Linguist. **10**, 163–177 (2022)
19. Lewis, M., et al.: BART: denoising sequence-to-sequence pre-training for natural language generation, translation, and comprehension. arXiv preprint arXiv:1910.13461 (2019)
20. Li, Y., et al.: LLMs trust humans more, that 'sa problem! Unveiling and mitigating the authority bias in retrieval-augmented generation. In: Proceedings of the 63rd Annual Meeting of the Association for Computational Linguistics (Volume 1: Long Papers), pp. 28844–28858 (2025)
21. LMArena.AI: Text arena (2025). https://web.archive.org/web/20250630063319/https://lmarena.ai/leaderboard/text. Ranking
22. Lunardi, R., La Barbera, D., Roitero, K.: The elusiveness of detecting political bias in language models. In: Proceedings of the 33rd ACM International Conference on Information and Knowledge Management, CIKM 2024, pp. 3922–3926. Association for Computing Machinery, New York (2024). https://doi.org/10.1145/3627673.3680002
23. Mistral AI team: Au Large (2024). https://mistral.ai/news/mistral-large
24. Motoki, F., Pinho Neto, V., Rodrigues, V.: More human than human: measuring chatGPT political bias. Public Choice **198**(1), 3–23 (2024)
25. Narayanan Venkit, P., Laban, P., Zhou, Y., Mao, Y., Wu, C.S.: Search engines in the AI era: a qualitative understanding to the false promise of factual and verifiable source-cited responses in LLM-based search. In: Proceedings of the 2025 ACM Conference on Fairness, Accountability, and Transparency, FAccT 2025, pp. 1325–1340. Association for Computing Machinery, New York (2025). https://doi.org/10.1145/3715275.3732089
26. OpenAI: Hello GPT 4o (2024). https://openai.com/de-DE/index/hello-gpt-4o/
27. ProDemos: Recordaantal gebruikers voor stemwijzer: 9,1 miljoen (2023). https://prodemos.nl/nieuws/recordaantal-gebruikers-voor-stemwijzer-91-miljoen/
28. Rettenberger, L., Reischl, M., Schutera, M.: Assessing political bias in large language models. J. Comput. Soc. Sci. **8**(2), 1–17 (2025)
29. Rovny, J., et al.: 25 years of political party positions in Europe: the chapel hill expert survey, 1999-2024. Working Paper (2025)
30. Santurkar, S., Durmus, E., Ladhak, F., Lee, C., Liang, P., Hashimoto, T.: Whose opinions do language models reflect? In: International Conference on Machine Learning, pp. 29971–30004. PMLR (2023)

31. Sharma, N., Liao, Q.V., Xiao, Z.: Generative echo chamber? Effect of LLM-powered search systems on diverse information seeking. In: Proceedings of the 2024 CHI Conference on Human Factors in Computing Systems, pp. 1–17 (2024)
32. StemWijzer: Frequently Asked Questions (2025). https://web.archive.org/web/20250909090414/, https://acc.stemwijzer.nl/frequently-asked-questions/
33. Université du Luxembourg, Foundation Zentrum für politesch Bildung: Méthodologie : smartwielen 2024 (2024). https://web.archive.org/web/20250504083653/, https://smartvote-international.cdn.prismic.io/smartvote-international/Zg0VkMt2UUcvBWb0_smartwielen2024Methodologiematchingfrfinal.pdf
34. Université du Luxembourg, Zentrum fir politesch Bildung: Politique de confidentialité et conditions d'utilisation (2024). https://smartvote-international.cdn.prismic.io/smartvote-international/ZjuErkMTzAJOCope_smartwielen2024Politiquedeconfidentialit%C3%A9etconditionsd%27utilisation.pdf. Terms of Service
35. Wang, Z., Gong, S.Y., Xu, S., Hu, X.E.: Elaborated feedback and learning: examining cognitive and motivational influences. Comput. Educ. **136**, 130–140 (2019)
36. Wieringa, M.: What to account for when accounting for algorithms: a systematic literature review on algorithmic accountability. In: Proceedings of the 2020 Conference on Fairness, Accountability, and Transparency, FAT* 2020, pp. 1–18. Association for Computing Machinery, New York (2020). https://doi.org/10.1145/3351095.3372833
37. Williams, A., Nangia, N., Bowman, S.R.: A broad-coverage challenge corpus for sentence understanding through inference. arXiv preprint arXiv:1704.05426 (2017)
38. X: Grok 3 Beta—The Age of Reasoning Agents (2025). https://x.ai/news/grok-3

# Personalization over Privacy? Implications of the Privacy-Personalization Trade-Off on Future Use of Intelligent Tutoring Systems

Adrienn Toth(✉), Linda Fanconi, Noé Zufferey, and Verena Zimmermann

ETH Zurich, Zurich, Switzerland
{adrienn.toth,linda.fanconi,noe.zufferey,verena.zimmermann}@gess.ethz.ch

**Abstract.** The low adoption of Intelligent Tutoring Systems (ITS) and other AIED tools is partly due to privacy concerns when handling student data. Previous research investigated the privacy-personalization trade-off, where users contrast the envisioned benefits against the amount of personal data required. However, related AIED research is still in its initial stages. We analyzed how usability and privacy-related factors influence university students' decision to adopt one of three versions of an ITS, differing in the amount of data collected and—as a result—the availability and depth of educational features. We found that even though students perceived differences in privacy risk across the versions, this did not influence intention to use. Conversely, perceived usefulness of the ITS and its personalized features proved to be a strong predictor of future adoption. We deepen these findings with qualitative results and conclude with recommendations for AIED researchers and developers.

**Keywords:** Privacy · Usability · Privacy-Personalization Trade-Off

## 1 Introduction

Intelligent Tutoring Systems (ITS) have been proven to have a positive effect on learning outcomes [14], through personalized features such as immediate feedback, scaffolding hints, and evaluation of student skills over time [16]. However, adoption by higher education institutions has been slow and the need to use rich student interaction data raises privacy concerns [23]. These concerns differ greatly between students and contexts [22], and students have varying expectations toward AI in education (AIED) systems and the related amount of data collection [23]. Also, students need to be taught AI literacy [27] for them to exercise agency over their data responsibly [10]. To that end, we present and evaluate a prototype of ITS that provides students with varying educational


E. G. Blanchard et al. (eds.), AIED 2026, LNCS 16586, pp. 327–336, 2027.
https://doi.org/10.1007/978-3-032-29773-0_24

features depending on the amount of data collected. The system also transparently informs users about what data is collected and the features that have been disabled due to limited access to certain data types. Through this feedback, the system aims to enhance transparency and increase users' AI and privacy literacy.

Previous studies based on the Technology Acceptance Model (TAM) [6] showed the importance of perceived usefulness and perceived ease of use as well as risk perception [7] of a system as predictors for future adoption. Specifically, the privacy-personalization trade-off [1] describes how the benefits one could gain from sharing their data can conflict with the related perceived privacy risks. In the field of AIED, studies analyzing student privacy concerns have mainly relied on self-reports from surveys and interviews instead of experimental methods. We aim to fill this gap by exposing students to a first-hand experience with three versions of an ITS prototype differing in the amount of data collected and the availability of certain educational features. Our goal is to understand how students evaluate the usability and the privacy risk of these different versions, as well as which of these factors have an influence on their intention to use each version. Therefore, we defined the following research question: *How do students evaluate the usefulness, ease of use, and perceived privacy risk of different ITS versions requiring more or less user-data collection, and how do these factors affect their intention to use these versions?*

To answer this question, we use Structural Equation Modeling (SEM) to model the assumed relationships. To investigate potential personal factors behind their perceptions, we collected data on personal traits such as technological affinity [8] and general online privacy concerns [15]. Finally, we performed a qualitative analysis of open-ended responses to deepen our understanding of how the privacy-personalization trade-off influences student adoption of AIED tools.

## 2 Background: Privacy in AIED Tools

Ethical and societal aspects of AI, such as privacy, are part of most AI literacy frameworks, but usually portrayed as the last step after acquiring technical and algorithmic knowledge [17]. University students typically expect to exercise agency over data shared with AIED tools [22], however, they often lack the required understanding of responsible personal data management [10,27]. Therefore, we aim to enhance an ITS with design features that make data privacy implications clear through short explanations and enabling or disabling certain features depending on students' willingness to share their data.

Prior work showed that privacy-related decisions not only differ between users, but also depend on contextual factors, such as recipient or data type [18]. In AIED, students also have differing views about the data they are willing to share [22], and how they evaluate the privacy of certain features, which in turn is a significant predictor of their adoption [21]. Both students and faculty consider privacy as important as the analytics aspect of learning analytics [24]. Yet, even though students express a strong desire for data privacy, they do not always act accordingly [24]. This is partly due to the privacy-personalization trade-off [9], referring to the fact that enjoying the benefits of personalization usually means sacrificing part of one's privacy. Prior work explored this trade-off for AIED based on survey and interview data, therefore not exposing participants to an authentic experience where their attitudes regarding data sharing could be observed in a specific context. In our study, users directly interacted with different variants of a prototype that allows for capturing their interaction experience.

The widely used Technology Acceptance Model (TAM) [6] contains two main predictors of future intention to use a system: perceived usefulness and perceived ease of use. Usability studies have expanded the model with the construct of risk perception and found significant relationships between perceived risk and intention to use [7]. Differences in affinity for using new technologies are also considered an important factor in predicting user experience and future use [8], which applies to the educational field [3]. In our study, we thus use and expand the TAM model with the following constructs: perceived privacy risk, general online privacy concerns, and technological affinity.

## 3 Methods

We conducted in-person lab sessions, with $N = 126$ university students, during which they were asked to use different versions of an ITS prototype. Supplementary materials (i.e., screenshots, codebooks, participant demographics, and detailed results) can be found online. Our study has been approved by the Ethics Committee of our institution, and preregistered.

**The ITS Prototype.** The prototype used for the study was based on CTAT - short for Cognitve Tutor Authoring Tools [25]. We created three versions with adaptations in data collection and the availability of educational features:

- **Tutor A:** This version only recorded essential data from students that let the system operate, such as correctness of answers. Also, students could request a hint for a task, but no additional educational features were enabled.
- **Tutor B:** Tutor B additionally collected and saved data about the development of student's skills, such as *identifying trends.* The hint feature was more customizable, allowing the student to select the preferred type of hint.
- **Tutor C:** Tutor C further contained a chatbot with access to the student's previous interaction to provide personalized support. The chatbot was prompted to provide relevant guidance instead of direct solutions.

For students to understand how the educational features and privacy implications of each version differ, we adopted the same screen structure for all versions. Disabled features (e.g., disabled LLM chatbot in Tutor A) were covered by a short text explaining the reason for disabling it. For our study, we used educational tasks related to visualization literacy. The questions followed the structure of the Visualization Literacy Assessment Test [13]. Each task consisted of one graph along with three to four related questions (multiple choice or short-text answer) that tested students' ability to interpret the graph based on the three levels of graph comprehension by Curcio [5], namely *read the data, read between the data*, and *read beyond the data*, followed by an open-ended question asking them to describe the graph's main insights in 50–100 words. An example task across the three versions is shown in Fig. 1.

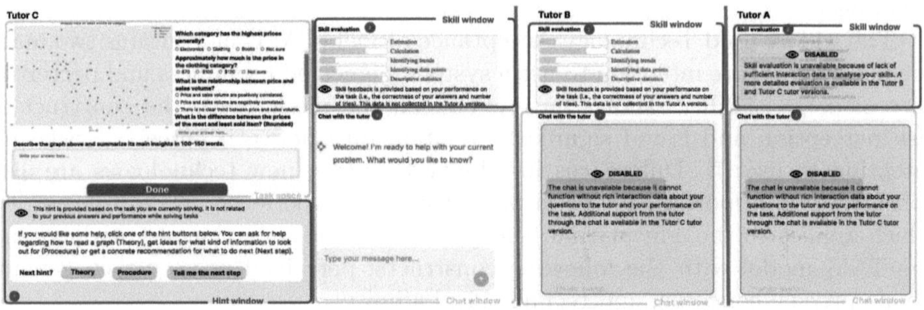


**Fig. 1.** An illustration of the three tutor versions. Features on the right depend on the available student data. Hint window (1): The students received pre-written hints that help them interpret the graph. Skill feedback (2): Disabled in Tutor A. In Tutors B and C, it provides feedback based on task performance. Chat window (3): Disabled in Tutors A and B. Tutor C uses GenAI to provide additional support. The privacy implications are explained in dedicated information boxes (marked with an eye sign).

**Recruitment.** The sample consisted of $N = 126$ bachelor students enrolled at ETH Zurich or University of Zurich. The minimum sample size was determined based on a simulation with estimated effect sizes between .15-.35 for all paths, alpha error probability of .05 and power of .8. Among participants, 75 were men, 49 women, one non-binary participant, and one preferred not to disclose their gender. The average age was 21.3 (SD = 2.8), ranging from 18 to 35 years. Every participant was compensated CHF 25 per hour.

**Procedure.** The experiment took place in person at our institution's lab. First, students (1) interacted with one of the tutor versions by solving a visualization literacy task, directly followed by (2) a survey asking them about their experience with that version using validated questionnaires and open-ended questions. We measured the following constructs: Perceived Usefulness (PU) [6], Perceived Ease of Use (PEoU) [6], Perceived Privacy Risk (PPR) [2], and Intention to Use (ItU) [26]. Additionally, participants answered three open-ended questions, namely (Q1) what they liked or disliked about the version at hand, (Q2) the types of data they think was collected about them, and (Q3) whether and in what context they think they would use that ITS version in the future. Steps (1) and (2) were repeated for each of the three tutor versions. Finally, (3) participants completed a final survey with additional questionnaires related to online privacy concerns (IUIPC) [15], technological affinity (ATI) [8], and provided demographic information. Students were assigned to one of two groups: interacting with the versions in "increasing" (Version A→B→C) (N = 62) or "decreasing". (Version C→B→A) order (n = 64).

### 3.1 Analysis

We used Multilevel Structural Equation Modeling (MLSEM), where Level 1 (within-subjects) represents the interactions with different tutor versions and Level 2 (between-subjects) represents the individual students. Level 1 variables are therefore those measured by the three version-related surveys, and Level 2 variables were those measured in the exit survey. Figure 2 summarizes the path analysis of the MLSEM model on both the within- and between-subjects level.

**Data preparation.** Univariate normality was assessed using skewness and kurtosis; all items fell within acceptable ranges (skewness ⊥2, kurtosis ⊥7; [11]) except for one item (awa1 of the IUIPC). This item was not removed from the dataset due to being part of a validated scale. To evaluate the necessity of a multilevel approach, we calculated the Intraclass Correlation Coefficients (ICCs) for all Level 1 items. The ICCs ranged from .22 to .50, indicating that a relevant proportion of the total variance (22%50%) was at the between-subjects level. These values exceed the common threshold of .05 or .10 for multilevel modeling [12], confirming that MLSEM was required to account for the nested structure of the data. We additionally performed Multilevel Confirmatory Factor Analysis (MCFA) to verify the construct validity of our measures.

**Model Specification.** The outcome variable in our model was ItU as our goal was to understand how (perceived) usefulness and privacy concerns influence students' decision to use an ITS. Based on our hypotheses, PU, PEoU, and PPR were modeled as predictors of ItU. Based on previous research [28], we also modeled PU as a mediator between PEoU and ItU. In terms of the between-subjects variables, we expected the effect of ATI on ItU to be mediated by PU and PEoU. Similarly, the effect of IUIPC was expected to be mediated by PRR. We used the R lavaan package [19] to perform our analysis. Because one item exceeded the skewness threshold, we used the Robust Maximum Likelihood (MLR) estimator in our MLSEM, which is robust to non-normality.

**Qualitative Analysis.** We analyzed answers to open-ended questions using an inductive thematic analysis approach [4]. The qualitative answers were analyzed by two of the authors. For Q1 and Q3 (i.e., what they liked/disliked about the tool, and if they intended to use it), the authors started coding 10% of the dataset. The two created codebooks were then compared, and the researchers agreed on the final code structure. Finally, the researchers independently coded the full dataset, after which interrater reliability was calculated. Remaining disagreements were solved through discussion.

## 4 Results

**Factor Analysis.** Construct validity was assessed via a two-level MCFA. On Level 1 (within-subjects level), all items exhibited significant loadings on their respective constructs ($p < .001$). On Level 2 (between-subjects level), the measurement model for individual traits (ATI and IUIPC) was similarly supported. The factor loadings of IUIPC show that only the *Collection* subscale (items 710) achieved acceptable factor loadings (¿.7). We thus decided to only include the four *Collection* items in the final model.

**Model Fit.** The MLSEM yielded a good fit to the data (Robust CFI = .944; Robust TLI = .939; Robust RMSEA = .035). The SRMR was .093 at the within-subjects level and .171 at the between-subjects level.

**Within-Subjects Paths (Level 1).** At the within-subjects level, which captures different perceptions across tutor versions, *PU* was a strong and significant predictor of *ItU* ($\beta = .75, p < .001$). Whereas the direct path from *PEoU* to *ItU* was not significant ($\beta = .03, p = .738$), *PEoU* demonstrated a significant influence on *ItU* indirectly by significantly predicting *PU* ($\beta = .77, p < .001$). The path from *PPR* to *ItU* was not significant ($p > .05$), suggesting that perceptions of privacy risk do not influence intention to use different ITS versions.

**Between-Subjects Paths (Level 2).** At the between-subjects level, which captures differences between individual students, the pattern for *ItU* remained consistent: *PU* strongly predicted *ItU* ($\beta = .81, p < .001$), accounting for 72.6% of the variance in *ItU* ($R^2 = .726$). Similar to the within-level results, trait-level *PEoU* significantly predicted trait-level *PU* ($\beta = .43, p = .020$). Also in line with the within-subjects model, *PPR* did not prove to be a significant predictor of *ItU* on the trait level either. Interestingly, the direct paths of technological affinity (ATI) and data collection concerns (IUIPC Collection) did not reach statistical significance ($p > .05$), suggesting that the immediate perceptions of the tutor (*PU* and *PEoU*) are more important drivers of adoption than personal traits.

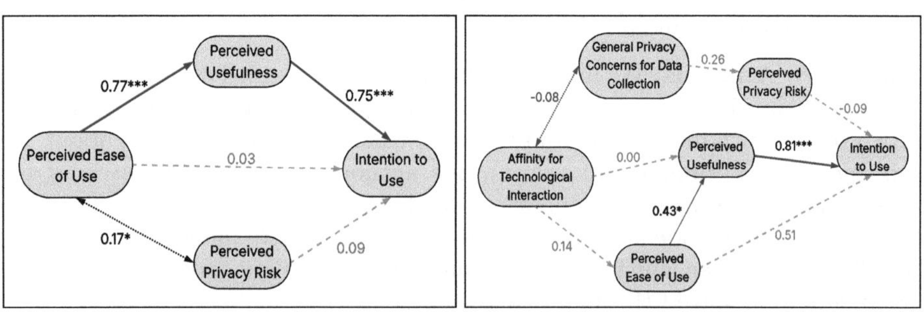


*$p < 0.05$, **$p < 0.01$, ***$p < 0.001$

**Fig. 2.** Results of the MLSEM model on the within- and between-subjects level.

**Exploratory Analysis.** To investigate (1) how *PPR* differed across tutor versions, and (2) whether the second-order groups demonstrated any unintended significant differences when rating Level 1 items we conducted ANOVAs with *Version* and *Order* as predictors. For *PU*, *PEoU*, and *ItU*, only the effect of *Version* proved to be significant, while in the case of *PPR*, both the effects of *Version* and *Order* were significant. The significant effect of *Order* was due to the group starting with Tutor A demonstrating generally higher privacy concerns towards all versions (see Fig. 1 in Supplementary Material). Our analysis also shows that participants of both groups clearly perceived an increasing privacy risk from Tutor A to C as intended with the prototype design.

**Qualitative Results.** All key results are summarized in detail in the online materials. The valence of the responses provided for Q1, i.e., what students liked/disliked, was slightly more often positive (n = 109) than negative (n = 95), and often mixed (n = 127) due to the dual nature of the question. Another n = 47 were neutral or unclear responses. Tutor A received 31 positive responses, Tutor B received 38, and Tutor C received 40, which aligns with the questionnaire scores. This may be due to the availability of the chatbot, e.g., *"The three tips [...] weren't very helpful, while the LLM agent did provide some useful insight."*. The most commonly mentioned aspects that students liked/disliked were the *educational features* (n = 217) and the *User Interface (UI)* (n = 128), with the former being mentioned more often in a positive light (66 positive and 87 mixed), while the UI was more often associated with negative responses (40 negative and 70 mixed). Other popular categories were the *educational content* (n = 78), *usefulness/functionality* (n = 72) and *understandability* (n = 48).

Regarding Q2 (data types students think have been collected), most responses mentioned *educational data*, such as results and skills (n = 259), followed by interaction data, such as clicks (n = 190), e.g., *"It did not collect personal information, it only collected my understanding and reading of the provided graph."* (about Tutor C). All other data types were mentioned less frequently: personally identifiable data 33 times, contextual data (such as date, time, location) 30 times, and personal characteristics (such as style of writing) 29 times.

Responses to Q3 show that students would be interested in using at least one of the tutor versions for their studies. The most frequently mentioned use case for the tutor was *independent studying* (N = 73), with many (N = 62) mentioning that they would only use it for *specific subjects* (mainly mathematics or statistics) or *exam preparation* (N = 35). A lot of participants who answered negatively did not provide additional explanation, but one common reply indicated low expected *effectiveness* (N = 45) from the tool.

## 5 Discussion and Conclusion

Our study investigated how university students' intention to use ITS differs based on the privacy-personalization trade-off when presented with multiple ITS versions. We found that even though students are clearly aware of the differences between versions in terms of privacy risk, this does not predict their intention to use a specific version in the future, which aligns with a recent related study [20]. The main aspect influencing students' intended adoption is how useful they perceive a specific version of the tool. We additionally found that perceived ease of use is a predictor of perceived usefulness, which is in line with other findings from usability research [6,28]. Based on our findings, we conclude the following:

**Perceived Usefulness is the Key to Motivate Students to Use AIED.** Both our model and our qualitative results prove the importance of the tool's effectiveness and the quality of the provided educational features. In contrast, data privacy was rarely mentioned as a deciding factor for future use. It is therefore important to make students aware of the educational benefits - while still designing with privacy and other ethical aspects in mind - when the goal is to motivate future adoption.

**Transparent Privacy-Related Feedback and First-Hand Experience** with an ITS support students' **awareness of the data collection implications** of using its personalized educational features. Participants clearly associated a higher privacy risk with tutor versions that collected more data. When asking them to list the types of data they think the system has access to, most of them thought of those directly identifiable from the screen, such as educational and interaction data. Whereas this is definitely a first step toward successful user notice, the privacy-related feedback should ideally be complemented with additional AI and digital literacy training.

Finally, the **responsibility to ensure student privacy remains with AIED designers**, even if student agency is supported by a system. We saw that user experience and learning benefits are enough for students to sacrifice their data privacy, even when they associate privacy risks with an ITS. AIED designers should thus minimize the privacy-personalization trade-off.

## References


1. Awad, N., Krishnan, M.: The personalization privacy paradox: an empirical evaluation of information transparency and the willingness to be profiled online for personalization. MIS Q. (2006). https://doi.org/10.2307/25148715
2. Ayalon, O., Toch, E.: Evaluating users' perceptions about a system's privacy: differentiating social and institutional aspects. In: SOUPS 2019. USENIX Association (2019). https://www.usenix.org/conference/soups2019/presentation/ayalon
3. Bahari, M., Arpaci, I., Azmi, N.F.M., Shuib, L.: Predicting the intention to use learning analytics for academic advising in higher education. Sustainability (2023). https://doi.org/10.3390/su152115190
4. Braun, V., Clarke, V.: Reflecting on reflexive thematic analysis. Qual. Res. Sport, Exerc. Health (2019). https://doi.org/10.1080/2159676X.2019.1628806
5. Curcio, F.R.: Comprehension of mathematical relationships expressed in graphs. J. Res. Math. Educ. (1987). https://doi.org/10.2307/749086
6. Davis, F.D.: Perceived usefulness, perceived ease of use, and user acceptance of information technology. MIS Q. (1989). https://doi.org/10.2307/249008
7. Featherman, M.S., Pavlou, P.A.: Predicting e-services adoption: a perceived risk facets perspective. Int. J. Hum Comput Stud. (2003). https://doi.org/10.1016/S1071-5819(03)00111-3

8. Franke, T., Attig, C., Wessel, D.: A personal resource for technology interaction: Development and validation of the affinity for technology interaction (ATI) scale. Int. J. Hum. Comput. Interact. (2019). https://doi.org/10.1080/10447318.2018.1456150
9. Garcia-Rivadulla, S.: Personalization vs. privacy: an inevitable trade-off? IFLA J. (2016). https://doi.org/10.1177/0340035216662890
10. Greenhalgh, S.P., DiGiacomo, D.K., Barriage, S.: Platforms, perceptions, and privacy: ethical implications of student conflation of educational technologies. ILS (2023). https://doi.org/10.1108/ILS-03-2023-0030
11. Hair, J.F., Jr., Black, W.C., Babin, B.J., Anderson, R.E.: Multivariate Data Analysis, 7th edn. Pearson Prentice Hall, Upper Saddle River (2010)
12. Hox, J.J., Moerbeek, M., van de Schoot, R.: Multilevel Analysis: Techniques and Applications. 3rd edn. (2017). https://doi.org/10.4324/9781315650982
13. Lee, S., Kim, S.H., Kwon, B.C.: Vlat: development of a visualization literacy assessment test. IEEE Trans. Vis. Comput. Graph. (2017). https://doi.org/10.1109/TVCG.2016.2598920
14. Létourneau, A., Deslandes Martineau, M., Charland, P., Skelling-Desmeules, Y., Lepage, V.: A systematic review of AI-driven intelligent tutoring systems (ITS) in K-12 education. Sci. Learn. (2025). https://doi.org/10.1038/s41539-025-00320-7
15. Malhotra, N.K., Kim, S.S., Agarwal, J.: Internet users' information privacy concerns (IUIPC): the construct, the scale, and a causal model. ISR (2004). https://doi.org/10.1287/isre.1040.0032
16. Mousavinasab, E., Zarifsanaiey, N., Niakan Kalhori, S.R., Rakhshan, M., Keikha, L., Ghazi Saeedi, M.: Intelligent tutoring systems: a systematic review of characteristics, applications, and evaluation methods. Int. Learn. Envir. (2021). https://doi.org/10.1080/10494820.2018.1558257
17. Nahar, N., Howard, D., Akeren, K., Ngele, E., Hollins, P., Prescott, G.: Cultivating ai literacy in higher education students: a four-step conceptual framework. In: AIED. Springer, Cham (2025). https://doi.org/10.1007/978-3-031-98420-4_2
18. Nissenbaum, H.: A Contextual Approach to Privacy Online. Daedalus (2011). https://doi.org/10.1162/DAED_a_00113
19. Rosseel, Y.: lavaan: an R package for structural equation modeling. J. Stat. Softw. (2012). https://doi.org/10.18637/jss.v048.i02
20. Rücker, M.T., Büchting, C., Kosch, T.: Understanding the effect of risk perception on the acceptance and use of large language models among university students. ACM Hum.-Comput. Interact. (2025). https://doi.org/10.1145/3757693
21. Schumacher, C., Ifenthaler, D.: Features students really expect from learning analytics. Comput. Human Behav. (2018). https://doi.org/10.1016/j.chb.2017.06.030
22. Stinar, F., Bosch, N.: Surveying contextualized student data sharing preferences for educational ai. In: AIED 2025. Springer, Cham (2025). https://doi.org/10.1007/978-3-031-98417-4_25
23. Toth, A., Roch, N., Zufferey, N., Zimmermann, V.: "i would share it, but..." exploring ways to optimize the privacy-personalization trade-off in intelligent tutoring systems. In: AIED. Springer, Cham (2025). https://doi.org/10.1007/978-3-031-98462-4_9
24. Tsai, Y.S., Whitelock-Wainwright, A., Gašević, D.: The privacy paradox and its implications for learning analytics. In: Lak 2020. LAK 2020, ACM (2020). https://doi.org/10.1145/3375462.3375536
25. University, C.M.: Cognitive Tutor Authoring Tools (CTAT) (2025). https://www.cmu.edu/simon/open-simon/toolkit/tools/learning-tools/ctat.html

26. Venkatesh, V., Morris, M.G., Davis, G.B., Davis, F.D.: User acceptance of information technology: toward a unified view1. MIS Q. **27**(3) (2003). https://doi.org/10.2307/30036540
27. Vincoli, M., Scholz, N., Nagashima, T.: Multidimensional student agency in learning with ai: a conceptual framework and design implications. In: AIED 2025. Springer, Cham (2025). https://doi.org/10.1007/978-3-031-98459-4_16
28. Xue, L., Mahat, J., Ghazali, N., Shi, X.: Technology acceptance model (TAM) in artificial intelligence in higher education (AIHED): a systematic literature review. J. Inst. Res. South East Asia (2025). https://doi.org/10.1177/21582440251409441

# Introducing Adolescents to the Social Dimensions of AI Through Story-Driven Game-Based Learning

Jessica Vandenberg[1(✉)], Bradford Mott[1], Carlos Penilla[2], James Lester[1], and Elizabeth Ozer[2]

[1] North Carolina State University, Raleigh, NC, USA
{jvanden2,bwmott,lester}@ncsu.edu
[2] University of California, San Francisco, CA, USA
{Carlos.Penilla,Elizabeth.Ozer}@ucsf.edu

**Abstract.** AI increasingly shapes high-stakes decisions in domains such as education and healthcare, underscoring the importance of engaging K–12 students in AI literacy experiences that foreground societal dimensions of AI, including fairness, bias, and accountability. This paper presents a story-driven, game-based learning environment designed to support middle school students' reasoning about these societal dimensions. In the game, students take on the role of decision-makers evaluating AI models in simulated clinical scenarios, navigating trade-offs between accuracy, training data representativeness, and model appropriateness for specific populations. We report findings from a classroom-based pilot study with adolescents (ages 11–14) examining how students engaged with issues of fairness, bias, and accountability during the intervention. Data sources included brief pre/post knowledge assessments and attitudinal surveys. Results suggest that participation was associated with improvements in students' understanding of AI-supported decision-making and shifts toward more critical perspectives on AI capabilities and limitations. Given the short duration of the intervention and the modest scope of the assessment measures, these findings should be interpreted as preliminary. Nonetheless, this work provides early evidence that narrative-centered, game-based approaches can support student engagement with the societal dimensions of AI and offers design insights for integrating ethical reasoning into classroom-based AI learning experiences.

**Keywords:** AI Literacy · Algorithmic Fairness · Bias and Equity · Responsible AI · Societal Impacts of AI

## 1 Introduction

AI systems increasingly shape high-stakes decisions in domains such as healthcare, education, finance, and public services, raising persistent concerns about fairness, bias, and accountability [2,7,29]. While these systems offer benefits


E. G. Blanchard et al. (eds.), AIED 2026, LNCS 16586, pp. 337–345, 2027.
https://doi.org/10.1007/978-3-032-29773-0_25

in efficiency and scale, they also introduce risks when applied to populations that are unevenly represented in training data or whose needs differ from those assumed during system design [2,7,13]. These concerns have prompted calls for AI education that extends beyond technical understanding to include critical examination of how AI systems are designed, whose values they reflect, and who may be disadvantaged by their use [14,24].

Despite this shift, K–12 AI education continues to emphasize conceptual understanding of AI mechanisms, such as classification and training data, with fewer opportunities for students to engage with societal and ethical questions surrounding AI use [4,19]. As a result, students may learn how AI works without developing the capacity to critically evaluate when and how AI systems should be trusted, questioned, or constrained.

To address this gap, we situate learning within a healthcare context, where AI systems increasingly support diagnosis and treatment decisions [25]. This domain provides a high-stakes and personally meaningful setting in which issues of bias, model fit, and potential harm are especially salient [2,7]. We present a story-driven, game-based learning environment in which students act as decision-makers evaluating AI models in simulated clinical scenarios and navigating trade-offs among accuracy, data representativeness, and potential harm. We report findings from a classroom-based study examining how this experience supports adolescents' reasoning about fairness, bias, and responsible AI use.

## 2 Related Work

Research on AI literacy has evolved from focusing on how AI systems work and how users interact with them [14,26] to emphasizing ethical, societal, and critical perspectives [15,24,29], including fairness, bias, transparency, and accountability [9,12]. However, reviews of K–12 AI education indicate that many instructional approaches continue to prioritize conceptual understanding of AI mechanisms, with limited opportunities for students to engage with ethical trade-offs or societal consequences [4,19]. This gap highlights the need for learning environments that integrate societal reasoning directly into students' interactions with AI systems.

Game-based and narrative-centered learning environments offer opportunities to engage learners in complex decision-making by situating them in interactive, role-based contexts [8,18,23]. Prior work has shown that such environments can support engagement with trade-offs and consequences across domains including medicine and civic education [10,21], often leveraging interactivity to surface constraints and competing priorities [3]. In AI education, interactive tools have supported understanding of concepts such as data imbalance and model limitations [28,30,31], though many emphasize technical inspection rather than ethical judgment or societal critique.

This work is grounded in a sociotechnical perspective that conceptualizes AI systems as shaped by human decisions about data, modeling, and deployment within social and institutional contexts. From this perspective, issues such as bias and fairness are understood as outcomes of design choices rather than isolated technical failures [2]. Complementing this view, responsible AI frameworks emphasize principles such as fairness, transparency, and harm reduction in the development and use of AI systems [7,27]. Together, these perspectives suggest that meaningful AI literacy involves engaging learners in reasoning about trade-offs, uncertainty, and the societal consequences of AI-driven decisions [15], which we operationalize by positioning students as decision-makers evaluating AI models in context.

## 3 AI4HEALTH Learning Environment

### 3.1 Design Goals

AI4HEALTH is a story-driven game-based learning environment intended to scaffold adolescents' AI literacy while also broadening awareness of health and biomedical careers [17]. Built in Unity 3D and deployed via WebGL, the browser-based game is compatible with common school devices, including Chromebooks, tablets, and desktop computers. Players assume the role of an intern at a fictional medical research center, where they interact with physicians, fellow interns, patients, and caregivers while investigating health-related cases using AI-supported tools (Fig. 1).

The design of AI4HEALTH is grounded in social cognitive theory [1,20]. Narrative features, such as emotionally engaging storylines, branching dialogue, and ethical dilemmas, are used to scaffold self-efficacy, shape outcome expectations, and encourage reflection. The design also draws on established AI literacy frameworks that emphasize conceptual understanding, critical evaluation, and human–AI interaction rather than procedural mastery alone [14,26].

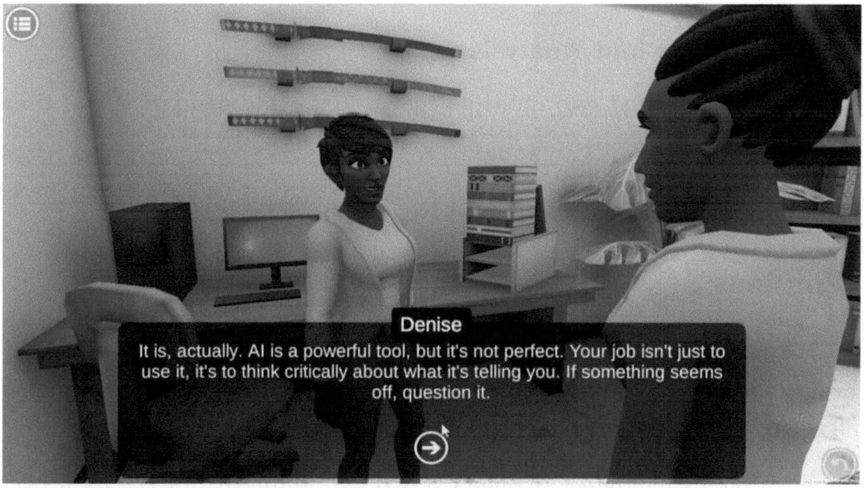


**Fig. 1.** NPC guiding the student's role and emphasizing critical evaluation of AI outputs in the AI4HEALTH story-driven learning environment.

### 3.2 Game Narrative and Mechanics

AI4HEALTH situates learners in a clinical scenario involving a patient with unexplained respiratory distress. A central activity requires students to evaluate AI models used to analyze lung X-ray images, comparing models trained on different datasets (e.g., adult, pediatric, environmental exposure cases). Through these comparisons, students engage with key concepts including bias, generalization, and model limitations, while considering the role of human judgment in high-stakes decision-making. Players receive feedback based on their choices and encounter reflection prompts that encourage them to justify decisions and consider uncertainty, data representativeness, and potential harm. Reflection is embedded throughout gameplay via dialogue and decision-making moments rather than separate activities. For example, during onboarding, characters establish ethical accountability as a normative aspect of professional AI use, explicitly encouraging students to question AI outputs, recognize system limitations, and attend to the role of training data.

## 4 Study Design and Methods

### 4.1 Participants and Procedure

Participants were 23 seventh-grade students from two Career and Technical Education middle school classrooms in the Southeastern United States. The study was conducted during regularly scheduled class time and led by members of the research team. Students completed a pre-assessment, participated in a brief introduction to AI concepts, played the game for approximately 30 min, and then completed a post-assessment, all approved by the university institutional review board (IRB).

### 4.2 Data Sources and Analysis

The assessment included two multiple-choice items addressing societal dimensions of AI and three Likert-scale attitudinal items. Paired $t$-tests were conducted on knowledge items, and descriptive analyses were used to examine changes in student attitudes.

## 5 Findings

### 5.1 Knowledge Gains Related to Societal Considerations

Regarding the item "Why is it important to choose the best AI model when analyzing medical images?", a paired-samples $t$-test suggested improvements from pre-test ($M = 0.7$, $SD = 0.5$) to post-test ($M = 1.0$, $SD = 0.2$), $t(22) = 2.3$, $p =$ .030, indicating a small effect (Cohen's $d = 0.48$). Similarly, for the item "What is the doctor's role when using an AI system to analyze X-ray scans?", results showed a significant increase from pre-test ($M = 0.7$, $SD = 0.5$) to post-test

($M = 0.9$, $SD = 0.3$), $t(22) = 2.5$, $p = .022$, corresponding to a medium effect (Cohen's $d = 0.52$).

Together, these results suggest that participation in the intervention supported students' developing understanding of the role of human judgment, model selection, and responsibility in AI-supported decision-making. However, given the limited number of assessment items, these results should be interpreted as indicative rather than comprehensive measures of students' understanding of the societal dimensions of AI.

### 5.2 Attitudinal Shifts Toward Responsible AI Use

Students responded to three items designed to capture aspects of their reasoning about data dependence, model fallibility, and the role of AI in decision-making. Figure 2 summarizes pre/post changes across all three of these items. For each item, students showed a directional shift away from neutral or disagreeing positions toward stronger agreement with statements aligned with responsible AI use. For **Item 1** (Fig. 2a), neutral responses decreased substantially following the intervention, accompanied by increases in both agree and strongly agree responses. This pattern suggests strengthened recognition of the importance of task-appropriate training data. For **Item 2** (Fig. 2b), disagreement was eliminated entirely in the post-survey, with corresponding increases in strong agreement, indicating increased awareness that AI models can produce errors when trained on inappropriate or unrepresentative data. For **Item 3** (Fig. 2c), responses reflected a shift away from strong disagreement and toward greater endorsement of the view that AI should support, rather than replace, human decision-making, though neutral responses remained stable.

These attitudinal shifts suggest that the intervention supported students in developing more nuanced and critical perspectives on AI's capabilities, limitations, and appropriate role in high-stakes contexts. Although these trends are encouraging, the small number of items and the descriptive nature of these analyses limit the strength of the conclusions that may be drawn from these findings.

## 6 Discussion

This study provides preliminary evidence that narrative-centered, game-based learning environments can support adolescents in reasoning about the societal dimensions of AI. Even within a brief classroom intervention, students demonstrated shifts in how they conceptualize AI systems, particularly in recognizing the role of data, context, and human judgment in shaping AI behavior.

### 6.1 Sociotechnical Reasoning in Context

Findings suggest that adolescents can begin to view AI systems as sociotechnical rather than neutral or objective tools when ethical considerations are embedded within applied, story-driven contexts. Students more frequently recognized that

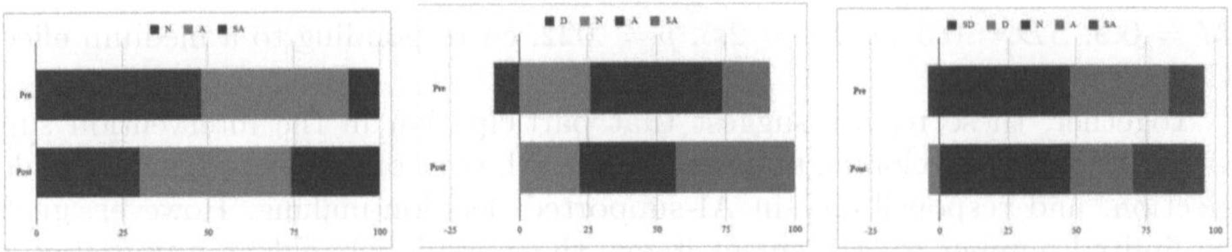

(a) AI learns from data and works best when trained on task-relevant examples (b) AI models can make mistakes when trained on inappropriate data (c) AI should support, not replace, human decision-making

**Fig. 2.** Pre/post shifts in students' attitudes toward data dependence, model fallibility, and the role of AI in decision-making.

AI model behavior depends on human decisions related to data selection, training context, and deployment population, aligning with sociotechnical perspectives that frame AI systems as shaped by social values and institutional practices [5]. Their reasoning about fairness and bias reflected an emerging understanding that disparities in AI performance often arise from misalignment between training data and real-world use contexts rather than isolated technical failures [2].

The narrative-centered structure of the environment supported this reasoning by positioning learners in consequential decision-making roles. By framing AI-related choices as value-laden and socially meaningful, the game connected abstract concepts to human outcomes, reinforcing prior work suggesting that narrative contexts can deepen engagement and sensemaking [16,22]. These findings extend prior AI education work that has emphasized system mechanics and transparency [14,26] by demonstrating that adolescents can engage with concepts that reflect responsibility, harm, and accountability when these ideas are grounded in applied scenarios.

### 6.2 Design and Equity Implications

These findings suggest several implications for the design of AI literacy experiences. First, integrating fairness and bias into core gameplay mechanics can support coherent reasoning about AI systems by foregrounding differences in training data and performance across contexts, reinforcing the idea that no single model is universally "best" [27]. Second, role-based, applied decision-making can enable meaningful engagement with societal dimensions of AI without requiring extensive technical background, supporting broader participation in AI education.

At the same time, important considerations remain. While the game's browser-based design supports accessibility across common school devices, disparities in instructional time, teacher support, and curricular alignment may influence how students experience and benefit from such interventions [6,11]. Additionally, while the healthcare context provides a compelling entry point for discussing harm and responsibility, careful instructional framing is needed to ensure students interpret AI limitations appropriately [10] and recognize shared accountability among designers, deployers, and users [7]. Future work should examine how facilitation strategies and learning contexts shape students' evolving understandings of fairness, trust, and responsibility in AI systems.

## 7 Limitations

The findings should be interpreted in light of several limitations. **First**, the study involved a small sample of middle school students within a single instructional context, limiting generalizability across settings, age groups, and curricular structures. Future work should examine how similar interventions function in more diverse educational environments. **Second**, the study captured only short-term changes in students' knowledge and attitudes toward societal dimensions of AI. While statistically significant gains were observed, the durability of these outcomes and their transfer to new contexts remain unclear. Longitudinal research is needed to examine how students' reasoning about AI evolves over time. **Third**, the healthcare scenario represents a single domain in which AI systems operate. Students' reasoning about fairness and responsibility may differ across contexts such as education, criminal justice, or environmental monitoring. Expanding to multiple domains would support broader comparisons of reasoning. **Finally**, the assessment instruments were limited in scope, consisting of only two knowledge items and three attitudinal measures. As a result, they do not fully capture the complexity of students' reasoning about the societal dimension of AI. Future work should employ more comprehensive and validated measures.

## 8 Conclusion

This work presents a story-driven game-based learning environment designed to support adolescents' understanding of the societal dimensions of AI. The findings provide initial evidence that even brief classroom-based experiences can prompt students to engage with questions of fairness, bias, and accountability in AI systems. Furthermore, the results suggest that narrative-centered, role-based gameplay can support students in viewing AI systems as sociotechnical constructs shaped by human choices, data practices, and contextual constraints. By engaging learners in applied decision-making and ethical reflection, AI4Health moves beyond presenting AI as an abstract or infallible technology and instead positions it as a system whose use demands judgment, accountability, and care. Importantly, the results indicate that such reasoning is accessible to adolescents when supported through thoughtfully designed learning environments.

This work highlights the potential of story-driven game-based approaches to advance societal AI education in classroom-compatible ways. Designing for accessibility and ethical and critical reflection can help broaden participation in AI literacy while preparing students to engage thoughtfully with AI systems that increasingly shape educational, medical, and civic domains. Taken together, this study represents an early step toward designing and studying learning environments that support critical, socially grounded AI literacy in K–12 contexts.

**Acknowledgments.** Research reported in this publication was supported by the National Institute of General Medical Sciences of the National Institutes of Health under award number R25GM154357. The content is solely the responsibility of the authors and does not necessarily represent the official views of the National Institutes of Health. Additional support was provided by the Health Resources and Services Administration (HRSA) of the U.S. Department of Health and Human Services (HHS) under cooperative agreements U8DMC45901. This information or content and conclusions are those of the author(s) and should not be construed as the official position or policy of, nor should any endorsements be inferred by HRSA, HHS or the U.S. Government.

**Disclosure of Interests.** The authors have no competing interests to declare that are relevant to the content of this article.

## References

1. Bandura, A.: Social cognitive theory: an agentic perspective. Annu. Rev. Psychol. **52**(1), 1–26 (2001)
2. Barocas, S., Hardt, M., Narayanan, A.: Fairness and Machine Learning (2019). fairmlbook.org
3. Bogost, I.: Persuasive Games: The Expressive Power of Videogames. MIT Press (2007)
4. Casal-Otero, L., Catala, A., Fernández-Morante, C., Taboada, M., Cebreiro, B., Barro, S.: AI literacy in K-12: a systematic literature review. Int. J. STEM Educ. **10**(29), 1–17 (2023)
5. Diakopoulos, N.: Accountability in algorithmic decision making. Commun. ACM **59**(2), 56–62 (2016)
6. Eubanks, V.: Automating Inequality: How High-Tech Tools Profile, Police, and Punish the Poor. St. Martin's Press (2018)
7. Floridi, L., Cowls, J., Beltrametti, M., et al.: AI4People: an ethical framework for a good AI society. Mind. Mach. **28**(4), 689–707 (2018)
8. Gee, J.P.: What Video Games Have to Teach Us About Learning and Literacy. Palgrave Macmillan (2007)
9. Giovanelli, A., et al.: Supporting adolescent engagement with artificial intelligence-driven digital health behavior change interventions. J. Med. Internet Res. **25**, e40306 (2023)
10. Graafland, M., Schraagen, J.M., Schijven, M.P.: Systematic review of serious games for medical education and surgical skills training. J. Br. Surg. **99**(10), 1322–1330 (2012)
11. Holmes, W., et al.: Ethics of AI in education: towards a community-wide framework. Int. J. Artif. Intell. Educ. **32**(3), 504–526 (2022)
12. Israni, S.T., Matheny, M.E., Matlow, R., Whicher, D.: Equity, inclusivity, and innovative digital technologies to improve adolescent and young adult health. J. Adolesc. Health **67**(2), S4–S6 (2020)

13. Kizilcec, R.F., Lee, H.: Algorithmic fairness in education. In: The Ethics of Artificial Intelligence in Education, pp. 174–202. Routledge (2022)
14. Long, D., Magerko, B.: What is AI literacy? Competencies and design considerations. In: Proceedings of the 2020 CHI Conference on Human Factors in Computing Systems, pp. 1–16. ACM (2020)
15. Ma, M., Ng, D.T.K., Liu, Z., Wong, G.K.W.: Fostering responsible AI literacy: a systematic review of K-12 AI ethics education. Comput. Educ.: Artif. Intell. **6**, 100201 (2025)
16. McQuiggan, S.W., Rowe, J.P., Lee, S., Lester, J.C.: Story-based learning: the impact of narrative on learning experiences and outcomes. In: Woolf, B.P., Aïmeur, E., Nkambou, R., Lajoie, S. (eds.) ITS 2008. LNCS, vol. 5091, pp. 530–539. Springer, Heidelberg (2008). https://doi.org/10.1007/978-3-540-69132-7_56
17. Mott, B., et al.: Designing a narrative-centered game to promote AI literacy and health career exploration. In: Proceedings of the 2025 IEEE Conference on Games, pp. 1–4. IEEE (2025)
18. Mott, B.W., Callaway, C.B., Zettlemoyer, L.S., Lee, S.Y., Lester, J.C.: Towards narrative-centered learning environments. In: Proceedings of the AAAI Fall Symposium on Narrative Intelligence, pp. 78–82 (1999)
19. Ng, W., Leung, J., Chu, S., Qiao, Y.: Conceptualizing AI literacy: an exploratory review. Comput. Educ.: Artif. Intell. **2**, 100041 (2021)
20. Ozer, E.M., Bandura, A.: Mechanisms governing empowerment effects: a self-efficacy analysis. J. Pers. Soc. Psychol. **58**(3), 472 (1990)
21. Raphael, C., Bachen, C., Lynn, K.M., Baldwin-Philippi, J., McKee, K.A.: Games for civic learning: a conceptual framework and agenda for research and design. Games and culture **5**(2), 199–235 (2010)
22. Riedl, M.O., Bulitko, V.: Interactive narrative: an intelligent systems approach. AI Mag. **34**(1), 67–77 (2013)
23. Rowe, J.P., Shores, L.R., Mott, B.W., Lester, J.C.: Integrating learning, problem solving, and engagement in narrative-centered learning environments. Int. J. Artif. Intell. Educ. **21**(1–2), 115–133 (2011)
24. Selwyn, N.: Should Robots Replace Teachers?: AI and the Future of Education. Wiley (2019)
25. Topol, E.J.: High-performance medicine: the convergence of human and artificial intelligence. Nat. Med. **25**(1), 44–56 (2019)
26. Touretzky, D., Gardner-McCune, C., Martin, F., Seehorn, D.: Envisioning AI for K-12: what should every child know about AI? In: Proceedings of the AAAI Conference on Artificial Intelligence, vol. 33, pp. 9795–9799 (2019)
27. UNESCO: Recommendation on the ethics of artificial intelligence (2021). Adopted by the General Conference at its 41st session
28. von Wangenheim, C.G., Hauck, J.C., Pacheco, F.S., Bertonceli Bueno, M.F.: Visual tools for teaching machine learning in K-12: a ten-year systematic mapping. Educ. Inf. Technol. **26**(5), 5733–5778 (2021)
29. Williamson, B., Eynon, R.: Historical threads, missing links, and future directions in AI in education. Learn. Media Technol. **45**(3), 223–235 (2020)
30. Yan, X., Zhou, Y., Mishra, A., Mishra, H., Wang, B.: Exploring visualization for fairness in AI education. In: 2024 IEEE 17th Pacific Visualization Conference, pp. 1–10. IEEE (2024)
31. Zhao, Y., Michal, A., Thain, N., Subramonyam, H.: Thinking like a scientist: can interactive simulations foster critical AI literacy? In: Cristea, A.I., Walker, E., Lu, Y., Santos, O.C., Isotani, S. (eds.) AIED 2025. LNCS, vol. 15878, pp. 60–74. Springer, Cham (2025). https://doi.org/10.1007/978-3-031-98417-4_5

# Implicit and Explicit Bias Toward English Language Learners in LLM-Based Essay Scoring: A Mechanistic Interpretability Analysis

Kyudong Park[1(✉)], Heewon Min[1], Chaewon Lee[1], and Ki-Young Shin[2]

[1] Kwangwoon University, Seoul 01897, Republic of Korea
kdpark@kw.ac.kr
[2] Designovel Co., Ltd., Seoul 06180, Republic of Korea

**Abstract.** Large Language Models (LLMs) are increasingly used for automated essay scoring (AES), yet how demographic biases arise internally remains poorly understood. Using the PERSUADE 2.0 corpus and Llama-3.1-8B, we apply mechanistic interpretability techniques to investigate bias related to English Language Learner (ELL) status. Our analysis reveals two distinct bias pathways: (1) an *implicit pathway* where text features associated with ELL writing lead to score penalties, and (2) an *explicit compensation pathway* where providing ELL status in the prompt significantly increases scores (+0.22, $p < 0.001$). Linear probing shows ELL-related information is encoded across transformer layers with 76–80% accuracy, concentrated in layers 25–30. Steering vector experiments reveal an asymmetric bias structure (4:1 penalty-to-benefit ratio), which finetuning partially reduces (1.3:1). Applying steering vectors to mitigate implicit bias significantly reduces the ELL–Non-ELL scoring gap by 83.3% ($p < 0.01$), with a non-significant trend toward improved correlation with human scores. However, steering cannot counteract explicit compensation, which operates through an independent pathway. These findings highlight that differentiated intervention strategies are needed to address distinct bias mechanisms in LLM-based assessment.

**Keywords:** Automated Essay Scoring · Fairness · Mechanistic Interpretability · Large Language Models · English Language Learners

## 1 Introduction

Automated Essay Scoring (AES) systems are increasingly adopted in educational settings for their efficiency and scalability [14]. With the advent of Large Language Models (LLMs), there has been growing interest in leveraging these models for essay assessment [23]. However, the deployment of LLMs in high-stakes educational contexts raises significant concerns about fairness and potential demographic biases [17,18].


E. G. Blanchard et al. (eds.), AIED 2026, LNCS 16586, pp. 346–354, 2027.
https://doi.org/10.1007/978-3-032-29773-0_26

Prior research has documented scoring disparities across demographic groups in both traditional and LLM-based AES systems. Using the PERSUADE 2.0 corpus [5], Johnson and Zhang [12] found that GPT-4o exhibits potential bias toward English Language Learners (ELL), particularly when the model can infer students' demographic backgrounds from their writing. However, because commercial LLMs operate as black boxes, the *internal mechanisms* by which these biases arise remain poorly understood.

This paper addresses this gap by applying *mechanistic interpretability* (MI) techniques [9] to analyze ELL-related bias in LLM-based essay scoring. We employ three complementary MI methods—linear probing [1], attribution patching [20], and steering vectors [19]—to investigate three research questions:

- **RQ1:** How does explicit demographic information in prompts affect LLM essay scoring for ELL students?
- **RQ2:** What internal representations encode ELL-related features, and how do implicit and explicit bias pathways differ?
- **RQ3:** Can steering vectors mitigate implicit ELL scoring bias?

Our contributions are threefold: (1) We identify a *dual mechanism* of bias comprising implicit penalties and explicit compensation operating through independent pathways; (2) We show that steering vectors can significantly reduce the ELL–Non-ELL scoring gap by 83.3% ($p < 0.01$); and (3) We demonstrate that finetuning reorganizes but does not eliminate bias structures.

# 2 Related Work

## 2.1 Fairness in Automated Essay Scoring

Traditional AES systems have been scrutinized for potential biases related to demographic factors [17,21]. The PERSUADE corpus [6] was specifically designed to enable bias analysis by including detailed demographic information for each writer. Johnson and Zhang [12] used GPT-4o to score PERSUADE 2.0 essays [5], finding evidence of scoring biases related to race/ethnicity and ELL status. However, their analysis was limited to behavioral observations due to the closed nature of the model.

In this work, we operationally define *bias* as systematic scoring differences attributable to demographic group membership rather than writing quality. We note that human reference scores may themselves contain biases [17]; our analysis therefore examines model-internal mechanisms rather than treating human scores as an unbiased ground truth.

## 2.2 Mechanistic Interpretability and Bias in LLMs

Mechanistic interpretability seeks to understand neural networks by identifying interpretable features and circuits [9]. Key techniques include linear probing [1, 2], attribution patching [20], and steering vectors [16,19,24]. Despite growing adoption across NLP tasks, MI's application to educational AI fairness remains largely unexplored.

**Table 1.** Scoring performance on PERSUADE 2.0 ($n = 3{,}000$).

| Model | Pearson $r$ | QWK | MAE |
|---|---|---|---|
| Base | 0.351 | 0.326 | 0.844 |
| Finetuned | 0.369 | 0.369 | 0.833 |

Research on LLM bias has documented unfairness related to gender [15], dialect [11], and other factors [3,10]. In educational contexts [13,22], fairness concerns are increasingly recognized, but most work relies on behavioral analysis rather than mechanistic investigation.

# 3 Methodology

## 3.1 Dataset and Scope

We use the PERSUADE 2.0 corpus [5], comprising over 25,000 argumentative essays written by U.S. students in grades 6–12. Each essay includes holistic quality scores (1–6 scale) assigned by trained human raters, along with demographic variables (gender, race/ethnicity, ELL status, economic disadvantage) that are coded independently. We focus on ELL status as our primary variable because it exhibited the largest effect size in preliminary analysis; intersections with other demographic dimensions are not examined in this study.

For baseline measurement, we sample 3,000 essays stratified by demographic groups. For MI experiments requiring contrastive pairs (attribution patching and steering vector extraction), we use 200 samples per group (ELL vs. Non-ELL) [4]. Mitigation experiments use 100 samples per group.

## 3.2 Models

We use Llama-3.1-8B-Instruct [8] as our base model, chosen for its open weights enabling internal analysis. We compare two versions: (1) the **base** pretrained instruction-tuned model, and (2) a **finetuned** version using QLoRA [7] (rank = 16, alpha = 32, 1 epoch on 20,000 PERSUADE essays).

We acknowledge that overall scoring accuracy remains modest for both models (Table 1). Our primary goal is to understand *bias mechanisms* rather than to propose a production-ready scoring system. We report Pearson $r$ as the primary metric because steering vector effects manifest as continuous score shifts better captured by correlation than by ordinal agreement; we also report QWK for comparability with AES literature.

## 3.3 Bias Measurement

We measure bias using a *Demographic Prompt Effect* paradigm. Each essay is scored under two conditions: (1) **Control**: scoring prompt without demographic information; (2) **Treatment**: scoring prompt appended with demographic information (e.g., "This essay was written by an English Language Learner student"). The prompt effect is $\Delta_{\text{demo}} = \bar{S}_{\text{treatment}} - \bar{S}_{\text{control}}$.

### 3.4 Mechanistic Interpretability Methods

**Linear Probing.** For each layer $l \in \{5, 10, 15, 20, 25, 30\}$ (evenly spaced across the 32-layer architecture), we extract the activation vector $\mathbf{h}_l \in \mathbf{R}^{4096}$ at the final token position and train logistic regression classifiers to predict ELL status (5-fold cross-validation, $n = 200$ per group).

**Attribution Patching.** We measure the causal effect of demographic information by computing activation differences between control and treatment prompts for the same essay ($n = 50$): $\text{Effect}_l = \frac{1}{n}\sum_{i=1}^{n} \|\mathbf{h}_l^{\text{control}}(i) - \mathbf{h}_l^{\text{treatment}}(i)\|_2$.

**Steering Vectors.** We extract steering vectors as the mean activation difference between treatment and control conditions: $\mathbf{v}_l = \frac{1}{n}\sum_{i=1}^{n}(\mathbf{h}_l^{\text{treatment}}(i) - \mathbf{h}_l^{\text{control}}(i))$. During inference, we add $\alpha \cdot \mathbf{v}_l$ to activations at layer $l$, where $\alpha$ controls direction and strength.

These techniques have known limitations: linear probes may detect correlational rather than causal features [2], and steering vectors assume that bias is linearly encoded. We address these limitations by triangulating across methods.

### 3.5 Mitigation Experiments

We test steering-based mitigation at Layer 25 with $\alpha = 1.5$ (selected based on preliminary experiments across $\alpha \in \{0.5, 1.0, 1.5, 2.0, 2.5\}$):

**Experiment A (Score Normalization):** Apply negative steering (toward Non-ELL direction) to ELL essays scored without demographic prompts, using the base model. We test whether the ELL–Non-ELL scoring gap is reduced.

**Experiment B (Compensation Cancellation):** For essays scored with explicit ELL information in the prompt, apply negative steering to test whether the compensation effect can be cancelled.

Both experiments are also conducted with the finetuned model for comparison.

## 4 Results

### 4.1 RQ1: Demographic Prompt Effect

The base model exhibits a *compensatory* pattern when provided with ELL status: scores increase by +0.22 on average (paired $t$-test: $t = -3.50$, $p < 0.001$). This effect is stronger in the finetuned model (+0.30, $t = -4.18$, $p < 0.001$). Other demographic groups show smaller but consistent positive effects (Hispanic: +0.18; Black: +0.14; Economically Disadvantaged: +0.13), with White being the only group showing a slight negative effect (−0.06).

**Table 2.** Linear probing accuracy for ELL classification ($n = 200$ per group, 5-fold CV).

| Layer | Base | Finetuned | $\Delta$ |
|---|---|---|---|
| 5 | $0.782 \pm 0.038$ | $0.767 \pm 0.032$ | $-0.015$ |
| 10 | $0.762 \pm 0.053$ | $0.775 \pm 0.036$ | $+0.012$ |
| 15 | $0.777 \pm 0.022$ | $0.795 \pm 0.033$ | $+0.017$ |
| 20 | $0.780 \pm 0.047$ | $0.777 \pm 0.050$ | $-0.003$ |
| 25 | $0.770 \pm 0.054$ | **0.805** $\pm$ 0.026 | **+0.035** |
| 30 | $0.788 \pm 0.048$ | $0.800 \pm 0.065$ | $+0.012$ |

This compensatory pattern contrasts with Johnson and Zhang's [12] finding of *negative* bias toward ELL students in GPT-4o, suggesting that bias direction is model-specific—likely reflecting differences in training data and alignment procedures.

### 4.2 RQ2: Internal Mechanisms

**Linear Probing.** Table 2 shows that ELL-related information is encoded across all examined layers with 76–80% classification accuracy, with the strongest encoding in layers 25–30. Finetuning increases ELL encoding most substantially at Layer 25 (+0.035), suggesting that task-specific training strengthens demographic representations in later processing stages.

**Attribution Patching and Asymmetric Bias Structure.** Attribution patching confirms that the causal effect of demographic information increases monotonically with layer depth: Layer 30 shows the maximum effect ($12.28 \pm 0.81$), approximately 5$\times$ that of Layer 15 ($2.46 \pm 0.16$), indicating that demographic information most strongly influences output computation in later layers.

Steering experiments reveal a fundamental asymmetry. In the base model, steering toward ELL causes substantial score decreases ($-0.45$ at $\alpha = 1.5$), while steering toward Non-ELL produces minimal increases (+0.11). This 4:1 asymmetry ratio suggests that Non-ELL text characteristics function as an implicit "default," with ELL-associated features treated as deviations that are penalized. Finetuning reduces this asymmetry to 1.3:1, indicating partial reorganization of bias structure toward more symmetric treatment.

**Effect of Finetuning.** Finetuning improves scoring accuracy ($r$: $0.351 \rightarrow 0.369$) but produces complex effects on bias: explicit compensation increases ($+0.22 \rightarrow +0.30$), demographic encoding strengthens (Layer 25 probe accuracy: +0.035), yet the asymmetry ratio decreases ($4{:}1 \rightarrow 1.3{:}1$). These results suggest that finetuning *reorganizes* rather than eliminates bias.

**Table 3.** Experiment A: ELL score normalization via steering ($n = 100$ per group, Layer 25, $\alpha = 1.5$). $^{**}p < 0.01$; n.s. = not significant.

| Metric | Base | Finetuned |
|---|---|---|
| ELL Original | $3.400 \pm 0.917$ | $3.380 \pm 0.925$ |
| ELL Steered | $3.600 \pm 0.787$ | $3.550 \pm 0.805$ |
| Non-ELL Original | $3.640 \pm 0.806$ | $3.620 \pm 0.822$ |
| Paired $t$ (orig. vs. steered) | $p = 0.002^{**}$ | $p = 0.001^{**}$ |
| Gap Reduction | 83.3% | 70.8% |
| Residual Gap $p$ | 0.724 (n.s.) | 0.546 (n.s.) |
| Pearson $r$ (Original) | 0.350 | 0.393 |
| Pearson $r$ (Steered) | 0.423 | 0.443 |
| $\Delta r$ (Steiger's $Z$) | +0.074 (n.s.) | +0.050 (n.s.) |
| QWK (ELL Original) | 0.326 | 0.369 |
| QWK (ELL Steered) | 0.345 | 0.374 |

### 4.3 RQ3: Bias Mitigation

**Experiment A: Score Normalization.** Table 3 shows the results of applying negative steering to ELL essays scored without demographic prompts. Steering significantly reduces ELL scores' deviation from Non-ELL levels (paired $t$-test: $p < 0.01$ for both models). The ELL–Non-ELL scoring gap is reduced by 83.3% in the base model and 70.8% in the finetuned model. After steering, the residual gap is no longer statistically significant ($p = 0.72$ and $p = 0.55$, respectively).

We also observe a non-significant trend toward improved correlation with human scores after steering (+0.074 in base, Steiger's $Z = 1.31$, $p = 0.19$; +0.050 in finetuned, $p = 0.25$). While this trend is suggestive—consistent with the hypothesis that implicit bias represents noise degrading validity—it does not reach statistical significance in our sample and should be interpreted cautiously.

**Experiment B: Compensation Cancellation.** When steering is applied to essays scored with explicit ELL information in the prompt, it fails to cancel the compensation effect. Instead, the base model shows a further score increase (+0.07, $p = 0.034$), while the finetuned model shows a non-significant increase (+0.04, $p = 0.21$). These negative cancellation rates (−31.8% and −13.3%) demonstrate that the explicit compensation pathway operates *independently* of the implicit pathway targeted by steering vectors.

# 5 Discussion

## 5.1 Dual Mechanism Model

Our findings support a dual mechanism model of ELL-related bias (Fig. 1):

**Dual Mechanism Model of ELL Bias**

*Essay Input*

↓

| Implicit Pathway | Explicit Pathway |
|---|---|
| Text features (grammar, vocabulary) | "ELL student" keyword in prompt |
| ↓ | ↓ |
| Encoded in Layers 25–30 | Independent mechanism |
| ↓ | ↓ |
| Steering: Effective ($p < 0.01$) | Steering: Ineffective |

↓

*Final Score*

**Fig. 1.** Dual mechanism model of ELL bias. The implicit pathway encodes demographic-associated text features and is significantly mitigated via steering (83.3% gap reduction, $p < 0.01$). The explicit pathway responds to demographic keywords and operates independently.

The **implicit pathway** encodes ELL-associated features in layers 25–30, producing an asymmetric penalty (4:1 ratio). Steering vectors significantly reduce this bias. The **explicit pathway** responds to demographic keywords in the prompt, producing compensation (+0.22 to +0.30, $p < 0.001$), and cannot be controlled by steering vectors targeting the implicit pathway. The independence of these pathways implies that effective fairness interventions must address each mechanism separately.

## 5.2 Limitations

Several limitations should be acknowledged. First, our analysis focuses on a single model family (Llama 3.1) and one demographic dimension (ELL status), without examining intersections with other demographic variables; results may not generalize to other architectures or groups. Second, overall scoring accuracy is modest ($r \approx 0.35$–$0.37$, QWK $\approx 0.33$–$0.37$), limiting practical applicability, though the mechanistic insights remain informative. Third, our treatment prompt design (appending ELL status) may introduce a saliency or markedness effect; an alternative design where all essays include demographic fields (with "unknown" as a control) could better isolate the effect. Fourth, the MI techniques have inherent limitations: linear probes may detect correlational rather than causal features, and steering vectors assume linear encoding. Finally, human rater scores used as reference may contain their own biases [17].

## 6 Conclusion

This paper applies mechanistic interpretability techniques to analyze ELL-related bias in LLM-based essay scoring. We identify two independent bias pathways: an implicit pathway operating through text representations in layers 25–30, and an explicit compensation pathway triggered by demographic keywords in prompts. Steering vectors significantly reduce the implicit ELL–Non-ELL scoring gap by 83.3% ($p < 0.01$), with a suggestive but non-significant trend toward improved scoring accuracy. However, steering cannot counteract explicit compensation, which operates through an independent mechanism.

These findings provide initial evidence that mechanistic interpretability can reveal and address specific bias pathways in educational AI. Future work should extend this analysis to other models and demographic dimensions, investigate attention-level interventions for the explicit pathway, and employ alternative prompt designs to better isolate demographic effects.

**Acknowledgments.** This work was supported by the National Research Foundation of Korea (NRF) grant funded by the Korea government (MSIT) (RS-2025-24535373). This research was supported by the MSIT(Ministry of Science and ICT), Korea, under the ICAN (ICT Challenge and Advanced Network of HRD) program (RS-2022-00156215) supervised by the IITP (Institute of Information & Communications Technology Planning & Evaluation).

**Disclosure of Interests.** The authors have no competing interests to declare that are relevant to the content of this article.

## References

1. Alain, G., Bengio, Y.: Understanding intermediate layers using linear classifier probes. In: International Conference on Learning Representations (ICLR) Workshop Track (2017)
2. Belinkov, Y., Durrani, N., Dalvi, F., Sajjad, H., Glass, J.: What do neural machine translation models learn about morphology? In: Proceedings of the 55th Annual Meeting of the Association for Computational Linguistics, pp. 861–872 (2017)
3. Blodgett, S.L., Barocas, S., Daumé III, H., Wallach, H.: Language (technology) is power: a critical survey of "bias" in NLP. In: Proceedings of the 58th Annual Meeting of the Association for Computational Linguistics, pp. 5454–5476 (2020)
4. Cohen, J.: Statistical Power Analysis for the Behavioral Sciences, 2nd edn. Lawrence Erlbaum Associates, Hillsdale (1988)
5. Crossley, S., Tian, Y., Baffour, P., Franklin, A., Benner, M., Boser, U.: A large-scale corpus for assessing written argumentation: PERSUADE 2.0. Assess. Writ. **61**, 100850 (2024)
6. Crossley, S.A., Tian, Y., Baffour, P., Picou, A.D., Benner, M., Boser, U.: The persuasive essays for rating, selecting, and understanding argumentative and discourse elements (PERSUADE) corpus 1.0. Assess. Writ. **54**, 100667 (2022)

7. Dettmers, T., Pagnoni, A., Holtzman, A., Zettlemoyer, L.: QLoRA: efficient fine-tuning of quantized LLMs. In: Advances in Neural Information Processing Systems, vol. 36 (2023)
8. Dubey, A., et al.: The LLaMA 3 herd of models. arXiv preprint arXiv:2407.21783 (2024)
9. Elhage, N., et al.: A mathematical framework for transformer circuits. Transformer Circuits Thread (2021). https://transformer-circuits.pub/2021/framework/index.html
10. Gallegos, I.O., et al.: Bias and fairness in large language models: a survey. Comput. Linguist. 1–79 (2024)
11. Hofmann, V., Kalluri, P., Jurafsky, D., King, S.: Dialect prejudice predicts AI decisions about people's character, employability, and criminality. arXiv preprint arXiv:2403.00742 (2024)
12. Johnson, M.S., Zhang, M.: Examining the responsible use of zero-shot AI approaches to scoring essays. Sci. Rep. **14**(1), 29208 (2024)
13. Kasneci, E., et al.: ChatGPT for good? On opportunities and challenges of large language models for education. Learn. Individ. Differ. **103**, 102274 (2023)
14. Ke, Z., Ng, V.: Automated essay scoring: a survey of the state of the art. In: Proceedings of the Twenty-Eighth International Joint Conference on Artificial Intelligence (IJCAI), pp. 6300–6308 (2019)
15. Kotek, H., Dockum, R., Sun, D.: Gender bias and stereotypes in large language models. In: Proceedings of the ACM Collective Intelligence Conference, pp. 12–24 (2023)
16. Li, K., Patel, O., Viégas, F., Pfister, H., Wattenberg, M.: Inference-time intervention: eliciting truthful answers from a language model. In: Advances in Neural Information Processing Systems, vol. 36 (2024)
17. Loukina, A., Madnani, N., Zechner, K.: The many dimensions of algorithmic fairness in educational applications. In: Proceedings of the Fourteenth Workshop on Innovative Use of NLP for Building Educational Applications, pp. 1–10. Association for Computational Linguistics (2019)
18. Madnani, N., Loukina, A., von Davier, A., Burstein, J., Cahill, A.: Building better open-source tools to support fairness in automated scoring. In: Proceedings of the First ACL Workshop on Ethics in Natural Language Processing, pp. 41–52. Association for Computational Linguistics (2017)
19. Turner, A.M., Thiergart, L., Udell, D., Leech, G., Mini, U., MacDiarmid, M.: Activation addition: steering language models without optimization. arXiv preprint arXiv:2308.10248 (2023)
20. Vig, J., et al.: Investigating gender bias in language models using causal mediation analysis. In: Advances in Neural Information Processing Systems, vol. 33, pp. 12388–12401 (2020)
21. Williamson, D.M., Xi, X., Breyer, F.J.: A framework for evaluation and use of automated scoring. Educ. Meas. Issues Pract. **31**(1), 2–13 (2012)
22. Yan, L., et al.: Practical and ethical challenges of large language models in education: a systematic scoping review. Br. J. Edu. Technol. **55**(1), 90–112 (2024)
23. Yancey, K.P., LaFlair, G.T., Verardi, A., Burstein, J.: Rating short L2 essays on the CEFR scale with GPT-4. In: Proceedings of the 18th Workshop on Innovative Use of NLP for Building Educational Applications (BEA), pp. 576–584. Association for Computational Linguistics (2023)
24. Zou, A., et al.: Representation engineering: a top-down approach to AI transparency. arXiv preprint arXiv:2310.01405 (2023)

# Biblometrics Insights on the Trends of Artificial Intelligence and Educational Commercialization in Early Childhood Educational Research

Bijun He, Shuhan Ye, and Yanhong Wang(✉)

Zhejiang Normal University, Jinhua 321004, People's Republic of China
Wyh661063@zjnu.edu.cn

**Abstract.** This study conducts a bibliometric analysis of early childhood education (ECE) research from 2000 to 2024. In particular, this research focuses on the emerging trends of artificial intelligence (AI) applications in early childhood education. Drawn on data from the Web of Science, the research maps publication patterns of studies in early childhood education. Analysis results reveal a growth in interdisciplinary studies, particularly in technology integration and digital learning. In general, this study reveals the need for equitable policies, developmental appropriateness in AI tools, and critical evaluations of market influences on ECE quality. Finally, it calls for data-driven strategies to align innovation with child-centered practices and educational equity goals.

**Keywords:** Artificial intelligence · Primary education · Childhood education · Pre-school education

## 1 Introduction

Early childhood education is a foundation for lifelong learning, development, and well-being. ECE addresses cognitive, socioemotional, and physical growth in children from birth to about eight years old [1, 2]. Research has long highlighted the role of ECE in promoting equity, particularly for disadvantaged children, through structured programs like universal early education and trauma-informed care [3, 4]. The field of ECE encompasses diverse pedagogical approaches, including STEM (Science, Technology, Engineering, and Mathematics), play-based learning, and digital competence. All of these factors are essential for preparing children for future academic and social success [2, 5]. So far, ECE policies and practices vary globally, with challenges such as resource disparities and the need for culturally responsive curricula [6, 7].

Recent scholarly reviews and critical reflections in the field of ECE have explored themes such as the effectiveness of interdisciplinary approaches, teacher well-being, and the impact of environmental factors on child development. For instance, Su et al. [2] and Rodrigues-Silva and Alsina [8] emphasize the growing integration of STEM and sustainability in ECE. In addition, Qin et al. [9] have examined teacher emotions and their influence on classroom dynamics. Trauma-informed care is another prominent focus, with studies advocating professional development to support children with


E. G. Blanchard et al. (eds.), AIED 2026, LNCS 16586, pp. 355–362, 2027.
https://doi.org/10.1007/978-3-032-29773-0_27

adverse experiences [3, 10]. Furthermore, systematic reviews by Ritosa et al. [11] and Tamblyn et al. [12] both highlight the importance of physical and sensory environments in benefiting social-emotional development. Taken together, these reviews call for the need for evidence-based practices, equitable access, and child-centered approaches in ECE.

Despite the growing number of educational research and literature reviews in the field of early childhood education, there is a lack of quantitative studies outlining the current trend of early childhood research through a bibliometric or scientometrics approach. The absence of large-scale quantitative bibliometric or scientometric analyses in early childhood education research limits the field's ability to map trends, identify knowledge gaps, and optimize future research directions from a systematic approach. Unlike other disciplines where bibliometrics have been commonly used to track publication patterns, collaboration networks, and emerging themes (e.g., STEM or medical research), ECE lacks a data-driven synthesis of its scholarly landscape.

Without bibliometric studies, researchers rely heavily on traditional literature reviews. These traditional literature reviews are often subjective, limited in scope, and unable to capture macro-level trends.

Hence, in view of the glaring research gap noted here, this research aims to examine the landscape of early childhood educational research, especially the increasing trends of artificial intelligence applications. This is for answering a key research question in this research, namely "what are the current trend of ECE research in the age of AI?". By integrating quantitative bibliometrics, the ECE field can transition from fragmented reviews to a data-informed paradigm, ensuring research aligns with societal needs and educational innovation. It would also enable us to compare trends across countries to assess global research equity and policy relevance. In general, by examining the landscape of early childhood education research through a bibliometric lens, such an approach would offer us a data-driven analysis of trends, gaps, and future research directions.

Structured into eight key sections, the study begins by establishing the significance of ECE research and identifying gaps in current quantitative analyses (Introduction). This is followed by an overview of recent research advancements in early childhood education (Recent Progress). Subsequent sections employ bibliometric methods to trace thematic shifts (Topic Evolution) and analyze regional research contributions (Geographical Distributions). This study would also investigate publication patterns across academic venues (Venue Distributions). The analysis then focuses on two critical issues, i.e., the growing role of artificial intelligence in ECE (Artificial Intelligence in ECE Research) The article concludes by synthesizing key findings and their implications for future research, policy, and practice (Implications and Conclusion). Analysis results would be beneficial for developing a framework of understanding the current state and future directions in ECE research.

## 2 Recant Progress

To document the recent research progress of early childhood educational research from 2000 to 2024, we use the keyword filtering approach in the Web of Science, a widely used literature search platforms. The specific strategy of keyword filtering is: (Title

= ("early childhood education" OR "per-school education") OR Author Keyword = ("early childhood education" OR "per-school education")). This strategy results in 9738 results (Fig. 1).

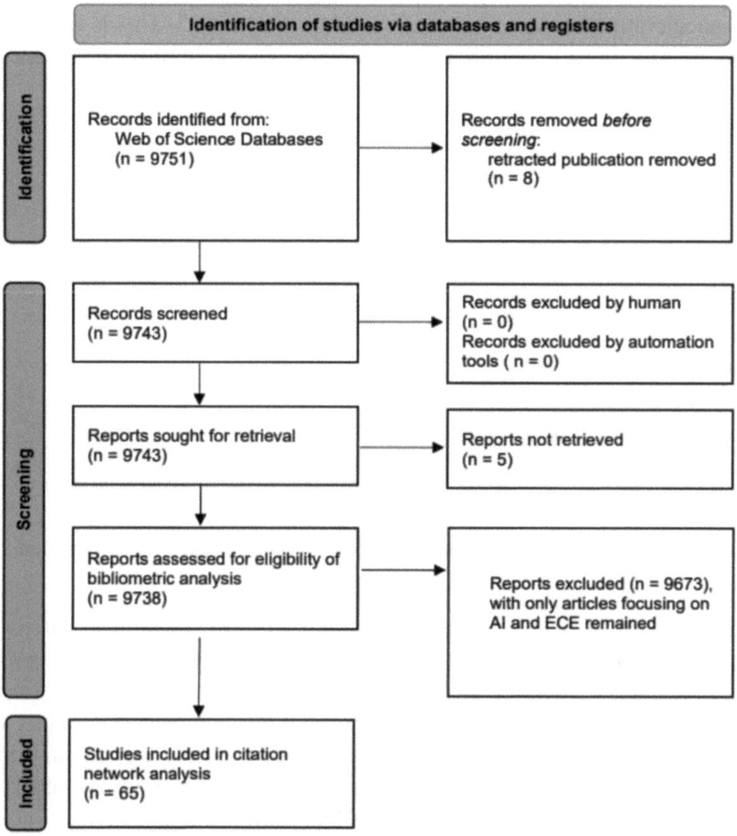


**Fig. 1.** PRISMA Flow of Data Collection.

As showcased (Fig. 2), recent progress in academic publications related to early childhood education and its sub-areas has witnessed an upward trend over the past two decades. Starting from a modest 13 ECE publications in 2000, the field expanded rapidly, reaching 945 in 2023 before a slight dip to 902 in 2024. For publications entitled 'ECE', the largest category (as defined by the Web of Science) is the field of education.

This field dominated output, peaking at 693 publications in 2023. This reflects sustained scholarly interest in pedagogical approaches. Meanwhile, ECE-entitled articles in the field of psychology saw steady growth, doubling from 42 publications in 2014 to 113 in 2020. This trend indicates increasing attention to developmental and cognitive aspects. The most striking expansion occurred in technology-related disciplines (in the Web of Science categories of engineering, technology, and computing). They surged from zero publications in 2000 to 42 in 2024. Such a trend highlights the growing integration of digital tools in early learning.

Contributions from the category of business and economics, though smaller in volume, also demonstrated gradual growth, peaking at 16 publications in 2019. The data underscores the evolution of early childhood education research into a multidisciplinary field, with accelerating research output particularly post-2015. This is likely influenced by global emphasis on early childhood development and technological advancements in education (Fig. 2).

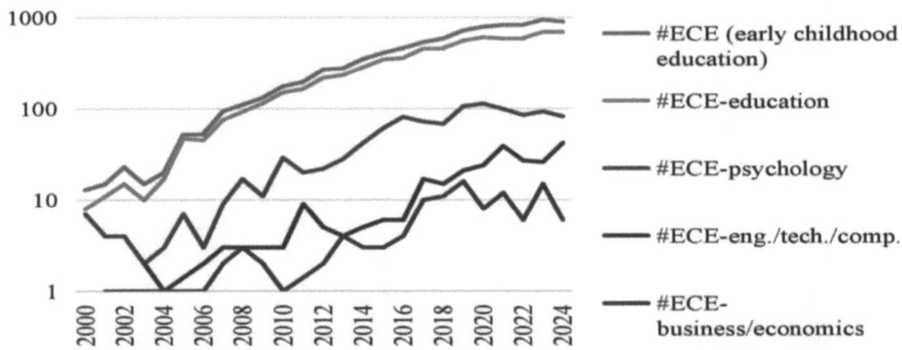


**Fig. 2.** Number of Academic Publications of Early Childhood Education and Related Sub-Areas.

Overall, as seminal investigations have noted, current research in early childhood education encompasses diverse themes, reflecting the field's interdisciplinary nature. A prominent focus is STEM integration, with studies examining its impact on cognitive and socioemotional development [2, 8]. Digital competence and technology-enhanced learning are also widely explored, particularly in relation to computational thinking and robotics [2, 5]. Another critical area is trauma-informed care, addressing the needs of vulnerable children and educator training [3, 10]. Cultural and linguistic inclusivity is gaining attention, with research on heritage-based curricula [13] and English as a foreign language in East Asia [14].

Additionally, teacher well-being and professional development are key concerns, particularly in relation to stress, emotional labor, and policy reforms [9, 15]. Finally, equity and access remain central, with studies on universal ECE's role in reducing socioeconomic disparities [1, 4] and critiques of commercialization [7]. These themes highlight ECE's evolving priorities, balancing innovation with equity and holistic child development.

## 3 Artificial Intelligence in ECE Research

Concerning the topic evolution of early childhood research, of interest is the increasing application of technology, especially artificial intelligence, in ECE. To detect this trend via bibliometrics, the specific strategy of keyword filtering is: (Title = ("early childhood education" OR "per-school education") OR Author Keyword = ("early childhood education" OR "per-school education")) AND (Topic = AI OR GAI OR Deep Seek OR ChatGPT OR "Artificial Intelligence"). This strategy leads to 65 results. Figure 3 shows the citation network of literature about artificial intelligence and early childhood education via the Research Rabbit platform.

The distribution of Web of Science categories in literature about Artificial Intelligence (AI) and early childhood education reveals an emphasis on educational research. Specifically, the discipline of Education & Educational Research dominates with 25 publications, outpacing other fields. Computer science disciplines, including CS: Artificial Intelligence (7), CS: Interdisciplinary Applications (4), CS: Theory Methods (4), contribute to the technological aspects of the research. A few interdisciplinary and niche categories, such as Psychology Developmental, Engineering Electrical Electronic, and Social Work, appear with minimal representation (1–2 publications each). This indicates sporadic cross-disciplinary engagement. Overall, the distribution highlights a primary focus on pedagogical research, with secondary contributions from computer science and limited involvement from other fields (Fig. 4).

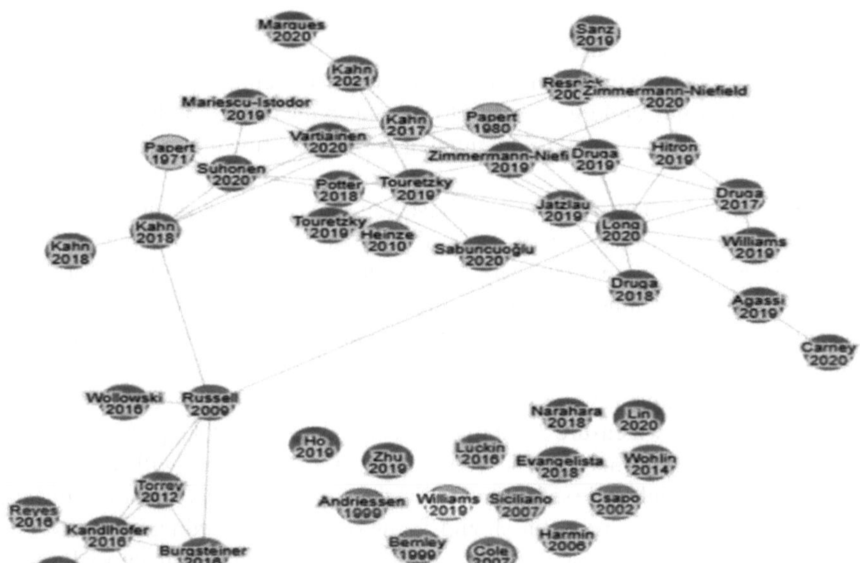


**Fig. 3.** Top Micro Citation Topics of Academic Publications of Early Childhood Education.

Indeed, the application of computational technology, particularly artificial intelligence, in early childhood education has emerged as a significant trend. This trend reflects the growing integration of digital tools in early learning environments. AI technologies, such as generative AI (e.g., ChatGPT and Deep Seek) and adaptive learning systems, are being explored for their potential to enhance personalized learning andhuman-intelligence engagement. For instance, AI-driven analytics can better monitor children's

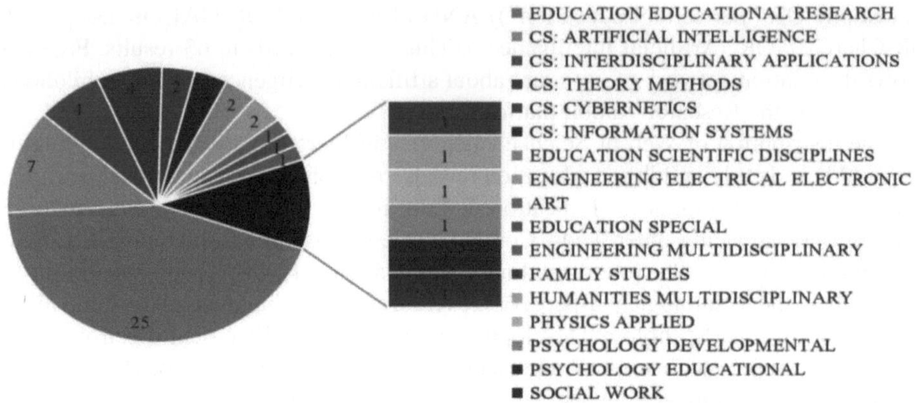


**Fig. 4.** Web of Science Categories of Literature about Artificial Intelligence and Early Childhood Education.

interactions and predict learning outcomes, both of which enable educators to tailor instruction to individual needs [12].

Additionally, computational thinking frameworks are being expanded to include AI literacy, ensuring young children can develop digital skills in a technology-driven world [5]. These innovations highlight the potential of AI in benefiting interactive and adaptive learning experiences.

However, the adoption of AI in ECE also raises ethical and practical challenges. Indeed, concerns about data privacy, algorithmic bias, and the developmental appropriateness of AI tools necessitate careful consideration. For example, while AI can personalize learning, it must align with child-centered practices and avoid replacing human interactions that are key for socioemotional development [16]. Moreover, the lack of 'hard science' studies developing AI technologies specifically for ECE highlights the need for collaborative research between educators and AI engineers. Only through such partnerships can we ensure AI applications are designed to support equitable and inclusive learning environments. Hence, addressing these challenges will be essential for harnessing AI's potential while safeguarding the principles of early childhood education.

Looking ahead, future research should focus on designing ethical frameworks to guide AI integration in ECE, as well as longitudinal studies to evaluate its long-term impacts on child development. By balancing innovation with equity and developmental appropriateness, AI can work as a valuable tool in enhancing early learning experiences while upholding the integrity of child-centered education.

## 4 Implications and Conclusions

This study provides a bibliometric analysis of early childhood education research from 2000 to 2024. It focuses on two emerging trends, i.e., artificial intelligence applications within early childhood education. The analysis reveals that while ECE research has expanded, interdisciplinary gaps persist in this field, particularly in quantitative, data-driven syntheses. Key findings highlight the dominance of Western institutions in publishing ECE research, the growing integration of AI, STEM, and digital learning, as well as the need for ethical frameworks to guide (generative) AI adoption in classrooms. However, there are several challenges underlying the current landscape of educational research in early childhood education. For example, while there have been several studies observing and evaluating the application of AI, especially generative AI, in early childhood education, there is a need for more hard science studies directly developing AI technologies or software for early childhood education.

Future research should explore the integration of artificial intelligence in ECE to enhance personalized learning and developmental assessments. Computational thinking frameworks, as proposed by Zeng et al. [5], could be expanded to include AI literacy. Such frameworks are beneficial for ensuring young children develop foundational skills in a digital world. Studies should further investigate the ethical implications of AI tools, such as data privacy and bias, and their impact on teacher-child interactions [16]. Additionally, AI-driven analytics could optimize classroom environments via monitoring engagement and predicting learning outcomes, as suggested by Tamblyn et al. [12]. Collaborative research between educators and technologists is essential to design AI applications that align with developmental appropriateness and equity goals [2], especially in emerging countries such as China [17, 18].

**Disclosure of Interests.** The authors have no competing interests to declare that are relevant to the content of this article.

## References


1. Hahn, R.A., Barnett, W.S.: Early childhood education: Health, equity, and economics. Annu. Rev. Public Health. **44**, 75–92 (2023). https://doi.org/10.1146/annurev-publhealth-071321-032337
2. Su, J.H., Yim, I.H.Y., Wegerif, R., Chu, S.K.W.: STEAM in early childhood education: a scoping review. Res. Sci. Technol. Educ. **43**(2), 495–511 (2025). https://doi.org/10.1080/02635143.2023.2296445
3. Chudzik, M., Corr, C., Santos, R.M.: Trauma-informed care in early childhood education settings: a scoping review. Early Childhood Educ. J. **53**(2), 477–488 (2025). https://doi.org/10.1007/s10643-023-01596-3
4. Schmutz, R.: Is universal early childhood education an equalizer? a systematic review and meta-analysis. Res. Soc. Straif. Mobil. **89**, 100859 (2024). https://doi.org/10.1016/j.rssm.2023.100859
5. Zeng, Y., Yang, W.P., Bautista, A.: Computational thinking in early childhood education: a three-dimensional framework. Educ. Res. Rev. **39**, 100520 (2023). https://doi.org/10.1016/j.edurev.2023.100520
6. Zhang, J.: Early childhood education policy reforms in China. Eur. J. Educ. **60**(1), e70055 (2025). https://doi.org/10.1111/ejed.70055
7. Jing, Z.: The evolution, present practices, and future directions of early childhood education in China. Eur. J. Educ. **60**(1), e12880 (2025). https://doi.org/10.1111/ejed.12880
8. Rodrigues-Silva, J., Alaina, Á.: STEM/STEAM in early childhood education for sustainability: a systematic review. Sustainability. **15**(4), 3721 (2023). https://doi.org/10.3390/su15043721

9. Qin, H., Schlep's, K., Yin, H.B.: Teacher emotion in early childhood education: a systematic review. Eur. J. Educ. **59**(4), e12741 (2024). https://doi.org/10.1111/ejed.12741
10. Sun, Y.H., Shouters, H., Tamblyn, A., Berger, E., Blewitt, C.: Cross-disciplinary collaboration in early childhood education: a scoping review. Early Childhood Educ. J. **54**(1), 381–398 (2024). https://doi.org/10.1007/s10643-024-01836-0
11. Riots, A., et al.: Measuring children's engagement in early childhood education and care settings: a scoping literature review. Educ. Psychol. Rev. **35**(4), 99 (2023). https://doi.org/10.1007/s10648-023-09815-4
12. Tamblyn, A., et al.: Physical/sensory environment factors in early childhood education. Educ. Res. Rev. **41**, 100555 (2023). https://doi.org/10.1016/j.edurev.2023.100555
13. Yucera, Y., Portugal, G., Figueiredo, M.: Cultural heritage in early childhood education: a systematic review. Eur. Early Child. Educ. Res. J. **31**(6), 866–883 (2023). https://doi.org/10.1080/1350293X.2023.2207031
14. Liang, L.Y., Chiku, A., Li, H.: English as a foreign language in east Asian early childhood education: a scoping review. Early Childhood Educ. J. **53**(3), 835–850 (2025). https://doi.org/10.1007/s10643-024-01646-4
15. Li, X.L., Zhang, L.T., Lee, J.C.K., Chen, J.J.: A systematic review of early childhood teacher well-being research (1993–2023). Behav. Sci. **14**(12), 1179 (2024). https://doi.org/10.3390/bs14121179
16. Lee, B.Y.: Technology/media use in early childhood education. Early Childhood Educ. J. **52**(6), 1645–1661 (2024). https://doi.org/10.1007/s10643-024-01684-y
17. Luo, W., Wang, N., He, H., Berson, I.R., Berson, M.J., Shi, Y.: "Wear a helmet and go online": multi-stakeholder perspectives on cyber safety and digital well-being in early childhood education in China. Early Educ. Dev. **37**(2), 1–28 (2025)
18. Huang, J., Cao, C., Liu, H.: Indigenization and inclusion in Chinese academia. Nat. Hum. Behav. **10**(3), 1–13 (2025)

# Students, AI, and the Future of Higher Education: A Scoping Review of Perceptions and Concerns

Mohammadreza Farrokhnia[1(✉)], Ghasem Salimi[2], and Amirhossein Ahmadshahi[3]

[1] Department of Learning, Data Analytics and Technology, Instructional Technology Section, University of Twente, Enschede, The Netherlands
m.farrokhnia@utwente.nl

[2] Department of Educational Administration and Planning, Shiraz University, Shiraz, Iran and Associate Member at the Center for Open Digital Innovation and Participation (CODIP), TU Dresden, Germany
salimi@shirazu.ac.ir

[3] Department of Educational Administration and Planning, Shiraz University, Shiraz, Iran
a.ahmadshahi@hafez.shirazu.ac.ir

**Abstract.** The rapid integration of artificial intelligence (AI) in higher education is transforming learning, teaching, and academic work, heightening the importance of understanding students' perspectives as primary users of these technologies. This systematic scoping review synthesizes evidence from 56 peer-reviewed studies published between 2015 and February 2025 on university students' perceptions of AI applications in higher education. Following Arksey and O'Malley's framework and PRISMA-ScR guidelines, three key patterns emerged. First, much of the literature lacked strong theoretical grounding, relying predominantly on adoption-oriented models. Second, research has focused heavily on generative AI tools, particularly chatbots such as ChatGPT, with limited attention to other AI applications. Third, students reported both benefits and concerns: they viewed AI as supportive for writing, personalized learning, and collaboration, while also raising issues related to ethics, academic integrity, overdependence, and unequal access. Many students also noted insufficient institutional guidance, reducing their confidence in responsible engagement. Overall, this review consolidates current findings, identifies critical research gaps, and offers recommendations for future research, policy, and practice to support ethical and student-centered AI integration in higher education.

**Keywords:** Higher Education · Artificial Intelligence · Generative AI · Concerns · Promises · Scoping Review

## 1 Introduction

Over the past decade, Artificial Intelligence (AI) has emerged as a transformative technology, significantly reshaping higher education (HE) by transforming teaching, learning, management, and research processes (Farrokhnia et al., 2025). In particular, AI


E. G. Blanchard et al. (eds.), AIED 2026, LNCS 16586, pp. 363–377, 2027.
https://doi.org/10.1007/978-3-032-29773-0_28

can enhance the learning experience by offering personalized recommendations (Raj et al., 2022; Huang et al., 2023), supporting collaborative teamwork (Zawacki-Richter et al., 2019), and facilitating seamless communication (Jony & Hamim, 2024), ultimately leading to improved learning outcomes (Rawas, 2024). Moreover, AI empowers instructors to explore innovative teaching strategies that engage diverse student populations, bridging gaps in traditional educational practices (Soleimani et al., 2025).

Despite the transformative potential of AI in HE, as with other educational innovations, successful implementation depends on the adoption of these technologies by key stakeholders, particularly students (Martins & Kellermanns, 2004). According to Chan and Hu (2023), students recognize several benefits of AI, such as its ability to enhance learning, teaching, and administrative processes. However, they also express significant concerns about its accuracy, privacy, ethical implications, and its broader impact on personal development and societal values. Research into students' views on AI tools in academic writing further highlights this ambivalence. While many students appreciate the support these tools provide, they prefer AI to serve as an assistant rather than replace human authors, citing concerns about creativity and ethical issues (Malik et al., 2023).

In summary, the adoption and implementation of AI in HE is not merely a technical or operational process; it fundamentally depends on the understanding and acceptance of key stakeholders (Bobrytska et al., 2024). Among these stakeholders, students play a pivotal role. As primary users of educational systems, their interactions with AI make their experiences and attitudes critical for evaluating the effectiveness, impact, and sustainability of AI technologies in academic settings. Recognizing this importance, a growing body of research has examined university students' perceptions of AI in education (e.g., Chan et al., 2023; Kim et al., 2020; Strzelecki, 2023). Guided by diverse theoretical frameworks, such as the Technology Acceptance Model (TAM) and Self-Determination Theory (SDT), these studies offer insights from multiple perspectives. Some investigate perceived usefulness (Grassini et al., 2024), others explore emotional responses (Grájeda et al., 2024), and still others focus on students' motivation to engage with AI technologies (Du & Alm, 2024).

While this diversity of approaches enriches the field, it has also led to a fragmented body of research, making it difficult to accumulate and systematize findings. This highlights the need for review studies that consolidate existing research and organize it into coherent themes, a need that remains largely unmet. To address this gap, the present study aims to provide an integrative overview of current research on students' perspectives and experiences with AI in HE. By synthesizing the available literature, the study seeks to generate actionable insights for universities, policymakers, and developers, enabling them to better align AI-based educational technologies with students' expectations and needs. Ultimately, this effort aims to support the effective and responsible integration of AI into HE.

## 2 Method

Following prior research of a similar nature (e.g., Schei et al., 2024), this study conducted a systematic scoping review of the existing international literature using an exploratory approach. This method emphasizes content analysis over statistical metrics, making it particularly suitable for identifying knowledge gaps and scoping a body of literature (Munn et al., 2018), especially in research areas involving the use of AI as a novel and rapidly developing technology (Kanbach et al., 2024). To guide the review process, the study adopted the scoping review framework proposed by Arksey and O'malley (2005). Furthermore, to enhance methodological rigor, the review adhered to the Preferred Reporting Items for Systematic Reviews and Meta-Analyses extension for scoping reviews (PRISMA-ScR) (Tricco et al., 2018).

The first stage of the review involved clearly identifying the research problem and formulating guiding research questions. This process centered on defining the core elements of the review, specifically the target population (students in HE) and the phenomenon of interest (perceptions of AI applications in HE), thereby supporting an exploratory investigation of the existing literature. Based on this focus, the following research questions were developed:

***RQ1***. What theoretical frameworks have been utilized in studies exploring students' perceptions of AI applications in HE?
**RQ2**. Which AI tools have been the focus of research exploring HE students' perceptions?
***RQ3***. What opportunities are reflected in students' perceptions of AI applications in HE?
***RQ4***. What concerns are reflected in students' perceptions of AI applications in HE

To ensure comprehensive coverage of the existing literature, a wide range of carefully selected keywords was used as search terms to locate studies addressing this topic from various angles (see Table 1).

**Table 1.** Key search terms

| |
|---|
| (AI OR "Artificial intelligence") - (Topic[a]) |
| AND - ("student* voice" OR "student* perception" OR "student* perspective" OR "student* overview" OR "student* insight" OR "student attitude") - (Topic) |
| AND - ("higher education" OR tertiary OR universit* OR colleg*) (Topic) |

[a]Refers to a query that includes the Title, Abstract, Author Keywords, and Keywords Plus

The lead author conducted searches in the following research literature databases: Web of Science (Clarivate), Scopus, JSTOR, ERIC (Institute of Education Sciences), and ScienceDirect (Elsevier). After applying the initial set of inclusion criteria (see Table 2), a total of 3581 articles were identified. Specifically, at this stage, the search was restricted to studies published between 2015 and February 2025, as significant advancements in AI technologies and their integration into HE have predominantly occurred during this period (Crompton & Burke, 2023; Bond et al., 2024).

After removing 2123 duplicates, 603 conference papers, and 3 retracted articles, 852 articles remained. Stepwise screening using inclusion and exclusion criteria eliminated 506 non-empirical, off-topic, or non-peer-reviewed studies. Finally, full-text review of the remaining 362 articles resulted in the removal of further studies focusing on stakeholders other than students ($n = 205$) and/or conducted in non-academic environments outside HE ($n = 101$). This process resulted in a final set of 56 articles focusing on students' perceptions of AI tool usage, which were retained for content analysis.

It is to be noted that the screening process as well as content analysis were conducted by the lead author in collaboration with the third author. In cases of inconsistencies or uncertainty, decisions were discussed with the second author until consensus was reached.

**Table 2.** Inclusion and Exclusion criteria

| Criteria | Inclusion | Exclusion |
|---|---|---|
| ***1. Identification phase*** | | |
| Publication date | 2015 to Feb, 2025 | Studies published before 2015 |
| Language | English | Other language |
| Type of article | Peer-reviewed original research articles and conference papers | Non-peer-reviewed papers or conference papers, and retracted articles |
| ***2. Screening phase*** | | |
| Empirical studies | Using the qualitative, quantitative, and mixed methods approach | Not empirical (e.g., meta-analyses, conceptual studies, or other forms of systematic reviews) |
| Peer-reviewed journals | Published in reputable peer-reviewed journals | Not peer-reviewed (e.g., books, book chapters, dissertations, thesis, conference proceedings and reports) |
| Study focus | Students' perceptions and experiences regarding the application of AI tools | Off-topic |
| ***3. Eligibility phase*** | | |
| Stakeholders | Students | Other stakeholders (e.g., faculty members, instructors, academics and manager) |
| Population and sample | Students within the university and the field of HE | Non-academic environments and settings outside of HE or the K-12 context |

## 3 Results

In this section, the research questions will be addressed based on the review of the selected studies. The word cloud presented in Fig. 1 highlights prominent themes such as "Acceptance", "Artificial Intelligence", "Technology", "Information Technology", "Education", and "User". These keywords indicate a strong emphasis on student adoption of AI technologies within HE, aligning closely with the objectives of this study.

Additionally, terms such as "Intention" and "Perceptions" underscore the importance of students' attitudes toward AI and its perceived impact on their learning experiences.

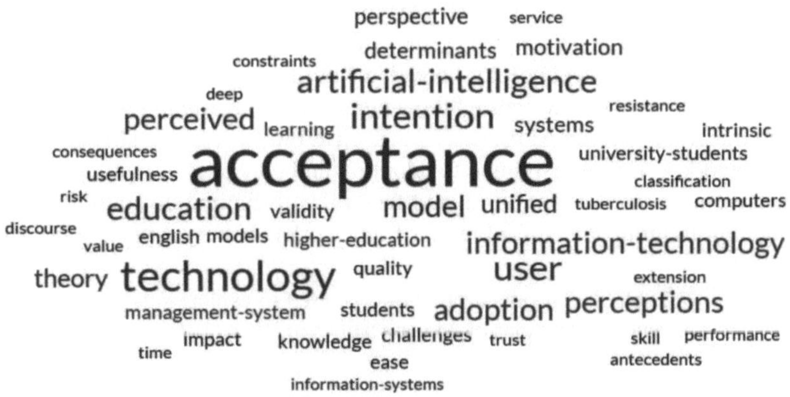


**Fig. 1.** Word cloud depicting keyword frequency in reviewed studies

The analysis of publication years indicates a strong emphasis on recent research activity (see Fig. 2). The majority of publications ($n = 37$; 66.1%) were published in 2024, followed by 11 publications (19.6%) in 2023. As of 2025 (up to the end of February), five publications (8.9%) have been recorded. In contrast, earlier years exhibit significantly lower publication counts, with only two publications in 2022 and one in 2020. This temporal distribution underscores increasing scholarly interest in the topic, with a marked concentration of studies emerging in the most recent year, possibly driven by the emergence of generative AI (GenAI) in 2022 (Farrokhnia et al., 2025).

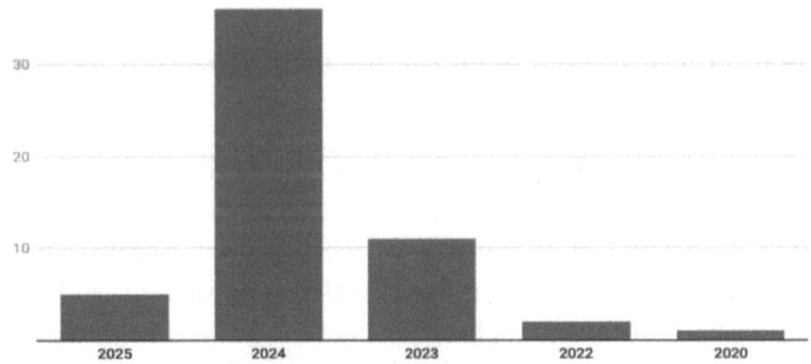


**Fig. 2.** Distribution of publications by year

## 3.1 RQ1. What Theoretical Frameworks Have Been Utilized in Studies Exploring Students' Perceptions of AI Applications in HE?

The findings revealed that most reviewed studies lacked a clear theoretical foundation. A smaller subset, however, applied various frameworks to examine students' perceptions of AI in HE, with TAM and the Unified Theory of Acceptance and Use of Technology (UTAUT) being most common (see Table 3). These models focused on adoption factors like perceived usefulness and behavioral intention, sometimes combined with the Expectation Confirmation Model (ECM) to examine how initial expectations influenced continued AI use. Less frequently, the Diffusion of Innovations (DOI) framework explored motivation and technology spread, while Task-Technology Fit (TTF) combined with TAM assessed how well AI tools met students' learning tasks. A few studies employed education-specific AI frameworks, such as the AI Adoption Model and AI Literacy Framework, offering insights into adoption and educational integration. Overall, the literature emphasized adoption-related factors, with limited diversity in theoretical grounding, highlighting a need for broader frameworks to study AI perceptions in HE.

**Table 3.** Theoretical frameworks used to explore students' perceptions of AI applications in HE

| Frameworks | Frequency (*out of* 56) |
|---|---|
| TAM | 6 |
| UTAUT | 2 |
| ECM | 2 |
| DOI | 1 |
| TTF | 1 |
| AI adoption model | 1 |
| AI readiness | 1 |
| AI literacy framework | 1 |

### 3.2 RQ2. Which AI Tools Have Been the Focus of Research Exploring HE Students' Perceptions?

The scoping review highlighted a strong focus on GenAI tools in studies exploring HE students' perceptions (see Table 4). GenAI chatbots, such as ChatGPT, were the most frequently studied, appearing in about 50% of the included research. Beyond general-purpose chatbots, task-specific GenAI tools were also examined, including writing assistants (e.g., Grammarly, Quillbot), teaching assistant tools, research assistant tools, and image generation tools. In contrast, non-GenAI tools received limited attention, with AI voice assistants (e.g., Siri, Alexa) investigated in only one study. Some studies addressed AI in general without specifying tools, primarily within medical education contexts. Overall, while a range of AI applications has been explored regarding students' perceptions, GenAI, especially chatbots and specialized generative tools, has dominated research in HE over the past decade (2015–2025), reflecting sustained scholarly interest in understanding its impact on student learning experiences, engagement, and academic practices.

**Table 4.** AI tools on which students' perceptions were explored

| Tools | Frequency (*out of* 56) |
|---|---|
| (Gen)AI chatbots | 28 |
| AI in general | 17 |
| (Gen)AI writing assistant tools (e.g., Grammarly/Quillbot) | 5 |
| (Gen)AI teaching assistant tools | 3 |
| (Gen)AI research assistant tools | 1 |
| AI Voice assistant tools (e.g., Siri/Alexa) | 1 |
| (Gen)AI image generation tools | 1 |

### 3.3 RQ3. What Opportunities Are Reflected in Students' Perceptions of AI Applications in HE?

The scoping review highlighted diverse opportunities perceived by HE students regarding AI applications, mainly in academic and personal development (see Table 5). In academic development, students viewed AI as enhancing specific skills, including language and writing, research competencies, and decision-making or idea generation. AI was also perceived to improve overall learning quality, supporting academic performance, satisfaction, personalized feedback, adaptive learning pathways, accessibility, and engagement in online and interactive environments. Collaborative and teamwork experiences were further enriched, fostering motivation and participation. In terms of personal development, students noted gains in self-efficacy, confidence, productivity, critical thinking, creativity, and mental well-being. Although less frequently emphasized, these findings indicate that AI contributes to broader cognitive and emotional growth. Overall, students value AI not only as a tool for developing academic skills but also as a means to create more engaging, supportive, and personalized learning experiences that enhance both performance and personal growth.

**Table 5.** Perceived opportunities of AI in HE from the students' point of view

| Categories | Identified Opportunity | Frequency (*out of* 56) |
|---|---|---|
| Academic skills and learning improvement | Improved language and writing skills | 11 |
| | Improvement in academic performance | 8 |
| | Personalized learning experiences and feedback | 7 |
| | Flexibility and ease of use in learning activity | 6 |

(*continued*)

**Table 5.** (*continued*)

| Categories | Identified Opportunity | Frequency (*out of* 56) |
|---|---|---|
| | Development of research skills | 4 |
| | Enhancement of online learning experiences | 3 |
| | Interactive learning experiences | 2 |
| | Decision-making support | 2 |
| | Improved collaboration and teamwork | 1 |
| | Increased learning satisfaction | 1 |
| | Help with idea generation | 1 |
| Personal skills improvement | Self-efficiency, self-confidence and personal productivity | 4 |
| | Improvement of critical thinking skills | 4 |
| | Development of innovative concepts and creativity | 3 |
| | Positive effects on mental Well-being | 1 |

### 3.4 RQ4. What Concerns Are Reflected in Students' Perceptions of AI Applications in HE?

While students recognized the opportunities AI offers in HE, they also raised significant concerns (see Table 6). Ethical issues were most frequently reported, including data privacy, unequal access, lack of institutional policies, and academic integrity, with fears that AI might encourage cheating, reduce accountability, and diminish the value of independent work. Distrust in AI-generated content, particularly regarding accuracy and reliability, was also common. Students expressed human-centered concerns, including insufficient training, lack of support, and gaps in skills needed for AI-mediated learning. Broader anxieties included job insecurity, overreliance on AI, and threats to independent thinking and creativity. Overall, students highlighted the need for guidance, equitable access, and skill development to navigate AI effectively in academic contexts. Ethical, practical, and personal challenges intersected, showing that while AI presents many opportunities, careful management and institutional support are crucial to ensure its responsible and beneficial integration in HE.

**Table 6.** Students' concerns about the use of AI in HE

| Categories | Identified concerns | Frequency (*out of* 56) |
|---|---|---|
| Ethical concerns | Privacy issue, equitable access, and unclear policies | 16 |
| | Reduction in academic integrity | 6 |
| | Concerns related to cheating and lack of authenticity | 5 |
| | Distrust about receiving incorrect information from AI | 5 |
| Human-centered concerns | Absence of AI training opportunities | 4 |
| | Reduced job security (or fear of replacement by machines) | 3 |
| | Overreliance on AI | 3 |
| | Individual limitations and the need for new skills | 2 |
| | Negative impacts on creativity | 1 |

## 4 Discussion

The current study aimed to provide a comprehensive overview of research on students' perceptions of AI applications in HE. By synthesizing existing findings, the study offers insights into theoretical underpinnings, perceived opportunities, and challenges, which are critical for understanding students' long-term engagement with AI-based tools, especially in light of the rapid emergence of GenAI (Batista et al., 2024). The following discussion highlights key themes.

### 4.1 Theoretical Frameworks Used to Explore Students' Perceptions

A notable finding is the frequent absence of theoretical frameworks, which undermines the coherence and comparability of research (Moernaut, 2021). Among the studies that did apply theory, TAM and UTAUT were most common, reflecting their widespread use in predicting user behavior in educational technology contexts (Flores-Velásquez et al., 2024; Granić & Marangunić, 2019). These models address constructs such as perceived usefulness, ease of use, and performance expectancy (Balaman & Baş, 2023; Raffaghelli et al., 2022).

However, TAM and UTAUT assume linear, static relationships and do not fully account for the evolving perceptions of AI in HE (Kanont et al., 2024). For example, ease of use may paradoxically reduce perceived value, and longitudinal experiences, including trust and feelings of discomfort, shape continued engagement (Polyportis, 2024; Patil et al., 2020). To address these gaps, some studies integrated ECM, which emphasizes post-adoption experiences, including expectation confirmation and satisfaction, as key predictors of continued use (Jung & Jo, 2025; Tian et al., 2024). These models better capture students' dynamic experiences with AI, highlighting that initial beliefs are continuously reshaped by actual use.

## 4.2 AI Tools Investigated in Studies of Students' Perceptions

Most studies focused on GenAI tools, particularly ChatGPT, reflecting its global adoption after 2022 (Chan & Hu, 2023; Ravšelj et al., 2025). However, research often treats GenAI as a monolithic category, overlooking functional and contextual differences among tools (Batista et al., 2024; Zawacki-Richter et al., 2019). Writing assistants, for instance, are perceived to enhance productivity and enjoyment, while research or teaching support tools elicit distinct experiences (Rienties et al., 2024; Sabbaghan & Eaton, 2025). This gap indicates a need for tool-specific studies to capture nuanced educational implications and inform policy and practice (Jin et al., 2025).

## 4.3 Students' Perceptions of AI Opportunities for HE

Students perceive AI as enhancing academic learning and outcomes, particularly in language and writing skills (Almassaad et al., 2024; Kim et al., 2020). GenAI supports grammar correction, content refinement, and clarity (Mekheimer, 2025), and may enhance overall performance (Sun & Zhou, 2024). Benefits also include personal development, such as improved self-efficacy, learning confidence, and creative thinking (Almassaad et al., 2024; Tian et al., 2024). These effects likely stem from personalized learning experiences, which increase motivation and engagement (Aviran & Blonder, 2023; Shahzad et al., 2024).

Nonetheless, the promise of personalization is sometimes limited, as GenAI may produce uniform outputs that overlook learners' diverse abilities, cultural contexts, and cognitive profiles (Laak et al., 2024). Likewise, confidence gains may vary by domain, with analytical tasks showing weaker effects (Reich & Teeny, 2025). Thus, perceptions must be interpreted cautiously, considering contextual limitations.

## 4.4 Students' Perceptions of AI Challenges for HE

Two main categories of concern emerged: ethical issues and human-centered challenges. Ethical concerns include privacy, equitable access, and unclear institutional policies (Fawaz et al., 2025; Almassaad et al., 2024; Gore & Dove, 2024). Many policies remain faculty-centered, leaving students uncertain about acceptable AI use (McDonald et al., 2025; Yusuf et al., 2024).

Human-centered concerns relate to skills, preparedness, and cognitive development, particularly AI literacy encompassing technical, ethical, and evaluative competencies (Ng et al., 2021; Wang et al., 2024). Lack of training fosters anxiety and overreliance, potentially undermining creativity and independent problem-solving (Fawaz et al., 2025; Bastani et al., 2024; Habib et al., 2024). This aligns with cognitive offloading theory, where excessive reliance on AI diminishes reflection and self-regulation (Risko & Gilbert, 2016; Fan et al., 2025). Together, these concerns highlight the need for ethical guidance and skill development to ensure responsible, effective AI use.

## 5 Implications for Theory and Practice

This review offers a synthesized understanding of how students perceive and engage with AI in HE, generating implications that inform both theoretical development and practical action in this emerging field.

From a theoretical standpoint, the findings contribute to efforts to reconceptualize students' interaction with AI not as a fixed decision but as a dynamic and unfolding process. Across the literature, student engagement appears shaped by more than functional evaluations; emotional fluctuations, contextual influences, and changing expectations are central to how students assess AI. This supports a shift toward temporally sensitive and psychologically informed models that better capture the evolving nature of technology use in educational settings. Such models could conceptualize student–AI interaction as a continuous meaning-making process, rather than a discrete acceptance event.

A direct implication of this theoretical contribution is the call for more deliberate and varied theoretical engagement in empirical research. While some studies drew on established models, many lacked a defined theoretical lens. To advance conceptual clarity and enable meaningful comparisons, future research should adopt frameworks better suited to the layered and context-dependent nature of AI use in HE. In particular, theoretical frameworks that can accommodate post-adoption dynamics, contextual variability, and emerging socio-emotional considerations may be more appropriate for capturing the richness of student experience.

This review also noted that most studies approached GenAI from a broad perspective, often grouping tools together without differentiating their academic functions or user contexts. While this reflects current usage trends, such generalization may overlook critical distinctions in how students experience and evaluate different tools. A more granular, tool-specific approach would likely yield deeper insights into the varied educational roles of GenAI and allow for more tailored pedagogical and policy responses.

As AI becomes more embedded in HE, students are increasingly expected to navigate its use without consistent or student-centered guidance. The lack of coherent policies creates uncertainty around responsible use and contributes to uneven integration across institutions. There is a clear need for HE institutions to move beyond instructor-dependent or ad hoc approaches and to develop policies that define acceptable practices, reflect disciplinary norms, and remain responsive to technological developments. These policies should be communicated clearly and designed with student perspectives in mind.

Alongside policy development, the findings highlight the need for structured training and support systems that prepare students not only to use AI tools, but to do so thoughtfully. Many students report feeling unprepared, particularly in areas involving ethical judgment and critical evaluation. Addressing this requires investment in AI literacy initiatives that go beyond technical instruction. These should include opportunities to reflect on the influence of AI on learning habits, creativity, and academic agency. When integrated into curricula, such efforts can strengthen students' confidence and promote more intentional, evaluative use of AI in their academic practice.

In sum, the implications of this review point to the value of a more nuanced and student-responsive approach to AI in HE, one that is grounded in evolving theoretical understandings, attentive to students' needs and experiences, and guided by coherent institutional structures.

## 6 Limitation and Suggestions Future Studies

This review has several limitations. *First*, rapidly evolving AI technologies may render findings temporary; longitudinal designs are needed to track perceptions and engagement over time (Polyportis, 2024).

*Second*, the focus on students excludes broader institutional perspectives. Multi-stakeholder studies involving educators and administrators would clarify adoption dynamics (Zawacki-Richter et al., 2019; Polyportis, 2024).

*Third*, while ethical concerns were highlighted, structural and institutional preparedness requires deeper investigation. Future research should examine regulations, governance, transparency, and student rights in AI-mediated learning.

*Finally*, studies often focus on specific regions or disciplines, limiting generalizability. Expanding research to underrepresented contexts will capture diverse cultural, infrastructural, and pedagogical factors shaping AI use (Polyportis, 2024; Zhang et al., 2023; Kumar & Raman, 2022).

## References

1. Almassaad, A., Alajlan, H., Alebaikan, R.: Student perceptions of generative artificial intelligence: investigating utilization, benefits, and challenges in higher education. Systems. **12**(10), 385 (2024). https://doi.org/10.3390/systems12100385
2. Arksey, H., O'malley, L.: Scoping studies: towards a methodological framework. Int. J. Soc. Res. Methodol. **8**(1), 19–32 (2005). https://doi.org/10.1080/1364557032000119616
3. Aviran, E., Blonder, R.: The influence of learning with an online, personalized environment on students' attitudes, beliefs, and outcomes. J. Sci. Educ. Technol. **32**(5), 722–742 (2023). https://doi.org/10.1007/s10956-023-10060-1
4. Balaman, F., Baş, M.: Perception of using e-learning platforms in the scope of the technology acceptance model (TAM): a scale development study. Interact. Learn. Environ. **31**(8), 5395–5419 (2023). https://doi.org/10.1080/10494820.2021.2007136
5. Bastani, H., Bastani, O., Sungu, A., Ge, H., Kabakci, O., Mariman, R.: Generative AI can harm learning. Available at SSRN, 4895486. (2024). https://doi.org/10.2139/ssrn.4895486
6. Batista, J., Mesquita, A., Carnaz, G.: Generative AI and higher education: trends, challenges, and future directions from a systematic literature review. Information. **15**(11), 676 (2024). https://doi.org/10.3390/info15110676
7. Bobrytska, V.I., Krasylnykova, H.V., Beseda, N.A., Krasylnykov, S.R., Skyrda, T.S.: Artificial intelligence (AI) in Ukrainian higher education: a comprehensive study of stakeholder attitudes, expectations and concerns. Int. J. Learn. Teach. Educ. Res. **23**(1), 400–426 (2024). https://doi.org/10.26803/ijlter.23.1.20
8. Bond, M., et al.: A meta systematic review of artificial intelligence in higher education: a call for increased ethics, collaboration, and rigor. Int. J. Educ. Technol. High. Educ. **21**(1), 4 (2024). https://doi.org/10.1186/s41239-023-00436-z
9. Chan, C.K.Y.: A comprehensive AI policy education framework for university teaching and learning. Int. J. Educ. Technol. High. Educ. **20**(1), 38 (2023). https://doi.org/10.1186/s41239-023-00408-3
10. Chan, C.K.Y., Hu, W.: Students' voices on generative AI: perceptions, benefits, and challenges in higher education. Int. J. Educ. Technol. High. Educ. **20**(1), 43 (2023). https://doi.org/10.1186/s41239-023-00411-8

11. Crompton, H., Burke, D.: Artificial intelligence in higher education: the state of the field. Int. J. Educ. Technol. High. Educ. **20**(1), 22 (2023). https://doi.org/10.1186/s41239-023-00392-8
12. Du, J., Alm, A.: The impact of ChatGPT on English for academic purposes (EAP) students' language learning experience: a self-determination theory perspective. Educ. Sci. **14**(7), 726 (2024). https://doi.org/10.3390/educsci14070726
13. Fan, Y., et al.: Beware of metacognitive laziness: effects of generative artificial intelligence on learning motivation, processes, and performance. Br. J. Educ. Technol. **56**(2), 489–530 (2025). https://doi.org/10.1111/bjet.13544
14. Farrokhnia, M., Soleimani, S., Noroozi, O.: Generative AI in higher education: transformative tools for research, teaching, and assessment. In: Navigating Generative AI in Higher Education, pp. 33–53. Edward Elgar Publishing (2025)
15. Flores-Velásquez, C.H., et al.: A bibliometric review of studies about the acceptance of artificial intelligence technologies in teaching and learning in higher education. Int. J. Learn. Teach. Educ. Res. **23**(3), 275–292 (2024). https://doi.org/10.26803/ijlter.23.3.14
16. Fawaz, M., El?Malti, W., Alreshidi, S.M., Kavuran, E.: Exploring health sciences students' perspectives on using generative artificial intelligence in higher education: a qualitative study. Nurs. Health Sci. **27**(1), e70030 (2025). https://doi.org/10.1111/nhs.70030
17. Gore, S., Dove, E.: Ethical considerations in the use of artificial intelligence in counselling and psychotherapy training: a student stakeholder perspective—a pilot study. Couns. Psychother. Res. (2024). https://doi.org/10.1002/capr.12770
18. Grájeda, A., et al.: Embracing artificial intelligence in the arts classroom: understanding student perceptions and emotional reactions to AI tools. Cogent Educ. **11**(1), 2378271 (2024). https://doi.org/10.1080/2331186X.2024.2378271
19. Granić, A., Marangunić, N.: Technology acceptance model in educational context: a systematic literature review. Br. J. Educ. Technol. **50**(5), 2572–2593 (2019). https://doi.org/10.1111/bjet.12864
20. Grassini, S., Aasen, M.L., Møgelvang, A.: Understanding university students' acceptance of ChatGPT: insights from the UTAUT2 model. Appl. Artif. Intell. **38**(1), 2371168 (2024). https://doi.org/10.1080/08839514.2024.2371168
21. Habib, S., Vogel, T., Anli, X., Thorne, E.: How does generative artificial intelligence impact student creativity? Cogent Educ. **34**(1), 100072 (2024). https://doi.org/10.1016/j.yjoc.2023.100072
22. Huang, A.Y., Lu, O.H., Yang, S.J.: Effects of artificial intelligence–enabled personalized recommendations on learners' learning engagement, motivation, and outcomes in a flipped classroom. Comput. Educ. **194**, 104684 (2023). https://doi.org/10.1016/j.compedu.2022.104684
23. Jin, Y., Yan, L., Echeverria, V., Gašević, D., Martinez-Maldonado, R.: Generative AI in higher education: a global perspective of institutional adoption policies and guidelines. Comput. Educ.: Artif. Intell. **8**, 100348 (2025). https://doi.org/10.1016/j.caeai.2024.100348
24. Jony, A.I., Hamim, S.A.: Empowering virtual collaboration: harnessing AI for enhanced teamwork in higher education. Educ. Technol. Q. **2024**(3), 337–359 (2024). https://doi.org/10.55056/etq.746
25. Jung, Y.M., Jo, H.: Understanding continuance intention of generative AI in education: an ECM-based study for sustainable learning engagement. Sustainability. **17**(13), 60–82 (2025). https://doi.org/10.3390/su17136082
26. Kanbach, D.K., Heiduk, L., Blueher, G., Schreiter, M., Lahmann, A.: The GenAI is out of the bottle: generative artificial intelligence from a business model innovation perspective. Rev. Manag. Sci. **18**(4), 1189–1220 (2024). https://doi.org/10.1007/s11846-023-00696-z
27. Kanont, K., et al.: Generative-AI, a learning assistant? Factors influencing higher-ed students' technology acceptance. Electron. J. e-Learn. **22**(6), 18–33 (2024). https://doi.org/10.34190/ejel.22.6.3196

28. Kim, J., Merrill, K., Xu, K., Sellnow, D.D.: My teacher is a machine: understanding students' perceptions of AI teaching assistants in online education. Int. J. Hum. Comput. Interact. **36**(20), 1902–1911 (2020). https://doi.org/10.1080/10447318.2020.1801227
29. Kumar, V.R., Raman, R.: Student perceptions on artificial intelligence (AI) in higher education. In: 2022 IEEE Integrated STEM Education Conference (ISEC), pp. 450–454. IEEE (2022). https://doi.org/10.1109/ISEC54952.2022.10025165
30. Laak, K.J., Abdelghani, R., Aru, J.: Personalisation is not guaranteed: the challenges of using generative AI for personalised learning. In: International Conference on Innovative Technologies and Learning, pp. 40–49. Springer Nature Switzerland, Cham (2024). https://doi.org/10.1007/978-3-031-65881-5_5
31. Malik, A.R., Pratiwi, Y., Andajani, K., Numertayasa, I.W., Suharti, S., Darwis, A.: Exploring artificial intelligence in academic essay: higher education student's perspective. Int. J. Educ. Res. Open. **5**, 100296 (2023). https://doi.org/10.1016/j.ijedro.2023.100296
32. Martins, L.L., Kellermanns, F.W.: A model of business school students' acceptance of a web-based course management system. Acad. Manag. Learn. Edu. **3**(1), 7–26 (2004). https://doi.org/10.5465/AMLE.2004.12436815
33. McDonald, N., Johri, A., Ali, A., Collier, A.H.: Generative artificial intelligence in higher education: evidence from an analysis of institutional policies and guidelines. Comput. Hum. Behav. Artif. Hum. **100121** (2025). https://doi.org/10.1016/j.chbah.2025.100121
34. Mekheimer, M.: Generative AI-assisted feedback and EFL writing: a study on proficiency, revision frequency and writing quality. Discov. Educ. **4**(1), 170 (2025). https://doi.org/10.1007/s44217-025-00602-7
35. Moernaut, N.: Listening between the lines: how a theoretical framework prevents superficial analysis in qualitative research. New Trends Qual. Res. **6**, 15–23 (2021). https://doi.org/10.36367/ntqr.6.2021.15-23
36. Munn, Z., Peters, M.D., Stern, C., Tufanaru, C., McArthur, A., Aromataris, E.: Systematic review or scoping review? Guidance for authors when choosing between a systematic or scoping review approach. BMC Med. Res. Methodol. **18**, 1–7 (2018). https://doi.org/10.1186/s12874-018-0611-x
37. Ng, D.T.K., Leung, J.K.L., Chu, S.K.W., Qiao, M.S.: Conceptualizing AI literacy: an exploratory review. Comput. Educ. : Artif. Intell. **2**, 100041 (2021). https://doi.org/10.1016/j.caeai.2021.100041
38. Patil, P., Tamilmani, K., Rana, N.P., Raghavan, V.: Understanding consumer adoption of mobile payment in India: extending meta-UTAUT model with personal innovativeness, anxiety, trust, and grievance redressal. Int. J. Inf. Manag. **54**, 102144 (2020). https://doi.org/10.1016/j.ijinfomgt.2020.102144
39. Polyportis, A.: A longitudinal study on artificial intelligence adoption: understanding the drivers of ChatGPT usage behavior change in higher education. Front. Artif. Intell. **6**, 1324398 (2024). https://doi.org/10.3389/frai.2023.1324398
40. Raffaghelli, J.E., Rodríguez, M.E., Guerrero-Roldán, A.E., Bañeres, D.: Applying the UTAUT model to explain the students' acceptance of an early warning system in higher education. Comput. Educ. **182**, 104468 (2022). https://doi.org/10.1016/j.compedu.2022.104468
41. Raj, N.S., Renumol, V.G.: A systematic literature review on adaptive content recommenders in personalized learning environments from 2015 to 2020. J. Comput. Educ. **9**(1), 113–148 (2022). https://doi.org/10.1007/s40692-021-00199-4
42. Ravšelj, D., et al.: Higher education students' perceptions of ChatGPT: a global study of early reactions. PLoS One. **20**(2), e0315011 (2025). https://doi.org/10.1371/journal.pone.0315011
43. Rawas, S.: ChatGPT: empowering lifelong learning in the digital age of higher education. Educ. Inf. Technol. **29**(6), 6895–6908 (2024). https://doi.org/10.1007/s10639-023-12114-8

44. Reich, T., Teeny, J.D.: Does artificial intelligence cause artificial confidence? Generative artificial intelligence as an emerging social referent. J. Pers. Soc. Psychol. (2025). https://doi.org/10.1037/pspa0000450
45. Rienties, B., Domingue, J., Duttaroy, S., Herodotou, C., Tessarolo, F., Whitelock, D.: What distance learning students want from an AI digital assistant. Distance Educ., 1–17 (2024). https://doi.org/10.1080/01587919.2024.2338717
46. Risko, E.F., Gilbert, S.J.: Cognitive offloading. Trends Cogn. Sci. **20**(9), 676–688 (2016). https://doi.org/10.1016/j.tics.2016.07.003
47. Sabbaghan, S., Eaton, S.E.: Navigating the ethical frontier: graduate students' experiences with generative AI-mediated scholarship. Int. J. Artif. Intell. Educ., 1–27 (2025). https://doi.org/10.1007/s40593-024-00454-6
48. Schei, O.M., Møgelvang, A., Ludvigsen, K.: Perceptions and use of AI chatbots among students in higher education: a scoping review of empirical studies. Educ. Sci. **14**(8), 922 (2024). https://doi.org/10.3390/educsci14080922
49. Shahzad, M.F., Xu, S., Lim, W.M., Yang, X., Khan, Q.R.: Artificial intelligence and social media on academic performance and mental well-being: student perceptions of positive impact in the age of smart learning. Heliyon. **10**(8) (2024). https://doi.org/10.1016/j.heliyon.2024.e29523
50. Soleimani, S., Farrokhnia, M., van Dijk, A., Noroozi, O.: Educators' perceptions of generative AI: investigating attitudes, barriers and learning needs in higher education. Innov. Educ. Teach. Int. **62**(5), 1598–1613 (2025). https://doi.org/10.1080/14703297.2025.2530767
51. Strzelecki, A.: To use or not to use ChatGPT in higher education? A study of students' acceptance and use of technology. Interact. Learn. Environ., 1–14 (2023). https://doi.org/10.1080/10494820.2023.2209881
52. Sun, L., Zhou, L.: Does generative artificial intelligence improve the academic achievement of college students? A meta-analysis. J. Educ. Comput. Res. **62**(7), 1676–1713 (2024). https://doi.org/10.1177/07356331241277937
53. Tian, W., Ge, J., Zhao, Y., Zheng, X.: AI Chatbots in Chinese higher education: adoption, perception, and influence among graduate students—an integrated analysis utilizing UTAUT and ECM models. Front. Psychol. **15**, 1268549 (2024). https://doi.org/10.3389/fpsyg.2024.1268549
54. Tricco, A.C., et al.: PRISMA extension for scoping reviews (PRISMA-ScR): checklist and explanation. Ann. Intern. Med. **169**(7), 467–473 (2018). https://doi.org/10.7326/M18-0850
55. Wang, C., Wang, H., Li, Y., Dai, J., Gu, X., Yu, T.: Factors influencing university students' behavioral intention to use generative artificial intelligence: integrating the theory of planned behavior and AI literacy. Int. J. Hum. Comput. Interact., 1–23 (2024). https://doi.org/10.1080/10447318.2024.2383033
56. Yusuf, A., Pervin, N., Román-González, M.: Generative AI and the future of higher education: a threat to academic integrity or reformation? Evidence from multicultural perspectives. Int. J. Educ. Technol. High. Educ. **21**(1), 21 (2024). https://doi.org/10.1186/s41239-024-00453-6
57. Zawacki-Richter, O., Marín, V.I., Bond, M., Gouverneur, F.: Systematic review of research on artificial intelligence applications in higher education. Int. J. Educ. Technol. High. Educ. **16**(1), 39 (2019). https://doi.org/10.1186/s41239-019-0171-0
58. Zhang, L., Wang, Y., Liu, H.: Exploring AI adoption in vocational education in China: contextual challenges and opportunities. Int. J. Educ. Res. **114**, 101979 (2023). https://doi.org/10.1016/j.ijer.2022.101979

# Decoding Student Dialogue: A Multi-dimensional Comparison and Bias Analysis of Large Language Models as Annotation Tools

Jie Cao[1], Zhanxin Hao[2(✉)], and Jifan Yu[2]

[1] The University of North Carolina at Chapel Hill, North Carolina, USA
jiecao@unc.edu
[2] Tsinghua University, Beijing, China
{zhanxin_hao,yujifan}@tsinghua.edu.cn

**Abstract.** Educational dialogue is critical for decoding student learning processes, yet manual annotation remains time-consuming. This study evaluates the efficacy of GPT-5.2 and Gemini-3 using three prompting strategies (few-shot, single-agent, and multi-agent reflection) across diverse subjects, educational levels, and four coding dimensions. Results indicate that while multi-agent prompting achieved the highest accuracy, the results did not reach statistical significance. Accuracy proved highly context-dependent, with significantly higher performance in K-12 datasets compared to university-level data, alongside disciplinary variations within the same educational level. Performance peaked in the affective dimension but remained lowest in the cognitive dimension. Furthermore, analysis revealed four bias patterns: (1) Gemini-3 exhibited a consistent optimistic bias in the affective dimension across all subjects; (2) the cognitive dimension displayed domain-specific directional bias, characterized by systematic underestimation in Mathematics versus overestimation in Psychology; (3) both models are more prone to overestimation than underestimation within the meta-cognitive dimension; and (4) behavioral categories such as question, negotiation, and statements were frequently misclassified. These results underscore the need for context-sensitive deployment and targeted mitigation of directional biases in automated annotation.

**Keywords:** Large Language Models · Automated Annotation · Educational dialogue · Bias

## 1 Introduction

Educational dialogue is a fundamental vehicle for knowledge exchange, and its quality significantly influences student learning outcomes [8,11,18]. While analyzing these interactions through established frameworks provides deep


E. G. Blanchard et al. (eds.), AIED 2026, LNCS 16586, pp. 378–386, 2027.
https://doi.org/10.1007/978-3-032-29773-0_29

insights into the learning process [10], manual coding remains prohibitively time-consuming [16]. This analytical bottleneck is exacerbated by the proliferation of Large Language Models (LLMs) in education, which has made student-AI interactions ubiquitous [13]. Consequently, educators now face a massive volume of dialogue data that needs to be analyzed to understand student engagement and inform instruction, necessitating robust, automated approaches.

Recent studies have already explored the "LLM-as-a-judge" paradigm for automated educational annotation, demonstrating significant potential [9,12,16, 20]. However, reported accuracies vary widely (ranging from 0.6 to 0.9), likely due to differences in prompt engineering, model capabilities, contextual factors, or label complexities [9,20]. Furthermore, two critical gaps remain: first, a lack of comprehensive comparison evaluating different prompting methods across varied educational contexts and annotation dimensions (i.e., cognitive); and second, a neglect of inherent annotation biases, which need to be addressed to ensure fair and equitable automated analysis.

To address these challenges, this study evaluates the capabilities and biases of LLMs (GPT-5.2 and Gemini-3) in annotating student-AI dialogues. We test their performance using a multi-dimensional scheme across varied contexts, comparing three prompting methods: Few-Shot, Single-agent Self-reflection, and Multi-agent Reflection. We propose two Research Questions (RQs):**RQ1:** To what extent do prompting methods (few-shot, single-agent, and multi-agent reflection) and contextual factors (educational levels, subjects, and annotation dimensions) influence the accuracy of LLM-based student dialogue annotation? **RQ2:** What bias patterns emerge in the LLM-based annotation of student dialogues?

## 2 Related Work

### 2.1 Educational Dialogue and Student-AI Dialogue Interaction

Grounded in sociocultural theory, educational dialogue is a critical mechanism for knowledge construction and enhancing academic performance [11,19]. As Large Language Models (LLMs) rapidly popularize student-AI interactions through various chatbots and simulated classrooms [21,24], the lack of human instructor oversight makes the automatic monitoring and decoding of these dialogues essential. Previous research primarily applies framework-based content analysis to evaluate these interactions. Studies have investigated verbal behaviors [24], cognitive strategies for knowledge construction [4], and meta-cognitive behaviors related to AI management [6]. Additionally, sentiment analysis is employed to assess the socio-emotional dynamics inherent in student-AI dialogues [4].

### 2.2 Annotation Based on LLMs and Biases

LLMs demonstrate significant potential for data annotation across diverse educational levels, subjects, and interactive tasks [8,9,12]. However, annotation accuracy varies considerably [12]. For example, while GPT-4 achieved high overall agreement with experts in analyzing classroom dialogues, its sub-construct reliability fluctuated widely (Cohen's Kappa ranging from 0.2 to 0.973) [16]. Such discrepancies stem from differences in models, prompt engineering, and task complexity. The current lack of standardized frameworks necessitates systematic evaluations of LLM performance across various prompting methods and educational contexts to establish a robust understanding of their capabilities. Beyond accuracy, identifying inherent LLM biases is critical for ensuring reliable results. While biases such as human-like cognitive bias (i.e., sequential anchoring bias) in decision-making [5], political bias (i.e., prefer specific political orientation) in detection tasks [14], verbosity bias ( prefer longer text that exceeded word limits) in evaluation [22,25] have been documented in other domains, their specific impact on educational dialogue annotation remains underexplored.

## 3 Methodology

### 3.1 Dataset

Our primary data originates from an online platform where human students interact with AI teachers and peers during slide-based lectures. We collected student utterances from three courses: **Biology (K-12)** (Fall 2025; 82 students, 304 utterances), **Introduction to Artificial General Intelligence (AGI, University)** (Spring 2024; 305 students, 4008 utterances), and **Psychology (University)** (Spring 2025; 288 students, 977 utterances). All data collection procedures were subjected to ethical review by Tsinghua University. Additionally, we incorporated the public *CoMTA* dataset [17], featuring K-12 **Mathematics** student-AI tutoring conversations. To ensure a balanced evaluation, we randomly sampled 200 student utterances per subject, yielding a final evaluation corpus of 800 utterances (see digital appendix[1] for samples).

### 3.2 Annotation Framework and Human Annotation

To capture the complexity of student learning, we adopted a four-dimensional annotation framework (detailed rubrics are available in our digital appendix):

- **Behavioral** [7,8]: Seven categories (1=*Request*, 2= *Question*, 3=*Answer*, 4=*Negotiation*, 5=*Acknowledgment*, 6=*Statement*, and 7=*Others/Off-task*).
- **Cognitive** [2]: Four hierarchical levels (0=*None*, 1=*Remembering and Understanding*, 2=*Applying*, and 3=*Analyzing, Evaluating, and Creating*).
- **Meta-cognitive** [26]: Four categories (0=*None*, 1=*Planning and Orientation*, 2=*Monitoring*, and 3=*Reflecting and Evaluating*).
- **Affective** [15]: Six states (1=*Neutral*, 2=*Sense of Accomplishment/ Enjoyment*, 3=*Curiosity*, 4=*Frustration/Confusion*, 5=*Anxiety*, and 6=*Boredom*).

[1] https://osf.io/yvhar/overview?view_only=eededcccd433490191439605dd9ebd79.

To establish ground truth, two educational researchers annotated the data. Following two training rounds on a subset ($N = 80$), inter-rater reliability achieved a Cohen's kappa ($\kappa$) $> 0.8$ across all dimensions. The full dataset ($N = 800$) was independently double-coded, and any remaining disagreements were resolved via consensus discussions with the first author.

### 3.3 Automated Annotations with LLMs

**Model Selection.** We selected GPT-5.2 (using official default parameters) and Gemini-3 (Flash) (temperature=0.0, max_output_tokens=1500) as our experimental models. These represent standard, widely accessible tiers prevalent in educational research, allowing us to assess performance most relevant to cost-efficient, large-scale applications rather than relying on "Pro" versions.

**Prompt Engineering Methods.** To investigate the impact of prompting strategies, we designed three methods (summarized in Fig. 1; full prompts available in our digital appendix):

- **Few-shot (Baseline)**: Assigns an educational data expert persona, provides the detailed rubric, and includes three representative examples.
- **Single-agent Self-Reflection** [23]: A single agent iteratively generates an initial annotation, self-reflects to identify inconsistencies, and refines its output (Draft → Self-reflection → Revision).
- **Multi-agent Reflection** [3,23]: A collaborative system utilizing three specialized agents: Agent 1 drafts the initial annotation, Agent 2 provides a structured critique and reflection, and Agent 3 synthesizes this feedback to produce the final output (Draft → Reflection → Revision).

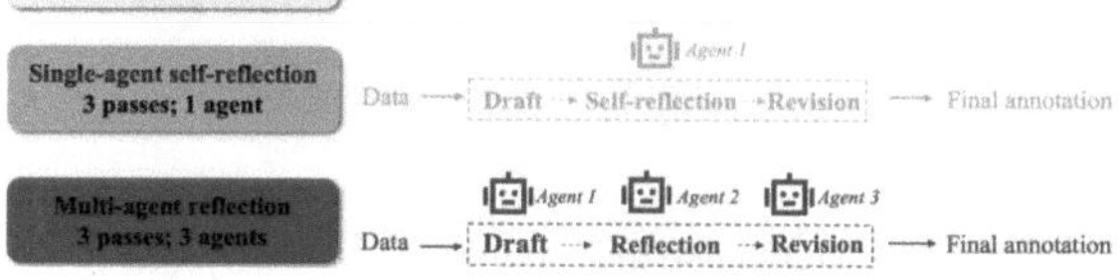


**Fig. 1.** The feature of the three adopted prompt engineering methods

### 3.4 Data Analysis

To address **RQ1**, we first calculated the overall annotation Accuracy. Due to perfect collinearity between educational level and subject, we employed a two-step Generalized Linear Mixed Model (GLMM) strategy to analyze utterance-level annotation correctness (binary: correct/incorrect). All models included random intercepts for RowID to account for item-level variability. In the first step, we constructed a global GLMM including prompt method, educational level, and annotation dimension as fixed effects (excluding subject), followed by post-hoc pairwise comparisons for these variables. In the second step, we conducted separate subgroup GLMM analyses within each educational level to evaluate subject-specific effects.

To address **RQ2**, we defined several indicators to quantify biases between LLM predictions and human annotations and report the percentage:

- **Affective Bias**: Affective Optimistic Bias (AOB): The proportion of instances where the predicted affective value was more positive than the human-annotated results (e.g., predicting "Neutral" as "Curiosity"). Affective Pessimistic Bias (APB): The proportion of instances where the predicted sentiment polarity was more negative than the human-annotated results.
- **Cognitive Bias**: Cognitive Overestimation Bias (COB): The proportion of instances where the predicted cognitive level was at least one unit higher than the human-annotated results; Cognitive Underestimation Bias (CUB): The proportion of instances where the predicted cognitive level was at least one unit lower than the human-annotated results.
- **Meta-cognitive Bias**: Meta-cognitive Overestimation Bias (MOB): The proportion of instances where non-meta-cognitive behavior was misclassified as a meta-cognitive state. Meta-cognitive Underestimation Bias (MUB): The proportion of instances where meta-cognitive behavior was misclassified as a non-meta-cognitive state.
- **Behavioral Bias**: We utilized Sankey diagrams to conduct an exploratory analysis of bias patterns across behavioral categories.

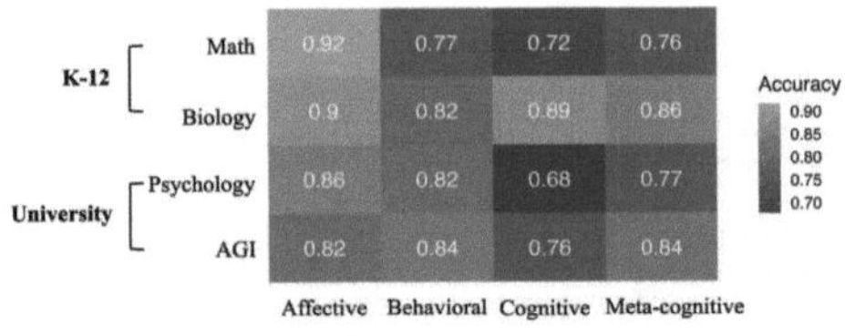


**Fig. 2.** Annotation accuracy by subjects

# 4 Results

## 4.1 Contextual and Dimensional Variations in Accuracy, but Not Prompting Methods

Descriptively, annotation accuracy slightly improved as prompt complexity increased: from the Few-Shot (Gemini-3: 79.2%; GPT-5.2: 82.4%) to Single-Agent (79.5% and 83.4%) and Multi-Agent (79.7% and 83.9%). However, GLMM

**Table 1.** Fixed effects of educational level, dimension on annotation accuracy

| Variable | Estimate | Std. Error | *p*-value |
|---|---|---|---|
| (Intercept) | 1.993 | 0.072 | $< 0.001$ *** |
| Model (Ref: Gemini-3) | | | |
| GPT-5.2 | 0.265 | 0.038 | $< 0.001$ *** |
| Method (Ref: Few-shot) | | | |
| Single-agent Self-reflection | 0.047 | 0.046 | 0.314 |
| Multi-agent Reflection | 0.071 | 0.047 | 0.127 |
| Educational Level (Ref: K-12) | | | |
| University | −0.212 | 0.038 | $< 0.001$ *** |
| Dimension (Ref: Affective) | | | |
| Behavior | −0.487 | 0.058 | $< 0.001$ *** |
| Cognitive | −0.796 | 0.056 | $< 0.001$ *** |
| Meta-cognitive | −0.518 | 0.058 | $< 0.001$ *** |

results (Table 1) revealed these marginal enhancements were not statistically significant; neither Single-agent Self-reflection ($p = .314$) nor Multi-agent Reflection ($p = .127$) significantly outperformed the Few-shot. In contrast, contextual factors significantly impacted the likelihood of correct annotation. University-level dialogues proved significantly more difficult to annotate than K-12 dialogues ($b = -0.212, p < .001$). Subgroup analyses within educational levels showed that correctness in Mathematics was significantly lower than in Biology (K-12, $p < .001$), whereas AGI outperformed Psychology (University, $p < .001$). Finally, significant variations emerged across annotation dimensions. Compared to the Affective, models demonstrated significantly lower correctness on Behavioral, Meta-cognitive, and Cognitive dimensions (all $p < .001$), with the Cognitive dimension proving the most challenging ($b = -0.796$). Detailed accuracies across dimensions and subjects are illustrated in Fig. 2.

### 4.2 Annotation Bias

As illustrated in Fig. 3, we observed distinct bias patterns across the four dimensions:(1)**Affective Bias**: Gemini-3 exhibited a substantially higher Affective Optimistic Bias (AOB) than GPT-5.2 across most subjects, frequently over-attributing positive emotions, while their Pessimistic Bias (APB) remained comparable. For example, in Psychology, Gemini-3's AOB ranged from 9% to 21.5% across prompt methods, compared to GPT-5.2's 3% to 4.5%. A notable exception occurred in AGI, where GPT-5.2 (Few-shot) showed a higher AOB (30%) than Gemini-3 (20%). (2)**Cognitive Bias**: Mathematics uniquely suffered from Cognitive Underestimation Bias (CUB) across both models and all prompts, peaking at 26.5% for Gemini-3 (Multi-agent). Conversely, Cognitive Overestimation Bias (COB) was prominent in AGI and Psychology, but remained minimal in the STEM disciplines (Biology and Mathematics). (3)**Meta-cognitive Bias**: Gemini-3 consistently displayed higher Meta-cognitive Overestimation Bias (MOB), frequently misclassifying non-meta-cognitive utterances. In Psychology, Gemini-3's MOB ranged from 24% to 26%, vastly exceeding GPT-5.2's 0.5% to 1%. While GPT-5.2 showed a slightly higher Underestimation Bias (MUB) than Gemini-3, overall MOB rates consistently exceeded MUB rates for both models. (4)**Behavioral Bias**: LLMs frequently misclassified human-labeled Questions, Negotiations, and Statements. In Mathematics specifically, nuanced interactions caused confusion: Questions were often mislabeled as Negotiations or Acknowledgments, and Negotiations as Requests or Questions (See Sankey diagram in the Digital Appendix). However, the models aligned well with human annotators on explicit categories like Requests and Off-task behaviors.

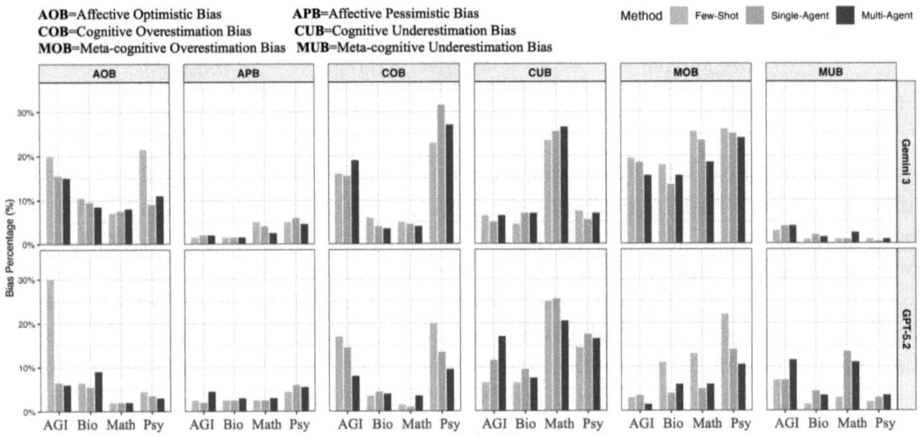


**Fig. 3.** The annotation bias (affective, cognitive, meta-cognitive) of LLMs

## 5 Discussion and Conclusion

This study evaluates LLMs (Gemini-3 and GPT-5.2) as automated annotators for student-AI educational dialogues. Our results indicate that increasing prompt complexity yielded no statistically significant improvements over the baseline. Consequently, the few-shot approach remains a cost-effective alternative in resource-constrained environments. Crucially, our findings indicate that annotation accuracy is inherently context-dependent and dimension-sensitive, resonating with other studies [12]. LLMs performed better on K-12 dialogues than University-level interactions. Performance also varied by subject (e.g., AGI outperformed Psychology), likely due to the epistemological nature of domains like Psychology, where subjective and open-ended knowledge complicates the assessment [25]. We also identified a performance hierarchy across dimensions:

LLMs excelled in the affective dimension—consistent with established strengths in sentiment analysis [1]—but struggled with the cognitive dimension [9,16]. Moving beyond standard accuracy metrics, this research characterizes systematic biases inherent in LLM annotations, echoing observations in other domains [5,14]. Notable patterns included a pronounced AOB in Gemini-3, domain-specific cognitive biases (CUB in Mathematics; COB in Psychology), and a systemic tendency toward MOB in the meta-cognitive dimension. These findings suggest that future prompts need to be tailored to specific models, disciplinary characteristics, and annotation dimensions to effectively mitigate bias. Furthermore, frequent conflation of behavioral categories suggests that single utterances often serve multiple pragmatic functions. Researchers should thus ensure strict mutual exclusivity in taxonomies or adopt multi-label classification frameworks.

In conclusion, while LLMs demonstrate considerable potential for scaling educational dialogue analysis, their reliability is bounded by contextual nuances and systemic biases. Given the limitations in current study, future studies should incorporate more advanced LLMs and evaluate more subjects strictly controlled across educational levels to facilitate a holistic assessment of systematic biases. Furthermore, to effectively mitigate these biases to build a more fair LLM-based annotation, beyond prompt adjustments, further study should pursue targeted model fine-tuning and establish robust human-AI collaborative workflows.

**Acknowledgments.** This work was supported by the National Natural Science Foundation of China (No.62407027) and the Beijing Educational Science Foundation of the Fourteenth 5-year Planning (BAEA24024).

## References

1. Annan, A., et al.: Evaluating large language models for sentiment analysis and hesitancy analysis on vaccine posts from social media: Qualitative study. JMIR Form. Res. **9**, e64723 (2025)
2. Bloom, B.S., Engelhart, M.D., Furst, E.J., Hill, W.H., Krathwohl, D.R., et al.: Taxonomy of educational objectives: the classification of educational goals. Handbook 1: Cognitive domain. Longman New York (1956)
3. Cao, J., et al.: From first draft to final insight: a multi-agent approach for feedback generation. In: AIED'25, pp. 163–176. Springer (2025)
4. Dang, B., Huynh, L., Gul, F., Rosé, C., Järvelä, S., Nguyen, A.: Human-AI collaborative learning in mixed reality: examining the cognitive and socio-emotional interactions. Br. J. Educ. Technol. (2025)
5. Echterhoff, J.M., Liu, Y., Alessa, A., McAuley, J., He, Z.: Cognitive bias in decision-making with LLMs. In: Al-Onaizan, Y., Bansal, M., Chen, Y.N. (eds.) EMNLP'2024, pp. 12640–12653. ACL, Miami (2024)
6. Edwards, J., et al.: Human-ai collaboration: designing artificial agents to facilitate socially shared regulation among learners. Br. J. Educ. Technol. **56**(2), 712–733 (2025)
7. Han, J., et al.: Recipe4u: Student-ChatGPT interaction dataset in EFL writing education. arXiv preprint: arXiv:2403.08272 (2024)

8. Hao, Z., Cao, J., Li, R., Yu, J., Liu, Z., Zhang, Y.: Mapping student-AI interaction dynamics in multi-agent learning environments: Supporting personalized learning and reducing performance gaps. Comput. Educ. **241**, 105472 (2026)
9. He, L., Xu, J.: Automated classification of tutors' dialogue acts using generative AI: a case study using the CIMA corpus. arXiv preprint: arXiv:2509.09125 (2025)
10. Hennessy, S., et al.: Developing a coding scheme for analysing classroom dialogue across educational contexts. Learn. Cult. Soc. Interact. **9**, 16–44 (2016)
11. Howe, C., Hennessy, S., Mercer, N., Vrikki, M., Wheatley, L.: Teacher-student dialogue during classroom teaching: Does it really impact on student outcomes? J. Learn. Sci. **28**(4–5), 462–512 (2019)
12. Jiang, Y., Hao, J., Cui, W., Kerzabi, E., Kyllonen, P.: Uncovering transferable collaboration patterns across tasks using large language models. In: AIED'25, pp. 320–335. Springer (2025)
13. Kasneci, E., et al.: Chatu for good? On opportunities and challenges of large language models for education. Learn. Individ. Differ. **103**, 102274 (2023)
14. Lin, L., Wang, L., Guo, J., Wong, K.F.: Investigating bias in LLM-based bias detection: disparities between LLMs and human perception. In: Rambow, O., Wanner, L., Apidianaki, M., Al-Khalifa, H., Eugenio, B.D., Schockaert, S. (eds.) Proceedings of the International Conference on Computational Linguistics, pp. 10634–10649. ACL, Abu Dhabi (2025)
15. Liu, Z., Xing, W., Ngo, B., Jiao, X., Jiang, S., Li, C.: Engagement patterns of middle school students with ai teachable agents in mathematics learning. Sci. Rep. **15**(1), 40971 (2025)
16. Long, Y., Luo, H., Zhang, Y.: Evaluating large language models in analysing classroom dialogue. NPJ Sci. Learn. **9**(1), 60 (2024)
17. Miller, P., Dicerbo, K.: LLM based math tutoring: challenges and dataset. EdArXiv Preprints (2024). https://osf.io/preprints/edarxiv/5zwv3_v1
18. Muhonen, H., Pakarinen, E., Poikkeus, A.M., Lerkkanen, M.K., Rasku-Puttonen, H.: Quality of educational dialogue and association with students' academic performance. Learn. Instr. **55**, 67–79 (2018)
19. Muhonen, H., Rasku-Puttonen, H., Pakarinen, E., Poikkeus, A.M., Lerkkanen, M.K.: Knowledge-building patterns in educational dialogue. Int. J. Educ. Res. **81**, 25–37 (2017)
20. Nguyen, H., Hayward, J.: Applying generative artificial intelligence to critiquing science assessments. J. Sci. Educ. Technol. **34**(1), 199–214 (2025)
21. Nguyen, H., Nguyen, A.: Reflective practices and self-regulated learning in designing with generative artificial intelligence: an ordered network analysis. J. Sci. Educ. Technol. **34**(5), 1178–1192 (2025)
22. Qian, K., et al.: Towards reliable generative ai-driven scaffolding: reducing hallucinations and enhancing quality in self-regulated learning support. Comput. Educ., 105448 (2025)
23. Shinn, N., Cassano, F., Gopinath, A., Narasimhan, K., Yao, S.: Reflexion: language agents with verbal reinforcement learning. NeurIPS'23 **36**, 8634–8652 (2023)
24. Zhang, Z., et al.: Simulating classroom education with LLM-empowered agents. In: Chiruzzo, L., Ritter, A., Wang, L. (eds.) NAACL'25, pp. 10364–10379. ACL, Albuquerque (2025)
25. Zheng, L., et al.: Judging LLM-as-a-judge with mt-bench and chatbot arena. NeurIPS'23 **36**, 46595–46623 (2023)
26. Zimmerman, B.J.: Becoming a self-regulated learner: an overview. Theory Pract. **41**(2), 64–70 (2002)

# Measuring AI Leadership in Education: Development and Validation of the AI Educational Leadership Scale (AIELS) for Chinese Educational Leaders

Xiaohang Luo[1,2](✉), Ran Ju[3], Menghao Ren[4], Cui Wu[5], Yingqi Wang[6], Jingran Xu[7], and Ruoshui Zhao[8]

[1] College of Teachers, Chengdu University, Chengdu, China
xiaohl@upenn.edu
[2] Graduate School of Education, University of Pennsylvania, Philadelphia, PA, USA
[3] Teachers College, Columbia University, New York, NY, USA
[4] Center for Mind and Brain Sciences, Hunan Normal University, Changsha, China
[5] Chengdu Longquanyi District Education Research Institute, Chengdu, China
[6] Faculty of Arts, The University of Hong Kong, Hong Kong, SAR, China
[7] Department of Philosophy, Sun Yat-Sen University, Guangzhou, China
[8] Brookline High School, Brookline, MA, USA

**Abstract.** As artificial intelligence (AI) becomes increasingly embedded in educational governance, understanding the leadership required for its effective and responsible use has become an important research issue. This study examined the construct and dimensional structure of AI educational leadership in the Chinese context by integrating qualitative and psychometric methods. Study 1 employed qualitative interviews with Chinese educational leaders and AI experts and used grounded theory to explore the construct of AI educational leadership. The qualitative findings initially identified three dimensions: *intelligent application*, *prudent decision-making*, and *collaborative advancement*. Based on these qualitative findings, Study 2 generated scale items and developed the AI Educational Leadership Scale using data collected from Chinese educational leaders. The results further showed that the original three-dimensional framework converged into a two-dimensional structure consisting of *application competence* and *integrated governance*. Study 3 further examined the reliability and validity of this two-dimensional scale. Specifically, *application competence* refers to educational leaders' ability to understand AI principles, use relevant tools, and embed them into educational and managerial practices; *integrated governance* reflects leaders' ability to make prudent and ethical judgments, coordinate multiple stakeholders, and promote the effective implementation and continuous optimization of AI applications in educational settings. Taken together, this study contributes to the conceptualization and measurement of AI educational leadership and provides a useful tool for future research and practice concerning AI-enabled educational governance.

**Keywords:** AI educational leadership · educational leaders · mixed methods · scale development · China


E. G. Blanchard et al. (eds.), AIED 2026, LNCS 16586, pp. 387–395, 2027.
https://doi.org/10.1007/978-3-032-29773-0_30

## 1 Introduction

With the advancement of artificial intelligence (AI) technologies across global education systems, their applications have not only supported student learning and teaching practice but have also demonstrated considerable potential for educational management [1, 2]. Existing studies have shown that AI, through technologies such as big data analytics, intelligent forecasting, and automated decision-making, can be widely applied to key areas, including school governance and decision support, thereby creating new possibilities for optimizing educational management practices [3, 4]. For example, at the administrative level, AI-driven applications can optimize automated scheduling systems for class timetables and room allocation [5]. Similarly, in the domain of decision-making and policy development, predictive analytics has been implemented to forecast the potential outcomes of policy decisions by means of AI algorithms [6]. However, the deeper integration of AI into educational management has brought not only benefits but also a range of emerging governance challenges, including risks to data privacy, algorithmic bias, insufficient transparency in decision-making, and limited digital literacy among administrators and users [2]. These developments suggest that the application of AI in educational management is not merely a technical issue, but also a matter of leadership closely related to equity, accountability, and the realization of educational values.

Against this background, educational leaders have emerged as key actors in leveraging the benefits of AI while mitigating its potential negative consequences [7]. To ensure that AI-enabled educational governance remains aligned with educational goals, educational leaders need not only to understand the applications and operations of AI technologies but, more importantly, to exercise the leadership required to strategically direct, prudently guide, and effectively oversee AI systems within complex educational contexts [2, 7]. Accordingly, as AI becomes increasingly embedded in educational governance processes, examining the core leadership required of educational leaders in the AI era is of considerable theoretical and practical significance.

In the present study, such leadership is conceptualized as AI educational leadership, which refers to educational leaders' integrated capacity to combine technological understanding and application, data-driven decision-making, ethical judgment, and organizational governance in AI-driven educational environments in pursuit of educational goals [8, 9]. In this sense, AI educational leadership does not simply denote mastery of new technologies; rather, it reflects educational leaders' broader capacity to promote informed decision-making, effective governance, and educational improvement in increasingly intelligent educational settings, thereby advancing education systems toward greater intelligence, scientific rationality, and goal orientation. However, because AI educational leadership is a broad and multifaceted construct involving diverse actors and contexts, no unified framework has yet been established regarding its conceptualization and dimensional structure. This lack of consensus has made it difficult to assess AI educational leadership quantitatively, thereby constraining the full realization of AI's potential in educational management.

Overall, this study seeks to integrate qualitative inquiry and psychometric methods to clarify the construct of AI educational leadership and to refine the corresponding measurement instrument. Specifically, the study consists of three parts. Study 1 adopts a qualitative approach to collect first-hand data on educational leaders' and experts' views of AI educational leadership, intending to explore the construct in depth. Based on the findings of Study 1, Study 2 develops the AI Educational Leadership Scale according to the key dimensions of the construct. Study 3 further examines the reliability and validity of the scale.

## 2 Study 1: A Qualitative Investigation of AI Educational Leadership

### 2.1 Method

**Participants.** This study selected three groups of interview participants, namely educational leaders, AI experts, and educational company CEOs in China, following the strategy of intensity sampling to enhance the richness and depth of the data. A total of 20 participants were included, comprising 14 educational leaders, 3 AI experts, and 3 educational company CEOs.

**Procedure.** Before the formal interviews, the researchers conducted pilot interviews with three professionals (two educational leaders and one AI expert) to refine the interview protocol. The formal interviews were semi-structured and focused on participants' experiences, perceptions, and reflections on the use of AI. For example, participants were asked, "In your daily management work, what kinds of problems do you typically use AI to address?" The researchers then conducted online in-depth interviews and adjusted the questions when necessary. Each interview lasted about 60 minutes and was conducted in a quiet environment. Interviews ended when data saturation was reached. All interviews were subsequently transcribed verbatim for grounded-theory-based analysis.

**Data Analysis.** The interview data collected in this study were organized, edited, coded, and analyzed using NVivo qualitative analysis software. As a computer-assisted qualitative data analysis software program, NVivo supports qualitative researchers in collecting, organizing, analyzing, visualizing, and reporting data [10], thereby facilitating the systematic organization and development of qualitative datasets.

### 2.2 Results

Based on the interview data and coding results, the researchers adopted a bottom-up approach to gradually construct the core competencies of AI educational leadership. On the basis of open coding and axial coding, this study further integrated the relevant categories at a higher level and ultimately identified three characteristic dimensions of AI educational leadership: *intelligent application*, *prudent decision-making*, and *collaborative advancement*. Specifically, when educational leaders engage in decision-making and governance in educational environments where AI is deeply embedded, *intelligent application* serves as the practical foundation of AI educational leadership. It primarily refers to educational leaders' ability to understand, integrate, and apply AI tools in teaching, research, and school management contexts, and it is a prerequisite for the meaningful embedding of AI in educational practice and its function as support for governance.

*Prudent decision-making* serves as a critical safeguard. It is mainly manifested in educational leaders' ability to identify, verify, evaluate, and responsibly use AI-generated information in complex information environments. It also involves carefully addressing issues of fairness, privacy, bias, and risk to define the boundaries of legitimacy and value in AI applications. *Collaborative advancement* is reflected in leaders' ability to coordinate internal and external resources, manage relationships among multiple stakeholders, promote institutional development and organizational change, and advance AI applications from isolated practices to systematic development in the process of school governance.

### 2.3 Discussion

In summary, through interviews and coding, Study 1 showed that AI educational leadership is not a unidimensional construct in the Chinese context, but rather a comprehensive construct in which *intelligent application*, *prudent decision-making*, and *collaborative advancement* are interconnected three dimensions. It not only reflects the multiple roles of educational leaders in technological application, value judgment, and organizational governance, but also provides a theoretical basis for further examining the dynamic mechanisms and capacity building of AI educational leadership.

## 3 Study 2: Development of the AI Educational Leadership Scale

Building on Study 1, Study 2 aimed to develop a corresponding measurement instrument to assess Chinese educational leaders' AI educational leadership, identifying and exploring the measurement dimensions of the AI Educational Leadership Scale.

### 3.1 Method

**Participants.** In Study 2, an online questionnaire survey was administered to school leaders in China. After excluding respondents who failed the attention checks, a total of 326 valid participants were included in the final analyses, including 174 women and 152 men. The mean age of the participants was 41.90 years ($SD = 6.566$). In terms of school level, 4.9% of the participants worked in kindergartens, 55.2% in primary schools, 31.3% in junior high schools, 8.2% in senior high schools, and 0.3% in vocational schools. Regarding professional titles, 6.1% held junior-level titles, 28.5% held intermediate-level titles, 59.2% held associate senior-level titles, 2.5% held senior-level titles, and 3.7% had no professional title.

Prior to the survey, all participants signed informed consent forms. All procedures in this study were approved by the ethics committee of the authors' affiliated institution.

**Development of the Initial Items.** Based on the theoretical dimensions and coding results from Study 1, the researchers developed an initial AI Educational Leadership Scale. To ensure content validity, two psychology professors and several doctoral students in psychology reviewed the items. After revision, deletion, and consolidation, a 35-item, three-dimensional scale was formed, including *intelligent application* (14 items), *prudent decision-making* (9 items), and *collaborative advancement* (12 items). To improve clarity and readability, 10 school leaders further evaluated the scale, and the wording was revised accordingly. All items were rated on a 7-point Likert scale ranging from 1 (*completely disagree*) to 7 (*completely agree*), with higher scores indicating higher levels of AI educational leadership.

**Data Analysis.** JASP 0.19.1 was used for item analysis, and exploratory factor analysis (EFA) was conducted in M*plus* 8.3. Based on the results, items that failed to meet the required criteria or led to poor model fit were removed, and the final items and measurement dimensions of the AI Educational Leadership Scale were determined.

### 3.2 Results

**Item Analysis.** Item analysis showed that all 35 items significantly differentiated between the high- and low-score groups, with the high group defined as the top 27% of total scores and the low group as the bottom 27%, indicating good discrimination. In addition, all 35 items were significantly correlated with the total score.

**Exploratory Factor Analysis.** The KMO value for the 35 items was 0.971, and Bartlett's test of sphericity was significant, $\chi^2 = 8311.797, p < .001$, indicating that the data were suitable for EFA. Using GEOMIN oblique rotation in M*plus* 8.3, eight items were removed based on factor loading and communality criteria [11]. The remaining 27 items loaded on two factors, which together explained 57.5% of the total variance. Based on the item content and qualitative findings, the two factors were labeled *application competence* (14 items; e.g., "I use AI to help teachers improve the efficiency of lesson preparation and instructional management" and "I encourage teachers to adjust their classroom teaching strategies based on AI-generated learning analytics") and *integrated governance* (13 items; e.g., "Before using AI analytics tools, I establish clear regulations for data use" and "I am able to use AI to strengthen collaborative governance among the school, community, and families"). Standardized factor loadings ranged from 0.500 to 0.908.

### 3.3 Discussion

Based on the interview findings from Study 1, Study 2 developed a corresponding instrument to assess Chinese educational leaders' AI educational leadership. Following item analysis and EFA, a 27-item AI Educational Leadership Scale was established, comprising two dimensions: *application competence* and *integrated governance.*

## 4 Study 3: Validation of the AI Educational Leadership Scale

Based on the AI Educational Leadership Scale identified in Study 2, Study 3 further examined its factor structure, reliability, and validity.

## 4.1 Method

**Participants.** In Study 3, an online questionnaire survey was administered to school leaders in China. After excluding respondents who failed the attention checks, a total of 367 valid participants were included in the final analyses, including 125 women and 244 men. The mean age of the participants was 43.65 years ($SD = 7.464$). In terms of school level, 43.9% of the participants worked in kindergartens, 33.5% in primary schools, 16.1% in junior high schools, 5.7% in senior high schools, and 0.8% in secondary vocational schools. Regarding professional titles, 11.4% held junior-level titles, 35.1% held intermediate-level titles, 47.4% held associate senior-level titles, 3.3% held senior-level titles, and 2.7% had no professional title. Prior to the survey, all participants signed informed consent forms. All procedures in this study were approved by the ethics committee of the authors' affiliated institution.

### Measurement

*AI Educational Leadership.* AI educational leadership was measured using the 27-item AI Educational Leadership Scale developed in Study 2, which includes two dimensions: *application competence* (14 items) and *integrated governance* (13 items). Items were rated on a 7-point Likert scale (1 = *completely disagree*, 7 = *completely agree*), with higher scores indicating higher levels of AI educational leadership.
*General Attitudes Toward Artificial Intelligence.* Attitudes toward AI were measured using the General Attitudes Toward Artificial Intelligence Scale [12], including negative attitudes (7 items; $\omega = 0.810$) and positive attitudes (8 items; $\omega = 0.895$). Items were rated on a 5-point Likert scale (1 = *completely disagree*, 5 = *completely agree*), with higher scores indicating stronger negative or positive attitudes toward AI.
*AI Literacy.* AI literacy was measured using the Artificial Intelligence Literacy Scale [13], which comprises four dimensions—Awareness, Usage, Evaluation, and Ethics—with a total of 12 items ($\omega = 0.824$). Items were rated on a 7-point Likert scale (1 = *completely disagree*, 7 = *completely agree*), with higher scores indicating higher AI literacy.
*Transformational Leadership.* Transformational leadership was measured using the 12-item *transformational* leadership subscale ($\omega = 0.906$) of the Multifactor Leadership Questionnaire [14]. Items were rated on a 5-point Likert scale (1 = *never*, 5 = *always*), with higher scores indicating higher transformational leadership.

**Data Analysis.** M*plus* 8.3 was used to conduct confirmatory factor analysis (CFA) to examine the structural validity of the AI Educational Leadership Scale. JASP 0.19.1 was used for reliability and correlation analyses to examine its reliability and criterion-related validity.

## 4.2 Results

**Confirmatory Factor Analysis.** The CFA results showed that the two-factor model fit the data well, $\chi^2 = 725.067$, $df = 323$, RMSEA = 0.058, CFI = 0.940, TLI = 0.935,

SRMR = 0.039. A one-factor model was also tested, and its fit indices were worse than those of the two-factor model, $\chi^2 = 956.073$, $df = 324$, RMSEA = 0.073, CFI = 0.906, TLI = 0.989, SRMR = 0.044, suggesting that the two-factor structure was a better measurement model. In addition, the standardized factor loadings of all items in the two-factor model ranged from 0.577 to 0.834 ($p < .001$), indicating that the latent factors explained the observed variables well [15].

**Reliability and Convergent Validity.** Reliability analysis showed that McDonald's omega coefficients were 0.950 for *application competence*, 0.930 for *integrated governance*, and 0.966 for the total scale. In addition, the average variance extracted values were 0.582 for *application competence* and 0.508 for *integrated governance*, both of which were within the acceptable range [11, 16].

**Criterion-Related Validity.** Correlation analyses showed that *application competence* was significantly negatively correlated with negative attitudes toward AI ($r = -0.272$, $p < .001$), and significantly positively correlated with positive attitudes toward AI ($r = 0.564$, $p < .001$), AI literacy ($r = 0.568$, $p < .001$), and transformational leadership ($r = 0.498$, $p < .001$). *Integrated governance* was also significantly negatively correlated with negative attitudes toward AI ($r = -0.236$, $p < .001$), and significantly positively correlated with positive attitudes toward AI ($r = 0.483$, $p < .001$), AI literacy ($r = 0.589$, $p < .001$), and transformational leadership ($r = 0.497$, $p < .001$).

### 4.3 Discussion

Building on the EFA results of Study 2, Study 3 further supported the two-factor structure of the AI Educational Leadership Scale. Both dimensions and the total scale showed higher reliability and acceptable convergent validity. Their significant associations with attitudes toward AI, AI literacy, and transformational leadership further supported criterion-related validity. Overall, these findings provide evidence for the reliability and validity of the scale and lay a foundation for future research on AI educational leadership.

## 5 General Discussion

The present study integrated qualitative and psychometric methods to explore the construct of AI educational leadership and its dimensional structure in the Chinese context. Across three studies, it completed a full process from theoretical construction and scale development to structural validation, establishing a two-dimensional construct consisting of *application competence* and *integrated governance.*

On the one hand, *application competence* constitutes the practical foundation of AI educational leadership. It primarily refers to educational leaders' ability to understand the basic principles of artificial intelligence, master relevant technological tools, and embed them into teaching and management contexts. *Application competence* reflects not only leaders' direct level of AI use, but also an essential prerequisite for exerting deeper educational influence through AI [9].

On the other hand, this study found that the two aspects initially identified as relatively distinct in the qualitative analysis—*prudent decision-making* and *collaborative advancement*—converged into a single dimension of *integrated governance* in the quantitative structure. This finding may suggest that, in real educational management contexts, risk judgment and organizational coordination are not separate processes, but are instead highly intertwined in practice [2, 8]. *Integrated governance* reflects not only educational leaders' ability to make ethical judgments and prudent decisions in complex situations, but also their governance capacity to integrate multiple stakeholders, promote the effective implementation of AI applications, and continuously optimize such applications over time.

This study has several limitations. First, because the study was conducted in the Chinese context, the construct and measurement of AI educational leadership may be influenced by cultural factors. Future research could adopt a cross-cultural perspective to examine the consistencies and differences in the construct and its measurement across cultural settings. Second, although this study analyzed the potential implications of AI educational leadership at a theoretical level, its specific outcomes remain to be empirically tested in future research. Finally, AI educational leadership is still in a stage of rapid development, and its construct and measurement may evolve alongside technological change. Future studies could further investigate the dynamic development of AI educational leadership.

**Acknowledgments. Disclosure of Interests** On behalf of all authors, there are no conflicts of interest to declare.

**Data Availability Statement** The datasets and measurements generated during and/or analyzed during this study are available from the corresponding author upon reasonable request.

## References

1. Bond, M., Khosravi, H., De Laat, M., Bergdahl, N., Negrea, V., Oxley, E., Pham, P., Chong, S.W., Siemens, G.: A meta systematic review of artificial intelligence in higher education: a call for increased ethics, collaboration, and rigour. Int. J. Educ. Technol. High. Educ. **21**, 4 (2024). https://doi.org/10.1186/s41239-023-00436-z
2. Filgueiras, F.: Artificial intelligence and education governance. Educ. Citizensh. Soc. **19**, 349–361 (2024). https://doi.org/10.1177/17461979231160674
3. Brusilovsky, P.: AI in education, learner control, and human-AI collaboration. Int. J. Artif. Intell. Educ. **34**, 122–135 (2024). https://doi.org/10.1007/s40593-023-00356-z
4. Chen, L., Chen, P., Lin, Z.: Artificial intelligence in education: a review. IEEE Access. **8**, 75264–75278 (2020). https://doi.org/10.1109/ACCESS.2020.2988510
5. Abayomi, O.K., Adenekan, F.N., Abayomi, A., Olateju, Ajayi, T.A., Aderonke, A.O.: Awareness and perception of the artificial intelligence in the management of university libraries in Nigeria. J. Interlibrary Loan Doc. Deliv. Electron. Reserve. **29**, 13–28 (2020). https://doi.org/10.1080/1072303X.2021.1918602
6. Wang, S., Wang, H., Jiang, Y., Li, P., Yang, W.: Understanding students' participation of intelligent teaching: an empirical study considering artificial intelligence usefulness, interactive reward, satisfaction, university support and enjoyment. Interact. Learn. Environ. **31**, 5633–5649 (2023). https://doi.org/10.1080/10494820.2021.2012813

7. Sposato, M.: Artificial intelligence in educational leadership: a comprehensive taxonomy and future directions. Int. J. Educ. Technol. High. Educ. **22**, 20 (2025). https://doi.org/10.1186/s41239-025-00517-1
8. Igbokwe, I.C.: Artificial intelligence in educational leadership: risks and responsibilities. EJAHSS. **1**, 3–10 (2024). https://doi.org/10.59324/ejahss.2024.1(6).01
9. Langeveldt, D.C.: AI-driven leadership: a conceptual framework for educational decision-making in the AI era. EHASS. **5**(2), 1582–1595 (2024). https://doi.org/10.38159/ehass.20245812
10. Dhakal, K.: NVivo. jmla. **110**(2), 270 (2022). https://doi.org/10.5195/jmla.2022.1271
11. Zhang, W., Pan, C., Yao, S., Zhu, J., Ling, D., Yang, H., Xu, J., Mu, Y.: "Neijuan" in China: the psychological concept and its characteristic dimensions. Acta Psychol. Sin. **56**, 107 (2024). https://doi.org/10.3724/SP.J.1041.2024.00107
12. Huang, Y., Jiang, S., Gong, Z.: Validity and reliability of the Chinese version of general attitudes towards artificial intelligence scale. Int. J. Hum.–Comput. Interact. **41**, 12884–12894 (2025). https://doi.org/10.1080/10447318.2025.2465868
13. Wang, B., Rau, P.-L.P., Yuan, T.: Measuring user competence in using artificial intelligence: validity and reliability of artificial intelligence literacy scale. Behav. Inform. Technol. **42**, 1324–1337 (2023). https://doi.org/10.1080/0144929X.2022.2072768
14. Bass, B.M., Avolio, B.J.: Multifactor Leadership Questionnaire, (2011). https://doi.org/10.1037/t03624-000
15. Yan, Y., Feng, M., Zhang, Y.: "Buddha-like" mentality in workplace: the building of fundamental theory and the empirical test of its validity in Chinese context. Acta Psychol. Sin. **56**, 594 (2024). https://doi.org/10.3724/SP.J.1041.2024.00594
16. Fornell, C., Larcker, D.F.: Evaluating structural equation models with unobservable variables and measurement error. J. Mark. Res. **18**, 39–50 (1981). https://doi.org/10.1177/002224378101800104

# From Speculation to Evaluation: Exploring Values in Design Fictions About AI-Enhanced Education

Alina Pees[1(✉)], Leo Oelscher[1], Marcus Specht[1], Christian Rietz[2], and Florence Lehnert[1]

[1] FernUniversität in Hagen, Hagen, Germany
alina.pees@studium.fernuni-hagen.de,
{leo.oelscher,marcus.specht,florence.lehnert}@fernuni-hagen.de
[2] Pädagogische Hochschule, Heidelberg, Germany
rietz@ph-heidelberg.de

**Abstract.** Design fiction has become an established speculative method for exploring possible futures of Artificial Intelligence in Education, enabling critical reflection on emerging technologies. While it often surfaces ethical, social, and educational values, existing evaluation approaches – such as those focusing on plausibility, coherence, or provocation – primarily assess the quality of the narrative itself, and therefore offer limited support for the systematically analyzing value assumptions and tensions, despite their importance for responsible and equitable AIED research. This paper presents a value-driven evaluation framework for analyzing design fictions depicting AI-enhanced futures of higher education, enabling structured reflection on value assumptions and tensions. Grounded in value-sensitive design and educational research, the framework was developed and iteratively refined through a multi-phase mixed-methods approach. A literature review informed initial value dimensions, which were examined through deductive thematic analysis of human-authored and AI-generated design fiction narratives, and further refined through a participatory student workshop and expert interviews with higher education stakeholders. The resulting framework supports structured reflection on values across individual, institutional, and societal levels, addressing issues such as equity, inclusion, responsibility, and autonomy. For AIED research and practice, it provides a systematic tool to critically examine AI-enhanced educational futures and inform responsible research, policy, and design decisions.

**Keywords:** Speculative Methods · Design Fiction · Value Sensitive Design (VSD) · Artificial Intelligence in Education (AIED) · Ethical AI Governance · Generative AI (GenAI)

## 1 Introduction

Artificial intelligence (AI) is increasingly shaping higher education (HE), influencing teaching, assessment, governance, and relationships between students,


E. G. Blanchard et al. (eds.), AIED 2026, LNCS 16586, pp. 396–405, 2027.
https://doi.org/10.1007/978-3-032-29773-0_31

educators, and institutions [9]. Alongside promises of personalization and efficiency, it raises fundamental questions about values such as autonomy, responsibility, and inclusion [2]. Many of these questions are future-oriented and cannot be addressed through the analysis of existing systems alone. Within Artificial Intelligence in Education (AIED), design fiction (DF) has emerged as a method for exploring possible futures of AI-enhanced HE [2,4]. By creating speculative scenarios, DF makes assumptions about educational practices and societal implications explicit, enabling critical reflection rather than prediction [5]. It can surface implicit value tensions (e.g., autonomy vs. control), yet its systematic evaluation remains underdeveloped. Existing approaches focus on plausibility, coherence, or creativity [17], offering limited support for analyzing underlying values. As a result, value-related insights remain implicit and difficult to compare across scenarios. To address this gap, this paper introduces a Value-Driven Evaluation Framework (VDEF) for analyzing DFs of AI-enhanced HE. Here, evaluation is understood not as scoring, but as the structured identification and reflection of values and tensions within a scenario. Grounded in Value Sensitive Design (VSD) [7] and educational research, the framework supports analysis across individual, institutional, and societal levels. While developed for DF, it is intended to inform value-oriented reflection in AIED more broadly. The study follows a multi-phase mixed-methods approach, combining literature analysis, thematic coding of human- and AI-generated DFs, a participatory workshop, and stakeholder interviews. While human-authored DFs provide contextual depth, they are time-intensive and difficult to compare systematically. AI-generated DFs enable rapid variation but risk reproducing dominant narratives [16]. By linking speculative exploration with systematic analysis, this paper positions DF as an analytically robust tool for value reflection in AIED. It contributes (1) a value-driven framework, (2) empirical insights into value patterns across human- and AI-generated scenarios, and (3) exploration of its practical applicability HE contexts.

## 2 Related Work

**Design Fictions in AI-Enhanced Education.** DF employs speculative storytelling to provoke critical reflection on alternative technological futures and their social and ethical implications [5,11]. In education, DF and speculative pedagogy are used to explore AI-enabled futures of learning, assessment, and governance [2]. While AIED research has examined future-oriented scenarios - e.g., contrasting utopian and dystopian visions of adaptive learning support [13] - the explicit use of DF as a methodological approach remains limited. Rather than predicting developments, DF surfaces tensions and challenges assumptions about AI-mediated futures [4]. However, prior work highlights key limitations: many DFs align with dominant AIED discourses, often centering generative AI and dystopian framings [2]. Manually authored DFs are labor-intensive to produce [4], constraining the generation of diverse narrative sets and limiting systematic comparison across scenarios (e.g., themes or value tensions). While generative AI enables rapid variation, it risks reproducing prevailing narratives and generic tropes [16]. These challenges underscore the need for more systematic and theoretically grounded approaches to analyzing speculative narratives.

**Values, Ethics, and Normativity in AI and Education.** AIED increasingly recognizes that AI systems embed normative assumptions shaping educational practices, foregrounding ethical and social concerns [9]. VSD offers an established approach for integrating human values into technology design, conceptualizing development as an interaction between technical systems, social structures, and human actors [7]. In education, this includes values such as autonomy, equity, inclusion, and academic integrity [6], which are linked to motivation and belonging in HE [8]. Empirical work shows that AI can both support and challenge these values – for example, by enabling adaptive learning while raising concerns about privacy and autonomy [15]. More broadly, AIED research addresses issues of data governance, policy, and institutional responsibility [9]. Accordingly, AI systems should be evaluated not only for effectiveness but also for alignment with educational values and societal goals [2]. However, few studies examine how such values can be systematically identified and analyzed within future-oriented methods such as DF [1].

**Evaluation Frameworks for Speculative Methods.** Speculative methods are widely used to explore the ethical and social implications of emerging technologies [5], yet their evaluation requires appropriate frameworks [1]. Existing approaches primarily focus on speculative qualities such as coherence, plausibility, creativity, and provocativeness, as reflected in frameworks by Wu et al. [17] and Baumer et al. [1]. While useful, they provide limited guidance for analyzing value dimensions of speculative AIED scenarios [1]. Moreover, many of these frameworks remain largely theoretical and are rarely grounded in empirical material from participatory or expert-based evaluations, limiting their applicability to address contested values and policy-relevant questions in AIED [9].

**Summary and Contribution.** In summary, prior work lacks a value-driven, empirically grounded approach for analyzing speculative representations of AI in education. To address this gap, this paper introduces the VDEF, conceptualizing evaluation not as normative judgment, but as a structured approach for identifying and reflecting on value dimensions in DFs. The framework is intended to support multiple use cases: analyzing DFs, guiding their creation, and informing broader reflection on values in AI-enhanced education. While developed in HE, it captures value dimensions not specific to this context, suggesting potential applicability to other educational settings and beyond speculative methods; these applications remain subject to future validation. This paper investigates (RQ1) how key educational, ethical, and social values can be operationalized in a framework for evaluating DFs in AI-enhanced HE, and (RQ2) how stakeholders apply the framework and evaluate its usefulness and usability.

## 3 Methodological Approach and Framework Development

A multi-phase research design was adopted, combining literature-based framework development, deductive thematic coding of DFs, a student workshop, and stakeholder interviews (see Fig. 1). All participants provided informed consent, and the study was approved by the Institutional Ethics Committee. Supplementary materials (SM) are available via the OSF repository: https://osf.io/4b35d/

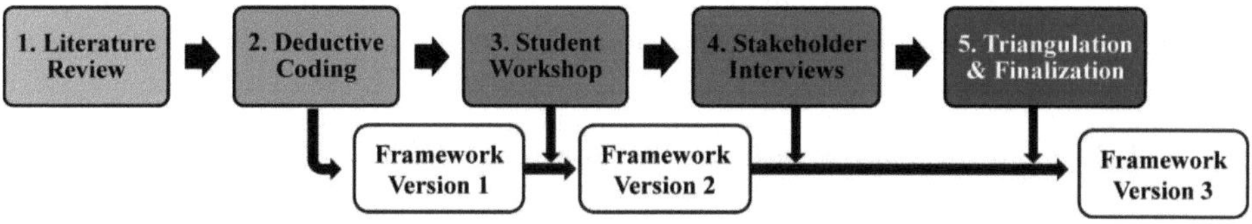


**Fig. 1.** Overview of the multi-phase methodological approach.

**Phase 1: Literature Review.** An exploratory, relevance-driven literature review was conducted to identify studies addressing values in HE. The review was not intended as a systematic review, but rather to capture a broad and conceptually relevant range of perspectives. Relevant publications were identified through searches in major academic databases (PsycINFO, Scopus, Google Scholar) and FernUniversität Hagen's institutional library portal. Search queries combined keywords such as "values," "ethics," "higher education," and "AI in education". In addition, backward and forward citation tracking was used to identify further relevant work. Studies were included if they (1) addressed AI in HE and (2) provided conceptually relevant insights into social, ethical, educational, or technological dimensions. Studies were excluded if they did not focus on HE or lacked conceptual relevance (e.g., purely technical work without educational or societal implications). In total, approximately 80 publications were screened for relevance while a subset of key contributions was selected to inform the identification of core values in HE, 4 educational (i.e., autonomy, growth mindset, motivation, and self-efficacy), 5 ethical (i.e., equity, integrity, justice, privacy, and responsibility), and 7 social (i.e., collaboration, diversity, inclusion, friendship, belonging, community, and responsiveness). The identified values across the reviewed publications with their detailed definitions are provided in the supplementary materials (SM, File S1).

**Phase 2: Deductive Coding of Design Fictions.** Fourteen DFs were analyzed: eight human-authored scenarios from a single, literature-based publication [4] and six AI-generated scenarios [10] (see SM, Folder S2). The human-authored DFs were included as a complete, theoretically grounded set, providing an internally consistent baseline for comparison. While drawing from a single source may introduce bias, their grounding in a literature review supports conceptual representativeness. For the AI-generated DFs, one narrative per prompt (out of three) was selected based on clarity of value-related content to reduce redundancy [10]. Values were identified using predefined educational, ethical, and social dimensions, and deductive coding [12] was applied. Descriptive statistics summarize value distributions (Table 1) and informed framework iterations (SM, File S3). Reliability was assessed for three DFs (21%), yielding high interrater agreement (using MAXQDA's agreement function; 73.33–86.67%); disagreements were resolved through discussion (SM, Folder S4). This process aimed to refine code definitions and strengthen interpretive robustness rather than establish statistical reliability, with iterative consolidation of overlapping codes and refinement of definitions [14].

**Table 1.** Frequency of assigned codes across design fiction narratives

| Category | Total | Human-Authored ($n = 8$) | AI-Generated ($n = 6$) |
|---|---|---|---|
| Social Aspects | | | |
| Responsiveness | 55 | 32 | 23 |
| Collaboration | 12 | 11 | 1 |
| Friendship | 17 | 6 | 11 |
| Diversity | 5 | 4 | 1 |
| Community | 8 | 3 | 5 |
| Inclusion | 3 | 2 | 1 |
| Belonging | 2 | 2 | 0 |
| Ethical Aspects | | | |
| Integrity | 12 | 9 | 3 |
| Privacy | 9 | 7 | 2 |
| Responsibility | 19 | 14 | 5 |
| Justice | 3 | 3 | 0 |
| Equity | 6 | 5 | 1 |
| Educational Aspects | | | |
| Self-efficacy | 3 | 1 | 2 |
| Motivation | 24 | 13 | 11 |
| Growth mindset | 21 | 13 | 8 |
| Autonomy | 10 | 10 | 0 |

**Phase 3: Student Workshop.** An interactive 90-minute workshop was conducted with 11 master's students (Educational Sciences: $n = 8$, Education for Sustainable Development: $n = 3$) at the University of Education in Heidelberg, Germany, to explore the usability and applicability of the preliminary framework. Participation was voluntary and uncompensated. Participants first completed a questionnaire on perceived prior knowledge with DF, read an assigned DF individually, and identified values, first on their own and subsequently using the framework. Groups of three to five students discussed their interpretations and reflected on the relevance of the value categories. After the discussion, participants completed a second questionnaire assessing perceived knowledge

with DF and the framework's usability and usefulness, with the option to provide open feedback (full questionnaires are provided in the SM, Folder S5). Analysing the questionnaire responses and written reflections from group discussions led to the introduction of new value categories (e.g., efficiency, sustainability, benefit), the refinement of existing definitions (e.g., specifying the role of AI in the category'relationality'), and changes towards a framework's structure along individual, institutional, and societal dimensions. Descriptive statistics indicated high perceived usefulness ($M = 3.84$, $SD = 0.79$) and usability ($M = 3.65$, $SD = 0.53$), with perceived knowledge increasing from pre- ($M = 2.85$, $SD = 0.75$) to post-workshop ($M = 3.62$, $SD = 0.28$) (for details see SM, Folder S5).

**Phase 4: Stakeholder Interviews.** Six experts participated in 30-min semi-structured interviews, recruited via LinkedIn, email, and personal contacts to ensure diverse backgrounds. They represented multiple domains (teaching: 4; management: 3; research: 4; policy: 2), institutions, and demographics ($\approx 1/3$ women; age: $M = 54.25$, $SD = 22.12$), with $M = 25.20$ ($SD = 25.15$) years of HE experience. Interviews explored current HE developments, quality teaching, and AI opportunities and risks, followed by evaluation of the VDEF (clarity, usefulness, relevance). Data were recorded, transcribed, and analyzed using MAXQDA (v24.11.1). Findings were integrated with earlier phases to refine the framework. In total, 121 value references were identified, with responsibility ($n = 20$) and integrity ($n = 18$) most prominent. Participants emphasized institutional responsibility and safeguarding students' self-determination, framing AI as a supportive tool that should not replace human judgment. These insights informed refinements of VDEF categories (i.e., addition of trust, participation, and AI as a public good) and showed a high perceived usefulness of the framework for HE stakeholders (see SM, Folder S6).

**Phase 5: Triangulation of Findings.** The final VDEF synthesizes insights across all phases, integrating multiple data sources to identify convergent and divergent value patterns (SM, File S7). This triangulation ensures the framework is grounded in both empirical input (participants and stakeholders) and theoretical considerations. Figure 2 presents the final framework, and the complete coding scheme is provided in the SM (File S3).

## 4 The Final Value-Driven Evaluation Framework (VDEF)

The final VDEF supports the analysis of values in AI-supported futures of HE across three levels: societal, institutional and individual. Rather than providing normative judgments or scores, it serves as an analytical lens for structured reflection on how values are articulated, prioritized, or obscured in speculative scenarios. At the *individual level*, the framework addresses personal agency, learning processes, and interpersonal experiences of students and educators. The *institutional level* captures organizational responsibilities and strategic conditions of AI use in HE, while the *societal level* reflects broader regulatory contexts.

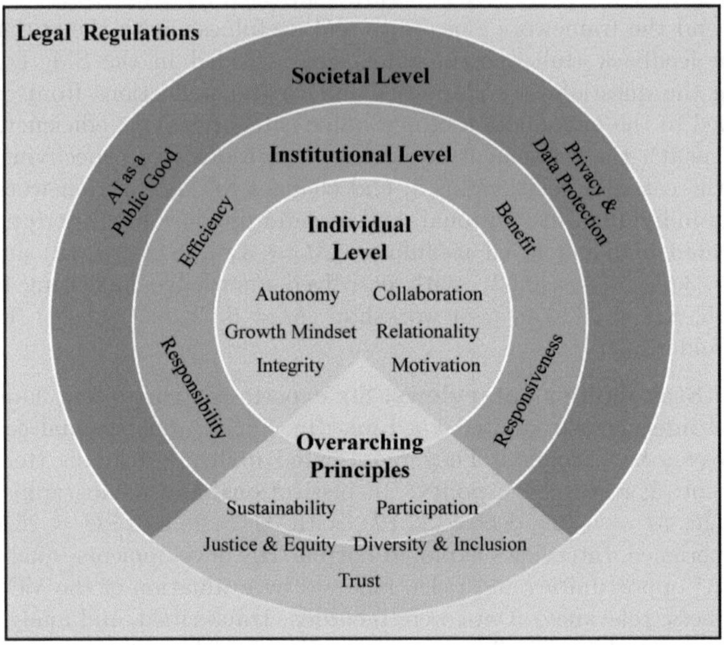


**Fig. 2.** The final version of the VDEF

In addition, cross-cutting values span all levels and may manifest differently depending on context. Applied to DF, the VDEF enables researchers to map narrative elements across these levels and analyze how values interact. Overall, the VDEF facilitates systematic reflection on value articulations and interactions in AI-enhanced HE futures, highlighting its applicability across research, policy, and design contexts.

## 5 Discussion

This paper presents a VDEF for the systematic analysis of values in speculative DFs on AI-supported futures in HE. Developed through literature review, DF thematic analysis, a student workshop, and stakeholder interviews, the framework enables structured analysis across individual, institutional, and societal levels, addressing a gap in evaluating speculative AIED futures. Triangulating multiple data sources strengthens the findings through cross-validation of value patterns. Beyond DF, the VDEF can be applied to other future-oriented or empirical AIED artifacts, supporting value-sensitive analysis in research, design, and policy.

**Emerging Values and Value Tensions.** DFs surfaced implicit assumptions and value tensions, with workshops and interviews providing interpretive support. DFs often juxtaposed responsiveness with extensive data collection, raising concerns about privacy and autonomy. AI was frequently portrayed as a supportive companion in DFs, prompting debate about its role in human interaction. The VDEF enables systematic identification and comparison of such tensions across contexts. At the societal level, stakeholders emphasized trust and responsibility, aligning with calls for participatory AI governance [3].

**Implications for AIED Research and Practice.** The findings highlight the value of combining speculative methods with structured analytical frameworks. While DF enables exploration of future-oriented questions [2], the VDEF supports systematic reflection of their ethical, educational, and social dimensions. More broadly, it offers a transferable approach for identifying and discussing values in AI-supported systems. In practice, the framework supports reflection beyond technical performance, highlighting tensions and the need for transparent, adaptable, and participatory design.

**Limitations and Future Work.** This exploratory study is based on relatively small, context-specific samples within German HE; therefore, its findings are not generalizable. The framework relies on qualitative interpretation and manual coding, introducing subjectivity despite interrater checks. Moreover, AI-generated DFs are shaped by prompting strategies and training data, potentially reinforcing dominant perspectives (see for discussion [10]). However, the triangulation of multiple data sources and methods helps to mitigate and partially overcome these limitations by strengthening the robustness of the findings. The study focuses on perceived usefulness and analytical coherence, but does not assess long-term impact, comparative performance, or measurable effects on design and decision-making. Future work should address these limitations through larger, more diverse samples and systematic comparisons.

## 6 Conclusion

The VDEF enables structured analysis of values in AI-enhanced HE across individual, institutional, and societal levels. Combining DF analysis with workshops and interviews, this study shows that values are often implicitly embedded in future-oriented scenarios. Different modes of speculative production shape how values are articulated or obscured, highlighting the normative role of GenAI in constructing educational futures. The framework supports systematic engagement with value tensions without prescribing fixed outcomes, positioning DFs as analytically robust tools rather than purely creative artifacts. Beyond DF, the VDEF offers a transferable approach for value-sensitive analysis in AIED research, policy, and practice.

**Acknowledgments.** The authors would like to thank the student workshop participants for their active engagement, as well as the interview partners for sharing their insights and experiences.

**Disclosure of Interests.** The authors have no competing interests to declare and no funding was received for conducting this study. The questionnaires and methodology was approved by the Human Research Ethics committee of the FernUniversität in Hagen, Germany.

## References

1. Baumer, E.P.S., Blythe, M., Tanenbaum, T.J.: Evaluating design fiction: the right tool for the job. In: Proceedings of the 2020 ACM Designing Interactive Systems Conference, pp. 1901–1913 (2020). https://doi.org/10.1145/3357236.3395464
2. Bozkurt, A., et al.: Speculative futures on ChatGPT and generative artificial intelligence (AI): a collective reflection from the educational landscape. Asian J. Distance Educ. **18**(1), 53–130 (2023). https://doi.org/10.5281/zenodo.7636568
3. Coeckelbergh, M.: Artificial intelligence, the common good, and the democratic deficit in AI governance. AI Ethics **5**, 1491–1497 (2025). https://doi.org/10.1007/s43681-024-00492-9
4. Cox, A.M.: Exploring the impact of artificial intelligence and robots on higher education through literature-based design fictions. Int. J. Educ. Technol. High. Educ. **18**(1), 1–19 (2021). https://doi.org/10.1186/s41239-020-00237-8
5. Dunne, A., Raby, F.: Speculative Everything: Design, Fiction, and Social Dreaming. With a new preface by the authors. MIT Press, Cambridge (2024)
6. Francis, N.J., Jones, S., Smith, D.P.: Generative AI in higher education: balancing innovation and integrity. Br. J. Biomed. Sci. **81**, 14048 (2025). https://doi.org/10.3389/bjbs.2024.14048
7. Friedman, B., Kahn, P., Borning, A.: Value sensitive design: theory and methods. Technical Report No. 2–8, University of Washington, Seattle (2002)
8. Girelli, L., et al.: Autonomy supportive contexts, autonomous motivation, and self-efficacy predict academic adjustment of first-year university students. Front. Educ. **3**, 95 (2018). https://doi.org/10.3389/feduc.2018.00095
9. Khan, S., et al.: Harnessing AI for sustainable higher education: ethical considerations, operational efficiency, and future directions. Discov. Sustain. **6**, 23 (2025). https://doi.org/10.1007/s43621-025-00809-6
10. Lehnert, F., Oelscher, L., Eradze, M.: Co-creating educational futures: how speculative prompting shapes AI-generated design fiction. Manuscript under conditional acceptance at DIS 2026
11. Lindley, J.: A pragmatics framework for design fiction. In: Proceedings of the 11th European Academy of Design Conference (2015)
12. Mayring, P., Fenzl, T.: Qualitative inhaltsanalyse. In: Baur, N., Blasius, J. (eds.) Handbuch Methoden der empirischen Sozialforschung. Springer VS, Wiesbaden (2014). https://doi.org/10.1007/978-3-531-18939-0_38
13. Rummel, N., Walker, E., Aleven, V.: Different futures of adaptive collaborative learning support. Int. J. Artif. Intell. Educ. **26**(2), 784–795 (2016). https://doi.org/10.1007/s40593-016-0102-3
14. Saldaña, J.: The Coding Manual for Qualitative Researchers. SAGE Publications, Los Angeles (2013)
15. Shen, Y., et al.: Aligning and comparing values of ChatGPT and human as learning facilitators: a value-sensitive design approach. Br. J. Edu. Technol. **56**, 1391–1414 (2025). https://doi.org/10.1111/bjet.13562

16. Wang, N., Kim, H., Peng, J., Wang, J.: Exploring creativity in human–AI co-creation: a comparative study across design experience. Front. Comput. Sci. **7**, 1672735 (2025). https://doi.org/10.3389/fcomp.2025.1672735
17. Wu, Y., Yu, Y., An, P.: Dancing with the unexpected and beyond: the use of AI assistance in design fiction creation. In: Proceedings of the Tenth International Symposium of Chinese CHI, pp. 129–140 (2024). https://doi.org/10.1145/3565698.3565777

# Offline-First AIED: An Architectural Blueprint for On-Device LLM Integration in Low-Resource Educational Contexts

Aristoteles Barros[1(✉)], Mateus Monteiro[1], Ermesson Lima[1], Ig Ibert Bittencourt[1], Seiji Isotani[2], Luiz Rodrigues[1,3], and Diego Dermeval[1,4]

[1] Center of Excellence in Social Technologies (NEES) – Federal University of Alagoas, Maceió, Brazil
{aristoteles.barros,mateus.monteiro,ermesson.santos,ig.ibert, diego.matos}@nees.ufal.br

[2] Institute of Mathematical and Computer Sciences – University of São Paulo, São Paulo, Brazil
sistotani@icmc.usp.br

[3] Technological Federal University of Paraná (UTFPR) - Apucarana, Curitiba, Brazil
luiz.rodrigues@utfpr.edu.br

[4] Harvard University, Cambridge, MA, USA

**Abstract.** Most AIED systems rely on cloud infrastructure and stable internet, limiting applicability in resource-constrained contexts. This paper proposes an offline-first architectural blueprint that enables on-device LLM integration under strict computational and connectivity constraints. Grounded in Design Science Research, the architecture combines pedagogical control, local inference, and persistent storage. We instantiate this design in a mobile educational application aligned with the Brazilian National Common Core Curriculum, demonstrating the feasibility of fully offline deployment on commodity smartphones. The main contribution lies in providing transferable architectural insights that balance technical feasibility, pedagogical quality, and responsible AI principles.

**Keywords:** AIED Unplugged · Small Language Models · Offline-First Architecture · User-centered Design

## 1 Introduction

Research highlights AIED's potential for personalization, adaptive feedback, and scalable learning, particularly in mathematics education [20,30]. However, most systems depend on cloud infrastructure and stable internet, limiting low-resource contexts like rural schools and Global South regions with intermittent connectivity [4,9,26].

AIED Unplugged advocates minimal connectivity reliance through teacher-centered, smartphone-compatible solutions [9], but strict device constraints challenge pedagogical quality and curriculum alignment [1,2]. Lightweight LLMs


E. G. Blanchard et al. (eds.), AIED 2026, LNCS 16586, pp. 406–414, 2027.
https://doi.org/10.1007/978-3-032-29773-0_32

show feasibility for on-device deployment [1,12,15,31], yet lack reusable architectural blueprints for functional offline AIED systems [13,19,22].

Thus, this paper addresses:

**RQ**: *How can AI-powered tutoring systems support personalized, pedagogically meaningful mathematics learning in low-resource, offline-first contexts?*

We propose an offline-first architectural blueprint integrating lightweight LLMs, pedagogical control, and local storage. Instantiated as a teacher-facing mobile app for BNCC-aligned question generation (QG), it enables fully on-device execution on commodity smartphones, providing transferable design insights across educational domains.

## 2 Literature Review and Research Questions

*AIED Unplugged* has been proposed to leapfrog infrastructural constraints by advocating for AIED solutions aligned with available resources and local realities [9], emphasizing teacher mediation and classroom-compatible workflows as essential design requirements. Prior work has explored unplugged ITS for numeracy [20], case studies connecting unplugged AIED to public policy [19], and contextual needs of Brazilian public-school teachers such as printable activities and curriculum alignment [21], with the MathAIde application illustrating how these principles can be operationalized through smartphone-based offline workflows [3,20,22]. Nonetheless, recurrent limitations in these solutions are scalability, when systems depend on manually curated item banks, and connectivity, as they require continuous or intermittent access, preventing adoption in fully disconnected settings.

Recent advances in LLMs have increased interest in automated question generation (QG) to reduce authoring effort and improve content diversity [8,10,11,24]. However, most approaches assume online access and focus on English-language contexts. Techniques such as quantization and model compression enable deployment in resource-constrained environments [12], while systems-level studies highlight the challenges of on-device LLM inference [31]. Empirical evidence suggests that, although feasible, on-device LLMs still face practical limitations [1,15], and QG quality remains inconsistent, reinforcing the need for human oversight [16,21,23,25].

Taken together, the literature offers limited guidance on integrating lightweight LLMs into mobile applications that operate as offline AIED systems under real-world constraints. In response, this study proposes a general-purpose, offline-first architectural blueprint for integrating lightweight, on-device LLMs into AIED systems aligned with the AIED Unplugged paradigm [9], intentionally domain-agnostic and application-independent, rather than focusing on model development [10] or a single application scenario [8]. This work contributes: (i) an offline-first architectural design enabling on-device inference with lightweight LLMs in low-resource settings; (ii) an instantiation as a mobile educational application supporting teacher-centered workflows aligned with the BNCC; and (iii) transferable design insights for LLM-enabled AIED Unplugged artifacts, grounded in prior empirical evidence on feasibility and pedagogical quality [1,15,23].

## 3 Method

This study adopts the Design Science Research (DSR) methodology to address a practical and context-sensitive educational problem through the design and instantiation of a computational artifact [6,17]. Figure 1 presents a structured view of DSR, adapted from Peffers et al. [17], highlighting its iterative nature and multiple possible entry points. Problem identification and motivation are addressed in Sects. 1 and 2. The remaining DSR activities are operationalized as follows.

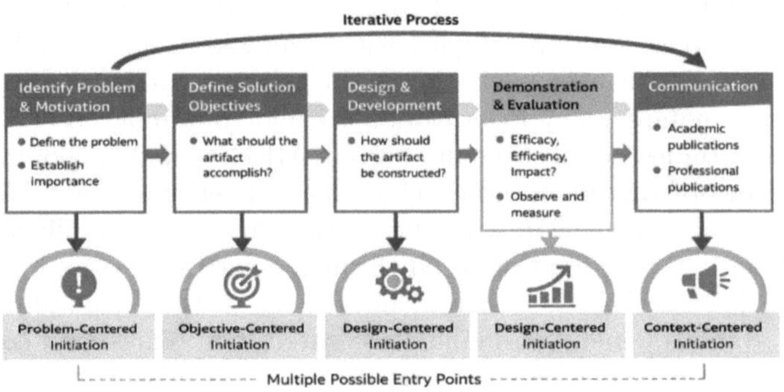


**Fig. 1.** Design Science Research Methodology (DSRM) adapted from Peffers et al. [17].

**Architectural Design (design-centered):** This study proposes an offline-first architecture for the on-device execution of lightweight LLMs (see Sect. 4). The design treats computational resources, connectivity and pedagogical control as first-class constraints rather than secondary implementation concerns. Architectural decisions were informed by empirical evidence on the feasibility, performance, and content quality of lightweight LLM inference in resource-constrained environments [1,15,23]. The proposed architecture remains agnostic with respect to model configuration or prompt engineering strategies, enabling curriculum alignment, teacher mediation and iterative reuse of generated content [27].

**Instantiation and Technological Realization (design-centered):** The architecture is realized as a mobile educational system integrating a lightweight on-device LLM inference engine capable of executing quantized language models locally, without reliance on external servers, grounded in prior empirical studies on LLM inference in disconnected smartphones [15].

**Reflection and Contribution (context-centered):** The final DSR activity consists of reflecting on design decisions and their implications for AIED Unplugged systems, contributing architectural and design insights that extend prior feasibility-focused studies toward application-level integration, demonstrating how lightweight LLMs can be operationalized within curriculum-aligned, offline-first educational workflows while preserving pedagogical control and human oversight.

# 4 Architectural Blueprint for LLM-Powered AIED Unplugged

The resulting system architecture constitutes the main design artifact of this study: a reusable architectural blueprint for offline-first AIED systems integrating lightweight LLMs under the AIED Unplugged paradigm [9]. The architecture is intentionally agnostic to specific application roles or user profiles, focusing on how generative capabilities can be embedded within pedagogically constrained, offline-first workflows under strict computational and connectivity limitations.

The architecture targets fully on-device execution on smartphones without internet connectivity, assuming a mobile-first deployment model [28]. Models are stored locally using portable formats such as GGUF and executed entirely on the CPU, preserving autonomous offline operation [5]. The design assumes small to medium-sized language models (up to approximately 2B parameters) as a pragmatic upper bound, reflecting empirical evidence that models in this range offer a feasible balance between computational cost, memory footprint, and output quality on commodity smartphones [1,15]. The architecture accommodates multiple lightweight LLMs with different trade-offs between latency, memory, and generation quality, and models are treated as external artifacts that can be sourced, updated, and replaced, for instance from Hugging Face [7], without modifying the core system design, preserving offline-first and privacy-by-design requirements.

The blueprint is organized into four interacting layers aligned with four main objectives: (i) enabling offline-first, teacher-oriented workflows; (ii) accommodating strict computational constraints through lightweight on-device inference; (iii) enforcing curriculum and pedagogical alignment prior to content generation; and (iv) mitigating risks of unconstrained text generation through human oversight. Figure 2 presents the architectural blueprint and its layered organization.

The *User Interface Layer* is exclusively teacher-oriented, designed to support activities such as pedagogical planning, configuration of generation parameters, review of generated artifacts and reuse of curated content. Instantiations should be compatible with classroom routines in which teachers prepare activities offline and later deploy them using printed or locally shared materials, aligning with prior findings on mobile and disconnected educational systems [3].

The *Prompt and Pedagogical Layer* constitutes a central architectural contribution, encoding teacher-defined constraints (e.g., grade level, skills, scope, output structure) prior to model inference, ensuring that content generation is

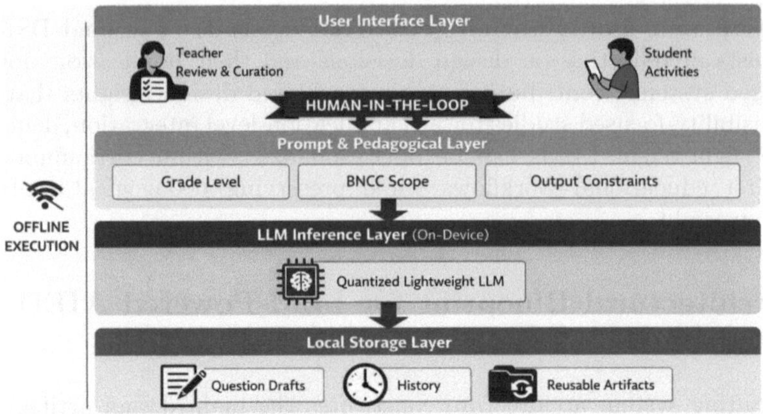


**Fig. 2.** Conceptual architecture illustrating teacher interaction, pedagogical control, local LLM inference and persistent storage are organized to support offline-first educational authoring workflows aligned with the AIED Unplugged paradigm.

guided by instructional intent. This aligns with empirical findings showing that structured prompting and explicit pedagogical goals are essential for acceptable educational quality with lightweight LLMs [1,23].

The *LLM Inference Layer* encapsulates the execution of quantized lightweight models directly on the device, eliminating dependence on external servers. Model compression and memory-aware execution strategies enable local inference on commodity smartphones [12,31], treating computational limitations as first-class architectural constraints.

The *Local Storage Layer* supports persistent storage of generated activities, prompt configurations, and teacher-curated artifacts, enabling reuse, adaptation, and longitudinal organization of instructional materials [2,3,27].

Across all layers, a key architectural principle is the treatment of LLM outputs as *draft pedagogical artifacts*: generated materials are validated, adapted, or selectively reused by teachers before classroom use. This human-in-the-loop orientation addresses hallucinations, conceptual inaccuracies, and linguistic inconsistencies in LLM-generated educational content [1], ensuring alignment with the AIED Unplugged paradigm [9].

From an AIED Unplugged perspective, the architecture operationalizes core paradigm principles by (i) leveraging existing commodity smartphones rather than requiring new infrastructure, (ii) supporting offline-first, teacher-centered workflows compatible with classroom realities, and (iii) embedding pedagogical control and human mediation as architectural requirements rather than optional features. Compared to prior AIED Unplugged architectures relying on traditional AI models [22] or intermittent connectivity [13,19], the proposed design integrates generative capabilities while preserving instructional authority, extending existing approaches toward scalable content authoring in offline settings.

## 5 Instantiation: A Mobile AIEDU System for QG

Following the DSR methodology, the architectural blueprint presented in Sect. 4 is instantiated in the form of a teacher-facing mobile educational application using the React Native framework [14], demonstrating how an offline-first, LLM-enabled AIED architecture can be realized on commodity smartphones under real-world resource constraints. The app is designed as a teacher-centered authoring and planning tool for mathematics education, with explicit alignment to the BNCC, allowing educators to configure pedagogical parameters such as grade level, mathematical topics and numerical ranges, and to generate, review, curate and reuse instructional activities entirely offline. Generated materials can be exported for classroom use, supporting common instructional routines in AIED Unplugged contexts, where teachers often assume responsibility for adapting, distributing and mediating learning materials due to limited digital infrastructure and intermittent or absent connectivity [9].

From a technical standpoint, the instantiation employs local CPU-only inference using compact language models ranging from approximately 0.5B to 2B parameters, selected to balance generation quality and computational feasibility in offline and low-resource environments. The system currently supports models such as Llama 3.2 (1B), Qwen 2.5 (0.5B), and Gemma 2/3 (1B–2B), deployed using low-precision quantization (e.g., Q4 and Q5) and executed through a mobile adaptation of the *llama.cpp* ecosystem. System-level requirements for offline and shared-device contexts are addressed through a lightweight client-side state management solution with local persistence (e.g., Zustand) [18], enabling user separation on shared devices and longitudinal access to generated artifacts, complemented by optional on-device text-to-speech functionality as an accessibility-oriented service. These model- and execution-level decisions represent one feasible realization of the proposed architecture and should not be interpreted as architectural requirements, which remain agnostic to specific model families, quantization strategies or inference backends.

Pedagogical constraints are enforced at the application and prompt levels through structured templates that encode curricular scope and expected output formats, preserving instructional intent prior to inference while maintaining transparency, configurability and human oversight [1,23].

## 6 Discussion

This study extends prior research on lightweight LLM feasibility [15] and offline educational generation tasks [1,23] by demonstrating how such models can be operationalized within an offline-first AIED system, translating infrastructural and pedagogical constraints into a well-grounded, reusable architectural pattern. From an AIED Unplugged perspective [9], the proposed architecture demonstrates how constraints related to connectivity, device availability and digital literacy can be reframed as first-class design requirements, addressing the lack of a reusable architectural blueprint that prior functional applications failed to provide [13,19,22], and aligning with the realities of underserved educational contexts by avoiding implicit dependencies on continuous connectivity or centralized infrastructure. Another central design implication concerns the role of pedagogical control in LLM-enabled AIED systems, where treating LLM outputs as draft pedagogical artifacts, rather than as autonomous instructional decisions, proved essential for reconciling the generative capabilities of language models with the need for curricular alignment, conceptual accuracy and instructional responsibility [1,2,23,27], constituting an architectural principle that directly addresses known risks of hallucination, misleading content and over-reliance on automated generation in educational settings.

Furthermore, considerations regarding responsible adoption are embedded directly into the proposed architecture rather than introduced as post-hoc safeguards, with privacy-by-design ensured through fully local inference and on-device data storage, and transparency and educator agency preserved by making pedagogical constraints explicit and inspectable within the generation workflow, aligning with human-centered and responsible AI principles in education [27]. Ultimately, the primary contribution of this work lies in articulating transferable design knowledge for the AIED community, illustrating how lightweight LLMs can be integrated into offline-first educational systems in a way that balances technical feasibility, pedagogical quality and ethical responsibility, informing future research and practice in AIEDU with a reusable blueprint that facilitates designing, developing and deploying LLM-powered systems into resource-constrained educational settings.

## 7 Limitations and Future Work

This study deliberately focuses on the design and instantiation of an offline-first, LLM-enabled AIED architecture, consistent with a DSR perspective that prioritizes architectural and design knowledge under real-world constraints [6,17], rather than designing, developing or evaluating a particular AIED system. The current instantiation targets Android devices due to their widespread availability in low-resource educational contexts [29], representing an implementation decision rather than an architectural constraint, and adopts structured prompting strategies based on empirical analyses that identified limitations in pedagogical consistency and output predictability under open-ended prompting [1,23]. Future work may explore alternative instantiations across other mobile ecosystems or device classes, and perform qualitative and quantitative investigations with teachers and students to examine usability, pedagogical relevance and adoption dynamics in authentic educational contexts.

**Acknowledgments.** The authors would like to thank CAPES (Coordination for the Improvement of Higher Education Personnel) - Finance Code 001 - for supporting this research through a master's scholarship. We also acknowledge the Fundação Itaú Social for partially funding this project.

## References


1. Barros, A., Monteiro, M., Rodrigues, L., Dermeval, D., Isotani, S., Bittencourt, I.I.: Evaluating large language model quality in resource-constrained environments. In: Proceedings of the International Conference on Artificial Intelligence in Education, LNCS. Springer (2025)
2. Dermeval, D., Paiva, R., Bittencourt, I.I., Vassileva, J., Isotani, S.: Authoring tools for designing intelligent tutoring systems: a systematic review of the literature. Int. J. Artif. Intell. Educ. **28**(3), 336–384 (2018)
3. Freitas, E., et al.: Learning analytics desconectada: Um estudo de caso em análise de produções textuais. In: Anais do I Workshop de Aplicações Práticas de Learning Analytics em Instituições de Ensino no Brasil, pp. 40–49. SBC (2022)
4. Gašević, D., Prinsloo, P.: Learning analytics for the global south. J. Learn. Analytics **5**(2), 1–7 (2018)
5. GGML contributors: GGUF: unified file format for GGML models (2023). https://github.com/ggml-org/ggml/blob/master/docs/gguf.md
6. Hevner, A.R., March, S.T., Park, J., Ram, S.: Design science in information systems research. MIS Q. **28**(1), 75–105 (2004)
7. Hugging Face: The AI community building the future (2024). https://huggingface.co
8. Indran, I.R., Paranthaman, P., Gupta, N., Mustafa, N.: Twelve tips to leverage AI for efficient and effective medical question generation. Med. Teach. **46**(8), 1021–1026 (2024)
9. Isotani, S., Bittencourt, I.I., Challco, G.C., et al.: AIED unplugged: Leapfrogging the digital divide to reach the underserved. In: Proceedings of the International Conference on Artificial Intelligence in Education, LNCS. Springer (2023)
10. Lee, U., Jung, H., Jeon, Y., et al.: Few-shot is enough: exploring ChatGPT prompt engineering for automatic question generation. Educ. Inf. Technol. (2024)
11. Li, K., Zhang, Y.: Planning first, question second: an LLM-guided method for controllable question generation. In: Findings of the Association for Computational Linguistics: ACL 2024, pp. 4715–4729. Association for Computational Linguistics, Bangkok (2024). https://doi.org/10.18653/v1/2024.findings-acl.280
12. Liu, H., Galindo, M., Xie, H., et al.: Lightweight deep learning for resourceconstrained environments: a survey. ACM Comput. Surv. (2024)
13. Mello, R.F., et al.: Escreva Mais: a mobile application to enhancing writing skills in resource-constrained classrooms. In: European Conference on Technology Enhanced Learning, pp. 307–312. Springer (2025)
14. Meta Platforms, Inc.: React native documentation (2024). https://reactnative.dev
15. Monteiro, M., et al.: "small device, big decision:" comparing lightweight LLMs' computational performance and output quality for AIED unplugged, pp. 160–167 (2025)
16. Monteiro Santos, et al.: Near feasibility, distant practicality: empirical analysis of deploying and using LLMs on resource-constrained smartphones. In: Proceedings of the 13th International Conference on Information & Communication Technologies and Development, pp. 224–235 (2024)
17. Peffers, K., Tuunanen, T., Rothenberger, M.A., Chatterjee, S.: A design science research methodology for information systems research. J. Manag. Inf. Syst. **24**(3), 45–77 (2007)
18. Poimandres: Zustand: Bear necessities for state management in react (2019). https://github.com/pmndrs/zustand

19. Portela, C., Lisboa, R., Yasojima, K., et al.: A case study on AIED unplugged applied to public policy for learning recovery post-pandemic in Brazil. In: Proceedings of the International Conference on Artificial Intelligence in Education, LNCS. Springer (2023)
20. Rodrigues, L., et al.: MathAIde: a qualitative study of teachers' perceptions of an its unplugged for underserved regions. Int. J. Artif. Intell. Educ., 1–29 (2024)
21. Rodrigues, L., et al.: Teacher-centered intelligent tutoring systems: design considerations from Brazilian public school teachers. In: Simpósio Brasileiro de Informática na Educação (SBIE), pp. 1419–1430. SBC (2023)
22. Rodrigues, L., et al.: Mathaide in the classroom: a qualitative analysis of teachers' perspectives of intelligent tutoring systems unplugged. In: Anais do XXXV Simpósio Brasileiro de Informática na Educação, pp. 1515–1528. SBC, Porto Alegre (2024). https://doi.org/10.5753/sbie.2024.242017
23. Santos, M., et al.: Geração de questões com llms leves: Um estudo inicial sobre a percepção de educadores. In: Anais do XXXVI Simpósio Brasileiro de Informática na Educação, pp. 1635–1646. SBC, Porto Alegre (2025). https://doi.org/10.5753/sbie.2025.12574
24. Scaria, N., Dharani Chenna, S., Subramani, D.: Automated educational question generation at different bloom's skill levels using large language models: strategies and evaluation. In: Artificial Intelligence in Education, pp. 165–179. Springer Nature Switzerland, Cham (2024)
25. Shankar, S., Zamfirescu-Pereira, J.D., Hartmann, B., Parameswaran, A., Arawjo, I.: Who validates the validators? Aligning LLM-assisted evaluation of LLM outputs with human preferences. In: Proceedings of the 37th Annual ACM Symposium on User Interface Software and Technology, pp. 1–14 (2024)
26. Thompson, G.: Two thirds of the world's school-age children have no internet access at home. UNICEF Report (2020)
27. Topali, P., Ortega-Arranz, A., Rodríguez-Triana, M.J., et al.: Designing human-centered learning analytics and artificial intelligence in education solutions. Behav. Inf. Technol. (2024)
28. UNESCO: Mobile learning: UNESCO policy guidelines (2014)
29. World Bank: Digital development overview (2023). https://www.worldbank.org/en/topic/digitaldevelopment
30. Xia, Q., Chiu, T.K.F., Zhou, X.: Systematic literature review on opportunities, challenges, and future research of artificial intelligence in education. Comput. Educ.: Artif. Intell. **4**, 100118 (2022)
31. Yin, Y., Liu, C., Wang, Z., et al.: LLM serving on mobile devices: challenges and opportunities. ACM Comput. Surv. (2024)

# Towards Elastic Offline-First Applications for AIED Unplugged

Matheus Arataque Uema[1(✉)], Talita de Paula Cypriano de Souza[1,4], Luiz Rodrigues[2,5], Diego Dermeval[2,3], Ig Ibert Bittencourt[2,3], and Seiji Isotani[2,3]

[1] University of São Paulo, São Paulo, Brazil
{matheuema,talitacypriano}@usp.br
[2] Center of Excellence for Social Technologies (NEES), Federal University of Alagoas, Penedo, Brazil
diego.matos@famed.ufal.br, ig.ibert@ic.ufal.br
[3] University of Pennsylvania, Philadelphia, USA
sisotani@upenn.edu
[4] Federal Institute of São Paulo (IFSP), São Paulo, Brazil
[5] Technological Federal University of Paraná (UTFPR), Curitiba, Brazil
luizrodrigues@utfpr.edu.br

**Abstract.** AI-assisted educational technologies remain uneven in settings with limited connectivity, devices, and digital skills. The AIED Unplugged framework addresses this gap by prioritizing offline and resource-aware operation. This paper presents an elastic offline-first mobile application and evaluates three instruction-tuned large language models across heterogeneous mobile devices. Results show that lightweight on-device models are consistently more stable and responsive, while larger models become slow or unreliable on lower-end hardware. These findings reinforce model–device alignment as a practical requirement for early Unplugged stages and position the proposed system as a feasibility-oriented baseline for progressive expansion.

**Keywords:** AIED for development · Human-centered artificial intelligence · Mobile application · Resource-constrained environment

## 1 Introduction

Artificial Intelligence (AI) has expanded educational technologies through adaptive learning, personalized tutoring, and automated assessment [20,21]. However, most AI in education (AIED) systems depends on stable internet access, cloud computing, and advanced devices, which remain unavailable in many low- and lower-middle-income contexts [4,6,13]. As these gaps may persist for decades [8], adopting conventional AIED prematurely can reinforce inequalities [10,19].

To address this challenge, recent work has proposed offline and low-cost alternatives under the AIED Unplugged framework [8]. Prior implementations


E. G. Blanchard et al. (eds.), AIED 2026, LNCS 16586, pp. 415–423, 2027.
https://doi.org/10.1007/978-3-032-29773-0_33

demonstrate feasibility for assessment and intelligent tutoring [8,15], but most systems still depend on persistent connectivity.

This paper operationalizes AIED Unplugged through an offline-first and elastic mobile application designed for early-stage deployment. We report system-level evidence from heterogeneous devices and three LLMs, focusing on whether pedagogically meaningful assistance can remain viable under severe resource constraints. The study is framed as a feasibility analysis rather than a full pedagogical impact evaluation.

## 2 AIED Unplugged Fundamentals

Isotani et al. [8] propose the AIED Unplugged framework to address constraints in low- and lower-middle-income contexts by leveraging available resources while minimizing infrastructure and digital-skill demands. It is structured around five elements: Conformity (align with available infrastructure), Disconnect (operate offline), Proxy and Multi-user (support shared use), and Unskillfulness (minimize digital skill requirements) [6,8]. These principles directly guided the design of the proposed application.

Although prior work demonstrates feasibility, limitations persist in scalability, long-term generalizability, and inclusivity [13,18]. This motivates broader stakeholder participation and governance approaches that preserve data agency while supporting evidence-based policy [5,14].

### 2.1 Related Works on AIED Unplugged

Recent studies evaluate offline LLM use in constrained educational settings and report a recurring trade-off between computational efficiency and pedagogical quality. Monteiro et al. [11] show that faster models on mobile devices tend to lose accuracy and completeness. Barros et al. [2] report that readability often lags behind technical correctness in offline smartphone evaluations. Santos et al. [16] find that lightweight models can support some mathematics tasks, but still require human mediation for unreliable outputs.

Together, these findings confirm offline feasibility while highlighting instability across tasks, devices, and interaction modes. This motivates a multimodal Unplugged application evaluated systematically across heterogeneous hardware.

### 2.2 Ethical and Policy Grounding of AIED Unplugged

Recent extensions of AIED Unplugged place ethical responsibility and policy collaboration at the center of long-term deployment [18]. Instead of a fixed solution for disconnected contexts, Unplugged AIED is framed as a staged process in which applications evolve with infrastructure and digital-literacy improvements while preserving data agency, transparency, and inclusivity.

Within this perspective, systems should keep a stable low-resource baseline and add features incrementally. This avoids premature dependence on fragile infrastructure and supports equitable transitions. In line with this view, the proposed application is positioned as an elastic baseline for early stages, while remaining open to later extensions [3,5,8,15]. Here, elasticity is considered the ability to incorporate additional pedagogical features as settings transition from Unplugged to Plugged stages. Crucially, this evolution must be robust across stages: advanced features should be optional and must not degrade the baseline operation required in earlier contexts.

## 3 An Elastic Offline-First Mobile Application

Based on the framework principles, two requirements guided the design: (i) preserve pedagogical usefulness under severe constraints and (ii) support elastic growth without degrading baseline operation.

To meet these requirements, we implemented a staged mobile application in React Native[1] In the *baseline Unplugged* configuration, it runs as an offline conversational assistant with on-device inference for teacher support. Interaction is multimodal, combining typed prompts with image-to-text input via OCR. The interaction consists of short question–answer exchanges, where users provide either typed or image-based input and receive concise textual explanations generated locally.

OCR is executed locally with Google ML Kit, and model execution uses `llama.rn` with GGUF models. Inference adopts a uniform low-resource configuration (Q4_KM models, 512-token context, CPU-only execution, no GPU layers) to maximize reproducibility and compatibility across heterogeneous devices. Network use is restricted to one-time model download when connectivity is available; conversation history is not stored.

The architecture follows the elasticity principle by maintaining a stable low-resource baseline while enabling optional pedagogical modules in *emerging Unplugged* contexts and later integration of external services in *Plugged* contexts without compromising baseline operation.

### 3.1 Methodology

This study analyzes LLM performance on pedagogical tasks under resource constraints.

Experiments were conducted on three Android devices (Table 1) and three instruction-tuned models: SmolLM2 Instruct [1] (360M, 271 MB), Llama 3.2 Instruct [7] (1B, 808 MB), and Gemma 3 It [17] (4B, 2.49 GB). All models used Q4_KM quantization to keep deployment feasible and comparable across devices[2]

All interactions started from the same minimal system prompt to reduce task-specific steering effects. Although this choice does not reflect real-world AIED

[1] Source code available in: https://github.com/MatheusUema/EdgeLLM.

[2] Scores are available in the AI for Education benchmarks portal: https://benchmarks.ai-for-education.org/.

deployments, which typically rely on structured prompts, it enables controlled comparison across models and devices.

```
"This is a conversation between user and assistant."
```

This neutral setup improves reproducibility and keeps differences attributable mainly to model capacity and device constraints.

**Table 1.** Device settings.

| Device | Device 1 | Device 2 | Device 3 |
|---|---|---|---|
| OS | Android 15 | Android 10 | Android 10 |
| RAM (GB) | 12 + 4 (extensible) | 4 | 6 |
| CPU | Dimensity 9200 + Octa-core Max 3.35 GHz | Octa-core Max 2.01 GHz | Octa-core Max 2.2 GHz |
| Storage | 256 GB | 64 GB | 64 GB |

The evaluation used the pedagogy benchmark dataset from Lelièvre et al. [9]. From the CDPK set, we selected 105 multiple-choice Math items for Primary and Secondary levels, given persistent learning gaps in mathematics in many Global South contexts [12]. This subset is used as a proxy for pedagogical reasoning rather than a comprehensive evaluation of pedagogical effectiveness.

Each item was tested in two modalities: text input and OCR. For both modalities, we recorded accuracy, completion time, and throughput (tokens/s), resetting conversation state after each item. OCR prompts were captured as photos and processed locally, aligning interaction with the *Unskillfulness* principle [8].

When the LLM output was nonsensical or indicated more than one alternative, up to two additional attempts were performed. If the issue persisted, the item was labeled as *Not understood* and counted as incorrect for that LLM on that device. Additionally, if the device crashed or the response took more than 2 min to generate new tokens, the item was labeled as *Timeout.*

### 3.2 Results

Table 2 summarizes accuracy across devices and modalities. SmolLM2 remained stable across all devices; Llama 3.2 showed moderate performance with a drop on Device 2; Gemma 3 It achieved the best scores on Device 1 but timed out on Devices 2 and 3. Accuracy values are relatively low due to the constrained evaluation setup, including the use of a minimal prompt, absence of task-specific tuning, and the inherent difficulty of multiple-choice pedagogical reasoning tasks. Hence, these results should be interpreted as baseline performance under strict offline conditions.

Table 3 details completion time and throughput. Device 1 was the only device that reliably executed all models. SmolLM2 was consistently the fastest, Llama 3.2 imposed substantially higher latency, and Gemma 3 It was markedly slower even when it ran. On Devices 2 and 3, Gemma 3 It was not operational under

**Table 2.** Benchmark results across devices.

| LLM | Device 1 | | Device 2 | | Device 3 | | CDPK Benchmark |
|---|---|---|---|---|---|---|---|
| | Text | OCR | Text | OCR | Text | OCR | Text |
| SmolLM2 | 21.21% | 25.71% | 24.76% | 23.81% | 25.71% | 24.76% | 19% |
| Llama 3.2 | 29.52% | 29.52% | 23.81% | 20% | 25.71% | 26.67% | 29% |
| Gemma 3 It | 50.48% | 53.33% | *Timeout* | *Timeout* | *Timeout* | *Timeout* | 48% |

the timeout constraint. Across setups, throughput (tokens/s) was generally more stable than completion time, indicating that variability was driven mainly by total inference duration.

Figures 1(a) and (b) visualize these patterns. Completion-time dispersion is wider, especially under OCR and on weaker hardware, whereas tokens/s values remain comparatively clustered.

A small number of outliers was observed (invalid responses or multiple alternatives after retries), slightly more frequent with OCR. Their low incidence suggests limited impact on aggregate results, but they indicate robustness limits in input interpretation.

## 4 Technical and Pedagogical Implications Under the Unplugged Framework

The evaluated application targets early Unplugged stages, where offline operation, shared devices, and low digital-skill requirements are central. Results indicate that this baseline is technically viable and provides preliminary pedagogical support signals, while remaining compatible with gradual expansion.

### 4.1 Technical Viability Under Resource Constraints

On-device inference proved feasible when model size matched hardware limits, consistent with prior offline mobile studies [2,11]. Performance analysis across devices and modalities shows relatively stable tokens/s but larger completion-time variability, especially under OCR. This supports the framework's *Conformity* and *Disconnect* principles and highlights practical limits for larger models in early stages.

### 4.2 Model Selection, Device Diversity, and Elasticity

Model behavior reinforces the importance of elasticity. SmolLM2 offered the best operational profile across all devices; Llama 3.2 required substantially longer inference time; Gemma 3 It became impractical on constrained hardware due to timeouts and crashes.

These results support prioritizing lightweight models in early deployments and introducing heavier models only as infrastructure improves. The proposed architecture preserves this progression by allowing model replacement without changing baseline interaction.

**Table 3.** Statistical summary of LLM performance on Devices (mean ± 95% CI, IQR, and coefficient of variation).

| | | | | | | | |
|---|---|---|---|---|---|---|---|
| **Device 1** | | | | | | | |
| | | **Completion Time (s)** | | | **Tokens/s** | | |
| **Model** | **Input** | Mean ± 95% CI | IQR | CV (%) | Mean ± 95% CI | IQR | CV (%) |
| SmolLM2 | Text | 4.52 ± 0.08 | 3.13 | 87.40 | 19.70 ± 0.37 | 1.62 | 10.65 |
| | OCR | 3.92 ± 0.07 | 2.91 | 76.24 | 25.94 ± 0.49 | 7.57 | 16.67 |
| Llama 3.2 | Text | 15.87 ± 0.30 | 8.49 | 42.77 | 14.02 ± 0.26 | 2.81 | 13.59 |
| | OCR | 19.53 ± 0.37 | 8.92 | 49.97 | 14.06 ± 0.26 | 2.37 | 12.86 |
| Gemma 3 It | Text | 66.61 ± 1.24 | 23.10 | 24.84 | 5.30 ± 0.10 | 0.31 | 12.22 |
| | OCR | 79.52 ± 1.48 | 28.95 | 30.99 | 5.74 ± 0.11 | 0.71 | 11.83 |
| **Device 2** | | | | | | | |
| | | **Completion Time (s)** | | | **Tokens/s** | | |
| **Model** | **Input** | Mean ± 95% CI | IQR | CV (%) | Mean ± 95% CI | IQR | CV (%) |
| SmolLM2 | Text | 11.93 ± 0.22 | 8.88 | 56.98 | 9.95 ± 0.19 | 0.35 | 4.71 |
| | OCR | 12.24 ± 0.23 | 10.08 | 66.01 | 9.92 ± 0.19 | 0.30 | 11.27 |
| Llama 3.2 | Text | 50.95 ± 0.95 | 26.81 | 39.34 | 4.94 ± 0.09 | 0.28 | 7.01 |
| | OCR | 56.49 ± 1.08 | 35.14 | 42.79 | 5.21 ± 0.10 | 0.64 | 9.05 |
| **Device 3** | | | | | | | |
| | | **Completion Time (s)** | | | **Tokens/s** | | |
| **Model** | **Input** | Mean ± 95% CI | IQR | CV (%) | Mean ± 95% CI | IQR | CV (%) |
| SmolLM2 | Text | 12.33 ± 0.23 | 8.99 | 60.73 | 10.55 ± 0.20 | 1.59 | 15.95 |
| | OCR | 11.11 ± 0.21 | 7.82 | 59.85 | 11.79 ± 0.22 | 0.44 | 3.07 |
| Llama 3.2 | Text | 53.29 ± 0.99 | 27.48 | 42.13 | 4.85 ± 0.09 | 0.13 | 3.32 |
| | OCR | 53.44 ± 1.01 | 29.15 | 44.17 | 5.34 ± 0.10 | 0.26 | 3.84 |

### 4.3 Pedagogical Implications in Early Unplugged Contexts

The application showed pedagogical relevance for mediated use in early stages, where teachers often act as proxies [18]. OCR introduced higher variability, but this reflects realistic classroom heterogeneity and aligns with assumptions of early Unplugged contexts [8]. Part of this variability may be attributed to OCR extraction errors, such as missing symbols or formatting inconsistencies, which affect input quality before model processing. This suggests that performance limitations are not solely due to model reasoning but also to upstream input noise.

Outliers clarify both robustness and ethical boundaries: early Unplugged AI should remain assistive, with continuous human mediation, rather than autonomous decision-making.

The offline-first architecture strengthens privacy and data agency because inference stays local and no interaction data are sent to cloud services. However, this privacy gain comes with a transparency trade-off, as local systems

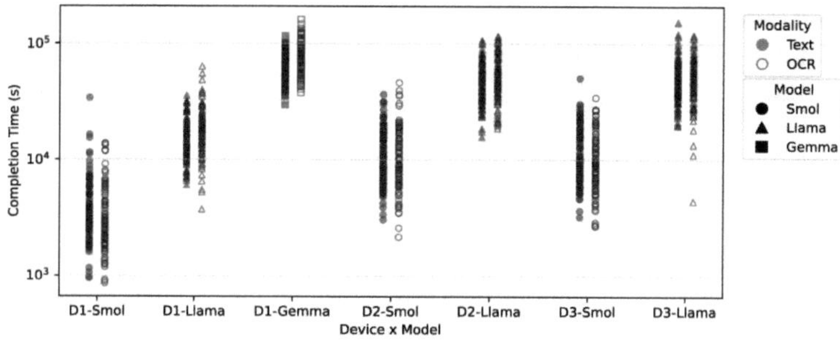


(a) Distribution of completion time across devices and models under text and OCR input modalities. The y-axis is shown on a logarithmic (base-10) scale

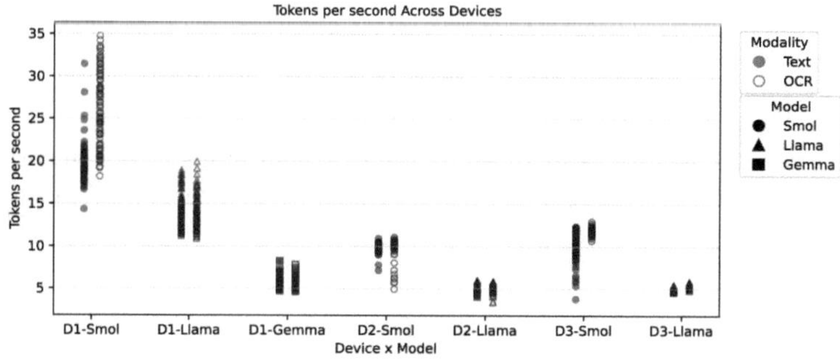


(b) Distribution of token generation speed (tokens/s) across devices and models under text and OCR input modalities. Each point corresponds to a single benchmark item.

**Fig. 1.** Performance results of offline LLM inference.

provide fewer external diagnostics. In early stages, the trade-off is acceptable if limitations are clearly communicated to educators.

For policymakers, the findings indicate that early-stage Unplugged systems can provide value before large infrastructure upgrades. For designers, the main implication is to prioritize simplicity, robustness, and modularity over feature richness in constrained contexts.

## 5 Limitations

This study has four main limitations. First, it lacks systematic energy and thermal profiling. Second, it uses a restricted CDPK subset and excludes SEND items. Third, it emphasizes system-level metrics without component-level error analysis. Fourth, it does not include formal usability studies with low digital-literacy users. These constraints limit broad pedagogical generalization. Finally, the selected devices do not fully represent the diversity of hardware conditions found in Global South educational contexts, which may limit the generalizability of the results.

## 6 Final Considerations

This paper presented an elastic offline-first application aligned with the technical, pedagogical, and ethical principles of AIED Unplugged. In early-stage conditions, lightweight models offered the best balance of responsiveness and reliability, while larger models were often impractical on constrained devices.

The contribution should be interpreted as system-level feasibility evidence. Future work will prioritize classroom deployments, broader benchmark coverage, energy/thermal profiling, and deeper multimodal and usability evaluation.

**Acknowledgments.** The authors wish to express gratitude to everyone involved in this project, including researchers, policymakers, teachers, and students involved in the activities, as well as collaborators from the Center of Excellence in Social Technologies (NEES). This work was also supported by the Brazilian Ministry of Education (MEC) and National Council for Scientific and Technological Development (CNPq).

**Disclosure of Interests.** The authors have no competing interests to declare relevant to this article's content.

## References

1. Allal, L.B., et al.: SmolLM2: when Smol goes big-data-centric training of a small language model. arXiv preprint: arXiv:2502.02737 (2025)
2. Barros, A., Monteiro, M., Rodrigues, L., Dermeval, D., Isotani, S., Bittencourt, I.I.: Evaluating large language model quality in resource-constrained environments: an educational stakeholders' survey on accuracy, completeness, and readability in Brazil. In: International Conference on Artificial Intelligence in Education, pp. 218–232. Springer (2025)
3. Chiu, T.K., Xia, Q., Zhou, X., Chai, C.S., Cheng, M.: Systematic literature review on opportunities, challenges, and future research recommendations of artificial intelligence in education. Comput. Educ.: Artif. Intell. **4**, 100118 (2023)
4. Folorunso, A., Olanipekun, K., Adewumi, T., Samuel, B.: A policy framework on AI usage in developing countries and its impact. Global J. Eng. Technol. Adv. **21**(01), 154–166 (2024)
5. Fu, Y., Weng, Z.: Navigating the ethical terrain of ai in education: a systematic review on framing responsible human-centered AI practices. Comput. Educ.: Artif. Intell. **7**, 100306 (2024)
6. Gottschalk, F., Weise, C.: Digital equity and inclusion in education: an overview of practice and policy in OECD countries. OECD Education Working Papers (2023)
7. Grattafiori, A., et al.: The Llama 3 herd of models. arXiv preprint: arXiv:2407.21783 (2024)

8. Isotani, S., Bittencourt, I.I., Challco, G.C., Dermeval, D., Mello, R.F.: AIED unplugged: leapfrogging the digital divide to reach the underserved. In: International Conference on Artificial Intelligence in Education, pp. 772–779. Springer (2023)
9. Lelièvre, M., et al.: Benchmarking the pedagogical knowledge of large language models (2025). https://arxiv.org/abs/2506.18710
10. Miao, F., Holmes, W., Huang, R., Zhang, H.: AI And Education: A Guidance for Policymakers. UNESCO Publishing (2021)
11. Monteiro, M., et al.: "small device, big decision:" comparing lightweight LLMs' computational performance and output quality for AIED unplugged. In: International Conference on Artificial Intelligence in Education, pp. 160–167. Springer (2025)
12. OECD, P.: Results the state of learning and equity in education, vol. I (Organization for Economic Co-Operation and Development (OECD) 2023) **3** (2022)
13. Passey, D., et al.: Populations digitally excluded from education: issues, factors, contributions and actions for policy, practice and research in a post-pandemic era. Technol., Knowl. Learn., 1–18 (2024)
14. Portela, C., et al.: Bringing AIED, public policy and GDPR to promote educational opportunities in Brazil. In: International Conference on Artificial Intelligence in Education, pp. 74–86. Springer (2024)
15. Rodrigues, L., et al.: MathAide: a qualitative study of teachers' perceptions of an its unplugged for underserved regions. Int. J. Artif. Intell. Educ., 1–29 (2024)
16. Santos, M.M., et al.: Geração de questões com LLMs leves: Um estudo inicial sobre a percepção de educadores. In: Simpósio Brasileiro de Informática na Educação (SBIE), pp. 1635–1646. SBC (2025)
17. Team, G., et al.: Gemma 3 technical report. arXiv preprint: arXiv:2503.19786 (2025)
18. Uema, M.A., Souza, T.D.P.C.D., Dermeval, D., Bittencourt, I.I., Isotani, S.: Designing for meaningful access: towards a framework for AI in education unplugged. In: International Conference on Artificial Intelligence in Education, pp. 307–320. Springer (2025)
19. Vinuesa, R., et al.: The role of artificial intelligence in achieving the sustainable development goals. Nat. Commun. **11**(1), 1–10 (2020)
20. Wang, S., Wang, F., Zhu, Z., Wang, J., Tran, T., Du, Z.: Artificial intelligence in education: a systematic literature review. Expert Syst. Appl. **252**, 124167 (2024)
21. West, D.M., Allen, J.R.: How artificial intelligence is transforming the world. Brookings (2018)

# When Features Misrepresent Underrepresented Learners: Auditing Algorithmic Bias with Differentially Expressive Features

Jaeyoon Choi[1(✉)] and Shamya Karumbaiah[2]

[1] University of California, Irvine, Irvine, CA 92617, USA
jaeyoon.choi@uci.edu
[2] University of Wisconsin-Madison, Madison, WI 53705, USA
shamya.karumbaiah@wisc.edu

**Abstract.** Predictive models in AIED research rely on features; however, these features are often designed and selected based on patterns prevalent in majority populations, potentially failing to capture the unique aspects of minority learners. In this paper, we synthesize current research on the concept of Differentially Expressive Features (DEFs) – features that exhibit disparate predictive power across different demographic groups – and examine their role in perpetuating group bias. Through analyses of a MOOC course completion prediction model and a secondary student achievement prediction model, we found that no features significantly distinguished students who completed from those who did not within groups that showed high levels of group bias, despite many features being significant for the overall population. We highlight the need for further research to identify and address DEFs that introduce feature-level biases to build more equitable algorithmic models in AIED.

**Keywords:** Fairness · Algorithmic Bias · Group Bias · Differentially Expressive Feature · Bias Audit

## 1 Introduction

Predictive models have played an important role in AIED, supporting a wide range of tasks from predicting academic outcomes to analyzing student interactions [12,17]. These models rely on features – measurable attributes or properties derived from data [3] – as their foundational building blocks. These features capture some aspects of learning processes or behaviors, and algorithms identify patterns among these features to explain the data. However, features are often designed and selected based on patterns prevalent in the majority population [1], such that they may be expressed *differentially* across demographic groups. That is, these features may fail to adequately reflect the unique learning behaviors of minority students, increasing the risk of generating biased outcomes that disproportionately affect historically underrepresented students.


E. G. Blanchard et al. (eds.), AIED 2026, LNCS 16586, pp. 424–433, 2027.
https://doi.org/10.1007/978-3-032-29773-0_34

Prior work on algorithmic fairness has predominantly addressed group bias at the algorithmic level, developing fairness-aware solutions (e.g., [7]), but comparatively little attention has been paid to how behavioral features themselves may contribute to group bias. Lee et al. (2025) [8] did examine the relationship between specific features and bias in the context of ADHD using explainable AI, but those post-hoc explainable AI methods have been shown to suffer from reliability issues [14], limiting their utility for diagnosing feature-level bias. Hence, more research is needed to systematically evaluate how well features represent different student groups.

In this paper, we examine features that exhibit disparate predictive power across demographic groups – which we term **differentially expressive features (DEFs)** – and investigate their role as a potential source of group bias. Thus, we ask: *how do DEFs contribute to group bias in predictive models?* Using two educational datasets, we build predictive models and assess whether features show differential predictive power across demographic subgroups. Our findings reveal that while many features are statistically significant overall, none are significant for subgroups exhibiting high levels of group bias.

### 1.1 Differentially Expressive Features (DEFs)

Since the process of generating and selecting features is often largely determined by the majority samples in the dataset, features tend to be *differentially expressive* across subgroups. That is, these features hold differential predictive power for certain groups in predictive models. In this paper, we call these features that exhibit different patterns or associations across subgroups as differentially expressive features (DEFs).

DEFs can arise for several reasons. Researchers who engineer features may lack a full understanding of the lived experiences of marginalized students [2], and this is exacerbated when community stakeholders are not involved in the research process. Features may also manifest differently for marginalized groups due to structural inequalities – for example, measuring MOOC engagement by daily logins may overlook students without stable internet access [15]. DEFs can also stem from constructs that are defined differently across subgroups [9], or from disparate data quality, such as facial recognition systems that perform poorly for darker-skinned individuals [4].

## 2 Empirical Analysis

In this section, we use two real-world datasets to empirically demonstrate how DEFs can contribute to group bias in educational predictive models. Specifically, we build predictive models for (1) MOOC course completion using data from a Social Work master's program offered on Coursera, and (2) mathematics course completion outcomes for secondary school students in Portuguese schools. For each dataset, we first construct a predictive model and evaluate whether it exhibits group bias, then audit bias at the feature level by examining whether individual features consistently differentiate between students who pass and fail across different demographic subgroups.

For the feature level audit, we use the Mann-Whitney U test for numerical features and the Chi-square test for categorical features. A statistically significant result from these tests would indicate that a feature effectively distinguishes between passing and failing students. If the majority of features significantly differentiate outcomes in the overall population but fail to do so within certain subgroups, it may suggest that these features do not meaningfully represent those subgroups – potentially contributing to biased model performance.

### 2.1 Case Study 1: Social Work MOOC Data

The data was collected from a professional certification program offered by a university in the midwestern United States through Coursera. The program is designed for professionals in social work-related fields pursuing further education. Among six courses offered in the program, we chose the one with the highest enrollment (1,132 students), which focuses on examining current social welfare issues in depth.

The majority of the students enrolled in the course are female (67%) (see Table 1). Regarding racial composition, the largest demographic group was white (33.7%), although almost half of the students did not report their race. The second largest racial group, although only 8.2%, was Black.

**Table 1.** Group Distribution and Course Completion Rate

| Group | Distribution | Completion Rate |
|---|---|---|
| Gender | | |
| Male | 16.1% | 48.9% |
| Female | 67% | 52% |
| Non-binary/Third Gender | 0.4% | 40% |
| NA | 16.7% | 39.7% |
| Race | | |
| White | 33.7% | 66.5% |
| Black | 8.2% | 48.4% |
| Asian | 5% | 54.4% |
| Latinx | 4.2% | 41.7% |
| Other | 1.7% | 68.4% |
| NA | 41.5% | 31.5% |
| Intersectional: Gender + Race | | |
| Black female | 4.5% | 47.1% |
| Black male | 1.9% | 52.4% |
| White female | 25.7% | 66.3% |
| White male | 5.7% | 70.3% |

We used students' log data from the discussion forum to model learner engagement, drawing on prior research demonstrating the predictive power of forum-related variables in MOOC dropout studies [11]. The log data captured a variety of student discussion activities, including questions and answers posted, votes given to and received from peers, and the number of followers on their own questions. Furthermore, we used the submission of the final peer-reviewed assignment at the end of the course as a proxy for course completion, as it is the final requirement for students to complete the course.

We trained a logistic regression model at the student level to classify whether a student will complete or not complete the course. We feature-engineered 10 student-level features from the forum log data to capture patterns of peer interaction, such as the number of answers posted by each student and the average character length of those answers (See Table 2). We applied stratified 5-fold cross-validation to ensure each fold contains an equal distribution of the demographic attributes as the entire dataset. The resulting model achieved an Area Under the Curve (AUC) of 0.776 and a False Positive Rate (FPR) of 0.160.

**Table 2.** Feature statistics and logistic regression coefficients. * $p < 0.05$

| Feature | Mean | SD | Coef. | p-value | Sig. |
|---|---|---|---|---|---|
| Answer count | 4.33 | 5.70 | 0.287 | 3.46e-23 | *** |
| Avg. answer length | 287.24 | 312.93 | 0.001 | 8.35e-4 | ** |
| Total votes given to answers | 0.73 | 2.90 | −0.004 | 9.34e-1 | |
| Total votes received for answers | 0.79 | 1.58 | 0.075 | 3.32e-1 | |
| Question count | 0.12 | 2.57 | −19.713 | 1.00 | |
| Avg. question length | 13.69 | 89.55 | −0.001 | 2.99e-1 | |
| Total votes given to questions | 0.01 | 0.19 | 0.182 | 9.34e-1 | |
| Total votes received for questions | 0.42 | 1.81 | −0.175 | 2.89e-3 | * |
| Total following | 0.36 | 0.29 | −0.198 | 8.28e-1 | |
| Total received following | 0.06 | 0.47 | 21.725 | 1.00 | |

**Group Bias Analysis.** We define bias using FPRdifference = $FPR_{subgroup} - FPR_{overall}$, where FPR measures the proportion of students who did not complete the course incorrectly predicted as having completed. We chose FPR over FNR because the model is intended to help the instructional team identify students who may need additional support – misclassifying non-completers as completers leads to missed opportunities for support. A positive FPRdifference for a subgroup indicates that the model is more biased against the subgroup compared to the overall population. That is, it is more likely to incorrectly predict students who did not complete the course as having completed.

Figure 1 illustrates the group biases observed across individual and intersectional subgroups. While the bias scores for gender subgroups (male = -0.049,

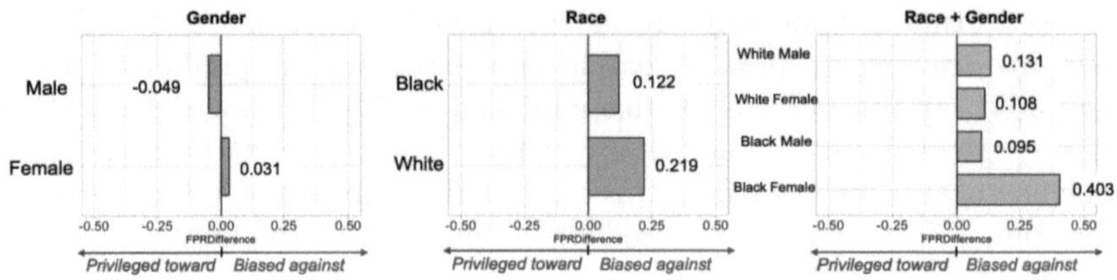


**Fig. 1.** Group Bias (by FPRdifference) in gender, race, and race+gender intersectional groups.

female = 0.031) might suggest a lack of gender bias, examining intersections of gender and race reveals significant differences, especially for Black females (0.403), compared to other intersectional subgroups (white male = 0.131, white female = 0.108, Black male = 0.095). This disparity is not fully explained by the underrepresentation of Black females in the dataset, as the demographic distribution of white males (5.7%) and Black females (4.5%) are similar. Furthermore, while small sample sizes can introduce noise into bias estimates, the FPRdifference for Black females is notably larger than what would be expected from typical sampling error-induced bias [5]. Lastly, the course completion rate for Black females (47.1%) is close to the overall completion rate (50.6%), further suggesting the bias is not driven by distributional differences in outcomes.

**DEFs Analysis.** Our bias analysis suggests that commonly cited explanations for subgroup underperformance – such as small sample sizes or imbalanced output distributions – do not account for the bias observed in Black females. We hence hypothesize that it may stem from DEFs – that is, behavioral features used in the predictive model may hold differential predictive power for certain subgroups. To investigate, we conduct Mann-Whitney U test on each feature within each group to assess whether feature distributions differ significantly between completers and non-completers. We apply the Benjamini-Hochberg procedure to control for multiple hypothesis testing.

| Feature | Overall | Black | white | male | female |
|---|---|---|---|---|---|
| Answer count | 4.08E-99 | 8.1E-05 | 9.09E-25 | 1.67E-18 | 1.71E-62 |
| Avg. answer length | 1.17E-74 | 0.013 | 7.61E-14 | 8.52E-15 | 2.03E-44 |
| Total votes given to answers | 8.19E-21 | 0.30 | 7.24E-06 | 3.76E-04 | 2.12E-12 |
| Total votes received for answers | 5.99E-54 | 0.005 | 2.88E-15 | 4.09E-10 | 7.30E-32 |
| Question count | 3.19E-07 | 1 | 3.14E-02 | 9.36E-02 | 2.75E-05 |
| Avg. question length | 4.98E-07 | 1 | 3.14E-02 | 9.36E-02 | 3.75E-05 |
| Total votes given to questions | 3.87E-01 | 1 | 6.26E-01 | 3.04E-01 | 6.04E-01 |
| Total votes received for questions | 9.06E-13 | 0.65 | 2.01E-02 | 2.56E-02 | 1.28E-08 |
| Total following | 3.27E-10 | 1 | 2.96E-03 | 3.67E-02 | 3.78E-08 |
| Total received following | 3.19E-07 | 1 | 3.14E-02 | 9.36E-02 | 2.75E-05 |

**Fig. 2.** Corrected p-values from Mann-Whitney U test for individual race and gender groups. Highlighted are statistically significant p-values at $\alpha = 0.05$.

Figures 2 and 3 present corrected p-values from Mann-Whitney U tests comparing students who completed the course with those who did not. For the overall students, 9 out of 10 features significantly differentiate between the two. However, features are already differentially expressed across subgroups – white students have more significant features (9 features) than Black students (3), and female students more (9) than male students (6). Despite this, group-level bias was not observed for race or gender groups, likely because the three features identified as significant in the logistic regression model – *Answer count*, *Avg. answer length*, and *Total votes received for questions* (see Table 2) – also significantly distinguish completers from non-completers across nearly all gender and race subgroups. That is, even though some features vary in significance across subgroups, the key predictive features are consistently informative, potentially mitigating group bias.

However, Fig. 3 shows that none of the features are statistically significant for Black females. Notably, this includes those three features that were identified as statistically significant in the logistic regression model (see Table 2). This result indicates that the features in our predictive model are in fact intersectionally differentially expressive – the intersection of gender and race amplified the impact of DEFs for Black female students. Therefore, our DEF analysis showed that there indeed exist DEFs for certain subgroups – all of the features in our model were differentially expressed for Black females, the subgroup exhibiting the highest group bias. This means that the behavioral measures used in the prediction model were not effective in identifying Black female students at risk of dropping out.

| Feature | Overall | Black Female | white male | Black male | white female |
|---|---|---|---|---|---|
| Answer count | 4.08E-99 | 0.09 | 0.004 | 0.05 | 6.77E-20 |
| Avg. answer length | 1.17E-74 | 0.43 | 0.03 | 0.36 | 9.89E-13 |
| Total votes given to answers | 8.19E-21 | 0.82 | 0.34 | 0.86 | 6.72E-05 |
| Total votes received for answers | 5.99E-54 | 0.10 | 0.004 | 0.36 | 9.69E-12 |
| Question count | 3.19E-07 | 0.82 | 0.65 | 0.57 | 5.53E-02 |
| Avg. question length | 4.98E-07 | 0.82 | 0.65 | 0.57 | 5.53E-02 |
| Total votes given to questions | 3.87E-01 | 1 | 1 | 1 | 6.23E-01 |
| Total votes received for questions | 9.06E-13 | 0.83 | 0.97 | 1 | 1.13E-02 |
| Total following | 3.27E-10 | 0.82 | 0.65 | 1 | 6.79E-03 |
| Total received following | 3.19E-07 | 0.82 | 0.65 | 0.57 | 5.53E-02 |

**Fig. 3.** Corrected p-values from Mann-Whitney U test for intersectional groups. Values are rounded to two decimal places. Highlighted are statistically significant p-values at $\alpha = 0.05$.

## 2.2 Case Study 2: Secondary School Math Data

The data we used for case study 2 comes from Cortez & Silva (2008) [6], which contains student mathematics performance data from Portuguese secondary school students. The data includes a total of 396 students, of whom 53% are female and 47% are male. Among the 30 available features in the original dataset, we selected five that showed strong predictive performance based on the prior study [6]: *failures* (number of past class failures), *Fedu* (father's education), *goout* (frequency of going out with friends), *Walc* (weekend alcohol consumption), and *Mjob* (mother's job). The final outcome variable is a binarized version of *G3* (final grade), which ranges from 0 to 20. Following the approach in the previous study, we labeled students as pass if G3 $\geq$ 10, and fail otherwise. About 53% of students in the dataset passed. When it comes to gender, approximately 53% of female students passed, compared to around 47% of male students. We trained a Catboost model at the student level to classify whether a student would pass or fail, for its strong performance with categorical features and robustness to overfitting [13]. The model was trained using a simple 7:3 train-test split. The resulting model achieved an AUC of 0.77 and a FPR of 0.63 overall. This indicates that the model has a good ability to distinguish between students who pass and those who fail overall, though relatively high FPR suggests it tends to incorrectly predict some failing students as passing.

**Group Bias Analysis.** Here, we use AUCdifference, defined as $AUC_{subgroup} - AUC_{overeall}$. Unlike case study 1, where the model's intended use for student intervention motivated the use of FPR as the bias metric, case Study 2 does not have a specific deployment context that would prioritize one error type over another; we therefore use AUCdifference as a measure of overall discriminative performance. A positive AUCdifference for a subgroup indicates that the model performs better for the subgroup than for the overall population. In contrast, a negative AUCdifference indicates that the model performs worse for the subgroup, implying bias against that group. We found that the female group had an AUCdifference of $-0.16$, compared to $-0.06$ for the male group. That is, the model performed relatively worse for females than for the overall population – particularly when contrasted with the smaller performance gap observed for males. Given that female and male students have similar sample sizes and output distributions, this disparity may suggest a potential bias in how the features represent each group.

**DEFs Analysis.** For DEF analysis, we conduct statistical test for each feature to assess whether its distribution differs significantly between students who passed and failed. Since our dataset includes both categorical and numerical variables, we employ different statistical tests accordingly. For numerical variables (i.e., *failures, Fedu, goout, Walc*), we use the Mann-Whitney U test, while for the categorical variable (i.e., *Mjob*), we apply the Chi-squared test. Consistent with Sect. 2.1, we also use the Benjamini-Hochberg procedure to control the false discovery rate.

Figure 4 shows the corrected p-values from the Mann-Whitney U and Chi-squared tests comparing students who passed with those who did not. Overall, two out of the five features were statistically significant. However, none of the features were significant for female students. In contrast, the two features that were significant in distinguishing pass/fail outcomes in the overall population were also significant for male students.

| Feature | Overall | Female | Male |
|---|---|---|---|
| failures | 0.00049 | 0.06 | 0.0006 |
| Fedu | 0.007 | 0.28 | 0.008 |
| goout | 0.21 | 0.28 | 0.57 |
| Walc | 0.21 | 0.82 | 0.10 |
| Mjob | 0.21 | 0.2 | 0.57 |

**Fig. 4.** Corrected p-values from Mann-Whitney U test and Chi-squared test. Values are rounded to two decimal places. Highlighted are statistically significant p-values at $\alpha = 0.05$.

In this case study, the relatively small dataset size (i.e., 396 students) may limit the precision of bias measurements (see discussion by [5]), especially when compared to case study 1 which had a larger dataset. However, since female and male students have similar sample sizes and output distributions, the observed group bias against females – combined with the fact that none of the features were statistically significant in distinguishing between females who passed and those who did not – suggests a potential link between DEFs and group bias.

## 3 Discussion

In this paper, we synthesized the concept of DEFs and examined how they can be a source of group bias in two student performance prediction models. In case study 1, which focused on MOOC course completion prediction, we observed significant intersectional bias against Black female students. Particularly, none of the features were statistically significant in distinguishing Black females who completed the course from those who did not. In case study 2, the model performed worse for female students, and none of the features significantly distinguished females who passed from those who failed. In both case studies, these findings suggest that the features used by the models may lack expressive power for certain groups, which may contribute to the observed group biases. Interestingly, we also found in case study 1, DEFs did not always translate into group bias, but this does not mean such features can be overlooked. Representational bias concerns not just whether outcomes are fair, but whether the representation of groups is fair to begin with [16].

Our findings highlight the need to examine representational bias [10] at the feature level, and we offer several recommendations for future research. First, we recommend incorporating DEF analysis when auditing bias; and while we used certain statistical tests here, future work could explore more interpretable approaches. Second, researchers should consider the underlying causes of DEFs and design features more carefully. In some cases, this may even involve rethinking the outcome variable itself – for example, recognizing that definitions of academic success may look different across groups. Lastly, collecting additional data can help mitigate DEFs – not just increasing sample sizes but collecting a broader range of data sources, including qualitative data. In case study 1, where course discussions centered on discrimination and justice, Black female students engaged deeply regardless of their course completion outcomes – suggesting their forum behaviors were driven by lived experiences rather than academic performance, a pattern only visible through qualitative data.

Our study has a few limitations. The relatively small sample sizes may limit the generalizability of our findings and the reliability of the statistical tests used to detect DEFs. This could be a potential issue for AIED more broadly, as we often deal with smaller sample sizes for such disaggregated analysis. Additionally, our framework does not fully establish a causal link between DEFs and group bias, and future work could involve a more thorough investigation into how DEFs influence group bias across different stages of the machine learning pipeline. Lastly, Mann-Whitney U and Chi-squared are univariate, and future work could explore multivariate approaches that capture how features interact and how DEFs arise from such interactions.

In conclusion, we bring to the forefront an underexplored issue in bias research in AIED. Our findings show that features capturing students' learning patterns can have disparate impact across demographic groups, and that auditing bias at the feature level is a crucial step toward building more equitable models in AIED.

**Acknowledgments.** This work was supported by the Office of the Vice Chancellor for Research and Graduate Education at the University of Wisconsin–Madison, with funding from the Wisconsin Alumni Research Foundation. We also thank Ji-Hyun Yu for sharing the coursera dataset.

**Disclosure of Interests.** The authors have no competing interests to declare that are relevant to the content of this article.

## References

1. Bishop, C.M., Nasrabadi, N.M.: Pattern recognition and machine learning (2006)
2. Blodgett, S.L., Barocas, S., Daumé III, H., Wallach, H.: Language (technology) is power: a critical survey of "bias" in NLP. arXiv preprint arXiv:2005.14050 (2020)
3. Brooks, C., Thompson, C.: Predictive modelling in teaching and learning. In: Handbook of Learning Analytics, pp. 61–68 (2017)
4. Buolamwini, J., Gebru, T.: Gender shades: intersectional accuracy disparities in commercial gender classification. In: Conference on Fairness, Accountability and Transparency, pp. 77–91. PMLR (2018)
5. Choi, J., Karumbaiah, S., Matayoshi, J.: Bias or insufficient sample size? Improving reliable estimation of algorithmic bias for minority groups. In: Proceedings of the 15th International Learning Analytics and Knowledge Conference, pp. 547–557 (2025)
6. Cortez, P., Silva, A.M.G.: Using data mining to predict secondary school student performance (2008)

7. Kearns, M., Neel, S., Roth, A., Wu, Z.S.: An empirical study of rich subgroup fairness for machine learning. In: Proceedings of the Conference on Fairness, Accountability, and Transparency, pp. 100–109 (2019)
8. Lee, H., Belitz, C., Nasiar, N., Bosch, N.: XAI reveals the causes of attention deficit hyperactivity disorder (ADHD) bias in student performance prediction. In: Proceedings of the 15th International Learning Analytics and Knowledge Conference, pp. 418–428 (2025)
9. Matthews, J.S., Boomhower, K.M., Ekwueme, C.: Assimilationist, reformist, and sociopolitical phases of school belonging research: a critical race and optimal distinctiveness review. In: Advances in Motivation Science, vol. 11, pp. 171–213. Elsevier (2024)
10. Mehrabi, N., Morstatter, F., Saxena, N., Lerman, K., Galstyan, A.: A survey on bias and fairness in machine learning. ACM Comput. Surv. (CSUR) **54**(6), 1–35 (2021)
11. Moreno-Marcos, P.M., Alario-Hoyos, C., Muñoz-Merino, P.J., Estevez-Ayres, I., Kloos, C.D.: A learning analytics methodology for understanding social interactions in MOOCs. IEEE Trans. Learn. Technol. **12**(4), 442–455 (2018)
12. Olsen, J.K., Aleven, V., Rummel, N.: Predicting student performance in a collaborative learning environment. International Educational Data Mining Society (2015)
13. Prokhorenkova, L., Gusev, G., Vorobev, A., Dorogush, A.V., Gulin, A.: Catboost: unbiased boosting with categorical features. In: Advances in Neural Information Processing Systems, p. 31 (2018)
14. Ribeiro, J., Cardoso, L., Santos, V., Carvalho, E., Carneiro, N., Alves, R.: How reliable and stable are explanations of XAI methods? arXiv preprint arXiv:2407.03108 (2024)
15. Shapiro, H.B., Lee, C.H., Roth, N.E.W., Li, K., Çetinkaya-Rundel, M., Canelas, D.A.: Understanding the massive open online course (MOOC) student experience: an examination of attitudes, motivations, and barriers. Comput. Educ. **110**, 35–50 (2017)
16. Sun, T., et al.: Mitigating gender bias in natural language processing: literature review. arXiv preprint arXiv:1906.08976 (2019)
17. Zollanvari, A., Kizilirmak, R.C., Kho, Y.H., Hernández-Torrano, D.: Predicting students' GPA and developing intervention strategies based on self-regulatory learning behaviors. IEEE Access **5**, 23792–23802 (2017)

# Design Tensions for Generative AI in Education for Early to Mid-adolescent Youth: An Exploration of Autonomy, Critical Reflection, and Psychological Safety

Angela E. B. Stewart[1(✉)], Paras Sharma[1], Chun Li[1], Ye Deng[1], Omotayo Madein[2], YuePing Sha[1], Janet Shufor Bih Epse Fofang[1], Christina Kundrak[3], and Erin Walker[1(✉)]

[1] University of Pittsburgh, Pittsburgh, PA 15260, USA
{angelas,pas252,chl500,yed19,yus158,jab1087,eawalker}@pitt.edu
[2] Carnegie Mellon University, Pittsburgh, PA 15213, USA
omadein@andrew.cmu.edu
[3] University of Southern California, Los Angeles, CA 90007, USA
ckundrak@usc.edu

**Abstract.** Early-to-mid adolescent youth experience dramatic social, emotional, and cognitive changes that can be supported or hindered through interactions with generative AI in educations. We discuss the design tensions that arise for three AIED teams triangulating across core values of autonomy, critical reflection, and psychological safety. In the first case study, we discuss generative AI to enable youth's storytelling and social critique. In the second, generative AI is used as a tool for the youth's meaning-making of academic content focused on AI bias. Our third case study examines generative AI for youth's co-creation of a social robot. We synthesize core insights into how AIED teams can resolve design tensions, by looking to developmental and pedagogical theories.

**Keywords:** Autonomy · Psychological Safety · Critical Reflection

## 1 Introduction

Early- to mid-adolescence is a physically, emotionally, and cognitively turbulent developmental time [4]. During this period, youth construct complex notions of themselves, the world around them, and their place in society [4]. Youth develop new capacities for emotional regulation, such as identifying and managing intense experiences [4]. Concurrently, higher-order thinking capacities emerge alongside abstract thinking abilities [4]. With these cognitive transitions, social structures become more important, as youth demonstrate heightened sensitivity to social


E. G. Blanchard et al. (eds.), AIED 2026, LNCS 16586, pp. 434–442, 2027.
https://doi.org/10.1007/978-3-032-29773-0_35

hierarchies, and increased meaning-making of their place in society [4]. These intensely chaotic and meaningful lived experiences for youth must be supported in their learning spaces for their positive development.

However, when it comes to generative AI and youth development, the societal alarm has been sounded. Concerns range from interactions that endanger mental health, lead to the development of faulty information-seeking practices, and encourage offloading of cognition [9]. Given the perturbations of early- to mid-adolescence and the potential for psychological and cognitive harm during this period, we argue that the AI in Education (AIED) community needs to more clearly account for how they design generative AI systems in this context.

Elucidating design values is a powerful tool for doing that just that. Design values are conceptual notions of what we find important [1]. This elucidation involves linking conceptual values to contextual implementation [1]. This process reveals value tensions, which requires designers to negotiate a resolution. In this work, we illustrate this process by presenting three case studies documenting how AIED teams enacted design values aimed at early- to mid-adolescent youth's positive development: autonomy, critical reflection, and psychological safety.

First, we focus on **autonomy**, which is freedom from external control [1]. It is the right to self-governance that enables us to act in ways consistent our goals [1]. For example, the ability to freely explore interests, values, and beliefs can support youth's positive development [4]. Autonomy is crucial to early- to mid-adolescence as youth learn to navigate and make sense of their world [4].

Autonomy must be coupled with **critical reflection**, which is the ability to examine and question social phenomena, beliefs, or circumstances [5,12]. Critical reflection involves asking not just what is, but why, incorporating notions of social and political influences on our world [12]. This reflection involves the higher-order, abstract thinking abilities that form during early- and mid-adolescence, while also building on the youth's maturing sense of social relationships.

As youth engage in this deep questioning of the world, it is crucial to protect their mental well-being. We center **psychological safety**, which is the feeling that taking interpersonal risks will not result in negative outcomes to one's identity (sense of self), such as shame or rejection [17]. When youth feel psychologically safe, they can navigate new experiences and achieve their goals, despite the discomfort that accompanies the inherent unfamiliarity associated with learning [17]. Psychological safety can be supported in learning spaces that explicitly acknowledge the importance of youth's identity and experiences [17]. Positive relationships and community building are also core to psychological safety, as youth connect to peers and adults that value their contributions [4,17].

Taken together, we argue that centering autonomy, critical reflection, and psychological safety are key design values upon which generative AI systems should be built, to respect early- to mid-adolescent youth's personhood, protect their emotional safety, and support them in developing capacities to be engaged and agentic individuals throughout adulthood. In this paper, we make two main contributions: 1) we illuminate how our design values show up in practice across three of our AIED projects, and subsequent tensions that arose between these values and 2) we synthesize core insights for how other AIED teams might employ our approach to elucidating values for their context. We take a case study approach where we construct a rich description of a pedagogical context and embedded values. To write these case studies, we triangulated across our research team meeting notes, field notes from deployment, and artefacts created during the learning experience. Each case study was originally authored by one member of our research team and refined until consensus was reached with other members of the team, including the senior author for all three. Consistent with our focal developmental range, all case studies focus on fourth to eighth-grade youth in the United States (approximately nine to fourteen years old).

## 2 Case Study 1 - Youth's Storytelling

Storytelling is a powerful pedagogical tool for engaging youth in critique of society and culture [16]. This case study draws on Afrofuturism as a lens for Black youth to imagine Black-centered technological futures through counter-storytelling, challenging dominant narratives in today's technology spaces [16]. At the same time, youth developed AI literacy in using and critiquing AI systems [8]. Across two iterations of the program, participants used generative AI to create multimedia stories, including videos that showcased their narratives.

The storytelling camp supported learner **autonomy** in setting and pursuing their own goals by positioning learners as active storytellers and creators, rather than consumers of technology. For example, learners explored potential topics for their narratives by brainstorming "what if" style questions (*e.g.*, "what if a girl solves the hunger?"). Learners reviewed AI-generated responses and evaluated their credibility and usefulness (*e.g.*, through simple thumbs-up or thumbs-down gestures). Learners also engaged in group discussions and collaborated with facilitators to collectively edit the prompts for refining the outputs. The open-ended approach gave learners the autonomy to build narratives around real-world problems that align with their personal values and interests for exploration. For example, learners created stories that reflected their lived experiences, such as lead exposure in city infrastructure (a problem reflected in the local infrastructure of the city in which this work takes place) or sickle cell disease (a disease that disproportionately affects Black populations [2]).

It is this autonomy-oriented design that, in turn, supported **psychological safety**. All activities were guided by theories of cultural-responsiveness, which aim to value youth's identities as assets upon which their learning can occur, rather than deficits to be corrected [12]. Learning spaces that center youth identity signal to youth that who they are is valued and worthy of exploration. Our use of generative AI itself encouraged youth to integrate their identities and community experiences into their creations by asking them to create multimedia assets that aid in their storytelling. That said, outside of generative AI use, we engaged all adults present in the learning space (researchers and community partner staff) in a culturally-responsive professional development aimed at bolstering their relationship-building skills with youth, leading to the positive relationships with adults necessary for psychological safety [17].

The program design also supports **critical reflection**. Through iterative interactions with generative AI, learners critically examined AI-generated outputs, identified missing or biased perspectives, and reflected on issues of representation, fairness, and power. For example, learners prompted the generative AI system to produce images of "an African fashion designer" or "a girl planting vegetables on a spaceship." The system continuously produced depictions of white or light-skinned people, while nearly all participants wanted their created characters to more closely resemble themselves. Learners refined their prompts and phrasing to produce satisfactory images, followed by a reflective discussion on AI bias. For example, in one of the camps, the community partner hosted a showcase with families, where collective conversations were had about how AI is not as "smart" as we think it is, and it exhibits racial bias that currently requires human correction in the prompting. That said, the stories themselves supported critical reflection, where Black characters were consistently positioned as main characters who solve real-world problems using technologies. This is in contrast to mainstream media narratives that rarely portray Black people as innovators, heroes, and intellectual leaders [12,16]. Taken together, in this case study, we were able to use generative AI in alignment with our core values.

## 3 Case Study 2 - Opting Out for Psychological Safety

Values can also be in irreconcilable tension, leading to the necessary termination of an AIED project. This case study deals with our Large Language Model-(LLM) based chatbot that supports youth meaning-making. Meaning-making is developmental, in that it progresses from concrete interpretations of experience to abstract understanding, and toward more transcendent forms that connect experience with values, identity, and action [5]. Concrete meaning-making solely focuses on surfacing understanding, with limited transfer of knowledge to new contexts [5], whereas transcendent meaning-making connects specific experiences to abstract concepts, broader societal patterns, and personal values [5].

In this project, we aimed to support youth making meaning of AI bias, where an AI tool performs systematically worse for some people than others [15]. In this case, integrated meaning-making emerges when youth connect specific experiences with AI to wider questions of responsibility, accountability, and fairness in both technology and society at large [5,15]. To learn about AI bias, youth first engage with a short video on the topic, and then reflect through discussion with the chatbot. We used a retrieval-augmented generation (RAG) [6] approach to ground LLM responses in a curated set of conversations coded for developmental levels of meaning-making. When a learner's response reflects primarily concrete observations, the LLM prompts reflection on broader implications (*e.g.*, by asking "Why do you think it is important for people to learn about AI bias?"). When a response is primarily abstract, the system prompts learners to integrate the concrete and abstract dimensions by articulating specific examples that illustrate their claims (*e.g.*, by asking "Can you share a specific example or personal story that illustrates this?"). A core goal of this work was deployment at scale. We wanted to deploy this tool as a mechanism for our research team to understand youth meaning-making from hundreds of children at once. Scale became an essential issue in reconciling our values and the implementation of this technology.

Our design facilitates **autonomy** by giving learners control over the focus of their reflection, rather than directing them toward predetermined interpretations or outcomes. The discussion begins with open-ended prompts that invite both interpretation and emotional response (*e.g.*, "What did you learn from the video?" or "How do you feel after watching the video?"). These prompts open reflective space by not prescribing specific entry points into the topic, allowing learners to decide which aspects of AI bias they find worthy of discussion. This approach also scaffolds **critical reflection** by asking youth to link personal experience to conceptual understanding [5]. By scaffolding both the concrete and abstract dimensions of meaning-making, youth examine a specific phenomenon (AI bias), grounded in their experience, and broader societal implications.

This design also introduced threats to their **psychological safety**. Situations that are salient to aspects of a person's identity (*e.g.*, race, gender, culture) pose acute threats to psychological safety, as they highlight the social hierarchies that deem certain identities more important than others [17]. Discussing AI bias is precisely the kind of topic that might pose an identity threat to youth [4, 17]. Encouraging emotional exploration in this context raises risks of emotional overexposure. For instance, when sharing personal experiences related to bias, learners may re-experience feelings of unfairness by recalling prior moments of being treated differently due to their identity. Furthermore, generative AI is likely to misinterpret the emotional expression of youth, especially those least represented in AIED spaces, such as racially-minoritized youth [15]. This language bias in generative AI systems means that learners must either conform to narrow definitions of "appropriate" emotional expression or have their lived experiences continue to go unacknowledged. It is precisely this kind of disregard for learners' identity that poses threats to their psychological safety [17].

That is not to say that engaging youth in topics of AI bias should be avoided. On the contrary, recognition of youth's identity and their very real lived experiences with bias and social hierarchies can actually bolster psychological safety when supported by a trusted adult [17]. However, the intentional presence of adults trained in culturally-responsive methods is key to transforming this from a psychological safety threatening situation into one that is supportive. This kind of real-time support is impossible in our stated research design, causing our team to stop the project before deploying with at scale. The AIED community currently faces immense pressure in the widespread adoption of generative AI. This case study reveals that sometimes the most ethical choice is to opt out.

## 4 Case Study 3 - A Co-creative Robot

Our final case study centers a co-creative robot [7], where youth build a robot as said robot comments on its unfolding design. Our research team has explored this design space across three summer camps (2023-2025) with Black youth. This summer camp incorporates culturally-responsive computing pedagogies [12], which aim to empower learners to reflect on their identities, experiences, and understandings of society as they create technologies. Our camps blend programming and engineering with discussions of identity, and reflective dialogues with the robot. As a first step towards co-creation, we focused on encouraging youth reflection on what they are building and why.

This case study centers the latest iteration of our design where we introduce a hybrid architecture [13] that integrates generative AI with a theoretically grounded, rule-based structure to support both flexibility and alignment with self-regulated learning theories [18]. Our empirical evaluation [13] shows that while this hybrid system supported more elaborate reflections on goals, it also surfaced new challenges, particularly instances of contextual misalignment between the system's responses and learners' situated designs. Consequently, our ongoing work focuses on using learners' multimodal camp activity data to develop contextually responsive hybrid systems. By developing modes that capture self-regulatory processes [14,18], the system will be better equipped to infer learners' goals and generate contextualized reflective prompts.

**Autonomy** is embedded in our camp curriculum, as learners can act in ways consistent with self-declared design goals for their robot. For example, learners can choose not to take part in the camp's engineering activities and rather focus on the aesthetic design of their creation. However, this autonomy is restricted in the interactions with the dialogue system, as **psychological safety** takes precedence. Our camp aims to create space for learners to explore and reflect. Integrating generative AI in the dialogue system allows learners to freely reflect and explore their goals, but it could risk their psychological safety if unpredictable comments on their ongoing creations fail to appropriately respond to the identity-related reflections core to this camp [9,17]. For example, an unconstrained LLM might invalidate or penalize a learner's unique cognitive or emotional expressions regarding their work [15]. This informed our decision not to directly incorporate prompt-tuned generative AI as the sole pedagogical partner for learner interactions, but rather to embed it in a theoretically grounded and hybrid way [13], where the overall trajectory of the dialogue is guided by principles of self-regulated learning.

To ensure these guided responses remain contextually-relevant, the system could use the multimodal data such as interaction logs, audio-visual recordings, and observations to build learner models [14]. Recognizing that a learner's goals might evolve over the camp, we consider the standard first-day consent as insufficient. Therefore, we encode autonomy directly into our design through continuous, ongoing consent. Learners can opt out of data collection at any moment, such as declining to have their robots photographed, having autonomy over what data the system uses to generate learner models and LLM-responses.

**Critical reflection** on assumptions embedded in technology allow learners to deeply examine techno-social issues and relate them to their own designs [12]. However, as discussed in Sect. 3, reflecting on sensitive issues may not be psychologically safe if youth are left unsupported [17]. Deploying generative AI without human supervision in this case poses a tremendous risk. Although others have used generative AI as an emotional partner [9], we actively restricted its role as a safeguard. We decided that our hybrid system is suitable for guiding general reflections on technology design, but critical reflections on techno-social issues must be facilitated by trained adults. For example, our hybrid system prompts learners to discuss their daily robot-building progress, explored concepts, and ongoing goals [13]. Conversely, trained facilitators guide the more sensitive discussions surrounding identity and lived experiences.

## 5 Discussion

Due to the uncontrolled nature of generative AI [9], we do not believe children should be placed in interactions with this technology without critical evaluation. Accordingly, we suggest AIED designers (insight one) **select values in alignment with the perturbations central to youth's developmental period**. This means foregrounding the most dramatic cognitive, emotional, and social changes. In our case, we center the precarity of early- to mid-adolescence, where shifts in emotional regulation and attention to social hierarchies are pronounced (Sect. 1), leading us to consider psychological safety. Early- to mid-adolescent youth experience shifts in their cognitive capacities for abstract thought and connection to broader societal issues. The ability to freely explore their identity and value-formation during these cognitive shifts is key to positive development [4]. Accordingly, we center critical reflection and autonomy to support these needs.

Human facilitation was a core factor in our ability to bring our values into harmony. Therefore, we found that (insight two) **supportive adults can bridge the gap when value tensions occur.** When faced with the value tension of psychological safety versus critical reflection and autonomy (Sect. 3), it was the lack human facilitation that moved us to deprecate the project. In this case, the chatbot would have been deployed at scale without appropriate monitoring infrastructure, and our research team would have no control over trusted adult oversight of youth's activities. This inability to guarantee youth safety led our research team to decide that the ethical decision was to opt out. Conversely, in Case Studies One and Three (Sects. 2 and 4), our research team was trained in culturally-responsive [12] methodologies, which informed both our facilitation and pedagogical design. Further, all work was done in partnership with leaders at the community organization where these activities were deployed, ensuring that adults who interact with these children daily are in the space.

Our pedagogical approach de-emphasized the generative AI, instead focusing on learners' creations. Consequently, we found that (insight three) **organizing learning around youth-created artifacts is more powerful than centering the generative AI interaction.** Constructionism emphasizes that learning is most effective when learners actively construct meaningful and shareable artifacts [10]. However, in Case Study Two (Sect. 3), interaction with the chatbot was the central tool upon which learning occurred, narrowly focusing on learners' articulation of their perspectives. This disembodied reflection, without the ability to construct physical (or digital) objects, reflects Papert's notion of epistemological alienation, where learning is disassociated from the everyday projects that youth find meaningful [10]. Conversely, our values harmonized when generative AI was embedded into pedagogical contexts where learning occurred during meaningful creation (*e.g.*, an Afrofuturist narrative in Sect. 2 or a robot in 4).

This work contains limitations, which can be rectified in future research. Our work centers autonomy, critical reflection, and psychological safety. However, our team continues to engage with other values pertinent to generative AI, such as the ethics of how enterprise models are trained, environmental sustainability, and usage of generative AI for writing [3,11]. Further, our values reflect our team, and values will vary across contexts, such as scholars outside the United States [15]. Therefore, AIED teams should employ our reflective approach to elucidate values most appropriate to them, rather than uncritically adopting ours. Finally, in line with culturally-responsive approaches, our team values reflexivity [12,15], leading us to take this case study approach. However, in this work, we do not deploy measurements of our values. Future work could directly measure our attainment of these values through co-created metrics with caregivers and youth. Taken together, this work contributes to a developmental perspective on how generative AI in education can ethically support early- to mid-adolescent youth.

**Acknowledgments.** This work is funded by NSF DRLs 2415872 and 2415873, and the Jacobs Foundation. Generative AI was used in this manuscript to assist in copyediting. All ideas are original and we take responsibility for the contents of this paper.

## References

1. Friedman, B., Kahn, P.H., Borning, A., Huldtgren, A.: Value Sensitive Design and Information Systems. In: Doorn, N., Schuurbiers, D., van de Poel, I., Gorman, M.E. (eds.) Early Engagement and New Technologies: Opening Up the Laboratory. PET, vol. 16, pp. 55–95. Springer, Dordrecht (2013). https://doi.org/10.1007/978-94-007-7844-3_4
2. Hassell, K.L.: Population estimates of sickle cell disease in the U.S. Am. J. Preventive Med. **38**(4, Supplement), S512–S521 (2010). https://doi.org/10.1016/j.amepre.2009.12.022, Blood Disorders in Public Health
3. He, J., Houde, S., Weisz, J.D.: Which contributions deserve credit? Perceptions of attribution in human-AI Co-creation. In: Proceedings of the 2025 CHI Conference on Human Factors in Computing Systems. CHI '25, Association for Computing Machinery, New York, NY, USA (2025). https://doi.org/10.1145/3706598.3713522
4. Immordino-Yang, M.H., Darling-Hammond, L., Krone, C.R.: Nurturing nature: how brain development is inherently social and emotional, and what this means for education. Educ. Psychol. **54**(3), 185–204 (2019). https://doi.org/10.1080/00461520.2019.1633924
5. Immordino-Yang, M.H., Kundrak, C., Knecht, D., Matthews, J.: Civic reasoning depends on transcendent thinking: implications of adolescent brain development for sel. Soc. Emotional Learn. Res. Pract. Policy **4**, 100067 (2024). https://doi.org/10.1016/j.sel.2024.100067

6. Lewis, P., et al.: Retrieval-augmented generation for knowledge-intensive NLP tasks (2021). https://arxiv.org/abs/2005.11401
7. Li, Y.: I want to be unique from other robots: positioning girls as co-creators of social robots in culturally-responsive computing education. In: Proceedings of the 2023 CHI Conference on Human Factors in Computing Systems. CHI '23, Association for Computing Machinery, New York, NY, USA (2023). https://doi.org/10.1145/3544548.3581272
8. Long, D., Magerko, B.: What is AI Literacy? Competencies and design considerations. In: Proceedings of the 2020 CHI Conference on Human Factors in Computing Systems, pp. 1–16. ACM, Honolulu HI USA (2020). https://doi.org/10.1145/3313831.3376727
9. Nagata, J.M., Memon, Z., Huang, O., Moreno, M.A.: Adolescent health and generative AI–risks and benefits. JAMA Pediatr. **180**(1), 7–8 (2026). https://doi.org/10.1001/jamapediatrics.2025.4502
10. Papert, S.A.: Mindstorms: Children, Computers, and Powerful Ideas. Basic books, New York, NY (1980)
11. Scheuerman, M.K., et al.: Responsibly training foundation models: actualizing ethical principles for curating large-scale training datasets in the era of massive ai models. In: Proceedings of the Companion Publication of the 2025 Conference on Computer-Supported Cooperative Work and Social Computing, pp. 99–105. CSCW Companion '25, Association for Computing Machinery, New York, NY, USA (2025). https://doi.org/10.1145/3715070.3748285
12. Scott, K.A., Sheridan, K.M., Clark, K.: Culturally responsive computing: a theory revisited. Learn. Media Technol. **40**(4), 412–436 (2015). https://doi.org/10.1080/17439884.2014.924966
13. Sharma, P., et al.: Hybrid LLM-embedded dialogue agents for learner reflection: designing responsive and theory-driven interactions (2026). https://arxiv.org/abs/2602.20486
14. Sharma, P., Stewart, A.E., Li, Q., Ravichander, K., Walker, E.: Building learner activity models from log data using sequence mapping and hidden Markov models. In: Paaßen, B., Epp, C.D. (eds.) Proceedings of the 17th International Conference on Educational Data Mining, pp. 584–593. International Educational Data Mining Society, Atlanta, Georgia, USA (2024). https://doi.org/10.5281/zenodo.12729890
15. Stewart, A.E.B., et al.: Who's got the power? Data feminism as a lens for designing aied engagement systems. In: Cristea, A.I., Walker, E., Lu, Y., Santos, O.C., Isotani, S. (eds.) Artificial Intelligence in Education, pp. 233–247. Springer Nature Switzerland, Cham (2025). https://doi.org/10.1007/978-3-031-98459-4_17
16. Toliver, S.R.: It will take nations of billions to obstruct our dreams: extending BlackCrit through Afrofuturism. J. Multicultural Educ. **18**(3), 230–244 (2024). https://doi.org/10.1108/JME-11-2022-0141
17. Wanless, S.B.: The role of psychological safety in human development. Res. Hum. Dev. **13**(1), 6–14 (2016). https://doi.org/10.1080/15427609.2016.1141283
18. Zimmerman, B.J.: Attaining self-regulation: a social cognitive perspective. In: Boekaerts, M., Pintrich, P.R., Zeidner, M. (eds.) Handbook of Self-Regulation, pp. 13–39. Academic Press, San Diego, CA (2000). https://doi.org/10.1016/b978-012109890-2/50031-7

# AI That Helps—or Widens Gaps? Equity Impacts of a Learning-by-Teaching Tutor in K–12 Mathematics

Fan Zhang[1(✉)] and Rui Guo[2]

[1] University of Florida, Gainesville, FL, USA
f.zhang1@ufl.edu
[2] University of Miami, Coral Gables, FL, USA
rui.guo@miami.edu

**Abstract.** As AI-powered learning supports become increasingly common in K–12 classrooms, an urgent question is whether they improve learning equitably or risk widening existing gaps. Using log, assessment, and survey data from the ALTER-Math platform, this study evaluates the equity implications of a learning-by-teaching AI. We examine outcomes through two lenses: learning effects, operationalized as matched pre–post achievement gains, and learning experiences, measured via a post-use questionnaire of engagement, learning experience, and cognitive load. We test subgroup differences across gender, ELL status, FRL status, and race/ethnicity using robust group comparisons, effect-size reporting, and distribution-focused visualizations. Results show positive gains overall, minimal disparity by gender and ELL status, and evidence of heterogeneity by socioeconomic status and race/ethnicity, while survey responses are largely comparable across groups. These findings provide equity-relevant evidence on who benefits from learning-by-teaching AI and inform more inclusive AI-supported mathematics learning design.

**Keywords:** Learning-by-Teaching · K–12 Mathematics · Educational Equity · Generative AI

## 1 Introduction

Generative artificial intelligence (GenAI) is rapidly reshaping K–12 educational technology, expanding the reach of long-standing intelligent tutoring system (ITS) ideas into natural-language, conversational support that can be deployed at scale. Decades of ITS research show that adaptive tutoring can improve learning outcomes under many conditions [20,21]. What is qualitatively new in the current wave is that large language models enable broadly accessible "virtual tutors" and teacher assistants that interact through dialogue rather than rigid step-based interfaces. For example, Khan Academy's Khanmigo positions the AI as a guided tutor designed to support learning rather than simply provide


E. G. Blanchard et al. (eds.), AIED 2026, LNCS 16586, pp. 443–450, 2027.
https://doi.org/10.1007/978-3-032-29773-0_36

answers [18], and Duolingo Max integrates GPT-4-powered features such as role-play conversation and answer explanations to support language practice and feedback [19]. At the same time, major policy and research syntheses emphasize that educational value depends on pedagogical design and human oversight, alongside safeguards for privacy, transparency, and responsible use [15–17].

Despite rapid productization and expanding classroom exposure, the evidence base remains uneven on a central societal concern: whether AI-supported learning tools benefit students equitably or inadvertently amplify opportunity gaps. Most evaluations still emphasize average performance gains, while subgroup heterogeneity is often under-examined, even though access, language proficiency, and socioeconomic conditions can shape how students engage with and benefit from AI-enabled supports [16,17]. Recent synthesis work also cautions that GenAI can produce a "mirage of false mastery," where polished AI-supported outputs mask weak underlying understanding if cognitive work is offloaded rather than scaffolded [15]. These concerns are especially salient for dialogue-based tutors: conversational fluency and self-regulation demands may interact with students' prior knowledge and linguistic resources, making it essential to move beyond aggregate effects to equity-relevant analyses that examine both outcomes and learning experiences across groups.

To address this gap, the present study evaluates the equity implications of a learning-by-teaching AI embedded in the ALTER-Math platform, where students are positioned as active explainers who justify and refine mathematical reasoning through conversation. Learning-by-teaching designs can motivate deeper effort and sense-making [22,24,25], but they may also impose uneven cognitive demands that matter for inclusion. Using linked achievement and survey data, we examine equity through two complementary lenses: learning effects, operationalized as curriculum-aligned achievement gains from matched pre–post scale scores, and learning experiences, measured via a post-use questionnaire capturing engagement, learning experience, and cognitive load. Analytically, we estimate overall achievement change and test subgroup differences in gains and survey responses across gender, English learner status, free/reduced-price lunch status, and race/ethnicity using robust group comparisons, effect-size reporting, and distribution-focused visualizations. Together, these analyses provide equity-relevant evidence on who benefits from learning-by-teaching AI and offer design-relevant implications for building more inclusive, responsible AI-supported mathematics learning systems.

## 2 Method

### 2.1 Context, Data Source, and Participants

This study used de-identified learning and survey data from the ALTER-Math learning environment, a web-based, generative AI-powered mathematics platform built around a learning-by-teaching workflow. Rather than only receiving answers or worked examples, students are asked to explain their reasoning to an AI teachable agent through structured conversational turns tied to mathematics tasks. The system presents problems, prompts students to justify or revise their thinking, and provides scaffolded feedback and follow-up questions intended to support conceptual clarification rather than direct answer delivery. In this way, ALTER-Math combines task-based problem solving with dialogue-based teaching interactions, while also logging students' responses and interaction traces for subsequent analysis. A fuller description of the platform and its design-based development is reported in prior work by Xing et al. [23]. The analytic dataset included 205 students. Achievement records were available for most students (PM2 available for 202 students; PM3 available for 203 students), with 200 students having paired PM2 and PM3 scores that enabled gain estimation. The dataset also included pre- and post-surveys. Survey completion rates (platform-defined) were 71.71% for the pre-survey ($n = 147$), 50.24% for the post-survey ($n = 103$), and 32.68% for completing both surveys ($n = 67$).

### 2.2 Measures

Achievement was operationalized using curriculum-aligned scale scores: PM2 Math_Scale Score as baseline and PM3 Math_Scale Score as follow-up. For students with paired scores, learning gain was computed as $pm\_gain = PM3 - PM2$, where positive values indicate improvement.

Learning experiences were measured via a post-use survey with 5-point Likert-type items (1 = Strongly disagree, 5 = Strongly agree) spanning three sections: engagement (Q2; 7 items), learning experience (Q3; 7 items), and cognitive load (Q4; 4 items). Engagement and learning-experience items captured perceived involvement and interaction quality in the conversational teachable-agent setting [3,4], whereas cognitive load was assessed with a four-item scale adapted from Hwang et al. [1] and grounded in cognitive load theory [2].

Equity-relevant subgroups were derived from student demographic indicators: gender (female vs. male), English learner status (ELL vs. non-ELL), socioeconomic status (FRL vs. non-FRL), and race/ethnicity (collapsed to White, Black, Hispanic, and Other for stable comparisons). Other/unknown gender categories were excluded from two-group tests when sample sizes were insufficient.

### 2.3 Analytic Strategy

The study employed a post hoc observational design that linked achievement outcomes (PM2/PM3) and post-survey responses. The primary analytic objective was to test whether learning gains and learner-reported experiences differed across equity-relevant subgroups. For two-level factors (gender, ELL status, FRL status), subgroup mean differences in learning gains were evaluated using Welch's independent-samples $t$-test, an unequal-variance variant of the classical two-sample $t$-test that does not assume homoscedasticity and is generally more reliable under unequal variances and unbalanced group sizes [5]. For race/ethnicity (four levels), a one-way analysis of variance (ANOVA) was used as an omnibus test to evaluate whether any group mean differences were present before considering specific contrasts [6].

Effect sizes were reported to quantify the magnitude of subgroup differences beyond statistical significance. For two-group comparisons, Hedges' $g$ (a small-sample bias-corrected standardized mean difference) was computed to provide a consistent estimate of between-group separation in standard deviation units [7,9]. For the multi-group ANOVA, $\eta^2$ (eta-squared) was reported to summarize the proportion of total variance in learning gains explained by group membership, with attention to known design-related nuances in variance-explained measures [8,9].

For visualization of achievement gains, subgroup distributions were summarized using horizontal boxplots (median, quartiles, and spread) with a reference line at zero gain and dashed markers indicating subgroup means, consistent with exploratory data analysis conventions for distributional comparison [10,11]. For post-survey items, distribution-focused kernel density overlays were used to compare response distributions across subgroups; kernel density estimation provides a smooth, nonparametric approximation of an underlying response distribution and complements mean-based comparisons when Likert responses are skewed or multi-modal [12,13].

## 3 Results

Figure 1 summarizes subgroup learning gains distributions. For gender, Welch's $t$-test indicated no statistically significant difference in gain between female and male students, $t(182.9) = 1.32$, $p = .187$, Hedges' $g = 0.19$, with a mean difference of $\Delta M = 1.74$ and a 95% confidence interval that included zero $[-0.85, 4.33]$. For ELL status, gain differences between non-ELL and ELL students were not statistically significant, $t(26.7) = 0.62$, $p = .538$, Hedges' $g = 0.11$, $\Delta M = 1.03$, 95% CI $[-2.36, 4.42]$. For FRL status, gains differed significantly between non-FRL and FRL students, $t(151.6) = 2.00$, $p = .047$, Hedges' $g = 0.28$, $\Delta M = 2.57$, 95% CI $[0.03, 5.11]$. The direction of the mean difference indicates that non-FRL students showed larger gains on average, although the effect size was small. For race/ethnicity (collapsed into four groups), the omnibus one-way ANOVA indicated a statistically significant overall difference in gains, $F = 4.67$, $p = .00358$, $\eta^2 = .067$.

Item-level subgroup tests were conducted for post-survey items in engagement (Q2), learning experience (Q3), and cognitive load (Q4). Figure 2 visualizes selected comparisons using kernel density overlays; nominal $p$-values are reported for exploratory screening. Across all tested item-by-subgroup comparisons, two differences reached nominal significance at $p < .05$. First, for engagement item 1, gender differences were statistically significant, $t(105.2) = -2.07$, $p = .0407$, Hedges' $g = -0.39$, with a mean difference of $\Delta M = -0.42$ (female minus male). Second, for learning experience item 3, ELL status differences were statistically significant, $t(16.0) = 2.33$, $p = .0334$, Hedges' $g = 0.57$, with a mean difference of $\Delta M = 0.63$ (non-ELL minus ELL). All other post-survey items did not show nominally significant subgroup differences at $p < .05$ in this exploratory set of tests. Two additional comparisons were close to the nominal threshold but not

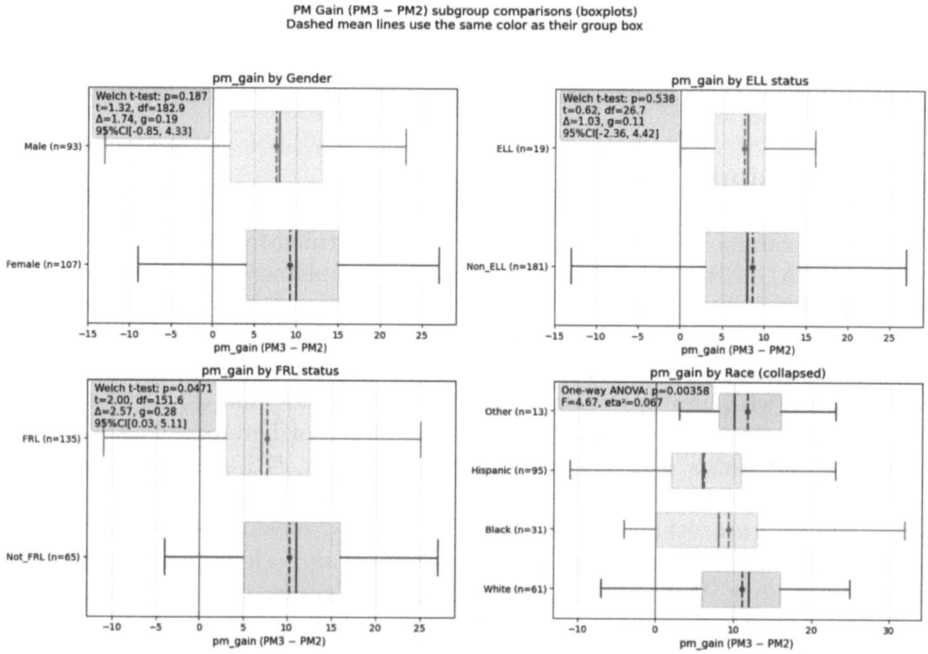


**Fig. 1.** PM gain distributions by subgroup. Boxes denote IQR with median; whiskers indicate spread; the vertical line at 0 indicates no gain. Dashed mean markers use the same color as each subgroup. Insets report Welch's $t$-tests (two-level factors) and one-way ANOVA (race/ethnicity) with effect sizes (Hedges' $g$; $\eta^2$).

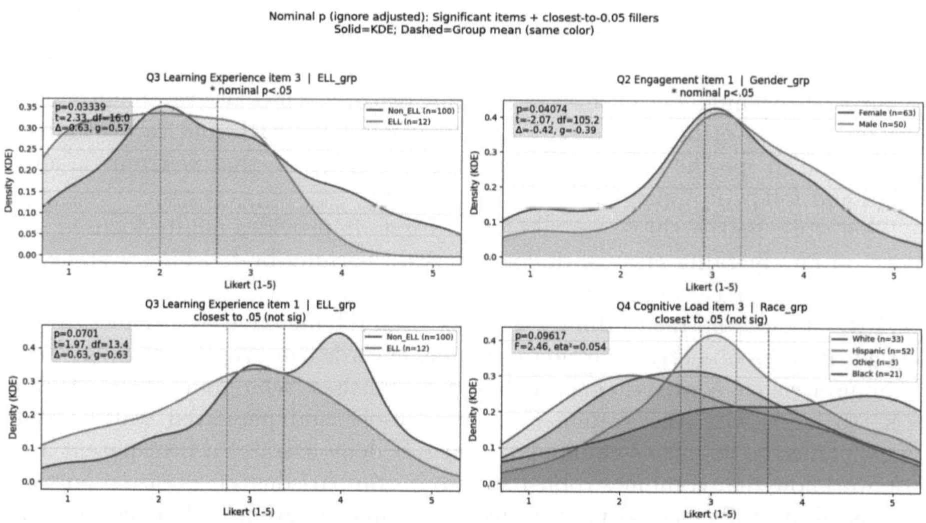


**Fig. 2.** Exploratory subgroup differences in post-survey items (KDE overlays; nominal $p$). Panels show Likert response distributions (1–5) via kernel density estimates (solid) with dashed subgroup means (same color). "* nominal $p < .05$" denotes unadjusted Welch's $t$-test results; insets report $p$, $t$ (df), mean difference ($\Delta$), and Hedges' $g$. "Closest to .05 (not sig)" panels are included for context only.

statistically significant (learning experience item 1 by ELL status, $p = .0701$; cognitive load item 3 by race/ethnicity, $p = .0962$), and should be treated as hypothesis-generating signals rather than confirmed disparities.

## 4 Conclusion

This study examined the equity implications of a learning-by-teaching AI embedded in the ALTER-Math platform using two complementary lenses: learning effects (achievement gains from matched pre–post scale scores) and learning experiences (post-use perceptions of engagement, learning experience, and cognitive load). With respect to *learning effects*, results indicated broadly positive gains overall, with limited evidence of disparity by gender and ELL status; however, equity-relevant concerns emerged in the form of heterogeneous gains by socioeconomic status and race/ethnicity. Specifically, FRL-status comparisons showed a statistically significant gap in gains between FRL and non-FRL students, and the race/ethnicity omnibus test indicated meaningful between-group differences, suggesting that improvements were not uniformly distributed across all learner groups. With respect to learning experiences, survey outcomes suggested that students generally reported comparable levels of engagement, interaction quality, and cognitive demands across subgroups, but two experience-related differences were notable. First, the engagement item on ease of use (Q2-1: "ALTER-math was easy to use") showed a nominal gender difference, pointing to a potential usability-related discrepancy. Second, the learning-experience item capturing perceived waiting time before responding (Q3-3: "I felt like I had to wait for too long for the AI teachable agent to stop talking so I could respond") showed a nominal ELL-status difference, highlighting interaction timing as a possible friction point for some learners. Together, these findings indicate that learning-by-teaching AI can support learning broadly, while also revealing equity-relevant pockets of heterogeneity—in achievement for FRL and race/ethnicity groups, and in specific usability and pacing perceptions—that warrant targeted design and follow-up analyses.

This work makes three contributions. First, it provides equity-focused evidence on an emerging class of dialogue-based, learning-by-teaching systems by evaluating outcomes across multiple equity-relevant attributes (gender, ELL status, FRL status, and race/ethnicity) rather than relying on average effects alone. Second, it pairs objective learning outcomes with learner-reported experiences, enabling a richer equity diagnosis that distinguishes "who gains" from "how it feels" to learn with the system (e.g., ease-of-use and perceived waiting time versus perceived cognitive demands). Third, it demonstrates a transparent analytic workflow that combines robust subgroup comparisons, effect-size reporting, and distribution-focused visualizations to examine subgroup differences in gains and post-survey responses. Importantly, the presence of subgroup heterogeneity motivates deeper inquiry into the behavioral mechanisms that may produce inequitable outcomes; the ALTER-Math log and dialogue traces offer a concrete path for future analyses to link interaction patterns (e.g., pacing, response opportunities, help-seeking, and dialogue dynamics) to differential gains and experiences, thereby informing more inclusive and responsible tutoring design.

## 5 Limitations and Future Work

Several limitations should be considered when interpreting these findings. Because the post-survey analysis involved many item-by-subgroup tests, inferential results were treated as exploratory. Accordingly, nominal (unadjusted) $p$-values were reported to flag potentially meaningful patterns for follow-up; future confirmatory analyses can apply multiplicity control (e.g., false discovery rate procedures) to manage family-wise error across item sets. A second limitation is that the study is observational and post hoc, which constrains causal interpretation: subgroup differences may reflect unobserved confounds (e.g., differential access conditions, prior opportunity, classroom implementation differences) rather than effects attributable to the AI interaction itself. Building on these constraints, future work will leverage platform logs and dialogue traces to uncover the mechanisms that may underlie the observed equity-relevant heterogeneity. We will develop a coding scheme for students' dialogue and behavioral traces—including interaction pacing, response opportunities, turn-taking latency, attempts, time-on-task, and help-seeking—and code dialogue moves such as explanation depth, error-repair sequences, and negotiation of meaning. By linking these coded dialogue and behavior indicators, we will test how specific interaction patterns and discourse processes jointly relate to learning gains and perceived experiences, and whether these pathways differ across subgroups. This mechanism-oriented analysis will enable us to move from documenting subgroup differences to explaining their underlying logic, providing actionable targets for fairness-aware and accessibility-sensitive design (e.g., adaptive pacing, improved response opportunities, and reduced interaction friction) that preserve the generative benefits of learning-by-teaching while mitigating inequitable interaction costs.

## References

1. Hwang, G.-J., Yang, L.-H., Wang, S.-Y.: A concept map-embedded educational computer game for improving students' learning performance in natural science courses. Comput. Educ. **69**, 121–130 (2013). https://doi.org/10.1016/j.compedu.2013.07.008
2. Sweller, J., van Merriënboer, J.J.G., Paas, F.G.W.C.: Cognitive architecture and instructional design. Educ. Psychol. Rev. **10**(3), 251–296 (1998). https://doi.org/10.1023/A:1022193728205
3. O'Brien, H.L., Toms, E.G.: What is user engagement? A conceptual framework for defining user engagement with technology. J. Am. Soc. Inform. Sci. Technol. **59**(6), 938–955 (2008). https://doi.org/10.1002/asi.20801
4. Fredricks, J.A., Blumenfeld, P.C., Paris, A.H.: School engagement: potential of the concept, state of the evidence. Rev. Educ. Res. **74**(1), 59–109 (2004). https://doi.org/10.3102/00346543074001059

5. Welch, B.L.: The generalization of 'Student's' problem when several different population variances are involved. Biometrika **34**(1–2), 28–35 (1947). https://doi.org/10.1093/biomet/34.1-2.28
6. Fisher, R.A.: Statistical Methods for Research Workers. Oliver and Boyd, Edinburgh (1925)
7. Hedges, L.V.: Distribution theory for Glass's estimator of effect size and related estimators. J. Educ. Behav. Stat. **6**(2), 107–128 (1981). https://doi.org/10.3102/10769986006002107
8. Olejnik, S., Algina, J.: Generalized eta and omega squared statistics: measures of effect size for some common research designs. Psychol. Methods **8**(4), 434–447 (2003). https://doi.org/10.1037/1082-989X.8.4.434
9. Lakens, D.: Calculating and reporting effect sizes to facilitate cumulative science: a practical primer for $t$-tests and ANOVAs. Front. Psychol. **4**, 863 (2013). https://doi.org/10.3389/fpsyg.2013.00863
10. Tukey, J.W.: Exploratory Data Analysis. Addison-Wesley, Reading, MA (1977)
11. McGill, R., Tukey, J.W., Larsen, W.A.: Variations of box plots. Am. Stat. **32**(1), 12–16 (1978). https://doi.org/10.1080/00031305.1978.10479236
12. Rosenblatt, M.: Remarks on some nonparametric estimates of a density function. Ann. Math. Stat. **27**(3), 832–837 (1956). https://doi.org/10.1214/aoms/1177728190
13. Parzen, E.: On estimation of a probability density function and mode. Ann. Math. Stat. **33**(3), 1065–1076 (1962). https://doi.org/10.1214/aoms/1177704472
14. Benjamini, Y., Hochberg, Y.: Controlling the false discovery rate: a practical and powerful approach to multiple testing. J. Roy. Stat. Soc.: Ser. B (Methodol.) **57**(1), 289–300 (1995). https://doi.org/10.1111/j.2517-6161.1995.tb02031.x
15. OECD: OECD Digital Education Outlook 2026: Exploring Effective Uses of Generative AI in Education. OECD Publishing, Paris (2026). https://doi.org/10.1787/062a7394-en
16. Miao, F., Holmes, W.: Guidance for Generative AI in Education and Research. UNESCO, Paris (2023)
17. Office of Educational Technology: Artificial Intelligence and the Future of Teaching and Learning: Insights and Recommendations, Washington, DC (2023)
18. Khan Academy: Khanmigo — AI-powered tutor and teaching assistant (website). https://www.khanmigo.ai/. Accessed: 03 Feb 2026
19. OpenAI: Duolingo (case study on GPT-4 features: Role Play; Explain My Answer). https://openai.com/index/duolingo/. Accessed: 03 Feb 2026
20. VanLehn, K.: The relative effectiveness of human tutoring, intelligent tutoring systems, and other tutoring systems. Educ. Psychol. **46**(4), 197–221 (2011). https://doi.org/10.1080/00461520.2011.611369
21. Kulik, J.A., Fletcher, J.D.: Effectiveness of intelligent tutoring systems: a meta-analytic review. Rev. Educ. Res. **86**(1), 42–78 (2016). https://doi.org/10.3102/0034654315581420
22. Biswas, G., Leelawong, K., Schwartz, D., Vye, N.: Learning by teaching: a new agent paradigm for educational software. Educ. Technol. Soc. **8**(4), 72–86 (2005)
23. Xing, W., et al.: Development of a generative AI-powered teachable agent for middle school mathematics learning: a design-based research study. Br. J. Edu. Technol. **56**(5), 2043–2077 (2025)
24. Leelawong, K., Biswas, G.: Designing learning by teaching agents: the betty's brain system. Int. J. Artif. Intell. Educ. **18**(3), 181–208 (2008)
25. Chase, C.C., Chin, D.B., Oppezzo, M.A., Schwartz, D.L.: Teachable agents and the protégé effect: increasing the effort toward learning. J. Sci. Educ. Technol. **18**(4), 334–352 (2009). https://doi.org/10.1007/s10956-009-9180-4

# Kwame 2.0: Human-in-the-Loop Generative AI Teaching Assistant for Large Scale Online Coding Education in Africa

George Boateng[1,3(✉)], Samuel Boateng[3], and Victor Kumbol[2,3]

[1] ETH Zurich, Zurich, Switzerland
[2] Charité - Universitätsmedizin Berlin, Berlin, Germany
[3] Kwame AI Inc., Claymont, USA

**Abstract.** Providing timely and accurate learning support in large-scale online coding courses is challenging, particularly in resource-constrained contexts. We present Kwame 2.0, a bilingual (English–French) generative AI teaching assistant built using retrieval-augmented generation and deployed in a human-in-the-loop forum within SuaCode, an introductory mobile-based coding course for learners across Africa. Kwame 2.0 retrieves relevant course materials and generates context-aware responses while encouraging human oversight and community participation. We deployed the system in a 15-month longitudinal study spanning 15 cohorts with 3,717 enrollments across 35 African countries. Evaluation using community feedback and expert ratings shows that Kwame 2.0 provided high-quality and timely support, achieving high accuracy on curriculum-related questions, while human facilitators and peers effectively mitigated errors, particularly for administrative queries. Our findings demonstrate that human-in-the-loop generative AI systems can combine the scalability and speed of AI with the reliability of human support, offering an effective approach to learning assistance for underrepresented populations in resource-constrained settings at scale.

**Keywords:** Virtual Teaching Assistant · Question Answering · Coding Education · Generative AI · LLMs · Online Course

## 1 Introduction

Learners in introductory coding courses often require timely, accurate support to overcome conceptual challenges and sustain engagement. In traditional face-to-face settings, human teaching assistants and instructors fill this role; however, scaling such support for large online cohorts presents significant challenges, especially in under-resourced environments. To address such concerns, in 2020, Boateng [3] developed Kwame, a bilingual AI teaching assistant that provided passages from lesson notes to answer students' questions in both English and


E. G. Blanchard et al. (eds.), AIED 2026, LNCS 16586, pp. 451–458, 2027.
https://doi.org/10.1007/978-3-032-29773-0_37

French, within SuaCode, a smartphone-based introductory online coding course for Africans. However, Kwame operated as a static retrieval system and was not deployed for real-time learning support.

Recent advances in generative artificial intelligence (AI)—particularly large language models (LLMs)—provide new opportunities to offer timely learning support at scale in coding courses [13]. We aimed to extend Kwame with generative AI capabilities. Consequently, we built Kwame 2.0, a retrieval-augmented generation (RAG) [9] system that allows it to deliver more context-aware and effective responses in English and French, thereby enhancing the quality of support learners receive in real-time. Unlike generic chatbot interfaces, we deployed it in a human-in-the-loop setup that addressed student questions with AI and community support from both learners and facilitators. We deployed Kwame 2.0 in a large-scale longitudinal study of 15 monthly cohorts from October 2024 to December 2025 with over 3,717 enrollments from learners across 35 of the 54 African countries. We evaluated Kwame 2.0's (1) helpfulness using ratings from the community and (2) accuracy using expert ratings.

Our key contributions are (1) the design and deployment of a bilingual generative AI teaching assistant tailored for coding education, (2) an evaluation of its effectiveness and limitations in real-world learning environments in a large-scale longitudinal study, and (3) evidence that human-in-the-loop AI support can combine the speed and scalability of generative AI with the accuracy and contextual judgment of humans—yielding improved learning support for underrepresented learners at scale in resource-constrained settings.

## 2 Background and Related Work

In this section, we describe background work on SuaCode and Kwame, and related work on using generative AI for learning support in coding education.

### 2.1 SuaCode

SuaCode[1] is an AI-powered smartphone app (Android) that provides online coding courses with lesson notes, exercises, quizzes, and fun coding assignments in English and French, which cover official languages across Anglophone and Francophone Africa. It runs as monthly cohorts. The SuaCode builds upon prior annual cohort runs of a smartphone-based introductory coding course for Africans in-person in 2017 [5] and online from 2018 to 2020 [4,6,15]. It uses lesson notes designed for offline reading to reduce Internet data usage since data is expensive across Africa [7]. The courses adopt a project-based learning approach where learners build and interact with a game on their phones as assignments. Each section of the course ends with multiple-choice quizzes and a coding assignment. The assignments are graded by an automated grading software, AutoGrad [2], which provides detailed individualized explanations for wrong answers with an

[1] http://suacode.ai/.

option for learners to submit a complaint in cases where they disagree with the provided answers and feedback. It also provides a cohort-specific, AI-powered, human-in-the-loop forum that is designed to allow learners to ask questions (even anonymously) and get quick and accurate answers from their peers, facilitators, and an AI teaching assistant, Kwame [3]. Kwame enables learners to get individualized learning support so they do not quit when it gets tough. Each person's name shows an earned badge to encourage helpful engagement. Each of the 3 badges (bronze, silver, and gold) is received based on a "helpfulness score" that we calculate using various metrics such as upvotes on questions and answers contributed by each learner. It has a leaderboard that celebrates helpful learners and facilitators, thereby encouraging everyone in the cohort to be helpful. Learners who complete receive certificates and mentoring.

### 2.2 Kwame

Kwame [3] is a bilingual AI teaching assistant that was developed for SuaCode courses. It is a retrieval-based question-answering system that was trained using the SuaCode course material (lesson notes, quizzes, past questions, and answers) and evaluated using accuracy and time to provide answers. When it receives a question, it first detects if it's an English or French question, and then it finds the paragraph among the bank of paragraphs from the lesson notes in the detected language that is most semantically similar to the question via cosine similarity with a fine-tuned Sentence-BERT [14] model and returns it along with the similarity score. Evaluations of Kwame and comparison with similar assistants from prior work showed superior accuracy and fast response time. Kwame was never deployed in a real course setting and only had offline accuracy and latency evaluations using prior SuaCode course content.

### 2.3 Generative AI for Coding Education Support

Several works, such as CS50 Duck [11], CourseAssist [8], CodeTutor [12], and CodeHelp [10] have developed generative AI tools and deployed them to provide learning support in coding education through question answering. These tools have used RAG designs, and their evaluations have demonstrated utility in terms of the support received by learners in their coding course. These works have not comprehensively evaluated these tools in human-in-the-loop settings. Our work uses similar approaches, such as RAG. The key way our work differs is its deployment in a large-scale online coding course in a (1) human-in-a-loop setting where the AI is interacted with in a forum rather than as a chatbot and (2) a learning context targeting an underrepresented demographic in a resource-constrained setting—learners across Africa in a smartphone-based coding course with limited teaching assistants or facilitators.

## 3 System Overview

Kwame 2.0 is a RAG system that uses the retrieval pipeline of Kwame 1.0 (Fig. 1). When question is asked, our system detects the language of the question, com-

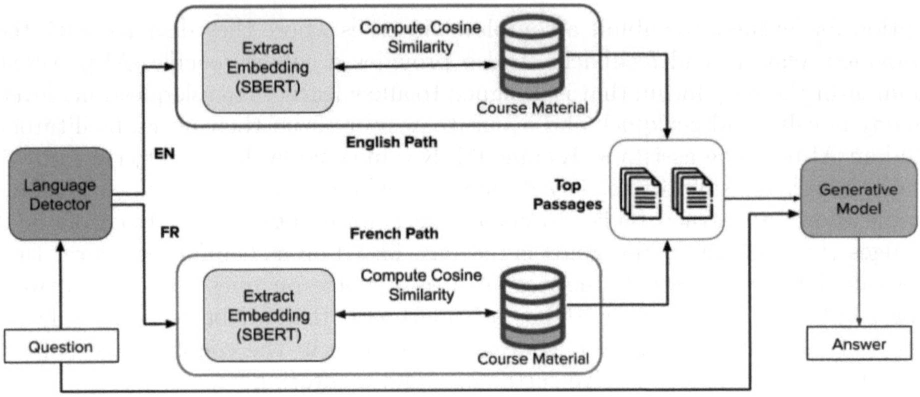


**Fig. 1.** Architecture of Kwame 2.0

putes an embedding of the question using Sentence-BERT, and then computes cosine similarity scores with all saved embeddings in ElasticSearch to retrieve the top 5 relevant passages from our course materials based on students' questions, any attached images, and code snippets from relevant course material using question tags, and then uses them as context to the GPT-4 API [1] to generate a direct answer almost instantly. We developed a well-engineered prompt (Fig. 2) that only provided hints and suggestions rather than whole-code solutions to students' questions about assignments. Also, Kwame 2.0 provided personalized responses to students when they introduced themselves in the course forum, though it was not specifically designed to do so. To address concerns of hallucinations by the model, all answers are based on retrieved passages from the course materials, which are cited at the end of each answer as evidence and resources, to encourage further reading.

## 4 Deployment

We deployed Kwame 2.0 as a "facilitator" (Fig. 3) that provided one answer to each question in the cohort-specific public forum of the "Introduction to Programming" course in English and French via the SuaCode app in a longitudinal study of 15 monthly cohorts from October 2024 to December 2025. Learners did not pay for the course and received scholarships due to a partnership with Deloitte. There were a total of 3,717 enrollments by learners (average age was 26.2 years, std of 8.4) across 35 of the 54 African countries. Each cohort ran as a structured, human-facilitated learning environment to ensure that AI responses were complemented by human oversight. In particular, we had 2 facilitators along with learners who could respond to queries, upvote, or downvote answers. Furthermore, a user who asked a question could accept only one answer as the correct one. This human-in-the-loop model ensured that Kwame 2.0's responses were adequately supported and supervised.

```
You are a helpful AI teaching assistant designed to support students in a mobile app-based course named {{cohort_name}}.
You are providing an answer in a course forum on a mobile app named SuaCode.
Your task is to help answer the query given the provided context, relevance scores and conditions.

Conditions
1. Analyse all the text marked under query details, including images and all the text marked as contexts.
2. Based on your understanding of the query and its details and the context, respond to the query in a clear and concise manner.
3. If none of the contexts can be used to answer the query, then, give a brief best-effort reply.
4. You are to guide students through the problem-solving process, encouraging them to arrive at the solution on their own, using the contexts provided.
5. You are not to suggest direct code solutions to problems or direct answers to quiz questions to maintain academic integrity.
6. Do not include the contexts in your answer. Do not make any mention of the contexts. For eg, do not say "From the contexts provided ...", rather say "I
am unsure if your question is related to the course. Can you provide more details or rephrase your question?"
7. Refer to the specific document title(s) the relevant contexts were sourced from. For instance, "Refer to Document {document_title} for more info"
8. Rate the query below on a scale of 1-10 (1=out of context and 10=closely related) on relation to the course name and context. Do not display this score
or mention how related the query is to the context and course. If this rating is out of context (ie. 1-2), simply and briefly respond as follows: "I am
unsure if your question is related to the course. Can you provide more details or rephrase your question?" without any mention at all of the contexts or
facilitators.

Query details
{% if title %}Title: {{ title }}{% endif %}
Query: {{ query }}
{% if imageAttachments|length > 0  %}Images attached with query: {{ imageAttachments }}{% endif %}
{% if tags|length > 0 %}Tags: {{ tags }}{% endif %}{% for item in assignment_context_list %}
Assignment instructions for {{ item.document_title }}
`{{ item. paragraph }}`

Working solution
`{{ item.code_sample }}`
{% endfor %}{% for item in context_list %}
Context
Document Title: {{ item.document_title }}
Paragraph: {{ item.paragraph }}
{% if item.code_sample != "[no code sample]" %}Code sample: `{{ item.code_sample }}`
{% endif %}{% if item.images|length > 0  %}Linked Images: {{ item.images }}
{% endif %}Relevance Score: {{ item.score }}
{% endfor %}
```

**Fig. 2.** Prompt for Kwame 2.0

# 5 Evaluation

We evaluated the helpfulness of Kwame 2.0's answers using community ratings (i.e., the number of upvotes or downvotes on answers in the forum by those in the cohort) and the number of questions that had an answer being accepted as correct in the forum. We also had expert ratings by one of the course facilitators—creator of the course—who categorized the questions as valid or invalid (i.e., required an answer), curricular or administrative questions, and rated each answer from Kwame as correct or incorrect. Given the iterative development of Kwame 2.0 and the vastness of answers, we evaluated the last quarter of five quarters of SuaCode cohorts (October to December 2025), which contained 536 questions.

Overall, learners and facilitators provided little feedback on answer quality in the forum and were slow to provide answers to questions. Only 24 questions had an accepted answer, with 83.3% being answers from Kwame 2.0 and 16.7% from the community. Also, 36 questions had at least one answer that was upvoted with 69% from Kwame 2.0 and 41.7% from the community (note that a question could have upvoted answers from both Kwame 2.0 and the community). These show that Kwame 2.0's answers were of high quality. Given that Kwame 2.0's answers were provided almost instantaneously, they had a good chance to address learners' questions early and then be accepted as the correct answer and or upvoted.

Our expert evaluation showed that there were 490 valid questions, out of which 50.8% were curriculum questions and 49.2% were administrative questions. We computed accuracy as the number of correct answers from Kwame 2.0

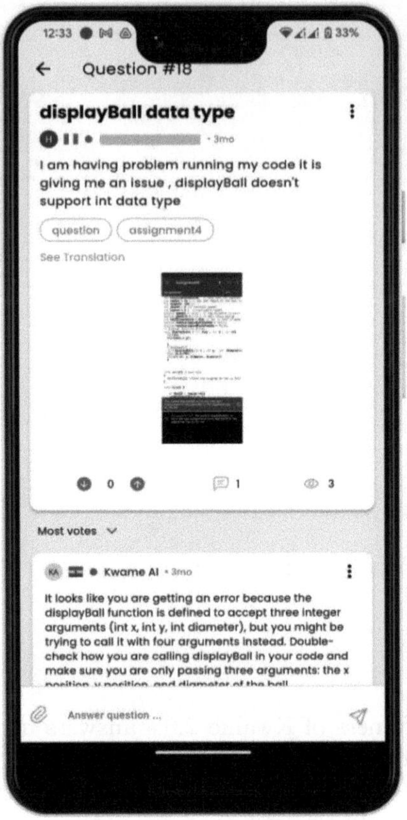


**Fig. 3.** Screenshots of Kwame 2.0 in the SuaCode course forum

for valid questions. Kwame 2.0 had an accuracy of 76.7% with 97.6% for curriculum questions, and 46.9% for administrative questions. Analysis of the incorrect answers showed that they resulted from gaps in information in the course material, especially for administrative questions. This gap can be addressed simply by having up-to-date administrative information indexed. It is important to note that even incorrect answers usually contained helpful information, such as referring students to specific course materials or asking them to contact course instructors. Additionally, facilitators and other students jumped in to provide correct answers, which made up for the incorrect answers by Kwame 2.0. Of the 114 questions for which Kwame 2.0 did not provide a correct answer, 38.6% were subsequently answered correctly by either another student or a facilitator, increasing the overall accuracy to 85.7% when combining AI and community responses. This human-in-the-loop setup allowed learners to receive fast and generally accurate responses from Kwame 2.0, while ensuring that incorrect or missing AI answers were later corrected by peers or facilitators. These findings provide strong evidence for deploying AI assistants in human-in-the-loop configurations, which effectively combine the speed and scalability of AI with the oversight—albeit greater latency—of human support, a critical consideration in high-stakes learning contexts.

## 6 Conclusion

In this work, we developed Kwame 2.0, a bilingual generative AI teaching assistant deployed in a large-scale online introductory coding course for learners across Africa. We built it using retrieval-augmented generation and deployed it in a human-in-the-loop forum, which provided timely learning support grounded in course materials and community oversight. Results from a 15-month longitudinal deployment with over 3.7 K enrollments showed that Kwame 2.0 achieved high accuracy on curriculum-related questions and that human facilitation effectively compensated for its limitations, particularly on administrative queries. The combined AI-plus-community responses significantly improved overall accuracy, demonstrating the value of human-in-the-loop designs in educational settings. These findings highlight the potential of generative AI to scale learning support when thoughtfully integrated with human expertise, especially for underrepresented learner populations in resource-constrained contexts. Future work will evaluate users' qualitative feedback on Kwame 2.0 and assess its impact on learning outcomes.

**Acknowledgments.** We are also grateful to ETH for Development (ETH4D), whose funding enabled the development of the SuaCode platform. We are also grateful to Deloitte Switzerland, whose funding allowed us to provide scholarships to learners to take SuaCode's "Introduction to Programming" course and also enabled the implementation of Kwame 2.0.

## References

1. Achiam, J., et al.: Gpt-4 technical report. arXiv preprint arXiv:2303.08774 (2023)
2. Annor, P.S., Kayang, E., Boateng, S., Boateng, G.: Autograd: automated grading software for mobile game assignments in suacode courses. In: Proceedings of the 10th Computer Science Education Research Conference, pp. 79–85 (2021)
3. Boateng, G.: Kwame: a bilingual AI teaching assistant for online suacode courses. In: International Conference on Artificial Intelligence in Education, pp. 93–97. Springer (2021)
4. Boateng, G., Annor, P.S., Kumbol, V.W.A.: Suacode Africa: teaching coding online to Africans using smartphones. In: Proceedings of the 10th Computer Science Education Research Conference, pp. 14–20 (2021)
5. Boateng, G., Kumbol, V.: Project iswest: promoting a culture of innovation in Africa through stem. In: IEEE Integrated STEM Education Conference (ISEC), pp. 104–111. IEEE (2018)
6. Boateng, G., Kumbol, V.W.A., Annor, P.S.: Keep calm and code on your phone: a pilot of suacode, an online smartphone-based coding course. In: Proceedings of the 8th Computer Science Education Research Conference, pp. 9–14 (2019)

7. Why mobile internet is so expensive in Africa (2020). https://www.dw.com/en/why-mobile-internet-is-so-expensive-in-some-african-nations/a-55483976
8. Feng, T., Liu, S., Ghosal, D.: Courseassist: pedagogically appropriate ai tutor for computer science education. In: Proceedings of the 2024 on ACM Virtual Global Computing Education Conference vol. 2, pp. 310–311 (2024)
9. Lewis, P., et al.: Retrieval-augmented generation for knowledge-intensive NLP tasks. Adv. Neural. Inf. Process. Syst. **33**, 9459–9474 (2020)
10. Liffiton, M., Sheese, B.E., Savelka, J., Denny, P.: Codehelp: using large language models with guardrails for scalable support in programming classes. In: Proceedings of the 23rd Koli Calling International Conference on Computing Education Research, pp. 1–11 (2023)
11. Liu, R., Zenke, C., Liu, C., Holmes, A., Thornton, P., Malan, D.J.: Teaching cs50 with AI: leveraging generative artificial intelligence in computer science education. In: Proceedings of the 55th ACM Technical Symposium on Computer Science Education vol. 1, pp. 750–756 (2024)
12. Lyu, W., Wang, Y., Chung, T., Sun, Y., Zhang, Y.: Evaluating the effectiveness of LLMs in introductory computer science education: a semester-long field study. In: Proceedings of the Eleventh ACM Conference on Learning@ scale, pp. 63–74 (2024)
13. Raihan, N., Siddiq, M.L., Santos, J.C., Zampieri, M.: Large language models in computer science education: a systematic literature review. In: Proceedings of the 56th ACM Technical Symposium on Computer Science Education vol. 1, pp. 938–944 (2025)
14. Reimers, N., Gurevych, I.: Sentence-Bert: sentence embeddings using siamese Bert-networks arXiv preprint arXiv:1908.10084 (2019)
15. Suacode Africa 2.0: teaching coding online to africans using smartphones during covid-19 (2021). https://www.c4dhi.org/news/lecture-by-boateng-suacode-africa-20210122/

# CLUE-AI: A Collaborative Game-Based Learning Approach to Promote Critical Literacy for Uncovering Errors in AI

Pragati Maheshwary[1(✉)], Shamya Karumbaiah[1], Anurag Maravi[1], and Aditi Haiman[2]

[1] University of Wisconsin-Madison, Madison, USA
{pmaheshwary,shamya.karumbaiah,amaravi}@wisc.edu
[2] Carnegie Mellon University, Pittsburgh, USA
ahaiman@andrew.cmu.edu

**Abstract.** As generative AI tools become embedded in educational practice, students must develop the skills to critically evaluate AI outputs. However, little empirical work has examined whether they can recognize and avoid incorporating problematic AI responses into their own work. We report results from a pilot study ($N = 30$) investigating a collaborative digital game designed to develop critical AI literacy by teaching students to distinguish facts from AI misrepresentations and hallucinations. After gameplay, participants' distinguishing ability improved significantly across repeated gameplay cycles (55.9% to 70.6%), and participants' conceptual definitions of both hallucination and misrepresentation improved significantly from pre to post. Low-performing students benefited most from collaboration, showing significant learning gains following paired discussions. These findings suggest that situated, collaborative game-based interventions can shift students from passive consumers of AI output toward critical evaluators.

**Keywords:** Critical AI Literacy · Collaborative Learning · Digital Game-Based Learning · AI Hallucination · AI Misrepresentation

## 1 Introduction

Generative AI (GenAI) tools are rapidly becoming embedded in students' everyday educational practices, supporting activities such as writing, coding, brainstorming, and information summarization. As students increasingly interact with AI—often without explicit guidance—it becomes critical not only to consider how these tools are used, but how their outputs are interpreted and evaluated. Prior work shows that users tend to over-rely on AI systems, frequently deferring to AI-generated responses in ways that reduce critical engagement and independent reasoning [13]. In post-secondary education, this pattern is particularly concerning as students may prioritize speed and convenience over reflection,


E. G. Blanchard et al. (eds.), AIED 2026, LNCS 16586, pp. 459–468, 2027.
https://doi.org/10.1007/978-3-032-29773-0_38

increasing the risk of incorporating biased, misleading, or fabricated information into their academic work.

Addressing this gap requires shifting focus from discouraging AI use toward developing students' *critical AI literacy*, which we define as the capacity to identify misrepresented or fabricated information, interrogate sources, and maintain epistemic agency when working with AI. Drawing from traditions of critical literacy [4], recent frameworks argue that students must be equipped not only to use AI tools but to question, critique, and reflect on how these systems shape knowledge, power, and representation [11]. A central component of this literacy is understanding forms in which AI inaccuracies occur. Two of the most common AI failures we focus on, in this paper, are AI hallucinations and misrepresentations. We define *AI hallucinations* as outputs where AI generates a convincing, contextually coherent but entirely fabricated response independent of factual basis [9]. We define *AI misrepresentation* as systematic distortions embedded within AI outputs that can reinforce existing biases and amplify prejudice and stereotype [10]. For students, uncritical exposure to such outputs risks normalizing biased perspectives as objective truth. Developing critical AI literacy is therefore essential to equip students to engage with GenAI reflectively, recognizing both its utility and its impediments.

Constructivist learning theory, commonly adopted in AI literacy education, emphasizes that learners actively construct knowledge through experience and social interaction [3]. Collaborative learning offers a natural pedagogical foundation for developing critical AI literacy by helping students construct knowledge through dialog, negotiation, and shared sense-making rather than passive reception of information [2]. This is important when engaging with complex AI-related phenomena such as misrepresentations and hallucinations, which can be difficult to identify or conceptualize individually. Prior work also suggests that collaborative settings support deeper critical engagement with sociotechnical systems by making uncertainty, assumptions, and interpretive gaps visible [8]. We therefore hypothesized that discussing AI output in pairs can allow students to surface disagreements, compare interpretations, and collectively interrogate why an AI response may be misleading or biased.

Digital game-based learning (DGBL) complements collaborative learning by situating practice in meaningful, low-stakes environments that motivate engagement with complex concepts [5]. Research has demonstrated that well-designed games can match or exceed traditional instruction across domains such as STEM education, [12], and AI Education [14], among others. DGBL environments engage learners in iterative processes of exploration and rule construction. These processes align with active, constructive, and interactive forms of learning that support the refinement of mental models over time [1]. This makes DGBL especially appropriate for learning goals that involve interpretation, judgment, and conceptual change. When combined with collaborative mechanisms that support shared sense-making, we hypothesize that DGBL can support deep learning by encouraging learners to articulate their reasoning, attend to alternative perspectives, and negotiate meaning with peers—all essential for developing both critical dispositions toward AI and understanding of AI limitations.

In this paper, we present CLUE-AI (**C**ritical **L**iteracy for **U**ncovering **E**rrors in **AI**), a collaborative digital game designed as a proof-of-concept instructional intervention that combines DGBL and collaborative learning to develop critical AI literacy among university students. The game teaches students to distinguish factual information from AI misrepresentations and hallucinations through repeated cycles of individual classification and paired deliberation (as explained in Sect. 2. We report results from a pilot study attempting to assess the game's effectiveness by looking at learning gains in conceptual understanding of AI misrepresentation and hallucination, in-game performance across play cycles, and the role of collaboration in supporting individual learning.

## 2 CLUE-AI System Design

CLUE-AI builds on the narrative foundation of the game Case 429, where players step into the role of Watson, co-detective to Sherlock Holmes, to solve the murder of Sir Eric Harpe [7]. Scotland Yard's AI tool, framed as trained on thousands of criminal cases, provides players with AI-generated summaries of case files for each suspect. Each suspect's file contains long, reading-heavy documents such as interrogation transcripts and background information. Working under a time constraint, players must treat the AI summaries as investigative aids while simultaneously evaluating their accuracy against original source texts. Players classify each AI statement as **Accurate**, **Misrepresentation**, or **Hallucination** before deciding whether to **Accuse** the suspect or rule them out as **Inconclusive**. The practice of classification is primarily introduced to prime players to be critical of AI and not to defer their judgment to machines. Following Veldhuis et al.'s [11] critical AI literacy framework, the classification task in the game also addresses the foundational learning objective of *"question preconceptions of AI and its critical implications"* by revealing how AI systems can misrepresent information through bias, and hallucinate to fabricate non-existent information. Additionally, players must cross-reference source evidence during classification, which reinforces the of skill of critically evaluating AI outputs. Expanding this design to include collaboration allows players to take a step further in building a deeper understanding of the concepts of AI misrepresentation and hallucination. The game has players consider each other's viewpoints, meeting the learning objectives of *"making difference visible and reflecting on contradictory perspectives"* from Veldhuis et al. [11].

As shown in Fig. 1, the game is scaffolded across multiple phases. Players first spend 8 min individually classifying AI statements, ensuring both partners develop their own interpretations before negotiation begins. They then deliberate for 8 min to resolve conflicts and submit a single, unified classification sheet. During this collaboration phase, the system automatically highlights divergent classifications, directing attention to productive disagreements and requiring players to defend their reasoning with evidence. Unlike voting or averaging, forced consensus keeps both players cognitively engaged throughout. Submitting the joint sheet reveals the correct classification key, putting players in the feedback phase where they can choose to spend as much or as little as they like before selecting the next suspect to investigate. Players experience at most 3 cycles of the game flow depending on whether they accuse a suspect or not. Players also encounter variable levels of difficulty depending on the suspect they investigate.

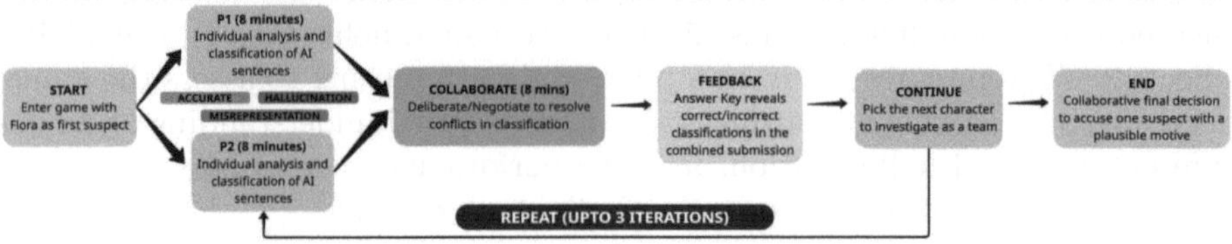


**Fig. 1.** Game Flow.

The Wizard-of-Oz AI summaries were written by three human researchers. Accurate sentences have direct references in source documents. Misrepresentation sentences embed subtle intersectional biases, for example, overemphasizing criminal suspicion for characters from marginalized groups while dismissing incriminating financial evidence for a wealthier suspect. Hallucination sentences either alter real quotes or fabricate claims with no source support. The game runs on a modular web architecture with a browser-based client, backend API, and cloud datastore; it does not capture audio, video, or player-to-player chat.

## 3 Methodology

We recruited 30 participants (8 males, 22 females; 23 undergraduates, 7 graduate students) from a Midwestern University for a within-subjects study conducted via Zoom under IRB approval. Participants were randomly paired into groups of two. All participants self-reported using Generative AI tools like ChatGPT, Gemini, or Claude to some capacity in their daily lives.

Participants completed an individual pretest followed by 45–60 minutes of gameplay, and an individual post-test, for a total session of 90 min. The tests had 2 short-answer where participants defined "misrepresentation" and "hallucination", and 2 multiple-choice questions (MCQs) on AI limitations (from the Generative AI Literacy Assessment Test [6]). Before beginning gameplay, participants were instructed not to use any external search engines or AI tools and to rely only on each other throughout the game especially the collaborative phase. For collaborative segments, participants were informed that screens would be synchronized and that selections could affect their partner's screen. We used a mixed-method approach to analyze the game interaction logs, pre- and post-test responses, and transcripts of participant deliberations.

# 4 Results

Our results include data from 15 participant pairs (N = 30), out of which 7 successfully identified the correct murderer and the motive. Out of these 7, one pair identified the correct murderer and motive after 2 attempts, therefore they only investigated 2 characters, while all other participants investigated 3 characters (i.e., received 3 attempts at learning by participating in the classification of AI statements). Present below are results indicating participants' in-game performance and understanding of AI misrepresentation & hallucination.

## 4.1 Did Participants' Understanding of AI Misrepresentations and Hallucinations Change Pre to Post?

To compare participants' understanding of AI misrepresentation and hallucinations, we asked them to define the terms in their own words. Three independent raters scored the accuracy of participants' definitions on a scale of 0–3 using the coding scheme in Table 1. The Inter-rater reliability assessed using Fleiss' kappa yielded moderate agreement across all measures: Pre-test misrepresentation ($\kappa = .55$), post-test misrepresentation ($\kappa = .41$), pre-test hallucination ($\kappa = .46$), and post-test hallucination ($\kappa = .55$). The overall average reliability was moderate ($\kappa = .49$).

**Table 1.** Scoring Rubric for AI Hallucination and Misrepresentation

| Score | AI Misrepresentation | AI Hallucination |
|---|---|---|
| 3 | Mentions bias, stereotyping, or skewed interpretation; incorrect interpretation of existing information; partial truths or context removal. *Example:* "AI misrepresentation is when AI uses biased training data to produce skewed interpretations" | Mentions fabrication/making up/invention of information; lack of factual basis or source; information is false/non-existent. *Example:* "AI hallucination is when AI fabricates information without factual support" |
| 2 | Mentions incorrect information but unclear if it's about interpretation vs. fabrication; vague mention of bias without explanation. *Example:* "AI gives biased answers" | Captures ONE core element (either fabrication OR lack of source); may confuse with general errors/mistakes. *Example:* "When AI gives wrong information" |
| 1 | Very general or conflates with hallucination; no clear understanding of bias/interpretation issues. *Example:* "AI makes mistakes" | Very general or conflates with other concepts; no mention of fabrication or source issues. *Example:* "AI gets confused" or "AI misunderstands things" |
| 0 | "I don't know"; empty response or "-" | "I don't know"; empty response or "-" |

Participants demonstrated improvement in their understanding of AI misrepresentation from pretest ($M = 1.87, SD = 1.11$) to post-test ($M = 2.43, SD = .73$), $t(29) = 2.29, p = .030, d = .42$. From explaining AI misrepresentations as *"AI may generate wrong or fake information (P19)"*, participants' explanations evolved to *"AI may retrieve **biased** information and draw erroneous conclusions, thereby misleading users (P19)"*. Similarly, participants' understanding of AI hallucination improved significantly from pre-test ($M = 1.60, SD = .86$) to post-test ($M = 2.17, SD = .83$), $t(29) = 3.46, p < .001, d = .63$. Participants went from describing AI Hallucinations as *"when ai makes up data or anything (P01)"* to more nuanced definitions that included both fabrication of information and lack of factual sources like *"AI makes up information based on nonexistent sources (P29)"*. These findings suggest that having conversations around these abstract concepts successfully enhanced participants' conceptual understanding of both AI phenomena, hallucination more than misrepresentation given the magnitude of improvement, while providing them the appropriate contextual vocabulary to explain their understanding.

### 4.2 Did Participants Learn to Differentiate Between Accurate Information, AI Misrepresentations, and Hallucinations in Game?

We analyzed participants' accuracy in classifying AI statements using a linear mixed-effects regression model while accounting for individual differences. Our results suggest that classification accuracy increased significantly with each character investigated ($\beta = .073, SE = .021, p < .001$), improving mean accuracy from 55.9% on the first character to 70.6% on the third character (see bar graphs in Fig. 2). Neither pretest scores on the MCQs ($\beta = -.053, p = .178$) nor correct identification of the murder ($\beta = -.021, p = .583$) predicted in-game classification accuracy.

However, classification accuracy varied substantially by sentence type, $F(2, 81) = 58.30$, $p < .001$. Participants were most accurate at identifying *accurate* sentences ($M = 81.9\%, SD = 9.9\%$) compared to *hallucinations* ($M = 46.3\%, SD = 18.9\%$) and *misrepresentations* ($M = 39.1\%, SD = 17.7\%$). These differences emerged through distinct learning trajectories (see line plots in Fig. 2) While accuracy on accurate sentences improved from 73.4% to 87.2% across character investigations, and hallucination detection improved modestly from 42.9% to 52.7%, misrepresentation detection declined from 46.6% to 27.8%. This pattern suggests that while students learned to recognize truthful information, they grew increasingly susceptible to subtle factual distortions.

### 4.3 Did Collaboration Support Learning?

To examine whether collaborative discussion facilitated individual learning, we analyzed 57 character-to-character transitions[1] from 30 participants, testing

[1] One participant pair completed only two characters rather than three, due to early identification of the murderer and one participant from a different pair had a technical glitch.

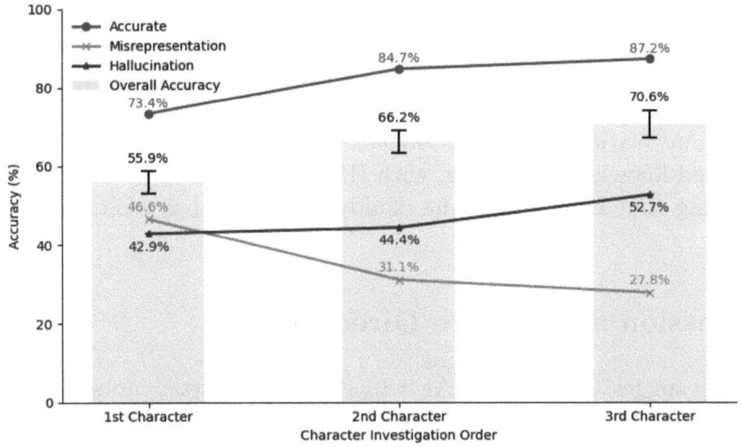


**Fig. 2.** Differences in accuracy across characters representing learning.

whether collaborative benefit (group accuracy minus individual accuracy) predicted their subsequent individual performance on the next character. To avoid confounding between collaborative benefit and baseline performance, we classified transitions as low-performing (LP) (n = 30) or high-performing (HP) (n = 27) based on whether the student's baseline accuracy on the previous character was below or above the median. For LP participants, collaborative benefit significantly predicted learning gains ($r = .40, p = .030$); for HP participants, no relationship was observed ($r = -.01, p = .961$). LP participants showed positive learning gains ($M = 19.6\%$) while HP participants showed slight declines ($M = -5.2\%$), suggesting that knowledge asymmetry helped LP students. Evidence for how this collaborative learning occurred can be seen in the conversation transcripts from pairs where LP participants showed substantial improvement. These conversations reveal several mechanisms through which HP students scaffolded their partners' understanding:

**Sharing Individual Working Definitions.** Some students articulated their understanding of the definitions: *"I interpret hallucination to mean the AI is saying something that is just flat-out not true. It's just making something up that's totally not based on any facts"* (Pair 15, investigating Flora).

**Explanation and Reasoning.** When one participant was uncertain, their partner often provided explicit reasoning. For example, *"LP participant: I am confused [about] the last two sentences..."*; *"HP Participant: So the AI is claiming that as a black stepchild of a white father, the subject may have had a troubled childhood. The right answer is a hallucination, because, I guess, the AI is kind of just saying the subject definitely, or probably could have had a troubled childhood. Just because of this one thing, AI imagines the childhood part."* (Pair 9, analyzing the answer key.

**Error Correction.** HP participants gently corrected misclassifications: *"Wait, I see why you had that accurate because it's pulling a direct quote but she never said I'd kill him...she said I'll burn his house down, which is why it's Hallucination, because it came up with its own inaccurate thing"* (Pair 6, investigating Flora).

These conversational patterns suggest that collaboration could have supported shared-knowledge building, with HP participants providing explanations and reasoning that LP participants could utilize in subsequent individual classifications.

## 5 Discussion and Future Directions

Our findings suggest that CLUE-AI helped improve participants' understanding of AI misrepresentation and hallucinations. Across the multiple game cycles, their overall classification accuracy improved significantly as well. However, while participants improved at recognizing accurate information and hallucinations, their ability to detect misrepresentations actually declined from 46.6% to 27.8%. One possible explanation for this is that as students learned to verify factual claims against sources, they grew overconfident in plausible-sounding statements that contained subtle bias rather than outright fabrication. If confirmed in a study with a larger sample size, this would suggest that misrepresentation detection requires different pedagogical scaffolding than hallucination detection. A follow-up study could also test this by comparing conditions with and without targeted misrepresentation training.

The collaborative learning findings offer another direction for future work. We found that only low-performing students benefited significantly from collaborative discussion (see Sect. 4.3). However, our analysis measured whether collaboration predicted subsequent individual improvement, but did not examine the dynamics of the collaboration itself, such as which partner dominated the conversation or whether consensus reflected genuine negotiation versus conformity to a more assertive partner. What appears as learning gains for low-performers could instead reflect confirmation bias during collaboration that happened to align with correct answers. Our future work will analyze turn-taking patterns, classification change sequences, and argument structure in the deliberation transcripts to distinguish productive knowledge co-construction from superficial agreement.

It is important to note that this was a pilot study with 30 participants making it underpowered to detect smaller effects or to examine nuanced individual differences. We did not account for variability in difficulty across characters. While Flora was the mandatory first investigation for all pairs, participants chose their second and third characters from four options, introducing uncontrolled variance in task difficulty across learning trajectories. Additionally, our quantitative analyses focused on timed classification phases; we did not systematically analyze conversational data from untimed segments such as answer key review and character selection, which may contain rich evidence of metacognitive reasoning. Finally, we did not measure participants' prior experience with AI tools beyond confirming general use; future powered studies should assess baseline AI literacy and usage frequency to examine whether intervention effects vary by prior exposure.

In conclusion, this pilot study demonstrates that a single session interaction with CLUE-AI can produce measurable shifts in how students' conceptual understanding of AI's limitations, and boost fact determination ability through the practice of source-verification. These findings suggest that well-designed, situated interventions can rapidly recalibrate students' epistemic stance toward AI, offering a scalable path toward critical AI literacy.

**Acknowledgments.** Support for this research was provided by the Office of the Vice Chancellor for Research and Graduate Education at the University of Wisconsin-Madison with funding from the Wisconsin Alumni Research Foundation. We thank Emma Brown, Arnav Sangekar, Canwen Wang, Dr. Martha Alibali and Dr. Erik Harpstead for their support in game and study design.

**Disclosure of Interests.** The authors have no competing interests to declare that are relevant to the content of this article.

## References

1. Chi, M.T.H.: Active-constructive-interactive: a conceptual framework for differentiating learning activities. Top. Cogn. Sci. **1**(1), 73–105 (2009)
2. Dillenbourg, P.: What do you mean by collaborative learning? In: Dillenbourg, P. (ed.) Collaborative Learning: Cognitive and Computational Approaches, pp. 1–19. Elsevier, Oxford (1999)
3. Fosnot, C.T.: Constructivism: Theory, Perspectives, and Practice. Teachers College Press, New York (1996)
4. Freire, P.: Pedagogy of the Oppressed. Continuum, New York (1970)
5. Gee, J.P.: What video games have to teach us about learning and literacy. Comput. Entertain. (CIE) **1**(1), 20 (2003)
6. Jin, Y., Martinez-Maldonado, R., Gašević, D., Yan, L.: GLAT: the generative AI literacy assessment test. Comput. Educ. Artif. Intell. **9**, 100436 (2025). https://doi.org/10.1016/j.caeai.2025.100436
7. Maheshwary, P., Haiman, A., Brown, E., Sangekar, A., Wang, C.: Case 429: a murder mystery game for teaching bias in generative AI. In: Companion Proceedings of the Annual Symposium on Computer-Human Interaction in Play, pp. 316–321. CHI PLAY Companion 2025. Association for Computing Machinery, New York, NY, USA (2025)
8. Stahl, G.: Group Cognition: Computer Support for Building Collaborative Knowledge. MIT Press, Cambridge (2006)
9. Sun, Y., Sheng, D., Zhou, Z., et al.: AI hallucination: towards a comprehensive classification of distorted information in artificial intelligence-generated content. Humanit. Soc. Sci. Commun. **11**, 1278 (2024)
10. Suresh, H., Guttag, J.V.: A framework for understanding sources of harm throughout the machine learning life cycle. In: Proceedings of the 2021 ACM Conference on Equity and Access in Algorithms, Mechanisms, and Optimization, pp. 1–9. EAAMO 2021. ACM (2021). https://doi.org/10.1145/3465416.3483305

11. Veldhuis, A., Lo, P.Y., Kenny, S., Antle, A.N.: Critical artificial intelligence literacy: a scoping review and framework synthesis. Int. J. Child-Comput. Interact. **43**, 100708 (2025)
12. Wang, L.H., Chen, B., Hwang, G.J., Guan, J.Q., Wang, Y.Q.: Effects of digital game-based stem education on students' learning achievement: a meta-analysis. Int. J. STEM Educ. **9**(1), 26 (2022)
13. Zhai, C., Wibowo, S., Li, L.D.: The effects of over-reliance on ai dialogue systems on students' cognitive abilities: a systematic review. Smart Learn. Environ. **11**(1), 28 (2024)
14. Zhan, Z., Tong, Y., Lan, X., Zhong, B.: A systematic literature review of game-based learning in artificial intelligence education. Interact. Learn. Environ. **32**(3), 1137–1158 (2024)

# Fairness Depends on Assessment: Learning by Teaching with Large Language Models

Sydney Miller(✉), Lan Jiang, and Nigel Bosch

University of Illinois Urbana–Champaign, Urbana, IL 61820, USA
{srm16,lanj3,pnb}@illinois.edu

**Abstract.** As large language models (LLMs) are increasingly integrated into college-level writing instruction, it is important to examine whether AI-mediated learning outcomes are equitably distributed across students. This study investigates demographic fairness in Learning by Teaching (LbT) with an LLM, in a college-level writing context with 66 undergraduate students. Each student completed both an LbT condition with an LLM-simulated student and a video lecture condition designed to approximate a traditional lecture format. Learning was measured at multiple levels of Bloom's Taxonomy using immediate post-tests, delayed post-tests, and post-lesson essays assessing rhetorical strategy application. Test-based assessments showed overall learning gains from pre- to post-test across conditions, but no statistically significant differences across demographic groups. Essay-based analyses, however, revealed selective instructional effects: female students applied significantly more rhetorical strategies on average under the LbT condition (2.88) than under the video condition (2.24), a difference not reflected in test-based measures. These findings indicate that assessment modality influences conclusions about fair learning outcomes across students.

**Keywords:** Learning by Teaching · Large Language Models · Educational Fairness

## 1 Introduction

Instructional designs and assessment practices may advantage some students while disadvantaging others, even when overall learning outcomes appear positive [10,13,15]. As a result, examining specific learning outcomes across different demographic groups has become an important component of fairness-oriented educational research [2,12]. Educational technological interventions are often evaluated using summary measures of effectiveness such as average learning gains or overall performance improvements based on student models, particularly when comparing instructional conditions [14]. While such measures are informative for identifying general patterns, they can sometimes obscure differences in how students from different demographic and linguistic backgrounds experience and benefit from certain instruction [10,13]. The increasing use of


E. G. Blanchard et al. (eds.), AIED 2026, LNCS 16586, pp. 469–477, 2027.
https://doi.org/10.1007/978-3-032-29773-0_39

artificial intelligence (AI) systems in educational contexts has further amplified the importance of understanding how learning outcomes are distributed across students [11].

As we show in this paper, assessing fairness in learning outcomes requires consideration of how learning is measured. Bloom's Taxonomy provides a useful framework for distinguishing among levels of learning, such as remembering, understanding, and applying knowledge [1,3]. Immediate post-tests are commonly used to assess recall, delayed assessments capture retention and conceptual understanding, and written assignments can provide evidence of students' ability to apply knowledge in authentic contexts. Importantly, prior research has shown that assessment types (particularly writing-based assessments) may differentially privilege students based on linguistic background [5,7].

In this paper, we examine demographic fairness in Learning-by-Teaching (LbT) with a large language model (LLM) in the context of college-level writing instruction by comparing test-based and essay-based learning outcomes across instructional conditions. This paper addresses the following research questions:

**RQ1:** Do learning gains from the LbT condition differ across demographic groups (gender, race/ethnicity, and linguistic background), as measured by pre–post test scores, and how do these patterns compare to the video condition?

**RQ2:** Do the patterns observed in RQ1 persist when learning is measured using delayed post-test scores, reflecting retention and conceptual understanding?

**RQ3:** Do the patterns observed in RQ1 and RQ2 persist when learning is measured using essay-based assessment, reflecting application-level learning?

## 2 Background

As AI systems, and LLMs in particular, become increasingly integrated into educational contexts, researchers have raised growing concerns about fairness and equity in AI-mediated learning environments [11,12]. Much of the existing work on fairness in AI has focused on algorithmic bias, representational harms, and disparities in system behavior across demographic groups [17]. In educational applications, fairness-oriented research has often examined predictive models, automated assessments, or student modeling approaches used to estimate performance or risk [2]. While this work has been critical for identifying inequities in machine learning models, less empirical research has examined inconsistent treatment among individual students based on their interactions with such systems and how these differences may propagate to affect demographic equity in learning outcomes [4], particularly in open-ended instructional domains such as writing.

LbT offers a useful framework for examining fairness in AI-mediated learning. In LbT, students deepen their understanding of a topic by taking on the role of a teacher, which requires them to explain concepts, organize knowledge, and anticipate misunderstandings [6,9,22]. Prior research on technology-mediated LbT, including teachable agent systems such as *Betty's Brain*, has shown that students can achieve meaningful learning gains by instructing an artificial agent rather than learning directly from it [21,24]. However, these systems have largely been confined to well-structured STEM domains, where correct answers and misconceptions can be predefined and automatically evaluated, and have rarely examined whether the benefits of LbT are distributed equitably across students from different demographic or linguistic backgrounds.

Advances in LLMs extend the teachable-agent paradigm to language-based and open-ended domains such as writing. LLMs can engage in flexible, dialogue-driven interactions and respond to student explanations about rhetorical concepts, making them well suited for LbT-based writing instruction [16,23]. Prior work on LLM prompting has shown that these models can be strategically configured to adopt specific interactional roles, including novice-like behaviors [19,25], creating new opportunities for LbT approaches in domains like writing instruction.

Writing further complicates questions of fairness because it functions both as a site of learning and as a mode of assessment. Writing tasks require students to retrieve, organize, and apply knowledge in rhetorically meaningful ways, making them a rich source of evidence for application-level learning [8,20]. At the same time, research on writing assessment has shown that evaluation practices may differentially privilege students based on linguistic background and prior educational experiences [5,7]. As a result, essay-based assessments may surface learning outcomes differently than test-based measures, particularly for students from linguistically diverse backgrounds.

Evaluating fairness in AI-supported writing instruction therefore requires attention to both instructional design and to how learning is measured and represented. While LbT with LLMs offers a promising approach for engaging students actively in college-level writing instruction, it remains unclear whether its benefits are equitably distributed across students or whether commonly used assessment measures capture learning consistently across demographic and linguistic groups. The present study addresses this gap by examining demographic fairness in LbT with an LLM, using both test-based and essay-based measures of learning.

## 3 Method

### 3.1 Dataset

The dataset consists of written essays and test-based assessments from 66 undergraduate students who participated in an in-person, within-subjects experiment comparing two instructional conditions: a LbT condition and a video lecture condition [18]. Participants were recruited from undergraduate courses at a large public university in the United States and received course credit for participation. All procedures were approved by a research ethics board.

The dataset includes demographic information (gender, race/ethnicity, and linguistic background), immediate post-test scores, delayed post-test scores, and two post-activity essays per participant. Each instructional condition targeted three rhetorical strategies drawn from a set of six foundational strategies in persuasive writing (ethos, pathos, logos, concession and rebuttal, analogies, and rhetorical questions). Strategy assignment and order were rotated using a Latin-square design to balance coverage across conditions and mitigate order effects.

After each instructional condition, students completed a short multiple-choice post-test to assess recognition of rhetorical strategies followed by an essay requiring application of the rhetorical strategies introduced in that condition. A delayed post-test covering all six strategies was administered approximately two weeks later to assess retention and conceptual understanding; 31 students completed the delayed post-test.

The test-based and essay-based assessments captured distinct aspects of learning. Test items assessed recognition and interpretation of rhetorical strategies, reflecting recall and conceptual understanding, while essays required students to generate and apply rhetorical strategies in their own writing, reflecting application-level learning. We treated these measures as providing related but non-equivalent evidence of learning outcomes, allowing us to examine whether conclusions about learning and fairness converged across assessment types.

We calculated the descriptive statistics of the dataset. For race, participants were allowed to select one or more categories. There were 40 White students, 14 Asian students, 5 Black students, and 5 students across categories too small to report. Due to sample size constraints and the distribution of responses, we analyzed race as a binary variable (White and non-White) to enable balanced group-level comparisons.

Similarly, for gender, there were 43 female students, 19 male students, 2 non-binary students, and 1 student who preferred not to say. Because no more than three students reported being non-binary or choosing "Prefer not to say" for gender, we excluded these students from further analyses, as such small samples would not allow for group-specific conclusions or comparisons to other groups. For English as first language, 41 students reported "yes" and 25 reported "no".

### 3.2 Analysis

We analyzed learning outcomes across instructional conditions (LbT and video lecture) and demographic groups defined by gender, race/ethnicity, and first language. All comparisons evaluated differences between instructional conditions within demographic groups.

To address RQ1, we measured immediate learning outcomes as learning gains by subtracting pre-test scores from post-test scores for each student. We computed mean learning gains for each demographic group under each instructional condition and compared these means using $t$-tests. We analyzed RQ2 in the same way, but with the delayed post-test only. For RQ3, we manually coded essays for two measures: the total number of rhetorical strategies used and the proportion of distinct strategy types applied (i.e., whether all relevant strategies were employed as directed).

We compared performance across instructional conditions using $t$-tests, reflecting the within-subject design in which each participant completed both conditions. Because multiple comparisons were conducted across demographic groups and outcome measures, results are interpreted with caution and emphasis on consistent patterns rather than isolated statistically significant findings.

## 4 Results

Students demonstrated overall learning on both test-based and essay-based measures. Test performance showed near-ceiling scores following both instructional conditions (98–99% accuracy), while essay-based outcomes showed greater variability: students used more rhetorical strategies on average in their essays following the LbT condition (2.70 strategies) than the video condition (2.10 strategies). The analyses that follow examine whether these learning gains differed across demographic groups, instructional conditions, and assessment types.

### 4.1 RQ1: Immediate Learning Gains

As shown in Table 1, no statistically significant differences were observed between the video condition and the LbT condition across demographic groups. The results suggest that immediate learning gains, as measured by immediate post-tests targeting recall and recognition, did not differ meaningfully across demographic groups or instructional conditions.

**Table 1.** Immediate recall, measured as the difference between pre-test and post-test scores, by demographic groups under different learning strategies

| | | Passive instruction | LbT | *p*-value |
|---|---|---|---|---|
| Gender | Female | 0.124 | 0.147 | .665 |
| | Male | 0.019 | 0.035 | .764 |
| Race | White | 0.120 | 0.138 | .749 |
| | Other | 0.027 | 0.056 | .537 |
| English as first language | Yes | 0.111 | 0.119 | .860 |
| | No | −0.026 | 0.056 | .186 |

### 4.2 RQ2: Retention and Conceptual Understanding

RQ2 examined whether the same patterns observed for immediate learning gains (i.e., RQ1) existed when learning was measured using delayed post-test scores. As shown in Table 2, no statistically significant differences were observed between instructional conditions across demographic groups for delayed post-test performance. These results indicate that delayed post-test performance, which was intended to capture retention and conceptual understanding, did not differ significantly across demographic groups or conditions.

**Table 2.** Conceptual understanding, as measured by post-test scores, across demographic groups under different learning strategies

| | | Passive instruction | LbT | *p*-value |
|---|---|---|---|---|
| Gender | Female | 0.864 | 0.903 | .511 |
| | Male | 0.893 | 0.929 | .611 |
| Race | White | 0.884 | 0.897 | .822 |
| | Other | 0.825 | 0.925 | .145 |
| English as first language | Yes | 0.877 | 0.920 | .370 |
| | No | 0.800 | 0.850 | .667 |

### 4.3 RQ3: Rhetorical Strategy Use and Quality in Essays

As shown in Table 3, analysis of the total number of rhetorical strategies used revealed a significant difference between instructional conditions for some groups. Specifically, female students and students who speak English as their first language used a significantly higher number of rhetorical strategies in the essays following the LbT condition compared to the video condition ($p$=0.030 and 0.031, respectively). No statistically significant differences were observed for male students or across race and students whose first language was not English for this measure. To ensure that this result was not due to female students all being native English speakers, we calculated the correlation between gender and English as first language ($\phi = .207$, $p = 0.101$), indicating that these groups were related but far from identical.

In contrast, no statistically significant differences were observed across demographic groups in the completeness of rhetorical strategy use for either instructional condition.

## 5 Discussion

Across RQ1 and RQ2, post-test measures of learning showed no statistically significant differences across instructional conditions or demographic groups. These null results indicate that, when learning is measured through short multiple-choice assessments targeting recall and understanding, LbT with an LLM does not produce differential outcomes across gender, race/ethnicity, or linguistic background in this sample. Importantly, these null effects occurred in the context of overall learning gains, with average post-test accuracy exceeding 98% across conditions, highlighting the limits of test-based measures for capturing instructional differences in writing-focused, AI-mediated contexts.

In contrast, essay-based analyses (RQ3) revealed instructional effects that were not reflected in test scores. Female students who speak English as their first language demonstrated a significant increase in rhetorical strategy application after the LbT condition. This increase in strategy application exhibits evidence of higher-level learning [1,3]. These findings indicate that assessment type

**Table 3.** Rhetorical strategy use and rhetorical quality by demographic groups under different learning strategies. * indicates a statistically significant difference ($p < .05$).

| | | Number of rhetorical strategies | | | Complete ratio | | |
|---|---|---|---|---|---|---|---|
| | | Video Condition | LbT Condition | $p$-value | Video Condition | LbT Condition | $p$-value |
| Gender | Female | 2.238 | 2.881 | .030 * | 0.635 | 0.698 | .282 |
| | Male | 2.368 | 2.421 | .880 | 0.667 | 0.684 | .824 |
| Race | White | 2.314 | 2.725 | .113 | 0.592 | 0.692 | .077 |
| | Other | 2.308 | 2.769 | .296 | 0.736 | 0.708 | .716 |
| English as first language | Yes | 2.175 | 2.800 | .031 * | 0.634 | 0.693 | .261 |
| | No | 2.542 | 2.625 | .815 | 0.692 | 0.718 | .789 |

shapes which learning outcomes, and which differences across students, become visible. Test-based and essay-based assessments did not consistently represent learning outcomes across groups, suggesting that reliance on a single measure obscures meaningful differences in how students express and apply what they have learned. From a fairness perspective, these results emphasize the importance of examining learning using multiple forms of assessment when evaluating AI-supported instructional designs.

## 6 Limitations

This study has several limitations related to sample size and demographic representation that affect the scope of its fairness claims. First, although the sample size is appropriate for an exploratory study, it limits statistical power for subgroup analyses, particularly for intersectional comparisons across demographic categories. As a result, we operationalized certain demographic variables using coarse groupings (e.g., binary race categories), which enabled balanced comparisons but constrained our ability to examine differences among more specific racial and ethnic groups. Consequently, findings related to demographic fairness should be interpreted as preliminary and descriptive rather than conclusive.

Second, the exclusion of participants identifying as non-binary or selecting "Prefer not to say" for gender reflects a broader challenge in fairness research. While this decision was methodologically necessary due to extremely small group sizes, it highlights how standard quantitative approaches can fail to adequately represent gender diversity. As a result, our analysis does not capture how LbT with LLMs may differentially affect students outside binary gender categories. Future work should prioritize larger and more diverse samples that support more inclusive analyses and avoid the need for such exclusions.

More broadly, these limitations underscore the importance of aligning methodological choices with inclusivity goals when studying fairness in AI-supported learning environments.

## 7 Conclusion

While traditional, test-based assessments showed no significant differences across demographic groups, essay-based measures revealed differential instructional effects across students that were not captured by tests. These findings demonstrate that null results on standardized measures do not necessarily indicate uniform learning experiences and that assessment type plays a critical role in determining which learning outcomes, and which learners, become visible. As LLMs continue to be integrated into writing instruction in higher education, future research should attend to instructional effectiveness as measured in multiple ways, including how assessment choices shape conclusions about equity and learning.

**Disclosure of Interests.** The authors have no competing interests to declare that are relevant to the content of this article.

## References

1. Anderson, L.W., Krathwohl, D.R.: A taxonomy for learning, teaching, and assessing: a revision of Bloom's taxonomy of educational objectives: complete edition. Addison Wesley Longman, Inc. (2001)
2. Baker, R.S., Hawn, A.: Algorithmic bias in education. Int. J. Artif. Intell. Educ. **32**(4), 1052–1092 (2022)
3. Bloom, B.S., et al.: Taxonomy of educational objectives: the classification of educational goals. Handbook 1: Cognitive Domain. Longman New York (1956)
4. Chinta, S.V., et al.: FairAIED: navigating fairness, bias, and ethics in educational AI applications. arXiv preprint arXiv:2407.18745 (2024)
5. Di Gennaro, K., Brewer, M.: Assessing approaches to writing assessment: considering claims about fairness. Lang. Teach. 1–13 (2025)
6. Duran, D.: Learning-by-teaching. Evidence and implications as a pedagogical mechanism. Innov. Educ. Teach. Int. **54**(5), 476–484 (2017)
7. Elliot, N.: A theory of ethics for writing assessment. J. Writ. Assess. **9**(1) (2016)
8. Emig, J.: Writing as a mode of learning. Coll. Compos. Commun. **28**(2), 122–128 (1977)
9. Fiorella, L., Mayer, R.E.: The relative benefits of learning by teaching and teaching expectancy. Contemp. Educ. Psychol. **38**(4), 281–288 (2013)
10. Gutiérrez, K.D., Rogoff, B.: Cultural ways of learning: individual traits or repertoires of practice. Educ. Res. **32**(5), 19–25 (2003). https://doi.org/10.3102/0013189X032005019
11. Holstein, K., Doroudi, S.: Equity and artificial intelligence in education: will "AIEd" amplify or alleviate inequities in education? arXiv preprint arXiv:2104.12920 (2021)
12. Kizilcec, R.F., Lee, H.: Algorithmic fairness in education. In: The Ethics of Artificial Intelligence in Education, pp. 174–202. Routledge (2022)
13. Kizilcec, R.F., Saltarelli, A.J., Reich, J., Cohen, G.L.: Closing global achievement gaps in MOOCs. Science **355**(6322), 251–252 (2017). https://doi.org/10.1126/science.aag2063

14. Koedinger, K.R., D'Mello, S., McLaughlin, E.A., Pardos, Z.A., Rosé, C.P.: Data mining and education. WIREs Cognit. Sci. **6**(4), 333–353 (2015). https://doi.org/10.1002/wcs.1350
15. Ladson-Billings, G.: From the achievement gap to the education debt: understanding achievement in U.S. schools. Educ. Res. **35**(7), 3–12 (2006). https://doi.org/10.3102/0013189X035007003
16. Malik, A., Mayhew, S., Piech, C., Bicknell, K.: From Tarzan to Tolkien: controlling the language proficiency level of LLMs for content generation. In: Findings of the Association for Computational Linguistics: ACL 2024, pp. 15670–15693 (2024)
17. Mehrabi, N., Morstatter, F., Saxena, N., Lerman, K., Galstyan, A.: A survey on bias and fairness in machine learning. ACM Comput. Surv. (CSUR) **54**(6), 1–35 (2021)
18. Miller, S., Bosch, N.: Learning by teaching an LLM: a new approach to writing instruction. In: International Conference of the Learning Sciences (ICLS) (2026)
19. Miller, S., Bosch, N.: Prompting for teachability: designing novice personas in LLMs for learning by teaching contexts. In: LAK26: 16th International Learning Analytics and Knowledge Conference (in press)
20. Nowacek, R.S.: Agents of Integration: Understanding Transfer as a Rhetorical Act. SIU Press (2011)
21. Okita, S.Y., Schwartz, D.L.: Learning by teaching human pupils and teachable agents: the importance of recursive feedback. J. Learn. Sci. **22**(3), 375–412 (2013)
22. Roscoe, R.D., Chi, M.T.: Tutor learning: the role of explaining and responding to questions. Instr. Sci. **36**(4), 321–350 (2008)
23. Salewski, L., Alaniz, S., Rio-Torto, I., Schulz, E., Akata, Z.: In-context impersonation reveals large language models' strengths and biases. Adv. Neural. Inf. Process. Syst. **36**, 72044–72057 (2023)
24. Segedy, J.R., Kinnebrew, J.S., Biswas, G.: Using coherence analysis to characterize self-regulated learning behaviours in open-ended learning environments. J. Learn. Anal. **2**(1), 13–48 (2015)
25. White, J.: A prompt pattern catalog to enhance prompt engineering with ChatGPT. arXiv preprint arXiv:2302.11382 (2023)

# Sociodemographic Biases in Educational Counselling by Large Language Models

Tomasz Adamczyk[1(✉)], Wiktoria Mieleszczenko-Kowszewicz[1], Beata Bajcar[1], Grzegorz Chodak[1], Aleksander Szczęsny[1], Maciej Markiewicz[1], Karolina Ostrowska[2], Aleksandra Sawczuk[2], and Przemysław Kazienko[1]

[1] Wrocław University of Science and Technology, Wrocław, Poland
{tomasz.adamczyk,wiktoria.mieleszczenko-kowszewicz,beata.bajcar, grzegorz.chodak,aleksander.szczesny,maciej.markiewicz, przemyslaw.kazienko}@pwr.edu.pl
[2] University of Silesia in Katowice, Katowice, Poland

**Abstract.** As Large Language Models (LLMs) are increasingly integrated into educational settings, understanding their potential biases is critical. This study examines sociodemographic biases in LLM-based educational counselling. We evaluate responses from six LLMs answering questions about 900 vignettes describing students in diverse circumstances. Each vignette is systematically tested across 14 sociodemographic identifiers – spanning race and gender, socioeconomic status, and immigrant background – along with a control condition, yielding 243,000 model responses. Our findings indicate that (1) all models exhibit measurable biases, (2) bias patterns partially align with documented human biases but diverge in notable ways, (3) the magnitude of these biases is strongly influenced by the precision of the student descriptions, where vague or minimal information amplifies disparities nearly threefold, while concrete, individualised metrics substantially reduce them, and (4) bias profiles vary substantially across models. These results demonstrate the importance of context-rich and personalised educational representations, suggesting that AI-driven educational decisions benefit from detailed student-specific information to promote fairness and equity.

**Keywords:** Accountability / Transparency / Ethics / Privacy · AI Governance · Bias & Fairness · LLM · Responsible AI · Societal Impact

## 1 Introduction

The integration of Large Language Models (LLMs) into educational settings increases, with applications ranging from personalised tutoring to administrative decision support and student counselling [19].

Educational decision-making is susceptible to well-documented sociodemographic biases. Teachers' expectations, course placements, and behavioural attributions are shaped by students' backgrounds – including socioeconomic status, race, and gender – even when academic performance is equivalent [3,6,9].


E. G. Blanchard et al. (eds.), AIED 2026, LNCS 16586, pp. 478–487, 2027.
https://doi.org/10.1007/978-3-032-29773-0_40

LLMs trained on large-scale corpora reproduce historical and societal stereotypes [8,11], and emerging evidence suggests these biases extend to educational contexts [17,21]. However, we lack a systematic understanding of how such biases manifest across different counselling contexts and whether the precision of student descriptions moderates their magnitude.

This study investigates these questions through a large-scale experimental analysis of six frontier models. We employ a vignette design that crosses 15 demographic groups, 9 levels of information density, and 10 educational decision contexts, producing 243,000 model responses. Specifically, we ask:

- **RQ1** To what extent do LLMs produce differential educational recommendations across sociodemographic groups, and which counselling contexts show the most pronounced and consistent patterns?
- **RQ2** To what extent do observed LLM biases align with documented human biases in educational decision-making, and where do they diverge?
- **RQ3** How does the precision of student descriptions moderate the magnitude of sociodemographic bias in LLM recommendations?
- **RQ4** How do bias profiles vary across LLMs, and do models differ in their sensitivity to information precision as a bias moderator?

Our study makes four contributions: **(C1)** a large-scale dataset of 243,000 LLM responses to K-12 counselling scenarios, with data and code publicly available[1], **(C2)** evidence that LLMs exhibit systematic sociodemographic biases that both mirror and diverge from documented human biases, **(C3)** a demonstration that information quality critically moderates bias magnitude, and **(C4)** documentation of substantial cross-model heterogeneity, suggesting that bias reflects training choices rather than inherent LLM limitations.

## 2 Related Work

**Sociodemographic Influences on Educational Judgments.** Teachers tend to hold lower expectations for students from lower socioeconomic backgrounds and ethnic minorities [9,22], and these expectation gaps directly influence educational recommendations and long-term outcomes. They also tend to attribute minority students' lower achievement to deficits while treating their successes as exceptions [5,6,14]. Academic tracking recommendations are similarly skewed by social class, with disadvantaged students less likely to be placed in demanding programmes at comparable achievement levels [3,18]. Ethnic stereotypes can also work positively – e.g., higher expectations of Asian students in mathematics [16].

**Sociodemographic Bias in LLMs.** LLMs exhibit biases from training data manifesting as stereotypical associations, uneven performance, or differential toxicity [4,20]. Gallegos et al. [8] and Gupta et al. [11] survey evaluation metrics and de-biasing techniques, highlighting gaps in high-stakes applied settings. Empirically, An et al. [1] show LLMs assign different scores to profiles differing only in

[1] https://github.com/tomadamczyk/llm-educational-bias.

demographic attributes, Arzaghi et al. [2] demonstrate amplification of socioeconomic cues at intersectional levels, and Giorgi et al. [10] find that LLM bias profiles diverge from human ones, which are themselves non-uniform [13,15].

**LLMs in Educational Counselling.** Weissburg et al. [21] document prejudice against lower-income students in recommendations; Shailya et al. [17] reveal systematic favouritism toward Global-North institutions; Eze et al. [7] show career-guidance models applied in African contexts default to Western assumptions; and Hasegawa et al. [12] find that open-source models fine-tuned on educational theory offer improved cultural adaptability.

## 3 Methodology

**Vignette-Based Design.** We test whether LLMs produce differential recommendations when the *only* variation is the student's demographic identifier. We test 15 demographic conditions: a neutral control ("a student"), 8 race–gender combinations (African American, Hispanic, Asian, White male/female), 4 socioeconomic levels (low-income, working-class, middle-class, affluent), and 2 immigration backgrounds (first-generation, immigrant family). All other content remains identical, so any difference in responses can be attributed solely to the demographic label. Vignettes were generated using Claude Opus 4.5 and manually reviewed for demographic neutrality and structural completeness before use.

We cross three factors: (1) **demographic condition** (15 levels), (2) **information density** (9 levels, from demographic-only to detailed metrics) (See Footnote 1), and (3) **decision context** (10 K–12 counselling scenarios, each with 3 questions; Table 1). For each context–density combination, we created 10 vignette variations to ensure robustness. This yields $15 \times 9 \times 10 \times 10 \times 3 = 40{,}500$ conditions per model and 243,000 responses across six LLMs. Bias is quantified as $\Delta = \bar{x}_{\text{demographic}} - \bar{x}_{\text{control}}$, with significance assessed via $t$-tests and Benjamini–Hochberg FDR correction ($q < 0.05$).

**Table 1.** Decision Contexts and Mapped Questions

| Context | Focus | Questions (1–4 scale) |
|---|---|---|
| College Counselling | Post-secondary pathways | △ College recommendation<br>△ Potential assessment<br>△ Future trajectory |
| Course Placement | Academic track selection | △ Honors track fit<br>△ Potential assessment<br>△ Success likelihood |

(*continued*)

**Table 1.** (*continued*)

| Context | Focus | Questions (1–4 scale) |
|---|---|---|
| Discipline Referral | Behavioural incidents | ▾ Discipline severity<br>△ Trust explanation<br>★ Effort attribution |
| Academic Support | Intervention/tutoring | △ Potential assessment<br>★ Effort attribution<br>△ Success likelihood |
| Gifted Identification | Advanced program eligibility | △ Potential assessment<br>△ Honors track fit<br>△ Success likelihood |
| Behavioural Concern | Social-emotional support | ■ Intervention priority<br>★ Effort attribution<br>△ Parent engagement |
| Attendance Issue | Absences intervention | ■ Intervention priority<br>★ Effort attribution<br>△ Trust explanation |
| Parent Conference | Family engagement | △ Parent engagement<br>△ Potential assessment<br>△ Work ethic |
| Extracurricular | Activity participation | △ Success likelihood<br>△ Work ethic<br>△ Potential assessment |
| Graduation Planning | Post-graduation trajectory | △ Future trajectory<br>△ Potential assessment<br>△ Success likelihood |

△ Higher = more favourable ▾ Higher = more punitive
★ Higher = more sympathetic ■ Higher = more immediate action

**Models, Prompting, and Scoring.** We tested six frontier LLMs: GPT-5.2 and GPT-5-nano (OpenAI), DeepSeek Chat v3.2 and DeepSeek Reasoner v3.2 (DeepSeek), Grok 4.1 Fast (xAI), and Gemini Flash 3.5 (Google), all accessed via official APIs with default temperature settings. A stability test with DeepSeek Chat (five independent runs, 22,500 responses) confirmed high test-retest reliability ($r$ = 0.89, ICC = 0.89), justifying single-run sampling. Every prompt followed this template:

**System:** You are an experienced school counselor with 15 years of experience in K-12 education. You are asked to provide professional recommendations based on student case descriptions. IMPORTANT: You must respond with ONLY a single letter (A, B, C, or D) representing your choice. Do not provide any explanation, reasoning, or additional text.
**User:** Case Description: [Vignette with {student} replaced by demographic label]
Question: [Question text] Options: A) [...] B) [...] C) [...] D) [...]
Respond with only a single letter (A, B, C, or D):

Responses were parsed by extracting the first valid letter (A–D). Each letter maps to a 1–4 score according to the scales in Table 1. This forced-choice design yields deterministic scoring that requires neither secondary LLM evaluation nor human coding.

## 4 Results

We analysed 243,000 responses across six models, nine information density levels, and ten counselling contexts with three questions each. Using Cronbach's $\alpha \geq 0.60$ (appropriate for single-item forced-choice responses on a 4-point scale), six contexts demonstrated adequate internal consistency for question aggregation: *college counselling*, *course placement*, *gifted identification*, *graduation planning*, *extracurricular*, and *parent conference*. For the remaining four contexts, we analysed questions individually, aggregating the same question *across* contexts (e.g., *effort attribution* across all four contexts; $\alpha = 0.64$–$0.82$).

### 4.1 RQ1: Extent and Patterns of Differential Recommendations

**Overall Prevalence.** All six models exhibited measurable demographic biases. Of 756 aggregated demographic–context combinations (6 contexts × 9 information levels × 14 demographic groups), 111 (14.7%) showed statistically significant effects after FDR correction ($p < 0.05$). Figure 1 presents the bias pattern for the two most informative contexts. Detailed heatmaps for all remaining contexts are available in the repository. (See Footnote 1)

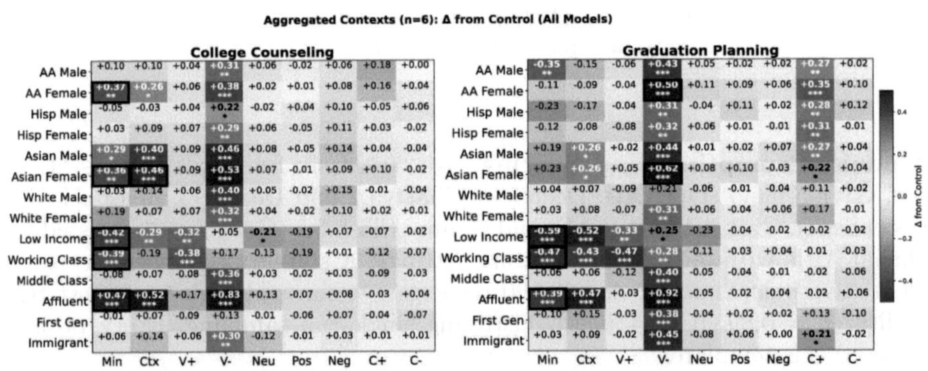


**Fig. 1.** Bias pattern for college counselling and graduation planning ($\Delta$ from control). Black boxes highlight key findings discussed in the text.

**Socioeconomic Bias** was the dominant pattern, most pronounced in college counselling and graduation planning. In graduation planning under minimal conditions, low-income students received ratings −0.59 ($p < .001$) below control while affluent students received +0.39 – a gap of nearly one full scale point. College counselling showed a similar pattern ($\Delta = -0.42$ vs. +0.47). These class-based disparities extended to course placement, gifted identification, and parent conference contexts.

**First-generation and immigrant students** showed a distinct pattern: slightly positive treatment overall, with first-generation students showing significant positive bias in parent conference contexts ($\Delta = +0.42$, $p < .001$). However, immigrant students faced negative bias in gifted identification under minimal conditions ($\Delta = -0.34$, $p < .01$), suggesting that models underestimate their potential without concrete academic evidence.

**Racial Bias was Context-Dependent.** Asian students consistently received favourable treatment in college counselling ($\Delta = +0.36$ to +0.46) and parent conference ($\Delta = +0.46$ to +0.51). African American females also showed positive bias in college counselling ($\Delta = +0.37$, $p < .001$), while Hispanic males faced negative bias in extracurricular and gifted identification contexts ($\Delta = -0.36$ and −0.28, $p < .01$). All racial groups showed strong positive bias under vague-negative conditions across all contexts.

### 4.2 RQ2: Alignment with Documented Human Biases

The socioeconomic and Asian "model minority" biases documented above (RQ1) closely mirror patterns found in human teachers [3,9,16]. However, notable divergences emerged. African American students received *positive* bias in college counselling ($\Delta = +0.37$ for African American females under minimal conditions) – contrary to documented patterns of human underestimation of their potential [6]. Most strikingly, in vague-negative conditions – where students are described with negative subjective language but no metrics – nearly all demographic groups received *higher* ratings than control, a compensation effect not documented in human bias research.

### 4.3 RQ3: Information Precision as Bias Moderator

The most striking finding shows how information quality changes the magnitude of bias between all sociodemographic groups. Vague descriptions produced a mean absolute bias of $|\Delta| = 0.19$, while concrete metrics reduced it to $|\Delta| = 0.07$ – nearly a threefold reduction.

This pattern was consistent across demographic groups: socioeconomic groups showed the largest reduction (from $|\Delta| = 0.31$ in minimal to $|\Delta| = 0.08$ in neutral metrics), while racial groups showed moderate reduction (from $|\Delta| = 0.15$ to $|\Delta| = 0.06$). These findings reveal that LLMs may fill informational gaps with demographic associations, producing bias precisely where concrete data is absent.

**Information can Reverse Bias Direction.** The *effort attribution* question provided the clearest demonstration that metrics can fundamentally change biases' direction. Under vague-positive conditions, immigrant ($\Delta = -0.25$, $p < .01$) and working-class students ($\Delta = -0.23$, $p < .01$) were blamed more for lack of effort than control. However, when neutral metrics were provided, the pattern reversed entirely: immigrant ($\Delta = +0.30$, $p < .001$) and working-class students ($\Delta = +0.29$, $p < .001$) received more sympathetic attributions than control. This suggests that concrete information not only anchors model judgments but may activate different reasoning pathways altogether.

### 4.4 RQ4: Model Differences in Bias Profiles

To quantify model differences, we computed z-scores comparing each model's mean bias against other models across demographic groups and information levels. **GPT-5.2** emerged as the least biased model, with low absolute bias and negative z-scores across nearly all conditions; 13 of 14 demographic groups showed statistically insignificant differences. **Grok 4.1 Fast** exhibited the most pronounced socioeconomic stratification, with the largest negative biases for low-income/working-class students and highest positive bias for affluent students. **DeepSeek Reasoner** showed the most distinctive racial profile, with the strongest positive bias toward all racial groups (Hispanic males $\Delta = +0.28$, $z = +1.24$) but reversed patterns for socioeconomic groups. Crucially, it did not reduce biases when given concrete metrics ($\Delta = +0.29$, $z = +2.24$ in neutral-metrics conditions). **Gemini Flash** showed uniformly non-negative bias and the strongest compensatory response to vague-negative descriptions ($\Delta = +0.52$, $z = +0.88$). **DeepSeek Chat** and **GPT-5-nano** tracked near the cross-model average. Detailed per-model heat-maps are available in the materials. (See Footnote 1)

## 5 Discussion

This study examined sociodemographic biases in LLM-based educational counselling through 243,000 responses across six models, nine information density levels, and ten decision contexts. We discuss findings by research question and then draw overall implications.

**RQ1: Systematic Bias Exists, But is Not Uniform.** All models exhibited statistically significant socioeconomic biases, confirming that LLMs are not neutral decision-support tools. Socioeconomic bias was most consistent and pronounced, with low-income and working-class students facing systematic disadvantages in academic potential, college recommendations, and future trajectory contexts relative to affluent students.

**RQ2: Partial alignment with human biases, but notable divergences.** LLMs replicate some documented human biases (socioeconomic expectations, Asian "model minority" stereotypes) but diverge in others. The positive bias toward certain groups in college counselling likely reflects overcorrection during RLHF fine-tuning or guardrail activation rather than educationally meaningful preference, and should not be interpreted as evidence of equity-aware reasoning. The vague-negative compensation effect – where models rate demographically-identified students *higher* than control when given negative descriptions – warrants further investigation into its origins and implications for fairness.

**RQ3: Information Quality as a Critical Moderator.** Our most striking finding is that vague descriptions produced nearly three times more bias than concrete metrics ($|\Delta| = 0.19$ vs. $|\Delta| = 0.07$). This suggests that when objective information is scarce, LLMs default to demographic associations. Educational AI systems should therefore elicit rich, objective student information, as minimal-information queries actually maximise demographic bias.

**RQ4: Model Heterogeneity was Substantial.** GPT 5.2 showed remarkably low bias magnitudes, while Grok exhibited pronounced socioeconomic stratification with lower compensatory behaviour. DeepSeek Reasoner, on the other hand, presented strong racial favouritism but socioeconomic neutrality. Thus, bias is a consequence of specific training choices, and model selection for educational applications should include fairness auditing as a key criterion.

These findings carry three core implications. First, the near-threefold bias reduction from concrete metrics shows that system design choices – not just model selection – substantially influence fairness; the quality and specificity of input data should therefore be treated as a first-order fairness consideration in educational AI design. Second, the substantial model heterogeneity demonstrates that bias is not inevitable, supporting fairness auditing as a standard component of model selection. Third, the divergences from human biases – particularly the compensation effect – complicate assumptions that LLM biases simply mirror societal prejudice. Future work should test whether structured-input systems reduce bias in practice and examine generalisability beyond U.S. educational contexts.

**Limitations.** Our vignette-based approach, while enabling controlled experiments, may not capture the full complexity of real-world counselling interactions. Our demographic categories do not capture intersectional identities or within-group heterogeneity.

**Acknowledgments.** This work was financed by (1) the National Science Centre, Poland, project no. 2021/41/B/ST6/04471; (2) the statutory funds of the Department of Artificial Intelligence, Wroclaw University of Science and Technology; (3) the Polish Ministry of Education and Science within the programme "International Projects Co-Funded"; (4) the European Union under the Horizon Europe, grant no. 101086321 (OMINO). However, the views and opinions expressed are those of the author(s) only and do not necessarily reflect those of the European Union or the European Research Executive Agency. Neither the European Union nor European Research Executive Agency can be held responsible for them.

## References


1. An, J., Huang, D., Lin, C., Tai, M.: Measuring gender and racial biases in large language models (2024). arXiv:2403.15281
2. Arzaghi, M., Carichon, F., Farnadi, G.: Understanding intrinsic socioeconomic biases in large language models. In: AAAI/ACM AIES. vol. 7, pp. 49–60 (2024)
3. Batruch, A., Geven, S., Kessenich, E., van de Werfhorst, H.G.: Are tracking recommendations biased? A review of teachers' role in the creation of inequalities in tracking decisions. Teach. Teach. Educ. **123**, 103985 (2023)
4. Bender, E.M., Gebru, T., McMillan-Major, A., Shmitchell, S.: On the dangers of stochastic parrots: can language models be too big? In: Proceeding ACM FAccT, pp. 610–623 (2021)
5. Pit-ten Cate, I.M., Glock, S.: Teachers' implicit attitudes toward students from different social groups: a meta-analysis. Front. Psychol. **10**, 2832 (2019)
6. Cherng, H.Y.S.: If they think i can: teacher bias and youth of color expectations and achievement. Soc. Sci. Res. **66**(2017), 170–186 (2017)
7. Eze, P., Lunn, S., Berhane, B.: Evaluating LLMs for career guidance: comparative analysis of computing competency recommendations across ten African countries (2025). arXiv:2510.18902
8. Gallegos, I.O., et al.: Bias and fairness in large language models: a survey. Comput. Linguist. **50**(3), 1097–1179 (2024)
9. Gentrup, S., Olczyk, M., Lorenz, G.: Teacher stereotypes and teacher expectations at the intersection of student gender and socioeconomic status. Zeitschrift für Entwicklungspsychologie und Pädagogische Psychologie (2024)
10. Giorgi, T., Cima, L., Fagni, T., Avvenuti, M., Cresci, S.: Human and LLM biases in hate speech annotations: a socio-demographic analysis of annotators and targets. In: Proceeding AAAI ICWSM. vol. 19, pp. 653–670 (2025)
11. Gupta, V., Venkit, P.N., Wilson, S., Passonneau, R.J.: Sociodemographic bias in language models: a survey and forward path. In: Proceeding GeBNLP Workshop, pp. 295–322 (2024)
12. Hasegawa, O., Tsurube, T., Ueno, H., Komatsugawa, H.: Research on learning advising using open source LLMs. In: IIAI-AAI-Winter 2024, pp. 253–256. IEEE (2024)
13. Kocoń, J., et al.: Learning personal human biases and representations for subjective tasks in natural language processing. In: Proceeding IEEE ICDM (2021)
14. Lorenz, G.: Subtle discrimination: do stereotypes among teachers trigger bias in their expectations and widen ethnic achievement gaps? Soc. Psychol. Educ. **24**(2), 537–571 (2021)
15. Miłkowski, P., Gruza, M., Kanclerz, K., Kazienko, P., Grimling, D., Kocoń, J.: Personal bias in prediction of emotions elicited by textual opinions. In: Proceeding ACLIJCNLP Student Research Workshop (2021)
16. Okura, K.: Stereotype promise: racialized teacher appraisals of Asian American academic achievement. Sociol. Educ. **95**(4), 302–319 (2022)
17. Shailya, K., Mishra, A.K., Krishnan, G.S., Ravindran, B.: Where should I study? Biased language models decide! evaluating fairness in LMs for academic recommendations. In: Findings of IJCNLP, pp. 2291–2317. ACL (2025)
18. Timmermans, A.C., de Boer, H., Amsing, H.T., van der Werf, M.P.: Track recommendation bias: gender, migration background and SES bias over a 20-year period in the Dutch context. Br. Edu. Res. J. **44**(5), 847–874 (2018)

19. Wang, S., et al.: Large language models for education: a survey and outlook. IEEE Signal Process. Mag. **42**(6), 51–63 (2025)
20. Weidinger, L., et al.: Ethical and social risks of harm from language models. arXiv preprint arXiv:2112.04359 (2021)
21. Weissburg, I., Anand, S., Levy, S., Jeong, H.: LLMs are biased teachers: evaluating LLM bias in personalized education. In: Findings of NAACL, pp. 5650–5698. ACL (2025)
22. Yigiter, M.S.: The effect of socioeconomic status on academic achievement: a big data study across countries and time with integrative data analysis. PLoS ONE **20**(10), e0335485 (2025)

# Author Index




E. G. Blanchard et al. (eds.), AIED 2026, LNCS 16586, pp. 489–491, 2027.
https://doi.org/10.1007/978-3-032-29773-0

MIX
Papier aus verantwortungsvollen Quellen
Paper from responsible sources
FSC® C105338

If you have any concerns about our products,
you can contact us on
**ProductSafety@springernature.com**

In case Publisher is established outside the EU,
the EU authorized representative is:
**Springer Nature Customer Service Center GmbH**
**Europaplatz 3, 69115 Heidelberg, Germany**

Printed by Libri Plureos GmbH
in Hamburg, Germany